LRC / LIBRARY
MORAINE VALLEY COMMUNITY COLLEGE
PALOS HILLS, ILLINOIS 60465

W9-COP-731

E185.86.B52 1986
Black American families, 1965-1984

3 5029 00004721 5

FOR REFERENCE

Do Not Take From This Room

BLACK AMERICAN FAMILIES, 1965-1984

RECENT TITLES IN
BIBLIOGRAPHIES AND INDEXES IN AFRO-AMERICAN AND AFRICAN STUDIES

BLACK AMERICAN FAMILIES, 1965-1984

A Classified, Selectively Annotated Bibliography

Walter R. Allen, *Editor-in-Chief*
Richard A. English *and* Jo Anne Hall, *Associate Editors*
David Carlson, *Database Programmer*
Bamidele Ade Agbasegbe Demerson, *Research Assistant*

Bibliographies and Indexes in Afro-American and African Studies, Number 16

GREENWOOD PRESS
New York • Westport, Connecticut • London

LIBRARY OF CONGRESS CATALOGING-IN-PUBLICATION DATA

Black American families, 1965-1984.

  (Bibliographies and indexes in Afro-American and
African studies, 0742-6925 ; no. 16)
  Includes index.
  1. Afro-American families—Bibliography.
I. Allen, Walter Recharde. II. English, Richard A.
(Richard Allyn) III. Hall, Jo Anne. IV. Series.
Z1361.N39B5 1986 [E185.86] 016.3068'08996073 86-14959
ISBN 0-313-25613-6 (U.S. : lib. bdg. : alk. paper)

Copyright © 1986 by Walter R. Allen

All rights reserved. No portion of this book may be
reproduced, by any process or technique, without the
express written consent of the publisher.

Library of Congress Catalog Card Number: 86-14959
ISBN: 0-313-25613-6
ISSN: 0742-6925

First published in 1986

Greenwood Press, Inc.
88 Post Road West, Westport, Connecticut 06881

Printed in the United States of America

The paper used in this book complies with the
Permanent Paper Standard issued by the National
Information Standards Organization (Z39.48-1984).

10 9 8 7 6 5 4 3 2 1

CONTENTS

TABLES

ACKNOWLEDGMENTS

        As is so often the case, this project has been valuably assisted
along the way by numerous individuals. Funding for research on another
project, the National Study of Black College Students, freed Walter
Allen's time and provided student research assistant resources as a by-
product to devote to the completion of this project. Without financial
assistance from the Ford and Mott Foundations, this project would not
have become a reality. We are grateful to Dr. Jo Anne Hall for her
magnificent work in organizing and directing the compilation and
indexing of source materials. A consummate professional, she was the
guiding light and spiritual resource throughout this process.   Thanks
also to Ahn Bui, Philip Cole, Ruby Gooley, Enos Grier, Arlene Mays, Paul
Newman, Aisha Ray, Jacqueline Smith, Tony West and Karen Wilson, for
their able assistance in the related tasks of identifying and retrieving
sources, photocopying materials, entering data into the system, typing
and filing. Special thanks to David Carlson and Jonathan Stern for
their work in designing this application of the Stanford Public Information Retrieval System (SPIRES) computer bibliographic system. Dr.
Blondell Strong assisted with the organization and compilation of source
materials. Bamidele Agbasegbe [Demerson] annotated 22 items, selected
and edited 239 abstracts, summaries and authors' texts, and conducted
library research. Garry Flemming supervised and coordinated student
assignments to the project while Vanessa Covington, Deborah Jones, and
Shalane Sheley typed related documents. Dr. Carlos Arce was instrumental in his suggestion of SPIRES as a reasonable way to accomplish
this task. Dr. Thomas Holt and Dr. Niara Sudarkasa, Center Directors,
were helpful for their willingness to lend support from the Center for
Afroamerican and African Studies to this task. Finally, a blanket
"thank you" to others too numerous to acknowledge. You know who you
are, what you contributed to this effort and how appreciative we feel
towards you.

INTRODUCTION

Currently no up-to-date, systematic summary of the published literature on Black American families is available. This work is intended to partially fill that void. It represents a partial response in that it is restricted, in this version, to the listing of works published between 1965 and 1984. The Bibliography is also restricted to works with a research orientation. Published research articles, books and book chapters, doctoral dissertations and master theses, government publications, and university publications, which address Black American families, are among the materials selected for inclusion. Coverage is interdisciplinary and extensive, encompassing the social sciences, the health sciences and the human service professions.

The explicit purpose of this work is to provide students of Black family life with a summary of the research record. Since 1965 there has been a virtual explosion of published literature on Black families. As is so often true during a proliferation of research on a topic, efforts to catalogue and codify findings have fallen behind the production of information. To be sure, there have been several excellent reviews of this literature published, each helpful in its own way. Some of these reviews have been published as free-standing articles or chapters while others have appeared as special issues of research journals or as theoretical review sections in books about Black family life. In still other cases, the literature on Black families has been reviewed or indexed as a subcomponent of a larger effort to examine or organize the general literature on families or children.

However, these various approaches to the codification of published research on Black families have only been partially satisfactory. Students of Black family life are still confronted by a terrain that is largely unmapped in regard to what is known about Black families. How are these families organized? How do they set their goals? How do they direct the activities of their members? These and a host of related questions persist. In a book to be published later, Beyond Pathology:

Research and Theory on Black Families, we hope to present answers to
many of these questions. In this work we are content, for the moment,
to organize the published sources into an accessible typology useful to
researchers working in the area.

We were convinced that research on Black families was impaired by
the absence of a large-scale, systematic, bibliographic effort. Often
researchers working on the same topics, or who have reported similar
findings, were not aware of one another. By the same token, students
and researchers new to the study of Black families were hard pressed to
locate reliable, comprehensive bibliographic sources from which to in
produce preliminary source lists. The sum total of these shortcomings
was to retard progress in an important area of research. Research on
Black families was hampered by the lack of a cumulative thrust, for such
a thrust can only emerge and be sustained where there is systematic
cataloguing and codification of findings. We see this work, and its
subsequent updates, as an important first step in this direction.

Background and History of Project

Walter Allen first developed an interest in the Black family
during his years as a graduate student at the University of Chicago.
This project had its genesis for Allen in a class entitled "Seminar on
Marriage and Family Research," taught by Dr. Reuben Hill. In line with
the course's emphasis, he undertook a review and codification of the
published literature. A much matured version of the resultant paper was
later published as a review/synopsis article in the Journal of Comparative Family Studies. More importantly, this experience illustrated to
Allen the necessity for systematic indexing of published literature if
an area is to solidify its gains and move forward to accumulate further
knowledge.

The University of Minnesota Family Research Inventory Project and
Dr. Robert Staples' annual Listing of Published Works on Black Families
provided important organizational models for the present work. The
former effort has grown into a large-scale operation which annually
publishes the Inventory of Marriage and Family Literature.1   To date,
[1]Volume I and Volume II, entitled International Bibliography of Research
in Marriage and the Family, were published by the University of Minnesota Press in 1967 and 1974 respectively. Volume I editors were Joan
Aldous and Reuben Hill and covered literature from 1900-1964. Volume II
editors were Joan Aldous and Nancy Dahl. Starting with Volume III,
there was a title change to Inventory of Marriage and Family Literature,
published by University of Minnesota, Department of Family Social
Science. Volumes III and IV (covering 1973-1974 and 1975-1976) were
edited by David H. Olson and Nancy Dahl. David H. Olson edited Volumes
V-VII, covering literature from 1977-1978, 1979, and 1980. Starting
with Volume V, the annual inventory was published by Sage Publications.
Volumes VIII-XI were edited by David H. Olson and Roxanne Markoff, and

this project has inventoried the published literature on family research from 1900 through 1984. The _Inventory_ with its author, subject, and keyword in title indexes provided the model for the current listing of published material on Black family life used in this text. Dr. Staples' much more modest effort (which continues today) provided further support for the idea and impetus for this work. His simple, alphabetical listing of published works on Black families proved to be an invaluable aid for teaching and research. In two articles published by the _Journal of Marriage and the Family_ (see entry numbers 1003 and 1005 in this Bibliography), Staples offered critical, integrative assessments of the Black family research literature from the decades 1960-1969 and 1970-1979. Together these articles provided invaluable assistance to a generation of students and researchers interested in the systematic study of Black family life. It is hoped that a wider audience will benefit from the availability of this bibliography on Black family research.

The idea of this bibliography of published research on Black families became a reality due to the work of Walter Allen and Richard English on a book in progress, titled _Beyond Pathology: Research and Theory on Black Families, 1965-1980._ The book is being written as a "state of the art" assessment. The study of Black family life has reached a vital crossroads. At this point in time, the study of Black family has reached a stage in development which would be greatly assisted by the creation of a volume which critically reviewed findings to date, organized these into a systematic typology, and outlined an agenda for future research. In the process of systematically reviewing the published literature and compiling source materials for the book, _Beyond Pathology,_ Allen and English naturally arrived at the decision to produce this Bibliography as a companion piece.

Online bibliographic searches in _Psychological Abstracts, Sociological Abstracts_ and the _Educational Resources Information Center (ERIC)_ system were conducted. Subject bibliographies, the Staples listings, the National Council on Family Resources Inventories and sources from the editors' private collections were consulted. Publications were collected, cataloged and the data entered onto a database management system. The work was examined again during the annotation selection stage. Where available, the author's abstract, summary or part of the text was edited and is so noted for 239 entries. Notes cited in the _National Union Catalog_ were used if a book was unavailable at the time of processing. Fifty original annotations were provided by one contributor and one editor, bringing the total of annotations to 289 entries.

The criteria used in selecting titles for annotation included: 1) significance of the work to the field based on how widely cited in the literature; 2) diversity of the subject matter regarding whether the covered literature from 1981-1984. Hereafter referred to as _Inventory_ or _Inventories_.

work demonstrated the variety of subjects (breadth of the field), and perspectives and methods that enrich or explain the various debates on the topic; and 3) reputation of the author(s). Items selected for annotating were to include established and widely recognized scholars as well as younger scholars involved in creative work.

Coverage of the Bibliography

This Bibliography of literature focuses primarily on Black American families within the United States. Several comparative studies concerning Black families in the Caribbean, Africa and the United States also appear. Coverage of the literature by publication type includes articles, books, essays in collected works, edited works, U.S. government documents and university publications/reports. The intended audience for this Bibliography includes undergraduates, research scholars, university faculty and any others interested in published research on Black family life.

The Bibliography is selective by nature and therefore by no means exhaustive. Articles cited in journals of a general or more popular nature were excluded. The Bibliography is restricted to works in English, though not restricted to United States or British publications. Included are works published between 1965 and 1984, although three articles and two books (published 1963-1964 and 1985 respectively) are included based on their diversity of subject matter and the termination date of this project for source collection and database entry. A list of the periodicals with publishers' names is included to suggest the interdisciplinary emphasis of source selection. (See page xxiii.)

Section 1 presents 1,153 citations, consecutively numbered and arranged alphabetically by author. Following the bibliographic citation, broad topic categories and specific subject headings are listed. Topic and subject assignments were based on the content of the work. An average of two topic/subject headings were assigned to each citation. The table of Contents outlines the topic categories and subject headings.

In Section 2, the works are organized by twelve broad topic categories and 120 subject headings. Within a subject heading listing, works are arranged numerically by entry number. Author(s) and title also are given. The complete bibliographic citation and related topic/subject headings are accessible in Section 1 by using the entry number.

Section 3 is a key word index with 924 words from the titles. Titles are listed numerically by entry number. Word plurals or derivations are shown with the word root. Word omissions include prepositions, conjunctions, selected adverbs and adjectives, and the words "Black," "United States," and "White." Names are included only if the title reflects a critique of a named theory or methodology, or if the work discusses a named family. See also references are provided for some words to indicate related terms or concepts.

In the last section, the names of 605 co-authors or co-editors are listed alphabetically. Entry numbers reflect co-authored publications only. The Bibliography section should be consulted to locate any single-authored publications by an individual or any publications authored by an organization, government body or university department.

Overview of the Literature

Works cited in the Bibliography include articles that appear in 175 journals, books (including edited volumes), doctoral dissertations and masters theses, U.S. government documents, and university publications. Journal articles had the largest number of citations, based on publication type; books and then dissertations/theses had the next highest number of citations. (See Table 1.) Almost 40 percent of the 612 articles were found in eleven journals. The National Council on Family Relations (NCFR) publication, Journal of Marriage and the Family was found to publish the most articles on the Black family. (See Table 2.)

Single or multiple authorship for the 1,153 publications is credited to 1,547 authors. (See Table 3.) Seven organizations (including university units and government departments) are listed as main authors. Three publications are cited without authors. Only one publication has over five authors. Almost three-fourths of the publications are written by single authors.

TABLE 1: NUMBER OF ENTRIES BY PUBLICATION TYPE

	Number	Percentage
Journal articles	612	54
Books	272	24
Dissertations/theses	174	15
Essays/book chapters	81	7
Government documents	11	1
University publications	3	3
Total	1,153	100

TABLE 2:   JOURNALS WITH ELEVEN OR MORE ARTICLES

		Number of Articles	Percentage[a]
1.	Journal of Marriage and the Family	85	13.9
2.	Phylon	23	3.8
3.	Family Coordinator	18	2.9
4.	Journal of Afro-American Issues	18	2.9
5.	Social Problems	16	2.6
6.	Western Journal of Black Studies	16	2.6
7.	Black Scholars	14	2.3
8.	Journal of Comparative Family Studies	14	2.3
9.	Journal of Negro Education	14	2.3
10.	Social Work	12	2.0
11.	Alternative Lifestyles	11	1.8
	Total	241	39.4

[a]Percentage of articles in each journal based on the total number of journal articles (n = 612).

TABLE 3:   NUMBER OF SINGLE-MULTIPLE-AUTHORED PUBLICATIONS

	Number of Publications	Percentage of Single and Multiple Authors[*]	Number of Authors[**]
Single	849	73.5	846
Two	224	19.4	448
Three	54	4.7	162
Four	15	1.3	60
Five or More	4	.3	21[***]
Anonymous and corporate authors	10	1.0	10
Total	1,153	100.0	1,547

[*] Percentage is rounded to the nearest percent to sum 100 percent.
[**] Authors may be counted in more than one category of publications.
[***] One publication had six authors and three publications had five authors.

A total of 1,206 named individuals are listed as authors. Over 86 percent of the authors listed have only one publication and over 13

percent are cited for two or more items. (See Table 4.) The large
majority of publications listed in this Bibliography, therefore, are
written by one author and each named writer has at least one publication
listed.

TABLE 4: NUMBER OF PUBLICATIONS BY NAMED AUTHORS

	Number of Authors	Percentage
1	1,041	86.4
2	97	8.0
3	35	2.9
4	15	1.3
5	9	.7
6-32	8	.7
Total	1,206	100.0

General Topic and Specific Subject Heading Trends

Broad topic categories and specific subject headings were
assigned to each work. The original classification scheme was developed
by the National Council on Family Resources (NCFR). For some topics,
subject headings were modified, deleted or added to effectively capture
the subject concentration of this publication. The NCFR classifications
were chosen based on their usage with the NCFR Family Resources Database, and to allow for user consistency across database management
systems related to family literature and family subject categories.

Table 5 is a listing of broad topic categories and the proportion
of entries per category. In addition, it shows the proportion of
article references that were listed in ten volumes of the Inventory.

The most often selected category, Family Relationships and Dynamics, accounted for over 28 percent of the references. Together with the
categories Trends and Change in Marriage and Family and Organizations
and Services to Families (12.6 percent each), these three categories
accounted for over 53 percent of all listings. (See Table 5.) According
to Olson and Markoff, at least 41 percent of the journal articles listed
in ten Inventories had been on topics indexed under Family Relationships
and Dynamics and/or Organizations and Services to Families.[2] The trend

---

[2]David H. Olson and Roxanne Markoff, "Introduction to Inventory of
Marriage and Family Literature," Inventory of Marriage and Family
Research, Volume X: 1983. Beverly Hills, CA: Sage Publications, 1984,
p. 13.

does not appear to vary much when the literature is focused on a specific family group such as the Black family. These same categories together accounted for about 41 percent of all references selected for this Bibliography.

The following four general categories accounted for almost 31 percent of the Black family literature: Aids for Theory and Research, Families with Special Problems, Family Counseling and Education, and Psychology and Sociology. The category Aids for Theory and Research gained in percentage of citations when compared to the history of the ten Inventories. (See Table 5.) The specific reason for gain may be attributed to the inclusion in this Bibliography of doctoral research and bibliographies in book format. Another reason for percentage gain may be the increased number of critiques and analyses on family theory and research methodology that focus on the Black family or that compare the Black family to other family groups.

TABLE 5: PROPORTIONS OF CITATIONS ASSIGNED TO TOPIC CATEGORIES

Subject Categories	Black Family Literature (1965-1984)		NCFR Inventory of Marriage and Family (1965-1983)	
	n	Percentage	n	Percentage
I. Trends and Change in Marriage and Family	294	12.6	4,751	9.4
II. Organizations and Services to Families	294	12.6	9,299	18.5
III. Family Relationships and Dynamics	661	28.3	1,837	23.5
IV. Mate Selection	38	1.6	680	1.4
V. Marriage and Divorce	94	4.0	2,426	4.8
VI. Issues Related to Reproduction	97	4.2	3,990	7.9
VII. Sexual Attitudes and Behavior	51	2.2	2,235	4.4
VIII. Families with Special Problems	153	6.6	7,022	14.1
IX. Psychology and Sociology	141	6.1	--	--
X. Family Counseling and Education	153	6.6	4,439	8.8
XI. Minority Groups	88	3.8	1,220	2.4
XII. Aids for Theory and Research	265	11.4	2,418	4.8
Total	2,329	100.0	50,317	100.0

The most frequently used key words used by authors when titling their works, is presented as an additional estimate of subjects covered in Black family literature. The assumption is made that authors attempt to include relevant concepts in the titles of publications. Table 6 is a listing of key words with thirty or more citations excluding terms such as "America", "Black", "White" or "United States".

The two words that appear in the Key Word Index most frequently are children (101 times) and women (94 times). Combined with the root word child, the concept children is used in 136 citations. The concept women is used in 124 citations when the words woman (30 times) and women (94 times) are combined. The four remaining concepts that are listed more than 50 times in the titles of publications are sex (64), race (54), marriage (53), and community (51).

Adding related concepts to the most frequently used terms, one finds three times the number of citations appear that relate to children (164) as to adolescents (30). There are more than twice the number of citations on female-oriented concepts (232) listed as there are citations on male-oriented concepts (101). Other related subject issues with over 50 citations include social issues (132), sex (103), class (91), education (82), urbanism (79), marriage (65), and community[ies] (51). (See Table 7.)

TABLE 6: KEY WORDS IN TITLES WITH OVER THIRTY CITATIONS

1.	Child, children	136
2.	Woman, women	124
3.	Sex, sexual, sexuality	64
4.	Race	54
5.	Marriage(s), married	53
6.	Community, communities	51
7.	Urban (ites, ism)	45
8.	Adolescence, adolescent(s)	41
9.	Mother(s)	41
10.	Male(s)	40
11.	Female(s)	39
12.	Attitude(s)	38
13.	Pattern(s)	32
14.	Relationship(s)	32
15.	Low(er) income	31

TABLE 7:   RELATED KEY WORDS COLLAPSED AS CONCEPTS

Female/Women   232

Female(s), female-head(ed, s), feminism(-ists), mother(s), mother-
(child, concept, headed, infant, led, son), motherhood, mothering,
woman, woman-lady, woman-to-woman, womanhood, women.

Children   164

Child, child care, childbirth, childhood, childrearing, childlessness,
children.

Social   132

Social, social and economic, social change, social class, social
ecological, social economic status, social movement, social psychology
(-ical), social science, social security, social work(-ers), socialization, socially, society(-ies), sociobehavioral, sociocultural,
socioeconomic, sociology(-ical).

Sex   103

Sex, sex differences, sex education, sex ratio, sex roles(s), sex typed,
sexism, sexist, sexual(ity, ly).

Male   101

Father(s), father absence (absent), father child, father identification,
father loss, father present, father role, father son, macho, male(s),
male dominated, man, manhood, masculine(-ity), men.

Class   91

Class, class differences, lower class, low(er) income, low(er) socioeconomic, middle class, social and economic, socioeconomic status,
upward(ly) mobile(-ity), working class.

Education   82

Academic(ally), college(s), college students, education(al), educators,
elementary schools, preschool(ers), school(s), scholastic, school(s),
school achievement, school performance, teacher(s), teaching, tenth
grade student.

Urbanism   79

City(-ies), ghetto(s), inner city, slum, urban(ism, ites).

TABLE 7: --Continued

LIST OF PERIODICALS

ADOLESCENCE Libra Publishers, Inc., Roslyn Heights, NY

ALTERNATIVE LIFESTYLES Human Sciences Press, New York, NY

AMERICAN ANTHROPOLOGIST American Anthropological Association,
Washington, DC

AMERICAN BEHAVIORAL SCIENTIST Sage Publications, Inc.,
Beverly Hills, CA

AMERICAN ETHNOLOGIST American Ethnological Society, Washington, DC

AMERICAN HISTORICAL REVIEW American Historical Association,
Washington, DC

AMERICAN JOURNAL OF COMMUNITY PSYCHOLOGY Plenum Press, New York, NY

AMERICAN JOURNAL OF MENTAL DEFICIENCY Boyd Printing Company, Albany, NY

AMERICAN JOURNAL OF ORTHOPSYCHIATRY American Orthopsychiatric
Association

AMERICAN JOURNAL OF PHYSICAL ANTHROPOLOGY Alan R. Liss, Inc.,
New York, NY

AMERICAN JOURNAL OF POLITICAL SCIENCE University of Texas Press,
Austin, TX

AMERICAN JOURNAL OF PSYCHIATRY American Public Health Association,
Washington, DC

AMERICAN JOURNAL OF PUBLIC HEALTH American Public Health Association,
Washington, DC

AMERICAN JOURNAL OF SOCIOLOGY University of Chicago Press, Chicago, IL

AMERICAN PSYCHOLOGIST American Psychological Association,
Washington, DC

AMERICAN SOCIOLOGICAL REVIEW American Sociological Association,
Washington, DC

AMERICAN SOCIOLOGIST American Sociological Association, Albany, NY

ANNALS OF THE AMERICAN ACADEMY OF POLITICAL AND SOCIAL SCIENCE Sage
Publications, Inc., Beverly Hills, CA

ARMED FORCES AND SOCIETY Sage Publications, Inc., Beverly Hills, CA

BEHAVIOR SCIENCE RESEARCH Human Services Press, New York, NY

BERKELY JOURNAL OF SOCIOLOGY Graduate Student Union, Dept. of
Sociology, University of California, Berkeley, Berkeley, CA

BLACKS BOOKS BULLETIN Institute of Positive Education, Chicago, IL

BLACK CHILD JOURNAL: A REVIEW OF BLACK CHILD DEVELOPMENT Black Child
Journal, Chicago, IL

BLACK MALE/FEMALE RELATIONSHIPS Black Think Tank, San Francisco, CA

BLACK SCHOLAR Black World Foundation, San Francisco, CA

BLACK WORLD Johnson Publishing Company, Chicago, IL

BULLETIN OF THE PSYCHONOMIC SOCIETY Psychonomic Society, Austin, TX

CHILD AND FAMILY National Commission on Human Life, Reproduction and
Rhythm, Oak Park, IL

CHILD DEVELOPMENT University of Chicago Press, Chicago, IL

CHILD PSYCHIATRY AND HUMAN DEVELOPMENT Human Services Press,
New York, NY

CHILD STUDY JOURNAL State University of New York, College at Buffalo,
Buffalo, NY

CHILD WELFARE Child Welfare League of America, New York, NY

COMMON MARKET LAW REVIEW Sijthoff and Noordhoff International
Publishers, Germantown, MD

CRIMINOLOGY Sage Publications, Inc., Beverly Hills, CA

CRISIS Crisis Publishing Company, Inc., New York, NY

CRJ REPORTER (COMMISSION FOR RACIAL JUSTICE REPORTER) United Church of Christ, Commission for Racial Justice, New York, NY

CURRENT Heldref Publications, Washington, DC

DAEDALUS American Academy of Arts and Sciences, Cambridge, MA

DEMOGRAPHY Population Association of America, Washington, DC

DEVELOPMENTAL PSYCHOLOGY American Psychological Association, Washington, DC

ECONOMIC INQUIRY California State University, Department of Economics, Long Beach, CA

ETHNIC GROUPS Gordon and Breach Science Publishers, Ltd., New York, NY

ETHNICITY Academic Press, Inc., New York, NY

ETHOS Victorian Association of Social Studies Teachers, Balaclava, Victoria, Australia

FAMILY COORDINATOR National Council of Family Relations, Minneapolis, MN

FAMILY PLANNING PERPSECTIVES Alan Guttmacher Institute, New York, NY

FAMILY RELATIONS National Council of Family Relations, Minneapolis, MN

FEMINIST STUDIES

FREEDOMWAYS Freedomways Associates, New York, NY

GERONTOLOGIST Gerontological Society, Washington, DC

HISTORY OF RELIGIONS University of Chicago Press, Chicago, IL

HOWARD LAW JOURNAL Howard University, School of Law, Washington, DC

HUMAN BIOLOGY Wayne State University Press, Detroit, MI

HUMAN LIFE REVIEW Human Life Foundations, Inc., New York, NY

HUMAN ORGANIZATION Society for Applied Anthropology, Washington, DC

INTEGRATED EDUCATION Integrated Education Associates, University of Massachusetts, School of Education, Amherst, MA

INTERNATIONAL JOURNAL OF INTERCULTURAL RELATIONS Pergamon Press, Inc., Elmsford, NY

INTERNATIONAL JOURNAL OF OFFENDER THERAPY AND COMPARATIVE CRIMINOLOGY Association for the Professional Treatment of Offenders, London, England

INTERNATIONAL JOURNAL OF SOCIAL PSYCHIATRY Avenue Publishing Company, London, England

INTERNATIONAL JOURNAL OF SOCIOLOGY OF THE FAMILY Vikas Publishing House, Pvt., Ltd., Ghazlabad, India

JOURNAL OF AFRO-AMERICAN ISSUES Educational and Community Counselors Associates Publications, Washington, DC

JOURNAL OF BIOSOCIAL SCIENCE Galton Foundation, Cambridge, England

JOURNAL OF BLACK PSYCHOLOGY University of Cincinnati, Cincinnati, Ohio

JOURNAL OF BLACK STUDIES Sage Publications, Inc., Beverly Hills, CA

JOURNAL OF BROADCASTING Broadcast Education Association, Washington, DC

JOURNAL OF CHILD PSYCHOLOGY AND PSYCHIATRY Pergamon Press, Inc., Elmsford, NY

JOURNAL OF CLINICAL PSYCHOLOGY Clinical Psychology Publishing Company, Inc., Brandon, VT

JOURNAL OF CONSULTING AND CLINICAL PSYCHOLOGY American Psychological Association, Washington, DC

JOURNAL OF CONTEMPORARY PSYCHOTHERAPY

JOURNAL OF COUNSELING PSYCHOLOGY American Psychological Association, Washington, DC

JOURNAL OF CROSS-CULTURAL PSYCHOLOGY Sage Publications, Inc., Beverly Hills, CA

JOURNAL OF ETHNIC STUDIES Western Washington University, Bellingham, WA

JOURNAL OF FAMILY HISTORY National Council of Family Relations, Minneapolis, MN

JOURNAL OF FAMILY WELFARE Family Planning Association of India, Bombay, India

JOURNAL OF GENETIC PSYCHOLOGY Journal Press, Provincetown, MA

JOURNAL OF HEALTH AND SOCIAL BEHAVIOR American Sociological
Association, Washington, DC

JOURNAL OF HUMAN RELATIONS Central State University, Wilberforce, OH

JOURNAL OF HUMAN RESOURCES University of Wisconsin Press, Madison, WI

JOURNAL OF INTERDISCIPLINARY HISTORY MIT Press, Cambridge, MA

JOURNAL OF MARKETING RESEARCH American Marketing Association,
Chicago, IL

JOURNAL OF MARRIAGE AND FAMILY COUNSELING American Association for
Marriage and Family Therapy, Upland, CA

JOURNAL OF MARRIAGE AND THE FAMILY National Council of Family
Relations, Minneapolis, MN

JOURNAL OF MINORITY AGING (FORMERLY CALLED BLACK AGING) National
Council on Black Aging, Inc., Durham, NC

JOURNAL OF NEGRO EDUCATION Howard University Press, Washington, DC

JOURNAL OF NEGRO HISTORY Association for the Study of Afro-American
Life and History, Inc., Washington, DC

JOURNAL OF NONWHITE CONCERNS IN PERSONNEL AND GUIDANCE American
Personnel and Guidance Association, Falls Church, VA

JOURNAL OF PERSONALITY AND SOCIAL PSYCHOLOGY American Psychological
Association, Washington, DC

JOURNAL OF POLITICS University of Florida, Department of Political
Science, Gainesville, FL

JOURNAL OF PSYCHOLOGY Journal Press, Provincetown, MA

JOURNAL OF RESEARCH IN CRIME AND DELINQUENCY National Council on Crime
and Delinquency, Hackensack, NJ

JOURNAL OF SEX RESEARCH Society for the Scientific Study, of Sex,
Philadelphia, PA

JOURNAL OF SOCIAL AND BEHAVIOR SCIENCES Association of Social Behavior
Scientists, Orangeburg, SC

JOURNAL OF SOCIAL HISTORY Carnegie-Mellon University Press,
Pittsburgh, PA

JOURNAL OF SOCIAL ISSUES Society for the Psychological Study of Social

Issues, Ann Arbor, MI

JOURNAL OF SOCIAL PSYCHOLOGY   Journal Press, Provincetown, MA

JOURNAL OF SOCIOLOGY AND SOCIAL WELFARE   Journal of Social Welfare
Incorporated, West Hartford, CT

JOURNAL OF SOUTHERN HISTORY   Southern Historical Association, University
of Georgia, Athens, GA

JOURNAL OF THE AMERICAN DIETETIC ASSOCIATION   American Dietetic
Association, Chicago, IL

JOURNAL OF THE NATIONAL MEDICAL ASSOCIATION   Appleton-Century-Crofts,
Norwalk, CT

JOURNAL OF TROPICAL PEDIATRICS AND ENVIRONMENTAL CHILD HEALTH   Oxford
University Press, Oxford, England

JOURNAL OF URBAN ECONOMICS   Academic Press, Inc., New York, NY

JOURNAL OF VOCATIONAL BEHAVIOR   Academic Press, Inc., New York, NY

JOURNAL OF YOUTH AND ADOLESCENCE   Plenum Press, New York, NY

JOURNALISM QUARTERLY   Association for Education in Journalism,
Columbia, SC

LAW AND CONTEMPORARY PROBLEMS   Duke University Press, Durham, NC

MICHIGAN DISCUSSIONS IN ANTHROPOLOGY   University of Michigan, Department
of Anthropology, Ann Arbor, MI

MILBANK MEMORIAL FUND QUARTERLY   Milbank Memorial Fund, New York, NY

NEGRO EDUCATIONAL REVIEW   Negro Educational Review, Inc.,
Jacksonville, FL

NEW SOCIETY   IPC Magazines, Ltd., London, England

NEW SOUTH   Southern Regional Council, Atlanta, GA

NURSE PRACTITIONER   Vernon Publications, Inc., Seattle, WA

OLD-TIME NEW ENGLAND   Society for the Preservation of New England
Antiquities, Boston, MA

PACIFIC SOCIOLOGICAL REVIEW   Sage Publications, Inc., Beverly Hills, CA

PERCEPTUAL AND MOTOR SKILLS   Dr. C. H. Ammons and Dr. R. B. Ammons,

Missoula, MT

PHYLON Atlanta University, Atlanta, GA

POLICY ANALYSIS John Wiley and Sons, Inc., New York, NY

POLITICS AND SOCIETY Geron-x, Inc. Publishers, Los Altos, CA

POPULATION STUDIES Johnson Reprint Corporation, New York, NY

PSYCHIATRIC ANNALS Charles B. Slack, Inc., Thorofare, NJ

PSYCHIATRY William Alanson White Psychiatric Foundation, Inc.,
  Washington, DC

PSYCHOLOGICAL REPORTS University of Montana, Box 9229, Missoula, Mt

PSYCHOLOGICAL STUDIES M.A. Faroqi, University of Calicut, Calicut,
  India

PSYCHOLOGY IN THE SCHOOLS Clinical Psychology Publishing Company, Inc.,
  Brandon, VT

PSYCHOLOGY OF WOMEN QUARTERLY Human Services Press, New York, NY

PSYCHOTHERAPY: THEORY, RESEARCH, AND PRACTICE American Psychological
  Association, Division of Psychotherapy, Los Angeles, CA

PUBLIC HEALTH REPORTS Public Health Service, Hyattsville, MD

PUBLIC INTEREST National Affairs, Inc., New York, NY

PUBLIC OPINION QUARTERLY Elsevier Science Publishing Company, Inc.,
  New York, NY

RACE AND CLASS Oxford University Press, London, England

RACE: THE JOURNAL OF THE INSTITUTE OF RACE RELATIONS (Name changed to
  RACE AND CLASS) Oxford University Press, London, England

RESEARCH PREVIEWS North Carolina University, Institute for Research in
  Social Science, Chapel Hill, NC

RQ: REFERENCE QUARTERLY American Library Association, Chicago, IL

RURAL SOCIOLOGY Rural Sociological Society, Knoxville, TN

SCIENCE American Association for the Advancement of Science,
  Washington, DC

SCIENCE NEWS Science Service, Inc., Washington, DC

SEX ROLES: A JOURNAL OF RESEARCH Plenum Press, New York, NY

SEXUAL BEHAVIOR

SIGNS: JOURNAL OF WOMEN IN CULTURE AND SOCIETY University of Chicago
   Press, Chicago, IL

SOCIAL BIOLOGY Society for the Study of Social Biology, Madison, WI

SOCIAL CASEWORK: THE JOURNAL OF CONTEMPORARY SOCIAL WORK Family
   Service Association of America, New York, NY

SOCIAL EDUCATION National Council for the Social Studies,
   Washington, DC

SOCIAL FORCES University of North Carolina Press, Chapel Hill, NC

SOCIAL POLICY Social Policy Corporation, New York, NY

SOCIAL POLICY AND ADMINISTRATION (Formerly titled SOCIAL AND ECONOMIC
   ADMINISTRATION) Basil Blackwell Publishers, Oxford, England

SOCIAL PROBLEMS Society for the Study of Social Problems, Buffalo, NY

SOCIAL SCIENCE AND MEDICINE Pergamon Press, Inc., Elmsford, NY

SOCIAL SCIENCE HISTORY Sage Publications, Inc., Beverly Hills, CA

SOCIAL SCIENCE QUARTERLY University of Texas Press, Austin, TX

SOCIAL SCIENCE RESEARCH Academic Press, Inc., New York, NY

SOCIAL SCIENCE REVIEW

SOCIAL SERVICE REVIEW University of Chicago Press, Chicago, IL

SOCIAL WORK National Association of Social Workers, New York, NY

SOCIETY (Formerly called SOCIAL SCIENCE AND MODERN SOCIETY) Transaction
   Periodicals Consortium, Rutgers University, New Brunswick, NJ

SOCIOLOGICAL FOCUS University of Cincinnati, Department of Sociology,
   Cincinnati, OH

SOCIOLOGICAL QUARTERLY Southern Illinois University, Department of
   Sociology, Carbondale, IL

SOCIOLOGICAL SYMPOSIUM (Name changed to SOCIOLOGICAL SPECTRUM)

Hemisphere Publishing Corporation, Washington, DC

SOCIOLOGY AND SOCIAL RESEARCH University of Southern California, Los Angeles, CA

SOCIOMETRY American Sociological Association, Washington, DC

STUDIES IN PUBLIC WELFARE American Public Welfare Association, Washington, DC

THE NUTRITION SOCIETY PROCEEDINGS Cambridge University Press, Cambridge, England; New York, NY

THE REVIEW OF BLACK POLITICAL ECONOMY Transaction Periodicals Consortium, Rutgers University, New Brunswick, NJ

THE URBAN AND SOCIAL CHANGE REVIEW   Boston College, Graduate Study of Social Work, Chestnut Hill, MA

THE WESTERN JOURNAL OF BLACK STUDIES Washington State University Press, Pullman, WA

TRANSACTION Transactions, Inc., Philadelphia, PA

UNIVERSITY OF NORTH CAROLINA NEWSLETTER University of North Carolina at Chapel Hill, Institute for Research in Social Science, Chapel Hill, NC

URBAN AFFAIRS QUARTERLY Sage Publications, Inc., Beverly Hills, NC

URBAN ANTHROPOLOGY Plenum Press, New York, NY

URBAN EDUCATION Sage Publications, Inc., Beverly Hills, CA

URBAN LEAGUE REVIEW Transaction Periodicals Consortium, Rutgers University, New Brunswick, NJ

URBAN RESEARCH REVIEW Howard University, Institute for Urban Affairs and Research, Washington, DC

VOCATIONAL GUIDANCE QUARTERLY American Personnel and Guidance Association, Falls Church, VA

YOUNG CHILDREN National Association for the Education of Young Children, Washington, DC

YOUTH AND SOCIETY Sage Publications, Inc., Beverly Hills, CA

BIBLIOGRAPHY

1 Abramson, Paul R. and Abramson, Seth D. "A Factorial Study of a Multidimensional Approach to Aggressive Behavior in Black Preschool Age Children." JOURNAL OF GENETIC PSYCHOLOGY 125, 1st Half (September 1974): 31-36. 6 pp., references.

Subjects: 1. Family Counseling and Education / Early Childhood Education; 2. Aids for Theory and Research / Statistics.

The Multidimensional Aggression Scale containing 34 variables of aggression, categorized along the dimension of intensity, agent, and directionality, was used to score the doll play responses of 123 black preschool age children. The 34 variables were factor-analyzed by Varimax rotation. Six factors were extracted on the basis of the amount of total variance contributed by each factor and the number of loadings exceeding .50. To assist in verbal reference, these factors were labelled as follows: Factor 1, Violent Aggression Toward the Family; Factor 2, Violent Aggression by the Family; Factor 3, Aggression by the Self; Factor 4, Aggression Directed Toward the Self; Factor 5, Assertion Directed Toward Others; and Factor 6, Assertion Directed Toward the Family. The data supported the authors' contention that aggression can be conceptualized along several dimensions. (Authors' summary)

2 Absuz, Robert H. "The Black Family During Reconstruction." In KEY ISSUES IN THE AFRO-AMERICAN EXPERIENCE. VOL 2: SINCE 1865, edited by Nathan Irvin Huggins, Martin Kilson and Daniel M. Fox, pp. 26-39. New York: Harcourt, Brace and Jovanovich, Inc., 1971. 14 pp.

Subjects: 1. Trends and Change in Marriage and Family / Family Life Prior to 1900.

3 Adams, Cora Marie Gaines. "The Black Family: Implications for Social Work Education and Practice." (D.S.W. dissertation, The University of Utah, 1977.) DISSERTATION ABSTRACTS INTERNATIONAL, 38, 10, April 1978, 6320A. (University Microfilms No. 7803862.) 237 pp.

Subjects: 1. Organizations and Services to Families / Social Work; 2. Family Relationships and Dynamics / Family Relationships; 3. Family Counseling and Education / Family Life Education.

4 Adams, Harold. "The Collective Black Family: Barriers to Community
Mental Health Services." (Ph.D. dissertation, The University of Utah,
1979.) DISSERTATION ABSTRACTS INTERNATIONAL, 40, 5, Nov. 1979, 2347B.
(University Microfilms No. 7924341.) 122 pp.

Subjects: 1. Organizations and Services to Families / Mental Health and
   the Family; 2. Psychology and Sociology / Psychology.

5 Addison, Donald P. BLACK FAMILIES: A COMPREHENSIVE BIBLIOGRAPHY.
Washington, DC: Howard University. Department of Sociology/Anthropology,
August 1979. 111 pp.

Subjects: 1. Trends and Change in Marriage and Family / Family Life in
   the United States; 2. Aids for Theory and Research / Classified
   Bibliographies of Family Literature.

   A listing, by author, of articles, books and essays on the Black
   family topic.

6 Agbasegbe, Bamidele Ade. "The Role of Wife in the Black Extended
Family: Perspectives from a Rural Community in the Southern United
States." In NEW RESEARCH ON WOMEN AND SEX ROLES AT THE
UNIVERSITY OF MICHIGAN: PAPERS, edited by Dorothy G. McGuigan, pp. 124-
138. Ann Arbor, MI: University of Michigan, Center for Continuing
Education of Women, 1976. 15 pp.

Subjects: 1. Trends and Change in Marriage and Family / Family Life in
   the United States; 2. Family Relationships and Dynamics / Extended
   Family and Kinship Groups; 3. / Family Roles and Sex Roles.

   This paper focuses on females in their affinal extended family
   compounds, and examines the stability of both the conjugal and
   consanguineal bonds in a rural community of the South Carolina Sea
   Islands.

7 Agbasegbe, Bamidele Ade. "Social Change and Extended Family in the
Black World: A Report on Research in Progress." MICHIGAN DISCUSSIONS IN
ANTHROPOLOGY 2, (Fall 1976): 46-54. 9 pp., bibliography.

Subjects: 1. Trends and Change in Marriage and Family / Family and
   Social Change; 2. Family Relationships and Dynamics / Extended Family
   and Kinship Groups.

8 Agbasegbe, Bamidele Ade. "Woman-to-Woman Marriages in Africa and
Afroamerica." BLACK MALE/FEMALE RELATIONSHIPS 2, 5 (Spring 1981): 13-
18. 6 pp., references, bibliography.

Subjects: 1. Trends and Change in Marriage and Family / Comparative
   Studies--International, Interclass, Sex, and Time Differences; 2.
   Marriage and Divorce / Marriage Customs and Forms; 3. Sexual Attitudes
   and Behavior / Homosexuality and the Family.

9 Agresti, Barbara Finlay. "The First Decades of Freedom: Black
Families in a Southern County, 1870 and 1885." JOURNAL OF MARRIAGE AND
THE FAMILY 40, 4 (November 1978): 697-706. 10 pp., references.

Subjects: 1. Trends and Change in Marriage and Family / Family Life
   Prior to 1900.

Data on family residential patterns for blacks in a Southern farming
county in 1870 and 1885 are presented. The 1870 data shows high
percentages of black families in nonfamily or non-nuclear family
households, which lends support to traditional sociological beliefs.
In 1885, however, the two-parent family was the norm and there were no
important family structural differences between blacks and whites in
the county. The findings are related to other recent writings on black
family history, to changes in the social and economic environment, and
to the prevailing system of agriculture which, it is argued, affected
the relationship of blacks to whites and the structure of black
families. (Author's abstract)

10 Aguirre, B. E. and Parr, W. C. "Husbands' Marriage Order and the
Stability of First and Second Marriages of White and Black Women."
JOURNAL OF MARRIAGE AND THE FAMILY 44, 3 (August 1982): 605-620. 16
pp., tables.

Subjects: 1. Family Relationships and Dynamics / Husband-Wife
   Relationships; 2. Marriage and Divorce / Marriage Satisfaction and
   Prediction Studies.

The effect of previous history--particularly the husband's marriage
order--on the stability of first and second marriages of white and
black women is evaluated. Data for analysis are a subset of the
National Survey of Family Growth, a stratified probability sample of
9797 civilian noninstitutionalized women. Multiple linear regressions
relate a marital-stability scale to a set of independent variables.
The most important predictor of the instability of first marriages of
women are the previous divorces of husbands. In comparison, all other
predictors of marital instability are unimportant. The stability of
second marriages of women presents different patterns. Husband's
marriage order is not an important predictor of marital stability.
Instead, stability is positively associated with religious endogamy,
and it is affected by the fertility experiences of the respondents.
The probability of stability in remarriages of black respondents
increases if husbands lived on a farm between the ages of six and
sixteen. For white women the stability of their remarriages is
inversely associated with the number of unwanted pregnancies, it also
diminishes if the women did not work for pay before their first
marriage. The effects of wife's marriage order on the stability of
first marriages and remarriages of men is briefly considered. The
paper concludes with a consideration of implications of theses
findings for theories of marital stability. (Authors' abstract)

11 Albanese, Anthony Gerald. THE PLANTATION SCHOOL. 1st ed. New York:
Vantage Press, 1976. 285 pp., bibliography; ISBN:0-533-01686-X; LC:76-
369825.

Subjects: 1. Trends and Change in Marriage and Family / Family Life
   Prior to 1900; 2. Organizations and Services to Families / Education
   and the Family.

Notes: Bibliography: pp. 257-285

12 Albin, Mel and Cavallo, Dominick, eds. FAMILY LIFE IN AMERICA, 1620-2000. New York: Revisionary Press, 1981.; ISBN:0960372606.

Subjects: 1. Trends and Change in Marriage and Family / Family Life 1900 to Present.

13 Alden, Lynn, Rappaport, Julian and Seidman, Edward. "College Students as Interventionists for Primary-Grade Children: A Comparison of Structured Academic and Companionship Programs for Children from Low-Income Families." AMERICAN JOURNAL OF COMMUNITY PSYCHOLOGY 3, 3 (September 1975): 261-271. 11 pp., references, tables.

Subjects: 1. Family Counseling and Education / Child Development; 2. / Early Childhood Education.

14 Aldous, Joan. "Wives' Employment Status and Lower-Class Men as Husband-Fathers: Support for the Moynihan Thesis." JOURNAL OF MARRIAGE AND THE FAMILY 31, 3 (August 1969): 469-476. 8 pp., references, tables.

Subjects: 1. Organizations and Services to Families / Employment and the Family; 2. / Working Mothers; 3. Family Relationships and Dynamics / Husband-Wife Relationships.

15 Aldridge, Delores P. "The Changing Nature of Interracial Marriage in Georgia: A Research Note." JOURNAL OF MARRIAGE AND THE FAMILY 35, 4 (November 1973): 641-642. 2 pp., references, tables.

Subjects: 1. Trends and Change in Marriage and Family / Family Life in the United States; 2. Marriage and Divorce / Inter-marriage.

16 Aldridge, Delores P. "Interracial Marriages: Empirical and Theoretical Considerations." JOURNAL OF BLACK STUDIES 8, 3 (March 1978): 355-368. 14 pp., references.

Subjects: 1. Marriage and Divorce / Inter-marriage; 2. Aids for Theory and Research / Family Theory.

17 Aldridge, Delores P. "Problems and Approaches to Black Adoptions." FAMILY COORDINATOR 23, 4 (October 1974): 407-410. 4 pp., references.

Subjects: 1. Organizations and Services to Families / Adoption and Adoption Services.

Some familiar phrases are "Blacks don't adopt" and "Black children are unadoptable." This work attempts to show that the real problem is not with black children or potential black adoptive parents but with agencies in the field of adoptions. Social agencies have to devise new and different approaches for becoming more responsive to the needs of black children. Policies and practices of agenices have to be refocused combined with reorientation and training of staff in the ethos of black people. The economic investment in new approaches is vital. (Author's abstract)

18 Aldridge, Delores P. "Teaching about Black American Families." SOCIAL EDUCATION 41, 6 (October 1977): 484-487. 4 pp., references, illustrations.

Subjects: 1. Organizations and Services to Families / Education and the
   Family; 2. Family Counseling and Education / Family Life Education.

19 Aldridge, Delores P.   "Toward an Understanding of Black Male/Female
Relationships." THE WESTERN JOURNAL OF BLACK STUDIES 8, 4 (Winter
1984): 184-91. 8 pp., references.

Subjects: 1. Aids for Theory and Research / Critiques and Analyses of
   Family Research Literature.

20 Allen, Richard L. and Chaffee, Steven H.   "Racial Differences in
Family Communication Patterns." JOURNALISM QUARTERLY 54, 1 (Spring
1977): 8-13,57. 7 pp., references, tables.

Subjects: 1. Family Relationships and Dynamics / Family Relationships;
   2. / Communication in the Family.

21 Allen, Walter R. "Black Family Research in the United States: A
Review, Assessment and Extension." JOURNAL OF COMPARATIVE FAMILY
STUDIES 9, 2 (Summer 1978): 167-189. 23 pp., references.

Subjects: 1. Aids for Theory and Research / Family Research Methodology;
   2. / Critiques and Analyses of Family Research Literature.

This paper reviews, assesses and suggests extensions of the research
on black families in the United States. Noting that there are as many
different findings and interpretations in the literature as there are
researchers and black families, the author attempts to contribute
towards clarification of extensive disagreements over the nature of
black family life in this society. Within the context of this paper,
major theoretical and methodological perspectives are identified, a
brief historical outline of the area is presented and central studies
in six substantive areas are reviewed. At its conclusion, the paper
suggests several strategies for systematizing research on black
families and proposes a list of salient issues in black family life
requiring further empirical investigation. (Author's abstract)

22 Allen, Walter R. "Class, Culture, and Family Organization: The
Effects of Class and Race on Family Structure in Urban America."
JOURNAL OF COMPARATIVE FAMILY STUDIES 10, 3 (Fall 1979): 301-313. 13
pp., references, tables.

Subjects: 1. Trends and Change in Marriage and Family / Family and
   Social Change; 2. / Comparative Studies--International, Interclass,
   Sex, and Time Differences; 3. Family Relationships and Dynamics /
   Family Relationships.

This paper investigates variations in one dimension of family
organization, namely family structural patterns, in urban areas with
100,000+ blacks using 1970 U.S. Census data. Cross-classification and
log-linear analyses are used to explore the effects of class and race
on family structure measured in terms of household headship (husband-
wife or female headed) and household composition (nuclear or
extended). Conventionally structured households (i.e., husband-wife,
nuclear) were more common among higher socioeconomic status and white
families than among lower SES and black families. It would appear that
economic moreso than cultural factors account for the adoption of

alternative structural patterns by black and poor families. However, final resolution of this question of relative effects must await further research on the other dimension of family organization, namely family processual style. (Author's abstract)

23 Allen, Walter R. "The Family Antecedents of Adolescent Mobility Aspirations." JOURNAL OF AFRO-AMERICAN ISSUES 4, 3/4 (Summer/Fall 1976): 295-314. 20 pp., references, illustrations.

Subjects: 1. Families with Special Problems / Achievement and the Family; 2. Family Counseling and Education / Adolescence.

24 Allen, Walter R. "Family Roles, Occupational Statuses, and Achievement Orientations among Black Women in the United States." SIGNS: JOURNAL OF WOMEN IN CULTURE AND SOCIETY 4, 4 (Summer 1979): 670-686. 17 pp., references, tables.

Subjects: 1. Organizations and Services to Families / Economics and the Family; 2. Family Relationships and Dynamics / Family Roles and Sex Roles; 3. Families with Special Problems / Achievement and the Family.

Census and survey data are employed to investigate differences in the occupational statuses of black women relative to white females and males of both races. . . Simply put, this paper asks whether the probable occupational status attainments of black women about to enter the labor force will accurately reflect their orientations toward achievement. The unequivocal conclusion is no. Some will, of course, argue that this conclusion holds for men and white women as well, to which the only reply is, "Yes, but not with the same force!" Black women have been, are, and will likely be in the near future disproportionately represented in menial, low-paying, low-prestige occupations. Where black women's achievement orientations did differ from those of other sex-race groupings, these differences were of insufficient consistency and magnitude to justify their large, persistent disadvantage in occupational status. . . A . . . viable approach to the study of continued black female occupational inequities involves scrutiny of institutions (their norms, personnel, and procedures) which impact on the achievement process. This information could then be combined with existing knowledge about black female socialization experiences and outcomes, thereby identifying critical personal and societal factors in the occupational achievement histories of black women. (From author's text)

25 Allen, Walter R. "Race and Sex Differences in the Socialization of Male Children." In BLACK MEN, edited by Lawrence E. Gary, pp. 99-114. Beverly Hill, CA: Sage Publications, Inc., 1981. 16 pp.

Subjects: 1. Family Relationships and Dynamics / Family Relationships; 2. / Socialization; 3. Aids for Theory and Research / Family Theory.

'This. . .is based on a study of family interpersonal dynamics and adolescent male socialization outcomes in a sample of Black and white middle-class families in Chicago, Illinois. . .The principle goals were (1) to challenge pathological conceptions of Black family life and Black child socialization; (2) to explore the family life and Black child socialization; (3) to shed light on the family roles of Black men; (4) to adopt an integrative view of Black child socialization outcomes; and (5) to accomplish these goals in the context of a comparative perspective by race, sex, and social class status of parents (and sons)' (From author's text, p. 99)

26 Allen, Walter R. "Race Differences in Husband-Wife Interpersonal Relationships during the Middle Years of Marriage." In BLACK MARRIAGE AND FAMILY THERAPY, edited by Constance E. Obudho, pp. 75-89. Westport, CT: Greenwood Press, 1983. 15 pp., references, tables.

Subjects: 1. Family Relationships and Dynamics / Husband-Wife Relationships; 2. / Middle Years.

27 Allen, Walter R. "Race, Family Setting and Adolescent Achievement Orientation." JOURNAL OF NEGRO EDUCATION 47, 3 (Summer 1978): 230-243. 14 pp., references, tables.

Subjects: 1. Family Relationships and Dynamics / Parent-Adolescent Relationships; 2. Families with Special Problems / Achievement and the Family.

The data for this paper [were] drawn from a 1974 citywide survey of Chicago, Illinois, male adolescents and their families. A stratified-cluster sample of 120 two-parent families, with at least one son aged 14-18 living in the home. . . An analysis of relationships existing between adolescent achievement orientation and family social status, parent aspirations, childrearing practices and parent-child relationships provided support for the hypothesis that the dynamics of achievement orientation development are different for Blacks and whites. Among Blacks, for example, the mother was the central figure in the determination of adolescent level of mobility aspirations, while among whites it was the father. The analysis also revealed. . . of the five components of achievement orientation [i.e., adolescent aspirations, academic self-concept, self-esteem, sense of environmental control and achievement values only], mobility aspirations and self-esteem, were strongly enough corelated with family factors to justify a view of the family as the deciding causal agent in their formation. Since achievement orientation is a multi-dimensional construct which results from a multiplicity of causes, it makes little sense to assign Black families--or any families for that matter--total responsiblity for the achievement attitudes and behaviors of their members. Instead, attention should be devoted to the full range of social, historical, economic and psychological factors in this society which interact to determine individual attitudes and attainments. (From author's text)

28 Allen, Walter R. "The Search for Applicable Theories of Black Family Life." JOURNAL OF MARRIAGE AND THE FAMILY 40, 1 (February 1978): 117-129. 13 pp., references.

Subjects: 1. Aids for Theory and Research / Family Theory; 2. / Critiques and Analyses of Family Research Literature.

29 Allen, Walter R. "The Social and Economic Statuses of Black Women in the United States." PHYLON 42, 1 (Spring 1981): 26-40. 15 pp., references, tables.

Subjects: 1. Organizations and Services to Families / Economics and the Family; 2. Family Relationships and Dynamics / Women's Issues.

30 Allen, Walter R. and Agbasegbe, Bamidele Ade. "A Comment on Scott's 'Black Polygamous Family Formation'." ALTERNATIVE LIFESTYLES 3, 4 (November 1980): 375-81. 7 pp.

Subjects: 1. Trends and Change in Marriage and Family / Alternative Family Forms; 2. Marriage and Divorce / Marriage Customs and Forms; 3. Aids for Theory and Research / Critiques and Analyses of Family Research Literature.

This brief article takes a critical look at Joseph W. Scott's article "Black Polygamous Family Formation". While Scott's research is seen as helpful, several problems in his treatment of plural mating and marriage arrangements among Black Americans are discussed. Major conceptual problems are created by Scott's use (or misuse) of the concept "polygyny." Significant methodological problems are also posed by his sampling approach, operationalization of concepts, and analytic strategies. Studies such as Scott's are of optimal value when their exploratory nature, and consequent limitation, are clearly acknowledged. (Author's abstract)

31 Allen, Walter R. and Stukes, Sandra. "Black Family Lifestyles and the Mental Health of Black Americans." In PERSPECTIVES ON MINORITY GROUP MENTAL HEALTH, edited by Faye V. Munoz and Russell Endo, pp. 43-52. Washington, DC: University Press of America, 1982. 10 pp.

Subjects: 1. Trends and Change in Marriage and Family / Family Life in the United States; 2. Organizations and Services to Families / Mental Health and the Family.

32 Almquist, Elizabeth M. "Untangling the Effects of Race and Sex: The Disadvantaged Status of Black Women." SOCIAL SCIENCE QUARTERLY 56, 1 (June 1975): 129-142. 14 pp., references, tables.

Subjects: 1. Family Relationships and Dynamics / Family Roles and Sex Roles.

33 American Psychopathological Association. CONTEMPORARY SEXUAL BEHAVIOR: CRITICAL ISSUES IN THE 1970'S, edited by Joseph Zubin and John Money. American Psychopathological Association Series. Baltimore, MD: The Johns Hopkins University Press, 1973. 468 pp., illustrations; ISBN:0-8018-1431-6; LC:72-4013.

Subjects: 1. Sexual Attitudes and Behavior / Sexual Attitudes and Behavior.

Notes: Based on the proceedings of the sixty-first annual meeting of the American Psychopathological Association. (From introduction)

34 An, Judy Yi-Bii Li. "Marital Satisfaction: A Comparative Study of Black and White College Students' Attitudes toward Marriage." (Ph.D. dissertation, Texas Woman's University, 1978.) DISSERTATION ABSTRACTS INTERNATIONAL, 40, 1, July 1979, 484A. (University Microfilms No. 7915861.) 186 pp.

Subjects: 1. Trends and Change in Marriage and Family / Comparative
   Studies--International, Interclass, Sex, and Time Differences; 2.
   Family Relationships and Dynamics / Family Roles and Sex Roles; 3.
   Marriage and Divorce / Marriage Satisfaction and Prediction Studies.

35 Anders, Sarah F. "New Dimensions in Ethnicity and Childrearing
Attitudes." AMERICAN JOURNAL OF MENTAL DEFICIENCY 73, 3 (November
1968): 505-508. 4 pp., references, tables.

Subjects: 1. Family Relationships and Dynamics / Parent-Child
   Relationships; 2. Family Counseling and Education / Value Education;
   3. Aids for Theory and Research / Family Research Methodology.

36 Anderson, Claud and Cromwell, Rue L. "'Black is Beautiful' and the
Color Preferences of Afro-American Youth." JOURNAL OF NEGRO EDUCATION
46, 1 (Winter 1977): 76-88. 13 pp., references, tables.

Subjects: 1. Trends and Change in Marriage and Family / Family and
   Social Change; 2. Family Relationships and Dynamics / Socialization;
   3. Family Counseling and Education / Adolescence.

37 Anderson, David C. CHILDREN OF SPECIAL VALUE: INTERRACIAL ADOPTION
IN AMERICA. New York: St. Martin's Press, 1971. 184 pp., bibliography;
LC:76-166172.

Subjects: 1. Organizations and Services to Families / Adoption and
   Adoption Services.

Notes: Bibliography: p. 184

38 Anderson, Elijah. A PLACE ON THE CORNER. Chicago and London:
University of Chicago Press, 1976. 237 pp., references, bibliography,
index; ISBN:0-226-01953-5; LC:78-1879.

Subjects: 1. Family Relationships and Dynamics / Men's Issues; 2.
   Minority Groups / Family and Social Class; 3. Aids for Theory and
   Research / Family Research Methodology.

Notes: Bibliography: pp. 227-234.

39 Anderson, John E. and Smith, Jack C. "Planned and Unplanned
Fertility in a Metropolitan Area: Black and White Differences." FAMILY
PLANNING PERSPECTIVES 7, 6 (November-December 1975): 281-285. 5 pp.,
references, illustrations, tables.

Subjects: 1. Issues Related to Reproduction / Fertility Rates.

   Since 1960, the total fertility rate has declined for both blacks and
   whites, with only slight change in group difference. The pattern has
   been very similar in the Atlanta area, in Georgia and in the United
   States as a whole: Black/white differences in fertility for women aged
   25 and older disappeared or became very small toward the end of the
   period surveyed. Between 1960 and 1970, non-marital fertility became
   the most important factor in the nationwide black/white difference in
   total fertility rate, while the importance of marital fertility
   decreased. Results of the 1965 and 1970 NFS suggest that much of the
   black/white convergence in marital fertility was a result of the

decrease in unwanted fertility among blacks. Data from the 1971 Atlanta Family Planning Survey document the difference for married women and show that the difference is due to higher levels of unplanned fertilitiy among blacks. (From author's summary and conclusions)

40 Andrew, Gwen. "Determinants of Negro Family Decisions in Management of Retardation." JOURNAL OF MARRIAGE AND THE FAMILY 30, 4 (November 1968): 612-617. 6 pp., references, tables.

Subjects: 1. Family Relationships and Dynamics / Decision Making; 2. Families with Special Problems / Families with Mentally Retarded.

41 Aronoff, Joel and Crano, William D. "A Re-examination of the Cross-Cultural Principles of Task Segregation and Sex Role Differentiation in the Family." AMERICAN SOCIOLOGICAL REVIEW 40, 1 (February 1975): 12-20. 9 pp., references, tables.

Subjects: 1. Trends and Change in Marriage and Family / Comparative Studies--International, Interclass, Sex, and Time Differences; 2. Family Relationships and Dynamics / Family Roles and Sex Roles.

42 Aschenbrenner, Joyce. "Extended Families among Black Americans." JOURNAL OF COMPARATIVE FAMILY STUDIES 4, 2 (Summer 1973): 257-268. 12 pp., references.

Subjects: 1. Family Relationships and Dynamics / Extended Family and Kinship Groups.

43 Aschenbrenner, Joyce. LIFELINES: BLACK FAMILIES IN CHICAGO. Case Studies in Cultural Anthropology. New York: Holt, Rinehart and Winston, Inc., 1975. 146 pp., bibliography, illustrations; ISBN:0-03-012826-9; LC:74-19871.

Subjects: 1. Family Relationships and Dynamics / Extended Family and Kinship Groups; 2. / Mother-Child Relationships; 3. Mate Selection / Mate Selection, Differential Patterns.

Ethnographic investigation of kinship and domestic groups among Chicago Blacks reveal that many have bilateral extended families skewed in the direction of maternal relations. The fragility of the conjugal bonds, it is suggested, result in part from the strength of the consanguineal bonds. Ethnographic data also highlight male/female love relationships, mother/daughter relationships, the father role, the importance of children, socialization, etc.

Notes: Bibliography: pp. 145-146.

44 Aschenbrenner, Joyce and Carr, Carolyn Hameedah. "Conjugal Relationships in the Context of the Black Extended Family." ALTERNATIVE LIFESTYLES 3, 4 (November 1980): 463-84. 22 pp.

Subjects: 1. Family Relationships and Dynamics / Extended Family and Kinship Groups; 2. / Family Relationships; 3. Aids for Theory and Research / Family Theory.

Black conjugal relationships are examined in relation to other kin relationships and contrasted with the Euro-American family pattern. In the latter, the fundamental relationship on which the nuclear family is based is the conjugal bond; the corresponding concept of family has a biological basis, seen as stemming from sexual intercourse and biological parenthood. In contrast, the Black family is grounded on the parent-child relationship--often involving shared (social) parenthood--and the social aspects of kinship take priority over a biological concept. Some descriptions and analyses of particular families demonstrate these ideas. (Authors' abstract)

45 Aseltine, Gwendolyn Pamenter. "Family Socialization Perceptions among Black and White High School Students." JOURNAL OF NEGRO EDUCATION 47, 3 (Summer 1978): 256-265. 10 pp., references, tables.

Subjects: 1. Family Relationships and Dynamics / Socialization; 2. Family Counseling and Education / Adolescence.

46 Ashburn, Elizabeth Alexander. "Influences and Motivations for Black and White Women to Attain Positions in a Male-Dominated Profession." (Ph.D. dissertation, State University of New York at Buffalo, 1979.) DISSERTATION ABSTRACTS INTERNATIONAL, 40, 4, Oct. 1979, 1870A-1871A. (University Microfilms No. 7921845.) 214 pp.

Subjects: 1. Organizations and Services to Families / Employment and the Family.

47 Austin, Roy L. "Race, Father-Absence, and Female Delinquency." CRIMINOLOGY 15, 4 (February 1978): 487-504. 18 pp., references, tables.

Subjects: 1. Family Relationships and Dynamics / Single Parent Families; 2. Families with Special Problems / Families with Juvenile Delinquents.

Discussions of the influence of father-absence on delinquency often show special concern for the relatively high rate of father absence among black Americans. However, for the four delinquent offenses studied, father- absence had detrimental effects only on whites, especially girls. The only significant effect among black girls was favorable to the father-absent girls. Further, contrary to Datesman and Scarpitti (1975), parental control has similar effects on delinquency and on the relationship between father-absence and delinquency for blacks and whites. It appears that policies which reduce the stigma of father-absence for white girls are more likely to succeed in reducing delinquency due to father-absence than policies of economic improvement. (Author's abstract)

48 Avery, Reginald Stanley. "The Impact of Court-Ordered Busing on Black Families in Boston, Massachusetts." (Ph.D. dissertation, Brandeis University, The F. Heller Graduate School for Advanced Study in Social Welfare, 1980.) DISSERTATION ABSTRACTS INTERNATIONAL, 41, 2, Aug. 1980, 578A-579A. (University Microfilms No. 8012752.) 396 pp.

Subjects: 1. Trends and Change in Marriage and Family / Family and Social Change; 2. Organizations and Services to Families / Education and the Family; 3. Families with Special Problems / Family Stress.

49 Axelson, Leland, Jr. "The Working Wife: Differences in Perception among Negro and White Males." JOURNAL OF MARRIAGE AND THE FAMILY 32, 3 (August 1970): 452-64. 13 pp.

Subjects: 1. Organizations and Services to Families / Employment and the Family; 2. Family Relationships and Dynamics / Men's Issues.

50 Babchuk, Nicholas and Ballweg, John A. "Black Family Structure and Primary Relations." PHYLON 33, 4 (Winter 1972): 334-47. 14 pp., references, tables.

Subjects: 1. Family Relationships and Dynamics / Family Relationships.

51 Badaines, Joel. "Identification, Imitation, and Sex-Role Preference in Father-Present and Father-Absent Black and Chicano Boys." JOURNAL OF PSCHOLOGY 92, 1 (January 1976): 15-24. 10 pp., references, tables.

Subjects: 1. Family Relationships and Dynamics / Family Roles and Sex Roles; 2. Families with Special Problems / Death, Bereavement and the Family; 3. Minority Groups / Ethnic Groups in the United States.

This two part study was concerned with identification and imitation in 52 black and Chicano seven-year-old boys. Part 1 investigated the effect of race of model and S on imitation of behavior. Part 2 investigated the effect of paternal status on choice of a male or female model and masculine sex-role preference. The Ss were exposed to filmed models. Black Ss expressed a significant preference for the black model, but for Chicano Ss no significant preferences among the black, white, and Chicano models were obtained. Father-present Ss had a significantly higher male sex-role preference score as compared to father-absent Ss. Both father-absent and father-present Ss imitated the male model significantly more than the female model, but these scores did not correlate significantly with the sex-role preference score. By age seven, masculine preference appeared well-established, but it was more marked for father-present Ss. (Author's summary)

52 Baldassare, Mark. "The Effects of Household Density on Subgroups." AMERICAN SOCIOLOGICAL REVIEW 46, 1 (February 1981): 110-118. 8 pp., references, tables.

Subjects: 1. Family Relationships and Dynamics / Environment (Space/ Housing).

53 Baldwin, Doris. "Poverty and the Older Woman: Reflections of a Social Worker." FAMILY COORDINATOR 27, 4 (October 1978): 448-50. 3 pp., references.

Subjects: 1. Organizations and Services to Families / Social Services and the Family; 2. / Economics and the Family; 3. Family Relationships and Dynamics / Later Years and Aging.

54 Baldwin, Joseph A. "Theory and Research Concerning the Notion of Black Self-Hatred: A Review and Reinterpretation." JOURNAL OF BLACK PSYCHOLOGY 5, 2 (February 1979): 51-77. 27 pp., references, tables.

Subjects: 1. Psychology and Sociology / Psychology; 2. Aids for Theory and Research / Family Theory.

55 Balkwell, Carolyn, Balswick, Jack and Balkwell, James W.   "On Black
and White Family Patterns in America: Their Impact on the Expressive
Aspect of Sex-Role Socialization." JOURNAL OF MARRIAGE AND THE FAMILY
40, 4 (November 1978): 743-47. 5 pp., references, tables.

Subjects: 1. Trends and Change in Marriage and Family / Family Life in
    the United States; 2. Family Relationships and Dynamics /
    Socialization; 3. / Family Roles and Sex Roles.

This research investigates the hypothesis that expressive aspects of
sex- roles are learned in the early socialization of the child.
Literature on the black family emphasizes the dominance and strength
of the mother as a model of behavior, hence, one might expect less
dimorphism in sex-roles among blacks than among whites if, indeed,
these behaviors are learned as the child internalizes the roles of the
parents. Expressiveness of fondness, sadness, pleasure, and antipathy
were operationalized by composite scales based upon responses to 16
Likert-type items which were administered to 1190 high school
students. Black students tended to have lower levels of expressiveness
of each of the four emotions than white students. Males were more
expressive of antipath, while females tended to be more expressive of
fondness, pleasure, and sadness. There was less sexual dimorphism
among blacks than among whites in the expressiveness of pleasure - but
not in the expressiveness of the other three emotions. (Authors'
abstract)

56 Ball, Richard E., Warheit, George J., Vandiver, Joseph S. and
Holzer, Charles E., III. "Friendship Networks: More Supportive of Low-
Income Black Women?" ETHNICITY 7, 1 (March 1980): 70-77. 8 pp.,
references, bibliography, tables.

Subjects: 1. Family Relationships and Dynamics / Extended Family and
    Kinship Groups; 2. / Socialization; 3. / Women's Issues.

57 Ball, Richard Everett. "Expressive Functioning and the Black
Family: Life and Domain Satisfaction of Black Women." (Ph.D.
dissertation, The University of Florida, 1980.) DISSERTATION ABSTRACTS
INTERNATIONAL, 41, 9, March 1981, 4179A. (University Microfilms
No. 8105556.) 233 pp.

Subjects: 1. Family Relationships and Dynamics / Family Relationships;
    2. Marriage and Divorce / Marriage Satisfaction and Prediction
    Studies; 3. Psychology and Sociology / Self-Esteem.

58 Baltes, Paul B. and Brim, Orville G., Jr., eds. LIFE-SPAN
DEVELOPMENT AND BEHAVIOR. VOLUME 2. New York: Academic Press, Inc.,
1979.; ISBN:0124318029.

Subjects: 1. Family Relationships and Dynamics / Stages in Family Life
    Cycle.

59 Bankde, Faola. "The Strategy of the Black Father's Council." BLACK
MALE/FEMALE RELATIONSHIPS 2, 5 (Spring 1981): 39-42. 4 pp.

Subjects: 1. Organizations and Services to Families / Community Groups
    and the Family; 2. Family Relationships and Dynamics / Extended Family
    and Kinship Groups.

60 Banks, William and Walker, Shelia, eds. AND AIN'T I A WOMAN
TOO! INTERACTION OF SEX AND ETHNICITY IN BLACK WOMEN. Berkeley, CA:
University of California Press, 1979.

Subjects: 1. Family Relationships and Dynamics / Women's Issues.

61 Barnes, Annie S. "An Urban Black Voluntary Association." PHYLON
40, 3 (September 1979): 264-69. 6 pp., references.

Subjects: 1. Organizations and Services to Families / Community Groups
and the Family.

Jack and Jill of America. . . is an urban black middle class
voluntary association [of families] that is nationally, regionally and
locally organized. . . Its membership consists of six thousand
mothers, four thousand teens, and numerous younger children. On the
local level, the mothers form the general chapter organization, while
their children, who are between two and twenty years of age, are
organized into subgroups, based on age. The fathers participate in
special activities and assist with the association's projects. . .
Interestingly enough, Jack and Jill continues to function in a society
that is much more integrated than at the inception of the organization
[in 1938]. However, in the second half of the twentieth century,
abrasive contacts, real and perceived insults, and slights, in the
wider society continue to plague blacks. Therefore, they must look to
the black subsociety to enhance their self-concept. The present
strategy of Jack and Jill has responded to this challenge by seeking
to provide opportunities for children beyond its own membership to
adapt effectively, particularly black children of lower socioeonomic
status, but also other deprived minorities as well. And for black
middle-class families, Jack and Jill still contributes to the positive
view they hold of themselves by providing membership, positions, and
activities that award status, self-expression, and decision-making
power. (From author's text)

62 Barnes, Annie Shaw. "The Black Family in Golden Towers." (Ph.D.
dissertation, University of Virginia, 1971.) DISSERTATION ABSTRACTS
INTERNATIONAL, 32, 8, Feb. 1972, 4367B. (University Microfilms
No. 727138.) 310 pp.

Subjects: 1. Organizations and Services to Families / Community Groups
and the Family; 2. Family Relationships and Dynamics / Socialization.

63 Barnes, Ben E. and Gay, Kathlyn. THE RIVER FLOWS BACKWARD. Port
Washington, NY: Ashley Books, Inc., 1975. 288 pp.; ISBN:0-87949-027-6;
LC:74-76645.

Subjects: 1. Trends and Change in Marriage and Family / Family Life in
the United States.

This is an autobiographical work.

64 Barnes, Edward J. "The Black Community as the Source of Children: A
Theoretical Perspective." In SCIENCE, MYTH, REALITY: THE BLACK FAMILY
IN ONE-HALF CENTURY OF RESEARCH, by Eleanor Engram, pp. 166-192.
Westport, CT: Greenwood Press, 1982. 27 pp.

Subjects: 1. Organizations and Services to Families / Community Groups and the Family; 2. Family Relationships and Dynamics / Socialization; 3. Aids for Theory and Research / Family Theory.

65 Barnes, Jimmie Franklin, Jr. "Factors Related to Deviant Health-Care Practices: A Study of Black Families in the Mississippi Delta." (Ph.D. dissertation, Mississippi State University, 1979.) DISSERTATION ABSTRACTS INTERNATIONAL, 40, 2, Aug. 1979, 1107A. (University Microfilms No. 7918518.) 81 pp.

Subjects: 1. Organizations and Services to Families / Physical Health and the Family.

66 Barnett, Larry D. "Research on International and Interracial Marriages." JOURNAL OF MARRIAGE AND THE FAMILY 25, 1 (February 1963): 105-107. 3 pp., bibliography.

Subjects: 1. Marriage and Divorce / Inter-marriage; 2. Aids for Theory and Research / Critiques and Analyses of Family Research Literature.

67 Barnett, Marguerite Ross and Hefner, James A., eds. PUBLIC POLICY FOR THE BLACK COMMUNITY: STRATEGIES AND PERSPECTIVES. Port Washington, NY: Alfred Publishing Co., 1976. 270 pp., references, illustrations; ISBN:0-88284-039-8; LC:76-24466.

Subjects: 1. Trends and Change in Marriage and Family / Family Policy; 2. Organizations and Services to Families / Economics and the Family; 3. Aids for Theory and Research / Collected Works.

68 Barney, William L. "Patterns of Crisis: Alabama White Families and Social Change 1850-1870." SOCIOLOGY AND SOCIAL RESEARCH 15, 63 (April 1979): 524-43. 20 pp.

Subjects: 1. Trends and Change in Marriage and Family / Family Life Prior to 1900; 2. / Family and Social Change.

69 Barron, Milton Leon, ed. THE BLENDING AMERICA: PATTERNS OF INTERMARRIAGE. Chicago, IL: Quadrangle Books, 1972. 357 pp., bibliography; ISBN:0-8129-0234-3; LC:78-182502.

Subjects: 1. Marriage and Divorce / Inter-marriage; 2. Aids for Theory and Research / Collected Works.

Twenty essays covering interracial, interethnic and religious intermarriage.

Notes: Bibliography: pp. 339-345

70 Bartz, Karen W. and Levine, Elaine S. "Childrearing by Black Parents: A Description and Comparison to Anglo and Chicano Parents." JOURNAL OF MARRIAGE AND THE FAMILY 40, 4 (November 1978): 709-19. 11 pp., references, bibliography, tables.

Subjects: 1. Trends and Change in Marriage and Family / Comparative Studies--International, Interclass, Sex, and Time Differences; 2. Family Relationships and Dynamics / Parent-Child Relationships.

This study describes the childrearing attitudes and behaviors of black parents living in a lower working-class neighborhood. Interview data from 160 black mothers and fathers compared to similar data from 152 Chicano and 143 Anglo parents living in the same neighborhood. Black parents are typified as expecting early autonomy, not allowing wasted time, being both highly supportive and controlling, valuing strictness and encouraging equalitarian family roles. The black parents differed from either the Anglo and/or Chicano parents on several dimensions of childrearing. Few differences by sex of parent or sex of child are reported. (Authors' abstract)

71 Bass, Barbara Ann, Wyatt, Gail Elizabeth and Powell, Gloria Johnson, eds. THE AFRO-AMERICAN FAMILY: ASSESSMENT, TREATMENT, AND RESEARCH ISSUES. Seminars in Psychiatry. New York: Grune and Stratton, Inc., 1982. 364 pp., references, index; ISBN:0-8089-1377-8; LC:81-13267.

Subjects: 1. Organizations and Services to Families / Mental Health and the Family; 2. Psychology and Sociology / Psychology; 3. Aids for Theory and Research / Collected Works.

Recognizing the 'growing need to offer information to mental health professionals about the assessment and psychiatric treatment of Afro-Americans and relevant research issues' (p. xiv), the editors have assembled 19 essays that represent a multidisciplinary focus. Grouped into four major areas of concern, the essays explore: (1) sociocultural variables and general background issues; (2) the assessment of children and adults; (3) psychotherapeutic treatment strategies and issues; and (4) self-concept and male/female relationships.

Notes: Papers presented at a series of seminars organized by the Neuropsychiatric Institute, UCLA Center for the Health Sciences, beginning in 1974.

72 Bates, James E., Lieberman, Harry H. and Powell, Rodney N. "Provisions for Health Care in the Ghetto: The Family Health Team." AMERICAN JOURNAL OF PUBLIC HEALTH 60, (July 1970): 1222-1225. 4 pp.

Subjects: 1. Organizations and Services to Families / Physical Health and the Family.

73 Baughman, Emmett Earl. BLACK AMERICANS: A PSYCHOLOGICAL ANALYSIS. New York: Academic Press, Inc., 1971. 113 pp., bibliography, illustrations; LC:70-152748.

Subjects: 1. Psychology and Sociology / Psychology; 2. / Racial Attitudes.

Notes: Bibliography: pp. 95-103.

74 Bauman, Karl E. and Udry, Richard J. "The Difference in Unwanted Births between Blacks and Whites." DEMOGRAPHY 10, 3 (August 1973): 315-28. 14 pp., bibliography, tables.

Subjects: 1. Issues Related to Reproduction / Birth Control; 2. / Illegitimacy.

75 Bauman, Karl E. and Udry, Richard J. "Powerlessness and Regularity of Contraception in an Urban Negro Male Sample: A Research Note." JOURNAL OF MARRIAGE AND THE FAMILY 34, 1 (February 1972): 112-114.   3 pp.

Subjects: 1. Issues Related to Reproduction / Birth Control.

76 Baumer-Mulloy, Marjorie. "A Study of the Relationship of Certain Home Environmental Factors to High or Low Achievement in Reading among Black Primary School Age Pupils of Low Socioeconomic Status." (Ph.D. dissertation, University of Maryland, 1977.) DISSERTATION ABSTRACTS INTERNATIONAL, 39, 2, Aug. 1978, 660A. (University Microfilms No. 7811945.) 152 pp.

Subjects: 1. Family Relationships and Dynamics / Family Relationships; 2. / Family Roles and Sex Roles; 3. Families with Special Problems / Achievement and the Family.

77 Baumrind, Diana and Black, Allen E. "Socialization Practices Associated with Dimension of Competence in Preschool Boys and Girls." CHILD DEVELOPMENT 38, 2 (June 1967): 291-327. 37 pp., references, bibliography, tables.

Subjects: 1. Family Relationships and Dynamics / Socialization; 2. Families with Special Problems / Achievement and the Family.

78 Bayerl, John Aloysius. "Transracial Adoption: White Parents Who Adopted Black Children and White Parents Who Adopted White Children." (Ph.D. dissertation, The University of Michigan, 1977.) DISSERTATION ABSTRACTS INTERNATIONAL, 38, 6, Dec. 1978, 3280A. (University Microfilms No. 7726200.) 151 pp.

Subjects: 1. Organizations and Services to Families / Adoption and Adoption Services; 2. Family Relationships and Dynamics / Decision Making.

79 Bayless, Vaurice G. "Selected Research Studies and Professional Literature Dealing with Physiological, Socioeconomic, Psychological, and Cultural Differences between Black and White Males with Reference to the Performance of Athletic Skills." (Ed.D. dissertation, North Texas State University, 1980.) DISSERTATION ABSTRACTS INTERNATIONAL, 41, 4, Oct. 1980, 1472A. (University Microfilms No. 8021883.) 189 pp.

Subjects: 1. Family Relationships and Dynamics / Men's Issues; 2. Aids for Theory and Research / Critiques and Analyses of Family Research Literature.

80 Bean, Frank D. and Aiken, Linda H. "Intermarriage and Unwanted Fertility in the United States." JOURNAL OF MARRIAGE AND THE FAMILY 38, 1 (February 1976): 61-72. 12 pp., references, bibliography, tables.

Subjects: 1. Marriage and Divorce / Inter-marriage; 2. Issues Related to Reproduction / Fertility Rates.

81 Bean, Frank D. and Wood, Charles H. "Ethnic Variations in the Relationship between Income and Fertility." DEMOGRAPHY 11, 4 (November 1974): 629-40. 12 pp., bibliography, tables.

Subjects: 1. Organizations and Services to Families / Economics and the Family; 2. Issues Related to Reproduction / Fertility Rates; 3. Minority Groups / Ethnic Groups in the United States.

The effects of husband's potential and relative incomes on completed fertility, as well as their effects on certain parity progression probabilities, are examined within samples of Anglos, Blacks and Mexican Americans. Relationships are estimated using data from the one-percent 1960 and 1970 U.S. Public Use Samples. The results reveal different patterns of relationship by ethnicity between the measures of income and the measures of fertility. The effects on completed fertility of the income measures are positive for Anglos and negative for Blacks, while in the case of Mexican Americans the effect of potential income is negative and that of relative income is positive. Income effects on the parity progression probabilities are similar in pattern to those from the analyses using completed fertility, although somewhat different patterns tend to appear at different birth orders, especially among Anglos. (Authors' abstract)

82 Beatt, Barbara Hamby and Wahlstrom, Barbara Berg. "A Developmental Approach to Understanding Families." SOCIAL CASEWORK: THE JOURNAL OF CONTEMPORARY SOCIAL WORK 57, 1 (January 1976): 3-8. 6 pp., references, charts.

Subjects: 1. Aids for Theory and Research / Family Theory.

83 Beckett, Joyce O. "Racial Differences in Why Women Work." In WORK, FAMILY ROLES AND SUPPORT SYSTEMS, edited by Susan Golden, pp. 31-50. Ann Arbor, MI: University of Michigan, Center for Continuing Education of Women, 1978. 20 pp.

Subjects: 1. Trends and Change in Marriage and Family / Comparative Studies--International, Interclass, Sex, and Time Differences; 2. Organizations and Services to Families / Employment and the Family; 3. Family Relationships and Dynamics / Women's Issues.

'Contemporary data indicate that factors important in determining the employment of Black wives are not the same as those relevant to whites, and the factors important to both groups have different influences on each race...There are important racial differences in why women work, in the salience of education, financial rewards, and the number of children to labor force participation.' (From author's text, p. 31.)

84 Beckett, Joyce O. "Working Wives: A Racial Comparison." SOCIAL WORK 21, 6 (November 1976): 463-71. 9 pp., references, tables.

Subjects: 1. Organizations and Services to Families / Employment and the Family.

85 Beckett, Joyce Octavia. "Working Wives: A Racial Analysis." (Ph.D. dissertation, Bryn Mawr College, 1977.) DISSERTATION ABSTRACTS INTERNATIONAL, 38, 10, April 1978, 6321A. (University Microfilms No. 7802584.) 276 pp.

Subjects: 1. Organizations and Services to Families / Employment and the Family; 2. Family Relationships and Dynamics / Women's Issues.

86 Bedrosian, Richard C. and Beck, Aaron T.   "Premature Conclusions
Regarding Black and White Suicide Attempters: A Reply to Steele."
JOURNAL OF CONSULTING AND CLINICAL PSYCHOLOGY 46, 6 (December 1978):
1498-99. 2 pp., references.

Subjects: 1. Families with Special Problems / Suicide and the Family.

87 Beglis, Jeanne F. and Sheikh, Anees A.   "Development of the Self-
Concept in Black and White Children."   JOURNAL OF NEGRO EDUCATION 43, 1
(Winter 1974): 104-10. 7 pp., references.

Subjects: 1. Psychology and Sociology / Self-Esteem; 2. Family
  Counseling and Education / Child Development.

88 Bell, Duran. "Why Participation Rates of Black and White Wives
Differ." JOURNAL OF HUMAN RESOURCES 9, 4 (Fall 1974): 465-479. 15 pp.,
references, bibliography, tables.

Subjects: 1. Organizations and Services to Families / Employment and the
  Family; 2. Family Relationships and Dynamics / Women's Issues.

Analysis of labor force participation of black and white wives by
family personal characteristics, from the 1967 Survey of Economic
Opportunity, revealed that 61.4 percent of black wives and 46.7
percent of white wives worked in 1966. Full-time work was more common
among black wives in better educated, more stable families, and among
white wives in less educated, poorer, unstable families. The reverse
applied to part-time employment. Results reflect the opening of white-
collar jobs to qualified black women, as an alternative to domestic
service. Strong sexist barriers to high-status employment of women
explain the relatively low participation of upper middle-class white
wives. (Author's abstract)

89 Bell, Duran Jr. "Indebtedness In Black And White Families."
JOURNAL OF URBAN ECONOMICS 1, 1 (January 1974): 48-60. 13 pp.,
references, bibliography, tables.

Subjects: 1. Organizations and Services to Families / Economics and the
  Family.

The greater incidence of short term debt among black families and the
lesser extent of total indebtedness are both reflections, in part, of
the relatively greater shortage of owner occupied housing available to
black families in metropolitan areas. Since housing is the form of
wealth which persons of modest incomes are able to generate over a
life time, barriers to homeownership are especially important in
limiting the wealth accumulation of black families. Additionally, the
lack of housing removes a possible symbol of social status, and there
is evidence that other commodities, such as automobiles and clothing,
are made to perform the same kind of task to which white families more
often assign their residential address. It is clear. . .that wealth
accumulation is limited by discrimination and segregation in housing
markets and in labor markets, both forms of racial discrimination
combine to limit wealth accumulation in black families. (From author's
conclusions)

90 Bell, Robert R. "Lower Class Negro Mothers and Their Children."
INTEGRATED EDUCATION 2, 6 (December-January 1965): 23-27. 5 pp.

Subjects: 1. Family Relationships and Dynamics / Mother-Child
   Relationships.

91 Bell, Robert R. "The Lower-Class Negro Family in the United States
and Great Britain: Some Comparisons." RACE AND CLASS 11, 2 (October
1969): 173-181. 9 pp., references.

Subjects: 1. Trends and Change in Marriage and Family / Comparative
   Studies--International, Interclass, Sex, and Time Differences.

92 Bell, Robert R. "Lower-Class Negro Mothers' Aspirations for Their
Children." SOCIAL FORCES 43, 4 (May 1965): 493-500. 8 pp., references.

Subjects: 1. Family Relationships and Dynamics / Mother-Child
   Relationships; 2. Minority Groups / Family and Social Class.

93 Bell, Winifred. "Relatives' Responsibility: A Problem in Social
Policy." SOCIAL WORK 12, 1 (January 1967): 32-39. 8 pp., references.

Subjects: 1. Trends and Change in Marriage and Family / Family Policy;
   2. Family Relationships and Dynamics / Extended Family and Kinship
   Groups.

94 Bengston, Vern L., Furlong, Michael J. and Lauffer, Robert S.
"Time, Aging and Continuity of Social Structure: Themes and Issues in
Generational Analysis." JOURNAL OF SOCIAL ISSUES 30, 2 (Spring 1974):
1-30. 30 pp.

Subjects: 1. Family Relationships and Dynamics / Stages in Family Life
   Cycle; 2. Aids for Theory and Research / Family Research Methodology.

95 Benjamin, Rommel. FACTORS RELATED TO CONCEPTIONS OF THE MALE
FAMILIAL ROLE BY BLACK YOUTH. Mississippi State University. Department
of Sociology and Anthropology. Sociology and Anthropology Series,
No. 15. State College, MS: Mississippi State University. College of Arts
and Sciences, 1971. 9 pp., references, illustrations; LC:72-104370.

Subjects: 1. Family Relationships and Dynamics / Family Roles and Sex
   Roles; 2. Family Counseling and Education / Adolescence.

96 Bequer, Marta Maria. "The Relationship of Parent Participation and
Selected Variables in Three Multi-Ethnic Elementary Schools in
Dade County, Florida." (Ed.D. dissertation, The University of Florida,
1977.) DISSERTATION ABSTRACTS INTERNATIONAL, 39, 1, July 1978, 34A.
(University Microfilms No. 7810921.) 129 pp.

Subjects: 1. Organizations and Services to Families / Education and the
   Family; 2. Family Relationships and Dynamics / Parent-Child
   Relationships.

97 Berger, Alan S. and Simon, William. "Black Families and the
Moynihan Report: A Research Evaluation." SOCIAL PROBLEMS 22, 2
(December 1974): 145-161. 17 pp., references, bibliography, tables.

Subjects: 1. Family Relationships and Dynamics / Family Relationships;
2. Aids for Theory and Research / Critiques and Analyses of Family
Research Literature.

The major hypothesis of the Moynihan Report posits that black family
socializes children very differently from the way that the white
family socializes children. It thus produces more antisocial behavior,
ineffective education, and lower levels of occupational attainment.
The current study employs data collected from a random sample of the
14-18 year old population of Illinois and examines the joint effects
of race, gender, social class, and family organization on a number of
indicators of family interaction, antisocial behavior   patterns,
educational aspirations, and gender role conceptions. Few differences
were found in the ways that families treat their children, and these
differences were not concentrated in the lower class. Even in the
lower-class broken family, there was no indication that black families
are dramatically different from white families. Thus, in terms of
delinquency, educational expectations, perceptions of the education
desired by the parents, self conceptions, and notions of appropriate
gender role behavior of adults, the empirircal evidence does not
provide adequate support for the conclusions of the Moynihan Report.
(Authors' abstract)

98 Bernard, Jessie. "Marital Stability and Patterns of Status
Variables." JOURNAL OF MARRIAGE AND THE FAMILY 28, 4 (November 1966):
421-439. 19 pp., references, tables, charts.

Subjects: 1. Marriage and Divorce / Marriage Satisfaction and Prediction
   Studies; 2. Minority Groups / Family and Social Class.

99 Bernard, Jessie. "Note On Educational Homogamy in Negro-White and
White-Negro Marriages, 1960." JOURNAL OF MARRIAGE AND THE FAMILY 28, 3
(August 1966): 274-76. 3 pp., tables.

Subjects: 1. Organizations and Services to Families / Education and the
   Family; 2. Marriage and Divorce / Inter-marriage.

100 Bernard, Jessie Shirley. MARRIAGE AND FAMILY AMONG NEGROES.
Englewood Cliffs, NJ: Prentice-Hall, 1966. 160 pp., references, tables,
charts, index; LC:66-16338.

Subjects: 1. Trends and Change in Marriage and Family / Family Life in
   the United States; 2. Marriage and Divorce / Marriage Satisfaction and
   Prediction Studies; 3. Aids for Theory and Research / Family Theory.

101 Bethel, Elizabeth Rauh. PROMISELAND: A CENTURY OF LIFE IN A NEGRO
COMMUNITY. Philadelphia, PA: Temple University Press, 1981. 329 pp.,
bibliography, index; ISBN:0-87722-211-8; LC:80-27732.

Subjects: 1. Trends and Change in Marriage and Family / Family Life in
   the United States.

Notes: Bibliography: pp. 317-324.

102 Bianchi, Suzanne M. "Racial Differences in Per Capita Income,
1960-76: The Importance of Household Size, Headship and Labor Force
Participation." DEMOGRAPHY 17, 2 (May 1980): 129-143.

Subjects: 1. Trends and Change in Marriage and Family / Comparative Studies--International, Interclass, Sex, and Time Differences; 2. Organizations and Services to Families / Economics and the Family; 3. Family Relationships and Dynamics / Nuclear Family.

Racial differences in average per capita income are decomposed, as are changes over time for both races. The 1960-76 decline in household size accounted for 13 percent of the per capita income improvement of both races. Whereas real increases in earnings of husbands contributed most to improvements in well-being in husband-wife households, increases in income from sources other than earnings were most important to female headed households. During a period in which a growing proportion of both races resided in female headed households and racial differences in living arrangements widened, the per capita income of female headed households relative to husband-wife households declined. (Author's abstract)

103 Bianchi, Suzanne M., Farley, Reynolds and Spain, Daphne. "Racial Inequalities in Housing: An Examination of Recent Trends." DEMOGRAPHY 19, 1 (February 1982): 37-51. 15 pp.

Subjects: 1. Family Relationships and Dynamics / Environment (Space/ Housing).

Changes in racial differences in homeownership and objective indicators of housing quality are examined using 1960 Census data and 1977 Annual Housing Survey data. Blacks, net of differences in socioeconomic status, family composition, and regional-metropolitan location, remained less likely than whites to own homes and somewhat more likely to live in older, crowded and structurally inadequate units in 1977. In general, however, net effects for race were much smaller in 1977 than in 1960. Racial differences in homeownership and crowding were smaller among recent movers than among the total sample in 1977, suggesting continued but gradual improvement in housing conditions for blacks in the latter 1970s. (Authors' abstract)

104 Bianchi, Suzanne M. and Farley, Reynolds. "Racial Differences in Family Living Arrangements and Economic Well-Being: An Analysis of Recent Trends." JOURNAL OF MARRIAGE AND THE FAMILY 41, 3 (August 1979): 537-551. 15 pp., references, tables, charts.

Subjects: 1. Trends and Change in Marriage and Family / Family Policy; 2. Organizations and Services to Families / Economics and the Family; 3. Family Relationships and Dynamics / Nuclear Family.

Among both races, recently, there has been a shift away from traditional living arrangements. Changes have been more significant among blacks and, thus, racial differences are now greater than at the time of the Moynihan [R]eport (1965). The economic consequences are described by analyzing trends in per capita income for types of families. Income has risen in all types of families but the improvements are greater in husband-wife families. Among both races, the gap which separates the economic well-being of those in husband-wife families from those in families headed by a woman has widened. A declining proportion of children and adults live in families with the greatest per capita income and in increasing fraction live in families

with the lowest income. Changes in living arrangements are related to
family welfare policies. (Authors' abstract)

105 Biller, Henry B. "A Note on Father Absence and Masculine
Development in Lower-Class Negro and White Boys." CHILD DEVELOPMENT 39,
3 (September 1968): 1003-1006. 4 pp., references, tables.

Subjects: 1. Trends and Change in Marriage and Family / Comparative
  Studies--International, Interclass, Sex, and Time Differences; 2.
  Family Relationships and Dynamics / Father-Child Relationships.

106 Biller, Henry B. and Meredith, Dennis. FATHER POWER. New York:
David McKay Company, Inc., 1975. 376 pp., bibliography, index; ISBN:0-
679-50520-2; LC:74-14018.

Subjects: 1. Family Relationships and Dynamics / Mother-Child
  Relationships; 2. / Parent-Child Relationships; 3. / Men's Issues.

  Notes: Originally copyrighted in 1974. Bibliography: pp 361-368.

107 Billingsley, Andrew. "Black Families and National Policy."
JOURNAL OF SOCIOLOGY AND SOCIAL WELFARE 2, 3 (Spring 1975): 312-325. 14
pp., references, tables.

Subjects: 1. Trends and Change in Marriage and Family / Family Policy.

108 Billingsley, Andrew. BLACK FAMILIES AND THE STRUGGLE FOR SURVIVAL.
New York: Friendship Press, 1974. 95 pp., references, illustrations;
ISBN:0-377-00001-9; LC:74-9839.

Subjects: 1. Trends and Change in Marriage and Family / Family Life in
  the United States.

  This book was published for the Commission on Ministries with Black
  Families, of the Black Christian Education Project of the National
  Council of Churches. The volume includes study questions and a guide
  for teaching purposes.

  Notes: Study Questions and Guides by Robert O. Dublin, Jr. and Edward
  L. Foggs.

109 Billingsley, Andrew. "Black Families and White Social Science."
JOURNAL OF SOCIAL ISSUES 26, 3 (Summer 1970): 127-142. 16 pp.,
references, tables.

Subjects: 1. Aids for Theory and Research / Critiques and Analyses of
  Family Research Literature.

110 Billingsley, Andrew. BLACK FAMILIES IN WHITE AMERICA. Englewood
Cliffs, NJ: Prentice-Hall, 1968. 218 pp., references, illustrations,
tables, charts, index; ISBN:0-13-077453-7; LC:68-54856.

Subjects: 1. Trends and Change in Marriage and Family / Family Policy;
  2. Family Relationships and Dynamics / Family Relationships; 3. Aids
  for Theory and Research / Family Theory.

A description of the major dimensions of Negro family life. The author seeks to contravene the Moynihan thesis of social disorganization of lower-class Negro families. Attention is given also to the small percentage of upper class Negro families--the present Negro elite.

Notes: The author was assisted by Amy Tate Billingsley.

111 Billingsley, Andrew. "Family Functioning in the Low-Income Black Community." SOCIAL CASEWORK: THE JOURNAL OF CONTEMPORARY SOCIAL WORK 50, 10 (December 1969): 563-572. 10 pp., references, tables.

Subjects: 1. Organizations and Services to Families / Community Groups and the Family; 2. Family Relationships and Dynamics / Family Relationships.

112 Billingsley, Andrew and Billingsley, Amy Tate. "Illegitimacy and Patterns of Negro Family Life." In THE UNWED MOTHER, edited by Robert W. Roberts, pp. 133-158. New York: Harper and Row, 1966. 26 pp.

Subjects: 1. Family Relationships and Dynamics / Family Relationships; 2. Issues Related to Reproduction / Illegitimacy; 3. Aids for Theory and Research / Family Research Methodology.

113 Billingsley, Andrew and Billingsley, Amy Tate. "Negro Family Life in America." SOCIAL SCIENCE REVIEW 39, 3 (September 1965): 310-319. 10 pp., bibliography.

Subjects: 1. Trends and Change in Marriage and Family / Family Life in the United States.

114 Billingsley, Andrew and Giovannoni, Jeanne M. CHILDREN OF THE STORM: BLACK CHILDREN AND AMERICAN CHILD WELFARE. New York: Harcourt, Brace and Jovanovich, Inc., 1972. 263 pp., bibliography, illustrations; ISBN:0-15-117340-0; LC:72-75593.

Subjects: 1. Organizations and Services to Families / Social Welfare.

Notes: Bibliography: pp. 253-256

115 Billingsley, Andrew and Greene, Marilyn Cynthia. "Family Life among the Free Black Population in the 18th Century." JOURNAL OF SOCIAL AND BEHAVIOR SCIENCES 20, 2 (Spring 1974): 1-18. 17 pp., references, bibliography, tables.

Subjects: 1. Trends and Change in Marriage and Family / Family Life in the United States.

When the first census of the United States was taken in 1790, there were approximately 750,000 persons of African descent enumerated in the returns for the 17 states and territories which comprised the continental United States at that time. Of that number, roughly 59,000 had legally free status. Despite the fact that the original census manuscript schedules for almost one-third of the states were destroyed in the War of 1812, our research in the remaining 12 states identifies almost 27,000 free Blacks living in family units in 1790. The present study focuses on the existence of family life among free Blacks. It is our view that the 18th century represents a critical period for the study of Blacks in America, for it was during this time that the basic structure of Black family life was developed, the broad outlines of which continue to the present time. (Authors' abstract)

116 Bird, Caroline and Briller, Sara Welles. BORN FEMALE: THE HIGH COST OF KEEPING WOMEN DOWN. New York: David McKay Company, Inc., 1968. 288 pp., references; LC:68-24496.

Subjects: 1. Organizations and Services to Families / Employment and the Family; 2. Family Relationships and Dynamics / Women's Issues.

Notes: Bibliographical references: pp. 251-271.

117 Bird, Caroline and Briller, Sara Welles. BORN FEMALE: THE HIGH COST OF KEEPING WOMEN DOWN. Revised ed. New York: David McKay Company, Inc., 1970. 302 pp., references; LC:71-134801.

Subjects: 1. Organizations and Services to Families / Employment and the Family; 2. Family Relationships and Dynamics / Women's Issues.

118 Bishop, John H. "Jobs, Cash Transfers and Marital Instability: A Review and Synthesis of the Evidence." JOURNAL OF HUMAN RELATIONS 15, 3 (Summer 1980): 301-334. 33 pp., references, bibliography, tables, charts.

Subjects: 1. Organizations and Services to Families / Employment and the Family; 2. Marriage and Divorce / Marriage Satisfaction and Prediction Studies.

119 "Black Age Lauded." CRISIS 86, 7 (August-September 1979): 302. 1 p., illustrations.

Subjects: 1. Family Relationships and Dynamics / Stages in Family Life Cycle.

120 Black Aged in the Future, San Juan, P.R., 1972. Proceedings. PROCEEDINGS OF 'BLACK AGED IN THE FUTURE'. s.l.: N.p., 1972. 140 pp.

Subjects: 1. Family Relationships and Dynamics / Later Years and Aging; 2. Aids for Theory and Research / Collected Works.

Notes: The proceedings were held on 15-16 December 1972, Caribe Hilton Hotel, San Juan, Puerto Rico under the auspices of the National Caucus on the Aged, Inc. and the Gerontological Society and directed by Jacqueline Johnson Jackson.

121 Black Child Development Institute. BLACK CHILDREN JUST KEEP ON GROWING: ALTERNATIVE CURRICULUM MODELS FOR YOUNG BLACK CHILDREN, edited by Madeleine Coleman. Washington, DC: Black Child Development Institute, 1977. 236 pp., bibliography, illustrations; LC:80-298301.

Subjects: 1. Organizations and Services to Families / Education and the Family; 2. Family Counseling and Education / Child Development.

122 Blackburn, George and Ricards, Sherman L. "The Mother-Headed
Family among Free Negroes in Charleston, South Carolina, 1850-1860."
PHYLON 42, 1 (Spring 1981): 11-25. 15 pp., references, tables.

Subjects: 1. Trends and Change in Marriage and Family / Family Life
   Prior to 1900; 2. Family Relationships and Dynamics / Single Parent
   Families.

   It is apparent that the free Negro women of Charleston lived under
   severe handicaps in the antebellum period. Not only were they, along
   with free males, subject to legal restrictions, but the census
   manuscripts show   that the free female had limited occupation
   opportunities; not surprisingly, free females were less successful in
   accumulating   wealth   than were males. In addition, there were
   substantially larger numbers of free Negro females than males in the
   adult years. One result was that female-headed families among free
   Negroes were more common than male-headed families. The census
   manuscripts also provide data which suggest that the female-headed
   families were stable. Thus stable, female-headed families among free?
   Negroes, despite difficulties, were a norm in antebellum Charleston,
   South Carolina. (From authors' text)

123 Blackburn, Regina Lynn. "Conscious Agents of Time and Self: The
Lives and Styles of African-American Women as Seen through Their
Autobiographical Writings." (Ph.D. dissertation, The University of New
Mexico, 1978.) DISSERTATION ABSTRACTS INTERNATIONAL, 39, 7, Jan. 1979,
4346A. (University Microfilms No. 7900935.) 348 pp.

Subjects: 1. Family Relationships and Dynamics / Family Relationships;
   2. / Women's Issues; 3. Psychology and Sociology / Self-Esteem.

124 Blair, Annie. "A Comparison of Negro and White Fertility
Attitudes." In SOCIOLOGICAL CONTRIBUTIONS TO FAMILY PLANNING RESEARCH,
edited by Donald Joseph Bogue, p. . Chicago, IL: University of Chicago
Community and Family Study Centers. University of Chicago Press, 1967.

Subjects: 1. Issues Related to Reproduction / Fertility Rates.

125 Blassingame, John W. THE SLAVE COMMUNITY: PLANTATION LIFE IN THE
ANTEBELLUM SOUTH. New York: Oxford University Press, 1972. 262 pp.,
bibliography, illustrations, index; LC:72-77495.

Subjects: 1. Trends and Change in Marriage and Family / Family Life
   Prior to 1900.

   Notes: Bibliography: pp. 239-254.

126 Blassingame, John W. THE SLAVE COMMUNITY: PLANTATION LIFE IN THE
ANTEBELLUM SOUTH. Revised and enl. ed. Oxford University Press, 1979.
414 pp., bibliography, illustrations, index; ISBN:0-19-502562-8; LC:78-
26890.

Subjects: 1. Trends and Change in Marriage and Family / Family Life
   Prior to 1900.

   Notes: Bibliography: pp. 383-402

127 Blau, Zena Smith. "Exposure to Childrearing Experts: A Structural Interpretation of Class-Color Differences." AMERICAN JOURNAL OF SOCIOLOGY 69, 6 (May 1964): 596-608. 13 pp., references, tables.

Subjects: 1. Family Relationships and Dynamics / Socialization; 2. Family Counseling and Education / Education for Parenthood; 3. Minority Groups / Family and Social Class.

128 Blau, Zena Smith, Oser, George T. and Stephens, Richard C. "Aging, Social Class, and Ethnicity: A Comparison of Anglo, Black and Mexican-American Texans." PACIFIC SOCIOLOGICAL REVIEW 22, 4 (October 1979): 501-25. 24 pp., references, tables.

Subjects: 1. Family Relationships and Dynamics / Later Years and Aging; 2. Minority Groups / Ethnic Groups in the United States; 3. / Family and Social Class.

129 Blaydon, Colin C. and Stack, Carol B. "Income Support Policies and the Family." DAEDALUS 106, 2 (Spring 1977): 147-162. 16 pp.

Subjects: 1. Trends and Change in Marriage and Family / Family Policy; 2. Organizations and Services to Families / Economics and the Family.

130 Blood, Robert O., Jr. and Wolfe, Donald M. "Negro-White Differences in Blue-Collar Marriages in a Northern Metropolis." SOCIAL FORCES 48, 1 (September 1979): 59-63. 5 pp., references, tables.

Subjects: 1. Marriage and Divorce / Differential Marriage Rates.

131 Bogue, Donald J. "Family Planning in the Negro Ghettos of Chicago." MILBANK MEMORIAL FUND QUARTERLY 48, 2 (April 1970): 283-299,300-307. 25 pp., tables.

Subjects: 1. Issues Related to Reproduction / Family Planning.

132 Bogue, Donald J. "A Long-Term Solution to the AFDC Problem: Prevention of Unwanted Pregnancy." SOCIAL SERVICE REVIEW 49, 4 (December 1975): 539-52. 14 pp., tables, appendices.

Subjects: 1. Issues Related to Reproduction / Birth Control.

133 Bogue, Donald Joseph, ed. SOCIOLOGICAL CONTRIBUTIONS TO FAMILY PLANNING RESEARCH. Community and Family Study Center, University of Chicago. Books and Monographs. Chicago, IL: University of Chicago Community and Family Study Centers. University of Chicago Press, 1967. 409 pp.; LC:70-12657.

Subjects: 1. Issues Related to Reproduction / Birth Control; 2. Psychology and Sociology / Sociology; 3. Aids for Theory and Research / Collected Works.

A collection of excerpts from graduate M.A. or Ph.D. theses originated in the Department of Sociology at the University of Chicago. (From author's introduction)

134 Bonner, Florence B. "Black Women and White Women: Comparative Analysis of Perceptions of Sex Roles for Self, Ideal Self and the Ideal

Male." JOURNAL OF AFRO-AMERICAN ISSUES 2, 3/4 (Summer 1974): 237-46.
11 pp., references, tables.

Subjects: 1. Family Relationships and Dynamics / Family Roles and Sex
   Roles.

Contemporary research on sex-role changes among Black women, in the
main, consists of polemical and informal discussions, communicated to
the general public as "the Black woman's position" on sex-role changes
and the related Feminist Movement. She is generally perceived to
differ markedly from the White female. This difference is perceived to
be linked to her race and to her inter-relationship to the Black male
which is believed to be "uniquely" different than   the   White
male/female   relationship.   The questionnaire, consisting of 104
stratements divided into three scales (self perception, ideal woman,
and ideal man) plus ten biographical questions, administered to the
sample of 34 Black women and 50 white women did not support this
position. It is not our intention to ignore differences between Black
and White females; rather, we suggest that neither group   is
homogeneous. Moreover, the impact of stereotypes on Black women's
attitudes toward "self" and "other(s)" remains questionable. Thus, we
suggest that this pilot study is a beginning. Further research is
necessary to adequately assess the complexities of the role network
and   the Black woman's attitudes about that network. (Author's
abstract)

135 Borland, Barry L. and Rudolp, Joseph P. "Relative Effects of
Low Socioeconomic Status, Parental Smoking and Poor Scholastic
Performance on Smoking among High School Students." SOCIAL SCIENCE AND
MEDICINE 9, 1 (January 1975): 27-30. 4 pp., references, tables.

Subjects: 1. Organizations and Services to Families / Physical Health
   and the Family; 2. Families with Special Problems / Achievement and
   the Family; 3. Minority Groups / Family and Social Class.

136 Bortner, R.W., Bohn, Claudia J. and Hultsch, David F. "A Cross-
Cultural Study of the Effects of Children on Parental Assessment of
Past, Present and Future." JOURNAL OF MARRIAGE AND THE FAMILY 36, 2
(May 1974): 370-378. 9 pp., references, tables.

Subjects: 1. Trends and Change in Marriage and Family / Comparative
   Studies--International, Interclass, Sex, and Time Differences; 2.
   Family Relationships and Dynamics / Parent-Child Relationships; 3.
   Issues Related to Reproduction / Childlessness.

137 Bould, Sally. "Black and White Families: Factors Affecting the
Wife's Contribution to the Family Income Where the Husband's Income is
Low to Moderate." SOCIOLOGICAL QUARTERLY 18, 4 (Autumn 1977): 536-547.
14 pp., references, tables.

Subjects: 1. Organizations and Services to Families / Dual Career
   Families; 2. / Working Mothers; 3. Family Relationships and Dynamics /
   Husband-Wife Relationships.

The economic role of the black wife in contrast to her husband's weak
economic position is a key assumption in Moynihan's thesis of a black
matriarchy. Using the National Longitudinal Survey of women, aged 30

to 44, in 1967, this paper examines the factors affecting the wife's contribution to the family income for both black and white families where the husband's income is below the median of all male-headed families. The results suggest that black wives and white wives respond similarly with respect to their overall contribution, the demand for female labor, and the effect of children. There is no support, moreover, for Moynihan's assumption that black wives are compensating for their husband's weak economic position. It appears, however, that the definition of the provider may differ among black families and white families. (Author's abstract)

138 Bould, Sally. "Female-Headed Families: Personal Fate Control and the Provider Role." JOURNAL OF MARRIAGE AND THE FAMILY 39, 2 (May 1977): 339-349. 11 pp., references, tables, charts.

Subjects: 1. Family Relationships and Dynamics / Single Parent Families; 2. / Family Roles and Sex Roles.

This paper examines black and white female heads of families who were interviewed in 1967 in a national longitudinal sample of women, age 30-44, for the Center for Human Resource Research. It was hypothesized that the source as well as the amount of income which these women received would affect their sense of personal fate control. The regression results suggest that poor women and women who must depend upon AFDC, child wupport and other stigmatizing or unstable sources of income feel less able to plan for their lives. (Author's abstract)

139 Bowie, Geraldine Robert Basley. "A Comparative Analysis of Vocabulary Diversity, Syntactic Maturity, and the Communicative and Cognitive Function of the Language of Black Four-Year-Old Children at Two Socioeconomic Levels." (Ph.D. dissertation, Southern Illinois University at Carbondale, 1979.) DISSERTATION ABSTRACTS INTERNATIONAL, 40, 8, Feb. 1980, 4395A. (University Microfilms No. 8004028.) 136 pp.

Subjects: 1. Family Counseling and Education / Early Childhood Education.

140 Bowser, Benjamin P. "The Contribution of Blacks to Sociological Knowledge: A Problem of Theory and Role to 1950." PHYLON 42, 2 (June 1981): 180-93. 14 pp., references.

Subjects: 1. Family Relationships and Dynamics / Family Roles and Sex Roles; 2. Psychology and Sociology / Sociology; 3. Aids for Theory and Research / Critiques and Analyses of Family Research Literature.

141 Boyd, Nancy Jeanne. "Clinicians' Perceptions of Black Families in Therapy." (Ph.D. dissertation, Columbia University, 1977.) DISSERTATION ABSTRACTS INTERNATIONAL, 38, 1, July 1978, 346B. (University Microfilms No. 7714783.) 193 pp.

Subjects: 1. Family Counseling and Education / Family Therapy; 2. Aids for Theory and Research / Family Theory.

142 Boykin, A. Wade, Franklin, Anderson J. and Yates, Jacques Frank, eds. RESEARCH DIRECTIONS OF BLACK PSYCHOLOGISTS. New York: Russell Sage Foundation, 1979. 440 pp., bibliography, illustrations, index; ISBN:0-87154-254-4; LC:79-7348.

Subjects: 1. Psychology and Sociology / Psychology; 2. Aids for Theory
and Research / Family Research Methodology.

143 Bracey, John H., Meier, August and Rudwick, Elliott, eds. BLACK
MATRIARCHY: MYTH OR REALITY? A Wadsworth Series: Explorations in the
Black Experience. Belmont, CA: Wadsworth Publishing Co., 1971. 217
pp., references; ISBN:0-534-00049-5; LC:77-154815.

Subjects: 1. Family Relationships and Dynamics / Women's Issues; 2.
  Aids for Theory and Research / Family Theory; 3. / Collected Works.

144 Braithwaite, Ronald. "A Paired Study of Self-Disclosure of Black
and White Inmates." JOURNAL OF NONWHITE CONCERNS IN PERSONNEL AND
GUIDANCE 1, 2 (January 1973): 86-94. 9 pp., references, tables.

Subjects: 1. Families with Special Problems / Families with Criminal
  Offenders; 2. Psychology and Sociology / Psychology.

145 Braithwaite, Ronald L. "Interpersonal Relations between Black
Males and Black Females." In BLACK MEN, edited by Lawrence E. Gary,
pp. 83-97. Beverly Hill, CA: Sage Publications, Inc., 1981. 15 pp.

Subjects: 1. Family Relationships and Dynamics / Family Relationships;
  2. / Men's Issues; 3. Mate Selection / Mate Selection, Differential
  Patterns.

[The author] identifies factors that influence the quality of
interaction between males and their families. Among the factors
discussed are the following: (1) the male sex role, (2) sexual
behavior, (3) the scarcity of eligible Black men, (4) the women's
liberation movement, and (5) class and family background. After
examining data from a national survey of over 600,000 Black people. .
. some specific suggestions for improving the relationships between
Black male and females [are noted]. (From editor's remarks)

146 Branson, Nathaniel William. "An Investigation of the Effects of
Work on the Families of Black, Female Registrants in the Baltimore City
Win Program, A Pilot Study." (Ph.D. dissertation, University of
Maryland, 1979.) DISSERTATION ABSTRACTS INTERNATIONAL, 40, 6,
Dec. 1980, 3525A. (University Microfilms No. 7926527.) 243 pp.

Subjects: 1. Organizations and Services to Families / Employment and the
  Family; 2. Psychology and Sociology / Self-Esteem.

147 Braxton, B. WOMEN, SEX AND RACE: A REALISTIC VIEW OF SEXISM AND
RACISM. Washington, D.C.: Verta Press, 1973. 227 pp., bibliography;
LC:72-91049.

Subjects: 1. Family Relationships and Dynamics / Family Roles and Sex
  Roles; 2. / Women's Issues; 3. Psychology and Sociology / Racial
  Attitudes.

Discusses women's issues ranging from witchcraft trials to the
Women's Liberation Movement.

Notes: Bibliography: pp. 218-224.

148 Brennan, Tim, Huizinga, David and Elliot, Delbert S. THE
SOCIAL PSYCHOLOGY OF RUNAWAYS. Lexington, MA: Lexington Books, 1978.
346 pp., bibliography, index; ISBN:0-669-00565-7; LC:75-42947.

Subjects: 1. Families with Special Problems / Runaways; 2. Psychology
   and Sociology / Psychology; 3. Family Counseling and Education /
   Adolescence.

Notes: Bibliography: pp. 325-335.

149 Brent, Linda, ed. INCIDENTS IN THE LIFE OF A SLAVE GIRL. New
York: Harcourt, Brace and Jovanovich, Inc., 1973. 210 pp.; LC:75-62285.

Subjects: 1. Trends and Change in Marriage and Family / Family Life
   Prior to 1900; 2. Family Relationships and Dynamics / Women's Issues.

Notes: Edited by Lydia Maria Child. New introduction and notes by
   Walter Teller.

150 Brigham, John C., Woodmansee, John J. and Cook, Stuart W.
"Dimensions of Verbal Racial Attitudes: Interracial Marriage and
Approaches to Racial Equality." JOURNAL OF SOCIAL ISSUES 32, 2 (Spring
1976): 9-21. 13 pp., references, tables.

Subjects: 1. Trends and Change in Marriage and Family / Family and
   Social Change; 2. Marriage and Divorce / Inter-marriage.

151 Brodber, Erma and Wagner, Nathaniel N. "The Black Family, Poverty,
and Family Planning: Anthropological Impressions." FAMILY COORDINATOR
19, 2 (August 1970): 168-72. 5 pp., references.

Subjects: 1. Issues Related to Reproduction / Family Planning; 2.
   Families with Special Problems / Family Stress.

152 Broderick, Carlfred B. "Social Heterosexual Development among
Urban Negroes and Whites." JOURNAL OF MARRIAGE AND THE FAMILY 27, 2
(May 1965): 200-203. 4 pp., references, tables, charts.

Subjects: 1. Family Relationships and Dynamics / Socialization; 2.
   Sexual Attitudes and Behavior / Sexual Attitudes and Behavior.

153 Broderick, Carlfred B. and Bernard, Jesse, eds. THE INDIVIDUAL,
SEX AND SOCIETY. Baltimore, MD: Johns Hopkins Press, 1969. 406 pp.,
references, bibliography, index; ISBN:0-8018-1036-1; LC:69-11934.

Subjects: 1. Sexual Attitudes and Behavior / Sexual Attitudes and
   Behavior; 2. Aids for Theory and Research / Collected Works.

Notes: A SIECUS (Sex Information and Education Council of the U.S.)
handbook for teachers and counselors.

154 Broderick, Carlfred Bartholomew, ed. A DECADE OF FAMILY RESEARCH
AND ACTION. Minneapolis, MN: National Council of Family Relations,
1971. 296 pp.; LC:74-103557.

Subjects: 1. Trends and Change in Marriage and Family / Family Life in
the United States; 2. Aids for Theory and Research / Critiques and
Analyses of Family Research Literature; 3. / Collected Works.

A number of articles that first appeared in The Journal of Marriage
and the Family.

155 Brody, Eugene B. et al. MINORITY GROUP ADOLESCENTS IN THE UNITED
STATES. Baltimore, MD: Williams and Wilkins, 1968. 243 pp.,
references; LC:68-11215.

Subjects: 1. Psychology and Sociology / Psychology; 2. Family Counseling
and Education / Adolescence; 3. Aids for Theory and Research /
Collected Works.

156 Brody, Eugene B., Ottey, Frank and Lagranade, Janet. "Early
Sex Education in Relationship Behavior: Evidence from Jamaican Women."
AMERICAN JOURNAL OF PSYCHIATRY 133, 8 (August 1976): 969-972. 4 pp.

Subjects: 1. Sexual Attitudes and Behavior / Sexual Attitudes and
Behavior; 2. Family Counseling and Education / Sex Education.

157 Brody, Gene H. and Endsley, Richard C. "Researching Children and
Families: Differences in Approaches of Child and Family Specialists."
FAMILY RELATIONS 30, 2 (April 1981): 275-280. 6 pp., references.

Subjects: 1. Family Relationships and Dynamics / Nuclear Family; 2.
Family Counseling and Education / Family Life Education; 3. Aids for
Theory and Research / Family Research Methodology.

158 Bromley, David G. and Longino, Charles F., Jr., eds. WHITE RACISM
AND BLACK AMERICANS. Cambridge, MA: Schenkman Publishing Co., 1972.
662 pp., bibliography; LC:72-81513.

Subjects: 1. Psychology and Sociology / Racial Attitudes; 2. Aids for
Theory and Research / Collected Works.

Notes: Forward by Shirley Chisholm.

159 Brook, Judith S., Lukoff, Irving F. and Whiteman, Martin. "Peer,
Family, and Personality Domains as Related to Adolescents' Drug
Behavior." PSYCHOLOGICAL REPORTS 41, 3 (December 1977): 1095-1102. 8
pp., references, bibliography, tables.

Subjects: 1. Family Relationships and Dynamics / Parent-Adolescent
Relationships; 2. Families with Special Problems / Drug Abuse.

160 Brook, Judith S., Whiteman, Martin, Peisach, Estelle and Deutsch,
Martin. "Aspiration Levels of and for Children: Age, Sex, Race,
Socioeconomic Correlates." JOURNAL OF GENETIC PSYCHOLOGY 124, 1 (March
1974): 3-16. 14 pp., references, bibliography, tables.

Subjects: 1. Organizations and Services to Families / Employment and the
Family; 2. Families with Special Problems / Achievement and the
Family; 3. Minority Groups / Family and Social Class.

One hundred sixty-five fifth-grade and 127 first-grade children and their parents were studied to examine correlates of the child's own occupational aspirations and of his parents' aspirations for him. Parents' educational and occupational aspirations for the child were related to (a) socioeconomic status (SES); (b) race in the educational area only; and (c) sex. The children's own occupational aspirations were associated with interactions of SES with grade and sex, and of grade with sex. The correlations between the parent's educational and occupational aspirations and between the parent and child aspirations were highest for the fifth-grade children, for the white parents irrespective of SES, and for the black parents of higher SES level. (Authors' summary)

161 Brookins, Geraldine Kearse. "Maternal Employment: Its Impact on the Sex Roles and Occupational Choices of Middle and Working Class Black Children." (Ph.D. dissertation, Harvard University, 1977.) DISSERTATION ABSTRACTS INTERNATIONAL, 38, 9, March 1978, 4441B. (University Microfilms No. 7801725.) 130 pp.

Subjects: 1. Organizations and Services to Families / Working Mothers; 2. Family Relationships and Dynamics / Family Roles and Sex Roles.

162 Brooks, Robert. SEX--BLACK AND WHITE. New York: Dell Books, 1971.; ISBN:440-07877-125.

Subjects: 1. Trends and Change in Marriage and Family / Comparative Studies--International, Interclass, Sex, and Time Differences; 2. Sexual Attitudes and Behavior / Sexual Attitudes and Behavior.

163 Broude, Gwen J. "Extramarital Sex Norms in Cross-Cultural Perspective." BEHAVIOR SCIENCE RESEARCH 15, 3 (July 1980): 181-218. 38 pp., references, bibliography, tables.

Subjects: 1. Trends and Change in Marriage and Family / Comparative Studies--International, Interclass, Sex, and Time Differences; 2. Sexual Attitudes and Behavior / Extramarital Sexual Behavior.

164 Broude, Gwen J. "Norms of Premarital Sexual Behavior: A Cross-Cultural Study." ETHOS 3, 3 (Fall 1975): 381-402. 21 pp., references, bibliography, tables.

Subjects: 1. Sexual Attitudes and Behavior / Premarital Sexual Behavior.

165 Brown, Alexander Lionel. "The Effects of Race, Intelligence and Maternal Employment Status of the Career/Occupational Role Stereotypes of Four-Year Old Girls." (Ed.D. dissertation, Indiana University, 1980.) DISSERTATION ABSTRACTS INTERNATIONAL, 41, 4, Oct. 1980, 1397A-1398A. (University Microfilms No. 8022706.) 81 pp.

Subjects: 1. Organizations and Services to Families / Working Mothers; 2. Families with Special Problems / Achievement and the Family; 3. Family Counseling and Education / Early Childhood Education.

166 Brown, Delindus R. and Anderson, Wanda F. "A Survey of the Black Woman and the Persuasion Process: The Study of Strategies of Identification and Resistance." JOURNAL OF BLACK STUDIES 9, 2 (December 1978): 233-48. 16 pp., references.

Subjects: 1. Family Relationships and Dynamics / Communication in the Family; 2. / Women's Issues.

167 Brown, George L. "Invisible Again: Blacks and the Energy Crisis." SOCIAL POLICY 7, 4 (January 1977): 39-42. 4 pp., illustrations.

Subjects: 1. Organizations and Services to Families / Consumerism; 2. Family Relationships and Dynamics / Environment (Space/Housing).

168 Brown, Josephine V., Bakeman, Roger, Snyder, Patricia A., Fredrickson, W. Timm, Morgan, Sharon T. and Hepler, Ruth. "Interactions of Black Inner-City Mothers with their Newborn Infants." CHILD DEVELOPMENT 46, 3 (September 1975): 677-86. 10 pp., references, tables.

Subjects: 1. Family Relationships and Dynamics / Mother-Child Relationships.

Interactions of 45 black inner-city mothers with their healthy full-term newborn infants were observed during a bottle-feeding on the third day after birth. An exhaustive catalog of some 100 mother and infant behaviors was used to describe objectively the interactions of mothers and infants. In addition to being observed with their mothers, infants were examined with the Rosenblith scale. The infant's birth weights, birth order, and sex and maternal medication were found to affect the infant's behaviors and/or the patterns of mother-infant interactions. (Authors' abstract)

169 Brown, Prudence, Perry, Lorraine and Harburg, Ernest. "Sex Role Attitudes and Psychological Outcomes for Black and White Women Experiencing Marital Dissolution." JOURNAL OF MARRIAGE AND THE FAMILY 39, 3 (August 1977): 549-61. 13 pp., references, tables.

Subjects: 1. Family Relationships and Dynamics / Family Roles and Sex Roles; 2. Marriage and Divorce / Divorce and Separation.

The mediating impact of sex role attitudes on psychological outcomes for black and white women experiencing dissolution is investigated. Findings are based on a sample of 253 women interviewed twice during the divorce process: when they first contacted a court-related marriage counseling service and then four months later. Findings indicated that black and white women did not differ in the degree of traditionality of their sex role attitudes on any of the three factors identified: (1) Women in the Home, (2) Traditional Family Roles, and (3) Job Inequality. Traditional white women reported significantly lower self-esteem, inner directedness and internal control, more distress and less well-being, and less personal growth than nontraditional white women. The relationship between sex role ideology and psychological outcomes during divorce was not evident for black women. Ethnic differences in women's psychological responses to divorce are discussed in the context of their different socialization experiences and historical family traditions in American society. (Authors' abstract)

170 Brown, Raeford. "The Relationship of Moral Conscience, Discipline and Culture among Black Children." (Ph.D. dissertation, The University of Michigan, 1978.) DISSERTATION ABSTRACTS INTERNATIONAL, 39, 2, Aug. 1978, 1042B. (University Microfilms No. 7813620.) 98 pp.

Subjects: 1. Family Relationships and Dynamics / Parent-Child
Relationships; 2. Family Counseling and Education / Value Education.

171 Brown, Steven E. "Sexuality and the Slave Community." PHYLON 42,
1 (Spring 1981): 1-10. 10 pp., references.

Subjects: 1. Trends and Change in Marriage and Family / Family Life
Prior to 1900; 2. Sexual Attitudes and Behavior / Sexual Attitudes and
Behavior.

Slaves could not completely control their sexual activities any more
than they could completely control any other phase of their existence.
Although masters were often able to compel submission and breeding,
blacks still managed to develop shared community values concerning
their sexual relationships. Although blacks were rather free in their
premarital sexual activities compared to whites, slaves did adhere to
clear codes of behavior. The slave testimonies [of the nineteenth
century] indicate that frequently there were standard procedures to be
followed regarding courtship. Furthermore,   the   slave   writings
convincingly demonstrate that families occupied a position of central
importance for slave life. Blacks were concerned with marriage despite
restrictions against the institution. Slaves considered fidelity and
caring for their loved ones a virtue. Perhaps the most telling
observation that may be noted is that slaves continued to develop love
for one another despite the circumscribed conditions imposed by
slavery. Blacks frequently exposed themselves to grave danger in order
to remain with their spouses, children and relatives. The slave
testimony eloquently attests to the efforts blacks underwent to
maintain a home and a family. (From author's text)

172 Brown, Waln K. "Black Gangs as Family Extensions." INTERNATIONAL
JOURNAL OF OFFENDER THERAPY AND COMPARATIVE CRIMINOLOGY 22, 1 (April
1978): 39-45. 7 pp., references.

Subjects: 1. Family Relationships and Dynamics / Extended Family and
Kinship Groups; 2. Families with Special Problems / Families with
Juvenile Delinquents.

[Researchers have often concluded] that delinquency among blacks is a
result of the disintegration and disorganization of the black lower-
class family. It is the purpose of this paper to go beyond these
findings and note the dynamics of lower-class black family life in
order to understand the context of black gang delinquency. Although
the complications of unstable family conditions cannot be dismissed as
a cause of delinquency, they cannot be considered the only factor.
More specifically, we would claim that the gang is an elementary form
of a survival technique where youths learn the rudiments of building
large personal networks of relationships that can be counted on for
aid when needed. This is a strong theme to be found in the dynamics of
black lower-class existence, and is a strategy employed by older males
and females alike who realize that mutual aid is a necessity for
survival in the ghetto. Gangs are thus the youth's early construct of
this network of relationships and through the gang the black youth
learns the intricacies of this survival technique and the other
nuances of this life-style that he must know if he is to function
safely and efficiently in the ghetto. (From author's text)

173 Brown, William Neal. "Strategies of Intervention with the Parents of 'Acting Out' Preschool Black Children." (D.S.W. dissertation, City University of New York, 1979.) DISSERTATION ABSTRACTS INTERNATIONAL, 40, 5, Nov. 1979, 2895A. (University Microfilms No. 7923710.) 130 pp.

Subjects: 1. Organizations and Services to Families / Education and the Family; 2. Family Relationships and Dynamics / Parent-Child Relationships; 3. Aids for Theory and Research / Family Research Methodology.

174 Brunswick, Ann F. "What Generation Gap? A Comparison of Some Generational Differences among Blacks and Whites." SOCIAL PROBLEMS 17, 3 (Winter 1970): 358-71. 12 pp., references, bibliography, tables.

Subjects: 1. Trends and Change in Marriage and Family / Family Life in the United States.

175 Bryant, Barbara Huddleston. "The Postdivorce Adjustment of Middle Class Black Women." (D.S.W. dissertation, University of California, Los Angeles, 1982.) DISSERTATION ABSTRACTS INTERNATIONAL, 43, 4, Oct. 1982, 1291A. (University Microfilms No. 8219648.) 232 pp.

Subjects: 1. Marriage and Divorce / Divorce and Separation.

176 Buehler, Marilyn H., Weigert, Andrew J. and Thomas, Darwin L. "Correlates of Conjugal Power: A Five Cultural Analysis of Adolescent Perceptions." JOURNAL OF COMPARATIVE FAMILY STUDIES 5, 1 (Spring 1974): 5-16. 12 pp., references, bibliography, tables.

Subjects: 1. Family Relationships and Dynamics / Husband-Wife Relationships; 2. / Parent-Adolescent Relationships; 3. / Men's Issues.

177 Bullard, Robert D. "Housing and the Quality of Life in the Urban Community: A Focus on the Dynamic Factor Affecting Blacks in the Housing Market." JOURNAL OF SOCIAL AND BEHAVIOR SCIENCES 25, 2 (Spring 1979): 46-52. 7 pp.

Subjects: 1. Family Relationships and Dynamics / Environment (Space/ Housing).

In recent years numerous discussions have been centered around the quality of housing in the black community. This study critically examines several conceptual and substantive areas which affect blacks in the housing market. To illustrate the fundamental problems of blacks in the housing market, six specific topics--governmental policies, homeownership, segregation, discrimination, migration and renewed interest in the inner city--were selected for intensive analysis. Market factors, in addition to discriminatory housing practices, continue to deny blacks a basic form of investment: namely, homeownership. (Author's abstract)

178 Bullard, Robert D. and Tryman, Donald L. "Competition for Decent Housing: A Focus on Housing Discrimination Complaints in a Sunbelt City." JOURNAL OF ETHNIC STUDIES 7, 4 (Winter 1980): 51-63. 11 pp., references, tables.

Subjects: 1. Family Relationships and Dynamics / Environment (Space/ Housing).

179 Burgess, Rebecca Bahr. "Effects of Attitudes about Premarital Sex on Contraceptive Risk-Taking among Low-Income Unmarried Teenagers." (Ph.D. dissertation, Emory University, 1979.) DISSERTATION ABSTRACTS INTERNATIONAL, 40, 1, July 1979, 485A. (University Microfilms No. 7916048.) 194 pp.

Subjects: 1. Issues Related to Reproduction / Teenage Pregnancy; 2. Sexual Attitudes and Behavior / Premarital Sexual Behavior.

180 Burgest, David R. "Afrocircular Child in a Eurocircular Society." BLACK CHILD JOURNAL: A REVIEW OF BLACK CHILD DEVELOPMENT 2, 1 (Fall 1980): 16-20. 5 pp.

Subjects: 1. Trends and Change in Marriage and Family / Family Life in Foreign Countries; 2. Family Relationships and Dynamics / Socialization.

181 Burgest, David R. and Bower, Joanna. "Erroneous Assumptions Black Women Make about Black Men." BLACK MALE/FEMALE RELATIONSHIPS 2, 5 (Spring 1981): 46-54. 9 pp.

Subjects: 1. Family Relationships and Dynamics / Women's Issues.

182 Burlew, Ann Kathleen. "Career Educational Choices Among Black Females." JOURNAL OF BLACK PSYCHOLOGY 3, 2 (February 1977): 88-106. 19 pp., references, charts.

Subjects: 1. Organizations and Services to Families / Education and the Family; 2. Family Relationships and Dynamics / Women's Issues.

183 Burnett-Epps, Martha Alma. "The Perceptions of the Black Aged and Their Relatives toward the Receipt of Care Components at Contracting Socioeconomic Levels." (Ph.D. dissertation, The Union for Experimenting Colleges and Universities, 1981.) DISSERTATION ABSTRACTS INTERNATIONAL, 42, 10, April 1982, 4390A-4391A. (University Microfilms No. 8205648.) 212 pp.

Subjects: 1. Organizations and Services to Families / Social Services and the Family; 2. Family Relationships and Dynamics / Later Years and Aging.

184 Burr, Wesley R., Hill, Reuben, Nye, F. I. and Reiss, Ira L. CONTEMPORARY THEORIES ABOUT THE FAMILY: VOLUME 1. RESEARCH-BASED THEORIES. New York: The Free Press, 1979.; ISBN:0-02-904940-7; LC:77-81430.

Subjects: 1. Aids for Theory and Research / Family Theory; 2. / Critiques and Analyses of Family Research Literature; 3. / Collected Works.

185 Burroughs, Louise Vitiello. "Occupational Preferences and Expectations as Related to Locus of Control, Sex-Role Contingency Orientation, Race and Family History among College Women." (Ed.D. dissertation, University of Massachusetts, 1981.) DISSERTATION

ABSTRACTS INTERNATIONAL, 42, 8, Feb. 1982, 3437A.   (University Microfilms No. 8201310.) 176 pp.

Subjects: 1. Organizations and Services to Families / Employment and the Family; 2. Family Relationships and Dynamics / Family Roles and Sex Roles.

186 Burwell, Sherri Lynn. "The Soul of Black Women: The Hermeneutical Method of Analysis as Applied to the Novel 'Corregidora'." (Ph.D. dissertation, California School of Professional Psychology, Berkeley, 1979.) DISSERTATION ABSTRACTS INTERNATIONAL, 39, 12, June 1979, 6111B. (University Microfilms No. 7914095.) 109 pp.

Subjects: 1. Family Relationships and Dynamics / Women's Issues; 2. Psychology and Sociology / Psychology.

187 Busse, Thomas V. and Seraydarian, Louisa. "Desirability of First Names, Ethnicity and Parental Education." PSYCHOLOGICAL REPORTS 40, 3, Part 1 (June 1977): 739-42. 4 pp., references, tables.

Subjects: 1. Family Counseling and Education / Education for Parenthood; 2. Minority Groups / Ethnic Groups in the United States.

188 Butler, Cynthia and Doster, Joseph A.   "Sex-Role Learning in the Black Male: Research and Clinical Implications." JOURNAL OF AFRO-AMERICAN ISSUES 4, 2 (Spring 1976): 121-38. 18 pp., references, charts.

Subjects: 1. Family Relationships and Dynamics / Family Roles and Sex Roles; 2. Aids for Theory and Research / Family Research Methodology.

189 Cade, Tinina Quick. "Black Parents' Beliefs about Appropriate Child Behaviors Relating to White Teachers." (Ph.D. dissertation, University of Pittsburgh, 1977.) DISSERTATION ABSTRACTS INTERNATIONAL, 38, 9, March 1978, 5314A. (University Microfilms No. 7801790.) 151 pp.

Subjects: 1. Organizations and Services to Families / Education and the Family; 2. Family Relationships and Dynamics / Socialization.

190 Cade, Toni, comp. THE BLACK WOMAN: AN ANTHOLOGY. New York: New American Library/A Signet Book, 1970. 256 pp.; LC:70-121388.

Subjects: 1. Family Relationships and Dynamics / Women's Issues; 2. Aids for Theory and Research / Collected Works.

191 Caldwell, John C. "Fertility and the Household Economy in Nigeria." JOURNAL OF COMPARATIVE FAMILY STUDIES 7, 2 (Summer 1976): 193-253. 60 pp., references, tables.

Subjects: 1. Trends and Change in Marriage and Family / Family and Social Change; 2. Issues Related to Reproduction / Fertility Rates.

192 Calhoun, Fred S. "Childrearing Practices of the Black Father." (M.S. thesis, California State University, Long Beach, 1977.) DISSERTATION ABSTRACTS INTERNATIONAL, 16, 3, Sept. 1978, 181. (University Microfilms No. 1311105.) 57 pp.

Subjects: 1. Family Relationships and Dynamics / Father-Child
Relationships.

193 Calhoun, Princess Diane. "Family Factors in Black Adolescent
Mental Health." (Ph.D. dissertation, George Peabody College for Teachers
of Vanderbilt University, 1981.) DISSERTATION ABSTRACTS INTERNATIONAL,
42, 11, May 1982, 4571B. (University Microfilms No. 8208440.) 95 pp.

Subjects: 1. Organizations and Services to Families / Mental Health and
the Family; 2. Family Relationships and Dynamics / Extended Family and
Kinship Groups; 3. Psychology and Sociology / Psychology.

194 Campbell, Randolph B. and Pickens, Donald K. "'My Dear Husband:' A
Texas Slave's Love Letter, 1862." JOURNAL OF NEGRO HISTORY 65, 4 (Fall
1980): 361-64. 4 pp., references.

Subjects: 1. Trends and Change in Marriage and Family / Family Life
Prior to 1900.

195 Carrington, Christine Hardy. "A Comparison of Cognitive and
Analytically Oriented Brief Treatment Approaches to Depression in Black
Women." (Ph.D. dissertation, University of Maryland, 1979.)
DISSERTATION ABSTRACTS INTERNATIONAL, 40, 6, Dec. 1979, 2829B.
(University Microfilms No. 7926513.) 201 pp.

Subjects: 1. Family Relationships and Dynamics / Women's Issues; 2.
Families with Special Problems / Families with Depressives; 3.
Psychology and Sociology / Psychology.

196 Carson, Josephine. SILENT VOICES: THE SOUTHERN NEGRO WOMAN TODAY.
New York: Delacorte Press, 1969. 273 pp.; LC:69-17530.

Subjects: 1. Family Relationships and Dynamics / Women's Issues.

197 Cazenave, Noel, ed. "Black Alternative Lifestyles: Special Issue
on Commentary and Reprise on Joseph Scott's Black Polygamous Family
Formation." ALTERNATIVE LIFESTYLES 3, 4 (November 1980): 371-503. 133
pp., references, bibliography.

Subjects: 1. Trends and Change in Marriage and Family / Alternative
Family Forms; 2. Aids for Theory and Research / Critiques and Analyses
of Family Research Literature.

A special issue devoted to discussions on black alternative
lifestyles. Includes three commentaries on Scott's black polygamous
family theory by Allen and Agbasegbe, McAdoo, and Jack (pp. 375-394),
a reprise by Scott (pp. 395-404) and five articles by Ericksen,
Cazenave, Staples, Aschenbrenner and Carr, and Rao and Rao. Concludes
with a tribute to alternative lifestyle researchers by Libby. See also
the individual listings by authors.

198 Cazenave, Noel A. "Alternative Intimacy, Marriage, and Family
Lifestyles among Low-Income Black Americans." ALTERNATIVE LIFESTYLES 3,
4 (November 1980): 425-44. 20 pp.

Subjects: 1. Trends and Change in Marriage and Family / Alternative
Family Forms; 2. Family Relationships and Dynamics / Family
Relationships; 3. Aids for Theory and Research / Family Theory.

This article describes nontraditional intimacy, marriage and family
structures, and patterns of interaction among low-income Black
Americans. Census data are reported to document trends in the
development of "alternative" family structures for American Blacks. An
explanation of why these lifestyles have heretofore been neglected in
alternative lifestyle research is suggested. The relation between
social structure and ethnic preferences in determining familial
lifestyle choices and options is explored. An attempt is made to
delineate the social, cultural, and economic forces associated with
their emergence. Finally, a theoretical approach to analyzing the
genesis of diverse ethnic family structure is explored. (Author's
abstract)

199 Cazenave, Noel A. "Family Violence and Aging Blacks: Theoretical
Perspectives and Research Possibilities." JOURNAL OF MINORITY AGING
(FORMERLY CALLED BLACK AGING) 4, 4 (September 1979): 99-108. 9 pp.,
references.

Subjects: 1. Family Relationships and Dynamics / Later Years and Aging;
2. Families with Special Problems / Family Violence; 3. Aids for
Theory and Research / Family Research Methodology.

Using a conflict approach, this article investigates various theories
of family violence as they may relate to aged blacks. Given the lack
of any studies in this particular area, a number of research
possibilities are suggested, including the study of the aged as
controllers, agitations, victims, or aggressors in familial violence.
(Author's abstract)

200 Cazenave, Noel A. "Middle Income Black Fathers: An Analysis of the
Provider Role." FAMILY COORDINATOR 28, 4 (October 1979): 583-93. 11
pp.

Subjects: 1. Organizations and Services to Families / Economics and the
Family; 2. Family Relationships and Dynamics / Family Roles and Sex
Roles; 3. / Men's Issues.

Interview data on 54 black letter carrier fathers were used for an
analysis of the provider role among middle-income black fathers. While
the provider role is found to be a very salient role identity for
these respondents, the conceptualization of the provider role common
in the popular sex-role literature as a one-dimensional, non-
expressive and restrictive escape from more involved patterns of
fathering does not apply. Instead, cross-generational data suggest
that these respondents are moving towards more developmental patterns
of fathering with increases in their ability to provide. The provider
role is viewed as an "interface phenomenon" which makes the execution
of other male familial roles possible. Proficiency in economic
provision is seen as essential to all paternal modalities and styles.
(Author's abstract)

201 Cazenave, Noel A. and Strauss, Murray A. "Race, Class, Network
Embeddedness and Family Violence: A Search for Potent Support Systems."

JOURNAL OF COMPARATIVE FAMILY STUDIES 10, 3 (Autumn 1979): 281-300.   20 pp., references, bibliography, tables.

Subjects: 1. Family Relationships and Dynamics / Socialization; 2. Families with Special Problems / Family Violence.

202 Chambers, Andrew Wade. "A Comparative Study of Black and White Homosexuals." (M.A. thesis, California State University, Fullerton, 1977.) DISSERTATION ABSTRACTS INTERNATIONAL, 16, 1, March 1978, 67. (University Microfilms No. 1310522.) 53 pp.

Subjects: 1. Sexual Attitudes and Behavior / Homosexuality and the Family; 2. Psychology and Sociology / Self-Esteem.

203 Chandler, Susan Meyers. "Self-Perceived Competency in Cross-Cultural Counseling." SOCIAL CASEWORK: THE JOURNAL OF CONTEMPORARY SOCIAL WORK 61, 6 (June 1980): 347-53.   7 pp., references, tables.

Subjects: 1. Trends and Change in Marriage and Family / Comparative Studies--International, Interclass, Sex, and Time Differences; 2. Psychology and Sociology / Self-Esteem; 3. Family Counseling and Education / Marital and Family Enrichment.

204 Chapman, Jane Roberts and Gates, Margaret, eds. WOMEN INTO WIVES: THE LEGAL AND ECONOMIC IMPACT OF MARRIAGE. Sage Yearbooks in Women's Policy Studies, No. 2. Beverly Hills, CA: Sage Publications, Inc., 1977. 320 pp., bibliography, charts, appendices; ISBN:0-8039-0700-1; LC:76-47070.

Subjects: 1. Family Relationships and Dynamics / Husband-Wife Relationships; 2. Marriage and Divorce / Marriage Satisfaction and Prediction Studies; 3. Aids for Theory and Research / Collected Works.

205 Chapman, Sabrina Coffey. "A Social-Psychological Analysis of Morale in a Selected Population: Low-Income Elderly Black Females." (Ph.D. dissertation, The Pennsylvania State University, 1979.) DISSERTATION ABSTRACTS INTERNATIONAL, 40, 5, Nov. 1979, 2922A. (University Microfilms No. 7922273.) 184 pp.

Subjects: 1. Family Relationships and Dynamics / Later Years and Aging; 2. Psychology and Sociology / Sociology; 3. Family Counseling and Education / Value Education.

206 Chappell, Earl Birges, III. "The Relationships between Socioeconomic Status, Sex, Self-Concept, Academic Achievement, and Course Selection of Urban Black Tenth-Grade Students." (Ed.D. dissertation, The College of William and Mary in Virginia, 1979.) DISSERTATION ABSTRACTS INTERNATIONAL, 40, 12, June 1980, 6180A. (University Microfilms No. 8014022.) 89 pp.

Subjects: 1. Organizations and Services to Families / Education and the Family; 2. Families with Special Problems / Achievement and the Family; 3. Psychology and Sociology / Self-Esteem.

207 Chauhan, Shri J.S. "Age at Marriage: A Study of 400 Mothers Obtaining Maternity Services at a Metropolitan Teaching Hospital."

JOURNAL OF FAMILY WELFARE 20, 4 (June 1974): 54-61.   8 pp., references, tables.

Subjects: 1. Marriage and Divorce / Differential Marriage Rates; 2.
   Issues Related to Reproduction / Fertility Rates.

208 Chavis, William M. and Lyles, Gladys J.   "Divorce Among Educated
Black Women." JOURNAL OF THE NATIONAL MEDICAL ASSOCIATION 67, 2 (March
1975): 128-34. 6 pp., references.

Subjects: 1. Organizations and Services to Families / Education and the
   Family; 2. Marriage and Divorce / Divorce and Separation.

   Selected through the gynecology practice of one of the investigators,
   50 married and 50 divorced educated Black women (i.e., those having at
   least 2 years of college or an equivalent level in business or
   technical training) from Detroit were interviewed regarding social and
   social-structural variables affecting their marriages. A comparison of
   the two groups revealed the following findings among others. Marriages
   were less stable when the wife's educational level superceded that of
   her husband. Although not significantly so, a greater percentage of
   married couples attended church more frequently than those couples
   whose marriages suffered a divorce. The most successful marriages were
   ones in which the prospective spouses knew each other for at least 36
   months prior to their wedding; whereas the prospective spouses in
   dissolved marriages were generally acquainted with each other less
   than 24 months prior to their wedding. It is further suggested that
   the presence of "relatives" in a couple's household for a long period
   of time may have a disturbing influence on the marital relationship.
   Based on the data generated in this study, some guidelines for
   premarital and marital counseling are offered.

209 Chermesh, Ran. "Internal Relations in Unemployed Families."
JOURNAL OF MARRIAGE AND THE FAMILY 37, 4 (November 1975): 978-984. 7
pp., references, tables, charts.

Subjects: 1. Organizations and Services to Families / Employment and the
   Family; 2. Family Relationships and Dynamics / Family Relationships.

210 Chestang, Leon. "The Dilemma of Biracial Adoption." SOCIAL WORK
17, 3 (May 1972): 100-105. 6 pp., references.

Subjects: 1. Organizations and Services to Families / Adoption and
   Adoption Services.

   Permanent homes must be found for the eighty thousand homeless black
   children in this country. Social work's solution has been biracial
   adoption. The author points up the dangers of such an approach both to
   the black child and the white adoptive parents. Although he does not
   advocate total abandonment of biracial adoption, he concludes that in
   this society only black families can assure an environment in which
   there is optimal opportunity for growth, development, and
   identification. (Author's abstract)

211 CHILD DEVELOPMENT FROM A BLACK PERSPECTIVE--CONFERENCE, JUNE 10-13,
1970, WASHINGTON, DC. Washington, DC: Black Child Development Education
Center, 1970. 94 pp., bibliography, illustrations; LC:73-23301.

Subjects: 1. Family Counseling and Education / Child Development; 2. Aids for Theory and Research / Collected Works.

Notes: Bibliography: p. 28

212 Chilman, Catherine S. "Families in Poverty in the Early 1970's: Rates, Associated Factors, Some Implications." JOURNAL OF MARRIAGE AND THE FAMILY 37, 1 (February 1975): 49-60. 11 pp., references, charts.

Subjects: 1. Organizations and Services to Families / Economics and the Family; 2. Families with Special Problems / Family Stress.

Analyses of recent Census data reveal that at least 12 per cent of the country's population was "below the poverty line" in 1970. This figure rises to 20 per cent when more realistic poverty measurements are used. It can be estimated that over one-fourth of the nation's children--over one-half of its black ones--are living in poverty. Factors most highly associated with poverty are female-headed families, large family size, minority group status, age (children, youth, the aged), unemployment and underemployment, region of residence, poor physical and mental health, little education, lack of income from sources other than wages. Structural problems in the economy and related social and political factors are shown to be far more causative of poverty than characteristics of individuals and families. It is unlikely that poverty can be reduced without improved income maintenance programs and creation of jobs in the public sector. (Author's abstract)

213 Chimezie, Amuzie. "Black Identity and the Grow-Shapiro Study on Transracial Adoption." JOURNAL OF AFRO-AMERICAN ISSUES 4, 2 (Spring 1976): 139-152. 13 pp., references, bibliography.

Subjects: 1. Organizations and Services to Families / Adoption and Adoption Services.

214 Chimezie, Amuzie. "Transracial Adoption of Black Children." SOCIAL WORK 20, 4 (July 1975): 296-301. 6 pp., references.

Subjects: 1. Organizations and Services to Families / Adoption and Adoption Services.

Objections against raising a black child in a white family are not based on doubts about the white parents' ability to meet the child's needs for food, clothing, and other material necesities; rather, they are based on the belief that the white family cannot equip the black child with the necessary psychosocial tools to develop an appropriate identity and deal appropriately with an oppressively racist society. This inability of white parents to help the black child in these respects could be in part because they are not black, because they probably tend to play down the harshness and inhumanity of oppressive racism, and because they live in a white neighborhood. . . Until much needed, direct, empirical studies are made of the adult personalities of white-raised blacks, placements of black children should not proceed as if it had already been ascertained that black-white transracial adoption is beneficial or even innocuous for black children. (From author's text)

215 Christensen, Harold T. and Johnson, Leanor B. "Premarital Coitus and the Southern Black: A Comparative View." JOURNAL OF MARRIAGE AND THE FAMILY 40, 4 (November 1978): 721-732. 11 pp.

Subjects: 1. Sexual Attitudes and Behavior / Premarital Sexual Behavior; 2. Aids for Theory and Research / Family Research Methodology.

Following procedures previously employed by the senior author in his ongoing cross-cultural sex research, this study focuses upon the sexuality of the southern black. Questionnaire data were gathered in 1968 from a southern black college, a midwestern white university, and a Swedish university; and again in 1973 from the first two of these. Black respondents were found to have higher premarital coital rates than their white counterparts, and to be less deterred by religiosity. But male-female differentials are greatest in the black samples, with black males inclining toward the permissive Scandinavian model and black females resembling the more conservative American model. Trends were generally in the direction of increased coital incidence coupled with decreased relationship commitment and decreased negative feelings following first coitus, and there is some evidence of both an intersex and intercultural convergence with respect to several of the items treated. Various ramifications of these and other comparisons are presented. The very striking gender gap which our data revealed for southern blacks, coupled with high sexual permissiveness in that culture, is pointed to as an anomaly that invites further study. (Authors' abstract)

216 Christian, Barbara. "Community and Nature: The Novels of Toni Morrison." JOURNAL OF ETHNIC STUDIES 7, 4 (Winter 1980): 65-78. 14 pp.

Subjects: 1. Trends and Change in Marriage and Family / Family Life in the United States; 2. Organizations and Services to Families / Community Groups and the Family.

217 Chunn, Jay Carrington, II. "A Comparison of Two Measures of Socioeconomic Status and Familial Factors as They Relate to Self Concept in Two Samples of Black Third and Fourth Grade Children." (Ph.D. dissertation, University of Maryland, 1978.) DISSERTATION ABSTRACTS INTERNATIONAL, 40, 1, July 1979, 149A. (University Microfilms No. 7915786.) 87 pp.

Subjects: 1. Family Relationships and Dynamics / Family Relationships; 2. Psychology and Sociology / Self-Esteem.

218 Chunn, Jay I., ed. THE SURVIVAL OF BLACK CHILDREN AND YOUTH. 1st edition Washington, DC: Nuclassics and Sciences Publishing Company, 1974. 196 pp., illustrations, tables; LC:77-94714.

Subjects: 1. Family Relationships and Dynamics / Socialization; 2. Family Counseling and Education / Child Development; 3. Aids for Theory and Research / Collected Works.

Notes: Papers presented at the first National Council for Black Child Development.

219 Clark, Candace. "Race, Motherhood, and Abortion." (Ph.D. dissertation, Columbia University, 1979.) DISSERTATION ABSTRACTS

INTERNATIONAL, 40, 10, April 1980, 5606A.   (University Microfilms
No. 8008711.) 316 pp.

Subjects: 1. Trends and Change in Marriage and Family / Family Policy;
    2. Issues Related to Reproduction / Abortion; 3. / Pregnancy and Child
    Birth.

220 Clark, Kenneth Bancroft. DARK GHETTO: DILEMMAS OF SOCIAL
POWER. 1st edition New York: Harper and Row, 1965.   251 pp., tables,
charts, index; ISBN:0-06-031470-2; LC:64-7834.

Subjects: 1. Trends and Change in Marriage and Family / Family and
    Social Change; 2. Aids for Theory and Research / Collected Works.

An exploration of the political, psychological and social problems of
an urban ghetto. The black family is discussed in the context of
psychological forces that are operative in the ghetto.

Notes: Forward by Gunnar Myrdal.

221 Clark, Reginald M. FAMILY LIFE AND SCHOOL ACHIEVEMENT: WHY POOR
BLACK CHILDREN SUCCEED OR FAIL. Chicago and London: University of
Chicago Press, 1983. 249 pp., references, bibliography, tables, charts;
ISBN:0-226-10769; LC:83-3481.

Subjects: 1. Organizations and Services to Families / Education and the
    Family; 2. Families with Special Problems / Achievement and the
    Family.

Notes: Bibliography: pp. 229-49.

222 Clark, Reginald Milton. "Black Families as Educators: A
Qualitative Inquiry." (Ph.D. dissertation, The University of Wisconsin-
Madison, 1977.) DISSERTATION ABSTRACTS INTERNATIONAL, 38, 8, Feb. 1978,
4642A. (University Microfilms No. 7719752.) 437 pp.

Subjects: 1. Organizations and Services to Families / Education and the
    Family; 2. Family Relationships and Dynamics / Family Relationships.

223 Clark, Reginald Milton. "The Dance Party as a Socialization
Mechanism for Black Urban Preadolescents and Adolescents." SOCIOLOGY
AND SOCIAL RESEARCH 58, 2 (January 1974): 145-54. 10 pp., references,
bibliography.

Subjects: 1. Family Relationships and Dynamics / Socialization; 2. Mate
    Selection / Mate Selection, Differential Patterns; 3. Family
    Counseling and Education / Adolescence.

An attempt has been made to show that as a socialization mechanism,
as a cultural ceremony, as an agent of cultural transmission, and as
an arena for Black cultural growth, the dance party is uniquely
equipped to serve its Black population. It offers an introduction to
Black unity and an introduction to ways of acting as an adult. . .
There is a "coming together" of people who have something in common.
The Black unity, the spirit of community, is expressed at the party
primarily in the dancing and in the "soul music." Through
conversations and interaction with peers and adults--who happen to be

the most important socializing influence among adolescents—the youngster learns standards of beauty, "appropriate" emotions for different situations and racial attitudes. It is clear also that certain patterns of interaction with members of the same sex and of the opposite sex can be seen developing in the social interaction between Black teens at these house parties. Elements of chauvinism and sexism, for example, are seen very readily. Finally, the dance party is a socially accepted vehicle for adolescent female/male interaction until they "outgrow" or "graduate" to lounges, bars, clubs or other adult social activities. (Author's conclusion)

224 Clark, Samuel D. "Sex, Contraception and Parenthood: Experience and Attitudes among Urban Black Young Men." FAMILY PLANNING PERSPECTIVES 16, 2 (March-April 1984): 77-82. 6 pp., tables.

Subjects: 1. Issues Related to Reproduction / Birth Control; 2. Sexual Attitudes and Behavior / Sexual Attitudes and Behavior; 3. Aids for Theory and Research / Statistics.

Examines the attitudes of Black urban adolescent males regarding sexual activity and contraception. (From author's text)

225 Clarke, James W. "Family Structure and Political Socialization among Urban Black Children." AMERICAN JOURNAL OF POLITICAL SCIENCE 17, 2 (May 1973): 302-15. 14 pp., references, tables.

Subjects: 1. Family Relationships and Dynamics / Family Relationships; 2. / Father-Child Relationships; 3. Psychology and Sociology / Racial Attitudes.

The results of this study of 94 urban black children suggest that father absence is an important variable in their political socialization. Father-absent children tend to be more cynical and also express much stronger preferences for a racially segregated environment. Beyond this, the results underscore the importance of intra-familial relationships in the political socialization process. (Author's abstract)

226 Clarke, John Henrik, ed. BLACK FAMILIES IN THE AMERICAN ECONOMY. Washington, DC: Educational and Community Counselors Associates Publications, 1975. 255 pp., references, tables; LC:77-100424.

Subjects: 1. Trends and Change in Marriage and Family / Family Life in the United States; 2. Organizations and Services to Families / Economics and the Family; 3. Aids for Theory and Research / Collected Works.

Published in the Journal of Afro-American Issues, Vol. 3, Nos. 3-4, 1975.

227 Clarke, John Henrik. "The Black Family in Historical Perspective." JOURNAL OF AFRO-AMERICAN ISSUES 3, 3/4 (Summer/Fall 1975): 336-42. 7 pp., references.

Subjects: 1. Trends and Change in Marriage and Family / Family Life in the United States; 2. Aids for Theory and Research / Critiques and Analyses of Family Research Literature.

228 Clay, Phillip L. "The Process of Black Suburbanization." URBAN
AFFAIRS QUARTERLY 14, 4 (June 1979): 405-24. 20 pp., references,
bibliography, tables.

Subjects: 1. Family Relationships and Dynamics / Socialization; 2.
Families with Special Problems / Family and Geographic Mobility.

229 Clayton, Richard R. and Voss, Harwin L. "Shacking Up: Cohabitation
in the 1970's." JOURNAL OF MARRIAGE AND THE FAMILY 39, 2 (May 1972):
273-84. 11 pp., references, bibliography, tables.

Subjects: 1. Mate Selection / Cohabiting.

230 Closs, Elizabeth Lee. "Isokinetic Measurement of Strength in Black
and White University Women." (Ph.D. dissertation, Texas Women's
University, 1977.) DISSERTATION ABSTRACTS INTERNATIONAL, 38, 9, March
1978, 5330A-5331A. (University Microfilms No. 7801749.) 156 pp.

Subjects: 1. Organizations and Services to Families / Physical Health
and the Family; 2. Family Relationships and Dynamics / Women's Issues.

231 Cogswell, Betty E. and Sussman, Marvin B. "Changing Family and
Marriage Forms: Complications for Human Service Systems." FAMILY
COORDINATOR 21, 4 (October 1972): 505-15. 12 pp., references,
bibliography.

Subjects: 1. Trends and Change in Marriage and Family / Alternative
Family Forms; 2. Organizations and Services to Families / Social
Services and the Family; 3. Marriage and Divorce / Marriage Customs
and Forms.

232 Cohen, Leland Bernard. "Interracial Families Adapt to Their
Marginality: Between Black and White." (Ph.D. dissertation, Washington
University, 1979.) DISSERTATION ABSTRACTS INTERNATIONAL, 40, 2,
Aug. 1979, 1100A. (University Microfilms No. 7918588.) 261 pp.

Subjects: 1. Organizations and Services to Families / Adoption and
Adoption Services; 2. Marriage and Divorce / Inter-marriage.

233 Cole, O. Jackson. "Scale Construction in the Assessment of Sex-Role
Stereotypes among Minorities." In RESEARCH DIRECTIONS OF BLACK
PSYCHOLOGISTS, edited by A. Wade Boykin, Anderson J. Franklin and
Jacques Frank Yates, pp. 57-73. New York: Russell Sage Foundation, 1979.
17 pp.

Subjects: 1. Family Relationships and Dynamics / Family Roles and Sex
Roles; 2. Aids for Theory and Research / Family Research Methodology.

234 Coleman, Willie Mae. "Keeping the Faith and Disturbing the
Peace. Black Women: From Anti-Slavery to Women's Suffrage." (Ph.D.
dissertation, University of California, Irvine, 1982.) DISSERTATION
ABSTRACTS INTERNATIONAL, 43, 2, Aug. 1982, 518A. (University Microfilms
No. 8216081.) 165 pp.

Subjects: 1. Family Relationships and Dynamics / Women's Issues.

235 Coley, Soraya Moore. "And Still I Rise: An Exploratory Study of
Contemporary Black Private Household Workers." (Ph.D. dissertation, Bryn
Mawr College, The Graduate School of Social Work and Social Research,
1981.) DISSERTATION ABSTRACTS INTERNATIONAL, 42, 8, Feb. 1982, 3758A.
(University Microfilms No. 8202839.) 353 pp.

Subjects: 1. Organizations and Services to Families / Employment and the
    Family.

236 Comer, James P. BEYOND BLACK AND WHITE. Chicago, IL: Quadrangle
Books, 1972. 272 pp., bibliography; LC:76-162812.

Subjects: 1. Psychology and Sociology / Psychology; 2. / Racial
    Attitudes.

Notes: Bibliography: pp. 258-64.

237 Comer, James P. THE BLACK FAMILY: AN ADAPTIVE PERSPECTIVE. New
Haven, CT: Yale University Press, 1970.

Subjects: 1. Trends and Change in Marriage and Family / Family Life in
    the United States; 2. Aids for Theory and Research / Critiques and
    Analyses of Family Research Literature.

238 Comer, James P. and Poussaint, Alvin F., Jr. BLACK CHILD CARE: HOW
TO BRING UP A HEALTHY BLACK CHILD IN AMERICA. A GUIDE TO EMOTIONAL AND
PSYCHOLOGICAL DEVELOPMENT. New York: Simon and Schuster, Inc., 1975.
408 pp., index; ISBN:0-671-21902-2; LC:74-28261.

Subjects: 1. Family Relationships and Dynamics / Parent-Child
    Relationships; 2. Family Counseling and Education / Adolescence; 3. /
    Child Development.

Two psychiatrists provide advice and a discussion on child
development

Notes: Bibliography: pp. 387-394.

239 Cone, James H. "Black Theology and the Black College Student."
JOURNAL OF AFRO-AMERICAN ISSUES 4, 3/4 (Summer/Fall 1976): 420-31. 12
pp.

Subjects: 1. Organizations and Services to Families / Religion and the
    Family.

240 Conference on Maryland History, 1st, Annapolis, 1974. LAW,
SOCIETY, AND POLITICS IN EARLY MARYLAND. PROCEEDINGS OF THE FIRST
CONFERENCE ON MARYLAND HISTORY, JUNE 14-15, 1974, edited by Aubrey C.
Land, Loris Green Carr and Edward C. Papenfuge. Baltimore, MD: The Johns
Hopkins University Press, 1977. 350 pp., illustrations, index; ISBN:0-
8018-1872-9; LC:76-47374.

Subjects: 1. Trends and Change in Marriage and Family / Family Life
    Prior to 1900; 2. Organizations and Services to Families /
    Governmental Units and the Family; 3. Aids for Theory and Research /
    Collected Works.

Notes: A bibliography of the writings of Morris Leon Radoff, compiled by Frank F. White, Jr, is on pages 333-335.

241 Conwill, William Louis. "A Conceptual Analysis of Black Family Instability." (Ph.D. dissertation, Stanford University, 1980.) DISSERTATION ABSTRACTS INTERNATIONAL, 41, 8, Feb. 1981, 3738A-3739A. (University Microfilms No. 8103497.) 212 pp.

Subjects: 1. Marriage and Divorce / Marriage Satisfaction and Prediction Studies; 2. Families with Special Problems / Family Disorganization.

242 Cooney, Rosemary Santana. "Changing Labor Force Participation of Mexican American Wives: A Comparison with Anglos and Blacks." SOCIAL SCIENCE QUARTERLY 56, 2 (September 1975): 252-61. 10 pp., references, tables.

Subjects: 1. Minority Groups / Ethnic Groups in the United States.

243 Cooney, Rosemary Santana. "Demographic Components of Growth in White, Black, and Puerto Rican Female-Headed Families: Comparison of the Cutright and Ross/Sawhill Methodologies." SOCIAL SCIENCE REVIEW 8, 2 (June 1979): 144-158. 15 pp., references, tables, appendices.

Subjects: 1. Family Relationships and Dynamics / Single Parent Families; 2. Minority Groups / Ethnic Groups in the United States; 3. Aids for Theory and Research / Family Research Methodology.

244 Cottle, Thomas J. BLACK CHILDREN, WHITE DREAMS. Boston, MA: Houghton Mifflin Co., 1974. 186 pp., bibliography; LC:73-14534.

Subjects: 1. Organizations and Services to Families / Governmental Units and the Family; 2. Family Relationships and Dynamics / Socialization; 3. Family Counseling and Education / Child Development.

Notes: Bibliography: pp. 177-187. Forward by Walter F. Mondale.

245 Craggett, Foster T. "A Form Critical Approach to the Oral Traditions of the Black Church as They Relate to the Celebration of Death." (D.Min. dissertation, School of Theology at Claremont, 1980.) DISSERTATION ABSTRACTS INTERNATIONAL, 41, 3, Sept. 1980, 1086A. (University Microfilms No. 8018684.) 80 pp.

Subjects: 1. Organizations and Services to Families / Religion and the Family; 2. Families with Special Problems / Death, Bereavement and the Family; 3. Aids for Theory and Research / Family Research Methodology.

246 Cramer, M. Richard. "Family Strength and Family Satisfaction: Some Racial Comparisons." UNIVERSITY OF NORTH CAROLINA NEWSLETTER 64, 2 (April 1979): 9-13. 5 pp., references, bibliography, tables.

Subjects: 1. Family Relationships and Dynamics / Family Relationships.

247 Cranford, Sharon Anita Hill. "An Expanded Case Study of Family Interaction and Transaction Roles of Middle-Class Black Mothers." (Ph.D. dissertation, Kansas State University, 1981.) DISSERTATION ABSTRACTS INTERNATIONAL, 42, 8, Feb. 1982, 3384A. (University Microfilms No. 8201596.) 177 pp.

Subjects: 1. Family Relationships and Dynamics / Mother-Child
Relationships; 2. / Family Roles and Sex Roles; 3. / Women's Issues.

248 Creecy, Robert F and Wright, Roosevelt. "Morale and Informal
Activity with Friends among Black and White Elderly." GERONTOLOGIST 19,
6 (December 1979): 544-47. 4 pp., references, tables.

Subjects: 1. Family Relationships and Dynamics / Later Years and Aging.

249 Creighton-Zollar, Ann. "A Member of the Family: Strategies for
Black Family Continuity." (Ph.D. dissertation, University of Illinois
at Chicago Circle, 1980.) DISSERTATION ABSTRACTS INTERNATIONAL, 41, 10,
April 1981, 4509A. (University Microfilms No. 8106863.) 167 pp.

Subjects: 1. Family Relationships and Dynamics / Family Relationships;
  2. Families with Special Problems / Family and Geographic Mobility.

250 Creswell-Betsch, Carol. "Comparison of a Family Microtraining
Program and a Reading Program to Enhance Empathic Communication by Black
Parents with Young Children." (Ed.D. dissertation, University of
Massachusetts, 1979.) DISSERTATION ABSTRACTS INTERNATIONAL, 40, 3,
Sept. 1979, 1275A. (University Microfilms No. 7920821.) 197 pp.

Subjects: 1. Organizations and Services to Families / Education and the
  Family; 2. Family Relationships and Dynamics / Parent-Child
  Relationships; 3. Family Counseling and Education / Education for
  Parenthood.

251 Cromwell, Ronald E., Vaughn, C. Edwin and Mindel, Charles H.
"Ethnic Minority Family Research in an Urban Setting: A Process of
Exchange." AMERICAN SOCIOLOGIST 10, 3 (August 1975): 141-50. 10 pp.

Subjects: 1. Minority Groups / Ethnic Groups in the United States; 2.
  Aids for Theory and Research / Critiques and Analyses of Family
  Research Literature.

252 Cromwell, Vicky L. and Cromwell, Ronald E. "Perceived Dominance in
Decision-Making and Conflict Resolution among Anglo, Black, and Chicano
Couples." JOURNAL OF MARRIAGE AND THE FAMILY 40, 4 (November 1978):
749-59. 11 pp., references, bibliography, tables.

Subjects: 1. Family Relationships and Dynamics / Conflict Resolution;
  2. / Men's Issues; 3. Minority Groups / Ethnic Groups in the United
  States.

  Subjective and theoretical works on ethnic minority groups frequently
  assign categorical and stereotypic labels to family structure without
  benefit of empirical tests. This investigation analyzes self-report
  perceptions of relative spousal dominance in decision-making and
  conflict resolution for an inner city neighborhood sample of 137
  marriages representing three ethnic groups (Anglo, N = 88; black, N =
  88; Chicano, N = 98). These comparative data illuminate perceived
  outcome of marital dynamics by husbands and wives within and across
  ethnicity. Results call into question stereotypic labeling of black
  families as matriarchal and Chicano families as   patriarchal.
  Ethnicity, by itself, controlling for social class, is not sufficient
  to account for the variance in self-perceptions of either conjugal

decision-making or conflict resolution. Discrepancies between husbands and wives within ethnic groups point to the need to look more closely inside the marriage. (Authors' abstract)

253 Cross, William E., Jr. "Black Family and Black Identity: A Literature Review." THE WESTERN JOURNAL OF BLACK STUDIES 2, 2 (Summer 1978): 111-24. 14 pp., bibliography.

Subjects: 1. Family Relationships and Dynamics / Socialization; 2. Aids for Theory and Research / Critiques and Analyses of Family Research Literature.

254 Crumbley, Joseph. "A Descriptive Analysis of Black and White Families Reported for Child Maltreatment." (D.S.W. dissertation, University of Pennsylvania, 1982.) DISSERTATION ABSTRACTS INTERNATIONAL, 43, 4, Oct. 1982, 1292A. (University Microfilms No. 8221914.) 280 pp.

Subjects: 1. Organizations and Services to Families / Social Services and the Family; 2. Families with Special Problems / Child Abuse.

255 Cuffaro, Sara Todd. "A Discriminant Analysis of Sociocultural, Motivation, and Personality Differences among Black, Anglo and Chicana Female Drug Abusers in a Medium Security Prison." (Ph.D. dissertation, United States International University, 1978.) DISSERTATION ABSTRACTS INTERNATIONAL, 39, 9, March 1979, 4572B-4573B. (University Microfilms No. 7906217.) 196 pp.

Subjects: 1. Families with Special Problems / Drug Abuse; 2. Psychology and Sociology / Psychology; 3. Minority Groups / Ethnic Groups in the United States.

256 Cummings, Scott. "Family Socialization and Fatalism among Black Adolescents." JOURNAL OF NEGRO EDUCATION 46, 1 (Winter 1977): 62-75. 14 pp., references, tables.

Subjects: 1. Family Relationships and Dynamics / Socialization; 2. / Parent-Adolescent Relationships.

257 Curtis, Lynn A. VIOLENCE, RACE AND CULTURE. Lexington, MA: Lexington Books, 1975. 168 pp., bibliography, illustrations, index; ISBN:0-669-96032-2; LC:74-15539.

Subjects: 1. Families with Special Problems / Family Violence; 2. / Families with Criminal Offenders.

Notes: Bibliography: pp. 133-158

258 Cutright, Phillips and Jaffe, Frederick S. "Family Planning Program Effects on the Fertility of Low-Income U.S. Women." FAMILY PLANNING PERSPECTIVES 8, 3 (May-June 1976): 100-10. 8 pp., references, tables.

Subjects: 1. Issues Related to Reproduction / Fertility Rates.

259 Cutright, Phillips and Madras, Patrik. "AFDC and the Marital and Family Status of Ever Married Women Aged 15-44: United States, 1950-

1970." SOCIOLOGY AND SOCIAL RESEARCH 60, 3 (April 1976): 314-27. 14
pp., references, bibliography, tables.

Subjects: 1. Organizations and Services to Families / Social Services
   and the Family.

260 D'Andrade, Roy G. "Father Absence, Identification, and Identity."
ETHOS 1, 4 (Winter 1973): 440-55. 16 pp., references, tables.

Subjects: 1. Families with Special Problems / Death, Bereavement and the
   Family.

261 Dancy, Joseph, Jr. THE BLACK ELDERLY: A GUIDE FOR PRACTITIONERS:
WITH COMPREHENSIVE BIBLIOGRAPHY. Ann Arbor, MI: University of Michigan;
Wayne State University. Institute of Gerontology, 1977. 56 pp.,
bibliography, illustrations; LC:77-152208.

Subjects: 1. Family Relationships and Dynamics / Later Years and Aging.

   Notes: Bibliography: pp. 41-55.

262 Darity, Evangeline Royall. "A Comparison of Fear-Of-Success
Imagery between Black Male and Female Undergraduates." (Ed.D.
dissertation, University of Massachusetts, 1978.) DISSERTATION
ABSTRACTS INTERNATIONAL, 38, 9, March 1978, 5316A. (University
Microfilms No. 7800566.) 244 pp.

Subjects: 1. Families with Special Problems / Achievement and the
   Family; 2. Psychology and Sociology / Self-Esteem.

263 Datcher, Linda. "Effects of Community, Family and Education on
Earnings of Black and White Men." THE REVIEW OF BLACK POLITICAL ECONOMY
10, 4 (Summer 1980): 341-94. 4 pp., references.

Subjects: 1. Organizations and Services to Families / Education and the
   Family; 2. / Economics and the Family; 3. Family Relationships and
   Dynamics / Men's Issues.

   [B]oth community and family background factors are important in
   determining the levels of education and earnings of black and white
   men. The community effects for Blacks operate largely through their
   moving into more integrated neighborhoods, so that many positive
   community externalities are apparently not available to families in
   predominantly black middle-class neighborhoods. While the effects of
   father's education, city origin, and community income are incomparable
   between Blacks and whites, white men's education is more affected by
   number of siblings, family income, and age of 1968 head of household
   than is black men's education. The relative sizes of the coefficients
   of these latter variables are consistent with steeper age-earnings
   profiles for older white men than older black men and higher prices
   paid for investing in children by black parents. . .[Further analysis
   confirms] that differences in backgrounds between Blacks and whites
   have large effects of achievement and that the principal source of the
   differences stem from differences in the type of community rather than
   from variations in individual family backgrounds. (Author's summary)

264 David, Paul A, Gutman, Herbert G., Sutch, Richard, Temin, Peter and Wright, Gavin, eds. RECKONING WITH SLAVERY: A CRITICAL STUDY IN THE QUANTITATIVE HISTORY OF AMERICAN NEGRO SLAVERY. New York: Oxford University.Press, 1976. 398 pp., bibliography, index; ISBN:0-19-502034-0; LC:75-38098.

Subjects: 1. Trends and Change in Marriage and Family / Family Life Prior to 1900.

Notes: With an introduction by Kenneth M. Stampp. Bibliography: pp. 358-382.

265 Davids, Anthony. "Self-Concept and Mother-Concept in Black and White Preschool Children." CHILD PSYCHIATRY AND HUMAN DEVELOPMENT 4, 1 (Fall 1973): 30-43. 14 pp., references, tables.

Subjects: 1. Family Relationships and Dynamics / Mother-Child Relationships; 2. / Socialization.

Utilizing objective psychological assessment instruments and projective techniques, measures of self-concept and mother-concept were obtained from young black children and white children. No significant differences were found between the self-concepts and mother-concepts of these two groups of children. As predicted, there was significant positive association between the self-concept and mother-concept in both groups. Consideration was given to contradictions between the present findings, plus some from other recent studies, and certain views presented in the older psychological literature. The need for longitudinal studies of self-esteem was emphasized. (Author's abstract)

266 Davis, Angela. "Reflections on the Black Woman's Role in the Community of Slaves." BLACK SCHOLAR 3, 4 (December 1971): 2-15. 14 pp., references.

Subjects: 1. Trends and Change in Marriage and Family / Family Life Prior to 1900; 2. Family Relationships and Dynamics / Family Roles and Sex Roles.

267 Davis, Angela Y. WOMEN, RACE AND CLASS. New York: Vintage Books, 1983. 271 pp., references; ISBN:0-394-71351-6; LC:82-20266.

Subjects: 1. Family Relationships and Dynamics / Women's Issues; 2. Psychology and Sociology / Racial Attitudes.

Notes: Originally published in 1981 by Random House.

268 Davis, Elizabeth B. "The American Negro: From Family Membership to Personal and Social Identity." JOURNAL OF THE NATIONAL MEDICAL ASSOCIATION 60, 2 (March 1968): 92-99. 7 pp.

Subjects: 1. Family Relationships and Dynamics / Family Relationships; 2. / Socialization; 3. Psychology and Sociology / General Attitudes.

269 Davis, Frank, G. "Impact of Social Security Taxes on the Poor." THE REVIEW OF BLACK POLITICAL ECONOMY 10, 2 (Winter 1980): 199-208. 10 pp., references.

Subjects: 1. Organizations and Services to Families / Social Services
and the Family.

270 Davis, George. LOVE, BLACK LOVE. 1st edition Garden City, NY:
Anchor Press, 1978. 254 pp.; ISBN:0-385-09788-3; LC:74-33636.

Subjects: 1. Mate Selection / Dating, Courtship, and Romanticism; 2.
Psychology and Sociology / Psychology.

271 Davis, Lenwood G. BLACK FAMILIES IN URBAN AREAS IN THE UNITED
STATES: A BIBLIOGRAPHY OF PUBLISHED WORKS ON THE BLACK FAMILY IN URBAN
AREAS IN THE UNITED STATES. Council of Planning Librarians. Exchange
Bibliography, No. 471. Monticello, IL: Council of Planning Librarians,
1973. 60 pp.; LC:74-160753.

Subjects: 1. Trends and Change in Marriage and Family / Family Life in
the United States; 2. Aids for Theory and Research / Classified
Bibliographies of Family Literature.

272 Davis, Lenwood G. THE BLACK FAMILY IN THE UNITED STATES: A
SELECTED BIBLIOGRAPHY OF ANNOTATED BOOKS, ARTICLES AND DISSERTATIONS ON
BLACK FAMILIES IN AMERICA. Westport, CT: Greenwood Press, 1978. 132
pp., index; ISBN:0-8371-9851-8; LC:77-89109.

Subjects: 1. Trends and Change in Marriage and Family / Family Life in
the United States; 2. Aids for Theory and Research / Classified
Bibliographies of Family Literature.

A selected annotated bibliography designed to be used as a reference
tool. The annotations are both descriptive and analytical.

273 Davis, Lenwood G. THE BLACK FAMILY IN URBAN AREAS IN THE UNITED
STATES: A BIBLIOGRAPHY OF PUBLISHED WORKS ON THE BLACK FAMILY IN URBAN
AREAS OF THE UNITED STATES. 2nd ed. Council of Planning
Librarians. Exchange Bibliography, No. 808-809. Monticello, IL: Council
of Planning Librarians, 1975. 84 pp.; LC:75-322342.

Subjects: 1. Aids for Theory and Research / Classified Bibliographies of
Family Literature.

274 Davis, Lenwood G. THE BLACK WOMAN IN AMERICAN SOCIETY: A SELECTED
ANNOTATED BIBLIOGRAPHY. Boston, MA: G. K. Hall Company, Inc., 1975.
159 pp., index; ISBN:0-8161-7858-5; LC:75-33275.

Subjects: 1. Family Relationships and Dynamics / Women's Issues; 2.
Aids for Theory and Research / Classified Bibliographies of Family
Literature.

275 Davis, Maria Susanne. "Sex-Role Factors in the Career Development
of Black Female High School Students." (Ph.D. dissertation, University
of Cincinnati, 1977.) DISSERTATION ABSTRACTS INTERNATIONAL, 38, 4,
Oct. 1977, 1874B. (University Microfilms No. 7721704.) 162 pp.

Subjects: 1. Family Relationships and Dynamics / Family Roles and Sex
Roles; 2. Families with Special Problems / Achievement and the Family.

276 Davis, Robert. "Suicide among Young Blacks: Trend and
Perspectives." PHYLON 41, 3 (September 1980): 223-29. 7 pp., tables.

Subjects: 1. Families with Special Problems / Suicide and the Family;
2. Aids for Theory and Research / Critiques and Analyses of Family
Research Literature.

Mortality statistics for 1970-1975 reveal that suicide among Blacks
is primarily a youthful phenomenon, i.e., 47 percent occuring among
those of the ages 20-34. A review of the literature indicates that
recent studies have suggested inadequate etiological explanations of
Black suicide as related to: the frustration and aggression stemming
from urban stress; the "cultural shock" correlated with social
mobilitiy and attempts to move into the American mainstream; and
certain conditions associated with female-male relationships. An
alternative paradigm suggests that as Black strong familial and
communal (i.e., church, social club, fraternal organization, etc.)
ties weaken OR as the Black young person removes himself or herself
from integration and reliance on these ties, the likelihood of self-
destruction increases.

277 Day, Beth Feagles. SEXUAL LIFE BETWEEN BLACKS AND WHITES: THE
ROOTS OF RACISM. New York: World, 1972. 376 pp., bibliography; ISBN:0-
529-04816-7; LC:72-85192.

Subjects: 1. Mate Selection / Dating, Courtship, and Romanticism; 2.
Marriage and Divorce / Inter-marriage; 3. Sexual Attitudes and
Behavior / Sexual Attitudes and Behavior.

Notes: Introduction by Margaret Mead. Bibliography: pp. 265-268.

278 Day, Dawn. THE ADOPTION OF BLACK CHILDREN: COUNTERACTING
INSTITUTIONAL DISCRIMINATION. Lexington, MA: Lexington Books, 1979.
156 pp., references, index; ISBN:0-699-02107-5; LC:77-18585.

Subjects: 1. Organizations and Services to Families / Adoption and
Adoption Services.

279 deAlmeida, Eleanor Engram. "A Descriptive and Analytical Study of
the Early Adult Roles of Black and White Women." (Ph.D. dissertation,
Duke University, 1977.) DISSERTATION ABSTRACTS INTERNATIONAL, 38, 4,
Oct. 1977, 2351A. (University Microfilms No. 7721869.) 123 pp.

Subjects: 1. Trends and Change in Marriage and Family / Comparative
Studies--International, Interclass, Sex, and Time Differences; 2.
Family Relationships and Dynamics / Family Roles and Sex Roles; 3. /
Women's Issues.

280 Dean, Dwight G., Braito, Rita, Powers, Edward A. and Bruton, Brent.
"Cultural Contradictions and Sex Roles Revisited: A Replication and a
Reassessment." SOCIOLOGICAL QUARTERLY 16, 2 (Spring 1975): 207-15. 9
pp., references, tables, appendices.

Subjects: 1. Trends and Change in Marriage and Family / Family and
Social Change; 2. Family Relationships and Dynamics / Family Roles and
Sex Roles; 3. Aids for Theory and Research / Family Research
Methodology.

281 Degler, Carl N. "Slavery in Brazil and the United States: An Essay in Comparative History." AMERICAN HISTORICAL REVIEW 75, 4 (April 1970): 1004-28. 25 pp.

Subjects: 1. Trends and Change in Marriage and Family / Family Life Prior to 1900; 2. / Comparative Studies--International, Interclass, Sex, and Time Differences.

282 Demerson, Bamidele Agbasegbe. "Some Aspects of Contemporary Rural Afro American Family Life in the Sea Islands of Southeastern United States." THE WESTERN JOURNAL OF BLACK STUDIES 6, 2 (Summer 1982): 60-65. 7 pp., references, bibliography, illustrations, tables, charts.

Subjects: 1. Trends and Change in Marriage and Family / Family Life in the United States; 2. Family Relationships and Dynamics / Extended Family and Kinship Groups; 3. / Environment (Space/Housing).

Known by their African derived ethnic designations, Gullah and Geechee, the Afroamericans of the Sea Islands have for generations had multihousehold compounds frequently established on land owned by paternally related heirs. The multigenerational family occupying a compound is built around a consanguineally related "core" of adult male household heads. Post-marital residence is virilocal. And the head of the extended family is usually the eldest male of the "core." Households are frequently neither the compositional nor functional equivalents of the so-called "nuclear" families idealized by Euroamerican society. Although exhibiting various degrees of self-sufficiency and autonomy, households are nevertheless interdependent such that the compound setting is the locus of much face-to-face interaction of its members. For example, socializing the young, caring for the infirm, assisting the elderly, working in the cultivation and marketing of truck crops, and exchanging reciprocal goods, services, and financial gifts are conducted within the compound setting. In contrast to the Euroamerican "nuclear"family, Sea Islander family structure is rooted in the principle of consanguinity which gives it a structural resemblance to the extended families of Africa, the Afrocaribbean, and other parts of Afro(north)america.

283 Dennis, Rutledge M. "Theories of the Black Family: The Weak-Family and Strong-Family Schools as Competing Ideologies." JOURNAL OF AFRO-AMERICAN ISSUES 4, 3,4 (Summer/Fall 1976): 315-28. 14 pp., references.

Subjects: 1. Aids for Theory and Research / Family Theory.

284 Derbyshire, Robert L. "The Uncompleted Negro Family: Suggested Research into the Hypotheses Regarding the Effect of the Negro's Outcaste Conditions upon His Own and Other American Sexual Attitudes and Behavior." JOURNAL OF HUMAN RESOURCES 15, 4 (1967): 458-68. 11 pp., references.

Subjects: 1. Sexual Attitudes and Behavior / Sexual Attitudes and Behavior; 2. Aids for Theory and Research / Family Research Methodology.

285 Desai, S. R. and Mehta, N. R. "The Impact of Health Education on Acceptance of Family Planning Methods for Spacing by Lower Socioeconomic

Primiparous Urban Women."   JOURNAL OF FAMILY WELFARE 22, 3 (December 1975): 3-9.   7 pp., references, tables, appendices.

Subjects: 1. Minority Groups / Family and Social Class.

286 Dickinson, George E.   "Dating Behavior of Black and White Adolescents Before and After Desegregation." JOURNAL OF MARRIAGE AND THE FAMILY 37, 3 (August 1975): 602-608.   7 pp., references, bibliography, tables.

Subjects: 1. Mate Selection / Dating, Courtship, and Romanticism.

Black and white adolescent dating behavior before and after desegregation in a Northeast Texas Community was analyzed. Questionnaires were administered in the segregated high schools in 1964 and the desegregated high school in 1974 (N's are 367 and 432, respectively). Eighteen multiple-choice questions were responded to by tenth, eleventh, and twelfth graders. Chi-square tests and one- and two-way analyses of variance were used in data analysis. Evidence was found to support the hypothesis that blacks' dating behavior has changed in the direction of whites, while whites have changed only slightly over time. It is suggested that reference group theory helps to explain this change. (Author's abstract)

287 Dietrich, Katheryn Thomas. "A Reexamination of the Myth of Black Matriarchy." JOURNAL OF MARRIAGE AND THE FAMILY 37, 2 (May 1975): 367-74.   8 pp., references, bibliography, tables.

Subjects: 1. Family Relationships and Dynamics / Single Parent Families; 2. / Decision Making; 3. Aids for Theory and Research / Family Research Methodology.

Previous arguments that matriarchy is a myth in the black lower classes are reviewed and an additional argument is presented: the irrelevance of heretofore employed decision-making measures for lower-class blacks. This study employs seemingly more relevant measures to examine conjugal decision-making and decision-implementation in predominantly lower-class black families in five metropolitan populations and two nonmetropolitan populations in the U.S. Role-patterning by specific decision-areas and composite power configurations based on the typologies of Wolfe and of Herbst are analyzed. The results call into question presumptions that matriarchy is normative in the black lower class. (Author's abstract)

288 Dill, Bonnie Thornton. "'The Means to Put My Children Through': Childrearing Goals and Strategies among Black Female Domestic Servants." In THE BLACK WOMAN, edited by La Frances Rodgers-Rose, pp. 107-23. Beverly Hills, CA: Sage Publications, Inc., 1980.   17 pp.

Subjects: 1. Organizations and Services to Families / Working Mothers; 2. Family Relationships and Dynamics / Parent-Child Relationships.

[The author] studied in depth the life histories of 26 women living in the United States who were household workers while raising their own children. The women, when interviewed, were between the ages of 60 and 80. [The data reveal]. . .that the relationship between the Black woman's family life and her work was shaped by four basic factors: (a) structure of the work; (b) tasks and duties assigned her; (c) degree of employer-employee intimacy; and (d) goals for her children. Those women who did not share much of their own lives with their employers appeared to minimize the interaction of work and family. (From the editor's remarks, p. 64.)

289 Dill, Bonnie Thornton. "Across the Boundaries of Race and Class: An Exploration of the Relationship between Work and Family among Black Female Domestic Servants." (Ph.D. dissertation, New York University, 1979.) DISSERTATION ABSTRACTS INTERNATIONAL, 40, 11, May 1980, 6024A-6025A. (University Microfilms No. 8010339.) 195 pp.

Subjects: 1. Organizations and Services to Families / Employment and the Family; 2. Family Relationships and Dynamics / Women's Issues; 3. Psychology and Sociology / Sociology.

290 Dill, Bonnie Thornton. "The Dialectics of Black Womanhood." SIGNS: JOURNAL OF WOMEN IN CULTURE AND SOCIETY 4, 3 (Spring 1979): 543-55. 13 pp., references, tables, charts.

Subjects: 1. Family Relationships and Dynamics / Women's Issues; 2. Aids for Theory and Research / Critiques and Analyses of Family Research Literature.

291 Dixon, Johanne C., comp. A SELECTED ANNOTATED BIBLIOGRAPHY ON BLACK FAMILIES. VOLUME 1. New York: National Urban League, 1977. 38 pp.

Subjects: 1. Trends and Change in Marriage and Family / Family Life in the United States; 2. Organizations and Services to Families / Social Services and the Family; 3. Aids for Theory and Research / Classified Bibliographies of Family Literature.

This volume includes sources identified as helpful aids to human service practitioners. The project was funded by the National Center on Child Abuse and Neglect, the National Urban League's Project THRIVE: Enhancing the Black Family and Protecting the Children.

292 Dixon, Richard D. "The Absence of Birth Order Correlations among Unwed and Married Black First-Conceptors." JOURNAL OF SEX RESEARCH 16, 3 (August 1980): 238-44. 7 pp., references, tables.

Subjects: 1. Family Relationships and Dynamics / Birth Order Differences; 2. Sexual Attitudes and Behavior / Premarital Sexual Behavior; 3. Aids for Theory and Research / Family Research Methodology.

Re-examination of the hypothesis that firstborns are overrepresented concerning premarital sexual activity was conducted with a sample of young, poor, black unwed and married first-conceptors. Contrary to confirming results obtained in earlier studies wherein all--or virtually all--respondents were white, the present study with black females did not support the hypothesis. U.S. black/white cultural differences were considered to account for the disparity of results found between this and earlier efforts. (Author's abstract)

293 Dobbins, Margaret Powell and Mulligan, James. "Black Matriarchy:
Transforming a Myth of Racism into a Class Model." JOURNAL OF
COMPARATIVE FAMILY STUDIES 11, 2 (Spring 1980): 195-217. 21 pp.,
references, bibliography, tables, charts.

Subjects: 1. Organizations and Services to Families / Employment and the
    Family; 2. Family Relationships and Dynamics / Single Parent Families;
    3. Aids for Theory and Research / Family Research Methodology.

Census data from Southern states demonstrate that the proportion of
households headed by females has continued to increase among Blacks,
and the ratio of female headed households to women of employable age
has increased significantly among whites as well as Blacks during each
of the four post World War II decades of the New South. [T]he authors
offer a class analysis of female headed households. They contend that
increases in female headed households are occassioned by changes in
the relation between capital and labor which create crises for working
class families and families becoming working class. They argue that
historically the legalization of racism has tended to buffer white
working class families from the effects of capital motion on working
class family life, while the effects on blacks have been intensified
and continuous. Hence for long periods of time white working class
families maintain or achieve family life styles and values which the
authors argue are only objectively realizable for the petty
bourgeoisie, which they see as rapidly and steadily disappearing.
During major crisis periods in capitalist economic cycles these
subjective values can no longer be sustained as white working class
families confront the conditions which account for the high incidence
of female headed households among Blacks. (Authors' abstract)

294 Dole, Arthur A. "Aspirations of Blacks and Whites for Their
Children." VOCATIONAL GUIDANCE QUARTERLY 22, 1 (September 1973): 24-31.
8 pp., references, tables.

Subjects: 1. Family Relationships and Dynamics / Parent-Child
    Relationships; 2. Families with Special Problems / Achievement and the
    Family; 3. Family Counseling and Education / Value Education.

295 Dorsett-Robinson, Jean, ed. THE BLACK ELDERS: WORKSHOP AND
CONFERENCE PROCEEDINGS. CONDUCTED BY THE COMMUNITY SERVICES PROGRAM TO
PROVIDE QUALITY CARE TO THE AGED. Carbondale?, IL: N.p., 1974. 192
pp., references, bibliography; LC:75-316605.

Subjects: 1. Family Relationships and Dynamics / Later Years and Aging;
    2. Aids for Theory and Research / Collected Works.

Proceedings of the workshop series on the Black Aging and Aged and
the Conference on the Black Aged and Aging. (NUC)

296 Dougherty, Molly Crocker. BECOMING A WOMAN IN RURAL BLACK
CULTURE. Case Studies in Cultural Anthropology. New York: Holt,
Rinehart and Winston, Inc., 1978. 111 pp., bibliography, illustrations;
ISBN:0-03-014921-5; LC:77-24218.

Subjects: 1. Trends and Change in Marriage and Family / Family Life in
    the United States; 2. / Family and Social Change; 3. Family
    Relationships and Dynamics / Women's Issues.

Notes: Bibliography: pp. 109-111.

297 Dowdall, George W. "Intermetropolitan Differences in Family Income Inequality: An Ecological Analysis of Total White and Nonwhite Patterns in 1960." SOCIOLOGY AND SOCIAL RESEARCH 61, 2 (January 1972): 176-91. 16 pp., references, tables, charts.

Subjects: 1. Trends and Change in Marriage and Family / Comparative Studies--International, Interclass, Sex, and Time Differences.

Proceeding from human ecological assumptions, this paper examines how variation in basic community dimensions affects the level and distribution of family income in metropolitan communities. A path model is presented which views income level and inequality as caused by ecological structure (age, racial composition, and regional location), industry mix (manufacturing and agricultural employment), and human capital factors (educational inequality and female labor force participation). Data for the total white and nonwhite populations of 197 SMSA's in 1960 are used in three parallel path analyses. The overall results demonstrate the utility of the ecological approach in explaining inequality. Considerable differences by color are found: roughly 74 percent of the intercommunity variation in income inequality for all families, 80 percent for whites and 17 percent for nonwhites are explained statistically. Regional location and median family income are of primary importance, and racial exploitation has a measurable effect. (Author's abstract)

298 Driskell, Judy A. and Price, Claudia S. "Nutritional Status of Preschoolers from Low-Income Alabama Families." JOURNAL OF THE AMERICAN DIETETIC ASSOCIATION 65, 3 (September 1974): 280-284. 5 pp., references, tables, charts.

Subjects: 1. Families with Special Problems / Family Stress.

299 Duberman, Lucile, ed. GENDER AND SEX IN SOCIETY. New York: Praeger Publishing Co., 1975. 274 pp., bibliography, index; ISBN:0-275-52110-9; LC:73-10658.

Subjects: 1. Trends and Change in Marriage and Family / Comparative Studies--International, Interclass, Sex, and Time Differences; 2. Family Relationships and Dynamics / Family Roles and Sex Roles; 3. Aids for Theory and Research / Collected Works.

Notes: There are chapters by Helen Mayer Hacker and Warren T. Farrell. Bibliography: pp. 253-268.

300 Duhon, Rose Marie. "An Analysis of Curriculum Offerings and Services Related to Child Abuse and Neglect in Early Childhood Teacher Preparation Programs at Historically Black Colleges and Universities." (Ph.D. dissertation, Kansas State University, 1980.) DISSERTATION ABSTRACTS INTERNATIONAL, 41, 5, Nov. 1980, 1937A. (University Microfilms No. 8024244.) 167 pp.

Subjects: 1. Families with Special Problems / Child Abuse; 2. Family Counseling and Education / Early Childhood Education.

301 Dukes, Phyllis Jean Carmack. "The Relationship between Paternal
Interaction Style and Infant Behavior as a Function of
Social Economic Status and Sex of Infant." (Ph.D. dissertation, The
University of Michigan, 1978.) DISSERTATION ABSTRACTS INTERNATIONAL,
39, 6, Dec. 1978, 2959B-2960B. (University Microfilms No. 7822891.) 222
pp.

Subjects: 1. Family Relationships and Dynamics / Father-Child
  Relationships.

302 Duncan, Beverly I. and Duncan, Otis Dudley. "Family Stability and
Occupational Success." SOCIAL PROBLEMS 16, 3 (Winter 1969): 273-85. 15
pp., references, tables.

Subjects: 1. Family Relationships and Dynamics / Family Relationships;
  2. Families with Special Problems / Achievement and the Family.

303 Dunmore, Charlotte J. BLACK CHILDREN AND THEIR FAMILIES: A
BIBLIOGRAPHY. San Francisco, CA: R and E Research Associates, Inc.,
1976. 103 pp.; ISBN:0-88247-378-6; LC:75-36566.

Subjects: 1. Family Relationships and Dynamics / Parent-Child
  Relationships; 2. Aids for Theory and Research / Classified
  Bibliographies of Family Literature.

304 Durbin, Elizabeth. "The Vicious Cycle of Welfare: Problems of the
Female-Headed Household in New York City." In SEX, DISCRIMINATION AND
THE DIVISION OF LABOR, edited by Cynthia B. Lloyd, pp. 313-45. New
York: Columbia University Press, 1975. 33 pp., references, tables,
appendices.

Subjects: 1. Organizations and Services to Families / Social Welfare;
  2. Family Relationships and Dynamics / Single Parent Families; 3. /
  Women's Issues.

305 Durrett, Mary Ellen, O'Bryant, Shirley and Pennebaker, James W.
"Childrearing Reports of White, Black and Mexican-American Families."
DEVELOPMENTAL PSYCHOLOGY 11, 6 (November 1975): 871. 1 p., references.

Subjects: 1. Family Relationships and Dynamics / Socialization.

306 Dynneson, Thomas L. "A Cross-Cultural Approach to Learning about
the Family." SOCIAL EDUCATION 46, 6 (October 1977): 482-83. 2 pp.,
references, tables.

Subjects: 1. Family Counseling and Education / Family Life Education.

307 Eberstein, Isaac W. and Frisbie, W. Parker. "Differences in
Marital Instability among Mexican Americans, Blacks, and Anglos: 1960
and 1970." SOCIAL PROBLEMS 23, 5 (June 1976): 609-21. 13 pp.,
references, bibliography, tables.

Subjects: 1. Marriage and Divorce / Marriage Satisfaction and Prediction
  Studies; 2. Families with Special Problems / Family Disorganization;
  3. Minority Groups / Ethnic Groups in the United States.

A comparative analysis of differences in marital instability, carried out over time as well as cross-sectionally, indicates that the relative frequency of marital disruption of ever-married women is low among Mexican Americans, followed by Anglos and Blacks in ascending order. Introduction of controls for age, age at first marriage, and other potential determinants of marital solidarity does not alter the ranking by ethnicity. The results suggest that conclusions, based on previous research, that the level of marital instability characteristic of Mexican Americans is higher than that of Anglos and that the trend in marital instability among Mexican Americans is converging with that of Blacks, are in need of revision. (Authors' abstract)

308 Edmonds, Mary McKinney. "Social Class and the Functional Health Status of the Aged Black Female." (Ph.D. dissertation, Case Western Reserve University, 1982.) DISSERTATION ABSTRACTS INTERNATIONAL, 43, 6, Dec. 1982, 2123A. (University Microfilms No. 8224688.) 201 pp.

Subjects: 1. Organizations and Services to Families / Physical Health and the Family; 2. Family Relationships and Dynamics / Later Years and Aging.

309 Edwards, Harry. "Black Muslim and Negro Christian Family Relationships." JOURNAL OF MARRIAGE AND THE FAMILY 30, 4 (November 1968): 604-11. 8 pp., references.

Subjects: 1. Organizations and Services to Families / Religion and the Family; 2. Family Relationships and Dynamics / Family Relationships.

This study compared families affiliated with the Nation of Islam to those matched families affiliated with various lower-class Negro Christian churches. The specific areas of family life covered included husband-wife relationships; family-extended kin relationships; parent-child relationships; and relationships between the families and various types of social groups and community agencies. The results indicated different patterns of family life existing between the two groups. Of particular interest was the tendency for the Muslim families to exhibit middle-class values and behavior patterns to a greater degree than did the Christian families. (Author's abstract)

310 Eigsti, Marilyn Ann H. "Interrelationships of Value Orientation, Decision-Making Mode and Decision-Implementing Style of Selected Low Socioeconomic Status Negro Homemakers." (Ph.D. dissertation, Michigan State University, 1973.) DISSERTATION ABSTRACTS INTERNATIONAL, 34, 6, Dec. 1973, 2758B-2759B. (University Microfilms No. 7329691.) 94 pp.

Subjects: 1. Family Relationships and Dynamics / Decision Making; 2. Psychology and Sociology / Sociology; 3. Minority Groups / Family and Social Class.

311 Elder, Glen H., Jr. "Approaches to Social Change and the Family." AMERICAN JOURNAL OF SOCIOLOGY 84, (1978): 1-38. 38 pp., references, bibliography.

Subjects: 1. Trends and Change in Marriage and Family / Family and Social Change; 2. Aids for Theory and Research / Family Theory.

312 Enberg, Lila E. "Household Differentiation and Integration as Predictors of Child Welfare in a Ghanaian Community." JOURNAL OF MARRIAGE AND THE FAMILY 36, 2 (May 1974): 389-99. 10 pp., references, tables.

Subjects: 1. Trends and Change in Marriage and Family / Family Life in Foreign Countries; 2. Organizations and Services to Families / Social Welfare.

313 Engerman, Stanley L. "Black Fertility and Family Structure in the U.S., 1880-1940." JOURNAL OF FAMILY HISTORY 2, 2 (Summer 1977): 117-38. 22 pp., references, tables, charts.

Subjects: 1. Trends and Change in Marriage and Family / Family Life in the United States; 2. Family Relationships and Dynamics / Family Relationships; 3. Issues Related to Reproduction / Fertility Rates.

314 Engerrand, Steven W. "Black and Mulatto Mobility and Stability in Dallas, Texas, 1880-1910." PHYLON 39, 3 (September 1978): 203-15. 13 pp., references, tables.

Subjects: 1. Trends and Change in Marriage and Family / Family Life in the United States; 2. Families with Special Problems / Family Disorganization; 3. Minority Groups / Family and Social Class.

315 English, Richard A. The Challenge for Mental Health Minorities and Their World Views. Austin, TX: Hogg Foundation for Mental Health and The University of Texas, 1984. 35 pp., bibliography, charts.

Subjects: 1. Organizations and Services to Families / Mental Health and the Family.

Notes: Presentation given as the Robert L. Sutherland Professor in Mental Health and Social Policy at The Second Annual Robert L. Sutherland Lecture, November 3, 1983. Lecture was sponsored by the School of Social Work at The University of Texas at Austin.

316 English, Richard H. "Beyond Pathology: Research and Theoretical Perspectives on Black Families." In SOCIAL RESEARCH AND THE BLACK COMMUNITY: SELECTED ISSUES AND PRIORITIES. A SELECTION OF PAPERS FROM A WORKSHOP ON DEVELOPING RESEARCH PRIORITIES FOR THE BLACK COMMUNITY HELD AT HOWARD UNIVERSITY IN WASHINGTON, D.C., JUNE 25-29, 1973, edited by Lawrence E. Gary, pp. 39-52. Washington, D.C.: Howard University, Institute for Urban Affairs and Research, 1974. 13 pp.

Subjects: 1. Trends and Change in Marriage and Family / Family Life in the United States; 2. Aids for Theory and Research / Critiques and Analyses of Family Research Literature.

317 Engram, Eleanor. SCIENCE, MYTH, REALITY: THE BLACK FAMILY IN ONE-HALF CENTURY OF RESEARCH. Contributions in Afro-American and African Studies, No. 64. Westport, CT: Greenwood Press, 1982. 216 pp., references, bibliography, charts, index; ISBN:0-313-22835-3; LC:81-1262.

Subjects: 1. Trends and Change in Marriage and Family / Family Life in the United States; 2. Aids for Theory and Research / Family Research

Methodology; 3. / Critiques and Analyses of Family Research Literature.

The empirical status of Black families is examined in a broad synthesis and methodological study of the primary research literature produced over the past fifty years. Major areas of focus include: theory, demography, mating, unwed motherhood, marriage, child rearing, and marital disruption. Methodological problems-- i.e., sampling, measurement, and data manipulation--in the study of Black families are also highlighted.

Notes: Bibliography: pp. 155-207.

318 Epps, Edgar G. "Impact of School Desegregation on Aspirations, Self-Concepts and Other Aspects of Personality." LAW AND CONTEMPORARY PROBLEMS 39, 2 (Spring 1975): 300-13. 14 pp., references.

Subjects: 1. Trends and Change in Marriage and Family / Family and Social Change; 2. Organizations and Services to Families / Education and the Family; 3. Psychology and Sociology / Psychology.

319 Epstein, Cynthia Fuchs. "Positive Effects of the Multiple Negative: Explaining the Success of Black Professional Women." AMERICAN JOURNAL OF SOCIOLOGY 78, 4 (January 1973): 912-35. 24 pp., references, bibliography, tables.

Subjects: 1. Family Relationships and Dynamics / Family Roles and Sex Roles.

320 Epstein, Cynthia Fuchs. "Women and Professional Careers: The Case of the Woman Lawyer." (Ph.D. dissertation, Columbia University, 1968.) DISSERTATION ABSTRACTS INTERNATIONAL, 30, 2, Aug. 1969, 824A. (University Microfilms No. 699188.) 413 pp.

Subjects: 1. Organizations and Services to Families / Employment and the Family; 2. Family Relationships and Dynamics / Women's Issues; 3. Families with Special Problems / Achievement and the Family.

321 Epstein, Ralph and Komorita, S.S. "Prejudice among Negro Children as Related to Parental Ethnocentrism and Punitiveness." JOURNAL OF PERSONALITY AND SOCIAL PSYCHOLOGY 4, 6 (December 1966): 643-647. 5 pp., references, tables.

Subjects: 1. Family Relationships and Dynamics / Socialization; 2. Psychology and Sociology / Racial Attitudes.

322 Eray, P. CHILDHOOD AND THE COSMOS: THE SOCIAL PSYCHOLOGY OF THE BLACK AFRICAN CHILD. New York: Black Orpheus Press, 1973.

Subjects: 1. Family Relationships and Dynamics / Socialization; 2. Psychology and Sociology / Psychology; 3. Family Counseling and Education / Child Development.

323 Ericksen, Julia A. "Race, Sex, and Alternative Lifestyle Choices." ALTERNATIVE LIFESTYLES 3, 4 (November 1980): 405-24. 21 pp.

Subjects: 1. Trends and Change in Marriage and Family / Alternative
Family Forms; 2. Family Relationships and Dynamics / Family
Relationships; 3. Psychology and Sociology / General Attitudes.

This article is a criticism of recent work on alternative life styles
both because of its lack of attention to structural constraints on the
ability of individuals to pursue personal growth as an important goal
in their lives and for its young, affluent, white male bias in the
choice of alternatives being researched. Using a sample of first year
students at a large urban university, we examined a range of lifestyle
choices by race and sex. Differences in the students' background
included larger families, lower levels of education, and more frequent
contacts with the extended family for Black students as compared to
their white counterparts. We were not surprised to find that, of the
four groups, white male students most approved the   types   of
alternatives usually discussed by alternative lifestyles researchers;
specifically, those concerning sexual freedom, since this is an area
traditionally more open to white males. On other alternatives, they
were the most conservative. The other three groups were more likely to
want egalitarian marriages and to be willing to raise an out of
wedlock child. More blacks than whites supported extended family
networks and radical political action. Women were more in favor of
egalitarian marriages than men. (Author's abstract)

324 Fadayomi, Theophilus Oyeyemi. "Black Women in the Labor Force: An
Investigation of Factors Affecting the Labor Force Participation of
Black Women in the United States." (Ph.D. dissertation, University of
Pennnsylvania, 1977.) DISSERTATION ABSTRACTS INTERNATIONAL, 38, 3,
Sept. 1977, 1679A-1680A. (University Microfilms No. 7719844.) 199 pp.

Subjects: 1. Organizations and Services to Families / Employment and the
Family; 2. Family Relationships and Dynamics / Women's Issues.

325 Farley, Reynolds. GROWTH OF THE BLACK POPULATION: A STUDY OF
DEMOGRAPHIC TRENDS. Chicago, IL: Markham Publishing Company, 1970.   286
pp.; ISBN:8410-4006-0; LC:72-111984.

Subjects: 1. Issues Related to Reproduction / Population Studies; 2.
Aids for Theory and Research / Statistics.

326 Farley, Reynolds and Hermalin, Albert I.   "Family Stability: A
Comparison of Trends between Blacks and Whites." AMERICAN SOCIOLOGICAL
REVIEW 36, 1 (February 1971): 1-17. 17 pp., references, bibliography,
tables.

Subjects: 1. Family Relationships and Dynamics / Family Relationships;
   2. Families with Special Problems / Family Disorganization.

327 Farmer, Bonnita May.   "Black Family Structure and Its Effects on
Adolescents." (Ph.D. dissertation, University of California, Riverside,
1979.) DISSERTATION ABSTRACTS INTERNATIONAL, 40A, 2, Aug. 1979, 1102A-
1103A. (University Microfilms No. 7918244.) 176 pp.

Subjects: 1. Family Relationships and Dynamics / Family Relationships;
   2. / Socialization; 3. Psychology and Sociology / Self-Esteem.

328   Farmer, James.   "The Plight of Negro Children in America Today."
CHILD WELFARE 47, 9 (November 1968): 508-15, 553.   9 pp.

Subjects: 1. Trends and Change in Marriage and Family / Family Life in
    the United States; 2. Family Relationships and Dynamics /
    Socialization.

329   Faulkes, Yolanda.   "Child Abuse in the Black Community."   BLACK
CHILD JOURNAL: A REVIEW OF BLACK CHILD DEVELOPMENT 2, 1 (September
1980): 24-26.   3 pp.

Subjects: 1. Families with Special Problems / Child Abuse.

330   Faust, Drew Gilpin.   "Culture, Conflict and Community: The Meaning
of Power on an Antebellum Plantation."   JOURNAL OF SOCIAL HISTORY 14, 1
(Fall 1980): 83-97.   15 pp.

Subjects: 1. Trends and Change in Marriage and Family / Family Life
    Prior to 1900.

331   Feagin, Joe R.   "The Kinship Ties of Negro Urbanites."   SOCIAL
SCIENCE QUARTERLY 49, 3 (December 1968): 660-65.   6 pp., references,
tables.

Subjects: 1. Family Relationships and Dynamics / Extended Family and
    Kinship Groups.

This paper has presented data on the extensity, intensity,
encapsulation, and types of kinship ties for a sample of Negro
urbanites, a sample most representative of the larger and poorer
families in [Roxbury] Boston's Negro ghetto area. The overwhelming
majority of these Negro respondents had relatives in the Boston area,
almost all of whom lived within the ghetto and its fringe. They
averaged 2.6 relatives each and a frequency of interaction score of
11.2. Almost half depended on relatives for aid in moving to their
present address; nearly a quarter had given financial aid to or
received advice from relatives in the past year. Given the relatively
recent migration of these respondents to the Boston area, this extent
of kinship interaction seems significant. Relatives were of some
importance to most of these Negro urbanites in terms of both mutual
visitation and reciprocal aid. . .[R]ough comparisons with certain
other studies. . .suggest more similarities than differences between
the kin contacts of these Negro urbanites and others so far studied.
(Author's summary and conclusions)

332   Feinman, Saul.   "Trends in Racial Self-Image of Black Children:
Psychological Consequences of a Social Movement."   JOURNAL OF NEGRO
EDUCATION 48, 4 (Fall 1979): 488-99.   12 pp., references.

Subjects: 1. Family Relationships and Dynamics / Socialization; 2.
    Psychology and Sociology / Racial Attitudes; 3. Family Counseling and
    Education / Child Development.

333   Ferman, Louis A., Kornbluh, Joyce L. and Haber, Alan, eds.   POVERTY
IN AMERICA: A BOOK OF READINGS. Revised edition Ann Arbor, MI:
Univeristy of Michigan Press, 1968.   669 pp., references, illustrations,
tables, charts, index; LC:68-29261.

Subjects: 1. Trends and Change in Marriage and Family / Family Life in the United States; 2. Minority Groups / Family and Social Class.

334 Ferranti, David Marc de. "Tests of Seven Hypotheses on Welfare Dependency and Family Disintegration." (Ph.D. dissertation, Princeton University, 1978.) DISSERTATION ABSTRACTS INTERNATIONAL, 39, 4, Oct. 1978, 2412A. (University Microfilms No. 7818325.) 370 pp.

Subjects: 1. Organizations and Services to Families / Social Welfare; 2. Families with Special Problems / Family Disorganization.

335 Fischer, Ann, Beasley, Joseph D. and Harter, Carl L. "Occurrence of the Extended Family at the Origin of the Family of Procreation: A Developmental Approach to Negro Family Structure." JOURNAL OF MARRIAGE AND THE FAMILY 30, 2 (May 1968): 290-300. 10 pp., references, tables, charts.

Subjects: 1. Family Relationships and Dynamics / Extended Family and Kinship Groups; 2. Issues Related to Reproduction / Illegitimacy.

A New Orleans sample of families are studied from a structural and developmental point of view. The significant differences between Negroes and whites in the distribution of family types in the sample is largely accounted for by the number of Negro families which begin with the birth of an illegitimate child. Various associations between race, class, age, and living with relatives at the origin of the family are explored. The sequences of family types in which women lived following the birth of an illegitimate child are given in detail. Age at pregnancy affects this sequence. (Authors' abstract)

336 Fisher, Jerilyn Beth. "The Minority Woman's Voice: A Cultural Study of Black and Chicana Fiction." (Ph.D. dissertation, The American University, 1978.) DISSERTATION ABSTRACTS INTERNATIONAL, 39, 3, Sept. 1978, 1565A. (University Microfilms No. 7814917.) 38 pp.

Subjects: 1. Family Relationships and Dynamics / Women's Issues; 2. Minority Groups / Ethnic Groups in the United States.

337 Fitzgerald, William A. "Pseudoheterosexuality in Prison and Out: A Study of the Lower Class Black Lesbian." (Ph.D. dissertation, City University of New York, 1977.) DISSERTATION ABSTRACTS INTERNATIONAL, 39, 4, Oct. 1978, 2582A. (University Microfilms No. 7818812.) 357 pp.

Subjects: 1. Sexual Attitudes and Behavior / Homosexuality and the Family; 2. Families with Special Problems / Families with Criminal Offenders.

338 Floyd, Russell F. "Marital Adjustment and Decision Making among Stable Black Married Couples." (Ed.D. dissertation, East Texas State University, 1981.) DISSERTATION ABSTRACTS INTERNATIONAL, 42, 12, June 1982, 5025A. (University Microfilms No. 8207868.) 99 pp.

Subjects: 1. Family Relationships and Dynamics / Decision Making; 2. Marriage and Divorce / Marriage Satisfaction and Prediction Studies; 3. Aids for Theory and Research / Family Theory.

339 Fogel, Robert. "Cliometrics and Culture: Some Recent Developments in the Historiography of Slavery." JOURNAL OF SOCIAL HISTORY 11, 1 (Fall 1977): 34-51. 18 pp.

Subjects: 1. Trends and Change in Marriage and Family / Family Life Prior to 1900.

340 Fogel, Robert William and Engerman, Stanley L. "Recent Findings in the Slave Demography and Family Structure." SOCIOLOGY AND SOCIAL RESEARCH 63, 3 (April 1979): 566-89. 24 pp., references, bibliography, tables, charts.

Subjects: 1. Trends and Change in Marriage and Family / Family Life Prior to 1900; 2. Family Relationships and Dynamics / Family Relationships; 3. Aids for Theory and Research / Statistics.

Recent works on the demographic patterns of slave and white populations in the U.S. and the slave population of the British West Indies are examined in order to summarize the principal new findings and to highlight several still unresolved issues. Studies presenting new data on fertility, mortality, and family structure are analyzed to determine the relative contributions of different factors to the differing demographic performance of U.S. slave and British West Indian slaves, and to point to certain similarities in patterns between U.S. slaves and southern whites. (Authors' abstract)

341 Fogel, Robert William and Engerman, Stanley L. TIME ON THE CROSS: THE ECONOMICS OF AMERICAN NEGRO SLAVERY. Boston, MA: Little, Brown and Company, 1974. 286 pp.; ISBN:0-316-28700-8; LC:73-18347.

Subjects: 1. Trends and Change in Marriage and Family / Family Life Prior to 1900.

In one section, the authors focused on the family. The authors maintained that planters assigned three functions to the slave family: distribution of food, clothing and provision of shelter; maintenance of labor discipline; and procreation of the slave population.

342 Folb, Edith A. RUNNING DOWN SOME LINES: THE LANGUAGE AND CULTURE OF BLACK TEENAGERS. Cambridge, MA: Harvard University Press, 1980. 260 pp., bibliography; ISBN:0-674-78039-6; LC:79-26708.

Subjects: 1. Family Relationships and Dynamics / Communication in the Family; 2. Family Counseling and Education / Adolescence.

Notes: Bibliography: pp. 219-221.

343 Foley, Vincent D. "Can a White Therapist Deal with Black Families?" In BLACK MARRIAGE AND FAMILY THERAPY, edited by Constance E. Obudho, pp. 233-249. Westport, CT: Greenwood Press, 1983. 17 pp.

Subjects: 1. Family Counseling and Education / Family Therapy.

344 Foley, Vincent D. "Family Therapy with Black, Disadvantaged Families: Some Observations on Roles, Communication and Technique." JOURNAL OF MARRIAGE AND FAMILY COUNSELING 1, 1 (January 1975): 29-38. 10 pp., references.

Subjects: 1. Family Counseling and Education / Family Therapy.

Within a system concept role delineation and communicational patterns of black, disadvantaged families are evaluated on the basis of 15 years experience. The observations made at best are suggestive and meant to highlight certain features of a black, disadvantaged family system. In the light of these observations some suggestions regarding technique are offered, notably the use of multiple family therapy as a way of increasing therapeutic effectiveness and facilitating movement in the system. (Author's abstract)

345 Ford, Beverly O. "Case Studies of Black Female Heads of Households in the Welfare System: Socialization and Survival." THE WESTERN JOURNAL OF BLACK STUDIES 1, 2 (June 1977): 114-18. 4 pp., bibliography.

Subjects: 1. Organizations and Services to Families / Social Welfare; 2. Family Relationships and Dynamics / Single Parent Families; 3. / Socialization.

Case study data is presented on eight young (mean age 27) Black females who head households with an average of three dependent children. Despite their low level of educational attainment and work history of menial jobs and unemployment, these women consistently view themselves as "resourceful" in managing their meager incomes—i.e., A.F.D.C. payments, financial assistance from males, monies accrued from illegal activities, and inkind reciprocal goods and services—thereby providing for the continued survival of their households. By observing older Black females, women are socialized to see strength and resourcefulness as integral to the cultural definition of their womanhood. Of course social disengagement and/or drug (including alcohol) dependent behavior have been observed in women for whom the physical strain and emotional stress of heading impoverished households have been overly burdensome. Case study data on the eight young women reveal that their ability to cope with stress lies, in part, in the moral support they receive from their mothers and a network of other adult female relatives—grandmothers, aunts, older sisters. Boyfriends, husbands, and peer groups are also other sources in the young women's support systems.

346 Fowler, Dale Eugene. "An Exploratory Investigation of the Relationship between Locus of Control and Parenting Tasks among Lower Socioeconomic Status Black Mothers." (Ph.D. dissertation, The University of Florida, 1978.) DISSERTATION ABSTRACTS INTERNATIONAL, 39, 10, April 1979, 5042B-5043B. (University Microfilms No. 7907743.) 114 pp.

Subjects: 1. Family Relationships and Dynamics / Parent-Child Relationships; 2. / Conflict Resolution; 3. Family Counseling and Education / Education for Parenthood.

347 Fowler, Irving A. "The Urban Middle Class Negro and Adoption: Two Series of Studies and Their Implications for Action." CHILD WELFARE 45, 9 (November 1966): 522-25. 4 pp., references.

Subjects: 1. Organizations and Services to Families / Adoption and Adoption Services.

Survey data from middle-income Blacks in Buffalo and Rochester, New
York indicated that the degree of interest in legal adoption varied
for childless couples and couples with parental experience. The former
were less interested than the later in adoption. Thus emerged the
perception that efforts to persuade middle-income childless Black
couples to adopt would not be massively successful in the immediate
future. To resolve the child welfare problems surrounding adoption, it
was suggested that financial assistance for significant parts of the
adoption process and for significant periods of time be provided to
working, lower-middle class Black couples whose parental experiences
have enhanced their interests in the needs of adoptive children.

348 Frankel, Barbara. CHILDBIRTH IN THE GHETTO: FOLK BELIEFS OF NEGRO
WOMEN IN A NORTH PHILADELPHIA HOSPITAL WARD. San Francisco, CA: R and E
Research Associates, Inc., 1977. 124 pp., references, bibliography,
appendices; ISBN:0-88247-4189; LC:76-27000.

Subjects: 1. Issues Related to Reproduction / Pregnancy and Child Birth.

  Notes: Bibliography: pp. 113-19.

349 Franklin, Clyde W., II. "White Racism as the Cause of Black Male/
Black Female Conflict: A Critique." THE WESTERN JOURNAL OF BLACK
STUDIES 4, 1 (Spring 1980): 42-49. 8 pp., references, bibliography.

Subjects: 1. Family Relationships and Dynamics / Conflict Resolution;
  2. Psychology and Sociology / Racial Attitudes.

  Black male-Black female conflict is a phenomenon existing on a large
  scale in the United States. . . It is suggested that the conflict
  stems from the diverse manner in which some Black males and Black
  females define situations, interpret each other's behaviors, and
  direct action toward each other. The familiar rationale offered for
  Black male-Black female [conflict], white racism, is deemed logically
  inadequate because of certain underlying assumptions. . .[that]
  violate basic canons of theory formulation and scientific scrutiny, as
  well as much of what is known about social interactions. The writer
  suggests that there is a need for logically adequate explanations of
  Black male-Black female conflict which are consistent and non-
  tautological. While a theoretical formulation is not offered in this
  paper, suggestions for reconceptualization of the problem using basic
  social interaction principles are posited as necessary to explain and
  ultimately control Black male-Black female conflict in a society that
  features white racism as a "setting" variable. (Author's conclusion)

350 Frate, Dennis Anthony. "Family Functioning and Hypertension in a
Black Population." (Ph.D. dissertation, University of Illinois at
Urbana-Champaign, 1978.) DISSERTATION ABSTRACTS INTERNATIONAL, 39, 12,
June 1979, 7408A. (University Microfilms No. 7913458.)

Subjects: 1. Organizations and Services to Families / Physical Health
  and the Family; 2. Family Relationships and Dynamics / Extended Family
  and Kinship Groups; 3. Families with Special Problems / Family Stress.

351 Frazier, Edward Franklin. THE NEGRO FAMILY IN THE UNITED STATES.
Chicago: University of Chicago Press, 1966. 372 pp.; ISBN:0-226-26141-
7; LC:66-13868.

Subjects: 1. Trends and Change in Marriage and Family / Family Life in the United States; 2. Family Relationships and Dynamics / Family Relationships.

352 Frazier, Edward Franklin. NEGRO YOUTH AT THE CROSSWAYS, THEIR PERSONALITY DEVELOPMENT IN THE MIDDLE STATES. New York: Schoeken Books, 1967. 299 pp.; LC:67-26987.

Subjects: 1. Psychology and Sociology / Psychology; 2. Family Counseling and Education / Adolescence.

Notes: This volume was prepared for the American Youth Commission, American Council on Education. This edition contains a new introduction by St. Clair Drake and the author.

353 Frazier, Edward Franklin, ed. ON RACE RELATIONS: SELECTED WRITINGS. Chicago: University of Chicago Press, 1968. 331 pp., references, bibliography; LC:68-8586.

Subjects: 1. Psychology and Sociology / Racial Attitudes; 2. Aids for Theory and Research / Collected Works.

Notes: Bibliography of E. Franklin Frazier: pp. 325-331.

354 Freeman, Harvey R., Schockett, Melanie R. and Freeman, Evelyn B. "Effects of Gender and Race on Sex-Role Preferences of Fifth-Grade Children." JOURNAL OF SOCIAL PSYCHOLOGY 95, First Half (February 1975): 105-108. 3 pp., references.

Subjects: 1. Family Relationships and Dynamics / Family Roles and Sex Roles.

Twenty-nine white and 14 black fifth-grade American students categorized 15 words as either masculine or feminine items. The subjects then rated the degree to which they liked each item. Results showed that girls significantly preferred items associated with their own sex, whereas boys were more ambiguous in their choices. Furthermore, girls assigned significantly more value to feminine items than boys assigned to masculine items and significantly less value to masculine items than boys assigned to feminine items. No significant effect due to race was found. (Authors' summary)

355 Freeman, Howard E., Ross, J. Michael, Armor, David and Pettigrew, Thomas F. "Color Gradation and Attitudes among Middle-Income Negroes." AMERICAN SOCIOLOGICAL REVIEW 31, 3 (June 1966): 365-74. 10 pp., references, tables.

Subjects: 1. Family Relationships and Dynamics / Socialization; 2. Psychology and Sociology / Self-Esteem.

356 Freeman, Janie Earlyn Andrews. "A Study of Black Middle-Class Feelings and Attitudes on Male/Female Role Identifications." (Ph.D. dissertation, United States International University, 1979.) DISSERTATION ABSTRACTS INTERNATIONAL, 40, 7, Jan. 1980, 4254A. (University Microfilms No. 7928689.) 175 pp.

Subjects: 1. Family Relationships and Dynamics / Parent-Adolescent
Relationships; 2. / Family Roles and Sex Roles.

357 Frey, Cecile P.   "The House of Refuge for Colored Children."
JOURNAL OF NEGRO HISTORY 66, 1 (Spring 1981): 10-25. 16 pp.,
references.

Subjects: 1. Organizations and Services to Families / Social Services
and the Family; 2. Psychology and Sociology / Self-Esteem.

358 Fu, Victoria R.   "A Longitudinal Study of the Self-Concepts of
Euro-American, Afro-American, and Mexican American Preadolescent Girls."
CHILD STUDY JOURNAL 9, 4 (Fall 1979): 279-88. 10 pp., references,
tables.

Subjects: 1. Psychology and Sociology / Self-Esteem; 2. Family
Counseling and Education / Adolescence.

359 Furlong, William Berry.   "Intermarriage is a Sometime Thing."   In
THE CONTEMPORARY AMERICAN FAMILY, edited by William Josiah Goode, p.   .
Chicago, IL: Quadrangle Books, 1971.

Subjects: 1. Marriage and Divorce / Inter-marriage.

360 Furstenberg, Frank F. Jr., Hershberg, Theodore and Modell, John.
"The Origins of the Female-Headed Black Family: The Impact of the Urban
Experience." JOURNAL OF INTERDISCIPLINARY HISTORY 6, 2 (Autumn 1975):
211-33. 23 pp., references, tables.

Subjects: 1. Trends and Change in Marriage and Family / Family Life
Prior to 1900; 2. Families with Special Problems / Death, Bereavement
and the Family.

This paper examines how family structure and family composition
varied by ethnic group in the second half of the nineteenth century in
Philadelphia, the nation's second largest city. Our analysis is based
on samples drawn from the decennial Federal population manuscript
schedules for 1850 through 1880. The black sample consists of all
black households; the white ethnic samples are drawn systematically
from the whole number of households headed by immigrants from Ireland
and Germany, and by native white Americans. None includes fewer than
2,000 households for each census year. . .The PSHP [Philadelphia
Social History Project] data indicate that the household structure in
1850, 1870, and 1880 was highly similar among each of the ethnic
groups. Black families were just as likely to be organized in nuclear
households, and, hence, were not more or less able to adapt to
conditions created by industrialization than other ethnic groups. A
somewhat higher proportion of black families were headed by a female
than was true for other ethnic groups. However, we argue that a
cultural explanation cannot account for this disparity. . .To the
extent that the female-headed family appeared during this period, it
emerged, not as a legacy of slavery, but as a result of the
destructive conditions of northern urban life. (From authors' text)

361 Gackenbach, Jayne.   "The Effect of Race, Sex and Career Goal
Differences on Sex Role Attitudes at Home and at Work." JOURNAL OF

VOCATIONAL BEHAVIOR 12, 1 (February 1978): 93-101.   9 pp., references, tables.

Subjects: 1. Organizations and Services to Families / Employment and the Family; 2. Family Relationships and Dynamics / Family Roles and Sex Roles; 3. Aids for Theory and Research / Family Research Methodology.

Male and female blacks and whites whose career goals differed as to sex role stereotypy were adminstered two sex role inventories. One measured attitudes toward women's expanding sex roles in the home/personal environment, while the other measured sex role attitudes in the working environment. The major finding of the present study is that black women had more traditional sex role attitudes in the home environment than white women but the same sex role attitudes about working, whereas both black and white women were more liberal in their sex role attitudes in both environments than black and white men. (Author's abstract)

362 Gardner, Coleman and Lea, Jacquelyn. "A Comparative Study on the Assertiveness of Black and White Women at the University Level." (Ph.D. dissertation, Southern Illinois University at Carbondale, 1977.) DISSERTATION ABSTRACTS INTERNATIONAL, 38, 10, April 1978, 5924A-5925A. (University Microfilms No. 7804256.) 79 pp.

Subjects: 1. Family Relationships and Dynamics / Women's Issues.

363 Gary, Lawrence E., ed. BLACK MEN. Sage Focus Editions, No. 31. Beverly Hill, CA: Sage Publications, Inc., 1981.   295 pp., bibliography, illustrations; ISBN:0-8039-1654-X; LC:81-9021.

Subjects: 1. Family Relationships and Dynamics / Men's Issues; 2. Aids for Theory and Research / Collected Works.

364 Gary, Lawrence E., ed. MENTAL HEALTH: A CHALLENGE TO THE BLACK COMMUNITY. Philadelphia, PA: Dorrance and Company, 1978.   365 pp., bibliography, illustrations, index; ISBN:0-8059-2493-0; LC:78-104789.

Subjects: 1. Organizations and Services to Families / Mental Health and the Family.

365 Gary, Lawrence E. "Policy Decisions in the Aid to Families with Dependent Children Program: A Comparative State Analysis." JOURNAL OF POLITICS 35, 4 (November 1973): 886-923.   38 pp.

Subjects: 1. Trends and Change in Marriage and Family / Family Policy; 2. Organizations and Services to Families / Social Welfare.

366 Gary, Lawrence E., ed. SOCIAL RESEARCH AND THE BLACK COMMUNITY: SELECTED ISSUES AND PRIORITIES. A SELECTION OF PAPERS FROM A WORKSHOP ON DEVELOPING RESEARCH PRIORITIES FOR THE BLACK COMMUNITY HELD AT HOWARD UNIVERSITY IN WASHINGTON, D.C., JUNE 25-29, 1973. Washington, D.C.: Howard University, Institute for Urban Affairs and Research, 1974. 216 pp., references; LC:74-195990.

Subjects: 1. Organizations and Services to Families / Community Groups and the Family; 2. Aids for Theory and Research / Critiques and Analyses of Family Research Literature.

367 Gary, Lawrence E. and Brown, Lee, P., eds. CRIME AND ITS IMPACT ON
THE BLACK COMMUNITY. Washington, DC: Howard University. Institute for
Urban Affairs and Research, 1975. 206 pp., references; LC:78-20233.

Subjects: 1. Families with Special Problems / Family Violence; 2. /
  Families with Criminal Offenders; 3. Aids for Theory and Research /
  Collected Works.

  Selection of papers presented at the 3d annual research conference
  sponsored by the Institute for Urban Affairs and Research, Howard
  University, held in Washington, D.C., June 4-6, 1975. (From authors'
  introduction)

368 Gaston, John C. "The Acculturation of the First-Generation Black
Professional Woman: A Denver, Colorado Area Study." THE WESTERN JOURNAL
OF BLACK STUDIES 4, 4 (Winter 1980): 256-60. 5 pp., references,
bibliography.

Subjects: 1. Mate Selection / Mate Selection, Differential Patterns.

  Fifty Black professional/business women from Denver, Colorado were
  interviewed regarding their expectations in male/female relationships.
  Some differences were found in the responses of those who were first
  generational professionals and those whose families of orientation had
  at least one professional parent. Whether single or divorced, women
  from professional families preferred men with similar status; whereas
  first generational professional women had no such preferences and were
  thus able to communicate with professional and nonprofessional males.
  Second generational women also appeared to be excessively tolerant of
  their mates' activities, whereas first generational professional women
  were more concerned about not being put through "a bunch of changes"
  by their mates. Nor surprisingly there were more divorces among the
  group of first generational professional women. At some point, the
  pursuit of career goals was perceived as contributing to marital
  conflict. However, the divorcees perceived their ex-husbands' lack of
  ambition and failure to accept the responsibilities of spouse and
  parent as key factors which undermined their marriages.

369 Gaston, John Coy. "The Denver, Colorado Area Black Professional/
Businesswoman's Perception of Her Communication with the Black
Male." (Ph.D. dissertation, University of Colorado at Boulder, 1979.)
DISSERTATION ABSTRACTS INTERNATIONAL, 40, 8, Feb. 1980, 4296A.
(University Microfilms No. 8002975.) 173 pp.

Subjects: 1. Family Relationships and Dynamics / Communication in the
  Family.

370 Geerken, Michael and Gove, Walter R. "Race, Sex, and Marital
Status: Their Effect on Mortality." SOCIAL PROBLEMS 21, 4 (April 1974):
567-80. 14 pp., references, bibliography, tables.

Subjects: 1. Families with Special Problems / Death, Bereavement and the
  Family.

371 Geismar, Ludwig L. and Gerhart, Ursula C. "Social Class,
Ethnicity, and Family Functioning: Exploring Some Issues Raised by the

Moynihan Report." JOURNAL OF MARRIAGE AND THE FAMILY 30, 3 (August 1968): 480-87. 8 pp., references, tables.

Subjects: 1. Minority Groups / Family and Social Class.

372 Gelles, Richard J. "Violence in the Family: A Review of Research in the Seventies." JOURNAL OF MARRIAGE AND THE FAMILY 42, 4 (November 1980): 873-85. 13 pp., references, bibliography, tables.

Subjects: 1. Families with Special Problems / Family Violence; 2. Aids for Theory and Research / Critiques and Analyses of Family Research Literature.

373 Genovese, Eugene D. "Husbands, Fathers, Wives and Mothers During Slavery." In FAMILY LIFE IN AMERICA, 1620-2000, edited by Mel Albin and Dominick Cavallo, pp. 237-51. New York: Revisionary Press, 1981. 15 pp., references.

Subjects: 1. Trends and Change in Marriage and Family / Family Life Prior to 1900; 2. Family Relationships and Dynamics / Family Relationships; 3. / Husband-Wife Relationships.

374 Genovese, Eugene D. ROLL, JORDAN, ROLL: THE WORLD THE SLAVES MADE. 1st edition New York: Pantheon Books, 1974. 823 pp., references; ISBN:0-394-49131-9; LC:74-4760.

Subjects: 1. Trends and Change in Marriage and Family / Family Life Prior to 1900.

375 George, Valerie Daring. "An Investigation of the Occupational Aspirations of Talented Black Adolescent Females." (Ph.D. dissertation, Case Western Reserve University, 1979.) DISSERTATION ABSTRACTS INTERNATIONAL, 40, 5, Nov. 1979, 2479A. (University Microfilms No. 7924816.) 201 pp.

Subjects: 1. Organizations and Services to Families / Employment and the Family; 2. Families with Special Problems / Achievement and the Family; 3. Family Counseling and Education / Adolescence.

376 Gerstman, Leslie Sue. "Withdrawal of Blacks and Whites from Public to Nonpublic Elementary Schools in Minneapolis." (Ph.D. dissertation, University of Minnesota, 1979.) DISSERTATION ABSTRACTS INTERNATIONAL, 40, 11, May 1980, 5665A-5666A. (University Microfilms No. 8011808.) 169 pp.

Subjects: 1. Organizations and Services to Families / Education and the Family; 2. Family Relationships and Dynamics / Decision Making.

377 Gibson, Geoffrey. "Kin Family Network: Overheralded Structure in Past Conceptualizations of Family Functioning." JOURNAL OF MARRIAGE AND THE FAMILY 34, 2 (February 1972): 13-23. 11 pp., references, tables.

Subjects: 1. Family Relationships and Dynamics / Extended Family and Kinship Groups.

378   Gibson, Rose C.   "Blacks at Middle and Late Life: Resources and Coping."   ANNALS OF THE AMERICAN ACADEMY OF POLITICAL AND SOCIAL SCIENCE 464, (Fall 1982): 79-90.   12 pp., references, illustrations, tables.

Subjects: 1. Family Relationships and Dynamics / Later Years and Aging; 2. / Middle Years; 3. Families with Special Problems / Family Stress.

379   Gibson, William.   FAMILY LIFE AND MORALITY: STUDIES IN BLACK AND WHITE.   Washington, D.C.: University Press of America, 1980.   116 pp.; ISBN:0-8191-0969-X; LC:79-57076.

Subjects: 1. Trends and Change in Marriage and Family / Family Life in the United States; 2. Family Counseling and Education / Value Education; 3. Aids for Theory and Research / Family Theory.

380   Gilbert, Gwendolyn C.   "Counseling Black Adolescent Parents." SOCIAL WORK 19, 1 (January 1974): 88-95.   8 pp., references.

Subjects: 1. Family Counseling and Education / Adolescence; 2. / Education for Parenthood.

381   Gilbert, Gwendolyn Cynthia.   "Patterns of Child Care among Black Families." (Ph.D. dissertation, Case Western Reserve University, 1979.) DISSERTATION ABSTRACTS INTERNATIONAL, 40, 7, Jan. 1980, 4236A. (University Microfilms No. 8001457.) 309 pp.

Subjects: 1. Organizations and Services to Families / Community Groups and the Family; 2. / Social Work; 3. Family Counseling and Education / Family Life Education.

382   Gilkes, Cheryl Louise Townsend.   "Living and Working in a World of Trouble: The Emergent Career of the Black Woman Community Worker." (Ph.D. dissertation, Northeastern University, 1979.) DISSERTATION ABSTRACTS INTERNATIONAL, 40, 9, March 1980, 5201A. (University Microfilms No. 8006385.) 437 pp.

Subjects: 1. Organizations and Services to Families / Social Work; 2. / Employment and the Family; 3. Family Relationships and Dynamics / Women's Issues.

383   Gilmore, Al-Tony, ed.   REVISITING BLASSINGAME'S "THE SLAVE COMMUNITY": THE SCHOLARS RESPOND.   Contributions in Afro-American and African Studies, No. 37. Westport, CT: Greenwood Press, 1978.   206 pp., references, index; ISBN:0-8371-9879-8; LC:77-84765.

Subjects: 1. Trends and Change in Marriage and Family / Family Life Prior to 1900; 2. Aids for Theory and Research / Family Theory; 3. / Critiques and Analyses of Family Research Literature.

A review of Blassingame's theory on the slave family structure and family interrelationships.

384   Giovannoni, Jeanne M. and Billingsley, Andrew.   "Child Neglect among the Poor: A Study of Parental Adequacy in Families of Three Ethnic Groups."   CHILD WELFARE 49, 4 (April 1970): 196-204.   9 pp., references.

Subjects: 1. Trends and Change in Marriage and Family / Comparative
Studies--International, Interclass, Sex, and Time Differences; 2.
Families with Special Problems / Family Disorganization; 3. Minority
Groups / Ethnic Groups in the United States.

This study was an attempt to elucidate additional factors that might
distinguish neglectful parents from more adequate ones, within a group
of mothers all of whom were of low-income status. One hundred and
eighty-six low-income, black, Caucasian, and Spanish-speaking mothers
[from the caseloads of public health nurses in the San Francisco
Department of Health and the caseloads of the Protective Services
Units at the Department of Social Services] were interviewed about
their past and current life situations. . .Ethnic variations noted
throughout, and particularly functioning in formal social systems, and
in childrearing practices, underscored the continuing importance of
evaluating and understanding families within the ethnic context. In
sum, the low-income neglectful parent is under greater environmental
and situational stress and has fewer resources and supports in coping
with these stresses than does the adequate mother. It is the current
situational strains that predominate among neglectful parents, not
those of their past life. (Authors' summary)

385 Glasser, Paul H. and Glasser, Lois N., eds. FAMILIES IN
CRISIS. Readers in Social Problems. New York: Harper and Row, 1970.
405 pp., references; ISBN:0-06-042349-8; LC:79-103916.

Subjects: 1. Trends and Change in Marriage and Family / Family and
Social Change; 2. Families with Special Problems / Family Stress; 3.
Aids for Theory and Research / Collected Works.

Twenty essays discussing various family problems.

386 Glick, Paul C. "Marriage and Marital Stability among Blacks."
MILBANK MEMORIAL FUND QUARTERLY 48, 2 (April 1970): 99-126. 27 pp.,
references, tables, charts.

Subjects: 1. Marriage and Divorce / Marriage Satisfaction and Prediction
Studies.

387 Gochros, Harvey L. and Gochros, Jean S., eds. THE SEXUALLY
OPPRESSED. New York: Association Press, 1977. 296 pp., bibliography;
ISBN:0-8096-1915-6; LC:76-49051.

Subjects: 1. Sexual Attitudes and Behavior / Sexual Attitudes and
Behavior; 2. Psychology and Sociology / Racial Attitudes; 3. Aids for
Theory and Research / Collected Works.

388 Golden, Herbert M. "Black Ageism." SOCIAL POLICY 7, 3 (November-
December 1976): 40-42. 3 pp., references.

Subjects: 1. Family Relationships and Dynamics / Stages in Family Life
Cycle.

389 Golden, Susan, ed. WORK, FAMILY ROLES AND
SUPPORT SYSTEMS. Continuing Education of Women (CEW) Series, New
Research on Women, No. 3. Ann Arbor, MI: University of Michigan, Center

for Continuing Education of Women, 1978. 143 pp., bibliography; LC:79-621526.

Subjects: 1. Organizations and Services to Families / Employment and the Family; 2. Family Relationships and Dynamics / Family Roles and Sex Roles; 3. / Women's Issues.

Papers presented at a conference sponsored by the Center for Continuing Education of Women at the University of Michigan, January 17, 1978

390 Goldenberg, Sheldon. "Kinship and Ethnicity Viewed as Adaptive Responses to Location in the Opportunity Structure." JOURNAL OF COMPARATIVE FAMILY STUDIES 8, 2 (Summer 1977): 149-165. 17 pp., references, charts.

Subjects: 1. Trends and Change in Marriage and Family / Social Mobility as it Affects the Family; 2. Family Relationships and Dynamics / Extended Family and Kinship Groups; 3. Minority Groups / Family and Social Class.

391 Goldstein, Rhoda L., ed. BLACK LIFE AND CULTURE IN THE UNITED STATES. New York: Thomas Y. Crowell, Co., 1971. 400 pp., bibliography, illustrations, tables; ISBN:0-690-14598-5; LC:74-146281.

Subjects: 1. Trends and Change in Marriage and Family / Family Life in the United States; 2. Aids for Theory and Research / Collected Works.

A collection of articles by various authors that was developed from lectures delivered at a course at Douglass College in the Spring of 1970. (NUC)

Notes: Bibliography: pp. 381-385.

392 Goode, William Josiah, ed. THE CONTEMPORARY AMERICAN FAMILY. Chicago, IL: Quadrangle Books, 1971. 302 pp., bibliography; ISBN:0-8129-0149-5; LC:79-124510.

Subjects: 1. Trends and Change in Marriage and Family / Family Life in the United States.

Notes: Bibliography: pp. 291-292.

393 Goodlett, Carlton B. "The Crisis of Youth and Adult Responsibility." BLACK SCHOLAR 10, 5 (January 1979): 19-30. 12 pp.

Subjects: 1. Family Relationships and Dynamics / Parent-Adolescent Relationships; 2. / Socialization; 3. / Conflict Resolution.

394 Gordon, Chad. LOOKING AHEAD: SELF CONCEPTIONS, RACE AND FAMILY AS DETERMINANTS OF ADOLESCENT ORIENTATION TO ACHIEVEMENT. The Arnold and Caroline Rose Monograph Series in Psychology. Washington, DC: American Sociological Association, 1972. 120 pp., bibliography, illustrations; ISBN:0-912764-02-3; LC:77-183121.

Subjects: 1. Families with Special Problems / Achievement and the Family; 2. Psychology and Sociology / Self-Esteem; 3. Family Counseling and Education / Adolescence.

Notes: Bibliography: pp. 111-120

395 Gordon, Vivian V. "The Methodologies of Black Self-Concept Research: A Critique." JOURNAL OF AFRO-AMERICAN ISSUES 4, 3/4 (Summer/Fall 1976): 373-381. 9 pp., references, tables.

Subjects: 1. Aids for Theory and Research / Family Research Methodology; 2. / Critiques and Analyses of Family Research Literature.

Throughout this review of the research we have found irregular patterns of results. There have even been differing reports about levels of black self-concept among studies reporting the use of the same instrument with comparable specific populations. We have found that there appears to be an association between findings of low self-concept and the time frame of the study; the research technique used and the geographical representation of the same. The data indicate that findings of low self-concept are most closely associated with the Forced Choice Identification Technique, and the preschool and elementary school age group. Moreover, there appears to be greater report of low self-concept among studies selecting Northeastern as opposed to Southeastern subjects. The extreme variability of these findings leads us to conclude that researchers have been studyng a widely shifting phenomenon or that there are serious validity problems in the study of the self-concept. The patterns of conflicting findings make generalized statements about low black self-concept highly questionable. The study results, taken as a whole, appear to be largely a function of the research instrument used; the theoretical orientation of the researcher and time and place of the study. Psychiatrists, convinced of damaged black psyches, find low self-concepts; while researchers less convinced of the psychic damage done by slavery and segregation find healthy black self-concepts. (From author's text)

396 Gordon, Vivian Verdell, ed. LECTURES: BLACK SCHOLARS ON BLACK ISSUES. Washington, DC: University Press of America, 1979. 308 pp., references; LC:80-289546.

Subjects: 1. Trends and Change in Marriage and Family / Family and Social Change; 2. Organizations and Services to Families / Education and the Family; 3. Aids for Theory and Research / Collected Works.

397 Gornick, Vivian and Moran, Barbara K., eds. WOMAN IN SEXIST SOCIETY: STUDIES IN POWER AND POWERLESSNESS. New York: Basic Books, Inc., 1971. 515 pp., bibliography; ISBN:0-465-09199-7; LC:70-157125.

Subjects: 1. Family Relationships and Dynamics / Women's Issues; 2. Aids for Theory and Research / Collected Works.

398 Gossett, Ruth. "Economics of Black Widowhood." JOURNAL OF AFRO-AMERICAN ISSUES 3, 3/4 (Summer/Fall 1975): 309-315. 7 pp., references, bibliography.

Subjects: 1. Organizations and Services to Families / Economics and the
    Family; 2. Families with Special Problems / Death, Bereavement and the
    Family.

399 Gossett, Ruth R.   "Black Widows."   In THE SEXUALLY OPPRESSED,
edited by Harvey L. Gochros and Jean S.   Gochros, pp. 84-95. New York:
Association Press, 1977.   12 pp.

Subjects: 1. Families with Special Problems / Death, Bereavement and the
    Family.

400 Gossett, Ruth Ross.   "So Few Men: A Study of Black
Widowhood."   (Ph.D. dissertation, Syracuse University, 1976.)
DISSERTATION ABSTRACTS INTERNATIONAL, 38, 5, Nov. 1977, 3086A.
(University Microfilms No. 7724539.) 148 pp.

Subjects: 1. Families with Special Problems / Death, Bereavement and the
    Family.

401 Graber, Anita Wine.   "Imagining the World: The Reflections and
Perceptions of Black Low-Income Mothers in Relation to Their
Involvements in the Educational Lives of Their Children." (Ed.D.
dissertation, Columbia University Teachers College, 1982.) DISSERTATION
ABSTRACTS INTERNATIONAL, 43, 5, Nov. 1982, 1459A.   (University
Microfilms No. 8223133.) 177 pp.

Subjects: 1. Organizations and Services to Families / Education and the
    Family; 2. Family Relationships and Dynamics / Mother-Child
    Relationships.

402 Graham, Lawrence O.   "Behind the Mask." CRISIS 86, (December
1979): 435-436.   2 pp.

Subjects: 1. Minority Groups / Ethnic Groups in the United States.

403 Graham, Richard.   "Slave Families on a Rural Estate in Colonial
Brazil." JOURNAL OF SOCIAL HISTORY 9, 3 (Spring 1976): 382-402.   21
pp., references, tables, charts.

Subjects: 1. Trends and Change in Marriage and Family / Family Life
    Prior to 1900.

404 Granger, Robert C. and Young, James C., eds. DEMYTHOLOGIZING THE
INNER CITY CHILD: PAPERS. Washington, DC: National Association for the
Education of Young Children, 1976.   138 pp., bibliography,
illustrations; ISBN:0-912674-50-4; LC:76-47135.

Subjects: 1. Organizations and Services to Families / Education and the
    Family; 2. Aids for Theory and Research / Collected Works.

    Papers of a conference held March 25-27, 1976. The conference was
    sponsored by the Urban Life Foundation of Georgia State University.
    (NUC)

405 Graves, Conrad.   "Family and Community Support Networks and Their
Utilization by the Black Elderly." (Ph.D. dissertation, New York

University, 1981.) DISSERTATION ABSTRACTS INTERNATIONAL, 43, 6,
Dec. 1982, 2092A. (University Microfilms No. 8210977.) 237 pp.

Subjects: 1. Organizations and Services to Families / Social Services
   and the Family; 2. Family Relationships and Dynamics / Later Years and
   Aging.

406 Graves, William L. and Bradshaw, Barbara R.   "Early Reconception
and Contraceptive Use among Black Teenage Girls After an Illegitimate
Birth." AMERICAN JOURNAL OF PUBLIC HEALTH 65, 7 (July 1975): 738-740.
3 pp., references, tables.

Subjects: 1. Issues Related to Reproduction / Birth Control; 2. /
   Teenage Pregnancy.

Contraceptive continuation and early reconception rates among a group
of low income, black, teenage primiparous women [N=289] were examined.
It was found that: 1. Subjects who subsequently married following
their first pregnancy were significantly more likely to conceive again
within 1 year, but, when the association was examined by method of
contraception chosen, the difference persisted only for those who
selected oral contraceptives. 2. There was no association between
method of contraception chosen and subsequent marriage within 2 years
postpartum, although patients who did not marry but reported at the
time of delivery that they had plans to marry were more likely to
choose oral contraceptives. 3. Selection of the IUD was associated
with a set of social situational factors which suggest that family
pressures may be an important factor in the choice of this method of
contraception. 4. Active use of contraception at 1 year does not
appear to be related to social situational factors in this population.
Psychological attributes seem to be more critical. It was shown that
passivity was related to continued use of the IUD and discontinued use
of oral contraceptives. (Authors' summary)

407 Gray, Naomi. "Sterilization and the Black Family: An Historical
Perspective." In MENTAL AND PHYSICAL HEALTH PROBLEMS OF BLACK WOMEN,
WASHINGTON, D.C., MARCH 29-30, 1974. PROCEEDINGS., by , pp. 80-90.
Washington, D.C.: Black Women's Community Development Foundation, 1975.
11 pp.

Subjects: 1. Family Relationships and Dynamics / Women's Issues; 2.
   Issues Related to Reproduction / Birth Control.

408 Greenberg, Edward S. "Black Children and the Political System."
PUBLIC OPINION QUARTERLY 34, 3 (Fall 1970): 333-345. 13 pp., tables,
charts.

Subjects: 1. Organizations and Services to Families / Governmental Units
   and the Family.

409 Greenberg, Edward S. "Black Children, Self-Esteem, and the
Liberation Movement." POLITICS AND SOCIETY 2, 3 (Spring 1972): 293-307.
15 pp., references, tables.

Subjects: 1. Trends and Change in Marriage and Family / Family and
   Social Change; 2. Psychology and Sociology / Self-Esteem.

410 Greenfield, Sidney M. ENGLISH RUSTICS IN BLACK SKIN: A STUDY OF MODERN FAMILY FORMS IN A PRE-INDUSTRIALIZED SOCIETY. New Haven, CT: College and University Press, 1966. 208 pp., bibliography; ISBN:0-8084-0121-1; LC:66-10484.

Subjects: 1. Trends and Change in Marriage and Family / Family Life in Foreign Countries; 2. Marriage and Divorce / Marriage Customs and Forms.

Combines a cultural-historical analysis with structural functions.

Notes: Bibliography: pp. 199-202.

411 Grier, William H. and Cobbs, Price M. BLACK RAGE. New York: Basic Books, Inc., 1968. 213 pp.; LC:68-29925.

Subjects: 1. Psychology and Sociology / Psychology.

Notes: Forward by Fred R. Harris.

412 Griffin, Don Quincy. "Personality Competence in Black Adolescents." (Ph.D. dissertation, University of California, Berkeley, 1978.) DISSERTATION ABSTRACTS INTERNATIONAL, 40, 1, July 1979, 491B. (University Microfilms No. 7914623.) 198 pp.

Subjects: 1. Psychology and Sociology / Psychology; 2. Family Counseling and Education / Adolescence.

413 Grigg, Ernest C. "Save the Children." CRISIS 86, 7 (August-September 1979): 287-289. 3 pp.

Subjects: 1. Organizations and Services to Families / Community Groups and the Family.

414 Grindstaff, Carl F. "Trend and Incidence of Childlessness by Race: Indicators of Black Progress Over Three Decades." SOCIOLOGICAL FOCUS 9, 3 (August 1976): 265-84. 20 pp., references, bibliography, tables, charts.

Subjects: 1. Issues Related to Reproduction / Childlessness.

This paper analyses the trends in childlessness of black and white ever-married women from 1940 through 1972, employing the trends as indicators of both cultural and institutional integration. It is hypothesized that rates of black and white childlessness have converged over the three decades, thus indicating that blacks have made progress into the basic structures of American society. The findings suggest two relatively distinct patterns of childlessness trends between the races by age groupings, and these patterns are somewhat at variance with one another. The implications of these findings are discussed within a cultural and institutional integration framework. Finally, trends for the future are discussed, and it is predicted that childlessness will continue to converge and increase for both racial groups in the 1970s. (Author's abstract)

415 Grow, Lucille J. and Shapiro, Deborah. "Adoption of Black Children by White Parents." CHILD WELFARE 54, 1 (January 1975): 57-59. 3 pp.

Subjects: 1. Organizations and Services to Families / Adoption and
  Adoption Services.

416 Grow, Lucille J. and Shapiro, Deborah. BLACK CHILDREN--WHITE
PARENTS: A STUDY OF TRANSRACIAL ADOPTION. New York: Child Welfare
League of America. Research Center, 1974. 239 pp., references; ISBN:0-
87868-177-9; LC:74-29169.

Subjects: 1. Organizations and Services to Families / Adoption and
  Adoption Services.

417 Gudeman, Stephen. "Herbert Gutman's THE BLACK FAMILY IN SLAVERY
AND FREEDOM, 1750-1925: An Anthropologist's View." SOCIAL SCIENCE
HISTORY 3, 3/4 (October 1979): 56-65. 10 pp., references.

Subjects: 1. Trends and Change in Marriage and Family / Family Life
  Prior to 1900.

418 Gump, Janice Porter. "Comparative Analysis of Black and White
Women's Sex-Role Attitudes." JOURNAL OF CONSULTING AND CLINICAL
PSYCHOLOGY 43, 6 (1975): 858-863. 6 pp., references, tables.

Subjects: 1. Trends and Change in Marriage and Family / Comparative
  Studies--International, Interclass, Sex, and Time Differences; 2.
  Family Relationships and Dynamics / Family Roles and Sex Roles; 3.
  Sexual Attitudes and Behavior / Sexual Attitudes and Behavior.

An assessment of the sex-role attitudes of 77 black college women and
40 white college women refuted the characterization of the black woman
as matriarchal and the white woman as home centerd and submissive.
Black women, in comparison with white women, were more likely to
define their identity with respect to the roles of wife and mother and
were more home centered and more submissive; white women expressed
significantly more interest in furthering their own development than
in fulfilling the traditional role. (Author's abstract)

419 Gump, Janice Porter. "Reality and Myth: Employment and Sex Role
Ideology in Black Women." In THE PSYCHOLOGY OF WOMEN: FUTURE DIRECTIONS
IN RESEARCH, edited by Julia A. Sherman and Florence L. Denmark,
pp. 349-80. New York: Psychological Dimensions, 1978. 32 pp.,
references, tables.

Subjects: 1. Organizations and Services to Families / Employment and the
  Family; 2. Family Relationships and Dynamics / Family Roles and Sex
  Roles; 3. / Women's Issues.

420 Gunthorpe, Wayne West. "Skin Color Recognition, Preference and
Identification in Interracial Children: A Comparative Study." (Ed.D.
dissertation, Rutgers University, The State University of New Jersey
(New Brunswick), 1977.) DISSERTATION ABSTRACTS INTERNATIONAL, 38, 7,
Jan. 1978, 3468B-3469B. (University Microfilms No. 7727946.) 113 pp.

Subjects: 1. Family Relationships and Dynamics / Socialization; 2.
  Psychology and Sociology / Psychology.

421 Gupta, Prithwis, Dasi. "A Period Analysis of Parity Distribution among White and Nonwhite Women in the United States, 1940-1974." SOCIAL BIOLOGY 24, 4 (Winter 1977): 303-15. 13 pp., references, tables.

Subjects: 1. Issues Related to Reproduction / Fertility Rates.

422 Gurin, Patricia and Epps, Edgar. BLACK CONSCIOUSNESS, IDENTITY AND ACHIEVEMENT: A STUDY OF STUDENTS IN HISTORICALLY BLACK COLLEGES. New York: John Wiley and Sons, Inc., 1975. 545 pp.; ISBN:0-471-33670X; LC:75-5847.

Subjects: 1. Families with Special Problems / Achievement and the Family; 2. Psychology and Sociology / Self-Esteem.

423 Gustavus, Susan O. and Mommsen, Kent G. "Black-White Differentials in Family Size Preferences among Youth." PACIFIC SOCIOLOGICAL REVIEW 16, 1 (January 1973): 107-19. 10 pp., references, bibliography, tables.

Subjects: 1. Issues Related to Reproduction / Family Planning.

In order to examine. . .questions [regarding the ideal family size preferences of black and white youth], information was obtained from sixth, ninth, and twelfth graders. A [non-random] stratified sample of 1,122 students was drawn from ten schools in Leon County, Florida, and Thomas County, Georgia. Of these students, 38% were black (n=430) and 62% were white (n=692). . .[T]he black youth in the present sample do desire to limit their family size and, more often than whites, think that their parents had too many children. Further, they are concerned with economic reasons for limiting family size, as are whites. Since 1957, both white and black fertility rates have declined, but there has been a slighly larger drop for blacks. If the present data on the family size preferences of black youth are at all representative, white and black fertility rates may continue to converge. (From authors' text)

424 Gutman, Herbert G. "Persistent Myths about the Afro-American Family." JOURNAL OF INTERDISCIPLINARY HISTORY 6, 2 (Autumn 1975): 181-210. 26 pp., references, tables.

Subjects: 1. Trends and Change in Marriage and Family / Family Life in the United States; 2. Aids for Theory and Research / Critiques and Analyses of Family Research Literature.

425 Gutman, Herbert George. THE BLACK FAMILY IN SLAVERY AND FREEDOM: 1750-1925. 1st ed. New York: Pantheon Books, 1976. 664 pp., references, bibliography, illustrations, tables, charts, index ; ISBN:0-394-47116-4; LC:76-7550.

Subjects: 1. Trends and Change in Marriage and Family / Family Life Prior to 1900; 2. / Family Life in the United States; 3. Family Relationships and Dynamics / Family Relationships.

An historical examination spanning the pre-Revolutionary Era (1750) to the post World War I Era (1925) and geographically touching South Carolina, Virginia, North Carolina, Alabama, Louisiana, and New York focuses specifically on: the development of family life in captivity and enlarged kin groups/kinship networks; sexual behavior and exogamy;

wedding ceremonies, interplantation marriage, involuntary marital dissolution; anthroponymic traditions; migrations, urban household structure, and sex roles; etc. Among the major conclusions reached are the following: (1) Enduring marital and familiar relationship during slavery derived their inner strength from norms and standards of the captives' community. (2) Following neither the initial adaptation to emancipation nor the early twentieth century northward migration was there a 'breakdown' in the households of rural and urban Blacks.

426 Gutman, Herbert George. SLAVERY AND THE NUMBERS GAME: A CRITIQUE OF TIME ON THE CROSS. Blacks in the New World. Urbana, IL: University of Illinois Press, 1975. 183 pp., references, index; ISBN:0-252-00564-3; LC:75-15899.

Subjects: 1. Trends and Change in Marriage and Family / Family Life Prior to 1900.

427 Gwaltney, John Langston, ed. DRYLONGSO: A SELF-PORTRAIT OF BLACK AMERICA. New York: Random House, Inc., 1980. 287 pp.; ISBN:0-394-51017-8; LC:79-5558.

Subjects: 1. Trends and Change in Marriage and Family / Family and Social Change; 2. Psychology and Sociology / Racial Attitudes; 3. Aids for Theory and Research / Collected Works.

428 Hacker, Helen M. "Class and Race Differences in Gender Roles." In GENDER AND SEX IN SOCIETY, edited by Lucile Duberman, pp. 134-184. New York: Praeger Publishing Co., 1975. 51 pp.

Subjects: 1. Family Relationships and Dynamics / Family Roles and Sex Roles.

429 Hahn, Andrew Barry. "The Voluntary Dimension in Work Effort: The Effects of Work and Leisure Orientations on the Work Patterns of Low Income Familyheads." (Ph.D. dissertation, Brandeis University, The Florence Heller Graduate School for Advanced Studies in Social Welfare, 1978.) DISSERTATION ABSTRACTS INTERNATIONAL, 39, 1, July 1978, 503A. (University Microfilms No. 7811012.) 291 pp.

Subjects: 1. Organizations and Services to Families / Employment and the Family.

430 Hale, Janice. "The Black Woman and Childrearing." In THE BLACK WOMAN, edited by La Frances Rodgers-Rose, pp. 79-87. Beverly Hills, CA: Sage Publications, Inc., 1980. 9 pp.

Subjects: 1. Trends and Change in Marriage and Family / Comparative Studies--International, Interclass, Sex, and Time Differences; 2. Family Relationships and Dynamics / Mother-Child Relationships.

[This discussion examines:] (1) those characteristics of Black child rearing that are on adaptation to the racism and oppression Black people have experienced in America; and (2) those characteristics of Black child rearing that are derived from. . .African culture. (From author's text)

431 Haley, Alex. ROOTS: THE SAGA OF AN AMERICAN FAMILY. 1st edition Garden City, NY: Doubleday and Co., Inc., 1976.   587 pp.; ISBN:0-385-03787-2; LC:72-76164.

Subjects: 1. Trends and Change in Marriage and Family / Family Life in the United States.

432 Hallowitz, David. "Counseling and Treatment of the Poor Black Family." SOCIAL CASEWORK: THE JOURNAL OF CONTEMPORARY SOCIAL WORK 56, 8 (October 1975): 451-59.   9 pp., references.

Subjects: 1. Family Counseling and Education / Family Therapy.

433 Halpern, Florence Cohn. SURVIVAL: BLACK/WHITE. Pergamon General Psychology Series, No. 15. New York: Pergamon Press, Inc., 1973.   238 pp., bibliography; ISBN:0-08-016994-5; LC:72-75372.

Subjects: 1. Trends and Change in Marriage and Family / Family and Social Change.

Notes: Bibliography: pp. 227-229.

434 Halsell, Grace. BLACK/WHITE SEX. New York: William Morrow and Co., Inc., 1972.   222 pp.; LC:74-182457.

Subjects: 1. Marriage and Divorce / Inter-marriage; 2. Sexual Attitudes and Behavior / Sexual Attitudes and Behavior; 3. Psychology and Sociology / Racial Attitudes.

435 Hammond, Boone E. and Ladner, Joyce. "Socialization into Sexual Behavior in a Negro Slum Ghetto." In THE INDIVIDUAL, SEX AND SOCIETY, edited by Carlfred B. Broderick and Jesse Bernard, pp. 41-51. Baltimore, MD: Johns Hopkins Press, 1969.   11 pp.

Subjects: 1. Family Relationships and Dynamics / Socialization; 2. Sexual Attitudes and Behavior / Sexual Attitudes and Behavior.

This paper deals with sexual socialization patterns of lower-class Negro preadolescents and adolescents, i.e., the attitudes and behavior patterns relating to sexuality and the ways in which they are formed as the child moves through adulthood. . .Although the project has an all-Negro population [of 150 males and females in the Pruitt-Igoe Housing Project in St. Louis, the researchers]. . .feel that much of the data are applicable to lower-class behavior in general. (From authors' text, pp. 41 and 42)

436 Hammond, Judith and Enoch, J. Rex. "Conjugal Power Relations among Black Working Class Families." JOURNAL OF BLACK STUDIES 7, 1 (September 1976): 107-28.   22 pp., references, bibliography, tables.

Subjects: 1. Family Relationships and Dynamics / Husband-Wife Relationships; 2. / Power in the Family.

The [52 Southern metropolitan] working class families involved in this study present a picture of husband and wife jointly working together in the maintenance of their families and in making decisions about their lives. In their discussions of family life they most often emphatically suppported the traditional normative prescription of the man as the head of the household; yet they, throughout the interviews, emphasized in many ways that an attitude of respect and consideration for their spouses' points of view prevail. . .Among families in this research, the wife dominant relationship involved the smallest percentage of families. . .[W]hen the husband is able to maintain his family in a respectable living condition—or he and wife together work to provide such maintenance for the family—the authority will rest in the hands of the husbands (as tradition dictates) or it will be shared in some form (supported by present day equalitarian attitudes), both of which patterns exist among working class families, black and white. (From authors' text)

437 Hammond, Lavinia Grace. "Differential Use of Reward and Punishment as a Function of Need Achievement and of Fear of Failure in Black Mothers." (Ph.D. dissertation, University of California, Berkeley, 1969.) DISSERTATION ABSTRACTS INTERNATIONAL, 30, 5, Nov. 1969, 1821A. (University Microfilms No. 6918930.) 111 pp.

Subjects: 1. Family Relationships and Dynamics / Parent-Child
   Relationships; 2. Families with Special Problems / Achievement and the
   Family; 3. Psychology and Sociology / Self-Esteem.

438 Hampton, Robert L. "Husband's Characteristics and Marital Disruption in Black Families." SOCIOLOGICAL QUARTERLY 20, 2 (Spring 1979): 255-266. 12 pp., references, tables, charts.

Subjects: 1. Family Relationships and Dynamics / Husband-Wife
   Relationships; 2. Marriage and Divorce / Marriage Satisfaction and
   Prediction Studies; 3. Families with Special Problems / Family
   Disorganization.

439 Hampton, Robert L. "Institutional Decimation, Marital Exchange, and Disruption in Black Families." THE WESTERN JOURNAL OF BLACK STUDIES 4, 2 (Summer 1980): 132-39. 8 pp., references, tables.

Subjects: 1. Families with Special Problems / Family Disorganization;
   2. Family Counseling and Education / Family Life Education.

440 Hampton, Robert Lewis. "Marital Disruption among Blacks." (Ph.D. dissertation, The University of Michigan, 1976.) DISSERTATION ABSTRACTS INTERNATIONAL, 38, 3, Sept. 1977, 1685A-1686A. (University Microfilms No. 7718018.) 203 pp.

Subjects: 1. Family Relationships and Dynamics / Stages in Family Life
   Cycle; 2. Marriage and Divorce / Marriage Satisfaction and Prediction
   Studies; 3. Families with Special Problems / Family Disorganization.

441 Haney, C. Allen, Michielutte, Robert, Vincent, Clark E. and Cochrane, Carl M. "Characteristics of Black Women in Male and Female Headed Households." JOURNAL OF BLACK STUDIES 6, 2 (December 1975): 136-57. 22 pp., references, bibliography, tables.

Subjects: 1. Family Relationships and Dynamics / Family Relationships;
   2. / Women's Issues.

442 Haney, C. Allen, Michielutte, Robert, Vincent, Clark E. and Cochrane, Carl M. "Factors Associated with the Poverty of Black Women." SOCIOLOGY AND SOCIAL RESEARCH 59, 1 (October 1974): 40-49. 10 pp., references, tables.

Subjects: 1. Organizations and Services to Families / Economics and the Family; 2. Families with Special Problems / Family Stress.

Data from a group of southern, black women reveal an association between a composite index of current life situation and educational attainment, age at first conception, emotional relationship with partner for first conception, and age first learned of contraception. These findings have implications in conflict with a "culture of poverty" or "evil-causes-evil" explanation for their economic and other problems. (Authors' abstract)

443 Haney, C. Allen, Michielutte, Robert, Cochrane, Carl M. and Vincent, Clark E. "Some Consequences of Illegitimacy in a Sample of Black Women." JOURNAL OF MARRIAGE AND THE FAMILY 59, 2 (May 1975): 359-66. 8 pp., references, tables.

Subjects: 1. Issues Related to Reproduction / Illegitimacy.

This research compares southern black women who have had illegitimate births with those who have had only legitimate births, with regard to their attitudes about the desired and ideal number of children, pregnancy, marriage, and abortion. Meaningful differences were found, by legitimacy status, for number of children desired, attitude toward pregnancy, and attitude toward marriage. The analysis suggests that it is the absence of a legal spouse rather than the definition of birth as illegitimate which exerts the most important effect on these attitudes among the women in our sample. (Authors' abstract)

444 Haney, C. Allen, Michielutte, Robert, Vincent, Clark E. and Cochrane, Carl M. "The Value Stretch Hypothesis: Family Size Preferences in a Black Population." SOCIAL PROBLEMS 21, 2 (Fall 1973): 206-220. 15 pp., references, bibliography, tables.

Subjects: 1. Issues Related to Reproduction / Population Studies.

445 Hannerz, Ulf. "Growing Up Male in a Black Ghetto." In FAMILY LIFE IN AMERICA, 1620-2000, edited by Mel Albin and Dominick Cavallo, pp. 220-33. New York: Revisionary Press, 1981. 14 pp., references.

Subjects: 1. Family Relationships and Dynamics / Men's Issues.

446 Hannerz, Ulf. "Roots of Black Manhood: Sex, Socialization and Culture in the Ghettos of American Cities." TRANSACTION 6, 11, Whole No. 49 (October 1969): 13-21. 9 pp., references, illustrations.

Subjects: 1. Family Relationships and Dynamics / Socialization; 2. / Men's Issues.

447 Hannerz, Ulf. SOULSIDE: INQUIRIES INTO GHETTO CULTURE AND COMMUNITY. New York: Columbia University Press, 1969. 236 pp., bibliography; ISBN:0-231-03363-X; LC:78-96865.

Subjects: 1. Organizations and Services to Families / Community Groups and the Family; 2. Psychology and Sociology / Sociology.

Notes: Bibliography: pp. 224-231.

448 Hannerz, Ulf. "What Ghetto Males Are Like: Another Look." In KEY ISSUES IN THE AFRO-AMERICAN EXPERIENCE. VOL 1.: TO 1877, edited by Nathan Irvin Huggins, Martin Kilson and Daniel M. Fox, pp. 313-27. New York: Harcourt, Brace and Jovanovich, Inc., 1971. 15 pp., references.

Subjects: 1. Family Relationships and Dynamics / Men's Issues.

449 Hardy, Kenneth Vandelle. "Attitudes toward Marriage Counseling: A Study. of Middle and Lower Class Blacks." (Ph.D. dissertation, The Florida State University, 1980.) DISSERTATION ABSTRACTS INTERNATIONAL, 41, 3, Sept. 1980, 1232A. (University Microfilms No. 8018840.) 176 pp.

Subjects: 1. Marriage and Divorce / Marriage Satisfaction and Prediction Studies; 2. Family Counseling and Education / Marriage Counseling and Therapy.

450 Hare, Bruce R. "Black and White Child Self-Esteem in Social Science: An Overview." JOURNAL OF NEGRO EDUCATION 46, 2 (Spring 1977): 141-56. 16 pp., references, charts.

Subjects: 1. Family Relationships and Dynamics / Socialization; 2. Psychology and Sociology / Self-Esteem.

451 Hare, Bruce R. Black Girls: A Comparative Analysis of Self-Perception and Achievement by Race, Sex and Socioeconomic Background. The Johns Hopkins University. Center for Social Organization of Schools. Report, No. 271. Baltimore, MD: The Johns Hopkins University, January 1979. 23 pp., references, tables.

Subjects: 1. Trends and Change in Marriage and Family / Comparative Studies--International, Interclass, Sex, and Time Differences; 2. Families with Special Problems / Achievement and the Family; 3. Psychology and Sociology / Self-Esteem.

452 Hare, Bruce R. "Racial and Socioeconomic Variations in Preadolescent Area-Specific and General Self-Esteem." INTERNATIONAL JOURNAL OF INTERCULTURAL RELATIONS 1, 3 (Fall 1977): 31-51. 21 pp., references, tables.

Subjects: 1. Family Relationships and Dynamics / Socialization; 2. Family Counseling and Education / Value Education; 3. Aids for Theory and Research / Family Theory.

This study of 210 fifth-grade students attempted to assess whether children of varying backgrounds differ in their levels of general and area-specific (school, peer, and home) self-esteem. It additionally investigated whether children are capable of maintaining differing levels of self-esteem across the different areas of experience, and whether the capacity to do so varies with their racial, SES, and/or sex characteristics. . .The study suggests that low SES exercises a greater "negative" influence on self-esteem than race, that the relationship of general self-esteem to the area-specific esteems, and the relationship of the area-specific esteems to each other varies across race and SES lines. Finally, the absence of significant differences in general self-esteem by race, or significant differences in home self-esteem by race or SES, suggests that both the black caste-like group and the family exercise considerable positive influence in protecting the child's sense of self-worth, despite the negative messages from outside others. (Author's abstract)

453 Hare, Bruce R. "Self-Perception and Academic Achievement: Variations in a Desegregated Setting." AMERICAN JOURNAL OF PSYCHIATRY 137, 6 (June 1980): 683-89. 7 pp., references, bibliography, tables.

Subjects: 1. Families with Special Problems / Achievement and the Family.

The author studied 101 black and 412 white fifth-grade students and found no significant racial differences on any measures of general or area-specific (i.e., school, peers, home) self-esteem when socioeconomic status (SES) was controlled but found significant differences by SES on most measures when race was controlled. There was a positive correlation between self-concept of ability and SES when race was controlled, but when SES was controlled black children scored significantly higher than did white children. Black and lower-SES subjects scored significantly lower than other subjects on academic achievement and achievement orientation. This study highlights the need to move from the current concern with the psychological consequences of desegregation for black children toward addressing the misfit relationship between all lower-SES children and the school. (Author's abstract)

454 Hare, J. and Hare, Nathan. "Coping with Male/Female Alienation in the Coming of Bad Years." BLACK MALE/FEMALE RELATIONSHIPS 1, 2 (1979): 15-21. 7 pp.

Subjects: 1. Family Relationships and Dynamics / Premarital Couples; 2. Mate Selection / Dating, Courtship, and Romanticism; 3. Families with Special Problems / Family Stress.

455 Hare, Nathan, ed. BLACK MALE/FEMALE RELATIONSHIPS 2, 1 (1979): 1-63. 63 pp.

Subjects: 1. Mate Selection / Mate Selection, Differential Patterns.

The articles in this issue discuss mate selection between black males and females.

Notes: The articles presented in this journal cover all issues dealing with the relationships between black men and black women. See issues from 1979 - 1983.

456 Hare, Nathan. "What Black Intellectuals Misunderstand about the Black Family." BLACK WORLD 25, 5 (March 1976): 4-14. 11 pp., references, illustrations.

Subjects: 1. Aids for Theory and Research / Critiques and Analyses of Family Research Literature.

457 Hareven, Tamara K., ed. TRANSITIONS: THE FAMILY AND THE LIFE
COURSE IN HISTORICAL PERSPECTIVE. Studies in Social Discontinuity. New
York: Academic Press, Inc., 1978. 304 pp., bibliography, illustrations,
index; ISBN:0-12-325150-8; LC:78-13208.

Subjects: 1. Trends and Change in Marriage and Family / Family and
  Social Change; 2. Family Relationships and Dynamics / Stages in Family
  Life Cycle; 3. Aids for Theory and Research / Collected Works.

  Notes: An outgrowth of a series of conferences sponsored by the
  Mathematics-Social Science Board of the National Science Foundation.
  (From the introduction)

458 Harley, Sharon and Terborg-Penn, Rosalyn, eds. THE AFRO-AMERICAN
WOMAN: STRUGGLES AND IMAGES. National University Publications. Series in
American Studies. Port Washington, NY: Kennikat Press, 1978. 137 pp.,
references, bibliography, index; ISBN:0-8046-9209-2; LC:78-9821.

Subjects: 1. Family Relationships and Dynamics / Women's Issues; 2.
  Aids for Theory and Research / Collected Works.

459 Harper, D. Wood, Jr. and Garza, Joseph M. "Ethnicity, Family
Generational Structure and Intergenerational Solidarity." SOCIOLOGICAL
SYMPOSIUM (NAME CHANGED TO SOCIOLOGICAL SPECTRUM) 2, (Spring 1969): 75-
82. 8 pp., bibliography, tables.

Subjects: 1. Family Relationships and Dynamics / Family Relationships.

460 Harrell-Bond, Barbara E. "Stereotypes of Western and African
Patterns of Marriage and Family Life." JOURNAL OF MARRIAGE AND THE
FAMILY 38, 2 (May 1976): 387-96. 10 pp., references, bibliography,
tables.

Subjects: 1. Trends and Change in Marriage and Family / Family and
  Social Change; 2. / Comparative Studies--International, Interclass,
  Sex, and Time Differences; 3. Marriage and Divorce / Marriage Customs
  and Forms.

461 Harrell, Jules P. "Analyzing Black Coping Styles: A Supplemental
Diagnostic System." JOURNAL OF BLACK PSYCHOLOGY 5, 2 (February 1979):
99-108. 11 pp., references, tables.

Subjects: 1. Family Relationships and Dynamics / Conflict Resolution;
  2. Families with Special Problems / Family Stress.

462 Harris, Clotiel J. "Alternative Planning for Foster Care and
Treatment of Children and Adolescents in Crises." (Ph.D. dissertation,
Union Graduate School (Ohio), 1976.) DISSERTATION ABSTRACTS
INTERNATIONAL, 39, 3, Sept. 1978, 1481B. (University Microfilms
No. 7816556.) 122 pp.

Subjects: 1. Organizations and Services to Families / Foster Care; 2.
  Families with Special Problems / Families with Emotionally Disturbed;
  3. Family Counseling and Education / Adolescence.

463 Harris, Joan Ricks. "Black/White and Socioeconomic Status as
Factors in Maternal Attitudes toward Childrearing Practices and the Use

of Health Care in Families with and without an Educable Mentally Retarded Child." (Ph.D. dissertation, Brandeis University, The Florence Heller Graduate School for Advanced Studies in Social Welfare, 1976.) DISSERTATION ABSTRACTS INTERNATIONAL, 38, 1, July 1977, 480A-481A. (University Microfilms No. 7715270.) 251 pp.

Subjects: 1. Family Relationships and Dynamics / Mother-Child Relationships; 2. Families with Special Problems / Families with Mentally Retarded; 3. Minority Groups / Family and Social Class.

464 Harris, Richard J.   "An Examination of the Effects of Ethnicity, Socioeconomic Status and Generation on Familism and Sex Role Orientation." JOURNAL OF COMPARATIVE FAMILY STUDIES 11, 1 (Spring 1980): 173-93. 21 pp.

Subjects: 1. Family Relationships and Dynamics / Family Roles and Sex Roles; 2. Minority Groups / Family and Social Class.

465 Harris, Roland Arsville, Jr.   "A Study of Black Aged Persons." (Ph.D. dissertation, The University of Tennessee, 1981.) DISSERTATION ABSTRACTS INTERNATIONAL, 42, 12, June 1982, 5263A. (University Microfilms No. 8208969.) 245 pp.

Subjects: 1. Family Relationships and Dynamics / Later Years and Aging.

466 Harris, William.   "Work and the Family in Black Atlanta, 1880." JOURNAL OF SOCIAL HISTORY 9, 3 (Spring 1976): 319-30. 12 pp., references, tables.

Subjects: 1. Trends and Change in Marriage and Family / Family Life Prior to 1900; 2. Organizations and Services to Families / Employment and the Family.

467 Harris, William G.   "Research on the Black Family: Mainstream and Dissenting Perspectives." JOURNAL OF ETHNIC STUDIES 6, 4 (Winter 1979): 45-64. 20 pp., references, tables.

Subjects: 1. Aids for Theory and Research / Critiques and Analyses of Family Research Literature.

468 Harrison-Ross, Phyllis and Wyden, Barbara. THE BLACK CHILD: A PARENT'S GUIDE TO RAISING HAPPY AND HEALTHY CHILDREN. New York: Peter H. Wyden, Inc., 1973. 360 pp., bibliography, illustrations; LC:73-75571.

Subjects: 1. Family Relationships and Dynamics / Parent-Child Relationships; 2. Family Counseling and Education / Child Development; 3. / Education for Parenthood.

Notes: Bibliography: pp. 353-354. Filmography: p. 354.

469 Harrison, Algea Othella and Minor, Joanne Holbert.   "Interrole Conflict, Coping Strategies, and Satisfaction among Black Working Wives." JOURNAL OF MARRIAGE AND THE FAMILY 40, 4 (November 1978): 799-806. 6 pp., references, tables.

Subjects: 1. Family Relationships and Dynamics / Family Roles and Sex
Roles; 2. Families with Special Problems / Family Stress; 3.
Organizations and Services to Families / Working Mothers.

The purpose of this study was to examine the relationships between
type of interrole conflict, choice of coping strategy, and overall
satisfaction with role performance of black employed wives with
children. Respondents (N = 104) completed a questionnaire on how
satisfied they were with their role performance and the type of coping
strategies used to handle marital conflicts. It was found that type of
conflict influenced the choice of coping strategy. However, choice of
coping strategy did not relate to satisfaction with role performance.
Professional and nonprofessional subjects differed in degree of worker
satisfaction. Husband's approval did not affect satisfaction with
worker role. (Author's abstract)

470 Hartnagel, Timothy F. "Father Absence and Self Conception among
Lower Class White and Negro Boys." SOCIAL PROBLEMS 18, 2 (Fall 1970):
152-63. 12 pp., references, tables.

Subjects: 1. Family Relationships and Dynamics / Father-Child
Relationships.

471 Harwood, Edwin. "Urbanism as a Way of Life." In LIFESTYLES IN THE
BLACK GHETTO (1st edition), by William M. McCord, pp. 19-35. New York:
W. W. Norton and Co., 1969. 17 pp.

Subjects: 1. Trends and Change in Marriage and Family / Family Life in
the United States.

472 Harwood, Edwin and Hodge, Claire C. "Jobs and the Negro Family: A
Reappraisal." PUBLIC INTEREST 23, (Spring 1971): 125-31. 7 pp.

Subjects: 1. Organizations and Services to Families / Employment and the
Family.

473 Hauser, Stuart T. BLACK AND WHITE IDENTITY FORMATION: STUDIES IN
THE PSYCHOSOCIAL DEVELOPMENT OF LOWER SOCIOECONOMIC CLASS ADOLESCENT
BOYS. New York: Wiley Interscience, 1971. 160 pp., bibliography;
ISBN:0-471-36150-X; LC:77-138910.

Subjects: 1. Families with Special Problems / Families with Mentally
Retarded; 2. Psychology and Sociology / Psychology; 3. Family
Counseling and Education / Adolescence.

Notes: Bibliography: pp. 143-152.

474 Havenstein, Louise. ATTITUDES OF MARRIED WOMEN TOWARD WORK AND
FAMILY: COMPARISON BY STRESS LEVEL, RACE AND WORK STATUS. Ann Arbor,
MI: University of Michigan, Department of Psychology, 1976.

Subjects: 1. Organizations and Services to Families / Employment and the
Family.

475 Havenstein, Louise S., Kasl, Stanislav V. and Harburg, Ernest.
"Work Status, Work Satisfaction, and Blood Pressure among Married Black

and White Women." PSYCHOLOGY OF WOMEN QUARTERLY 1, 4 (Summer 1977): 334-49. 16 pp., references, tables.

Subjects: 1. Organizations and Services to Families / Physical Health and the Family; 2. / Employment and the Family.

476 Hawkins, Brin D. "Formal and Informal Support Systems for the Black Elderly." URBAN RESEARCH REVIEW 8, 2 (1982): 5-7. 3 pp.

Subjects: 1. Family Relationships and Dynamics / Later Years and Aging.

Short version of a paper originally presented at the Minority Research Associates Conference, Washington, DC, February 1982. Summarizes the formal (i.e., federal, state and local social service programs) and informal (e.g., family, friends, church and community groups) supports systems. Identifies research areas that might provide data for improving both social and health care delivery to the Black aged: aging in the Black family, informal support systems in the community, Black lifestyle/culture and health, institutional care, and social services for the healthy aged. (From author's text)

477 Hawkins, Homer C. "Urban Housing and the Black Family." PHYLON 37, 1 (March 1976): 73-84. 12 pp., references.

Subjects: 1. Family Relationships and Dynamics / Environment (Space/ Housing).

478 Hawkins, Ioma LaNell. "Achievement Motivation, Race, and Social Class Influences upon Female Attributions." (Ph.D. dissertation, California School of Professional Psychology, Los Angeles, 1979.) DISSERTATION ABSTRACTS INTERNATIONAL, 41, 2, Aug. 1980, 733B-734B. (University Microfilms No. 8017815.) 138 pp.

Subjects: 1. Family Relationships and Dynamics / Women's Issues; 2. Families with Special Problems / Achievement and the Family; 3. Minority Groups / Family and Social Class.

479 Hawkins, James L., Weisberg, Carol and Ray, Dixie L. "Marital Communication Style and Social Class." JOURNAL OF MARRIAGE AND THE FAMILY 39, 3 (August 1977): 479-90. 12 pp., references, tables, charts.

Subjects: 1. Family Relationships and Dynamics / Communication in the Family; 2. Minority Groups / Family and Social Class.

480 Hays, William C. and Mindel, Charles H. "Extended Kinship Relations in Black and White Families." JOURNAL OF MARRIAGE AND THE FAMILY 35, 1 (February 1973): 51-57. 7 pp., references, tables.

Subjects: 1. Trends and Change in Marriage and Family / Comparative Studies—International, Interclass, Sex, and Time Differences; 2. Family Relationships and Dynamics / Extended Family and Kinship Groups.

This study is an attempt to compare and explain differences in extended family cohesion of black and white families. The black family is not approached as deviant or pathological, but from the view of a separate subculture within a pluralistic society. Comparisons were made in terms of both intensity and extensity of interaction of black and white families with their extended kin. Specific comparisons were made of contact and help patterns, number of kin living in the household, and salience of kin. It is shown that the extended kin network is a more salient structure for black families than it is for white families. (Authors' abstract)

481 Hays, William C. and Mindel, Charles H. "Parental Perceptions for Children: A Comparison of Black and White Families." ETHNIC GROUPS 1, 4 (September 1977): 281-95. 15 pp., references, tables.

Subjects: 1. Family Relationships and Dynamics / Parent-Child Relationships; 2. Psychology and Sociology / Psychology; 3. Family Counseling and Education / Education for Parenthood.

This exploratory study of 23 matched black and white families indicates that there is very little difference in the behavior of children as perceived by their parents, the parental wishes and expectations of the children's behavior and life chances, and the parental goals and aspirations for their children. The lack of clear-cut differences indicate little support for viewing the black family as a social problem or as "pathological". The findings in this study tend to support a view of differential family structures and family organization acting, not in a deviant or "pathological" manner, but rather producing types of behavior and goals very similar to those found in the ideal type of the middle class family. (Authors' abstract)

482 Heer, David M. "Negro-White Marriage in the United States." JOURNAL OF MARRIAGE AND THE FAMILY 28, 3 (August 1966): 262-73. 12 pp., tables.

Subjects: 1. Marriage and Divorce / Inter-marriage.

483 Heer, David M. "Negro-White Marriage in the United States." NEW SOCIETY 6, 152 (26 August 1965): 7-9. 3 pp., illustrations, charts.

Subjects: 1. Marriage and Divorce / Inter-marriage.

484 Heer, David M. "The Prevalence of Black-White Marriage in the United States, 1960 and 1970." JOURNAL OF MARRIAGE AND THE FAMILY 36, 2 (May 1974): 246-58. 13 pp., references, tables.

Subjects: 1. Marriage and Divorce / Inter-marriage.

485 Heiss, Jerold. THE CASE OF THE BLACK FAMILY: A SOCIOLOGICAL INQUIRY. New York: Columbia University Press, 1975. 246 pp., bibliography, index; ISBN:0-231-03782-1; LC:74-34418.

Subjects: 1. Trends and Change in Marriage and Family / Family Life in the United States; 2. Family Relationships and Dynamics / Family Relationships; 3. Psychology and Sociology / Sociology.

Notes: Bibliography: pp. 233-239

486 Heiss, Jerold. "On the Transmission of Marital Instability in
Black Families." AMERICAN SOCIOLOGICAL REVIEW 37, 1 (February 1972):
82-92. 11 pp., references, bibliography, tables.

Subjects: 1. Marriage and Divorce / Marriage Satisfaction and Prediction
   Studies; 2. Families with Special Problems / Family Disorganization.

487 Hemming, R. C. L. "The Net Resource Distribution of Two Parent
Low Income Families: A Regional Comparison." SOCIAL POLICY AND
ADMINISTRATION (FORMERLY TITLED SOCIAL AND ECONOMIC ADMINISTRATION) 9, 3
(Fall 1975): 207-19. 13 pp., references, tables.

Subjects: 1. Organizations and Services to Families / Economics and the
   Family.

488 Hempel, Donald J. "Family Buying Decisions: A Cross-Cultural
Perspective." JOURNAL OF MARKETING RESEARCH 11, 3 (August 1974): 295-
302. 8 pp., references, tables.

Subjects: 1. Trends and Change in Marriage and Family / Comparative
   Studies--International, Interclass, Sex, and Time Differences; 2.
   Organizations and Services to Families / Economics and the Family; 3.
   Family Relationships and Dynamics / Men's Issues.

489 Hendin, Herbert. BLACK SUICIDE. New York: Basic Books, Inc.,
1969. 176 pp., illustrations; LC:72-92476.

Subjects: 1. Families with Special Problems / Suicide and the Family;
   2. Psychology and Sociology / Psychology.

490 Hendricks, Leo E. "Black Unwed Adolescent Fathers." In BLACK MEN,
edited by Lawrence E. Gary, pp. 131-40. Beverly Hill, CA: Sage
Publications, Inc., 1981. 10 pp.

Subjects: 1. Family Relationships and Dynamics / Father-Child
   Relationships; 2. Issues Related to Reproduction / Teenage Pregnancy;
   3. Family Counseling and Education / Adolescence.

   [This] exploratory study [seeks] to identify and describe the
   perceptions of a select population of Black unwed adolescent fathers
   toward fatherhood and their relationships with the mothers of their
   first children. The purpose of this study was to document information
   that will be helpful to social service agencies in meeting the needs
   of adolescent parents, both male and female. (From author's text)

491 Hendricks, Leo E. "Sexual Knowledge, Attitudes, and Practices of
Black Unwed Fathers." CRJ REPORTER (COMMISSION FOR RACIAL JUSTICE
REPORTER) , (Summer 1980): 27-29. 3 pp.

Subjects: 1. Family Relationships and Dynamics / Men's Issues; 2.
   Sexual Attitudes and Behavior / Sexual Attitudes and Behavior.

492 Hendricks, Leo E. Unmarried Adolescent Fathers: Problems They Face
and the Ways They Cope with Them. Final Report. Washington, D.C.:
Howard University, Institute for Urban Affairs and Research, Mental
Health Research and Development Center, September 1979.

Subjects: 1. Family Relationships and Dynamics / Men's Issues; 2.
Issues Related to Reproduction / Teenage Pregnancy.

493 Hendricks, Leo Edward, Jr. "The Effect of Family Size, Child
Spacing and Family Density on Stress in Low Income Black Mothers and
Their Preadolescent Children." (Ph.D. dissertation, The University of
North Carolina at Chapel Hill, 1977.) DISSERTATION ABSTRACTS
INTERNATIONAL, 38, 12, June 1978, 5844B. (University Microfilms
No. 7807136.)

Subjects: 1. Organizations and Services to Families / Mental Health and
the Family; 2. Family Relationships and Dynamics / Women's Issues; 3.
Families with Special Problems / Family Stress.

494 Henning, Rita Claiborne. "The Ecology of Childrearing Patterns of
Low to Moderate Income Black Families: The Development of
Sociobehavioral Competencies in Black Children." (Ph.D. dissertation,
George Peabody College for Teachers of Vanderbilt University, 1981.)
DISSERTATION ABSTRACTS INTERNATIONAL, 42, 4, Oct. 1981, 1526A.
(University Microfilms No. 8121581.) 255 pp.

Subjects: 1. Family Relationships and Dynamics / Parent-Child
Relationships.

495 Henri, Florette. BLACK MIGRATION: MOVEMENT NORTH, 1890-1920.
Garden City, NY: Anchor Books, 1975. 419 pp., bibliography, index;
ISBN:0-385-04030-X; LC:74-9453.

Subjects: 1. Trends and Change in Marriage and Family / Family Life 1900
to Present; 2. Families with Special Problems / Family and Geographic
Mobility.

Notes: Bibliography: pp. 395-408.

496 Henry, Sheila E. "Family Structures, Social Class and Cultural
Values." JOURNAL OF COMPARATIVE FAMILY STUDIES 8, 3 (Fall 1977): 291-
99. 9 pp., references, tables.

Subjects: 1. Families with Special Problems / Family Stress; 2. Family
Counseling and Education / Value Education; 3. Minority Groups /
Family and Social Class.

497 Hernton, Calvin C. SEX AND RACISM IN AMERICA. 1st ed. Garden
City, NY: Doubleday and Co., Inc., 1965. 180 pp., references; LC:64-
20576.

Subjects: 1. Marriage and Divorce / Inter-marriage; 2. Sexual Attitudes
and Behavior / Sexual Attitudes and Behavior; 3. Psychology and
Sociology / Racial Attitudes.

498 Hershey, Marjorie Randon. "Racial Differences in Sex-Role
Identities and Sex Stereotyping: Evidence against a Common Assumption."
SOCIAL SCIENCE QUARTERLY 58, 4 (March 1978): 583-96. 14 pp.,
references, bibliography, tables.

Subjects: 1. Trends and Change in Marriage and Family / Family and
   Social Change; 2. Family Relationships and Dynamics / Stages in Family
   Life Cycle.

[A 1976 survey of Indiana University students including Blacks
(n=122) and whites (n=175)] provides evidence against the widespread
assumption that blacks are more androgymous than whites in their sex-
role identities and more egalitarian in their sex-role attitudes. Sex-
typing and traditional sex stereotypes are at least as common among
the black respondents in this study as among the whites. Regression
analysis demonstrates that racial differences in sex-role identities
are barely perceptible; the tendency for women to identify more
strongly with qualities such as compassion and warmth while men rate
themselves higher on dominance and assertiveness is characteristic of
both blacks and whites. In short, the expectation that race is a major
determinant of differences in sex-role identities and attitudes has
not been fulfilled. (From author's text)

499 Herson, Jay, Crocker, Cyril L. and Butts, Ernest. "Comprehensive
Family Planning Services to an Urban Black Community." JOURNAL OF THE
NATIONAL MEDICAL ASSOCIATION 67, 1 (January 1975): 61-65. 5 pp.,
references, tables.

Subjects: 1. Organizations and Services to Families / Social Services
   and the Family; 2. Issues Related to Reproduction / Family Planning;
   3. / Birth Control.

500 Herzog, Elizabeth. "Is There a 'Break-Down' of the Negro Family?"
SOCIAL WORK 11, 1 (January 1966): 3-10. 7 pp., references, tables.

Subjects: 1. Trends and Change in Marriage and Family / Family Life in
   the United States; 2. Aids for Theory and Research / Family Theory.

501 Hetherington, E. Mavis. "Effects of Paternal Absence on Sex-Typed
Behaviors in Negro and White Preadolescent Males." JOURNAL OF
PERSONALITY AND SOCIAL PSYCHOLOGY 4, 1 (July 1966): 87-91. 5 pp.,
references, tables.

Subjects: 1. Family Relationships and Dynamics / Single Parent Families;
   2. Sexual Attitudes and Behavior / Sexual Attitudes and Behavior;
   3. Family Counseling and Education / Adolescence.

502 Hiday, Virginia Aldige. "Parity and Well-Being among Low-Income
Urban Families." JOURNAL OF MARRIAGE AND THE FAMILY 37, 4 (November
1975): 789-797. 9 pp., references, tables, charts.

Subjects: 1. Families with Special Problems / Family Stress.

503 Higginbotham, Elizabeth Starr. "Educated Black Women: An
Exploration into Life Chances and Choices." (Ph.D. dissertation,
Brandeis University, 1980.) DISSERTATION ABSTRACTS INTERNATIONAL, 41,
1, July 1980, 407A-408A. (University Microfilms No. 8013630.) 362 pp.

Subjects: 1. Organizations and Services to Families / Education and the
   Family; 2. Family Relationships and Dynamics / Women's Issues; 3.
   Minority Groups / Family and Social Class.

504 Higman, B. W. "Household Structure and Fertility on Jamaican Slave
Plantations: A Nineteenth-Century Example." POPULATION STUDIES 27, 3
(November 1973): 527-50. 25 pp., references, tables, charts.

Subjects: 1. Trends and Change in Marriage and Family / Family Life
   Prior to 1900; 2. Issues Related to Reproduction / Fertility Rates; 3.
   Minority Groups / Blacks in the Caribbean.

505 Higman, B. W. "The Slave Family and Household in the British
West Indies, 1800-1834." JOURNAL OF INTERDISCIPLINARY HISTORY 6, 2
(Autumn 1975): 261-87. 27 pp., references, tables.

Subjects: 1. Trends and Change in Marriage and Family / Family Life
   Prior to 1900; 2. Minority Groups / Blacks in the Caribbean.

506 Hill, Herbert. "Of Blacks, Whites and Family Stability." CURRENT
188, (December 1976): 11-12. 2 pp.

Subjects: 1. Trends and Change in Marriage and Family / Comparative
   Studies--International, Interclass, Sex, and Time Differences; 2.
   Families with Special Problems / Family Disorganization.

507 Hill, Robert B. and Godley, Carol J. AN INVENTORY OF SELECTED
NATIONAL DATA SOURCES ON THE SOCIAL AND ECONOMIC CHARACTERISTICS OF
BLACK FAMILIES. Washington, DC: Bureau of Social Science Research,
Inc., 1982. 243 pp., references.

Subjects: 1. Aids for Theory and Research / Family Research Methodology;
   2. / Classified Bibliographies of Family Literature; 3. / Statistics.

Notes: Prepared for The Foundation for Child Development.

508 Hill, Robert Bernard. BLACK FAMILIES IN THE 1974-1975 DEPRESSION:
SPECIAL POLICY REPORT. New York: National Urban League, July 1975. 29
pp., references, tables; LC:78-84421.

Subjects: 1. Trends and Change in Marriage and Family / Family Policy;
   2. Organizations and Services to Families / Economics and the Family;
   3. Aids for Theory and Research / Statistics.

A report of the effects of the 1974-1975 economic depression on the
Black family. Covers the declining work experience of Black men,
women, and teenagers. Also reports the various poverty levels of
Blacks and their standard of living.

509 Hill, Robert Bernard. INFORMAL ADOPTION AMONG BLACK FAMILIES.
Washington, DC: National Urban League, Research Department, 1977. 130
pp., references, bibliography, tables.

Subjects: 1. Organizations and Services to Families / Foster Care; 2.
   Family Relationships and Dynamics / Extended Family and Kinship
   Groups.

[O]ne of the key functions performed by the black extended family is
the informal adoption or foster care of children by grandparents,
aunts and uncles and other kin. . . .Although informally adopted
children are more likely to be economically disadvantaged, most of

them are not on public assistance. (From author's 'Summary of Major Findings')

Notes: Bibliography: pp. 120-30.

510 Hill, Robert Bernard. THE STRENGTHS OF BLACK FAMILIES. 1st edition New York: Emerson Hall Publishers, Inc., 1972. 76 pp., bibliography; ISBN:0-87829-008-7; LC:70-188563.

Subjects: 1. Family Relationships and Dynamics / Family Relationships; 2. Families with Special Problems / Family Stress; 3. Aids for Theory and Research / Family Theory.

Examination of the literature on Black families reveals that the following characteristics have been functional for their survival, development, and stability: 1. Strong kinship bonds 2. Strong work orientation 3. Adaptability of family roles 4. Strong achievement orientation 5. Strong religious orientation. Although these traits [strengths] can be found among white families, they are manifested quite differently in the lives of Black families because of the unique history of racial oppression experienced by Blacks in America. (From author's introduction)

Notes: Originally published by The National Urban League in 1971. Preface is by Vernon E. Jordan, Jr. and foreword by Andrew Billingsley. Bibliography: pp. 61-76.

511 Hill, Robert Bernard and Shackleford, Lawrence. "The Black Extended Family Revisited." URBAN LEAGUE REVIEW 1, 2 (Fall 1975): 18-24. 7 pp., references.

Subjects: 1. Family Relationships and Dynamics / Extended Family and Kinship Groups.

Extended family households are frequently created by the "informed" adoption of minors, most likely at very early ages, by older relatives. Illness, death, separation, and divorce of parents, the immaturity of unwed mothers, the proximity of relatives to a school, a feeling of familial responsibility, and the desire of adults to rear children and thus experience parenting have been cited as motivating factors underlying informal adoptions. Often intended as a temporary arrangement, some of these adoptions become long term. Two-thirds of informally adopted children live with their grandparents; and one-fifth reside with uncles and aunts. Informally, adopted children are usually aware that their parental "surrogates" are not their natural parents. Indeed many have periodic contact with their birth parents. Three-fifths of the households with informally adopted minors are above the poverty line. More than one-half of the female-headed households with informally adopted children are poor, whereas only three-tenths of couple-headed households with informally adopted children share a similar condition.

512 Hine, Darlene C. "Female Slave Resistance: The Economics of Sex." THE WESTERN JOURNAL OF BLACK STUDIES 3, 2 (Summer 1979): 123-27. 5 pp., references.

Subjects: 1. Trends and Change in Marriage and Family / Family Life
Prior to 1900; 2. Family Relationships and Dynamics / Women's Issues.

[Women] constituted an important and necessary part of the work force
and they were, through their child-bearing function, the one group
most responsible for the size and indeed the maintenance of the slave
labor pool. Therefore, when they resisted sexual exploitation through
such means as sexual abstention, abortion, and infanticide, they were,
at the same time, rejecting their vital economic function as breeders.
This resistance, of course, became especially important after 1808,
when it was no longer legal to import slaves into the United States
from Africa. (From author's text)

513 Hirsch, Carl. "Primary Group Supports among a Sample of Elderly
Black and White Ethnic Residents of Urban, Working-Class
Neighborhoods." (Ph.D. dissertation, The Pennsylvania State University,
1979.) DISSERTATION ABSTRACTS INTERNATIONAL, 40, 11, May 1980, 6031A.
(University Microfilms No. 8010066.) 225 pp.

Subjects: 1. Organizations and Services to Families / Community Groups
and the Family; 2. Family Relationships and Dynamics / Extended Family
and Kinship Groups; 3. / Later Years and Aging.

514 Hirsch, Seth Lewis. "Home Climate in the Black Single-Parent
Mother-Led Family: A Social-Ecological Interactional Approach." (Ph.D.
dissertation, United States International University, 1979.)
DISSERTATION ABSTRACTS INTERNATIONAL, 40, 9, March 1980, 4485B.
(University Microfilms No. 8007637.)

Subjects: 1. Family Relationships and Dynamics / Single Parent Families;
2. / Family Relationships; 3. Psychology and Sociology / General
Attitudes.

515 Hobbs, Daniel F., Jr. and Wimbish, Jane Maynard. "Transition to
Parenthood by Black Couples." JOURNAL OF MARRIAGE AND THE FAMILY 39, 4
(November 1977): 677-89. 13 pp., references, tables.

Subjects: 1. Family Counseling and Education / Education for Parenthood.

The present study replicates, using black parents, two earlier
studies of the amount of difficulty reported by white parents in
adjusting to their first infant. Mothers reported significantly more
difficulty than fathers in adjusting to their infants, as had been
found earlier with white parents and mean difficulty scores were
slightly higher for black parents than for white parents. Of 15
potential predictor variables, postbirth marital satisfaction, age of
self, whether pregnancy was planned and/or desired, number of
additional children desired, and preference for sex of baby were
associated with fathers' adjustment to their first child, while age of
self and age of baby were associated with adjustment by mothers. It
was concluded that black parents' difficulties in adjusting to their
first child were slightly greater than and somewhat different from
difficulties reported in the prior studies of white parents, but their
difficulties were not of crisis proportions. (Authors' abstract)

516 Holly, Ellen. "The Role of Media in the Programming of an
Underclass." BLACK SCHOLAR 10, 5 (February 1979): 31-37. 7 pp.

Subjects: 1. Families with Special Problems / Family Stress; 2. Family
Counseling and Education / Media and the Family.

517   "Homicide among Black Males: Highlights of the Symposium Sponsored
by the Alcohol, Drug Abuse, and Mental Health Administration,
Washington, D.C. May 13-14, 1980." PUBLIC HEALTH REPORTS 95, 6 (12
November 1980): 549-61. 13 pp., references, tables, charts.

Subjects: 1. Family Relationships and Dynamics / Men's Issues; 2.
  Families with Special Problems / Death, Bereavement and the Family.

518   Hook, Bell. AIN'T I A WOMAN: BLACK WOMEN AND FEMINISM. Boston,
MA: South End Press, 1981. 205 pp., bibliography; ISBN:0-89608-128-1;
LC:81-51392.

Subjects: 1. Family Relationships and Dynamics / Women's Issues.

  Notes: Bibliography: pp. 197-202.

519   Hopkins, Thomas J. "The Role of Community Agencies as Viewed by
Black Fathers." AMERICAN JOURNAL OF ORTHOPSYCHIATRY 42, 3 (April 1972):
508-16. 9 pp., references.

Subjects: 1. Organizations and Services to Families / Community Groups
  and the Family; 2. Family Relationships and Dynamics / Men's Issues.

520   Hopkins, Thomas J. "The Role of the Agency in Supporting Black
Manhood." SOCIAL WORK 18, 1 (January 1973): 53-58. 6 pp., references.

Subjects: 1. Organizations and Services to Families / Community Groups
  and the Family; 2. Family Relationships and Dynamics / Men's Issues.

521   Hopper, Columbus B. SEX IN PRISON: THE MISSISSIPPI EXPERIMENT WITH
CONJUGAL VISITING. Baton Rouge, LA: Louisiana State University Press,
1969. 160 pp., bibliography, illustrations; ISBN:8071-0905-3; LC:70-
86491.

Subjects: 1. Sexual Attitudes and Behavior / Sexual Attitudes and
  Behavior; 2. Families with Special Problems / Families with Criminal
  Offenders.

  Notes: Bibliography: pp. 149-155.

522   Horton, Carrell P., Gray, Billie B. and Roberts, S. Oliver.
"Attitudes of Black Teenagers and Their Mothers toward Selected
Contemporary Issues." JOURNAL OF AFRO-AMERICAN ISSUES 4, 2 (Spring
1976): 172-92. 21 pp., references, tables.

Subjects: 1. Family Relationships and Dynamics / Parent-Adolescent
  Relationships; 2. Psychology and Sociology / General Attitudes; 3.
  Family Counseling and Education / Adolescence.

523   Horton, James Oliver and Horton, Lois E. BLACK BOSTONIANS: FAMILY
LIFE AND COMMUNITY STRUGGLE IN THE ANTEBELLUM NORTH. New York: Holmes
and Meier Publishers, Inc., 1979. 175 pp., bibliography, illustrations,
index; ISBN:0-8419-0445-6; LC:78-24453.

Subjects: 1. Trends and Change in Marriage and Family / Family Life
Prior to 1900.

Notes: Bibliography: pp. 155-169.

524 Houten, Warren D. Ten. "The Black Family: Myth and Reality."
PSYCHIATRY 33, 2 (May 1970): 145-73. 29 pp., references, bibliography,
tables.

Subjects: 1. Family Relationships and Dynamics / Family Relationships;
2. Aids for Theory and Research / Critiques and Analyses of Family
Research Literature.

525 Howard, Alicia, Royse, David D. and Skerl, John A. "Transracial
Adoption: The Black Community Perspective." SOCIAL WORK 22, 3 (May
1977): 184-89. 6 pp., references, tables.

Subjects: 1. Organizations and Services to Families / Adoption and
Adoption Services.

While any generalized conclusions drawn from this [survey] research
of [150 households selected by systematic random sampling] can only be
applied to the population from which the sample was drawn [i.e., the
nine census tracts containing the highest concentration of blacks],
the data suggest that the majority of blacks do not oppose the idea of
transracial adoptions and a large majority could be described as
favorable to this alternative under certain conditions. The majority
of respondents felt that it is more important that a black child
receive love from white parents than be placed in foster care or in an
institution. While the respondents were concerned about the child's
possible loss of identification with the black community, the needs of
the individual child were seen to be of prime importance. (Authors'
conclusions)

526 Howard, Cleopatra S., comp. A RESOURCE GUIDE ON BLACK FAMILIES IN
AMERICA. Washington, DC: Howard University, Institute for Urban Affairs
and Research, Mental Health Research and Development Center, 1980. 154
pp., references, tables, charts; LC:80-80664.

Subjects: 1. Aids for Theory and Research / Classified Bibliographies of
Family Literature.

527 Howell, C. Diane. "Black Concepts of the Ideal Black Woman." (Ph.D.
dissertation, University of California, Berkeley, 1978.) DISSERTATION
ABSTRACTS INTERNATIONAL, 39, 8, Feb. 1979, 4103B-4104B. (University
Microfilms No. 7904483.) 137 pp.

Subjects: 1. Family Relationships and Dynamics / Women's Issues.

528 Hu, Teh-Wei and Knaub, Norman. "Effects of Cash and In-Kind
Welfare Payments on Family Expenditures." POLICY ANALYSIS 2, 1 (Winter
1976): 71-92. 22 pp., references, tables, charts.

Subjects: 1. Organizations and Services to Families / Economics and the
Family.

529 Hoffman, Louis Wladis and Manis, Jean Denby. "The Value of
Children in U.S.: A New Approach to the Study of Fertility." JOURNAL OF
MARRIAGE AND THE FAMILY 41, 3 (August 1979): 583-96. 14 pp.,
references, tables.

Subjects: 1. Family Relationships and Dynamics / Family Relationships;
   2. Issues Related to Reproduction / Fertility Rates; 3. Aids for
   Theory and Research / Critiques and Analyses of Family Research
   Literature.

530 Huggins, Nathan Irvin, Kilson, Martin and Fox, Daniel M., eds. KEY
ISSUES IN THE AFRO-AMERICAN EXPERIENCE. VOL 1.: TO 1877. New York:
Harcourt, Brace and Jovanovich, Inc., 1971. 272 pp., references,
bibliography, illustrations, tables, index; ISBN:0-15-548371-4; LC:76-
141607.

Subjects: 1. Trends and Change in Marriage and Family / Family Life
   Prior to 1900; 2. / Family Life 1900 to Present; 3. Aids for Theory
   and Research / Collected Works.

531 Huggins, Nathan Irvin, Kilson, Martin and Fox, Daniel M., eds. KEY
ISSUES IN THE AFRO-AMERICAN EXPERIENCE. VOL 2: SINCE 1865. New York:
Harcourt, Brace and Jovanovich, Inc., 1971. 320 pp., references,
bibliography, illustrations, tables, index; ISBN:0-15-548372-2; LC:76-
141607.

Subjects: 1. Trends and Change in Marriage and Family / Family Life
   Prior to 1900; 2. / Family Life 1900 to Present; 3. Aids for Theory
   and Research / Collected Works.

532 Hunt, Janet G. and Hunt, Larry L. "Race, Daughters and Father-
Loss: Does Absence Make the Girl Grow Stronger?" SOCIAL PROBLEMS 25, 1
(October 1977): 90-102. 13 pp., references, tables.

Subjects: 1. Family Relationships and Dynamics / Father-Child
   Relationships; 2. Families with Special Problems / Death, Bereavement
   and the Family.

This research examines some of the consequences of father absence for
female children within the existing framework of both sexual and
racial stratification. An analysis of survey data collected by Morris
Rosenberg and Roberta Simmons (1972) shows that father-loss has mixed
implications for girls and a differing patterns of effects by race.
Among whites, the absence of fathers appears to slightly weaken sex-
role identification but 'release' girls for higher achievement. This
is explained in terms of probable changes attendant with father-loss
in the normal process of family socialization, which allocates girls
to supportive rather than personal achievement roles. The long-term
significance of the achievement advantage if fatherless white girls is
questioned, however, in light of remaining structural barriers to
female status attainment and the girls' own lack of optimism regarding
future success. Among blacks, the effects of father absence are less
dramatic but more uniformly negative. They may be linked to the unique
role of black women in assuming responsibility for the family under
structurally-induced conditions of poverty and family breakdown.
(Authors' abstract)

533 Hunt, Janet G. and Hunt, Larry L. "The Sexual Mystique: A Common Dimension of Racial and Sexual Stratification." SOCIOLOGY AND SOCIAL RESEARCH 59, 3 (April 1975): 231-42. 12 pp., references, bibliography, tables.

Subjects: 1. Sexual Attitudes and Behavior / Sexual Attitudes and Behavior.

In this essay low-status black males and "high status" white females are compared, and some propositions concerning similar personal consequences of racial and sexual stratification are presented. The view formulated draws extensively on the ideas of Elliot Liebow (1967) and Betty Friedan (1963) and suggests that, while many dimensions of their circumstances and the content of their personal identities may differ radically, low-status black males and high-status white females may evidence similar responses to structural barriers to achievement on the level of identity integration and in the compensatory nature of sex-role identification. (Authors' abstract)

534 Hunt, Larry L. and Hunt, Janet G. "Family Structure and Educational Attainment: Sex Differences among Urban Blacks." SOCIOLOGICAL FOCUS 12, 2 (April 1979): 103-11. 9 pp., references, tables.

Subjects: 1. Trends and Change in Marriage and Family / Comparative Studies--International, Interclass, Sex, and Time Differences; 2. Organizations and Services to Families / Education and the Family.

535 Hunt, Larry L. and Hunt, Janet G. "Race and the Father-Son Connection: The Conditional Relevance of Father Absence for the Orientations and Identities of Adolescent Boys." SOCIAL PROBLEMS 23, 1 (October 1975): 35-52. 18 pp., references, bibliography, tables.

Subjects: 1. Family Relationships and Dynamics / Father-Child Relationships; 2. Families with Special Problems / Death, Bereavement and the Family.

This study investigates how structural circumstances condition the meaning of the father-son connection and the effects of father absence. Examining a sample of white and black adolescents, the research sought father-present/father-absent differences in personal identity and orientation toward the conventional success goals of early adulthood. The results indicate that father absence has quite different consequences by race, with father absence being associated with damaging effects only among white boys. By contrast, father absence seems to have some slightly positive effects on black boys. This pattern of "costs" for whites and "gains" for blacks is general across social class levels. The lack of evidence of detrimental effects of father absence among black boys raises questions about the role of the black family in sustaining intergenerational patterns of racial inequality. (Authors' abstract)

536 Hunt, Larry L. and Hunt, Janet G. "Race, Father Identification and Achievement Orientation: The Subjective Side of the Father-Son Connection, A Research Note." YOUTH AND SOCIETY 9, 1 (September 1977): 113-120. 7 pp., references, tables.

Subjects: 1. Family Relationships and Dynamics / Father-Child
Relationships; 2. Families with Special Problems / Achievement and the
Family.

A pervasive theme in the social science literature is that racial
stratification perpetuates--or is perpetuated by--race differences in
the father-son connection. . .Examining. . .boys in. . .[a] Baltimore
sample living in intact families, we assess race differences in the
degree of father identification and the contribution, if any, of
father identification to adolescent achievement orientation. . .The
data observed in this research support the notion that the father-son
connection is a structurally conditional sponsorship relationship,
which whites--for whom it tends to work--emphasize and tend to
perceive as operating independently of the broader realities of racial
stratification and, which blacks--for whom it tends not to work--
deemphasize in their own subcultural explanations of destiny. Yet, the
findings also suggest that identification may vary systematically
within the racial communities. . .[I]n the lower class. . .high
achievement orientation is most negatively correlated with father
identification. At the other end of the class spectrum, while the
overall level of identification is still markedly lower than among
middle-class whites, the association between identification and
orientation become less positive. . .[A]lthough the black middle-class
may remain less father-central than the white world, father
identification tends to be compatible with, maybe even conducive to,
success orientations in sons at this class level. (From authors' text)

537 Hunter, Virginia. "The Impact of Adolescent Parenthood on Black
Teenage Mothers and Their Families and the Influence of Two Alternative
Types of Child Care." (Ph.D. dissertation, University of California,
Los Angeles, 1982.) DISSERTATION ABSTRACTS INTERNATIONAL, 43, 4,
Oct. 1982, 1034A-1035A. (University Microfilms No. 8219694.) 481 pp.

Subjects: 1. Family Relationships and Dynamics / Family Relationships;
   2. Issues Related to Reproduction / Teenage Pregnancy; 3. Family
   Counseling and Education / Education for Parenthood.

538 Husbands, Ann. "The Developmental Task of the Black Foster Child."
SOCIAL CASEWORK: THE JOURNAL OF CONTEMPORARY SOCIAL WORK 51, 7 (July
1970): 406-09. 4 pp., references.

Subjects: 1. Organizations and Services to Families / Foster Care; 2.
   Family Counseling and Education / Child Development.

Problems of biological, racial, and social identity are shared by all
children to a varying degree. These problems are intensified in the
black child, however, by the special restrictions imposed on him in
our society. This article observes the psychosocial dynamics central
to the problem of establishing ego identity in the black foster child
and offers a few suggestions for caseworkers in helping foster parents
cope with this problem. (From author's text)

539 Hutchinson, Ira W., III. "The Significance of Marital Status for
Morale and Life Satisfaction among Lower-Income Elderly." JOURNAL OF
MARRIAGE AND THE FAMILY 37, 2 (May 1975): 287-93. 7 pp., references,
bibliography, tables.

Subjects: 1. Family Relationships and Dynamics / Stages in Family Life
Cycle; 2. Marriage and Divorce / Marriage Satisfaction and Prediction
Studies; 3. Family Counseling and Education / Value Education.

540 Hyde, Janet Shibley and Rosenberg, Benjamin George. HELP THE HUMAN
EXPERIENCE: THE PSYCHOLOGY OF WOMEN. Lexington, MA: D. C. Heath Co.,
1976. 306 pp., bibliography, illustrations, index; ISBN:0-669-93641-3;
LC:75-7207.

Subjects: 1. Family Relationships and Dynamics / Women's Issues; 2.
Psychology and Sociology / Psychology.

Notes: Bibliography: pp. 279-299.

541 Hyman, Herbert H. and Reed, John Shelton. "'Black Matriarchy'
Reconsidered: Evidence from Secondary Analysis of Sample Surveys."
PUBLIC OPINION QUARTERLY 33, 3 (Fall 1969): 346-54. 9 pp., references,
tables.

Subjects: 1. Family Relationships and Dynamics / Single Parent Families;
2. / Women's Issues; 3. Aids for Theory and Research / Family Research
Methodology.

542 Hynes, Winifred Joyce. "Single Parent Mothers and Distress:
Relationships between Selected Social and Psychological Factors and
Distress in Low-Income Single Parent Mothers." (D.S.W. dissertation, The
Catholic University of America, 1979.) DISSERTATION ABSTRACTS
INTERNATIONAL, 40, 3, Sept. 1979, 1686A. (University Microfilms
No. 7920551.) 223 pp.

Subjects: 1. Family Relationships and Dynamics / Single Parent Families;
2. Families with Special Problems / Family Stress.

Notes: Studies in Social Work No. 132

543 Idusogie, E. O. "Role of Maternal Nutritional Health and Care in
the Development and Personality of Children in Africa." JOURNAL OF
TROPICAL PEDIATRICS AND ENVIRONMENTAL CHILD HEALTH 21, 1B (February
1975): 31-35. 5 pp.

Subjects: 1. Trends and Change in Marriage and Family / Family Life in
Foreign Countries; 2. Organizations and Services to Families /
Physical Health and the Family; 3. Family Counseling and Education /
Child Development.

544 Iglitzin, Lynne B. "A Case Study in Patriarchal Politics: Women on
Welfare." AMERICAN BEHAVIORAL SCIENTIST 17, 4 (March-April 1974): 487-
506. 20 pp., references.

Subjects: 1. Organizations and Services to Families / Social Welfare;
2. Family Relationships and Dynamics / Husband-Wife Relationships; 3.
/ Family Roles and Sex Roles.

545 Indiana University. Libraries. THE BLACK FAMILY AND THE BLACK
WOMAN: A BIBLIOGRAPHY, edited by Phyllis Rauch Klotman and Wilmer
H. Baatz. New York: Arno Press, 1978. 231 pp.; ISBN:0-405-10523-1;
LC:77-20144.

Subjects: 1. Family Relationships and Dynamics / Family Relationships;
2. / Women's Issues; 3. Aids for Theory and Research / Classified
Bibliographies of Family Literature.

This is a bibliography of the holdings in the Indiana University
Library. (NUC)

546   Institute of Society, Ethics and the Life Sciences. Research Group
on Ethics and Population. POPULATION POLICY AND ETHICS: THE AMERICAN
EXPERIENCE. A PROJECT OF THE RESEARCH GROUP ON ETHICS AND POPULATION OF
THE INSTITUTE OF SOCIETY, ETHICS AND THE LIFE SCIENCES, edited by Robert
M. Veatch. Population and Demography Series. New York: Irvington
Publishers, Inc., 1977. 501 pp., bibliography, index; ISBN:0-470-15170-
6; LC:76-18887.

Subjects: 1. Trends and Change in Marriage and Family / Family Policy;
2. Issues Related to Reproduction / Population Studies; 3. Aids for
Theory and Research / Collected Works.

Notes: Distributed by Halsted Press.

547   International Conference on Love and Attraction. Swansea, Wales,
1977. LOVE AND ATTRACTION: AN INTERNATIONAL CONFERENCE, edited by Mark
Cook and Glenn Wilson. 1st ed. Oxford; New York: Pergamon Press, Inc.,
1979. 554 pp., references, illustrations, index; ISBN:0-08-022234-X;
LC:78-40286.

Subjects: 1. Marriage and Divorce / Marriage Satisfaction and Prediction
Studies; 2. Sexual Attitudes and Behavior / Sexual Attitudes and
Behavior; 3. Aids for Theory and Research / Collected Works.

548   International Family Research Seminar, 9th, Tokyo, 1965. FAMILIES
IN EAST AND WEST: SOCIALIZATION PROCESS AND KINSHIP TIES, edited by
Reuben Hill and Rene Konig. The Hague: Mouton, 1970. 630 pp.,
references, illustrations; ISBN:90-2796-429-2; LC:76-122526.

Subjects: 1. Trends and Change in Marriage and Family / Comparative
Studies--International, Interclass, Sex, and Time Differences; 2.
Family Relationships and Dynamics / Parent-Child Relationships; 3.
Aids for Theory and Research / Collected Works.

Notes: A seminar sponsored jointly by the Japan Sociological Society,
the Japanese National Commission for UNESCO,and the International
Sociological Association.

549   Intons-Peterson, M. J. and Samuels, Arlene K.   "The Cultural Halo
Effect: Black and White Women Rate Black and White Men." BULLETIN OF
THE PSYCHONOMIC SOCIETY 11, 4 (May 1978): 309-12. 4 pp., references,
charts.

Subjects: 1. Family Relationships and Dynamics / Stages in Family Life
Cycle; 2. Mate Selection / Mate Selection, Differential Patterns.

In an explanatory study, black and white college women rated black
and white men on traits associated with masculinity, femininity, and
social desirability using the Bem scale. Black women rated black men
as more masculine than white men, whereas white women characterized

both black and white men as less masculine than the ratings assigned by black women to black men but as more masculine than the ratings assigned by black women to white men. Both black and white women attributed feminine socially desirable traits to black and white men in approximately equal proportions. These data were consistent with a "cultural hero" hypothesis. (Authors' abstract)

550   Iowa. State University of Science and Technology, Ames. College of Home Economics. FAMILIES OF THE FUTURE. Ames, IA: Iowa State University Press, 1972. 145 pp., bibliography, illustrations; ISBN:0-8138-0620-8; LC:72-58.

Subjects: 1. Trends and Change in Marriage and Family / Family Life in the United States; 2. Aids for Theory and Research / Collected Works.

Notes: Papers presented at a conference, Families of the Future: A Search for Meaning, held at Iowa State University, Oct. 4-7, 1971, as one of the Centennial Programs of the College of Home Economics.

551   Irvine, Russell W. "The Black Family and Community: Some Problems in the Development of Achievement Values." NEGRO EDUCATIONAL REVIEW 29, 3/4 (July-October 1978): 249-54. 6 pp., references.

Subjects: 1. Organizations and Services to Families / Community Groups and the Family; 2. Families with Special Problems / Achievement and the Family.

552   Iscoe, Ira, Williams, Martha and Harvey, Jerry. "Age, Intelligence and Sex as Variables in the Conformity Behavior of Negro and White Children." CHILD DEVELOPMENT 35, 2 (June 1964): 451-60. 10 pp., references, bibliography, tables, charts.

Subjects: 1. Family Relationships and Dynamics / Socialization.

553   Jack, Lenus, Jr. "Kinship and Residential Propinquity: A Case Study of a Black Extended Family in New Orleans." (Ph.D. dissertation, University of Pittsburgh, 1980.) DISSERTATION ABSTRACTS INTERNATIONAL, 41, 1, July 1980, 352A. (University Microfilms No. 8015312.) 214 pp.

Subjects: 1. Family Relationships and Dynamics / Extended Family and Kinship Groups; 2. / Environment (Space/Housing).

554   Jackman, Norman and Dodson, Jack. "Negro Youth and Direct Action." PHYLON 28, 1 (Spring 1967): 5-15., references, tables.

Subjects: 1. Family Counseling and Education / Adolescence.

555   Jackson, Agnes Durham. "Militancy and Black Women's Competitive Behavior in Competitive vs. Non-Competitive Conditions." (Ph.D. dissertation, Rutgers University, The State University of New Jersey, 1978.) DISSERTATION ABSTRACTS INTERNATIONAL, 39, 7, Jan. 1979, 3519B. (University Microfilms No. 7901272.) 90 pp.

Subjects: 1. Trends and Change in Marriage and Family / Comparative Studies--International, Interclass, Sex, and Time Differences; 2. Family Relationships and Dynamics / Women's Issues; 3. Psychology and Sociology / Psychology.

556 Jackson, Anthony W., ed. BLACK FAMILIES AND THE MEDIUM OF
TELEVISION. Ann Arbor, MI: University of Michigan, Bush Program for
Child Development and Social Psychology, 1982. 108 pp.

Subjects: 1. Trends and Change in Marriage and Family / Family Policy;
2. Family Counseling and Education / Children and Television; 3. Aids
for Theory and Research / Collected Works.

In May, 1980, over 150 scholars, advocates, television artists and
decision makers, and representatives from concerned governmental and
private agencies met [at The University of Michigan] to examine the
television images of Blacks, and especially Black families. . .[The
eleven chapters comprising the proceedings considers wide ranging
issues related to queries such as the following:] What is the
potential impact of television images of Black families? Where do
ideas about Black families come from and what are the marketing
considerations television executives face in translating these ideas
into images? Are there roles for social scientists and other
professionals, advocates, and the government in affecting
programming?. . .[I]ncluded are a number of alternatives for future
action which were suggested at the close of the meeting. (From the
'Introduction' by Anthony Jackson and Deborah Cherniss)

557 Jackson, Harrisene. THERE'S NOTHING I OWN THAT I WANT. Englewood
Cliffs, NJ: Prentice-Hall, 1974. 168 pp.; ISBN:0-13-914697-0; LC:74-
8801.

Subjects: 1. Family Relationships and Dynamics / Women's Issues.

558 Jackson, Jacquelyne. MINORITIES AND AGING. Belmont, CA: Wadsworth
Publishing Co., 1980. 256 pp., bibliography, index; ISBN:0-534-00779-1;
LC:79-21807.

Subjects: 1. Family Relationships and Dynamics / Later Years and Aging.

  Notes: Bibliography: pp. 226-244.

559 Jackson, Jacquelyne Johnson, ed. AGING BLACK WOMEN: SELECTED
READINGS FOR NCBA. Washington, DC: College and University Press, 1975.
449 pp., references, bibliography, illustrations; LC:77-155041.

Subjects: 1. Family Relationships and Dynamics / Later Years and Aging;
2. / Women's Issues; 3. Aids for Theory and Research / Collected
Works.

A compilation to provide related background material for participants
in the 3d annual conference of the National Caucus on the Black Aged,
held in Washington, DC, April 13-15, 1975. (NUC)

Notes: The editor was assisted by Faith Hampton Childs and Robin
Ficker

560 Jackson, Jacquelyne Johnson. RESEARCH CONFERENCE ON MINORITY GROUP
AGED IN THE SOUTH, DURHAM, NC, 1971. PROCEEDINGS. Durham, NC: Duke
University Medical Center. Center for the Study of Aging and Human
Development, 1972. 233 pp., bibliography; LC:73-172038.

Subjects: 1. Family Relationships and Dynamics / Later Years and Aging;
2. Aids for Theory and Research / Family Research Methodology.

561 Jackson, Jacquelyne Johnson, Childs, Faith Hampton and Ficker,
Robin, eds. AGING BLACK WOMEN: SELECTED READINGS FOR NCBA. Washington,
D.C.: National Caucus on the Black Aged, 1975. 449 pp., bibliography,
illustrations; LC:77-69629.

Subjects: 1. Family Relationships and Dynamics / Later Years and Aging;
2. / Women's Issues; 3. Aids for Theory and Research / Collected
Works.

562 Jackson, Jacquelyne J. "Family Organization and Ideology." In
COMPARATIVE STUDIES OF BLACKS AND WHITES IN THE UNITED STATES, edited by
Kent S. Miller and Ralph Mason Dreger, pp. 405-445. New York and London:
Seminar Press, 1973. 41 pp.

Subjects: 1. Trends and Change in Marriage and Family / Family Life in
the United States; 2. Aids for Theory and Research / Family Theory.

563 Jackson, Jacquelyne Johnson. "But Where Are the Men?" BLACK
SCHOLAR 3, 4 (December 1971): 30-41. 12 pp., references, tables.

Subjects: 1. Mate Selection / Mate Selection, Differential Patterns.

564 Jackson, Jacquelyne Johnson. "Comparative Lifestyles and Family
and Friend Relationships among Older Black Women." FAMILY COORDINATOR
21, 4 (October 1972): 477-85. 9 pp., references, bibliography, tables.

Subjects: 1. Family Relationships and Dynamics / Family Relationships;
2. / Socialization; 3. / Later Years and Aging.

Subdividing the sample by those with and those without spouses,
kinship data collected principally in 1968-1969 interviews with older,
Southern urban black women were employed in describing and analyzing
selected instrumental and affective relationships with, where present,
their oldest child and closest friend, in an exploratory effort aimed
toward reducing gaps in knowledge about older black women, their
normal family and friend relationships, and effects of spouse presence
or spouse absence upon those relationships. While those relationships
are probably considerably more complex than suggested by these data,
perhaps the most striking hypothesis is the amazing similarity
characterizing those relationships irrespective of spouse presence or
absence. A major implication is the need for much more relevant data
about normal and variant marital, family, and friendship patterns
among older black women. (Author's abstract)

565 Jackson, Jacquelyne Johnson. "Marital Life among Aging Blacks."
FAMILY COORDINATOR 21, 1 (January 1972): 21-27. 7 pp., references,
tables.

Subjects: 1. Family Relationships and Dynamics / Later Years and Aging;
2. Marriage and Divorce / Marriage Satisfaction and Prediction
Studies.

566 Jackson, Jacquelyne Johnson. "The Plight of Older Black Women in
the United States." BLACK SCHOLAR 7, 7 (April 1976): 47-55. 9 pp.

Subjects: 1. Family Relationships and Dynamics / Stages in Family Life
   Cycle; 2. / Women's Issues.

567 Jackson, Lorraine B. "The Attitudes of Black Females toward Upper
and Lower Class Black Males." JOURNAL OF BLACK PSYCHOLOGY 1, 2
(February 1975): 53-64. 12 pp., references, tables.

Subjects: 1. Family Relationships and Dynamics / Singles (Lifestyle);
   2. Mate Selection / Mate Selection, Differential Patterns; 3.
   Psychology and Sociology / General Attitudes.

   Sarbin's adjective word list was administered to 100 Black female
   college students. The subjects were asked to select adjectives which
   they thought described upper and lower class Black and white males,
   and to assign favorability ratings to the adjectives. Both groups of
   Black males were assigned more favorable traits than both groups of
   white males. (Author's abstract)

568 Jackson, Maurice and Wood, James. IMPLICATIONS FOR THE BLACK
AGED. Aging in America, No. 5. Washington, D.C.: National Council on the
Aging, 1976. 38 pp., tables.

Subjects: 1. Family Relationships and Dynamics / Later Years and Aging.

569 Jackson, Roberta H. "Some Aspirations of Lower Class Black
Mothers." JOURNAL OF COMPARATIVE FAMILY STUDIES 6, 2 (Autumn 1975):
171-81. 11 pp., references, tables.

Subjects: 1. Family Relationships and Dynamics / Mother-Child
   Relationships.

   This report is focused toward determining whether family size,
   education and income have any influence upon the aspirations for
   offspring of lower class black mothers. The sample consisted of 441
   subjects randomly selected from lower class black female parents who
   lived in low-income housing projects in a small southeastern city with
   a population of almost 100,000. Several conclusions may be derived
   from the analysis of data which dealt with the relationship of family
   size, education and income to the aspirations for offspring of lower
   class black mothers. First, contrary to some allegations, the majority
   of indigent black mothers have positive aspirations for their
   children. Second, contrary to common expectation, indigent black
   female parents in families of above average size tend to think more
   positively about the future success of their offspring than mothers in
   smaller families. Third, black mothers of low socioeconomic status who
   have attained an educational level of nine or more years of formal
   training appear to be more positive in their aspirations for children
   than mothers with less formal training. Fourth, the percentage of
   positive aspirations for offspring increases as levels of income and
   education become higher in the families of lower class black mothers.
   Fifth, female parents in low socioeconomic black families have become
   increasingly aware of the necessity of encouraging their children,
   regardless of sex, to obtain an education. Finally, the findings in
   this report should provide a more objective basis for future
   examination of the relationship of family size, education, and income
   to some of the problems which confront low income black families.
   (From author's text)

570   Jacob, Theodore, Fagin, Robert, Perry, Joseph and Dyke, Ruth Ann
Van. "Social Class, Child Age, and Parental Socialization Values."
DEVELOPMENTAL PSYCHOLOGY 11, 3 (May 1975): 393. 1 p., references.

Subjects: 1. Family Relationships and Dynamics / Socialization; 2.
   Family Counseling and Education / Value Education; 3. Minority Groups
   / Family and Social Class.

571   Jacobs, James Harris. "Black/White Interracial Families: Marital
Process and Identity Development in Young Children." (Ph.D.
dissertation, The Wright Institute, 1977.) DISSERTATION ABSTRACTS
INTERNATIONAL, 38, 10, April 1978, 5023B. (University Microfilms
No. 7803173.) 362 pp.

Subjects: 1. Family Relationships and Dynamics / Socialization; 2.
   Marriage and Divorce / Inter-marriage; 3. Psychology and Sociology /
   Psychology.

572   Jacques, Jeffrey M. "Self-Esteem among Southeastern Black American
Couples." JOURNAL OF BLACK STUDIES 7, 1 (September 1976): 11-28. 18
pp., references, tables.

Subjects: 1. Family Relationships and Dynamics / Husband-Wife
   Relationships; 2. Psychology and Sociology / Self-Esteem.

From a study of 98 randomly selected black-American couples living in
a moderately large Southeastern city, it was concluded that the
overwhelming majority of those sampled had positive self-esteem
scores. Both measures of self-esteem--Kuhn and McPartland's Twenty
Statements Test and Rosenberg's Self-Esteem Scale--showed the
consistency in which the current black sample reported positive self-
esteem. These findings cast considerable doubt on the current validity
of generalizations made from earlier studies. . .[regarding] the
reported notion of negative self-esteem among black-Americans. .
.Further, the notion that spouse's self-esteem was related to other
spouse's color was not substantiated. Specifically, wives who were
physically lighter than their husbands did not have husbands who had
poor self-esteem. Also, husbands who were physically darker than their
wives did not have wives with poor self-esteem. One of the possible
explanations for the differences between the findings and inferences
of the current study and the previous studies may be found in the
changes that have taken place in American society. (Author's
conclusions)

573   James, W. F. Bernell, James, Pauline M. and Walker, Edgar. "Some
Problems of Sexual Growth in Adolescent Underprivileged Unwed Black
Girls." JOURNAL OF THE NATIONAL MEDICAL ASSOCIATION 69, 9 (September
1977): 631-33. 3 pp., references, tables.

Subjects: 1. Family Counseling and Education / Adolescence; 2. / Sex
   Education.

574   Janowitz, Barbara S. "The Impact of AFDC on Illegitimate Birth
Rates." JOURNAL OF MARRIAGE AND THE FAMILY 38, 3 (August 1976): 485-94.
10 pp., references, bibliography, tables.

Subjects: 1. Organizations and Services to Families / Social Welfare;
2. Issues Related to Reproduction / Illegitimacy.

575 Jantz, Richard K. and Sciara, Frank J. "Does Living with a
Female Head of Household Affect the Arithmetic Achievement of Black
Fourth-Grade Pupils?" PSYCHOLOGY IN THE SCHOOLS 12, 4 (October 1975):
468-72. 4 pp., references.

Subjects: 1. Organizations and Services to Families / Education and the
Family.

It was the purpose of this investigation to examine the effects of
living with a male or female head-of-household upon the arithmetic
performance of fourth graders. No significant differences were found
in mean scores between male and female pupils. Significant differences
were found favoring those pupils living with male heads-of-households,
particularly for female pupils and for pupils with IQ scores greater
than 100. These findings should not be considered as simple cause and
effect relationships, but rather as indicative of potential difficulty
for some pupils. (Authors' abstract)

576 Jeffers, Camille. LIVING POOR: A PARTICIPANT OBSERVER STUDY OF
PRIORITIES AND CHOICES. Ann Arbor, MI: Ann Arbor Publishers, 1967. 123
pp., references; LC:67-24378.

Subjects: 1. Organizations and Services to Families / Economics and the
Family; 2. Minority Groups / Family and Social Class; 3. Aids for
Theory and Research / Family Research Methodology.

577 Jenkins, Clyde Elbert. "The Profile Analysis of Parent-Child
Interaction in Families' Purchasing Decisions: A Cross-Cultural
Study." (D.B.A. dissertation, Texas Tech University, 1981.)
DISSERTATION ABSTRACTS INTERNATIONAL, 42, 8, Feb. 1982, 3732A-3733A.

Subjects: 1. Organizations and Services to Families / Consumerism; 2.
Family Relationships and Dynamics / Nuclear Family; 3. / Decision
Making.

578 Jenkins, Joyce Odessa. "To Make a Woman Black: A Critical Analysis
of the Women Characters in the Fiction and Folklore of Zora Neale
Hurston." (Ph.D. dissertation, Bowling Green State University, 1978.)
DISSERTATION ABSTRACTS INTERNATIONAL, 39, 7, Jan. 1979, 4257A-4258A.
(University Microfilms No. 7901444.) 228 pp.

Subjects: 1. Family Relationships and Dynamics / Women's Issues.

579 Jensen, Arthur R. "Cumulative Deficit: A Testable Hypothesis."
DEVELOPMENTAL PSYCHOLOGY 10, 6 (November 1974): 996-1019. 24 pp.,
references, bibliography, tables, charts.

Subjects: 1. Aids for Theory and Research / Family Research Methodology.

580 Jewell, K. Sue. "Use of Social Welfare Programs and the
Disintegration of the Black Nuclear Family." THE WESTERN JOURNAL OF
BLACK STUDIES 8, 4 (Winter 1984): 192-98. 8 pp., references.

Subjects: 1. Organizations and Services to Families / Social Welfare;
   2. Family Relationships and Dynamics / Nuclear Family.

581 Jiobu, J. and Marshall, H. "Minority Status and Family Size: A
Comparison of Explanations." POPULATION STUDIES 31, 3 (November 1977):
509-17. 9 pp., references, tables.

Subjects: 1. Trends and Change in Marriage and Family / Family and
   Social Change; 2. Issues Related to Reproduction / Fertility Rates.

582 John, Craig St. "Race Differences in Age at First Birth and the
Pace of Subsequent Fertility: Implications for the Minority Group Status
Hypothesis." DEMOGRAPHY 19, 3 (August 1982): 301-14. 14 pp.

Subjects: 1. Issues Related to Reproduction / Fertility Rates.

We examine race differences in the effects of age at first birth on
the pace of subsequent fertility. If race differences in the pace of
fertility persist net of age at first birth and socioeconomic
variables, they will be taken as new support for the minority group
status hypothesis. Data from the 1973 National Survey of Family Growth
are analyzed with the finding that race differences in the pace of
fertility are real, giving support to the hypothesis. Implications are
drawn suggesting that the proper points at which to examine group
differences in fertility are the different stages in the process which
culminates in completed fertility, rather than limiting investigation
to the final product. (Author's abstract)

583 Johnson, Audrey Louise. "The Perceptions and Social
Characteristics Related to Occupational Mobility of Black Women and
Intraracial Assimilation of Blacks in America." (Ph.D. dissertation, New
School for Social Research, 1977.) DISSERTATION ABSTRACTS
INTERNATIONAL, 39, 2, Aug. 1978, 1146A-1147A. (University Microfilms
No. 7811867.) 241 pp.

Subjects: 1. Family Relationships and Dynamics / Women's Issues; 2.
   Families with Special Problems / Achievement and the Family; 3.
   Psychology and Sociology / Sociology.

584 Johnson, C. Lincoln. "Transracial Adoption: Victim of Ideology."
SOCIAL WORK 21, 3 (May 1976): 241-242. 2 pp., references, tables.

Subjects: 1. Organizations and Services to Families / Adoption and
   Adoption Services.

585 Johnson, Clara L. "Adolescent Pregnancy: Intervention into the
Poverty Cycle." ADOLESCENCE 9, 35 (Fall 1974): 391-406. 16 pp.,
references, bibliography.

Subjects: 1. Issues Related to Reproduction / Teenage Pregnancy.

586 Johnson, Cynthia Elaine. "Factors Influencing the
Marital Stability of Older Black Couples." (Ph.D. dissertation, The
Ohio State University, 1980.) DISSERTATION ABSTRACTS INTERNATIONAL, 41,
4, Oct. 1980, 1793A. (University Microfilms No. 8022296.) 152 pp.

Subjects: 1. Family Relationships and Dynamics / Stages in Family Life
   Cycle; 2. / Later Years and Aging; 3. Marriage and Divorce / Marriage
   Satisfaction and Prediction Studies.

587 Johnson, Leanor B.   "The Search for Values in Black Family
Research." THE WESTERN JOURNAL OF BLACK STUDIES 1, 2 (June 1977): 98-
104. 7 pp., references.

Subjects: 1. Family Counseling and Education / Value Education; 2. Aids
   for Theory and Research / Critiques and Analyses of Family Research
   Literature.

588 Johnson, Leanor Boulin and Staples, Robert E.   "Family Planning of
the Young Minority Male: A Pilot Project." FAMILY COORDINATOR 28, 4
(October 1979): 535-43. 9 pp., references, tables, charts.

Subjects: 1. Family Relationships and Dynamics / Family Roles and Sex
   Roles; 2. Issues Related to Reproduction / Family Planning; 3. Family
   Counseling and Education / Family Life Education.

This paper is a report of the first coordinated program of its kind
aimed at young Black, Spanish speaking, Asian and American Indian
males in relation to family life education, family planning and
parental concerns. The project sought to develop an approach to the
promotion of sexual responsibility and the reduction of repetition of
unwanted, out-of-wedlock pregnancy through goal-directed support and
assistance to unwed fathers and potential unwed fathers, 14 to 24
years of age. (Authors' abstract)

589 Johnson, Leon Johanson, Sr.   "A Comparative Study of the Womanhood
Experiences of Black Young Adult Females and White Young Adult
Females." (Ph.D. dissertation, University of South Carolina, 1976.)
DISSERTATION ABSTRACTS INTERNATIONAL, 38, 1, July 1977, 177A.
(University Microfilms No. 7713890.) 97 pp.

Subjects: 1. Trends and Change in Marriage and Family / Comparative
   Studies--International, Interclass, Sex, and Time Differences; 2.
   Family Relationships and Dynamics / Women's Issues.

590 Johnson, Leonor Bonlin.   "The Sexual Oppression of Blacks." In THE
SEXUALLY OPPRESSED, edited by Harvey L. Gochros and Jean S. Gochros,
pp. 173-191. New York: Association Press, 1977. 19 pp.

Subjects: 1. Sexual Attitudes and Behavior / Sexual Attitudes and
   Behavior.

591 Johnson, Nan E.   "A Response to Rindfuss." AMERICAN JOURNAL OF
SOCIOLOGY 86, 2 (September 1980): 375-77. 3 pp., references.

Subjects: 1. Aids for Theory and Research / Critiques and Analyses of
   Family Research Literature.

592 Johnson, Otis Samuel.   "The Social Welfare Role of the Black
Church." (Ph.D. dissertation, Brandeis University, The F. Heller
Graduate School for Advanced Study in Social Welfare, 1980.)
DISSERTATION ABSTRACTS INTERNATIONAL, 41, 5, Nov. 1980, 2293A.
(University Microfilms No. 8024554.) 231 pp.

Subjects: 1. Organizations and Services to Families / Religion and the
Family; 2. / Social Welfare.

593 Johnson, Robert C. "The Black Family and Black Community
Development." JOURNAL OF BLACK PSYCHOLOGY 8, 1 (August 1981): 23-40.
18 pp., references.

Subjects: 1. Organizations and Services to Families / Community Groups
and the Family.

Black family life is discussed in the context of Black community
development. The author contends that mutual, interactive actions by
Black families and Black community institutions could benefit both.
The familial functions of socialization (including racial
consciousness) and economic functioning are reviewed, and the ways
that Black families can assist in the development of the Black
community through efficient use of family resources are explored. The
author argues that more judicious resource utilization and allocation
by Black organizations could contribute to increased family well-
being. Discussion also focuses upon the theoretical relationship
between the Black family and the Black community, emphasizing the
centrality of Black family life in the Black community. Other topics
explored in this article include the relationship between Black self-
concept and consumer behavior; the interrelation among racial
awareness, consumerism, and community development; and the
contemporary bond between Black families and Black institutions.
(Author's abstract)

594 Johnson, Shirley B. "The Impact of Women's Liberation on Marriage,
Divorce and Family Lifestyles." In SEX, DISCRIMINATION AND THE DIVISION
OF LABOR, edited by Cynthia B. Lloyd, pp. 401-26. New York: Columbia
University Press, 1975. 26 pp., references, tables.

Subjects: 1. Family Relationships and Dynamics / Family Relationships;
2. / Women's Issues; 3. Marriage and Divorce / Marriage Satisfaction
and Prediction Studies.

595 Johnson, Willa D. and Green, Thomas L., eds. PERSPECTIVES ON AFRO-
AMERICAN WOMEN. Washington, DC: Educational and Community Counselors
Associates Publications, 1975. 197 pp.; LC:76-73767.

Subjects: 1. Family Relationships and Dynamics / Women's Issues.

596 Jones, Allan P. and Demaree, R. G. "Family Disruption, Social
Indices, and Problem Behavior: A Preliminary Study." JOURNAL OF
MARRIAGE AND THE FAMILY 37, 3 (August 1975): 497-502. 6 pp.,
references, tables.

Subjects: 1. Family Relationships and Dynamics / Environment (Space/
Housing); 2. Families with Special Problems / Family Disorganization;
3. Minority Groups / Family and Social Class.

Family functioning patterns have been found to be related to various
demographic characteristics. Data on 46 demographic variables were
gathered from 159 census tracts in Tarrant County, Texas. Based on a
principal components analysis and varimax rotation, seven components
were extracted - Family Disruption, Young Families, Suburban Growth,

Socioeconomic Status, Residence Patterns, Black Ethnicity, and Black Change. Index scores computed on each component were related to incidence rates of a wide range of social problem behaviors. Strong positive relationships were found between family disruption and the problem behaviors. Implications for future research are discussed. (Authors' abstract)

597 Jones, Bobby Frank. "A Cultural Middle Passage: Slave Marriage and Family in the Antebellum South." (Ph.D. dissertation, The University of North Carolina at Chapel Hill, 1965.) DISSERTATION ABSTRACTS INTERNATIONAL, 26, 7, Jan. 1966, 3886. (University Microfilms No. 6514357.) 273 pp.

Subjects: 1. Trends and Change in Marriage and Family / Family Life Prior to 1900; 2. Family Relationships and Dynamics / Family Relationships; 3. / Men's Issues.

598 Jones, Clarence B. "Perspective on the Black Family." FREEDOMWAYS 19, 4 (1979): 234. 1 p.

Subjects: 1. Trends and Change in Marriage and Family / Family Life in the United States.

599 Jones, Jacqueline. "'My Mother Was Much of A Woman': Black Women, Work, and the Family under Slavery." FEMINIST STUDIES 8, 2 (Summer 1982): 235-69. 35 pp.

Subjects: 1. Trends and Change in Marriage and Family / Family Life Prior to 1900; 2. Family Relationships and Dynamics / Women's Issues.

The purpose of this article is to suggest that the burdens shouldered by slave women actually represented in extreme form the dual nature of all women's labor within a patriarchal, capitalist society: the production of goods and services and the reproduction and care of members of a future work force. The antebellum plantation brought into focus the interaction between notions of women qua "equal" workers and women qua unequal reproducers; hence a slaveowner just as "naturally" put his bondwomen to work chopping cotton as washing, ironing, or cooking. Furthermore, in seeking to maximize the productivity of his entire labor force while reserving certain domestic tasks for women exclusively, the master demonstrated how patriarchal and capitalist assumptions concerning women's work could reinforce one another. The "peculiar institution" thus involved forms of oppression against women that were unique manifestations of a more universal condition. The . . . discussion focuses on female slaves in the American rural South between 1830 and 1860--cotton boom years that laid bare the economic and social underpinnings of slavery and indeed all of American society. (From author's text)

600 Jones, Jacqueline. LABOR OF LOVE, LABOR OF SORROW: BLACK WOMEN, WORK, AND THE FAMILY FROM SLAVERY TO THE PRESENT. New York: Basic Books, Inc., 1985. 432 pp., references, bibliography, illustrations, index; ISBN:0-465-03756-9; LC:84-24310.

Subjects: 1. Trends and Change in Marriage and Family / Family Life in the United States; 2. Organizations and Services to Families /

Employment and the Family; 3. Family Relationships and Dynamics /
Women's Issues.

Notes: Selected Bibliography: pp. 406-15.

601 Jones, Mary Elaine. "An Anthropological Assessment of Bonding:
Mother Infant Attachment Behavior in a Study of Forty Adolescent Black
and White Mothers from Delivery through Six Months." (Ph.D.
dissertation, Southern Methodist University, 1981.) DISSERTATION
ABSTRACTS INTERNATIONAL, 42, 3, Sept. 1981, 1229A. (University
Microfilms No. 8119859.) 255 pp.

Subjects: 1. Organizations and Services to Families / Community Groups
    and the Family; 2. Family Relationships and Dynamics / Mother-Child
    Relationships; 3. Issues Related to Reproduction / Teenage Pregnancy.

602 Jones, Reginald Lanier, ed. BLACK PSYCHOLOGY. New York: Harper
and Row, 1972. 432 pp., bibliography, tables, charts, index; ISBN:0-06-
043431-7; LC:72-190660.

Subjects: 1. Psychology and Sociology / Psychology; 2. Aids for Theory
    and Research / Family Research Methodology; 3. / Collected Works.

603 Jones, Reginald Lorrin. "The Impact of Newborn Sickle Cell Testing
on Maternal Attitudes toward Childrearing: A Simulation Study." (Ph.D.
dissertation, University of Cincinnati, 1980.) DISSERTATION ABSTRACTS
INTERNATIONAL, 41, 6, Dec. 1980, 2325B-2326B. (University Microfilms
No. 8021036.) 125 pp.

Subjects: 1. Organizations and Services to Families / Physical Health
    and the Family; 2. Family Relationships and Dynamics / Mother-Child
    Relationships.

604 Jordan, Ernest E. "A Study of the Social and Maternal
Responsibility of a Group of Negro Unwed Mothers." (Ed.D. dissertation,
University of Pennsylvania, 1969.) DISSERTATION ABSTRACTS
INTERNATIONAL, 30, 7, Jan. 1970, 2802A-2803A. (University Microfilms
No. 6921641.) 151 pp.

Subjects: 1. Family Relationships and Dynamics / Mother-Child
    Relationships; 2. / Family Roles and Sex Roles; 3. Issues Related to
    Reproduction / Illegitimacy.

605 Jordan, Winthrop D. WHITE OVER BLACK: AMERICAN ATTITUDES TOWARD
THE NEGRO, 1550-1812. Institute of Early American History and Culture
Series. Durham, NC: University of North Carolina Press, 1968. 651 pp.,
bibliography, illustrations; LC:68-13295.

Subjects: 1. Trends and Change in Marriage and Family / Family Life
    Prior to 1900; 2. Psychology and Sociology / Psychology.

Notes: Published for the Institute of Early American History and
Culture at Williamsburg, VA by the University of North Carolina Press.
Bibliography: pp. 610-614.

606 Josephson, Eric. "The Matriarchy: Myth and Reality." FAMILY
COORDINATOR 18, 3 (July 1969): 268-76. 9 pp., references.

Subjects: 1. Family Relationships and Dynamics / Single Parent Families;
2. Aids for Theory and Research / Family Theory.

607 Kamii, Constance K. and Radin, Norma L. "Class Differences in the
Socialization Practices of Negro Mothers." JOURNAL OF MARRIAGE AND THE
FAMILY 29, 2 (May 1967): 302-10. 9 pp., references, tables, charts.

Subjects: 1. Trends and Change in Marriage and Family / Comparative
Studies--International, Interclass, Sex, and Time Differences; 2.
Family Relationships and Dynamics / Socialization; 3. Minority Groups
/ Family and Social Class.

608 Kammeyer, Kenneth C., Yetman, Norman R. and McClendon, Mckee J.
"Family Planning Services and the Distribution of Black Americans."
SOCIAL PROBLEMS 21, 5 (June 1974): 674-90. 17 pp., references,
bibliography, tables.

Subjects: 1. Organizations and Services to Families / Social Services
and the Family; 2. Issues Related to Reproduction / Family Planning.

609 Kandel, Denise B. "Race, Maternal Authority and Adolescent
Aspiration." AMERICAN JOURNAL OF SOCIOLOGY 76, 6 (May 1971): 999-1020.
22 pp., references, bibliography, tables, appendices.

Subjects: 1. Family Relationships and Dynamics / Parent-Adolescent
Relationships; 2. / Power in the Family.

610 Kanno, Nellie B. "Comparative Lifestyles of the Black Female in
the United States and the Black Female in Lesotho." JOURNAL OF AFRO-
AMERICAN ISSUES 2, 3 (1974): 212-17. 6 pp.

Subjects: 1. Trends and Change in Marriage and Family / Comparative
Studies--International, Interclass, Sex, and Time Differences; 2.
Family Relationships and Dynamics / Stages in Family Life Cycle; 3. /
Women's Issues.

This paper. . .concentrate[s] on the styles of the black female in
the United States and in Lesotho, Southern Africa. [T]he twin
"adversities" of being both female and black have produced a group of
women determined to succeed in societies which practice the most
blatant form of oppression and in which it is assumed that the black
female   presides   over   a family structure which is undergoing
progressive deterioration. (From author's text)

611 Kapsis, Robert E. "Black Streetcorner Districts." SOCIAL FORCES
57, 4 (June 1979): 1212-1228. 17 pp., references, bibliography, tables,
charts.

Subjects: 1. Family Relationships and Dynamics / Environment (Space/
Housing); 2. Sexual Attitudes and Behavior / Sexual Attitudes and
Behavior; 3. / Prostitution.

612 Karge, Bernadine. "Constitutional Law-Municipal Ordinance Limiting
Occupancy of Homeowners Dwelling to Certain Family Members Violative of
Fourteenth Amendment Due Process Clause: Moore v. City of East
Cleveland, Ohio." HOWARD LAW JOURNAL 21, 2 (1978): 645-660. 16 pp.,
references.

Subjects: 1. Organizations and Services to Families / Governmental Units
and the Family; 2. Family Relationships and Dynamics / Environment
(Space/Housing).

613 Keller, Ella Tates. "Black Families in the Military
System." (Ph.D. dissertation, Mississippi State University, 1980.)
DISSERTATION ABSTRACTS INTERNATIONAL, 41, 3, Sept. 1980, 1233A.
(University Microfilms No. 8021115.) 288 pp.

Subjects: 1. Organizations and Services to Families / Military Families;
2. Family Relationships and Dynamics / Decision Making.

614 Kelley, Michael Robert. "Some Psychological and Sociological
Factors Influencing Motivation for Interracial Marriage." (Ph.D.
dissertation, California School of Professional Psychology, 1976.)
DISSERTATION ABSTRACTS INTERNATIONAL, 37, 9, March 1977, 4686B-4687B.
(University Microfilms No. 776304.) 250 pp.

Subjects: 1. Mate Selection / Mate Selection, Differential Patterns; 2.
Marriage and Divorce / Inter-marriage.

615 Kennedy, Theodore R. YOU GOTTA DEAL WITH IT: BLACK FAMILY
RELATIONS IN A SOUTHERN COMMUNITY. New York: Oxford University Press,
1980. 215 pp.; ISBN:0-19-502591-1; LC:79-14476.

Subjects: 1. Family Relationships and Dynamics / Family Relationships.

616 Khalesi, Mohammad Reza. "Comparison of the Parenting Attitudes,
Conflict Management Styles, and Interpersonal Behavior Patterns of
Anglo, Black and Mexican-American Parents." (Ph.D. dissertation,
University of Colorado at Boulder, 1980.) DISSERTATION ABSTRACTS
INTERNATIONAL, 41, 8, Feb. 1981, 3426A. (University Microfilms
No. 8103110.) 232 pp.

Subjects: 1. Family Relationships and Dynamics / Parent-Child
Relationships; 2. / Power in the Family; 3. Minority Groups / Ethnic
Groups in the United States.

617 Kilpatrick, Allie C. "Future Directions for the Black Family."
FAMILY COORDINATOR 28, 3 (July 1979): 347-52. 6 pp., references.

Subjects: 1. Trends and Change in Marriage and Family / Futuristic
Studies of the Family; 2. Aids for Theory and Research / Family
Theory.

618 King, James R. "African Survivals in the Black American Family:
Key Factors in Stability." JOURNAL OF AFRO-AMERICAN ISSUES 4, 2 (Spring
1976): 153-67. 15 pp.

Subjects: 1. Trends and Change in Marriage and Family / Family Life in
the United States.

619 King, Jerry Glenn. "A Study of Strengths in Black
Families." (Ph.D. dissertation, The University of Nebraska-Lincoln,
1980.) DISSERTATION ABSTRACTS INTERNATIONAL, 41, 07, Jan. 1981, 3282A.
(University Microfilms No. 8100434.) 153 pp.

Subjects: 1. Family Relationships and Dynamics / Family Relationships;
2. Marriage and Divorce / Marriage Satisfaction and Prediction
Studies; 3. Psychology and Sociology / Self-Esteem.

620 King, Karl. "Adolescent Perception of Power Structure in the Negro
Family." JOURNAL OF MARRIAGE AND THE FAMILY 31, 4 (November 1969): 751-
55. 5 pp., references, tables.

Subjects: 1. Family Relationships and Dynamics / Power in the Family;
2. Family Counseling and Education / Adolescence.

621 King, Karl. "A Comparison of the Negro and White Family Structure
in Low Income Families." CHILD AND FAMILY 6, 2 (Spring 1967): 65-74.
10 pp., references, tables.

Subjects: 1. Family Relationships and Dynamics / Power in the Family.

622 King, Karl, Abernathy, Thomas J. and Chapman, Ann H. "Black
Adolescents' Views of Maternal Employment as a Threat to the Marital
Relationship, 1963-1973." JOURNAL OF MARRIAGE AND THE FAMILY 38, 4
(November 1976): 733-37. 4 pp., references.

Subjects: 1. Organizations and Services to Families / Working Mothers;
2. Marriage and Divorce / Marriage Satisfaction and Prediction
Studies; 3. Family Counseling and Education / Adolescence.

Two surveys of ninth-grade black adolescents, one in 1963 and in
1973, were conducted in two metropolitan areas in the Southeast using
the same procedures to determine adolescent attitudes toward working
wives as a threat to the marital relationship. In general, hypotheses
were supported that adolescents whose mothers were employed viewed
employment as less threatening, adolescents from higher status
families perceived mother employment as less threatening, as did
females when compared to males in 1963 and 1973. (Authors' abstract)

623 King, Mae C. "Oppression and Power: The Unique Status of the Black
Woman in the American Political System." SOCIAL SCIENCE QUARTERLY 56, 1
(June 1975): 116-28. 13 pp., references.

Subjects: 1. Organizations and Services to Families / Governmental Units
and the Family; 2. Family Relationships and Dynamics / Women's Issues.

624 Kokonis, Nicholas. "Three Wishes of Black American Children:
Psychosocial Implications." PERCEPTUAL AND MOTOR SKILLS 38, 2 (June
1974): 1335-38. 4 pp., references, tables.

Subjects: 1. Family Relationships and Dynamics / Socialization; 2.
Family Counseling and Education / Education for Parenthood.

The present study investigated the wishes of black American children
aged 7 to 12 years (63 boys, 74 girls), to obtain normative data and
to compare these children with other cultural groups. Ss wished for
material things more often than anything else, boys tended to wish for
money and material things more strongly than girls, and girls were
more interested in personal attributes and skills than boys. No
developmental trends were noted. Findings were compared with those of
studies dealing with white American and Greek-American children,

emphasizing   psychosocial   change   in   human   development.   (Author's summary)

625 Kriesberg, Lewis. "Rearing Children for Educational Achievement in Fatherless Families." JOURNAL OF MARRIAGE AND THE FAMILY 29, 2 (May 1967): 288-301. 14 pp., references, tables.

Subjects: 1. Organizations and Services to Families / Education and the Family; 2. Family Relationships and Dynamics / Single Parent Families.

626 Kronus, Sidney J. THE BLACK MIDDLE CLASS. Columbus, OH: Charles E. Merrill, 1971. 182 pp., bibliography; ISBN:0-675-09218-3; LC:79-148247.

Subjects: 1. Trends and Change in Marriage and Family / Family and Social Change; 2. Minority Groups / Family and Social Class.

Notes: Bibliography: pp. 172-177

627 Kulikoff, Allan. "The Beginnings of the Afro-American Family in Maryland." In LAW, SOCIETY, AND POLITICS IN EARLY MARYLAND. PROCEEDINGS OF THE FIRST CONFERENCE ON MARYLAND HISTORY, JUNE 14-15, 1974, edited by Aubrey C. Land, Loris Green Carr and Edward C. Papenfuge, pp. 171-196. Baltimore, MD: The Johns Hopkins University Press, 1977. 26 pp.

Subjects: 1. Trends and Change in Marriage and Family / Family Life Prior to 1900.

628 Kunkel, Peter H. and Kennard, Sara Sue. SPOUT SPRING: A BLACK COMMUNITY. Case Studies in Cultural Anthropology. New York: Holt, Rinehart and Winston, Inc., 1971. 99 pp., bibliography, illustrations; ISBN:0-03-085751-1; LC:76-166105.

Subjects: 1. Organizations and Services to Families / Community Groups and the Family; 2. Family Relationships and Dynamics / Family Relationships; 3. Aids for Theory and Research / Kinship Terminology.

The ethnographic description of Spout Spring neighborhood in the city of Sequoyah and state of Ozarka (each name is of course a pseudonym) focuses on race-relations, economics, leadership styles, families and households, non-kin groups, and social change. Not unlike other Black communities in other parts of the United States, Spout Spring Blacks have variable household compositions and organizational patterns. Conjugal family households, matrilateral multi-household extended families, 'matrifocal' households with no resident husband-father, and 'patrifocal' households with no resident wife-mother are discussed in relation to case study data. Also discussed are kin terms and exogamy, husband-wife relations, parent-child relations, sibling relations, and socialization.

Notes: Bibliography: pp. 95-99.

629 Kunz, Phillip R. "Black and Mormonism: A Social Distance Change." PSYCHOLOGICAL REPORTS 45, 1 (August 1979): 81-82. 2 pp., tables.

Subjects: 1. Trends and Change in Marriage and Family / Family and
Social Change; 2. Organizations and Services to Families / Religion
and the Family.

630 Kushnick, Louis. "The Negro Family in the United States: A
Review." RACE: THE JOURNAL OF THE INSTITUTE OF RACE RELATIONS (NAME
CHANGED TO RACE AND CLASS) 8, 4 (April 1967): 409-14. 6 pp.,
references.

Subjects: 1. Trends and Change in Marriage and Family / Family Life in
the United States; 2. Aids for Theory and Research / Critiques and
Analyses of Family Research Literature.

631 Kutner, Nancy G. "The Poor Vs. the Non-poor: An Ethnic and
Metropolitan-Non-metropolitan Comparison." SOCIOLOGICAL QUARTERLY 16, 2
(Spring 1975): 250-63. 14 pp., references, bibliography, tables.

Subjects: 1. Families with Special Problems / Family Stress.

632 Labinjoh, Justin. "The Sexual Life of the Oppressed: An
Examination of the Family Life of Antebellum Slaves." PHYLON 35, 4
(December 1974): 375-97. 23 pp., references, tables.

Subjects: 1. Trends and Change in Marriage and Family / Family Life
Prior to 1900.

Through the use of primary sources such as narratives of the formerly
enslaved population and plantation records, an examination is made
into the conjugal life of antebellum captives. While conjugal family
life was threatened by disorganizing factors during slavery, many
captives managed to have a "fairly stable" domestic life. The data
suggest that the captives' sense of family consciousness and mutual
respect for conjugal bonds as well as the planters' vested economic
interests in keeping families together were factors that contributed
to the degrees of stability in black domestic groups in captivity.
Among the various topics discussed are: the comparative statuses of
enslaved families in Latin America and British North America; the non-
legally recognized nuptial bonding; interplantation marriages; length
of marriages; wedding ceremonies; social stratification and mate
selection; consciousness of kinship; the question of matrifocality;
family headship; and so forth.

633 Labovitz, Eugene M. "Race, SES Contexts and Fulfillment of College
Aspirations." SOCIOLOGICAL QUARTERLY 16, 2 (Spring 1975): 241-49. 10
pp., references, bibliography, tables.

Subjects: 1. Organizations and Services to Families / Education and the
Family; 2. Families with Special Problems / Achievement and the
Family.

The differential effects of social contexts and race on educational
behavior are examined in terms of a causal process model. Based on
data from San Diego, the role of social contexts are found to be
important through a causal process in which SES contexts affect
personal characteristics which, in turn, influence educational
aspirations and attainment. Utilizing both correlational and tabular
techniques, the basic model holds for all racial (ethnic) groups;

however, race does affect the level of the individual variables. The findings from this study suggest that the importance of SES contexts are mediated by race and contingent upon the common relations of these contexts and educational behavior to individual characteristics. (Authors's abstract)

634 Labrecque, Suzanne Volin. "Childrearing Attitudes and Observed Behaviors of Black Fathers with Kindergarten Daughters." (Ph.D. dissertation, The Florida State University, 1976.) DISSERTATION ABSTRACTS INTERNATIONAL, 37, 7, Jan. 1977, 4646A-4647A. (University Microfilms No. 7629458.) 121 pp.

Subjects: 1. Family Relationships and Dynamics / Father-Child Relationships; 2. / Parent-Child Relationships; 3. Aids for Theory and Research / Family Research Methodology.

635 Ladner, Joyce A., ed. THE DEATH OF WHITE SOCIOLOGY. New York: Vintage Books, 1973. 476 pp., references, tables; ISBN:0-394-71868-2; LC:72-10449.

Subjects: 1. Psychology and Sociology / Sociology.

636 Ladner, Joyce A. "Labeling Black Children: Social-Psychological Implications." JOURNAL OF AFRO-AMERICAN ISSUES 3, 1 (Winter 1975): 43-52. 10 pp., references.

Subjects: 1. Family Relationships and Dynamics / Socialization; 2. Family Counseling and Education / Education for Parenthood.

637 Ladner, Joyce A. "Mixed Families: White Parents and Black Children." SOCIETY (FORMERLY CALLED SOCIAL SCIENCE AND MODERN SOCIETY) 14, 6 (10 September-October 1977): 70-78. 9 pp., references, illustrations.

Subjects: 1. Trends and Change in Marriage and Family / Alternative Family Forms; 2. Organizations and Services to Families / Adoption and Adoption Services.

638 Ladner, Joyce A. TOMORROW'S TOMORROW: THE BLACK WOMAN. 1st edition Garden City, N.Y.: Doubleday and Co., Inc., 1971. 304 pp., bibliography; LC:78-139038.

Subjects: 1. Family Relationships and Dynamics / Family Relationships; 2. / Women's Issues; 3. Issues Related to Reproduction / Illegitimacy.

A review of the status of the Black woman and her progress, this book is a revision of the author's dissertation thesis.

Notes: Bibliography: pp. 289-297.

639 Ladner, Joyce Ann. "On Becoming a Woman in the Ghetto: Modes of Adaptation." (Ph.D. dissertation, Washington University, 1968.) DISSERTATION ABSTRACTS INTERNATIONAL, 29, 6, Dec. 1968, 1970A. (University Microfilms No. 6817190.) 272 pp.

Subjects: 1. Family Relationships and Dynamics / Family Roles and Sex
Roles; 2. / Women's Issues; 3. Sexual Attitudes and Behavior / Sexual
Attitudes and Behavior.

640 Lammermeier, Paul J.   "The Urban Black Family of the 19th Century:
A Study of Black Family Structure in the Ohio Valley, 1850-1880."
JOURNAL OF MARRIAGE AND THE FAMILY 35, 3 (August 1973): 440-56.   17 pp.,
references, bibliography, tables, charts.

Subjects: 1. Trends and Change in Marriage and Family / Family Life
Prior to 1900.

This study of the black family structure in seven Ohio Valley cities
is an effort to fill the void in historical literature on the origins
of the present-day urban black family, especially the phenomenon of
the lower-class "black- matriarchy." Based on the manuscript census,
all male- and female-headed families are compared with such
demographic data as the age, sex, and family structures; size and
number of children; and socioeconomic data of real-estate ownership
and occupations. The basic conclusions are twofold: (1) the urban
black family structure during the nineteenth century was basically a
two-parent, male-headed family that showed little evidence of
retaining structural characteristics of the slave family, and (2)
despite the increasing trend towards residential segregation, the only
sign of a lessening of the two-parent family is a rise in the
proportion of female-headed extended families. (Author's abstract)

641 Landry, Bart and Jendrek, Margaret Platt.   "The Employment of Wives
in Middle-Class Black Families." JOURNAL OF MARRIAGE AND THE FAMILY 40,
4 (November 1978): 787-97. 11 pp., references, tables.

Subjects: 1. Organizations and Services to Families / Employment and the
Family; 2. Aids for Theory and Research / Family Research Methodology.

Prior studies of the employment of black and white wives have
compared rates and patterns among all black and white wives. The
present study focuses primarily upon wives in black middle-class
families, with comparisons made to wives in middle-class white and
working-class black families. A model with 11 independent variables is
presented, and multiple regression analysis used to predict the
probability that a wife will be employed. Findings support the
hypothesis of both race and class effects upon the employment of
wives. Black middle-class wives were found to have higher employment
rates than both white middle- and black working-class wives. At the
same time, patterns of influence among factors affecting employment
differed between black and white middle-class wives, as well as
between black middle- and working-class wives. Results of the
regression analysis and contingency analysis of relevant data suggest
that black middle-class wives have higher employment rates because of
economic need. (Authors' abstract)

642 Lane, Ellen A.   "Childhood Characteristics of Black
College Graduates Reared in Poverty." DEVELOPMENTAL PSYCHOLOGY 8, 1
(January 1973): 42-45. 4 pp., references, tables.

Subjects: 1. Organizations and Services to Families / Education and the
Family.

Childhood records of 22 black college graduates from poverty backgrounds were studied. IQ scores from the second grade were below national averages and showed no differences from school norms, siblings, and matched controls. By eighth grade, however, subjects' scores were significantly higher than all three controls. School progress, birth order, family stability, and family composition also were examined. (Author's abstract)

643 Lantz, Herman R. and Hendrix, Lewellyn. "The Free Black Family at the Time of the U.S. Census: Some Implications." INTERNATIONAL JOURNAL OF SOCIOLOGY OF THE FAMILY 7, 1 (January 1977): 37-44. 6 pp., references, tables.

Subjects: 1. Trends and Change in Marriage and Family / Family Life
   Prior to 1900.

This paper reports on an examination of Black family size in the federal census of 1790. The data reveal that Black family size reported is smaller than the White. Those racial differences are found consistently in every category and in all regions. Explanations for such findings are discussed. These include the possibility of an undercount for Blacks, higher infant mortality for Black children, and higher rates of Black illegitimacy which were not reported. None of these reasons appears to provide a satisfactory reason for differences in family size. The hypothesis that voluntary constraints on Black fertility were presented in the eighteenth century is introduced as possible explanation. This hypothesis is supported with evidence from Puritan influences present in the north, and the hypothesis is further supported by evidence on the existence of stable Black communities in the South. Several limitations inherent in this analysis are presented. These include problems with early census data especially in the areas of Black infant mortality and Black fertility. The possibility that several different types of Black family structures may have existed in the past is suggested. These different Black family structures are still to be identified. (Authors' abstract)

644 Lantz, Herman R. "A Research Note on the Free Black Family in Our Early History." FAMILY COORDINATOR 24, 3 (July 1975): 363-65. 2 pp., references.

Subjects: 1. Trends and Change in Marriage and Family / Family Life
   Prior to 1900.

645 Lawder, Elizabeth A., Hoopes, Janet L., Andrews, Roberta G., Lower, Katherine D. and Perry, Susan Y. A STUDY OF BLACK ADOPTION FAMILIES: A COMPARISON OF A TRADITIONAL AND QUASI-ADOPTION PROGRAM. New York: Child Welfare League of America, 1971. 77 pp., bibliography; ISBN:0-87868-089-6; LC:71-170922.

Subjects: 1. Organizations and Services to Families / Adoption and
   Adoption Services.

Notes: Bibliography: pp. 75-77

646 Lawrence, Margaret Morgan. YOUNG INNER CITY FAMILIES: DEVELOPMENT OF EGO STRENGTH UNDER STRESS. New York: Behavioral Publications, Inc., 1975. 139 pp., bibliography; ISBN:0-87705-156-9; LC:74-8153.

Subjects: 1. Organizations and Services to Families / Mental Health and the Family; 2. Families with Special Problems / Family Stress; 3. Psychology and Sociology / Psychology.

Notes: Bibliography: pp. 137-139

647 Leashore, Bogart Raymond. "Interracial Households in 1850-1880 Detroit, Michigan." (Ph.D. dissertation, The University of Michigan, 1979.) DISSERTATION ABSTRACTS INTERNATIONAL, 40, 2, Aug. 1979, 1077A-1078A. (University Microfilms No. 7916755.) 242 pp.

Subjects: 1. Trends and Change in Marriage and Family / Family Life Prior to 1900; 2. Marriage and Divorce / Inter-marriage.

648 Lebsock, Suzanne. "Free Black Women and the Question of Matriarchy: Petersburg, Virginia, 1784-1820." FEMINIST STUDIES 8, 2 (Summer 1982): 271-92. 22 pp.

Subjects: 1. Trends and Change in Marriage and Family / Family Life Prior to 1900; 2. Family Relationships and Dynamics / Women's Issues.

Women are called matriarchs when the power they exercise relative to men of their own group is in some respect greater than that defined as appropriate by the dominant culture. [Data gleaned from Federal census records and archival sources on free Blacks in Petersburg, Virginia from 1784 to 1820 reveal that:] [t]he "matriarch" and the victim . . .were usually the same woman. . . . . In a slave society of the early nineteenth century, there developed among free blacks a relatively high degree of equality between the sexes. . .For free black women, the high rate of gainful employment and the high incidence of female-headed households were symptoms of oppression. Neither was chosen from a position of strength; both were products of a shortage of [Black] men and of chronic economic deprivation. The high incidence of female property holding, meanwhile, was largely the consequences of a system that limited the achievement of black men. (From author's text)

649 Lee, Irene Kathy. "Intergenerational Interaction among Black Limited-Resource Middlescent Couples, Adult Children, Aging Parents." (Ph.D. dissertation, Kansas State University, 1977.) DISSERTATION ABSTRACTS INTERNATIONAL, 39, 1, July 1978, 163A-164A. (University Microfilms No. 7811426.) 299 pp.

Subjects: 1. Trends and Change in Marriage and Family / Family Life in the United States; 2. Family Relationships and Dynamics / Extended Family and Kinship Groups; 3. / Later Years and Aging.

650 Lefcowitz, Myron Jack. DIFFERENCES BETWEEN NEGRO AND WHITE WOMEN IN MARITAL STABILITY AND FAMILY STRUCTURE: A MULTIPLE REGRESSION ANALYSIS. Wisconsin. University. Institute for Research on Poverty. Discussion Papers, No. 13-68. Madison, WI: Institute for Research on Poverty, 1968. 71 pp.; LC:70-29275.

Subjects: 1. Family Relationships and Dynamics / Family Relationships; 2. / Women's Issues; 3. Marriage and Divorce / Marriage Satisfaction and Prediction Studies.

651 Lefever, Harry G.   "'Playing the Dozens': A Mechanism for Social
Control."   PHYLON 42, 1 (Spring 1981): 73-85.   13 pp., references.

Subjects: 1. Trends and Change in Marriage and Family / Family and
   Social Change; 2. Psychology and Sociology / Sociology.

652 Lenus, Jack, Jr.   "Friendship: A Refutation."   ALTERNATIVE
LIFESTYLES 3, 4 (November 1980): 398-94.   6 pp.

Subjects: 1. Trends and Change in Marriage and Family / Alternative
   Family Forms; 2. Marriage and Divorce / Marriage Customs and Forms; 3.
   Aids for Theory and Research / Critiques and Analyses of Family
   Research Literature.

   This article questions the definition of man-sharing arrangements of
   11 legal and 11 consensual wives as polygamy. The holistic approach of
   anthropology   would negate Scott's definition of man-sharing as
   polygyny. The article concludes that though a deviant form of   family
   formation exists, American culture does not socially or legally
   recognize polygyny. (Author's abstract)

653 Lerner, Gerda, comp. BLACK WOMEN IN WHITE AMERICA: A DOCUMENTARY
HISTORY. 1st edition New York: Pantheon Books, 1972.   630 pp.,
references; ISBN:0-394-47540-2; LC:77-173892.

Subjects: 1. Family Relationships and Dynamics / Women's Issues; 2.
   Aids for Theory and Research / Collected Works.

654 Lesi, F. E. A. and Bassey, Expo E. E. "Family Study in Sickle Cell
Disease in Nigeria."   JOURNAL OF BIOSOCIAL SCIENCE 4, 3 (July 1972):
307-13.   7 pp., references, tables.

Subjects: 1. Trends and Change in Marriage and Family / Family Life in
   Foreign Countries; 2. Organizations and Services to Families /
   Physical Health and the Family.

655 Levin, Herman. "Income Alternatives for Poor Families."   FAMILY
COORDINATOR 24, 3 (July 1975): 303-13.   11 pp., references, tables.

Subjects: 1. Organizations and Services to Families / Economics and the
   Family; 2. Families with Special Problems / Family Stress.

656 LeVine, Robert A.   "Intergenerational Tensions and Extended
Family Structures in Africa."   In SYMPOSIUM ON THE FAMILY,
INTERGENERATIONAL RELATIONS AND SOCIAL STRUCTURE. DUKE UNIVERSITY,
1963. SOCIAL STRUCTURE AND THE FAMILY: GENERATIONAL RELATIONS, edited by
Ethel Shanas and Gordon Franklin Streib, pp. 188-204. Englewood Cliffs,
NJ: Prentice-Hall, 1965.   17 pp.

Subjects: 1. Trends and Change in Marriage and Family / Family Life in
   Foreign Countries; 2. Family Relationships and Dynamics / Extended
   Family and Kinship Groups.

657 Levitt, Morris. "Negro Student Rebellion against Parental
Political Beliefs."   SOCIAL FORCES 45, 3 (March 1967): 438-39.   2 pp.,
references, tables.

Subjects: 1. Family Relationships and Dynamics / Parent-Child
Relationships; 2. Psychology and Sociology / Sociology.

658 Lewis, Diane K. "The Black Family: Socialization and Sex Roles."
PHYLON 36, 3 (Fall September 1975): 221-37. 17 pp., references, tables.

Subjects: 1. Family Relationships and Dynamics / Family Roles and Sex
Roles.

659 Lewis, Diane K. "A Response to Inequality: Black Women, Racism,
and Sexism." SIGNS: JOURNAL OF WOMEN IN CULTURE AND SOCIETY 3, 2
(Winter 1977): 339-61. 23 pp., references, tables.

Subjects: 1. Family Relationships and Dynamics / Women's Issues; 2.
Psychology and Sociology / Sociology.

660 Lewis, Hylan. "Agenda Paper No. V: The Family: Resources for
Change-Planning Session for the White House Conference 'To Fulfill These
Rights'." In BLACK FAMILIES AND THE MEDIUM OF TELEVISION, edited by
Anthony W. Jackson, pp. 314-43. Ann Arbor, MI: University of Michigan,
Bush Program for Child Development and Social Psychology, 1982. 30 pp.,
references, charts.

Subjects: 1. Trends and Change in Marriage and Family / Family and
Social Change.

661 Lewis, Hylan. "The Changing Negro Family." In SCHOOL CHILDREN IN
THE URBAN SLUM: READINGS IN SOCIAL SCIENCE RESEARCH, edited by Joan
I. Roberts, pp. 397-405. New York: The Free Press, 1967. 9 pp.,
references.

Subjects: 1. Trends and Change in Marriage and Family / Family and
Social Change.

662 Lewis, Hylan. "Childrearing among Low-Income Families." In
POVERTY IN AMERICA: A BOOK OF READINGS (Revised edition), edited by
Louis A. Ferman, Joyce L. Kornbluh and Alan Haber, pp. 433-444. Ann
Arbor, MI: Univeristy of Michigan Press, 1968. 12 pp.

Subjects: 1. Family Relationships and Dynamics / Parent-Child
Relationships; 2. Minority Groups / Family and Social Class.

663 Lewis, Hylan. "Culture, Class and Family Life among Low-Income
Urban Negroes." In EMPLOYMENT, RACE AND POVERTY (1st ed.), edited by
Arthur Max Ross and Herbert Hill, pp. 149-172. New York: Harcourt, Brace
and World, Inc., 1967. 24 pp.

Subjects: 1. Trends and Change in Marriage and Family / Family and
Social Change; 2. Family Relationships and Dynamics / Family
Relationships; 3. Minority Groups / Family and Social Class.

664 Lichtman, Allan J. and Challinor, Joan R., eds. KIN AND
COMMUNITIES: FAMILIES IN AMERICA. Smithsonian International Symposia
Series. Washington, D.C.: Smithsonian Institution Press, 1979. 335
pp., bibliography, illustrations, index; ISBN:0-87474-608-6; LC:78-
24246.

Subjects: 1. Family Relationships and Dynamics / Extended Family and
Kinship Groups; 2. Aids for Theory and Research / Family Theory; 3. /
Collected Works.

Proceedings of a Smithsonian Institution Symposium held in
Washington, DC, June 14-17, 1977.

Notes: Bibliography: pp. 319-324.

665 Lieberman, Leonard. "The Emerging Model of the Black Family."
INTERNATIONAL JOURNAL OF SOCIOLOGY OF THE FAMILY 3, 1 (January-June
1973): 10-22. 13 pp., references, bibliography.

Subjects: 1. Aids for Theory and Research / Family Theory.

666 Lieberson, Stanley. "Generational Differences among Blacks in the
North." AMERICAN JOURNAL OF SOCIOLOGY 79, 3 (November 1973): 550-65.
16 pp., references, tables.

Subjects: 1. Family Relationships and Dynamics / Nuclear Family.

A generational classification is virtually a standard procedure for
research on European and Asian migrants and their descendants in the
United States. An analogous distinction is rarely applied to the
southern- and northern-born components of the black population living
in the North. Analysis of educational attainment among northern black
residents indicates the existence of substantial differences between
these two generations with respect to this important characteristic.
Likewise, decomposition of the effect of population increase on
changes in urban racial segregation indicates that growth in the
northern- and southern-born generations has opposite consequences.
Therefore, changes in the southern-born proportion among the black
population of the North may greatly distort inferences about the
causes of long-term shifts in the conditions of blacks living in that
region. There are certain implicit theoretical assumptions made when
generation is overlooked in research on blacks or any other racial or
ethnic group. Although these assumptions may be valid in some contact
settings--particularly for later generations--their validity can
usually be resolved through empirical research. (Author's abstract)

667 Liebow, Elliot. "Attitudes toward Marriage and Family among Black
Males in Tally's Corner." MILBANK MEMORIAL FUND QUARTERLY 48, 2 (April
1970): 151-182. 30 pp., references.

Subjects: 1. Family Relationships and Dynamics / Family Roles and Sex
Roles; 2. Marriage and Divorce / Marriage Satisfaction and Prediction
Studies.

668 Liebow, Elliot. "Fathers Without Children." PUBLIC INTEREST 2-5,
5 (Fall 1966): 13-25. 13 pp.

Subjects: 1. Family Relationships and Dynamics / Father-Child
Relationships; 2. / Men's Issues; 3. Marriage and Divorce / Custody
and Child Support.

669 Liebow, Elliot. TALLY'S CORNER: A STUDY OF NEGRO STREETCORNER
MEN. 1st ed. Boston, MA: Little, Brown and Company, 1967. 260 pp.,
bibliography; ISBN:0-316-52513-8; LC:67-18106.

Subjects: 1. Family Relationships and Dynamics / Father-Child
  Relationships; 2. Aids for Theory and Research / Family Research
  Methodology.

  A study of the relationships between lower-income men, their jobs,
  their women, and their children. This edition is a revision of the
  author's thesis.

  Notes: Bibliography: pp. 257-260.

670 Lightfoot, Sara Lawrence. WORLDS: RELATIONSHIPS BETWEEN FAMILIES
AND SCHOOLS. New York: Basic Books, Inc., 1978. 257 pp., references,
bibliography, index.

Subjects: 1. Organizations and Services to Families / Education and the
  Family.

  Chapter 4: 'Black Dreams and Closed Doors' pp. 125-75. This chapter
  discusses the historical and contemporary relationships between Blacks
  and public schooling.

  Notes: Bibliography: pp. 235-43.

671 Lincoln, Charles Eric, ed. THE BLACK EXPERIENCE IN RELIGION.
Garden City, NY: Anchor Press, 1974. 369 pp., references; ISBN:0-385-
01884-3; LC:73-16508.

Subjects: 1. Organizations and Services to Families / Religion and the
  Family.

672 Lindblad, Marion Barr. "A Study of the Relationships between
Family Interaction Patterns and Imaginativeness in Disadvantaged
Preschool Children." (Ph.D. dissertation, Temple University, 1977.)
DISSERTATION ABSTRACTS INTERNATIONAL, 38, 4, Oct. 1977, 1861B.
(University Microfilms No. 7721825.) 143 pp.

Subjects: 1. Family Relationships and Dynamics / Parent-Child
  Relationships; 2. Psychology and Sociology / Psychology.

673 Lindsay, Beverly, ed. COMPARATIVE PERSPECTIVES OF THIRD WORLD
WOMEN: THE IMPACT OF RACE, SEX, AND CLASS. Praeger Special Studies. New
York: Praeger Publishing Co., 1980. 318 pp., bibliography, index;
ISBN:0-03-046651-2; LC:78-19793.

Subjects: 1. Trends and Change in Marriage and Family / Comparative
  Studies--International, Interclass, Sex, and Time Differences; 2.
  Family Relationships and Dynamics / Women's Issues; 3. Minority Groups
  / Ethnic Groups in the United States.

674 Linn, Margaret W., Hunter, Kathleen I. and Perry, Priscilla R.
"Differences by Sex and Ethnicity in the Psychosocial Adjustment of the
Elderly." JOURNAL OF HEALTH AND SOCIAL BEHAVIOR 20, (September 1979):
273-81. 9 pp., references, tables.

Subjects: 1. Family Relationships and Dynamics / Later Years and Aging;
2. Psychology and Sociology / General Attitudes; 3. Aids for Theory
and Research / Statistics.

Elderly men and women from white, black, and Cuban groups were
studied in terms of their psychosocial adjustment. Essentially no sex
differences were found in overall adjustment. However, strong cultural
differences were observed. Elderly blacks showed the best adjustment
when social class and level of disability were held constant.
Disability had more of an effect on level of adjustment than did
social class in the sample studied. Cubans showed the most negative
adjustment, most likely because of their cultural displacement from
Cuba to the United States. The fact that many whites in the sample
were also "displaced persons," having moving from other areas of the
country to Miami when they retired, and the fact that most blacks were
natives may account for the black elderly having the best overall
adjustment. (Authors' abstract)

675 Little, Monroe H.   "Class and Culture: A Reassessment of
E. Franklin Frazier's Black Experience."   THE WESTERN JOURNAL OF BLACK
STUDIES 4, 2 (Summer 1980): 122-31. 10 pp., references, tables.

Subjects: 1. Minority Groups / Family and Social Class.

676 Littlefield, Robert P.   "Self-Disclosure among Some Negro, White,
and Mexican American Adolescents."   JOURNAL OF COUNSELING PSYCHOLOGY 21,
2 (March 1974): 133-36. 4 pp., references, tables.

Subjects: 1. Family Relationships and Dynamics / Parent-Adolescent
  Relationships; 2. Minority Groups / Ethnic Groups in the United
  States.

677 Lloyd, Cynthia B., ed.   SEX, DISCRIMINATION AND THE DIVISION OF
LABOR.   New York: Columbia University Press, 1975.   431 pp.,
bibliography, illustrations; ISBN:0-231-03750-3; LC:74-32175.

Subjects: 1. Organizations and Services to Families / Employment and the
  Family; 2. Family Relationships and Dynamics / Women's Issues; 3.
  Aids for Theory and Research / Family Research Methodology.

Notes: Bibliography: pp 427-31.

678 Loewenberg, Bert and Bogin, Ruth, eds.   BLACK WOMEN IN
NINETEENTH CENTURY AMERICAN LIFE: THEIR WORDS, THEIR THOUGHTS, THEIR
FEELINGS.   University Park, PA: Pennsylvania State University Press,
1976.   355 pp., bibliography, index; ISBN:0-271-01207-2; LC:75-27175.

Subjects: 1. Trends and Change in Marriage and Family / Family Life
  Prior to 1900; 2. Family Relationships and Dynamics / Women's Issues.

Notes: Bibliography: pp. 338-346

679 Logan, Sadye L.   "Race, Identity, and Black Children: A
Developmental Perspective."   SOCIAL CASEWORK: THE JOURNAL OF
CONTEMPORARY SOCIAL WORK 62, 1 (January 1981): 47-56.   10 pp.,
references.

Subjects: 1. Family Relationships and Dynamics / Socialization; 2.
   Family Counseling and Education / Child Development.

680   Long, Charles H.   "Perspectives for a Study of Afro-American
Religion in the United States."   HISTORY OF RELIGIONS 11, 1 (August
1971): 54-66.   13 pp., references.

Subjects: 1. Organizations and Services to Families / Religion and the
   Family.

681   Lorde, Audre.   "Scratching the Surface: Some Notes on Barriers to
Women and Loving."   BLACK SCHOLAR 9, 7 (April 1978): 31-35.   5 pp.,
references.

Subjects: 1. Family Relationships and Dynamics / Women's Issues; 2.
   Mate Selection / Dating, Courtship, and Romanticism.

682   Love, Bette Bonder.   "Self-Esteem in Women Related to Occupational
Status: A Biracial Study."   (Ph.D. dissertation, Northwestern University,
1974.)   DISSERTATION ABSTRACTS INTERNATIONAL, 35, 6, Dec. 1974, 3427A.
(University Microfilms No. 7428675.) 200 pp.

Subjects: 1. Organizations and Services to Families / Employment and the
   Family; 2. Family Relationships and Dynamics / Women's Issues; 3.
   Psychology and Sociology / Self-Esteem.

683   Lowry, Waldra Greene.   "Sex-Role Attitudes and Stereotypes among
Black College Students."   (Ph.D. dissertation, The Florida State
University, 1981.)   DISSERTATION ABSTRACTS INTERNATIONAL, 42, 11, May
1982, 4945A.   (University Microfilms No. 8208744.) 114 pp.

Subjects: 1. Family Relationships and Dynamics / Family Roles and Sex
   Roles.

684   Luckraft, Dorothy, ed.   BLACK AWARENESS: IMPLICATIONS FOR BLACK
PATIENT CARE.   New York: American Journal of Nursing Company, 1976.   43
pp., bibliography; LC:75-25321.

Subjects: 1. Organizations and Services to Families / Physical Health
   and the Family; 2. Aids for Theory and Research / Collected Works.

   Papers presented at a conference held October 18-19, 1974 at Palo
   Alto, California and coordinated by Continuing Education in Nursing,
   the University of California, San Francisco. (NUC)

685   Lyles, Michael R. and Carter, James H.   "Myths and Strengths of the
Black Family: A Historical and Sociological Contribution to Family
Therapy."   JOURNAL OF THE NATIONAL MEDICAL ASSOCIATION 74, 11 (November
1982): 1119-1123.   5 pp., references.

Subjects: 1. Family Counseling and Education / Family Therapy; 2. Aids
   for Theory and Research / Critiques and Analyses of Family Research
   Literature.

686   Mabrey, Wilbert Gene.   "African-American Polygynous Relatedness: An
Exploratory Study Utilizing Phenomenological Techniques."   (Ph.D.
dissertation, California School of Professional Psychology, 1978.)

DISSERTATION ABSTRACTS INTERNATIONAL, 39, 7, Jan. 1979, 3528B.
(University Microfilms No. 7901751.) 119 pp.

Subjects: 1. Trends and Change in Marriage and Family / Alternative
Family Forms; 2. Family Relationships and Dynamics / Husband-Wife
Relationships; 3. Marriage and Divorce / Marriage Customs and Forms.

687 MacDonald, Mairi T. and Stewart, J. B. "Nutrition and Low-Income
Families." THE NUTRITION SOCIETY PROCEEDINGS 33, 1 (May 1974): 75-78.
4 pp., references, tables.

Subjects: 1. Organizations and Services to Families / Physical Health
and the Family.

688 Mack, Delores E. "The Power Relationship in Black Families and
White Families." JOURNAL OF PERSONALITY AND SOCIAL PSYCHOLOGY 30, 3
(September 1974): 409-13. 5 pp., references, tables.

Subjects: 1. Trends and Change in Marriage and Family / Comparative
Studies--International, Interclass, Sex, and Time Differences; 2.
Family Relationships and Dynamics / Power in the Family.

This study focused on the power relationship in 80 married couples
selected to vary by race (40 black, 40 white), and class (40 middle
class, 40 working class). Marital power was measured by three tasks: a
questionnaire, which couples first filled out individually, then
jointly; a discussion, in which couples attempted to arrive at a joint
statement about two topics; and a bargaining situation, which reqired
couples to bargain over four items imported from Africa. The results
indicated that working-class husbands were significantly more powerful
than middle-class husbands in the questionnaire situation. No other
important racial or class differences were found. (Author's abstract)

689 Macke, Anne Statham and Morgan, William R. "Maternal Employment,
Race, and Work Orientation of High School Girls." SOCIAL FORCES 57, 1
(September 1978): 187-204. 18 pp., references, bibliography, tables,
charts.

Subjects: 1. Organizations and Services to Families / Employment and the
Family; 2. Family Counseling and Education / Adolescence.

Socialization by mothers, a key determinant of daughters' work
orientation, has generally been thought to operate via positive role-
modeling. But socialization also occurs through negative modeling,
normative influence, and conditional modeling. Using a sample of
Louisville high school senior girls and their mothers, we tested
whether the differential presence of these processes helps to explain
why higher percentages of black than white women work. Other than
negative modeling for black girls whose mothers hold blue-collar jobs,
both groups of girls have strong similarities, with conditional
positive modeling predominating. To the extent that these racial
patterns can be generalized, they predict that expanded economic
opportunities for black families will reduce racial differences in
rates at which mothers are employed. These and other findings suggest
that at least for the near future, current family roles, in which
breadwinning is primarily the husband's responsibility, are not likely

to be radically altered by married women's increasing propensity to work. (Authors' abstract)

690 Mackinlay, Peter W. "The New England Puritan Attitude toward Black Slavery." OLD-TIME NEW ENGLAND 63, 3 (Winter 1973): 81-87. 7 pp., references.

Subjects: 1. Trends and Change in Marriage and Family / Family Life Prior to 1900.

691 Madison, Bernice Q. and Schapiro, Michael. "Black Adoption-Issues and Policies: Review of the Literature." SOCIAL SERVICE REVIEW 47, 4 (December 1973): 531-60. 28 pp., references, bibliography, tables.

Subjects: 1. Organizations and Services to Families / Adoption and Adoption Services; 2. Aids for Theory and Research / Critiques and Analyses of Family Research Literature.

This paper discusses developments in black adoption from 1945 to the present. Special attention is given to efforts of the social work profession to increase and improve adoptive services for black children. These efforts are related both to the broad social forces that influence this area of child welfare practice and to quantitative outcomes. Factors that increase or decrease effectiveness in reaching desired objectives are also analyzed. (Authors' abstract)

692 Mahone, Jack Randall. "The Influence of Family Relations upon Socially Desiring Behavior of Black and Caucasian Preschool Children." (M.S. thesis, California State University, Long Beach, 1977.) DISSERTATION ABSTRACTS INTERNATIONAL, 15, 2, June 1977, 84. (University Microfilms No. 139580.) 126 pp.

Subjects: 1. Family Relationships and Dynamics / Parent-Child Relationships; 2. / Socialization; 3. Family Counseling and Education / Child Development.

693 Mahoney, E. R. "Premarital Coitus and the Southern Black: A Comment." JOURNAL OF MARRIAGE AND THE FAMILY 41, 4 (November 1979): 694-95. 2 pp., references, tables.

Subjects: 1. Family Relationships and Dynamics / Premarital Couples; 2. Mate Selection / Cohabiting.

694 Markides, Kyriakos S. and Hazuda, Helen P. "Ethnicity and Infant Mortality in Texas Counties." SOCIAL BIOLOGY 4, 27 (Winter 1980): 261-271. 11 pp., references, bibliography, tables.

Subjects: 1. Issues Related to Reproduction / Population Studies; 2. Families with Special Problems / Death, Bereavement and the Family; 3. Minority Groups / Ethnic Groups in the United States.

695 Malina, Robert M., Mueller, William H. and Holman, John D. "Parent-Child Correlations and Heritability of Stature in Philadelphia Black and White Children 6-12 Years of Age." HUMAN BIOLOGY 48, 3 (September 1976): 475-86. 12 pp., references, tables.

Subjects: 1. Family Relationships and Dynamics / Parent-Child
Relationships.

696 Malone, Rubie M. "The Relationship of Family--Non-Family Support
to the Academic Performance of Urban Black Disadvantaged
College Students." (D.S.W. dissertation, Columbia University, 1982.)
DISSERTATION ABSTRACTS INTERNATIONAL, 43, 5, Nov. 1982, 1704A.
(University Microfilms No. 8222440.) 154 pp.

Subjects: 1. Organizations and Services to Families / Education and the
Family; 2. Families with Special Problems / Achievement and the
Family.

697 Markides, Kyriakos S. "Mortality among Minority Populations: A
Review of Recent Patterns and Trends." PUBLIC HEALTH REPORTS 98, 3
(Summer 1983): 252-60. 9 pp., references, tables.

Subjects: 1. Families with Special Problems / Death, Bereavement and the
Family.

698 Martin, Elmer P. and Martin, Joanne Mitchell. THE BLACK EXTENDED
FAMILY. Chicago: University of Chicago Press, 1978. 129 pp.,
references, bibliography, illustrations, tables, charts, index ; ISBN:0-
226-50796-3; LC:77-17058.

Subjects: 1. Trends and Change in Marriage and Family / Family Life in
the United States; 2. Family Relationships and Dynamics / Extended
Family and Kinship Groups.

A study that focuses on describing the composition of the black
extended family; major functions and goals of the family; survival
techniques used by the black extended family; the relationships
between   young/old,   male/female,   lower-/middle-class   members;
urban/rural dwellers; the affects of social change; and the prospects
for   survival   of   the   black   extended family. (From authors'
introduction)

Notes: Bibliography: pp. 121-124.

699 Martindale, Melanie and Poston, Dudley L., Jr. "Variations in
Veteran/Nonveteran Earnings Patterns among WWII, Korea, and Vietnam War
Cohorts." ARMED FORCES AND SOCIETY 5, 2 (February 1979): 219-43. 25
pp., references, tables, charts.

Subjects: 1. Organizations and Services to Families / Economics and the
Family.

700 Martineau, William H. "Informal Social Ties among Urban Black
Americans: Some New Data and a Review of the Problem." JOURNAL OF BLACK
STUDIES 8, 1 (September 1977): 83-104. 22 pp., references,
bibliography, tables.

Subjects: 1. Minority Groups / Family and Social Class; 2. Aids for
Theory and Research / Critiques and Analyses of Family Research
Literature.

701 Mathis, Arthur. "Contrasting Approaches to the Study of Black
Families." JOURNAL OF MARRIAGE AND THE FAMILY 40, 4 (November 1978):
667-76. 10 pp., references, bibliography.

Subjects: 1. Aids for Theory and Research / Family Research Methodology.

   This paper examines two competing perspectives which have influenced
   the study of black families. The first perspective is related to the
   early research by E. Franklin Frazier and has subsequently impacted
   the formulation of social policy. This view assumes that black
   families are patterned after the dominant culture. Whereas, the other
   perspective holds that at least part of black family life is linked to
   African forms of culture. Theoretical and empirical studies are
   presented in an attempt to show where future research would be most
   useful in developing a cohesive view of the nature of black families.
   (Author's abstract)

702 Matthews, Basil. CRISIS OF THE WEST INDIAN FAMILY: A SAMPLE STUDY.
Westport, CT: Greenwood Press, 1971. 117 pp., bibliography; ISBN:0-
8371-3127-8; LC:75-98782.

Subjects: 1. Marriage and Divorce / Marriage Satisfaction and Prediction
   Studies; 2. Minority Groups / Blacks in the Caribbean.

   Notes: Reprint of 1953 edition. First published in 1947 under the
   title: THE NEGRO FAMILY IN TRINIDAD. Bibliography: pp. 115-117.

703 Maxwell, Joseph W. "Rural Negro Father Participation in Family
Activities." RURAL SOCIOLOGY 33, 1 (March 1968): 80-83. 4 pp.,
references.

Subjects: 1. Family Relationships and Dynamics / Power in the Family;
   2. / Men's Issues.

704 Mayo, Julia. "The New Black Feminism: A Minority Report." In
CONTEMPORARY SEXUAL BEHAVIOR: CRITICAL ISSUES IN THE 1970'S, edited by
Joseph Zubin and John Money, pp. 175-186. Baltimore, MD: The Johns
Hopkins University Press, 1973. 12 pp.

Subjects: 1. Family Relationships and Dynamics / Women's Issues; 2.
   Sexual Attitudes and Behavior / Sexual Attitudes and Behavior.

705 Mays, Rose M. "Primary Health Care and the Black Family." NURSE
PRACTITIONER 4, 6 (November-December 1979): 13,15,20-21. 4 pp.,
references, charts.

Subjects: 1. Organizations and Services to Families / Physical Health
   and the Family.

706 McAdoo, Harriette. "Family Therapy in the Black Community."
AMERICAN JOURNAL OF ORTHOPSYCHIATRY 47, 1 (January 1977): 75-79. 5 pp.,
references.

Subjects: 1. Family Counseling and Education / Family Therapy.

   Black, upwardly mobile families face all the stresses experienced by
   other families dealing with development crises and economic changes,

but are subject to the additional strain of discrimination. Support, often unavailable from the community, is received instead from the family and others involved in the kinship network. Treatment strategies designed for the unique situation of the black family are proposed. (Author's abstract)

707 McAdoo, Harriette P. "A Review of the Literature Related to Family Therapy in the Black Community." JOURNAL OF CONTEMPORARY PSYCHOTHERAPY 9, 1 (Summer 1977): 15-19. 5 pp., references.

Subjects: 1. Family Counseling and Education / Family Therapy; 2. Aids for Theory and Research / Critiques and Analyses of Family Research Literature.

708 McAdoo, Harriette P. "Stress Absorbing Systems in Black Families." FAMILY RELATIONS 31, 4 (October 1982): 479-88. 10 pp.

Subjects: 1. Trends and Change in Marriage and Family / Social Mobility as it Affects the Family; 2. Family Relationships and Dynamics / Extended Family and Kinship Groups; 3. Families with Special Problems / Family Stress.

Upwardly mobile black families were examined in an attempt to ascertain the possible relationships between stress, economic mobility and kin network support within their social/interactional systems. Despite high ratings on stress and high frequencies of major life change events, most families studied exhibited high levels of satisfaction with family life situations. Families upwardly mobile over three generations and in the highest social status classification had the lowest stress scores. Kin support systems greatly facilitated stress management. (Author's abstract)

709 McAdoo, Harriette Pipes, ed. BLACK FAMILIES. Sage Focus Editions, No. 41. Beverly Hills, CA: Sage Publications, Inc., 1981. 303 pp., bibliography; ISBN:0-8039-1741-4; LC:81-14442.

Subjects: 1. Trends and Change in Marriage and Family / Family Life in the United States; 2. Family Relationships and Dynamics / Family Relationships; 3. Aids for Theory and Research / Collected Works.

Addressing some unresolved issues regarding Black families, this interdisciplinary anthology of twenty essays focuses on: diverse conceptualizations of Black families; demographic characteristics, economics, and mobility; Black attitudes toward pair-bonding; socialization in Black families; Black family policies and advocacy.

710 McAdoo, Harriette Pipes. "Black Women and the Extended Family Support Network." In THE BLACK WOMAN, edited by La Frances Rodgers-Rose, pp. 125-44. Beverly Hills, CA: Sage Publications, Inc., 1980. 20 pp.

Subjects: 1. Family Relationships and Dynamics / Extended Family and Kinship Groups; 2. / Women's Issues.

[The author] explores the differential involvement and support given Black mothers who are single parents and those mothers who have husbands. The. . .sample was 175 mothers; 26% were single and 74% were

married. The mothers. . .were involved extensively in the kin-help
exchange network. The kin exchange took the form of child care,
financial assistance, and emotional support. All the mothers were
middle class. Single mothers received more help than married mothers.
However, both groups of mothers felt obligated to help poorer members
of the family and they in turn, expected someone in the family who was
substantially better off than they were to help them. The data support
the importance of the extended family system in maintaining economic
and emotional stability. (From the editor's remarks)

711 McAdoo, Harriette Pipes. "Commentary on Joseph Scott's 'Black
Polygamous Family Formation'." ALTERNATIVE LIFESTYLES 3, 4 (November
1980): 383-88. 6 pp.

Subjects: 1. Trends and Change in Marriage and Family / Alternative
    Family Forms; 2. Family Relationships and Dynamics / Women's Issues;
    3. Mate Selection / Cohabiting.

The essay critiques the polygny model of Joseph Scott in terms of the
pressures felt by young, poor, Black women with children who often
enter into extramarital unions with married men as they attempt to
find economic and emotional security. (Author's abstract)

712 McAdoo, Harriette Pipes, proj. dir. EXTENDED FAMILY SUPPORT OF
SINGLE BLACK MOTHERS: FINAL REPORT. Columbia, MD: Columbia Research
Systems, Inc., March 1983. 217 pp., bibliography, tables.

Subjects: 1. Family Relationships and Dynamics / Extended Family and
    Kinship Groups; 2. / Single Parent Families; 3. Aids for Theory and
    Research / Family Theory.

Notes: A report submitted to the National Institute of Mental Health,
Public Health Service, Human Services. Bibliography: pp. 142-45.

713 McAdoo, Harriette Pipes. "Factors Related to Stability in
Upwardly Mobile Black Families." JOURNAL OF MARRIAGE AND THE FAMILY 40,
4 (November 1978): 761-68. 16 pp., references, tables, charts.

Subjects: 1. Trends and Change in Marriage and Family / Social Mobility
    as it Affects the Family; 2. Minority Groups / Family and Social
    Class; 3. Aids for Theory and Research / Family Research Methodology.

The impact of upward mobility over three generations, on the extended
kin network of black parents in the mid-Atlantic area was examined.
Extensive involvement had been maintained by those born in both the
middle and working classes and those living in urban and suburban
sites. The reciprocal obligations of the help exchange patterns were
not perceived as excessive, but were stronger for those born in the
working class. Educational achievement and maternal employment peaked
in the generation in which mobility occurred. Kin interaction was high
with low geographic mobility. Results indicate that extended help
patterns are culturally rather than solely economically based.
(Author's abstract)

714 McAdoo, Harriette Pipes. "Minority Families." In BLAMING THE
VICTIM, by William Ryan, pp. 176-195. New York: Pantheon Books, 1971.
20 pp.

Subjects: 1. Family Relationships and Dynamics / Family Relationships.

715 McAdoo, John. "Black Father and Child Interactions." In BLACK MEN, edited by Lawrence E. Gary, pp. 115-30. Beverly Hill, CA: Sage Publications, Inc., 1981. 16 pp.

Subjects: 1. Family Relationships and Dynamics / Father-Child Relationships; 2. Aids for Theory and Research / Family Research Methodology.

The purposes of this study were (1) to determine the patterns of verbal interaction that take place between the Black father and his child, (2) to determine the types of nonverbal interaction that take place between the Black father and his child, (3) to explore the father's attitudes toward child-rearing. The goal was to observe the process of interaction that takes place between a Black father and his preschool child, using methodologies developed by observing other ethnic-group fathers. (From author's text)

716 McBroom, Patricia. "The Black Matriarchy: Healthy or Pathological?" SCIENCE NEWS 94, (October 1968): 393-95. 3 pp., illustrations.

Subjects: 1. Family Relationships and Dynamics / Single Parent Families; 2. / Power in the Family; 3. Aids for Theory and Research / Family Theory.

717 McConahay, Shirley A. and McConahay, John B. "Sexual Permissiveness, Sex Role Rigidity, and Violence Across Cultures." JOURNAL OF SOCIAL ISSUES 33, 2 (Spring 1977): 134-43. 10 pp., references.

Subjects: 1. Family Relationships and Dynamics / Family Roles and Sex Roles; 2. Sexual Attitudes and Behavior / Sexual Attitudes and Behavior; 3. Families with Special Problems / Family Violence.

718 McCord, William M. et al. LIFESTYLES IN THE BLACK GHETTO. 1st edition New York: W. W. Norton and Co., 1969. 334 pp., references; LC:69-18479.

Subjects: 1. Trends and Change in Marriage and Family / Family and Social Change; 2. Family Relationships and Dynamics / Stages in Family Life Cycle; 3. Aids for Theory and Research / Family Research Methodology.

719 McCormick, E. Patricia. ATTITUDES TOWARD ABORTION: EXPERIENCES OF SELECTED BLACK AND WHITE WOMEN. Lexington, MA: Lexington Books, 1975. 160 pp., bibliography, appendices, index; ISBN:0-669-96594-4; LC:74-25054.

Subjects: 1. Issues Related to Reproduction / Abortion.

The focus of this study was on the attitudes toward abortion and not on the abortion behavior of the study population. . .The sample comprised 200 women who were applying for an abortion at three facilities in the Baltimore-Washington metropolitan area. . . There is a substantial differential in racial attitudes toward abortion, with black women being less receptive to the use of induced abortion either as a supplement or as an alternative to contraception. This difference persisted throughout controls for contraceptive use, religion, education of respondent, education of respondent's mother, current economic status, marital status, future child desired, and number of siblings, although at times the differences appeared minimal. Only when education of respondent's father and parity were introduced did the black women respond more favorably than the white respondents, and then only within certain categories. (From author's 'Summary and Conclusions')

Notes: Bibliography: pp. 140-151.

720 McCummings, Le Verne, comp. THE BLACK FAMILY: A CONSOLIDATION OF PAPERS PRESENTED TO THE NATIONAL CONFERENCE OF BLACK SOCIAL WORKERS, FEBRUARY 21-23, 1969. Philadelphia, PA: N.p., 1969. 159 pp., bibliography, charts; LC:75-105472.

Subjects: 1. Trends and Change in Marriage and Family / Family Life in the United States; 2. / Family and Social Change; 3. Psychology and Sociology / Racial Attitudes.

Notes: Bibliography: pp. 158-159.

721 McCurdy, Paula Carol Kresser. "Sex Role, Decision Making Practices, Marital Satisfaction and Family Problems with Economically Disadvantaged Anglo, Black, and Chicano Couples." (Ph.D. dissertation, University of Missouri-Kansas City, 1978.) DISSERTATION ABSTRACTS INTERNATIONAL, 38, 11, May 1978, 6970A. (University Microfilms No. 7805663.) 110 pp.

Subjects: 1. Family Relationships and Dynamics / Family Roles and Sex Roles; 2. Marriage and Divorce / Marriage Satisfaction and Prediction Studies; 3. Minority Groups / Ethnic Groups in the United States.

722 McDonald, Robert L. and Gynther, Malcolm D. "Relationship of Self and Ideal-Self: Descriptions with Sex, Race and Class in Southern Adolescents." JOURNAL OF PERSONALITY AND SOCIAL PSYCHOLOGY 1, 1 (January 1965): 85-88. 4 pp., references, tables.

Subjects: 1. Psychology and Sociology / Self-Esteem; 2. Family Counseling and Education / Adolescence.

This study evaluated the effects of sex, race, and social class on the self- and ideal-self-concepts of adolescent Ss. Interpersonal Check List data were obtained from 261 Negro and 211 white high school seniors from urban segregated schools whose social class was determined on the basis of parental occupations as reported by the students. Sex and race markedly influenced the results, but class was not found to have any effect. Negro students obtained higher dominance and love scores than the white students for self-ratings, but lower scores on ideal descriptions. Male's self- and ideal-self-ratings yielded higher scores on dominance while females' ratings yielded higher scores on the love variable. There was less discrepancy between ideal and self-ratings of: (a) Negroes compared with whites, (b) males compared with females on dominance, and (c) females compared with males on love. (Authors' abstract)

723 McFadden, Johnnie. "Stylistic Counseling of the Black Family." In
BLACK MARRIAGE AND FAMILY THERAPY, edited by Constance E. Obudho,
pp. 209-226. Westport, CT: Greenwood Press, 1983. 18 pp.

Subjects: 1. Family Counseling and Education / Family Therapy; 2. /
  Marital and Family Enrichment.

724 McGuigan, Dorothy G., ed. NEW RESEARCH ON WOMEN AND SEX ROLES AT
THE UNIVERSITY OF MICHIGAN: PAPERS. Ann Arbor, MI: University of
Michigan, Center for Continuing Education of Women, 1976. 403 pp.,
bibliography, index; LC:76-375522.

Subjects: 1. Family Relationships and Dynamics / Women's Issues; 2.
  Sexual Attitudes and Behavior / Sexual Attitudes and Behavior; 3. Aids
  for Theory and Research / Family Research Methodology.

Regarding work, family, and social change, Black women are examined
cross-culturally in three studies (one each on): the Sea Islands of
Southeastern United States [see the essay by Agbasegbe]; Cauca Valley,
Columbia, South America; and West Africa.

Notes: Papers presented at a conference sponsored in the Spring of
1975 by the Center for Continuing Education of Women. (JAH)

725 McLaughlin, Clara J., Frisby, Donald R., McLaughlin, Richard A. and
Williams, Melvin W. THE BLACK PARENTS HANDBOOK: A GUIDE TO HEALTHY
PREGNANCY, BIRTH AND CHILD CARE. 1st edition New York: Harcourt, Brace
and Jovanovich, Inc., 1976. 220 pp., illustrations, index; ISBN:0-15-
113185-6; LC:75-43986.

Subjects: 1. Issues Related to Reproduction / Pregnancy and Child Birth;
  2. Family Counseling and Education / Education for Parenthood.

A discussion on aspects of parenthood ranging from the period of
conception until the sixth year of the child.

726 McMillan, Sylvia R. "Aspirations of Low-Income Mothers." JOURNAL
OF MARRIAGE AND THE FAMILY 29, 2 (May 1967): 282-87. 6 pp., tables,
charts.

Subjects: 1. Family Relationships and Dynamics / Mother-Child
  Relationships.

727 McNair, Charles L. "The Black Family Is Not a Matriarchal Family
Form." NEGRO EDUCATIONAL REVIEW 26, 2/3 (March-July 1975): 93-100. 8
pp., references.

Subjects: 1. Aids for Theory and Research / Family Theory.

728 McPherson, James M. et al. "The Black Family in Urban America."
In BLACKS IN AMERICA: BIBLIOGRAPHIC ESSAYS (1st ed.), by James M.
McPherson, Lawrence B. Holland, James M. Banner, Jr., Nancy J. Weiss and
Michael D. Bell, pp. 364-72. Garden City, NY: Doubleday and Co., Inc.,
1971. 9 pp., references.

Subjects: 1. Trends and Change in Marriage and Family / Family Life in
  the United States; 2. / Family and Social Change.

729 McPherson, James M., Holland, Lawrence B., Banner, James M., Jr.,
Weiss, Nancy J., Bell, Michael D. et al. BLACKS IN AMERICA:
BIBLIOGRAPHIC ESSAYS. 1st ed. Garden City, NY: Doubleday and Co., Inc.,
1971. 430 pp.; LC:70-164723.

Subjects: 1. Aids for Theory and Research / Classified Bibliographies of
   Family Literature.

730 McQueen, Adele Bolden. "The Influence of Increased Parent-Child
Verbal Interaction on the Language Facility of Preschool Inner-City
Black Children." (Ph.D. dissertation, The Catholic University of
America, 1979.) DISSERTATION ABSTRACTS INTERNATIONAL, 40, 11, May 1980,
5719A-5720A. (University Microfilms No. 8008352.) 181 pp.

Subjects: 1. Family Relationships and Dynamics / Mother-Child
   Relationships; 2. Family Counseling and Education / Early Childhood
   Education.

731 McQueen, Albert J. "The Adaptations of Urban Black Families:
Trends, Problems and Issues." In THE AMERICAN FAMILY: DYING OR
DEVELOPING?, edited by David Reiss and Howard A. Hoffman, pp. 79-101.
New York: Plenum Press, 1979. 23 pp.

Subjects: 1. Trends and Change in Marriage and Family / Family Life in
   the United States; 2. Aids for Theory and Research / Family Theory.

732 McRoy, Ruth Gail Murdock. "A Comparative Study of the Self-Concept
of Transracially and Inracially Adopted Black Children." (Ph.D.
dissertation, The University of Texas at Austin, 1981.) DISSERTATION
ABSTRACTS INTERNATIONAL, 42, 3, Sept. 1981, 1318A-1319A. (University
Microfilms No. 8119339.) 394 pp.

Subjects: 1. Organizations and Services to Families / Adoption and
   Adoption Services; 2. Family Relationships and Dynamics /
   Socialization; 3. Psychology and Sociology / Self-Esteem.

733 Meeker, Edward. "Freedom, Economic Opportunity, and Fertility:
Black Americans, 1860-1910." ECONOMIC INQUIRY 15, 3 (July 1977): 397-
412. 16 pp., references, bibliography, tables.

Subjects: 1. Trends and Change in Marriage and Family / Family Life
   Prior to 1900; 2. Organizations and Services to Families / Economics
   and the Family; 3. Issues Related to Reproduction / Fertility Rates.

Black fertility declined sharply following Reconstruction.
Demographers argue that explanations of post-bellum white fertility
behavior are inapplicable to blacks. This paper hypothesizes that the
reduced fertility was due to economic factors. An economic model of
fertility is developed and estimated econometrically; it is consistent
with the fertility experience of both races . It is concluded that
several products of emancipation, including urbanization, increased
literacy levels, and a shift in the economic burden of child
maintenance from the slave owner to the family, were instrumental in
increasing the opportunity cost of black children to their parents.
(Author's abstract)

734 Meggerson-Moore, Joyce Ann. "A Survey of a Sample of Black
Families' Views of the Counseling Profession." (Ph.D. dissertation,
Saint Louis University, 1979.) DISSERTATION ABSTRACTS INTERNATIONAL,
40, 5, Nov. 1979, 2484A. (University Microfilms No. 7923655.) 153 pp.

Subjects: 1. Family Counseling and Education / Family Therapy.

735 Melton, Willie and Otto, Lothen B.   "Antecedents of Self-
Satisfaction and Marital Stability among Black Males." JOURNAL OF
SOCIAL AND BEHAVIOR SCIENCES 25, 4 (Fall 1979): 106-17.   12 pp.,
references, bibliography, tables, charts.

Subjects: 1. Marriage and Divorce / Marriage Satisfaction and Prediction
    Studies.

Structural equation models are estimated to determine the relative
effects of labor force participation, income, and selected demographic
characteristics of black husbands and wives on husband's self-
satisfaction and, subsequently, on marital stability. The analysis is
based on five-wave panel data (1968-1972) from a sub-sample of black
heads of households (N=460) drawn from two national probability
samples. The theoretically derived models are not powerful predictors
of either variation in self-satisfaction or marital   stability.
Examination of the relative effects of the antecedents reveals that
neither wife's income nor her employment has adverse consequences for
the black husband's self-satisfaction, but husband's steady employment
proves to be an important source for his self-satisfaction. Increases
in wife's earnings produce negative effects on marital stability;
husband's sense of self-satisfaction has a small positive effect on
the stability of his marriage, and black marital stability increases
with husband's age. The implications of these and related findings for
previous explanation of the relatively high rate of marital
instability among blacks are discussed and directions for future
research on marital stability of blacks are suggested. (Authors'
abstract)

736 Melton, Willie and Thomas, Darwin. "Instrumental and Expressive
Values in Mate Selection of Black and White College Students." JOURNAL
OF MARRIAGE AND THE FAMILY 38, 3 (August 1976): 509-17.   9 pp.,
references, tables.

Subjects: 1. Mate Selection / Mate Selection, Differential Patterns.

The objective of this study is to investigate differences between
black and white college students' values concerning mate selection.
The relative importance of 12 desired traits in a potential mate,
divided equally into what are termed instrumental and expressive
traits, is examined. The general conclusions are: (1)black respondents
tend to attach greater importance to the instrumental dimension than
white respondents; (2)there is little difference between black and
white respondents in the degree of importance of the expressive
dimension; (3) black males place considerably more emphasis on
instrumental traits than white males; and (4) the importance of
instrumental traits is inversely related to socioeconomic status.
(Author's abstract)

737 Melton, Willie, III. "Self-Satisfaction and Marital Stability
among Black Males: Socioeconomic and Demographic Antecedents." (Ph.D.
dissertation, Washington State University, 1976.) DISSERTATION
ABSTRACTS INTERNATIONAL, 37, 8, Feb. 1977, 5387A-5388A. (University
Microfilms No. 772872.) 107 pp.

Subjects: 1. Family Relationships and Dynamics / Husband-Wife
   Relationships; 2. / Men's Issues; 3. Marriage and Divorce / Marriage
   Satisfaction and Prediction Studies.

738 MENTAL AND PHYSICAL HEALTH PROBLEMS OF BLACK WOMEN, WASHINGTON,
D.C., MARCH 29-30, 1974. PROCEEDINGS. Washington, D.C.: Black Women's
Community Development Foundation, 1975. 136 pp., illustrations; LC:75-
325602.

Subjects: 1. Organizations and Services to Families / Mental Health and
   the Family; 2. / Physical Health and the Family; 3. Family
   Relationships and Dynamics / Women's Issues.

Notes: The Library of Congress main entry is by title:
Miniconsultation on the Mental and Physical Health Problems of Black
Women, Washington, D.C., March 29-30, 1974. Proceedings.

739 Mercer, Charles V. "Interrelations among Family Stability, Family
Composition, Residence and Race." JOURNAL OF MARRIAGE AND THE FAMILY
29, 3 (August 1967): 456-60. 5 pp., references, tables.

Subjects: 1. Family Relationships and Dynamics / Family Relationships;
   2. Aids for Theory and Research / Statistics.

740 Miller, Elizabeth W. and Fisher, Mary L., comps. THE NEGRO IN
AMERICA: A BIBLIOGRAPHY. 2nd edition, revised and enlarged Cambridge,
MA: Harvard University Press, 1970. 351 pp.; ISBN:674-60703-1; LC:71-
120319.

Subjects: 1. Trends and Change in Marriage and Family / Family Life in
   the United States; 2. Aids for Theory and Research / Classified
   Bibliographies of Family Literature.

Notes: Forward by Thomas H. Pettigrew. Materials appropriate for
grades 10-12.

741 Miller, Kent S. and Dreger, Ralph Mason, eds. COMPARATIVE STUDIES
OF BLACKS AND WHITES IN THE UNITED STATES. New York and London: Seminar
Press, 1973. 572 pp., bibliography; ISBN:0-12-873650-X; LC:72-82126.

Subjects: 1. Trends and Change in Marriage and Family / Family and
   Social Change; 2. / Comparative Studies--International, Interclass,
   Sex, and Time Differences; 3. Aids for Theory and Research / Collected
   Works.

742 Miller, Randall M., ed. "DEAR MASTER": LETTERS OF A SLAVE FAMILY.
Ithaca, NY: Cornell University Press, 1978. 281 pp., bibliography,
illustrations, index; ISBN:0-8014-1134-3; LC:77-90907.

Subjects: 1. Trends and Change in Marriage and Family / Family Life
   Prior to 1900.

This book relates the story of an American slave family, the Skipwiths, a family separated by time, place, and circumstance from their Virginia home. Some members of the family were freed to emigrate to Liberia, a frontier society in Africa; others were settled on an absentee-owned plantation in Alabama, then the frontier of the cotton South. . .Ironically, the slave owner who separated them also joined them: he established a correspondence with two generations of Skipwiths, and through him the family bridged the two continents of their residence. This correspondence--probably the largest and fullest epistolary record left by an American slave family--traces the history of the planter, the freedman, and the slaves. It is the substance of this book. (From author's 'Preface')

Notes: Bibliography: pp. 265-269.

743 Milner, Christina and Milner, Richard. BLACK PLAYERS: THE SECRET WORLD OF BLACK PIMPS. Boston, MA: Little, Brown and Company, 1972.   329 pp., bibliography, illustrations; ISBN:0-316-57411-2; LC:72-175475.

Subjects: 1. Sexual Attitudes and Behavior / Prostitution.

Notes: A revision of Christina Milner's thesis, University of California, Berkeley, 1970. Bibliography: pp. 325-329.

744 Mindel, Charles H. and Habenstein, Robert Wesley, eds. ETHNIC FAMILIES IN AMERICA: PATTERNS AND VARIATIONS. New York: Elsevier North-Holland, Inc., 1976.   429 pp., bibliography; ISBN:0-444-99022-4; LC:75-40654.

Subjects: 1. Trends and Change in Marriage and Family / Family and Social Change; 2. Minority Groups / Ethnic Groups in the United States; 3. Aids for Theory and Research / Collected Works.

745 Mindel, Charles H. and Habenstein, Robert Wesley, eds. ETHNIC FAMILIES IN AMERICA: PATTERNS AND VARIATIONS. 2nd ed. New York: Elsevier North-Holland, Inc., 1981.   432 pp., bibliography; ISBN:0-444-99090-9; LC:81-7787.

Subjects: 1. Trends and Change in Marriage and Family / Family and Social Change; 2. Minority Groups / Ethnic Groups in the United States; 3. Aids for Theory and Research / Collected Works.

746 Mirowsky, John, II and Ross, Catherine E. "Minority Status, Ethnic Culture, and Distress: A Comparison of Blacks, Whites, Mexicans, and Mexican Americans." AMERICAN JOURNAL OF SOCIOLOGY 86, 3 (November 1980): 479-95. 17 pp., references, bibliography, tables, charts.

Subjects: 1. Families with Special Problems / Family Stress; 2. Minority Groups / Ethnic Groups in the United States.

747 Misra, B. D. "Correlates of Males Attitudes toward Family Planning." In SOCIOLOGICAL CONTRIBUTIONS TO FAMILY PLANNING RESEARCH, edited by Donald Joseph Bogue, pp. 161-271. Chicago, IL: University of Chicago Community and Family Study Centers. University of Chicago Press, 1967. 111 pp.

Subjects: 1. Family Relationships and Dynamics / Men's Issues; 2.
   Issues Related to Reproduction / Family Planning; 3. Aids for Theory
   and Research / Family Research Methodology.

748 Mitchell, J. Marcus. "The Paul Family." OLD-TIME NEW ENGLAND 63, 3
(Winter 1973): 73-77. 5 pp., illustrations.

Subjects: 1. Trends and Change in Marriage and Family / Family Life
   Prior to 1900.

749 Mitchell, Jacquelyn. "Strategies for Achieving One-Upsmanship: A
Descriptive Analysis of Afro-American Siblings in Two Speech
Events." (Ed.D. dissertation, Harvard University, 1979.) DISSERTATION
ABSTRACTS INTERNATIONAL, 40, 12, June 1980, 6258A. (University
Microfilms No. 8012834.) 324 pp.

Subjects: 1. Family Relationships and Dynamics / Sibling Relationships.

750 Mithun, Jacqueline S. "Cooperation and Solidarity as Survival
Necessities in a Black Urban Community." URBAN ANTHROPOLOGY 2, 1
(Spring 1973): 25-34. 10 pp., references.

Subjects: 1. Organizations and Services to Families / Community Groups
   and the Family; 2. Family Relationships and Dynamics / Socialization;
   3. Families with Special Problems / Family Stress.

   This study explores the "cooperative" networks in an urban Afro-
   American community to discover to what extent "cooperation and
   solidarity" representr "survival necessities" for a community.
   Cooperation is viewed herein in the larger context of cultural
   adaptation. Some cultural traits such as etiquette and polite codes of
   behavior, larger familial and friendship networks, mutual aid
   associations, and the behavior suggested in the concept of "soul
   brother," which have been suggested in the literature, will be
   described and analyzed. (Author's abstract)

751 Modell, John. "Herbert Gutman's THE BLACK FAMILY IN SLAVERY AND
FREEDOM, 1750-1925: Demographic Perspectives." SOCIAL SCIENCE HISTORY
3, 3/4 (October 1979): 45-55. 11 pp., references.

Subjects: 1. Trends and Change in Marriage and Family / Family Life
   Prior to 1900.

752 Mogey, John M. "The Negro Family System in the United States." In
FAMILIES IN EAST AND WEST: SOCIALIZATION PROCESS AND KINSHIP TIES,
edited by Reuben Hill and Rene Konig, pp. 442-53. The Hague: Mouton,
1970., references, tables.

Subjects: 1. Trends and Change in Marriage and Family / Family Life in
   the United States.

753 Moles, Oliver C. "Marital Dissolution and Public Assistance
Payments: Variations among American States." JOURNAL OF SOCIAL ISSUES
32, 1 (Winter 1976): 87-101. 15 pp., references, bibliography, tables.

Subjects: 1. Organizations and Services to Families / Family Law; 2.
   Marriage and Divorce / Divorce and Separation.

754 Molofed, Martin. COLLOQUIUM ON STRESS AND CRIME. McLean, VA: The Mitre Corporation, 1980.

Subjects: 1. Families with Special Problems / Family Stress; 2. / Families with Criminal Offenders; 3. Aids for Theory and Research / Collected Works.

755 Monahan, Thomas P. "Are Interracial Marriages Really Less Stable?" SOCIAL FORCES 48, 4 (June 1970): 461-73. 13 pp., references, bibliography, tables, charts.

Subjects: 1. Marriage and Divorce / Inter-marriage.

756 Monahan, Thomas P. "Illegitimacy by Race and Mixture of Race." INTERNATIONAL JOURNAL OF SOCIOLOGY OF THE FAMILY 7, 1 (January-June 1977): 45-54. 10 pp., references, tables.

Subjects: 1. Minority Groups / Ethnic Groups in the United States; 2. Issues Related to Reproduction / Illegitimacy.

757 Monahan, Thomas P. "Interracial Parentage as Revealed by Birth Records in the United States, 1970." JOURNAL OF COMPARATIVE FAMILY STUDIES 8, 1 (Spring 1977): 65-77. 13 pp., references, bibliography, tables.

Subjects: 1. Trends and Change in Marriage and Family / Alternative Family Forms; 2. Marriage and Divorce / Inter-marriage.

758 Monahan, Thomas P. "Marriage Across Racial Lines in Indiana." JOURNAL OF MARRIAGE AND THE FAMILY 35, 4 (November 1973): 632-40. 9 pp., references, tables.

Subjects: 1. Marriage and Divorce / Inter-marriage.

759 Monahan, Thomas P. "The Occupational Class of Couples Entering into Interracial Marriages." JOURNAL OF COMPARATIVE FAMILY STUDIES 7, 2 (Summer 1976): 175-92. 18 pp., references, tables, charts.

Subjects: 1. Marriage and Divorce / Inter-marriage; 2. Minority Groups / Family and Social Class.

760 Monahan, Thomas P. "An Overview of Statistics on Interracial Marriage in the United States with Data on Its Extent from 1963-1970." JOURNAL OF MARRIAGE AND THE FAMILY 32, 2 (May 1976): 223-31. 9 pp., references, tables.

Subjects: 1. Marriage and Divorce / Inter-marriage; 2. Aids for Theory and Research / Statistics.

The increasing extent of interracial marriage between three racial groups, White, Negro, and Other Races, and the variations from state to state, is examined by using sample marriage record data from the U.S. Marriage Registration Area for the years 1963-1970. The differential proclivity of males and females towards interracial marriage is established for the three racial groups. Although marriage records have deficiencies, they are nevertheless the most relevant source of data upon interracial unions. Unfortunately the social usefulness of such data is being greatly undermined by moves to delete the racial item from the marriage records in many states. (Author's abstract)

761 Monroe, Ben, III. "The Effects of Mode of Presentation on the Comprehension of Sickle Cell Disease Information of Black Parents." (Ph.D. dissertation, The University of New Mexico, 1976.) DISSERTATION ABSTRACTS INTERNATIONAL, 37, 8, Feb. 1977, 3771B. (University Microfilms No. 7625673.) 111 pp.

Subjects: 1. Organizations and Services to Families / Physical Health and the Family; 2. Aids for Theory and Research / Family Research Methodology.

762 Moody, Anne. COMING OF AGE IN MISSISSIPPI. New York: Dial Press, 1968. 348 pp.; LC:65-55153.

Subjects: 1. Trends and Change in Marriage and Family / Family Life in the United States.

Notes: An autobiographical work.

763 Moore, William. THE VERTICAL GHETTO: EVERYDAY LIFE IN AN URBAN PROJECT. New York: Random House, Inc., 1969. 265 pp., bibliography; LC:69-20029.

Subjects: 1. Trends and Change in Marriage and Family / Family and Social Change; 2. Organizations and Services to Families / Social Services and the Family; 3. Family Relationships and Dynamics / Environment (Space/Housing).

A study of life patterns of households within an urban housing project. Described also are the roles of service institutions, father-child relationships and sibling relationships.

Notes: Bibliography: pp. 251-253.

764 Morgan, Elizabeth Ruth Pryor. "The Process of Parenting among Twenty-Four Black Families in Berkeley, California." (Ph.D. dissertation, University of California, Berkeley, 1981.) DISSERTATION ABSTRACTS INTERNATIONAL, 42, 7, Jan. 1982, 3317A. (University Microfilms No. 8200218.) 150 pp.

Subjects: 1. Family Counseling and Education / Education for Parenthood.

765 Morin, Rita J. "Black Child, White Parents: A Beginning Biography." CHILD WELFARE 56, 9 (November 1977): 576-83. 8 pp., bibliography.

Subjects: 1. Trends and Change in Marriage and Family / Alternative Family Forms; 2. Organizations and Services to Families / Adoption and Adoption Services.

766 Morisey, Patricia Garland. "Professional Advocacy, Community Participation and Social Planning: The Case of the Unmarried Mother from the 'Inside the Ghetto' Perspective." (D.S.W. dissertation, Columbia

University, 1970.) DISSERTATION ABSTRACTS INTERNATIONAL, 31, 10, April 1971, 5522A-5523A. (University Microfilms No. 716229.) 560 pp.

Subjects: 1. Organizations and Services to Families / Social Welfare; 2. Issues Related to Reproduction / Illegitimacy.

767 Morris, Roger Baxter. "Strengths of the Black Community: An Investigation of the Black Community and 'Broken Homes'." (Ed.D. dissertation, Columbia Teachers College, 1977.) DISSERTATION ABSTRACTS INTERNATIONAL, 38, 4, Oct. 1977, 1960A. (University Microfilms No. 7722276.) 75 pp.

Subjects: 1. Trends and Change in Marriage and Family / Alternative Family Forms; 2. Organizations and Services to Families / Community Groups and the Family; 3. Family Relationships and Dynamics / Single Parent Families.

768 Morrison, Toni. THE BLUEST EYE: A NOVEL. 1st edition New York: Holt, Rinehart and Winston, Inc., 1970. 164 pp.; ISBN:0-03-085074-6; LC:79-117270.

Subjects: 1. Organizations and Services to Families / Community Groups and the Family; 2. Family Relationships and Dynamics / Parent-Child Relationships; 3. Family Counseling and Education / Child Development.

A novel of childhood that portrayed the growth of three black girls. The perceptions and relationships within two black families and their community are also portrayed.

769 Morrow, Betty Hearn. "A Comparison of Eight-Year-Old Children Born to Young Black Adolescents and Those Born to Comparable Mothers in Their Early Twenties." (Ph.D. dissertation, University of Miami, 1978.) DISSERTATION ABSTRACTS INTERNATIONAL, 39, 4, Oct. 1978, 2151A-2152A. (University Microfilms No. 7818713.) 138 pp.

Subjects: 1. Family Relationships and Dynamics / Family Relationships; 2. Issues Related to Reproduction / Teenage Pregnancy; 3. Minority Groups / Family and Social Class.

770 Mortimer, Jeylan T. "Social Class, Work and the Family: Some Implications of the Father's Occupation for Familial Relationships and Sons' Career Decisions." JOURNAL OF MARRIAGE AND THE FAMILY 38, 2 (May 1976): 241-56. 16 pp., references, bibliography, tables.

Subjects: 1. Organizations and Services to Families / Employment and the Family; 2. Family Relationships and Dynamics / Father-Child Relationships; 3. Minority Groups / Family and Social Class.

771 Mott, Frank L. "Racial Differences in Female Labor-Force Participation: Trends and Implications for the Future." THE URBAN AND SOCIAL CHANGE REVIEW 11, 1/2 (1978): 21-27. 7 pp., references, illustrations, tables.

Subjects: 1. Trends and Change in Marriage and Family / Family and Social Change; 2. Organizations and Services to Families / Employment and the Family.

772 Mott, Frank L. and Sandell, Steven H. WOMEN, WORK AND FAMILY:
DIMENSIONS OF CHANGE IN AMERICAN SOCIETY. Lexington, MA: Lexington
Books, 1978. 153 pp., bibliography, illustrations, tables, index;
ISBN:0-669-02092-3 ; LC:77-18329.

Subjects: 1. Organizations and Services to Families / Employment and the
   Family; 2. Family Relationships and Dynamics / Women's Issues; 3.
   Aids for Theory and Research / Family Research Methodology.

   Notes: A project of the staff of the Center for Human Resources
   Research of Ohio State University. Bibliography: pp. 147-152.

773 Moynihan, Daniel Patrick. "Employment, Income, and the Ordeal of
the Negro Family." DAEDALUS 94, 4 (Fall 1965): 745-70. 26 pp.,
references, tables, charts.

Subjects: 1. Organizations and Services to Families / Employment and the
   Family.

774 Mueller, Charles W. and Campbell, Blair G. "Female Occupational
Achievement and Marital Status: A Research Note." JOURNAL OF MARRIAGE
AND THE FAMILY 39, 3 (August 1977): 587-93., references, bibliography,
tables.

Subjects: 1. Organizations and Services to Families / Employment and the
   Family; 2. Marriage and Divorce / Marriage Satisfaction and Prediction
   Studies.

   The influence of early occupational achievement of single never-
   married women on subsequent marital status is examined for a national
   sample of U.S. females, aged 30-44 in 1967. For white females, a
   positive relationship is observed between occupational achievement and
   the likelihood to remain single; for black females, the relationship
   is much weaker. (Authors' abstract)

775 Mueller, William H. and Malina, Robert M. "Differential
Contribution of Stature Phenotypes to Assortative Mating in Parents of
Philadelphia Black and White School Children." AMERICAN JOURNAL OF
PHYSICAL ANTHROPOLOGY 45, 2 (September 1976): 269-76. 7 pp.,
references, tables.

Subjects: 1. Mate Selection / Mate Selection, Differential Patterns.

776 Mullings, Leith. "On Women, Work and Society." FREEDOMWAYS 20, 1
(1980): 15-24. 10 pp., bibliography.

Subjects: 1. Organizations and Services to Families / Employment and the
   Family; 2. Family Relationships and Dynamics / Women's Issues.

777 Mumbauer, Corrine C. and Gray, Susan W. "Resistance to Temptation
in Young Negro Children." CHILD DEVELOPMENT 41, 4 (December 1970):
1203-1207. 5 pp., references.

Subjects: 1. Family Relationships and Dynamics / Decision Making; 2.
   Family Counseling and Education / Value Education.

A game-like situation was used to investigate the resistance to temptation of disadvantaged 5-year-old Negro children. Sex of the experimenter, sex of the child, and father absence or presence were varied. Expectations based on potential influences of father absence were not confirmed. Boys and girls from father-absent homes did not differ significantly in their resistance to temptation. Boys from father-present homes resisted temptation more with a female while girls resisted temptation more with a male rule giver. Findings were discussed in light of previous research by other investigators. A satiation-deprivation of social reinforcement explanation was suggested to account for the findings. (Authors' abstract)

778 Munick, Warren A. and Sullivan, Dennis. "Race, Age, and Family Status Differentials in Metropolitan Migration of Households." RURAL SOCIOLOGY 42, 4 (Winter 1977): 536-43. 8 pp., references, tables.

Subjects: 1. Families with Special Problems / Family and Geographic Mobility; 2. Minority Groups / Family and Social Class.

779 Munoz, Faye V. and Endo, Russell, eds. PERSPECTIVES ON MINORITY GROUP MENTAL HEALTH. Washington, DC: University Press of America, 1982. 192 pp.; ISBN:0-81912343-9; LC:81-40848.

Subjects: 1. Trends and Change in Marriage and Family / Family Life in the United States; 2. Organizations and Services to Families / Mental Health and the Family; 3. Aids for Theory and Research / Collected Works.

780 Murray, Pauli. "The Liberation of Black Women." In VOICES OF THE NEW FEMINISM, edited by Mary Lou Thompson, pp. 87-102. Boston, MA: Beacon Press, Inc., 1970. 16 pp., references.

Subjects: 1. Family Relationships and Dynamics / Women's Issues.

781 Murray, Robert F., Jr. "The Ethical and Moral Values of Black Americans and Population Policy." In POPULATION POLICY AND ETHICS: THE AMERICAN EXPERIENCE. A PROJECT OF THE RESEARCH GROUP ON ETHICS AND POPULATION OF THE INSTITUTE OF SOCIETY, ETHICS AND THE LIFE SCIENCES, edited by Robert M. Veatch, pp. 197-209. New York: Irvington Publishers, Inc., 1977. 13 pp., references.

Subjects: 1. Issues Related to Reproduction / Family Planning.

782 Murray, Saundra Rice and Mednick, Martha Tamara Shuch. "Black Women's Achievement Orientation: Motivational and Cognitive Factors." PSYCHOLOGY OF WOMEN QUARTERLY 1, 3 (Spring 1977): 247-59. 13 pp., references.

Subjects: 1. Families with Special Problems / Achievement and the Family.

The literature on motivational and cognitive factors related to the achievement orientation of black women is reviewed. Achievement motivation and fear of success are discussed, and the inconclusiveness of the findings for black women is noted. The limited data concerning black women's expectations for and causal attributions about achievement outcomes are also examined. Directions for future research are discussed with emphasis on the necessity of considering sex role concerns as mediators of black women's achievement behavior. (Authors' abstract)

783 Myers, Hector F. "Research on the Black Family: A Critical Review." In THE AFRO-AMERICAN FAMILY: ASSESSMENT, TREATMENT, AND RESEARCH ISSUES, edited by Barbara Ann Bass, Gail Elizabeth Wyatt and Gloria Johnson Powell, p. . New York: Grune and Stratton, Inc., 1982.

Subjects: 1. Aids for Theory and Research / Critiques and Analyses of Family Research Literature.

784 Myers, Hector F., Gabriel-Rana, Phyllis, Harris-Epps, Ronee and Jones, Rhonda J., comps. RESEARCH IN BLACK CHILD DEVELOPMENT: DOCTORAL DISSERTATION ABSTRACTS, 1927-1979. Westport, CT: Greenwood Press, 1982. 737 pp., bibliography, index; ISBN:0-313-22631-8; LC:81-13425.

Subjects: 1. Family Counseling and Education / Child Development; 2. Aids for Theory and Research / Classified Bibliographies of Family Literature.

785 Myers, Hector F., Rana, Phyllis G. and Harris, Marcia, eds. BLACK CHILD DEVELOPMENT IN AMERICA: 1927-1977: AN ANNOTATED BIBLIOGRAPHY. Westport, CT: Greenwood Press, 1979. 470 pp., index; ISBN:0-313-20719-4; LC:78-20028.

Subjects: 1. Family Relationships and Dynamics / Socialization; 2. Family Counseling and Education / Child Development; 3. Aids for Theory and Research / Classified Bibliographies of Family Literature.

786 Myers, Lena Wright. BLACK WOMEN: DO THEY COPE BETTER? Englewood Cliffs, NJ: Prentice-Hall, 1980. 118 pp., bibliography, index; ISBN:0-13-077834-6; LC:80-21595.

Subjects: 1. Family Relationships and Dynamics / Women's Issues; 2. Psychology and Sociology / Psychology.

Based on interviews with 400 Black women (200 from Grand Rapids, Michigan and 200 from Jackson, Mississippi), the study examines how these females develop and maintain positive self-images in a racist and sexist society that is designed to thwart their growth potential. The discussion particularly notes the Black woman's alternative ways of dealing with the pressures of society, social support systems, roles, and relationships with males.

787 Myers, Lena Wright. "On Marital Relations: Perceptions of Black Women." In THE BLACK WOMAN, edited by La Frances Rodgers-Rose, pp. 161-72. Beverly Hills, CA: Sage Publications, Inc., 1980. 12 pp.

Subjects: 1. Family Relationships and Dynamics / Women's Issues; 2. Marriage and Divorce / Marriage Satisfaction and Prediction Studies.

[The author] gives an account of the social interaction among Black couples as perceived by 400 Black women. Half the sample was from Michigan and half from Mississippi. The women ranged in age from 20 to 81 years; they were either presently married for at least five years or they were separated or divorced. The author looked at the perceptions of cathectic affection, the opportunity to relate to their husbands, and perceived degree of satisfaction with companionships. . .[T]he women still married were more satisfied with the cathectic aspect of their marriages than the separated or divorced women. Also, the married women felt freer than the separated or divorced women to communicate with their spouses. (From the editor's remarks)

788 N'Namdi, George Richard. "Analysis of Parent-Child Interaction in the Two-Child Black Family." (Ph.D. dissertation, The University of Michigan, 1978.) DISSERTATION ABSTRACTS INTERNATIONAL, 39, 6, Dec. 1978, 3052B-3053B. (University Microfilms No. 7822975.) 80 pp.

Subjects: 1. Family Relationships and Dynamics / Parent-Child Relationships; 2. Family Counseling and Education / Child Development.

789 Nail, Richard L., Gunderson, Eric and Arthur, Ransom J. "Black-White Differences in Social Background and Military Drug Abuse Patterns." AMERICAN JOURNAL OF PSYCHIATRY 131, 10 (October 1974): 1097-1102. 6 pp., references, tables.

Subjects: 1. Families with Special Problems / Drug Abuse.

790 Nanjundappa, G. "Occupational Differences among Black Male Cross-Regional Migrants from and to the South." PHYLON 42, 1 (Spring 1981): 52-59. 9 pp., references, tables.

Subjects: 1. Organizations and Services to Families / Employment and the Family.

791 Neilson, Jacqueline. "Tayari: Black Homes for Black Children." CHILD WELFARE 55, 1 (January 1976): 41-50. 10 pp.

Subjects: 1. Organizations and Services to Families / Adoption and Adoption Services; 2. Family Relationships and Dynamics / Environment (Space/Housing).

792 Nichols, Robert C. "Black Children Adopted by White Families." AMERICAN PSYCHOLOGIST 32, 8 (August 1977): 678-80. 3 pp., references, tables.

Subjects: 1. Organizations and Services to Families / Adoption and Adoption Services.

793 Nobbe, Charles E., Ebanks, G. Edward and George, P. M. "A Re-exploration of the Relationship between Types of Sex Unions and Fertility: The Barbadian Case." JOURNAL OF COMPARATIVE FAMILY STUDIES 7, 2 (Summer 1976): 295-308. 14 pp., references, tables, charts.

Subjects: 1. Mate Selection / Mate Selection, Differential Patterns; 2. Issues Related to Reproduction / Fertility Rates.

794 Noble, Jeanne L. BEAUTIFUL, ALSO, ARE THE SOULS OF MY BLACK SISTERS: A HISTORY OF THE BLACK WOMAN IN AMERICA. Englewood Cliffs, NJ: Prentice-Hall, 1978. 353 pp., references, index; ISBN:0-13-066555-X; LC:77-27408.

Subjects: 1. Family Relationships and Dynamics / Women's Issues.

795 Nobles, Wade and Nobles, Grady. "African Roots in Black Families: The Social-Psychological Dynamics of Black Family Life and the Implications for Health Care." In BLACK AWARENESS: IMPLICATIONS FOR BLACK PATIENT CARE, edited by Dorothy Luckraft, pp. 6-11. New York: American Journal of Nursing Company, 1976. 6 pp.

Subjects: 1. Trends and Change in Marriage and Family / Family Life in the United States; 2. Organizations and Services to Families / Physical Health and the Family.

796 Nobles, Wade W. "African Root and American Fruit: The Black Family." JOURNAL OF SOCIAL AND BEHAVIOR SCIENCES 20, 2 (Spring 1974): 52-64. 12 pp.

Subjects: 1. Trends and Change in Marriage and Family / Comparative Studies--International, Interclass, Sex, and Time Differences; 2. Aids for Theory and Research / Family Theory.

797 Nobles, Wade W. "Africanity: Its Role in Black Families." BLACK SCHOLAR 5, 9 (June 1974): 10-17. 8 pp., references.

Subjects: 1. Aids for Theory and Research / Family Theory.

798 Nobles, Wade W. et al., proj. dir. A FORMULATIVE AND EMPIRICAL STUDY OF BLACK FAMILIES. FINAL REPORT. San Francisco, CA: Westside Community Mental Health Center, Inc., Research Department, 1976. 316 pp., bibliography, appendices.

Subjects: 1. Aids for Theory and Research / Family Research Methodology; 2. / Family Theory.

  Notes: Bibliography: pp. 187-97.

799 Nobles, Wade W. "Toward an Empirical and Theoretical Framework for Defining Black Families." JOURNAL OF MARRIAGE AND THE FAMILY 40, 4 (November 1978): 679-688. 10 pp., references, charts.

Subjects: 1. Aids for Theory and Research / Family Theory.

800 Nobles, Wade W. and Goddard, Lawford V. "Consciousness, Adaptability and Coping Strategies. Socioeconomic Characteristics and Ecological Issues in Black Families." THE WESTERN JOURNAL OF BLACK STUDIES 1, 2 (June 1977): 105-113. 9 pp., references, appendices.

Subjects: 1. Family Relationships and Dynamics / Environment (Space/ Housing); 2. Families with Special Problems / Family Stress.

801 Nolle, David B. "Changes in Black Sons and Daughters: A Panel Analysis of Black Adolescents' Orientations toward Their Fathers." JOURNAL OF MARRIAGE AND THE FAMILY 34, 3 (August 1972): 443-47. 5 pp., references, tables.

Subjects: 1. Family Relationships and Dynamics / Father-Child Relationships; 2. Family Counseling and Education / Adolescence.

802 Norris, Wessie Lavon. "A Path Model for Feelings of Personal Efficacy for Black Employed Male and Female Familyheads, Employed Female

Non-Familyheads, and Housewives." (Ph.D. dissertation, The University of
Michigan, 1980.) DISSERTATION ABSTRACTS INTERNATIONAL, 41, 2,
Aug. 1980, 738B. (University Microfilms No. 8017330.) 138 pp.

Subjects: 1. Organizations and Services to Families / Employment and the
   Family; 2. Family Relationships and Dynamics / Socialization; 3.
   Psychology and Sociology / Psychology.

803 North, George E. and Buchanan, O. Lee. "Maternal Attitudes in a
Poverty Area." JOURNAL OF NEGRO EDUCATION 37, 4 (Fall 1968): 418-26.   8
pp., references, tables.

Subjects: 1. Family Relationships and Dynamics / Mother-Child
   Relationships; 2. Psychology and Sociology / General Attitudes.

804 O'Connell, Martin. "Comparative Estimates of Teenage Illegitimacy
in the United States, 1940-44 to 1970-74." DEMOGRAPHY 17, 1 (February
1980): 13-23. 11 pp., references, tables.

Subjects: 1. Issues Related to Reproduction / Teenage Pregnancy.

805 Oberle, Wayne H. "Role Models of Black and White Rural Youth at
Two States of Adolescence." JOURNAL OF NEGRO EDUCATION 43, 2 (Spring
1974): 234-44. 11 pp., references, tables.

Subjects: 1. Family Relationships and Dynamics / Family Roles and Sex
   Roles; 2. Family Counseling and Education / Adolescence.

806 Obudho, Constance E., ed. BLACK MARRIAGE AND FAMILY THERAPY. Afro-
American and African Studies, No. 72. Westport, CT: Greenwood Press,
1983. 269 pp., references, tables, appendices, index; ISBN:0-313-22119-
7; LC:82-20967.

Subjects: 1. Marriage and Divorce / Marriage Satisfaction and Prediction
   Studies; 2. Family Counseling and Education / Family Therapy; 3. Aids
   for Theory and Research / Collected Works.

807 Okonkwo, Rina. "Adelaide Casely Hayford: Cultural Nationalist and
Feminist." PHYLON 42, 1 (Spring 1981): 41-51. 11 pp., references.

Subjects: 1. Family Relationships and Dynamics / Women's Issues.

808 Oliver, Mamie O. "Elderly Blacks and the Economy: Variables of
Survival: 'Personal Integration', 'Style', 'Pride and Positive Spirit'."
JOURNAL OF AFRO-AMERICAN ISSUES 3, 3/4 (Summer/Fall 1975): 316-23.   8
pp., references.

Subjects: 1. Organizations and Services to Families / Economics and the
   Family; 2. Family Relationships and Dynamics / Later Years and Aging.

809 Oliver, William. "Black Males and the Tough Guy Image: A
Dysfunctional Compensatory Adaptation." THE WESTERN JOURNAL OF BLACK
STUDIES 8, 4 (Winter 1984): 199-203. 5 pp., references.

Subjects: 1. Family Relationships and Dynamics / Men's Issues.

810   Oppel, Wallace Churchill. "Illegitimacy: A Comparative Follow-Up Study. A Matched Group of 120 Six to Eight Year-Old Negro Illegitimate Children and Their Mothers Is Compared to a Group of 120 Legitimate Six to Eight Year-Old Negro Children and Their Mothers on Measures of Child Development and Mothering Behavior." (D.S.W. dissertation, The Catholic University of America, 1969.) DISSERTATION ABSTRACTS INTERNATIONAL, 30, 5, Nov. 1969, 2159A-2160A. (University Microfilms No. 6917861.) 188 pp.

Subjects: 1. Family Relationships and Dynamics / Mother-Child Relationships; 2. Issues Related to Reproduction / Illegitimacy.

Notes: Studies in Social Work No. 54

811   Orive, Ruben and Gerard, Harold B. "Social Contact of Minority Parents and Their Children's Acceptance by Classmates." SOCIOMETRY 38, 4 (December 1975): 518-24. 7 pp., references, tables.

Subjects: 1. Family Relationships and Dynamics / Socialization; 2. Minority Groups / Family and Social Class.

812   Orum, Anthony M., Cohen, Roberta S., Grasmuck, Sherri and Orum, Amy W. "Sex, Socialization and Politics." AMERICAN SOCIOLOGICAL REVIEW 39, 2 (April 1974): 197-209. 13 pp., references, tables.

Subjects: 1. Family Relationships and Dynamics / Communication in the Family; 2. / Family Roles and Sex Roles.

813   Osmond, Marie Withers. "Marital Organization in Low-Income Families: A Cross-Race Comparison." INTERNATIONAL JOURNAL OF SOCIOLOGY OF THE FAMILY 7, 2 (July-December 1977): 143-56. 14 pp., references, tables, charts.

Subjects: 1. Family Relationships and Dynamics / Family Roles and Sex Roles; 2. Minority Groups / Family and Social Class.

Patterns of marital interaction, that are associated with differential probabilities of marital dissolution, are analyzed in a black and in a white subsample of 277 low-income families. Structured interviews with one or the other of the spouses were conducted in a sample of welfare applicants/recipients in the states of Florida, Georgia, West Virginia, and New Jersey. In a multivariate analysis of the data, two "family polity" variables emerge as of overriding importance in predicting marital intactness: mode of decision making and strategy of conflict resolution. Marital decision making, or who actually makes the decisions, has the highest association with marital intactness for whites. For blacks, however, the most important indicator of family "power" is conflict resolution, or whose decision prevails when the spouses' interests conflict. A greater number of black respondents report husband dominance in marriage and about equal numbers of blacks and whites report "democratic" decision making. There is no evidence of "black matriarchy," neither normative nor behavioral. There is a greater polarization of significant others for black spouses than for white. Background variables (degree of homogamy in terms of fathers' occupation and spouses' educational attainment) are differentially related to marital intactness for blacks and whites. Conclusions underscore the variety of conditions which can be

associated with both intact and dissolved marriages for   each   racial
group. (Author's abstract)

814 Osmond, Marie Withers and Martin, Patricia Yancey. "A Contingency
Model of Marital Organization in Low Income Families." JOURNAL OF
MARRIAGE AND THE FAMILY 40, 2 (May 1978): 315-29. 15 pp., references,
tables, charts.

Subjects: 1. Minority Groups / Family and Social Class; 2. Aids for
  Theory and Research / Family Research Methodology.

815 Owens, Leslie Howard. THIS SPECIES OF PROPERTY: SLAVE LIFE AND
CULTURE IN THE OLD SOUTH. New York: Oxford University Press, 1976. 291
pp., references, index; LC:75-38110.

Subjects: 1. Trends and Change in Marriage and Family / Family Life
  Prior to 1900.

(Chapter: 'A Family Folk' pp. 182-213, 276-83). An extensive
examination of the testimonies of those who experienced slavery
provides a wealth of data on such subjects, as: wedding ceremonies,
marriage, maternal-child bonding, sex-linked role activies, 'hiring-
out', intergenerational transference of lore, social stratification,
enculturation, children, domestic and work roles of youth, discipline,
and family holiday gatherings. While 'natural' (i.e., conjugal)
families were certainly visible in the community of captives, co-
rending 'extended' families were known to have evolved from the sales
separating conjugal family members. Thus minors were adopted or
fostered in domestic settings other than that of their natural
parents; and new adult arrivals on a plantation were absorbed into
familial settings to which they were expected to contribute.

816 Painter, Dianne Holland. "Black Women and the Family." In WOMEN
INTO WIVES: THE LEGAL AND ECONOMIC IMPACT OF MARRIAGE, edited by Jane
Roberts Chapman and Margaret Gates, pp. 151-67. Beverly Hills, CA: Sage
Publications, Inc., 1977. 17 pp.

Subjects: 1. Organizations and Services to Families / Employment and the
  Family; 2. Family Relationships and Dynamics / Women's Issues; 3.
  Marriage and Divorce / Marriage Satisfaction and Prediction Studies.

817 Parker, Maude I. "Growing Up Black." In SEX IN THE CHILDHOOD
YEARS: EXPERT GUIDANCE FOR PARENTS, COUNSELORS AND TEACHERS, compiled by
Isadore Rubin and Lester A. Kirkendall, pp. 161-168. New York:
Association Press, 1970. 8 pp.

Subjects: 1. Family Relationships and Dynamics / Socialization; 2.
  Family Counseling and Education / Child Development; 3. / Sex
  Education.

818 Parker, Seymour and Kleiner, Robert J. "Characteristics of Negro
Mothers in Single-Headed Households." JOURNAL OF MARRIAGE AND THE
FAMILY 28, 4 (November 1966): 507-13. 7 pp., references.

Subjects: 1. Family Relationships and Dynamics / Single Parent Families.

819 Parker, Seymour and Kleiner, Robert J. "Social and Psychological
Dimensions of the Family Role Performance of the Negro Male." JOURNAL
OF MARRIAGE AND THE FAMILY 31, 3 (August 1969): 500-06. 7 pp.,
references, tables.

Subjects: 1. Family Relationships and Dynamics / Family Roles and Sex
    Roles.

820 Parris, Percival J. "Pedro Tovookan Parris." OLD-TIME NEW ENGLAND
63, 3 (Winter 1973): 61-68. 8 pp., references, illustrations.

Subjects: 1. Trends and Change in Marriage and Family / Family Life
    Prior to 1900.

821 Parron, Delores Louise. "Black Parents' Concept of Parenthood: A
Study of Parental Role Definition and Parenting Style." (D.S.W.
dissertation, The Catholic University of America, 1977.) DISSERTATION
ABSTRACTS INTERNATIONAL, 38, 9, March 1978, 5717A. (University
Microfilms No. 7802096.) 168 pp.

Subjects: 1. Family Relationships and Dynamics / Parent-Child
    Relationships; 2. Family Counseling and Education / Education for
    Parenthood; 3. Aids for Theory and Research / Family Theory.

Notes: Number 120 of the series titled Studies in Social Work.

822 Parron, Eugenia Mary. "Relationships of Black and White Golden
Wedding Couples." (Ph.D. dissertation, Rutgers University, The State
University of New Jersey (New Brunswick), 1979.) DISSERTATION ABSTRACTS
INTERNATIONAL, 40, 10, April 1980, 5039B. (University Microfilms
No. 8008912.) 150 pp.

Subjects: 1. Trends and Change in Marriage and Family / Comparative
    Studies--International, Interclass, Sex, and Time Differences; 2.
    Family Relationships and Dynamics / Stages in Family Life Cycle; 3.
    Marriage and Divorce / Marriage Satisfaction and Prediction Studies.

823 Patterson, Orlando. "Persistence, Continuity and Change in the
Jamaican Working-Class Family." JOURNAL OF FAMILY HISTORY 7, 2 (Summer
1982): 135-61. 27 pp.

Subjects: 1. Organizations and Services to Families / Employment and the
    Family; 2. Minority Groups / Blacks in the Caribbean.

824 Pavenstedt, Eleanor, ed. THE DRIFTERS: CHILDREN OF DISORGANIZED
LOWER-CLASS FAMILIES, BY CHARLES A. MALONE AND OTHERS. Boston: Little,
Brown and Company, 1967. 345 pp., bibliography; LC:67-27513.

Subjects: 1. Families with Special Problems / Family Disorganization;
    2. Minority Groups / Family and Social Class; 3. Aids for Theory and
    Research / Collected Works.

Notes: Contains a foreword by Bernard Bandler.

825 Pepper, Gerald Wesley. "Interracial Adoptions: Family Profile,
Motivation and Coping Methods." (D.S.W. dissertation, University of

Southern California, 1966.) DISSERTATION ABSTRACTS INTERNATIONAL, 27, 8, Jan. 1967, 2621A. (University Microfilms No. 67420.) 311 pp.

Subjects: 1. Organizations and Services to Families / Adoption and Adoption Services; 2. Family Relationships and Dynamics / Family Roles and Sex Roles.

826 Peres, Yochanan and Schrift, Ruth. "Intermarriage and Interethnic Relations: A Comparative Study." ETHNIC AND RACIAL STUDIES 1, 4 (October 1978): 428-51. 24 pp., references, bibliography, tables.

Subjects: 1. Marriage and Divorce / Inter-marriage; 2. Minority Groups / Ethnic Groups in the United States.

827 Peretti, Peter O. "'Woman-Lady' Concept in the Dating Process among Black College Youth." PSYCHOLOGICAL STUDIES 20, 2 (July 1975): 62-70. 9 pp., references, tables.

Subjects: 1. Mate Selection / Dating, Courtship, and Romanticism.

In a science, the serendipity effect sometimes leads to interesting and valuable results. The present research motivated by serendipity focused on "woman" and "lady" roles existing in premarital dating among black college students. Both "woman" and "lady" have specific attributes which make them unique dating partners. Significant differences were found between the various attributes associated with each role as well as between male and female responses on varying criteria related to them. (Author's abstract)

828 Perkins, Eugene. HOME IS A DIRTY STREET: THE SOCIAL OPPRESSION OF BLACK CHILDREN. 1st edition Chicago, IL: Third World Press, 1975. 193 pp., bibliography; ISBN:0-88378-048-8; LC:74-78322.

Subjects: 1. Trends and Change in Marriage and Family / Family and Social Change; 2. Psychology and Sociology / Psychology; 3. Family Counseling and Education / Child Development.

Notes: Bibliography: pp. 189-193.

829 Perkins, Useni Eugene, ed. BLACK CHILD JOURNAL: A REVIEW OF BLACK CHILD DEVELOPMENT 2, 1 (Fall 1980): 4-44. 41 pp., references, illustrations.

Subjects: 1. Family Counseling and Education / Child Development.

830 Perkins, Useni Eugene, ed. BLACK CHILD JOURNAL: A REVIEW OF BLACK CHILD DEVELOPMENT 2, 2 (Winter 1981): 4-38. 35 pp.

Subjects: 1. Family Counseling and Education / Child Development.

831 Perkowski, Stefan. "Some Observations Concerning Black Children Living in a Residential Care Agency." INTERNATIONAL JOURNAL OF SOCIAL PSYCHIATRY 20, 1/2 (Spring/Summer 1974): 89-93. 5 pp., bibliography, tables.

Subjects: 1. Organizations and Services to Families / Foster Care.

832   Perrucci, Carolyn Cummings and Targ, Dena B., eds. MARRIAGE AND
THE FAMILY: A CRITICAL ANALYSIS AND PROPOSALS FOR CHANGE.   New York:
David McKay Company, Inc., 1974.   457 pp., references; ISBN:0-679-30248-
4; LC:73-93038.

Subjects: 1. Trends and Change in Marriage and Family / Family Life in
    the United States; 2. Marriage and Divorce / Marriage Satisfaction and
    Prediction Studies; 3. Aids for Theory and Research / Collected Works.

833   Perry, Lorraine. "Strategies of Black Community Groups." SOCIAL
WORK 21, 3 (May 1976): 210-215.   6 pp., references, tables, charts.

Subjects: 1. Organizations and Services to Families / Community Groups
    and the Family.

834   Perry, Robert L.   "The Black Matriarchy Controversy and Black Male
Delinquency." JOURNAL OF AFRO-AMERICAN ISSUES 4, 3/4 (Summer/Fall
1976): 362-72.   11 pp., references.

Subjects: 1. Family Relationships and Dynamics / Mother-Child
    Relationships; 2. Families with Special Problems / Families with
    Juvenile Delinquents.

835   Peters, Marie F., ed. "Special Issue: Black Families." JOURNAL OF
MARRIAGE AND THE FAMILY 40, 4 (November 1978): 655-862.   208 pp.,
references, tables, charts.

Subjects: 1. Trends and Change in Marriage and Family / Family Life in
    the United States; 2. Aids for Theory and Research / Family Theory; 3.
    / Critiques and Analyses of Family Research Literature.

An issue devoted to current research on black families including
lifestyles, relationships and behavior patterns. The special issue
includes sixteen articles contributed by twenty-seven authors. Book
reviews of four books dealing with the topics, black families and
interracial adoption, are found on pages 829-835.

836   Peters, Marie Ferguson. "The Black Family--Perpetuating the Myths:
An Analysis of Family Sociology Textbook Treatment of Black Families."
FAMILY COORDINATOR 23, 4 (October 1974): 349-57.   9 pp., references.

Subjects: 1. Psychology and Sociology / Sociology; 2. Family Counseling
    and Education / Family Life Education.

837   Peters, Marie Ferguson. "Nine Black Families: A Study of Household
Management and Childrearing in Black Families with Working
Mothers." (Ed.D. dissertation, Harvard University, 1976.) DISSERTATION
ABSTRACTS INTERNATIONAL, 37, 7, Jan. 1977, 4648A-4649A. (University
Microfilms No. 77321.) 339 pp.

Subjects: 1. Organizations and Services to Families / Working Mothers;
    2. Family Relationships and Dynamics / Husband-Wife Relationships; 3.
    / Parent-Child Relationships.

838   Pettapiece, Mervyn Arthur. "Interpersonal Relationships and
Affection Needs of Black, Teenage, Inner-City, Unwed Mothers." (Ed.D.
dissertation, Wayne State University, 1980.) DISSERTATION ABSTRACTS

INTERNATIONAL, 41, 4, Oct. 1980, 1526A. (University Microfilms
No. 8022819.) 126 pp.

Subjects: 1. Issues Related to Reproduction / Teenage Pregnancy.

839 Phillips, Mona Taylor. "The Black Family and Community: Their Role
in the Formation of Positive Self-Concept of Working-Class Black
Youth." (Ph.D. dissertation, The University of Michigan, 1982.)
DISSERTATION ABSTRACTS INTERNATIONAL, 43, 6, Dec. 1982, 2116A.
(University Microfilms No. 8225019.) 138 pp.

Subjects: 1. Organizations and Services to Families / Community Groups
   and the Family; 2. Family Relationships and Dynamics / Extended Family
   and Kinship Groups; 3. Psychology and Sociology / Self-Esteem.

840 Pierce, Chester M. "Problems of the Negro Adolescent in the Next
Decade." In INFORMAL ADOPTION AMONG BLACK FAMILIES, by Robert Bernard
Hill, pp. 17-47. Washington, DC: National Urban League, Research
Department, 1977. 31 pp.

Subjects: 1. Family Counseling and Education / Adolescence.

841 Pierre, Thelma. "The Relationship between Hypertension and
Psychosocial Functioning in Young Black Men." JOURNAL OF AFRO-AMERICAN
ISSUES 4, 3/4 (Summer/Fall 1976): 408-19. 12 pp., references.

Subjects: 1. Organizations and Services to Families / Physical Health
   and the Family; 2. Family Relationships and Dynamics / Men's Issues.

842 Pinderhughes, Elaine B. "Family Functioning of Afro-Americans."
SOCIAL WORK 27, 1 (Winter 1982): 91-96. 6 pp., references.

Subjects: 1. Family Relationships and Dynamics / Family Relationships;
   2. Psychology and Sociology / Sociology.

843 Pleck, Elizabeth H. "The Two-Parent Household: Black
Family Structure in Late Nineteenth-Century Boston." JOURNAL OF SOCIAL
HISTORY 6, 1 (Fall 1972): 3-31. 29 pp., references, tables.

Subjects: 1. Trends and Change in Marriage and Family / Family Life
   Prior to 1900; 2. Family Relationships and Dynamics / Nuclear Family.

The most typical black household in late nineteenth-century Boston
included the husband and wife, or husband, wife and children. This
predominant household form prevailed among all occupational levels and
among families of both urban and rural origins. By enlarging the
household to include boarders, families from all occupational strata
augmented the family income and provided homes for the large numbers
of migrants in the population. This evidence from the [1880 federal]
manuscript census contradicts the commonly held association between
"the tangle of pathology," "family disorganization" and the black
family. (Author's text)

844 Pohlmann, Vernon C. and Walsh, Robert H. "Black Minority Racial
Status and Fertility in the United States, 1970." SOCIOLOGICAL FOCUS 8,
2 (April 1975): 97-109. 13 pp., references, bibliography, tables.

Subjects: 1. Issues Related to Reproduction / Fertility Rates; 2. Minority Groups / Family and Social Class.

Reversal in the trend toward convergence of black and white fertility rates in the United States between 1940 and 1970 has given rise to the theory of independent effect of minority racial status. The 1970 Public Use Sample is used in this study to extract data on a 1/1000 sample of all black and white women (excluding Spanish Americans) ages 15 to 59 in order to analyze relationships between fertility and other census variables. The results tend to support the theory of independent effect of minority racial status on fertility. The relationship is more pronounced for women under 35 than for women 40 and over. Distinctive patterns emerge by race and age cohorts. (Authors' abstract)

845   Point, Velma De Vonne La.   "A Descriptive Survey of Some Perceptions and Concerns of Black Female Single Parent Families in Lansing, Michigan." (Ph.D. dissertation, Michigan State University, 1977.) DISSERTATION ABSTRACTS INTERNATIONAL, 38, 3, Sept. 1977, 1231A. (University Microfilms No. 7718504.) 140 pp.

Subjects: 1. Family Relationships and Dynamics / Single Parent Families; 2. Psychology and Sociology / General Attitudes; 3. Family Counseling and Education / Family Life Education.

846   Polgar, Steven and Hiday, Virginia A.   "The Effect of an Additional Birth on Low-Income Urban Families." POPULATION STUDIES 23, 3 (November 1974): 463-71.   9 pp., references, tables, charts.

Subjects: 1. Family Relationships and Dynamics / Environment (Space/ Housing); 2. Issues Related to Reproduction / Fertility Rates.

847   Pope, Hallowell.   "Negro-White Differences in Decisions Regarding Illegitimate Children." JOURNAL OF MARRIAGE AND THE FAMILY 31, 4 (November 1969): 756-64.   8 pp., references, tables, charts.

Subjects: 1. Trends and Change in Marriage and Family / Comparative Studies--International, Interclass, Sex, and Time Differences; 2. Issues Related to Reproduction / Illegitimacy.

848   Pope, Hallowell.   "Unwed Mothers and Their Sex Partners." JOURNAL OF MARRIAGE AND THE FAMILY 29, 3 (August 1967): 555-567.   13 pp., references, tables.

Subjects: 1. Family Relationships and Dynamics / Single Parent Families; 2. Sexual Attitudes and Behavior / Premarital Sexual Behavior.

849   Pope, Hallowell and Mueller, Charles W.   "The Intergenerational Transmission of Marital Instability: Comparisons by Race and Sex." JOURNAL OF SOCIAL ISSUES 32, 1 (Winter 1976): 49-66.   18 pp., references, tables.

Subjects: 1. Marriage and Divorce / Marriage Satisfaction and Prediction Studies; 2. Families with Special Problems / Family Disorganization.

The intergenerational transmission of marital instability was examined with the use of data from five surveys, four of them from national samples. Among blacks, whites, males, and females, respondents from parental homes that were disrupted by death or divorce during their childhood had higher rates of divorce or separation in their own first marriages. Except for black males, a greater transmission effect was found among respondents from childhood homes disrupted by divorce or separation rather than by death. Implications from the literature on sex-role learning in children were examined by comparing the transmission effect for respondents who, after having their parental homes disrupted, were reared in households of different composition. The results indicated that the role model rationale for the transmission of marital instability must be elaborated before it can successfully account for the findings from existing national surveys. (Authors' abstract)

850 Porter, Dorothy B. "Family Records, A Major Resource for Documenting the Black Experience in New England." OLD-TIME NEW ENGLAND 63, 3 (Winter 1973): 69-72. 4 pp.

Subjects: 1. Aids for Theory and Research / Classified Bibliographies of Family Literature.

851 Porter, John R. DATING HABITS OF YOUNG BLACK AMERICANS: AND ALMOST EVERYBODY ELSE'S TOO. Dubuque, IA: Kendall Hunt Publishing Company, 1979. 253 pp., bibliography, index; ISBN:0-8403-2024-8; LC:79-84220.

Subjects: 1. Mate Selection / Dating, Courtship, and Romanticism; 2. Family Counseling and Education / Adolescence.

Notes: Bibliography: pp. 247-249.

852 Porter, Judith D. R. BLACK CHILD, WHITE CHILD: THE DEVELOPMENT OF RACIAL ATTITUDES. Cambridge, MA: Harvard University Press, 1971. 278 pp., bibliography, illustrations; ISBN:0-674-07610-9; LC:76-133213.

Subjects: 1. Psychology and Sociology / Psychology; 2. / Racial Attitudes; 3. Family Counseling and Education / Child Development.

Originally presented as the author's thesis, this study reports the empirical results related to children's racial attitudes and children's awareness of race as a social phenomenon.

Notes: Bibliography: pp. 265-273.

853 Porterfield, Ernest. BLACK AND WHITE MIXED MARRIAGES. Chicago, IL: Nelson-Hall Publishing, 1978. 189 pp., bibliography, index; ISBN:0-88229-131-9; LC:77-8796.

Subjects: 1. Marriage and Divorce / Inter-marriage.

This study presents a systematic ethnographic description of forty black-white families. It focuses attention on intrafamilial relations, interactional patterns between families and their kin network, and relations between these unions and larger society. A secondary aim is to generate greater understanding of the possibilities of, as well as the difficulties in, developing an egalitarian multiracial society (such as the United States) through large-scale miscegenation. (From author's 'Preface')

Notes: Bibliography: p. 73.

854   Poussaint, Alvin F. WHY BLACKS KILL BLACKS. New York: Emerson
Hall Publishers, Inc., 1972. 126 pp., bibliography; ISBN:0-87829-004-4;
LC:74-188564.

Subjects: 1. Families with Special Problems / Family Violence; 2.
   Psychology and Sociology / Psychology; 3. / Racial Attitudes.

Notes: An introduction by Jesse Jackson. Bibliography: pp. 125-126.

855   Powell, Frances LaJune Johnson. "A Study of the Structure of the
Freed Black Family in Washington, D.C., 1850-1880." (D.A. dissertation,
The Catholic University of America, 1980.) DISSERTATION ABSTRACTS
INTERNATIONAL, 41, 3, Sept. 1980, 1174A. (University Microfilms
No. 8018913.) 122 pp.

Subjects: 1. Trends and Change in Marriage and Family / Family Life
   Prior to 1900; 2. Family Relationships and Dynamics / Nuclear Family;
   3. Aids for Theory and Research / Family Research Methodology.

856   Prather, Jeffrey Lynn. A MERE REFLECTION: THE PSYCHODYNAMICS OF
BLACK AND HISPANIC PSYCHOLOGY. Philadelphia, PA: Dorrance and Company,
1977. 167 pp., bibliography, index; ISBN:0-8059-2428-0; LC:77-372571.

Subjects: 1. Psychology and Sociology / Psychology; 2. Minority Groups /
   Ethnic Groups in the United States.

Notes: Bibliography: pp. 161-162.

857   Presser, Harriet B. and Salsberg, Linda S. "Public Assistance and
Early Family Formation: Is There a Pronatulist Effect?" SOCIAL PROBLEMS
23, 2 (December 1975): 226-41. 16 pp., references, bibliography,
tables.

Subjects: 1. Organizations and Services to Families / Social Welfare.

858   Preston, Samuel H. "Differential Fertility, Unwanted Fertility and
Racial Trends in Occupational Achievement." AMERICAN SOCIOLOGICAL
REVIEW 39, 4 (August 1974): 492-506. 15 pp., references, bibliography,
tables.

Subjects: 1. Organizations and Services to Families / Employment and the
   Family; 2. Issues Related to Reproduction / Fertility Rates.

This paper estimates the effects on future occupational achievement
and mobility levels of maintaining current class differences in
fertility. Separate computations are made for the white and non-white
populations, under the assumption that both groups are henceforth
subject to the mobility regime of all men recorded in the 1962 Current
Population Survey. Because fertility differentials are larger in the
non-white population, maintaining them has a greater impact on this
group. Differential fertility reduces the proportion of non-white men
in the top three occupational groups by 10-11% in the second
generation and beyond, and raises the proportion in the bottom three
groups by 21-23%. Eliminating unwanted fertility from recorded class

differences largely removes the effect of differential fertility on occupational distributions. (Author's abstract)

859 Price-Bonham, Sharon and Skeen, Patsy. "A Comparison of Black and White Fathers with Implications for Parent Education." FAMILY COORDINATOR 28, 1 (January 1979): 53-59. 7 pp.

Subjects: 1. Family Relationships and Dynamics / Father-Child Relationships; 2. Family Counseling and Education / Education for Parenthood.

860 Proctor, Samuel D. "Stability of the Black Family and the Black Community." In CHILDBIRTH IN THE GHETTO: FOLK BELIEFS OF NEGRO WOMEN IN A NORTH PHILADELPHIA HOSPITAL WARD, by Barbara Frankel, pp. 104-15. San. Francisco, CA: R and E Research Associates, Inc., 1977. 12 pp.

Subjects: 1. Organizations and Services to Families / Community Groups and the Family.

861 Radin, Norma and Kamii, Constance K. "The Childrearing Attitudes of Disadvantaged Negro Mothers and Some Educational Implications." JOURNAL OF NEGRO EDUCATION 34, 2 (Spring 1965): 138-46. 9 pp., references, bibliography, tables.

Subjects: 1. Organizations and Services to Families / Education and the Family; 2. Family Relationships and Dynamics / Mother-Child Relationships.

862 Rainwater, Lee. BEHIND GHETTO WALLS: BLACK FAMILIES IN A FEDERAL SLUM. Chicago, IL: Aldine Publishing Company, 1970. 446 pp., bibliography; ISBN:202-30113-3; LC:77-113083.

Subjects: 1. Trends and Change in Marriage and Family / Family Life in the United States; 2. Family Relationships and Dynamics / Environment (Space/Housing).

Notes: Bibliography: pp. 427-440.

863 Rainwater, Lee. "Crucible of Identity: The Negro Lower Class Family." DAEDALUS 95, 1 (Winter 1966): 172-216. 45 pp., references, tables.

Subjects: 1. Family Relationships and Dynamics / Family Relationships; 2. Aids for Theory and Research / Family Theory.

864 Rainwater, Lee and Yancey, William L. "Black Families and the White House." TRANSACTION 3, 5 (July-August 1966): 48-53. 13 pp., illustrations.

Subjects: 1. Organizations and Services to Families / Governmental Units and the Family.

865 Rainwater, Lee and Yancey, William L., eds. THE MOYNIHAN REPORT AND THE POLITICS OF CONTROVERSY: A TRANSACTION SOCIAL SCIENCE AND PUBLIC POLICY REPORT. Cambridge, MA: MIT Press, 1967. 493 pp., references, illustrations; LC:67-15238.

Subjects: 1. Organizations and Services to Families / Governmental Units and the Family.

Notes: Includes the full text of THE NEGRO FAMILY: THE CASE FOR NATIONAL ACTION by Daniel Patrick Moynihan.

866 Ramirez, Manuel, III and Price-Williams, Douglas R. "Cognitive Styles of Children of Three Ethnic Groups in the United States." JOURNAL OF CROSS-CULTURAL PSYCHOLOGY 5, 2 (June 1974): 212-19. 8 pp., references, tables.

Subjects: 1. Psychology and Sociology / Psychology.

Children of three subcultural groups in the United States—Anglos, Blacks, and Mexican-Americans were tested with the Portable Rod and Frame Test. The results showed that Black and Mexican-American children, and females in all three groups, scored in a significantly more field-dependent direction than Anglo children. The results confirmed previous findings that members of groups which emphasize respect for family and religious authority and group identity and which are characterized by shared-function family and friendship groups tend to be field-dependent in cognitive style. Members of groups which encourage questioning of convention and an individual identity and are characterized by formally organized family and friendship groups, on the other hand, tend to be more field-dependent. (Authors' abstract)

867 Rao, V.V. Prakakasa and Rao, V. Nandini. "Alternatives in Intimacy, Marriage, and Family Lifestyles: Preferences of Black College Students." ALTERNATIVE LIFESTYLES 3, 4 (November 1980): 485-98. 13 pp., references, bibliography, tables.

Subjects: 1. Family Relationships and Dynamics / Family Relationships; 2. Marriage and Divorce / Marriage Customs and Forms; 3. Sexual Attitudes and Behavior / Sexual Attitudes and Behavior.

This study investigated a sample of southern Black students' willingness to engage in 16 alternative intimacy, marriage, and family forms and examined the relation between demographic, familial, and social psychological variables and alternative lifestyles chosen. Data were obtained from a random sample of 230 Black students of marriageable age. In general, the subjects expressed relatively less willingness to experiment with the nontraditional lifestyles compared to conventional family forms; but theoretically relevant correlates of their predisposition were different for each sex. Year in college, major areas, parental love, family income, parental authority, and parental permissiveness with regard to dating relationships were significantly related to females' willingness, while residence and fathers' education were related to males' willingness to engage in alternative lifestyes. (Authors' abstract)

868 Rao, V.V. Prakakasa and Rao, V. Nandini. "Family Size and Sex Preferences of Children: A Biracial Comparison." ADOLESCENCE 16, 62 (Summer 1981): 385-401. 17 pp., references, bibliography, tables.

Subjects: 1. Family Relationships and Dynamics / Family Roles and Sex
Roles; 2. Issues Related to Reproduction / Population Studies; 3. Aids
for Theory and Research / Statistics.

869 Rao, V.V. Prakakasa and Rao, V. Nandini. "Instrumental and
Expressive Values in Mate Selection among Black College Students." THE
WESTERN JOURNAL OF BLACK STUDIES 4, 1 (Spring 1980): 50-56. 7 pp.,
references, tables.

Subjects: 1. Mate Selection / Mate Selection, Differential Patterns.

The study is designed to compare the values of Black male and female
students [from Jackson State University, Jackson, Mississippi (n=206)]
regarding mate selection. Six hypotheses are developed to investigate
the differences on the relative importance of the instrumental and
expressive traits of a potential mate by sex and socioeconomic status
variables. Data reveal that females assign greater importance to
instrumental traits in selecting a mate than do males. There is also a
tendency for female respondents to give more importance to the
expressive characteristics in a future spouse when compared with
males. Analysis of variance produced no significant differences
between socioeconomic status variables (parents'   education   and
parents' occupation) and two dimensions of family life. However,
father's education seems to explain the variance in the instrumental
and expressive values in higher proportion than the father's
occupation. (Authors' summary)

870 Rathbone, McCuan Eloise. "Elderly Victims of Family Violence and
Neglect." SOCIAL CASEWORK: THE JOURNAL OF CONTEMPORARY SOCIAL WORK 61,
5 (May 1980): 296-304. 9 pp., references.

Subjects: 1. Family Relationships and Dynamics / Stages in Family Life
Cycle; 2. Families with Special Problems / Family Violence.

871 Rawick, George P., ed. THE AMERICAN SLAVE: A COMPOSITE
AUTOBIOGRAPHY. VOL. 1: FROM SUNDOWN TO SUNUP: THE MAKING OF THE BLACK
COMMUNITY. Contributions in Afro-American and African Studies, No. 11.
Westport, CT: Greenwood Press, 1972. 208 pp., bibliography; ISBN:0-
8371-3314-9; LC:71-38591.

Subjects: 1. Trends and Change in Marriage and Family / Family Life
Prior to 1900.

A discussion of the Black family during slavery is presented in
chapter five.

Notes: Bibliography: pp. 179-200.

872 Reed, Fred W. and Udry, J. Richard. "Female Work, Fertility and
Contraceptive Use in a Biracial Sample." JOURNAL OF MARRIAGE AND THE
FAMILY 35, 4 (November 1973): 597-602. 6 pp., references, bibliography,
tables.

Subjects: 1. Organizations and Services to Families / Employment and the
Family; 2. Issues Related to Reproduction / Fertility Rates; 3. /
Birth Control.

873 Reed, Fred W., Udry, J. Richard and Ruppert, Maxine. "Relative
Income and Fertility: The Analysis of Individuals' Fertility in a
Biracial Sample." JOURNAL OF MARRIAGE AND THE FAMILY 37, 4 (November
1975): 799-805. 7 pp., references, tables.

Subjects: 1. Organizations and Services to Families / Economics and the
Family; 2. Issues Related to Reproduction / Fertility Rates.

  This research tested the hypothesis that fertility is directly
  related to the husband's relative income. Separate samples of blacks
  and whites were analyzed. Two measures of husband's relative income
  were found to be directly related to fertility for both blacks and
  whites even after controls are introduced for female's age at
  marriage, female's age at first birth, and duration of marriage. The
  statistical model we used explained about 45 per cent of the variance
  in the fertility of blacks and whites. (Authors' abstract)

874 Reed, Julia. "Marriage and Fertility in Black Female Teachers."
BLACK SCHOLAR 1, 3/4 (January-February 1970): 22-28. 7 pp., references,
tables.

Subjects: 1. Marriage and Divorce / Differential Marriage Rates; 2.
Issues Related to Reproduction / Fertility Rates.

  [C]ensus data for the United States (1960) suggest that, while black
  female teachers are more middle-class in some characteristics than
  their white counterparts, their adherence to (or achievement of)
  middle-class goals may produce a problem for them in their adjustment
  to marital and family life. Data also provided evidence for subsidiary
  hypotheses revolving around contradictions and dilemmas of status and
  roles: (1) that black female teachers are more middle class than their
  white counterparts in characteristics reflecting a large degree of
  individual initiative (years of school completed, propensity for
  marriage, patterns of fertility), and (2) less middle class in those
  characteristics which other persons or/and the social system may wield
  an impact strongly resistant to personal initiative (family income,
  occupation of spouse, marital stability). (From author's text)

875 Reid, Inez Smith. "TOGETHER" BLACK WOMEN. 1st edition New York:
Emerson Hall Publishers, Inc., 1972. 383 pp.; ISBN:0-87829-003-6;
LC:73-188561.

Subjects: 1. Family Relationships and Dynamics / Women's Issues.

  Notes: Prepared for the Black Women's Community Development
  Foundation. Distributed by Independent Publishers' Group.

876 Reiner, Beatrice Simcox. "The Real World of the Teenage Negro
Mother." CHILD WELFARE 47, 7 (July 1978): 391-96. 6 pp., references.

Subjects: 1. Issues Related to Reproduction / Teenage Pregnancy.

877 Reiss, David and Hoffman, Howard A., eds. THE AMERICAN FAMILY:
DYING OR DEVELOPING? New York: Plenum Press, 1979. 246 pp.,
bibliography, index; ISBN:0-306-40117-7; LC:78-24447.

Subjects: 1. Trends and Change in Marriage and Family / Family Life in the United States; 2. Family Relationships and Dynamics / Family Relationships; 3. Aids for Theory and Research / Collected Works.

Proceedings of the conference held in Washington, DC on   June   10-11, 1978.

878 Richardson, Barbara Blayton.   "Racism and Childrearing: A Study of Black Mothers." (Ph.D. dissertation, Claremont Graduate School, 1981.) DISSERTATION ABSTRACTS INTERNATIONAL, 42, 1, July 1981, 125A. (University Microfilms No. 8114049.) 385 pp.

Subjects: 1. Family Relationships and Dynamics / Mother-Child Relationships; 2. Psychology and Sociology / Racial Attitudes.

879 Riessman, Frank. THE INNER-CITY CHILD. 1st ed. New York: Harper and Row, 1976.   130 pp., references, index; ISBN:0-06-013567-0; LC:76-8414.

Subjects: 1. Organizations and Services to Families / Education and the Family.

880 Rindfuss, Ronald R.   "Minority Status and Fertility Revisited Again: A Comment on Johnson." AMERICAN JOURNAL OF SOCIOLOGY 86, 2 (September 1980): 372-75.   4 pp., references, charts.

Subjects: 1. Trends and Change in Marriage and Family / Family and Social Change; 2. Issues Related to Reproduction / Fertility Rates.

881 Ripley, C. Peter. "The Black Family in Transition: Louisiana, 1860-65." JOURNAL OF SOUTHERN HISTORY 41, 3 (August 1975): 369-80.   12 pp., references, tables.

Subjects: 1. Trends and Change in Marriage and Family / Family Life Prior to 1900.

Despite abuses inherent in the institution of slavery, marriage with strong   commitments existed between bonds persons in antebellum Louisiana. Interestingly, the Civil War generated its own set of problems for Black families. Thus when Union troops advanced, many fleeing planters took enslaved husbands and fathers with them to Texas AND abandoned wives, mothers, and children. The separation of enslaved conjugal families was furthermore a correlate of the Confederate military impressment of slave labor. Of course escape to Federal lines or liberation by the advancing Union army did not ensure that Black conjugal families would be exempted from forced separations. Hence in an effort to reduce the labor shortage in the areas of public works, fortifications, and plantations, Black laborers were moved about with an apparent little regard for keeping families intact. Even the quasi-"shanghaiing" of Blacks into military duty produced involuntary marital familial separations. Nevertheless, the various protests and actions that Blacks took to reunify their domestic and kin groups, both during slavery and in freedom, indicates the strong commitments that Blacks had to their families in Louisiana, 1860-1865.

882 Ritchey, P. Neal. "The Effect of Minority Group Status on Fertility: A Re-examination of Concepts." POPULATION STUDIES 29, 2 (July 1975): 249-57. 9 pp., references, tables, charts.

Subjects: 1. Issues Related to Reproduction / Fertility Rates; 2. Minority Groups / Family and Social Class.

883 Roberts, Joan I., ed. SCHOOL CHILDREN IN THE URBAN SLUM: READINGS IN SOCIAL SCIENCE RESEARCH. New York: The Free Press, 1967. 626 pp., bibliography, index; LC:67-12519.

Subjects: 1. Organizations and Services to Families / Education and the Family; 2. Psychology and Sociology / Sociology; 3. Aids for Theory and Research / Collected Works.

Notes: Produced through Project TRUE at Hunter College.

884 Roberts, Robert W., ed. THE UNWED MOTHER. New York: Harper and Row, 1966. 270 pp.; ISBN:0-448-12951-5; LC:66-12562.

Subjects: 1. Issues Related to Reproduction / Illegitimacy; 2. / Teenage Pregnancy; 3. Aids for Theory and Research / Collected Works.

885 Robertson, Diana Conway. "Parental Socialization Patterns in Interracial Adoption." (Ph.D. dissertation, University of California, Los Angeles, 1974.) DISSERTATION ABSTRACTS INTERNATIONAL, 35, 8, Feb. 1975, 5553A-5554A. (University Microfilms No. 751998.) 277 pp.

Subjects: 1. Organizations and Services to Families / Adoption and Adoption Services; 2. Family Relationships and Dynamics / Socialization; 3. Psychology and Sociology / Racial Attitudes.

886 Robertson, Leon S., Kosa, John, Alpert, Joel J. and Heagarty, Margaret C. "Race, Status and Medical Care." PHYLON 28, 4 (Winter 1967): 353-60. 8 pp., references, tables.

Subjects: 1. Organizations and Services to Families / Physical Health and the Family.

887 Robins, Lee N., West, Patricia A. and Herjanie, Barbara L. "Arrests and Delinquency in Two Generations: A Study of Black Urban Families and Their Children." JOURNAL OF CHILD PSYCHOLOGY AND PSYCHIATRY 16, 2 (April 1975): 125-40. 16 pp., references, tables, charts.

Subjects: 1. Families with Special Problems / Families with Juvenile Delinquents.

In interviews[,] a cohort of 223 young black urban-born men [from St. Louis] were asked for names and ages of their children and the children's mothers. Police and juvenile court records were obtained for both parents and all offspring past the age of official designation as a juvenile--145 children of 76 men qualified. A comparison of juvenile records of parents and children showed similar rates and types of offenses. Parental arrest histories were powerful predictors of their children's delinquency. Other family characteristics that might modify the risks of delinquency in children of arrested parents were explored. (Authors' summary)

888 Robins, Lee N. and Wish, Eric. "Childhood Deviance as a Development Process: A Study of 223 Urban Black Men from Birth to 18." SOCIAL FORCES 56, 2 (December 1977): 448-71. 24 pp., references, tables, charts.

Subjects: 1. Psychology and Sociology / Psychology; 2. Family Counseling and Education / Child Development.

Can one view deviance as a developmental process in which one type of deviant act leads to another? This paper proposes a number of criteria that would need to be met if there is such a process and applies them to data from records and retrospective interviews about the ages at which 13 kinds of childhood behaviors began. Results appear consistent with both a quantitative developmental process, i.e., one in which the probability ? of committing a new type of deviance is in part a function of the variety of acts previously committed, and a qualitative one, i.e., one in which having committed one particular type of deviant act makes more probable initiating another particular type of deviance thereafter. (Authors' abstract)

889 Rodgers-Rose, La Frances, ed. THE BLACK WOMAN. Sage Focus Editions, No. 21. Beverly Hills, CA: Sage Publications, Inc., 1980. 316 pp., references, bibliography, illustrations; ISBN:0-8039-1311-7; LC:79-28712.

Subjects: 1. Family Relationships and Dynamics / Family Relationships; 2. / Women's Issues; 3. Aids for Theory and Research / Collected Works.

The original works of sixteen Black female authors from the fields of sociology, social psychology, political science, demography and history. The volume is divided into four sections: social demographic characteristics of the Black woman; the Black woman and her family; political, educational, and economic institutions of the Black woman; and the social psychology of the Black woman. A total of nineteen pieces plus an historical overview are presented.

890 Rodman, Hyman. "Family and Social Pathology in the Ghetto." SCIENCE 161, 3843 (August 1968): 756-62. 7 pp., references.

Subjects: 1. Organizations and Services to Families / Physical Health and the Family.

891 Rodman, Hyman. LOWER-CLASS FAMILIES: THE CULTURE OF POVERTY IN NEGRO TRINIDAD. New York: Oxford University Press, 1971. 242 pp., references; LC:77-146953.

Subjects: 1. Trends and Change in Marriage and Family / Family and Social Change; 2. Minority Groups / Blacks in the Caribbean; 3. / Family and Social Class.

892 Rodman, Hyman and Crams, Paul. "Juvenile Delinquency and the Family: A Review and Discussion in the United States President's Commission on Law Enforcement and Administration of Justice." In A

FORMULATIVE AND EMPIRICAL STUDY OF BLACK FAMILIES. FINAL REPORT, by Wade
W. Nobles et al., pp. 188-221. San Francisco, CA: Westside Community
Mental Health Center, Inc., Research Department, 1976.   34 pp.

Subjects: 1. Families with Special Problems / Families with Juvenile
   Delinquents.

893   Romer, Nancy and Cherry, Debra.   "Ethnic and Social Class
Differences in Children's Sex-Role Concepts."   SEX ROLES: A JOURNAL OF
RESEARCH 6, 2 (April 1980): 245-63.   19 pp., references, tables.

Subjects: 1. Family Relationships and Dynamics / Family Roles and Sex
   Roles; 2. Minority Groups / Family and Social Class.

   Differences in sex-role concepts of 360 Black, Italian, and Jewish
   children, ages 10 through 17, from middle- and working-class families
   (as defined by parents' education) were examined through a modified
   version of the Sex Role Questionnaire, yielding descriptions of the
   self and the male and female sex-role stereotypes on both competence
   and expressive dimensions. . .In general, Black children describe the
   male sex-role stereotype as extremely expressive and perceive the two
   sex roles as fairly similar in expressiveness. Social class status has
   an opposite effect on sex-role definitions for Blacks than it does for
   Whites: Black middle-class children view the sex roles as clearly
   distinct on the competence dimension, describing the male stereotype
   as extremely competent; Black working-class children see the sex-role
   stereotypes as more blended on the competence dimension, describing
   the male sex role stereotype as relatively noncompetent. Ethnic and
   social class differences are cast in their historical and cultural
   contexts. (Authors' abstract)

894   Rooks, Evelyn and King, Karl.   "A Study of the Marriage Role
Expectations of Black Adolescents."   ADOLESCENCE 8, 31 (Fall 1973): 317-
24.   9 pp., references.

Subjects: 1. Marriage and Divorce / Marriage Satisfaction and Prediction
   Studies; 2. Family Counseling and Education / Adolescence.

895   Rosaldo, Michelle Zimbalist, Lamphere, Louise and Bamberger, Joan,
eds.   WOMAN, CULTURE, AND SOCIETY.   Stanford, CA: Stanford University
Press, 1974.   352 pp., bibliography; ISBN:0-8047-0850-9; LC:73-89861.

Subjects: 1. Family Relationships and Dynamics / Women's Issues; 2.
   Aids for Theory and Research / Collected Works.

   Notes: Bibliography: pp. 321-339.

896   Rosen, Lawrence.   "Matriarchy and Lower Class Negro Male
Delinquency."   SOCIAL PROBLEMS 17, 2 (Fall 1969): 175-89.   15 pp.,
references, bibliography, tables.

Subjects: 1. Family Relationships and Dynamics / Mother-Child
   Relationships; 2. Families with Special Problems / Families with
   Juvenile Delinquents; 3. Aids for Theory and Research / Family Theory.

897   Rosenberg, Morris and Simmons, Roberta G.   BLACK AND WHITE SELF-
ESTEEM: THE URBAN SCHOOL CHILD. The Arnold and Caroline Rose Monograph

Series in Sociology. Washington, DC: American Sociological Association,
1971. 160 pp.; ISBN:0-912764-05-8; LC:78-183124.

Subjects: 1. Psychology and Sociology / Psychology; 2. / Self-Esteem;
3. Family Counseling and Education / Child Development.

Notes: Bibliography: pp. 151-160.

898 Rosenfeld, Rachel A. "Race and Sex Differences in Career
Dynamics." AMERICAN SOCIOLOGICAL REVIEW 45, 4 (August 1980): 583-609.
27 pp., references, bibliography, tables, charts.

Subjects: 1. Organizations and Services to Families / Employment and the
Family.

899 Ross, Arthur Max and Hill, Herbert, eds. EMPLOYMENT, RACE AND
POVERTY. 1st ed. New York: Harcourt, Brace and World, Inc., 1967. 598
pp., references; LC:65-23537.

Subjects: 1. Organizations and Services to Families / Economics and the
Family; 2. / Employment and the Family; 3. Psychology and Sociology /
Racial Attitudes.

900 Ross, Joel A. "Influence of Expert and Peer upon Negro Mothers of
Low Socioeconomic Status." JOURNAL OF SOCIAL PSYCHOLOGY 89, First Half
(February 1973): 79-84. 6 pp., references.

Subjects: 1. Minority Groups / Family and Social Class.

The effectiveness of a white expert (psychologist) and that of a peer
in influencing Negro mothers of low socioeconomic status were
compared. Each subject was given advice by the expert after her young
child had been evaluated by him. Subjects then received a positive,
neutral, or negative opinion of the expert's advice from a confederate
peer. Results indicated that the expert was more effective than the
peer. While both sources had a significant immediate effect, the
expert was also significantly influential in having subjects act after
having left the testing situation. It was concluded that expertness
was the strongest factor, even though other factors like race and
referent-group membership might have worked against it. (Author's
summary)

901 Rosser, Pearl L. and Hamlin, Joyce Fite, eds. RESEARCH ON THE
BLACK CHILD AND FAMILY AT HOWARD UNIVERSITY: 1867-1978. Washington, DC:
Howard University, Institute for Child Development and Family Life,
1979. 42 pp., bibliography; LC:79-52708.

Subjects: 1. Family Relationships and Dynamics / Parent-Child
Relationships; 2. Aids for Theory and Research / Classified
Bibliographies of Family Literature.

Notes: Bibliography: p. 42.

902 Rowland, Glovioell Winsmore. "Early Effects of Postpartum
Intervention on Black Adolescent Mother-Infant Interaction." (Ph.D.
dissertation, Boston University Graduate School, 1980.) DISSERTATION

ABSTRACTS INTERNATIONAL, 41, 5, Nov. 1980, 1944B-1945B. (University Microfilms No. 8024217.) 131 pp.

Subjects: 1. Family Relationships and Dynamics / Parent-Child
  Relationships; 2. Issues Related to Reproduction / Teenage Pregnancy.

903 Rubin, Dorothy. "Parental Schemata of Negro Primary School
Children." PSYCHOLOGICAL REPORTS 25, 1 (August 1969): 60-62. 3 pp.,
references, tables.

Subjects: 1. Family Relationships and Dynamics / Parent-Child
  Relationships; 2. Family Counseling and Education / Education for
  Parenthood.

904 Rubin, Isadore. SEXUAL LIFE IN THE LATER YEARS. SIECUS Study
Guides, No. 12. New York: Sex Information and Education Council of the
U.S., 1970. 33 pp., bibliography; LC:73-17156.

Subjects: 1. Family Relationships and Dynamics / Later Years and Aging;
  2. Sexual Attitudes and Behavior / Sexual Attitudes and Behavior; 3.
  Family Counseling and Education / Sex Education.

905 Rubin, Isadore and Kirkendall, Lester A., comps. SEX IN THE
ADOLESCENT YEARS. New York: Association Press, 1968. 223 pp.; LC:68-
11492.

Subjects: 1. Sexual Attitudes and Behavior / Sexual Attitudes and
  Behavior; 2. Family Counseling and Education / Sex Education.

A collection of articles originally published in Sexology Magazine.

906 Rubin, Isadore and Kirkendall, Lester A., comps. SEX IN THE
CHILDHOOD YEARS: EXPERT GUIDANCE FOR PARENTS, COUNSELORS AND TEACHERS.
New York: Association Press, 1970. 190 pp.; ISBN:8096-1716-1; LC:69-
18849.

Subjects: 1. Family Counseling and Education / Child Development; 2. /
  Sex Education; 3. Aids for Theory and Research / Collected Works.

The articles in this collection originally appeared in the magazine
Sexology.

907 Rubin, Roger H. "Matriarchal Themes in Black Family Literature:
Implications for Family Life Education." FAMILY COORDINATOR 27, 1
(January 1978): 33-41. 9 pp., references, bibliography, tables.

Subjects: 1. Family Counseling and Education / Family Life Education;
  2. Aids for Theory and Research / Critiques and Analyses of Family
  Research Literature.

908 Rubin, Roger H. MATRICENTRIC FAMILY STRUCTURE AND THE SELF-
ATTITUDES OF NEGRO CHILDREN. San Francisco, CA: R and E Research
Associates, Inc., 1976. 75 pp., bibliography; ISBN:0-88247-391-3;
LC:75-41668.

Subjects: 1. Family Relationships and Dynamics / Family Relationships;
  2. Psychology and Sociology / Self-Esteem.

Notes: Bibliography: pp. 62-65.

909 Rutledge, Essie Manuel. "Marital Interaction Goals of Black Women:
Strengths and Effects." In THE BLACK WOMAN, edited by La Frances
Rodgers-Rose, pp. 145-59. Beverly Hills, CA: Sage Publications, Inc.,
1980. 15 pp.

Subjects: 1. Family Relationships and Dynamics / Husband-Wife
   Relationships; 2. Marriage and Divorce / Marriage Satisfaction and
   Prediction Studies.

The purpose of the study is to interpret marital 'strength' on the
basis of marital interaction goals. The study is based on a sample of
256 Black women [living in Detroit]. The findings indicate that the
most valued interaction goals were being a good wife, understanding
how the husband thinks, and helping to make big decisions. . .[T]hese
findings are quite contrary to the notion of Black female dominance
which has traditionally saturated the family literature. . .[T]he
least valued among the goals was having the kind of sex life desired.
The one variable which was most consistent in its impact on marital
interaction goals was the chance for extrafamilial activities. .
.[T]he marital relations of the Black women in. . .[this] study are
much more characteristic of 'strengths' than of weaknesses. (From the
editor's remarks)

910 Ryan, Vernon and Warland, Rex H. "Race and the Effect of Family
Status among Male Agricultural Laborers." RURAL SOCIOLOGY 43, 3 (Fall
1978): 335-47. 13 pp., references, bibliography, tables.

Subjects: 1. Minority Groups / Family and Social Class.

Daniel Patrick Moynihan's thesis that males in low income black
families do not adequately meet the economic demand of their nuclear
families was examined by investigating the effects of marital and
parental status positions on male agricultural workers' earnings.
Comparisons of these effects by race were also made to see how the
earnings of black male workers compared with the earnings of white
male workers. Generally the findings showed that black males earn more
if they have a wife and child (or children). The effect of the marital
position on earnings was significantly lower for blacks than for
whites, however. No difference was found in the case of the parental
position. In spite of minor differences by race, we conclude that the
findings question Moynihan's thesis, since higher earnings were
associated with the black males' family status. (Authors' abstract)

911 Ryan, William. BLAMING THE VICTIM. New York: Pantheon Books,
1971. 299 pp., references, index; ISBN:0-394-41726-7; LC:69-15476.

Subjects: 1. Trends and Change in Marriage and Family / Family and
   Social Change.

Notes: A revised, updated edition was published by Random House in
1976.

912 Safa, Helen Icken. AN ANALYSIS OF UPWARD MOBILITY IN LOW-INCOME
FAMILIES: A COMPARISON OF FAMILY AND COMMUNITY LIFE AMONG AMERICAN

NEGROES AND PUERTO RICAN POOR. Syracuse, NY: Syracuse University. Youth Development Center, 1967. 141 pp., references, tables; LC:70-77112.

Subjects: 1. Trends and Change in Marriage and Family / Family and Social Change; 2. / Social Mobility as it Affects the Family; 3. Organizations and Services to Families / Community Groups and the Family.

Notes: References cited on leaves 138-141.

913 Sager, Clifford J., Brayboy, Thomas L. and Waxenberg, Barbara R. BLACK GHETTO FAMILY IN THERAPY: A LABORATORY EXPERIENCE. New York: Grove Press Inc., 1970. 245 pp.; LC:71-111015.

Subjects: 1. Organizations and Services to Families / Mental Health and the Family; 2. Family Counseling and Education / Family Therapy.

Notes: A report of a laboratory conducted by the authors at the 26th annual conference of the American Group Psychotherapy Association, February 8, 1969. (From authors' introduction)

914 Samuels, Douglas D. and Griffore, Robert. "Ethnic Differences in Mothers' Anxiety." PSYCHOLOGICAL REPORTS 40, 3, Part Two (December 1977): 1270. 1 p., references, tables.

Subjects: 1. Family Relationships and Dynamics / Mother-Child Relationships.

915 Samuels, Shirley C. "An Investigation into the Self-Concepts of Lower and Middle-Class Black and White Kindergarten Children." JOURNAL OF NEGRO EDUCATION 42, 4 (Fall 1973): 467-72. 6 pp., references.

Subjects: 1. Family Relationships and Dynamics / Socialization; 2. Psychology and Sociology / Self-Esteem.

[Two child self concept tests, the Clark U-Scale and the Brown test, were administered to 93 randomly chosen subjects from a heterogenous kindergarten of a New York City suburb.] The white lower-class children and the black lower-class children were not significantly different from one another in either test. The black middle-class children had higher self concepts at a statistically significant level than the black lower-class children on both tests (p=.01). The same results were found for the white middle-class children, who had higher self concepts than the white lower-class children, only on the Clark U-Scale (p=.01). There were no significant differences on the Brown Test between the white middle- and lower-class children. No significant differences were found between the self concepts of the middle-class white and the middle-class black children. . .There was no relationship between the sex of the child, nursery school attendance, intactness of the home, the age of the mother, whether she worked or not or the family's mobility, and child self concept. . .This study provides evidence to substantiate the fact that the family's social status, which in our society is primarily dependent on the education and occupation of the father, has a bearing on how children feel about themselves. (From author's text)

916 Sanderson, P. Rhonne. "Black and White Single Parents' Attitudes toward Traditional Family Relations." (Ph.D. dissertation, The University of Florida, 1980.) DISSERTATION ABSTRACTS INTERNATIONAL, 41, 9, March 1981, 3890A. (University Microfilms No. 8105608.) 120 pp.

Subjects: 1. Family Relationships and Dynamics / Single Parent Families;
    2. / Family Relationships.

917 Sanderson, Warren C. "Herbert Gutman's THE BLACK FAMILY IN SLAVERY AND FREEDOM, 1750-1925: A Cliometric Reconsideration." SOCIAL SCIENCE HISTORY 3, 3/4 (October 1979): 66-85. 20 pp., references, tables.

Subjects: 1. Trends and Change in Marriage and Family / Family Life
    Prior to 1900.

918 Saunders, Marie Teresa. "Disciplinary Techniques of Black Mothers of Higher and Lower Socioeconomic Status: A Questionnaire and Interview Study." (Ed.D. dissertation, Columbia University Teachers College, 1980.) DISSERTATION ABSTRACTS INTERNATIONAL, 41, 1, July 1980, 194A. (University Microfilms No. 8015099.) 305 pp.

Subjects: 1. Family Relationships and Dynamics / Mother-Child
    Relationships.

919 Savage, James E. Jr., Adair, Alvis V. and Friedman, Philip. "Community-Social Variables Related to Black Parent-Absent Families." JOURNAL OF MARRIAGE AND THE FAMILY 40, 4 (November 1978): 779-85. 7 pp., references, bibliography.

Subjects: 1. Trends and Change in Marriage and Family / Alternative
    Family Forms; 2. Organizations and Services to Families / Social
    Services and the Family; 3. Family Relationships and Dynamics /
    Socialization.

    Psychological and systemic variables affecting black single-parent families were studied. An attempt was made to describe some of the forces that maintain or impede the functioning of the black single-parent family. Two hundred black parent-absent families divided into five groups (male-headed, parent-incarcerated, separated, divorced and widowed) responded to a series of questionnaires. Significant differences among these groups were observed with respect to their attitudes and feelings about family role structure, family cohesion and parent-child relationships. The impact of various societal systems were also perceived differently by the parent-absent groups. (Authors' abstract)

920 Scanzoni, John. "Sex Roles, Economic Factors, and Marital Solidarity in Black and White Marriages." JOURNAL OF MARRIAGE AND THE FAMILY 37, 1 (February 1975): 130-44. 15 pp., references, tables, charts.

Subjects: 1. Marriage and Divorce / Marriage Satisfaction and Prediction
    Studies; 2. Family Relationships and Dynamics / Family Roles and Sex
    Roles.

    Based on a five-state probability sample of households, black and white marriages are compared in terms of sex role norms, and influences on economic and marital satisfactions. Divergences appear by race with regards to measures of sex role egalitarianism. Basic processes are similar in both racial categories with respect to factors accounting for marital solidarity. (Author's abstract)

921 Scanzoni, John and Fox, Greer Litton. "Sex Roles, Family and Society: The Seventies and Beyond." JOURNAL OF MARRIAGE AND THE FAMILY 42, 4 (November 1980): 743-56. 15 pp., references, bibliography.

Subjects: 1. Family Relationships and Dynamics / Family Roles and Sex Roles.

922 Scanzoni, John H. THE BLACK FAMILY IN MODERN SOCIETY. Boston, MA: Allyn and Bacon, Inc., 1971. 353 pp., bibliography; LC:74-138817.

Subjects: 1. Trends and Change in Marriage and Family / Family Life in the United States; 2. Organizations and Services to Families / Economics and the Family; 3. Family Relationships and Dynamics / Family Relationships.

Notes: Bibliography: pp. 335-345.

923 Scarr, Sandra and Weinberg, Richard A. "I.Q. Test Performance of Black Children Adopted by White Families." AMERICAN PSYCHOLOGIST 31, 10 (October 1976): 726-39. 14 pp., references, tables.

Subjects: 1. Organizations and Services to Families / Education and the Family; 2. / Adoption and Adoption Services; 3. Families with Special Problems / Achievement and the Family.

The poor performance of black children on IQ tests and in school has been hypothesized to arise from (a) genetic racial differences or (b) cultural/environmental disadvantages. To separate genetic factors from rearing conditions, 130 black/interracial children adopted by advantaged white families were studied. The socially classified black adoptees, whose natural parents were educationally average, scored above the IQ and the school achievement mean of the white population. Biological children of the adoptive parents scored even higher. Genetic and environmental determinants of differences among the black/interracial adoptees were largely confounded. The high IQ scores of the socially classified black adoptees indicate malleability for IQ under rearing conditions that are relevant to the tests and the schools. (Authors' abstract)

924 Schab, Fred. "Work Ethic of Gifted Black Adolescents." JOURNAL OF YOUTH AND ADOLESCENCE 7, 3 (Summer 1978): 295-99. 5 pp., references, bibliography, tables.

Subjects: 1. Families with Special Problems / Achievement and the Family; 2. Family Counseling and Education / Adolescence.

The attitudes and opinions of 15 gifted Black male and 152 Black female adolescents toward their future in the world of work were surveyed. Under headings of self-determination on the job, rewards, and work philosophy, significant differences were found between the sexes. Males demanded more freedom and independence, yet would be more willing to unionize. They also believed men to be the main breadwinners and marriage more important to females. Gifted males wanted to surpass the successes of their parents more than did their gifted female peers. The latter would not put up with poor working conditions as often as would the males. Thus, among gifted Black adolescents the world of work is still the domain of the male. (Author's abstract)

925 Schneller, Donald P. "Prisoners' Families: A Study of Some Social and Psychological Effects of Incarceration on the Families of Negro Prisoners." CRIMINOLOGY 12, 4 (February 1975): 402-12. 11 pp., references, tables.

Subjects: 1. Families with Special Problems / Families with Criminal Offenders.

This study examines the effects of imprisonment on the families of inmates. Likert scaling procedures were used to measure three components of change occurring in 93 families subsequent to the incarceration of the family head. These are: change in social acceptance, change in economic status, and change in the degree of sexual and emotional frustration of the wife. Findings indicate that finances and sexual-emotional frustrations underwent significant change and became problematic for a majority of families. Contrary to expectations, changes in social acceptance of the families were neither significant nor problematic except for a small minority. (Author's abstract)

926 Schulz, David A. "Variations in the Father Role in Complete Families of the Negro Lower Class." SOCIAL SCIENCE QUARTERLY 49, 3 (December 1968): 651-59. 9 pp., references.

Subjects: 1. Family Relationships and Dynamics / Father-Child Relationships; 2. / Family Roles and Sex Roles.

927 Schulz, David Allen. COMING UP BLACK: PATTERNS OF GHETTO SOCIALIZATION. Englewood Cliffs, NJ: Prentice-Hall, 1969. 209 pp., bibliography; LC:69-15340.

Subjects: 1. Family Relationships and Dynamics / Extended Family and Kinship Groups; 2. / Family Roles and Sex Roles; 3. Issues Related to Reproduction / Illegitimacy.

928 Schwartz, Michael. "The Northern United States Negro Matriarchy: Status Versus Authority." PHYLON 26, 1 (Spring 1965): 18-24. 7 pp., references.

Subjects: 1. Family Relationships and Dynamics / Women's Issues; 2. Minority Groups / Family and Social Class; 3. Aids for Theory and Research / Family Theory.

929 Schweninger, Loren. "A Slave Family in the Antebellum South." JOURNAL OF NEGRO HISTORY 60, 1 (January 1975): 29-44., references, charts.

Subjects: 1. Trends and Change in Marriage and Family / Family Life Prior to 1900.

An investigation of one slave family will not end the controversy [on the impact of the peculiar institution on Black family life]. In a limited sense it can only tell us about A family, and one that was in many respects very fortunate. The members of the Thomas-Rapier slave family received an education; achieved a degree of economic independence; and eventually became free or at least "quasi-free." Moreover, they belonged to extremely permissive and beneficient masters. They lived in an urban environment (as did only 10% of the South's slave population), and hired out, though it was against the law. But, like many other Blacks in the ante bellum South, they too suffered the pains of separation (living in Alabama, Tennessee, and Canada); sexual exploitation (the slave mother bore three sons by three different white men); and the legal denial of the slave family. Yet, in spite of these institutional barriers or perhaps because of them, the members of the Thomas-Rapier family maintained their integrity. Indeed, as seen in a rare collection of slave letters, notes, and autobiographical reminiscences, they preserved a cohesive family unit for three generations. In a larger sense, then, an investigation of one slave family can perhaps shed some light on the family experiences of many slaves in the ante bellum South. (From author's text)

930 Sciara, Frank J. "Effects of Father Absence on the Educational Achievement of Urban Black Children." CHILD STUDY JOURNAL 5, 1 (Winter 1975): 45-55. 11 pp., references, tables.

Subjects: 1. Family Relationships and Dynamics / Father-Child Relationships; 2. Families with Special Problems / Achievement and the Family.

Achievement test scores in reading and arithmetic of 300 children from father absent homes and 773 children from father present homes were collected over a two year period and analyzed by utilizing the variables of year, sex, family status, and intelligence. These test scores were from fourth grade Black youngsters from eight Model Cities schools located in a low income area of a large midwestern metropolitan school system. Consistency of the test scores was established over the two year period. The analysis of variance revealed significant differences favoring the academic achievement of both boys and girls from father present homes in the two test areas. Father absence had a much greater effect on the achievement scores of boys and girls in this study whose measured I.Q. was above 100. (Author's abstract)

931 Sciara, Frank J. and Jantz, Richard K. "Father Absence and Its Apparent Effect on the Reading Achievement of Black Children from Low-Income Families." JOURNAL OF NEGRO EDUCATION 43, 2 (Spring 1974): 221-27. 7 pp., references, tables.

Subjects: 1. Organizations and Services to Families / Education and the Family; 2. Family Relationships and Dynamics / Father-Child Relationships; 3. Families with Special Problems / Achievement and the Family.

932 Scott-Jones, Diane. "Family Variables Associated with School Achievement in Low-Income Black First-Graders." (Ph.D. dissertation, The University of North Carolina at Chapel Hill, 1979.)

DISSERTATION ABSTRACTS INTERNATIONAL, 40, 8, Feb. 1980, 3986B.
(University Microfilms No. 8005072.) 139 pp.

Subjects: 1. Organizations and Services to Families / Education and the
     Family; 2. Family Relationships and Dynamics / Parent-Child
     Relationships; 3. Family Counseling and Education / Child Development.

933 Scott, James F.   "Police Authority and the Low-Income Black Family:
An Area Needed Research." In CRIME AND ITS IMPACT ON THE BLACK
COMMUNITY, edited by Lawrence E. Gary and Lee Brown, P., pp. 155-164.
Washington, DC: Howard University. Institute for Urban Affairs and
Research, 1975. 10 pp.

Subjects: 1. Organizations and Services to Families / Governmental Units
     and the Family; 2. Aids for Theory and Research / Critiques and
     Analyses of Family Research Literature.

934 Scott, Joseph W.   "Black Polygamous Family Formation: Case Studies
of Legal Wives and Consensual 'Wives'." ALTERNATIVE LIFESTYLES 3, 1
(February 1980): 41-64.   24 pp.

Subjects: 1. Trends and Change in Marriage and Family / Alternative
     Family Forms; 2. Marriage and Divorce / Marriage Customs and Forms; 3.
     Issues Related to Reproduction / Teenage Pregnancy.

This study examines how eleven legal wives and eleven consensual
wives drifted into polygamous (man-sharing) relationships. The study
also examines how the declining sex ratio may be influencing these and
other demographic developments in the black communities across the
United States. A case in point is the rising number of out-of-wedlock
births among black teenagers and their subsequent drift into man-
sharing arrangements due to the circumstances of the rating-dating-
mating marketplace. (Author's abstract)

935 Scott, Joseph W.   "Conceptualizing and Researching American
Polygyny--And Critics Answered." ALTERNATIVE LIFESTYLES 3, 4 (November
1980): 395-404.   10 pp.

Subjects: 1. Trends and Change in Marriage and Family / Alternative
     Family Forms; 2. Marriage and Divorce / Marriage Customs and Forms; 3.
     Aids for Theory and Research / Family Theory.

This article attempts to offer a rebuttal to some of the criticisms
advanced by the authors of the three rejoinders to my article "Black
Polygamous Family Formation." It focuses on the nature, meaning, and
conceptualization of a polygamous practice whereby a legally married
man takes on a second consensual mate, begins a second family, and
lives with it in coexistence with the first family. Both African and
African-American patterns are explored to see what the fundamental
differences or similarities are between these two patterns of plural
marriages--or what I call "polygynous relationships".   (Author's
abstract)

936 Scott, Joseph W.   "Polygamy: A Futuristic Family Arrangement for
African-Americans." BLACK BOOKS BULLETIN 4, 2 (Summer 1976): 13-19,25.
8 pp., references, illustrations.

Subjects: 1. Trends and Change in Marriage and Family / Alternative
Family Forms.

937 Scott, Joseph W. "The Sociology of the Other Woman." BLACK MALE/
FEMALE RELATIONSHIPS 2, 1 (January 1979): 30-32. 3 pp.

Subjects: 1. Family Relationships and Dynamics / Women's Issues; 2.
Sexual Attitudes and Behavior / Extramarital Sexual Behavior.

938 Scott, Mona Claire Vaughn. "Ethnic Differences in the Impact of
Family Background Factors on Level of Education and College
Completion." (Ph.D. dissertation, Stanford University, 1977.)
DISSERTATION ABSTRACTS INTERNATIONAL, 38, 6, Dec. 1977, 3757A.
(University Microfilms No. 7725722.) 204 pp.

Subjects: 1. Trends and Change in Marriage and Family / Comparative
Studies--International, Interclass, Sex, and Time Differences; 2.
Organizations and Services to Families / Education and the Family; 3.
Families with Special Problems / Achievement and the Family.

939 Scott, Patricia Bell. "Sex Roles Research and Black Families: Some
Comments on the Literature." JOURNAL OF AFRO-AMERICAN ISSUES 4, 3/4
(Summer/Fall 1976): 349-61. 13 pp., references.

Subjects: 1. Family Relationships and Dynamics / Family Roles and Sex
Roles; 2. Aids for Theory and Research / Critiques and Analyses of
Family Research Literature.

940 Scott, Patricia Bell and McKenry, Patrick C. "Some Suggestions for
Teaching about Black Adolescence." FAMILY COORDINATOR 26, 1 (January
1977): 47-51. 5 pp., references.

Subjects: 1. Family Counseling and Education / Adolescence; 2. / Family
Life Education.

This paper seeks to explore a neglected area in family life
education--that area being black adolescence. The influence that black
culture has upon the maturation process is discussed. Some suggestions
for exploring black adolescent experience are outlined for educators
and other helping professionals. (Authors' abstract)

941 Scott, Patricia Bell and Weddle, Karen. "Bringing Outsiders into
the Legislative Process: A Brief Report from a Pilot Project in the
Black Community." FAMILY COORDINATOR 26, 4 (October 1977): 478-80. 2
pp.

Subjects: 1. Organizations and Services to Families / Family Law.

942 Scott, Ralph. "Home Start: Family-Centered Preschool Enrichment
for Black and White Children." PSYCHOLOGY IN THE SCHOOLS 10, 2 (April
1973): 140-46. 7 pp., references, tables.

Subjects: 1. Family Counseling and Education / Marital and Family
Enrichment.

943 Scott, Ralph and Kobes, David A. "The Influence of Family Size on
Learning Readiness Patterns of Socioeconomically Disadvantaged Preschool

Blacks." JOURNAL OF CLINICAL PSYCHOLOGY 31, 1 (January 1975): 85-88. 4 pp., references, tables.

Subjects: 1. Organizations and Services to Families / Education and the Family; 2. Issues Related to Reproduction / Family Planning; 3. Family Counseling and Education / Early Childhood Education.

Preschool readiness measures were secured on 35 pairs of disadvantaged 2- to 3-year-old lower-SES black children, who represented large and small families, to determine the impact of family size on readiness profiles. The findings reveal that blacks from small families achieved significantly higher scores on three of the nine skill areas: Visual Memory, Expressive Language, and Expressive Concepts. The results were reviewed in the context of Inhelder-Piaget formulations that concern the early growth of the intellect, which provide a possible explanation of how intra-family dynamics may depress the learning of black lower-SES preschool children. It is suggested that replication and longitudinal studies are needed to ascertain better the long-term social and educational implications of these findings. (Authors' summary)

944 Sebald, Hans. "Patterns of Interracial Dating and Sexual Liaison of White and Black College Men." INTERNATIONAL JOURNAL OF SOCIOLOGY OF THE FAMILY 4, 1 (Spring 1974): 23-27. 5 pp.

Subjects: 1. Mate Selection / Dating, Courtship, and Romanticism; 2. Sexual Attitudes and Behavior / Sexual Attitudes and Behavior.

945 Semaj, Leahcim Tufani. "Meaningful Male/Female Relationships in a State of Declining Sex-Ratio." BLACK BOOKS BULLETIN 6, 4 (Winter 1978): 4-10. 7 pp., references, illustrations.

Subjects: 1. Family Relationships and Dynamics / Premarital Couples; 2. Mate Selection / Dating, Courtship, and Romanticism.

946 Shade, Barbara J. "Regional Differences in Personality of Afro-American Children." JOURNAL OF SOCIAL PSYCHOLOGY 107, First Half (February 1979): 71-76. 6 pp., references.

Subjects: 1. Psychology and Sociology / Psychology; 2. Family Counseling and Education / Child Development.

This study was designed to determine whether regional differences could be found in an Afro-American population as they had been in previous studies of the general population. With the use of the Coan-Cattell Early School Questionnaire, 120 children from two different cities were compared by region, sex, and age. An analysis of variance revealed no differences within groups but found differences according to regions, along with some expected age differences. It was concluded that if geographical differences are considered along with those usually found for socioeconomic status, age, and sex, perhaps ethnicity is not nearly as important a variable as is currently maintained. (Author's summary)

947 Shanas, Ethel. "Family-Kin Networks and Aging in Cross-Cultural Perspective." JOURNAL OF MARRIAGE AND THE FAMILY 35, 3 (August 1973): 505-11. 8 pp., references, tables.

Subjects: 1. Family Relationships and Dynamics / Extended Family and
Kinship Groups; 2. / Later Years and Aging.

948 Shanas, Ethel and Streib, Gordon Franklin, eds. SYMPOSIUM ON THE
FAMILY, INTERGENERATIONAL RELATIONS AND SOCIAL
STRUCTURE. DUKE UNIVERSITY, 1963. SOCIAL STRUCTURE AND THE FAMILY:
GENERATIONAL RELATIONS. Prentice-Hall Sociology Series. Englewood
Cliffs, NJ: Prentice-Hall, 1965. 394 pp., bibliography; LC:65-25258.

Subjects: 1. Trends and Change in Marriage and Family / Comparative
Studies--International, Interclass, Sex, and Time Differences; 2.
Family Relationships and Dynamics / Later Years and Aging; 3. Aids for
Theory and Research / Collected Works.

Notes: A report of a symposium sponsored by the Program in
Socioeconomic Studies of Aging, Duke University, and the Special
Projects Committee, the Psychological and Social Sciences Section of
the Gerontological Society. (NUC)

949 Shannon, Lyle W. "The Changing World View of Minority Migrants in
an Urban Setting." HUMAN ORGANIZATION 38, 1 (Spring 1972): 56-62. 11
pp., references, bibliography, tables.

Subjects: 1. Trends and Change in Marriage and Family / Family and
Social Change; 2. Family Relationships and Dynamics / Socialization;
3. Families with Special Problems / Family and Geographic Mobility.

950 Shell, Juanita. "Familial, Situational, and Cognitive Determinants
of Sharing Behavior in African American Children." (Ph.D. dissertation,
City University of New York, 1977.) DISSERTATION ABSTRACTS
INTERNATIONAL, 38, 6, Dec. 1977, 2949B. (University Microfilms
No. 7727626.) 126 pp.

Subjects: 1. Family Relationships and Dynamics / Family Relationships;
2. Psychology and Sociology / Psychology; 3. Family Counseling and
Education / Child Development.

951 Sherman, Julia A. and Denmark, Florence L., eds. THE PSYCHOLOGY OF
WOMEN: FUTURE DIRECTIONS IN RESEARCH. New York: Psychological
Dimensions, 1978. 758 pp., bibliography, index; ISBN:0-88437-009-7;
LC:78-31824.

Subjects: 1. Family Relationships and Dynamics / Women's Issues; 2.
Psychology and Sociology / Psychology.

Notes: Based on the proceedings of a conference sponsored by the
Department of Curriculum and Instruction, School of Education,
University of Wisconsin.

952 Sherman, Roger Holmes. "Portraits of Family and Kinship Relations
among Black Americans: A Study in the Properties, Structures and
Functions of Primary Groups." (Ph.D. dissertation, Columbia University,
1980.) DISSERTATION ABSTRACTS INTERNATIONAL, 43, 5, Nov. 1982, 1709A-
1710A. (University Microfilms No. 8222487.) 789 pp.

Subjects: 1. Family Relationships and Dynamics / Extended Family and Kinship Groups; 2. Aids for Theory and Research / Critiques and Analyses of Family Research Literature.

953 Shifflet, Crandall A. "The Household Composition of Rural Black Families: Louisa County, Virginia, 1880." JOURNAL OF INTERDISCIPLINARY HISTORY 6, 2 (Autumn 1975): 235-60. 26 pp., references, tables, charts.

Subjects: 1. Trends and Change in Marriage and Family / Family Life Prior to 1900.

954 Shimkin, Demitri P., Shimkin, Edith M. and Frate, Dennis, eds. THE EXTENDED FAMILY IN BLACK SOCIETIES. The Hague: Mouton and Company, 1978. 526 pp., references, illustrations, tables, charts, index; ISBN:90-279-7590-6.

Subjects: 1. Family Relationships and Dynamics / Extended Family and Kinship Groups.

Growing out of presentations to the IXth International Congress of Anthropological and Ethnological Sciences, the sixteen essays in this volume focus on Afroamerican multi-household extended families. More specifically, the theoretical, conceptual, and/or interpretive essays, the ethnographic studies focusing on various locales in the United States, and the comparative papers based on the field investigations of Caribbeanists and Africanists, explore the continuity and variation in Black kinship and domestic groups. The implications of such data for policy implications are addressed in a final essay.

955 Shin, Eui Hang. "Correlates of Intercounty Variations in Net Migration Rates of Blacks in the Deep South, 1960-1970." RURAL SOCIOLOGY 44, 1 (Spring 1979): 39-55. 17 pp., references, tables, charts.

Subjects: 1. Families with Special Problems / Family and Geographic Mobility; 2. Psychology and Sociology / Sociology; 3. Aids for Theory and Research / Statistics.

956 Sickels, Robert J. RACE, MARRIAGE AND THE LAW. Albuquerque, NM: University of New Mexico Press, 1972. 167 pp., bibliography; ISBN:0-8263-0256-4; LC:72-86815.

Subjects: 1. Organizations and Services to Families / Family Law; 2. Marriage and Divorce / Inter-marriage; 3. Psychology and Sociology / Racial Attitudes.

Notes: Bibliography: pp. 162-164.

957 SIECUS Conference on Religion and Sexuality, St. Louis, 1971. SEXUALITY AND HUMAN VALUES: THE PERSONAL DIMENSION OF SEXUAL EXPERIENCE, edited by Mary Calderone. New York: Association Press, 1974. 158 pp., bibliography; ISBN:0-8096-1891-5; LC:74-22119.

Subjects: 1. Sexual Attitudes and Behavior / Sexual Attitudes and Behavior; 2. Family Counseling and Education / Sex Education; 3. Aids for Theory and Research / Collected Works.

Notes: Bibliography: pp. 157-158.

958 Siegel, Jacob S. "Estimates of Coverage of the Population by Sex, Race and Age in the 1970 Census." DEMOGRAPHY 11, 1 (February 1974): 1-23.

Subjects: 1. Trends and Change in Marriage and Family / Comparative Studies--International, Interclass, Sex, and Time Differences; 2. Aids for Theory and Research / Statistics.

959 Silverstein, Barry and Krate, Ronald. CHILDREN OF THE DARK GHETTO: A DEVELOPMENTAL PSYCHOLOGY. New York: Praeger Publishing Co., 1975. 271 pp., references, index; ISBN:0-275-50370-4; LC:74-23264.

Subjects: 1. Trends and Change in Marriage and Family / Family and Social Change; 2. Family Relationships and Dynamics / Socialization; 3. Psychology and Sociology / Racial Attitudes.

960 Simmons, Joe Louis. "A Study of the Relationship between Father-Absent Homes and Father-Present Homes and the Academic Performance and Social Adjustment of Black Middle School Students." (Ed.D. dissertation, The College of William and Mary in Virginia, 1981.) DISSERTATION ABSTRACTS INTERNATIONAL, 43, 3, Sept. 1982, 618A. (University Microfilms No. 8218005.) 141 pp.

Subjects: 1. Organizations and Services to Families / Education and the Family; 2. Family Relationships and Dynamics / Father-Child Relationships; 3. Families with Special Problems / Achievement and the Family.

961 Simmons, Roberta G., Brown, Leslie, Bush, Diane Mitsch and Blyth, Dale A. "Self-Esteem and Achievement of Black and White Adolescents." SOCIAL PROBLEMS 26, 1 (October 1978): 89-96. 11 pp., references, tables.

Subjects: 1. Families with Special Problems / Achievement and the Family; 2. Psychology and Sociology / Self-Esteem.

962 Simon, Rita J. "Black Attitudes toward Transracial Adoption." PHYLON 39, 2 (June 1978): 135-42. 8 pp., references, tables.

Subjects: 1. Organizations and Services to Families / Adoption and Adoption Services.

The purpose of the survey was to assess the attitudes and predict the behavior of middle-class, young, educated black men and women on two themes: 1) their willingness to adopt and 2) their attitudes toward the practice of transracial adoption. [W]hile many of the respondents showed a strong interest in limiting the size of their families as manifest both by the number of children they had and by the number they planned to have, almost one out of five said they would be willing to and interested in adopting a child if the government offered even minimal financial incentives. [Such incentives] would place most of the black children with families who wanted them, and on the other, it would resolve the current anger and objections that black social workers and leaders of black social movements have toward the practice of transracial adoption. As the results of this survey demonstrate, it is not only black leaders who object to and attack the practice, but rank and file, middle-class blacks as well. Between 60 and 70 percent believe that white parents do not know how to rear black children and that those black children who are adopted by whites will be lost to the black community. (Author's conclusion)

963 Simon, Rita James. "An Assessment of Racial Awareness, Preference, and Self-Identity among White and Adopted Non-White Children." SOCIAL PROBLEMS 22, 1 (October 1974): 43-57., references, tables.

Subjects: 1. Psychology and Sociology / Racial Attitudes.

This article reports levels of racial awareness, racial preferences, and racial identities among non-white children (American Negro, Korean, American Indian), who have been adopted by white families, and their white siblings who have been born into those families. The respondents are all children between the ages of three and eight. The basic question addressed in the research is how similar or different are the reactions of these children compared to those of the same sex, age range, and race who have been reared in typical family settings. The major findings are that black children who are reared in the special setting of multi-racial families do not acquire the ambivalence toward their own race that has been reported among all other groups of young black children and that there are no significant differences in the racial attitudes of any of the categories of children. (Author's abstract)

964 Simon, Rita James and Altstein, Howard. TRANSRACIAL ADOPTION. New York: John Wiley and Sons, Inc., 1977. 197 pp., references, index; ISBN:0-471-79208-X; LC:76-44817.

Subjects: 1. Organizations and Services to Families / Adoption and Adoption Services; 2. Family Relationships and Dynamics / Socialization; 3. Minority Groups / Ethnic Groups in the United States.

[The researchers] provide empirical data on the adjustments of the nonwhite adopted children to their new family, on the quality of the relationships among white and nonwhite children in those families, and on how the children's racial preferences, awareness, and identities have been affected by unusual family composition. [Finally subsidized and single-parent adoptions are discussed as alternatives to transracial adoption]. (From authors' 'Preface')

965 Sims, Edward, Jr. and Snowden, Thomas Gayle. BLACK NOMADS IN THE URBAN CENTERS: THE EFFECTS OF RACISM AND URBANISM ON THE BLACK FAMILY. Washington, DC: University Press of America, 1978. 185 pp., bibliography; LC:79-132302.

Subjects: 1. Trends and Change in Marriage and Family / Family and Social Change; 2. Family Relationships and Dynamics / Environment (Space/Housing); 3. Psychology and Sociology / Racial Attitudes.

Notes: Bibliography: pp. 175-185.

966 Sims, Janet L., comp. THE PROGRESS OF AFRO-AMERICAN WOMEN: A
SELECTED BIBLIOGRAPHY AND RESOURCE GUIDE. Westport, CT: Greenwood
Press, 1980.   378 pp.; ISBN:0-313-22083-2; LC:79-8948.

Subjects: 1. Family Relationships and Dynamics / Women's Issues; 2.
  Aids for Theory and Research / Classified Bibliographies of Family
  Literature.

967 Sitgraves, Mary Elizabeth. "Recent Life Event Stress and Patterns
of Mother-Son Interaction in High Risk Versus Low Risk Black
Mothers." (Ph.D. dissertation, Boston University Graduate School, 1980.)
DISSERTATION ABSTRACTS INTERNATIONAL, 40, 12, June 1980, 5832B.
(University Microfilms No. 8013300.) 275 pp.

Subjects: 1. Family Relationships and Dynamics / Mother-Child
  Relationships; 2. Families with Special Problems / Family Stress.

968 Skerry, Peter. "The Black Family Revisited." HUMAN LIFE REVIEW 7,
1 (Winter 1981): 78-89. 12 pp., references.

Subjects: 1. Family Relationships and Dynamics / Family Relationships.

969 Slaughter, Diana T. "The Black Child: Issues and Priorities."
JOURNAL OF BLACK PSYCHOLOGY 10th Anniversary Edition IV, 1/2 (August
1977-Feb. 1978): 119-33. 15 pp., references.

Subjects: 1. Family Counseling and Education / Child Development.

970 Slovenko, Ralph, ed. SEXUAL BEHAVIOR AND THE LAW. Springfield,
IL: Charles C. Thomas Publishers, 1965. 886 pp., references; LC:64-
18728.

Subjects: 1. Sexual Attitudes and Behavior / Sexual Attitudes and
  Behavior; 2. Families with Special Problems / Families with Criminal
  Offenders; 3. Aids for Theory and Research / Collected Works.

971 Smallwood, James. "Emancipation and the Black Family: A Case Study
in Texas." SOCIAL SCIENCE QUARTERLY 57, 4 (March 1977): 849-57. 9 pp.,
references, bibliography, tables.

Subjects: 1. Trends and Change in Marriage and Family / Family Life
  Prior to 1900.

  [Reviewing the testimonies of captives, letters, documents pertaining
  to complaints and litigation actions, and the 1870 Federal manuscript
  census   for   three   rural Texas counties--Matagorah, Smith, and
  Grayson:], this survey would suggest that by 1870 the black family in
  Texas had acquired a remarkable degree of stability. Excepting the
  differences. . . such as the high percentage of black women and
  children working and varied occupational patterns based largely on
  racial lines, the black family closely resembled the white. Households
  and individual families were approximately the same size, with about
  the same percentage headed by males. While. . .the tendency toward
  matriarchy in slave households was not as strong as some scholars had
  previously supposed, this study suggests that the trend toward
  patriarchy evolved into the norm in the black community   in
  Reconstruction Texas, as men headed most black households.

Legalization of marriages along with the actions of well-intentioned bureau agents and preachers and teachers, both black and white, helped stabilize the black family. In addition, most freedmen apparently had strong familial instincts--at least as strong as their white cunterparts. (From author's text)

972 Smith, Daniel Scott, Dahlin, Michel and Friedberger, Mark. "The Family Structure of the Older Black Population in the American South in 1880 and 1900." SOCIAL SCIENCE RESEARCH 63, 3 (April 1979): 544-65. 22 pp., references, tables.

Subjects: 1. Trends and Change in Marriage and Family / Family Life Prior to 1900.

This paper explores the relations between southern black and white old people and their adult children. The data derive from samples of persons over age 65 taken from the U.S. manuscript censuses for 1880 and 1900. The families of older blacks and whites were similar in several important ways. Only half of old blacks, however, lived with children compared to nearly seventy percent of whites. Co-residence of adult generations was related to family economic activity and to the provision of welfare to needy kin. Economic factors account for part of the black-white differential and for differentials within the black population. Both black and white families served welfare functions, but welfare in the black family flowed more from older to younger generations. (Authors' abstract)

973 Smith, Larry J. BLACK-WHITE REPRODUCTIVE BEHAVIOR: AN ECONOMIC INTERPRETATION. San Francisco, CA: R and E Research Associates, Inc., 1977. 132 pp., bibliography, charts; ISBN:0-88247-453-7; LC:76-56467.

Subjects: 1. Issues Related to Reproduction / Family Planning; 2. / Fertility Rates; 3. Aids for Theory and Research / Family Research Methodology.

Notes: Bibliography: pp. 128-132.

974 Smith, Virginia Ware. "The Impact of Selected Internal and External Influences on Successful Coping among Mothers of Children with Sickle Cell Disease." (Ph.D. dissertation, Saint Louis University, 1980.) DISSERTATION ABSTRACTS INTERNATIONAL, 42, 4, Oct. 1981, 1798A. (University Microfilms No. 8120648.) 235 pp.

Subjects: 1. Organizations and Services to Families / Physical Health and the Family; 2. Families with Special Problems / Family Stress.

975 Snell, Dee. HOW TO GET AND HOLD YOUR BLACK MAN IN SPITE OF WOMEN'S LIB. Baltimore, MD: Ceehul Publishing Company, 1974.

Subjects: 1. Family Relationships and Dynamics / Women's Issues; 2. Mate Selection / Mate Selection, Differential Patterns.

976 Snow, Jacquelyn E. "A Heuristic Study of Black Female Heads of Households and Black Females Who Are Not Heads of Households and Their Involvement with Their Children's Educational Development in Camden, New Jersey." (Ed.D. dissertation, Rutgers University, The State University of New Jersey (New Brunswick), 1976.) DISSERTATION ABSTRACTS

INTERNATIONAL, 37, 12, June 1977, 8002A. (University Microfilms
No. 7713291.) 139 pp.

Subjects: 1. Organizations and Services to Families / Education and the
   Family; 2. Family Relationships and Dynamics / Nuclear Family; 3. /
   Single Parent Families.

977 Sobol, Marion G. and Beck, William W. "Perceptions of Black
Parents in an Undesegregated Subdistrict of an Integrated School
System." URBAN EDUCATION 12, 4 (January 1978): 411-22. 12 pp.,
references, tables.

Subjects: 1. Organizations and Services to Families / Education and the
   Family.

978 Solomon, Barbara Bryant and Mendes, Helen A. "Black Families: A
Social Welfare Perspective." In THIS SPECIES OF PROPERTY: SLAVE LIFE
AND CULTURE IN THE OLD SOUTH, by Leslie Howard Owens, pp. 271-95. New
York: Oxford University Press, 1976. 25 pp., references.

Subjects: 1. Organizations and Services to Families / Social Welfare.

979 Spaights, Ernest. "Some Dynamics of the Black Family." NEGRO
EDUCATIONAL REVIEW 24, 3/4 (July-October 1973): 127-37. 11 pp.,
references.

Subjects: 1. Family Relationships and Dynamics / Family Relationships.

980 Spain, Johnny. "The Black Family and the Prisons." BLACK SCHOLAR
4, 2 (October 1972): 18-31. 14 pp., references.

Subjects: 1. Families with Special Problems / Families with Criminal
   Offenders.

981 Spurlock, Jeanne. "Introduction: Children and Families -- Cultural
Differences and Mental Health." PSYCHIATRIC ANNALS 6, 5 (May 1976): 11-
12. 2 pp., bibliography, illustrations.

Subjects: 1. Organizations and Services to Families / Mental Health and
   the Family; 2. Family Relationships and Dynamics / Family
   Relationships.

982 Stack, Carol B. ALL OUR KIN: STRATEGIES FOR SURVIVAL IN A BLACK
COMMUNITY. 1st ed. New York: Harper and Row, 1974. 175 pp.,
bibliography, index; ISBN:0-06-013974-9; LC:73-4126.

Subjects: 1. Organizations and Services to Families / Economics and the
   Family; 2. Family Relationships and Dynamics / Extended Family and
   Kinship Groups; 3. Families with Special Problems / Family Stress.

   Black families in The Flats [an urban midwestern ghetto] and the non-
   kin they regard as kin have evolved patterns of co-residence, kinship-
   based exchange networks linking multiple domestic units, elastic
   household boundaries, lifelong bonds of three-generational households,
   social controls against the formation of marriage that could endanger
   the network of kin, the domestic authority of women, and limitations
   on the role of the husband or male friend within a woman's kin

network. These highly adoptive structural features of urban black families comprise a resilient response to the social-economic conditions of poverty, the inexorable unemployment of black women and men, and the access to scarce economic resources of a mother and her children as AFDC recipients. (From author's 'Conclusion' written in collaboration with John R. Lombardi)

Notes: Bibliography: pp. 160-67.

983 Stack, Carol B.   "Sex Roles and Survival Strategies in an Urban Black Community."   In WOMAN, CULTURE, AND SOCIETY, edited by Michelle Zimbalist Rosaldo, Louise Lamphere and Joan Bamberger, pp. 113-128. Stanford, CA: Stanford University Press, 1974. 16 pp.

Subjects: 1. Family Relationships and Dynamics / Family Roles and Sex Roles; 2. Families with Special Problems / Family Stress.

Notes: Adapted from Chapter 7 of the author's monograph, ALL OUR KIN.

984 Stack, Carol B. and Semmel, Herbert.   "The Concept of Family in the Poor Black Community."   STUDIES IN PUBLIC WELFARE 12, 2 (November 1973): 275-305. 31 pp., references, tables.

Subjects: 1. Trends and Change in Marriage and Family / Family Life in the United States; 2. Family Relationships and Dynamics / Family Relationships.

985 Staples, Robert.   "Beyond the Black Family: The Trend toward Singlehood."   THE WESTERN JOURNAL OF BLACK STUDIES 3, 3 (Fall 1979): 150-156. 7 pp., references, illustrations.

Subjects: 1. Trends and Change in Marriage and Family / Alternative Family Forms; 2. Family Relationships and Dynamics / Singles (Lifestyle).

986 Staples, Robert.   "The Black American Family."   In ETHNIC FAMILIES IN AMERICA: PATTERNS AND VARIATIONS (2nd ed.), edited by Charles H. Mindel and Robert Wesley Habenstein, pp. 221-47. New York: Elsevier North-Holland, Inc., 1981. 27 pp., references.

Subjects: 1. Trends and Change in Marriage and Family / Family Life in the United States; 2. Aids for Theory and Research / Family Research Methodology; 3. / Family Theory.

987 Staples, Robert.   "The Black Family in Evolutionary Perspective." BLACK SCHOLAR 5, 9 (June 1974): 2-9. 8 pp., references.

Subjects: 1. Family Relationships and Dynamics / Family Relationships; 2. Aids for Theory and Research / Family Theory.

988 Staples, Robert.   "The Black Family Revisited: A Review and Preview."   JOURNAL OF SOCIAL AND BEHAVIOR SCIENCES 20, 2 (Spring 1974): 65-78. 14 pp.

Subjects: 1. Trends and Change in Marriage and Family / Family Life in the United States; 2. Family Relationships and Dynamics / Family

Relationships; 3. Aids for Theory and Research / Critiques and
Analyses of Family Research Literature.

989 Staples, Robert. BLACK MASCULINITY: THE BLACK MALE'S ROLE IN
AMERICAN SOCIETY. San Francisco: Black Scholar Press, 1982. 182 pp.,
references; ISBN:0-933296-07-X; LC:81-69452.

Subjects: 1. Family Relationships and Dynamics / Family Roles and Sex
  Roles; 2. / Men's Issues.

990 Staples, Robert. "Black Singles in America." In SINGLE LIFE:
UNMARRIED ADULTS IN SOCIAL CONTEXT, by Peter J. Stein, pp. 40-51. New
York: St. Martin's Press, 1981. 12 pp.

Subjects: 1. Family Relationships and Dynamics / Singles (Lifestyle).

991 Staples, Robert. "Intimacy Patterns among Black, Middle-Class
Single Parents." ALTERNATIVE LIFESTYLES 3, 4 (November 1980): 445-62.
18 pp.

Subjects: 1. Trends and Change in Marriage and Family / Alternative
  Family Forms; 2. Family Relationships and Dynamics / Single Parent
  Families; 3. Mate Selection / Dating, Courtship, and Romanticism.

  Based on a study of college-educated, Black, single parents living in
  urban areas, the author explores the problems and experiences peculiar
  to women with children who must fulfill roles of worker, parent, and
  romantic companion. While the existence of children complicates the
  normative problems associated with heterosexual intimacy, they also
  give these women a mechanism for coping with their single status.
  Children do impose a different single lifestyle on single mother and
  impose constraints on their time, sexual behavior, desirability, and
  mate selection standards. (Author's abstract)

992 Staples, Robert. "Male/Female Sexual Variations: Functions of
Biology or Culture." JOURNAL OF SEX RESEARCH 9, 1 (February 1973): 11-
20. 10 pp., references.

Subjects: 1. Mate Selection / Mate Selection, Differential Patterns; 2.
  Sexual Attitudes and Behavior / Sexual Attitudes and Behavior.

993 Staples, Robert. "Masculinity and Race: The Dual Dilemma of Black
Men." JOURNAL OF SOCIAL ISSUES 34, 1 (Winter 1978): 169-83. 15 pp.,
references, bibliography.

Subjects: 1. Family Relationships and Dynamics / Men's Issues.

994 Staples, Robert. "The Matricentric Family System: A Cross-Cultural
Exploration." JOURNAL OF MARRIAGE AND THE FAMILY 34, 1 (February 1972):
156-166. 11 pp.

Subjects: 1. Trends and Change in Marriage and Family / Comparative
  Studies--International, Interclass, Sex, and Time Differences; 2.
  Family Relationships and Dynamics / Family Relationships; 3. Aids for
  Theory and Research / Family Theory.

995 Staples, Robert. "The Mexican-American Family: Its Modifications Over Time and Space." PHYLON 32, (Summer 1971): 179-193. 15 pp.

Subjects: 1. Trends and Change in Marriage and Family / Comparative Studies--International, Interclass, Sex, and Time Differences; 2. Minority Groups / Ethnic Groups in the United States.

996 Staples, Robert. "The Myth of Black Macho: A Response to Angry Black Feminists." BLACK SCHOLAR 10, 6/7 (March-April 1979): 24-33. 10 pp., references.

Subjects: 1. Family Relationships and Dynamics / Men's Issues; 2. Mate Selection / Mate Selection, Differential Patterns; 3. Psychology and Sociology / General Attitudes.

997 Staples, Robert. "The Myth of the Black Matriarchy." BLACK SCHOLAR 1, 3 (January 1970): 8-16. 9 pp.

Subjects: 1. Trends and Change in Marriage and Family / Family Life in the United States; 2. Family Relationships and Dynamics / Women's Issues; 3. Aids for Theory and Research / Family Theory.

998 Staples, Robert. "The New Majority: Black Singles in America." In SINGLES AND SOCIETY, edited by P. Stein and R. Hilty, p. . New York: St. Martin's Press, 1981.

Subjects: 1. Family Relationships and Dynamics / Singles (Lifestyle).

999 Staples, Robert. "Public Policy and the Changing Status of Black Families." FAMILY COORDINATOR 22, 3 (July 1973): 345-51. 7 pp., references.

Subjects: 1. Organizations and Services to Families / Governmental Units and the Family.

1000 Staples, Robert. "Race, Liberalism-Conservatism and Premarital Sexual Permissiveness: A Biracial Comparison." JOURNAL OF MARRIAGE AND THE FAMILY 40, 4 (November 1978): 733-42. 10 pp., references, tables.

Subjects: 1. Sexual Attitudes and Behavior / Premarital Sexual Behavior; 2. Psychology and Sociology / General Attitudes; 3. Aids for Theory and Research / Family Research Methodology.

Data were gathered by means of questionnaires administered to 429 black and white, male and female college students in Florida and California. The purpose of this investigation was to test Ira Reiss' proposition that a liberal or conservative attitude differentially affects groups that are traditionally high or low on premarital sexual permissiveness. Using blacks and whites as comparison groups, the data confirm that liberalism, along with other social forces, has a greater effect on the permissiveness level of whites than blacks. (Author's abstract)

1001 Staples, Robert. "Race, Stress and Family Violence." In COLLOQUIUM ON STRESS AND CRIME, by Martin Molofed, pp. 73-86. McLean, VA: The Mitre Corporation, 1980. 14 pp.

Subjects: 1. Families with Special Problems / Family Violence; 2. /
  Family Stress.

1002 Staples, Robert. "The Sexuality of Black Women." SEXUAL BEHAVIOR
2, 6 (June 1972): 2-18. 17 pp.

Subjects: 1. Family Relationships and Dynamics / Women's Issues; 2.
  Sexual Attitudes and Behavior / Sexual Attitudes and Behavior.

1003 Staples, Robert. "Towards a Sociology of the Black Family: A
Theoretical and Methodological Assessment." JOURNAL OF MARRIAGE AND THE
FAMILY 33, 1 (February 1971): 119-138. 20 pp., references.

Subjects: 1. Psychology and Sociology / Sociology; 2. Aids for Theory
  and Research / Critiques and Analyses of Family Research Literature.

This paper is a summary and analysis of research and theory on black
families in the past decade. In the macro-sociological section the
theories on black family life are critically analyzed for their
theoretical and methodological validity. The second section presents
micro-sociological research findings on black family life and is more
of a summary of the research literature on this subject. These
research findings are presented according to the typical family stage
sequences of black family life, from dating behavior to parental roles
and socialization processes. In his overall assessment of works on the
black family the author concludes that the imposition of ethnocentric
values on the analysis of black family life preclude the application
of much of the current research and theory to the development of a
viable sociology of the black family. (Author's abstract)

1004 Staples, Robert. THE WORLD OF BLACK SINGLES: CHANGING PATTERNS OF
MALE/FEMALE RELATIONS. Contributions in Afro-American and African
Studies, No. 57. Westport, CT: Greenwood Press, 1981. 259 pp.,
bibliography, index; ISBN:0-313-22478-1; LC:80-1025.

Subjects: 1. Family Relationships and Dynamics / Singles (Lifestyle);
  2. Mate Selection / Mate Selection, Differential Patterns.

Notes: Bibliography: pp. 247-252.

1005 Staples, Robert and Mirande, Alfredo. "Racial and Cultural
Variations among American Families: A Decennial Review of the Literature
on Minority Families." JOURNAL OF MARRIAGE AND THE FAMILY 42, 4
(November 1980): 1-41. 41 pp., references, bibliography.

Subjects: 1. Trends and Change in Marriage and Family / Family and
  Social Change; 2. Minority Groups / Ethnic Groups in the United
  States; 3. Aids for Theory and Research / Critiques and Analyses of
  Family Research Literature.

This article is a review and assessment of the past decade's
literature on Asian-American, black, Chicano, and Native American
families. The authors report that, prior to 1970, minority families
were subject to negative stereotypes which were not empirically
supported. In the case of blacks and Chicanos, the family literature
of the 1970s represented an improvement because it depicted the
positive aspects of their family life. Theory and research on Asian

and Native American families remained too limited to make any generalizations about their family lifestyles. The insider-outsider perspective continued to be a source of controversy in the study of minority families. (Authors' abstract)

1006 Staples, Robert E. "Black Family Life and Development." In MENTAL HEALTH: A CHALLENGE TO THE BLACK COMMUNITY, edited by Lawrence E. Gary, pp. 73-94. Philadelphia, PA: Dorrance and Company, 1978. 22 pp.

Subjects: 1. Organizations and Services to Families / Mental Health and the Family.

[This discussion focuses on] how the family promotes emotional well-being in individuals. [Indeed]. . .the Black family has been a sanctuary which has buttressed individuals from the pervasiveness of white racism, provided needed support systems that were unavailable in other majority group institutions, and socialized and nurtured the young. . .[A]s the Black population has dispersed from its original location in the rural South to urban ghettos and differentiated into. . .class strata, new values--alien values--replaced traditional ones about the family and the role of Blacks in it. Hence culture is a dichotomous phenomenon: it enables a people to adopt to oppressive conditions, but the imposition of new institutions and value modalities can stabilize their oppression in the colonial context. (From author's text)

1007 Staples, Robert E., comp. THE BLACK FAMILY: ESSAYS AND STUDIES. The Wadsworth Series in Sociology. Belmont, CA: Wadsworth Publishing Co., 1971. 393 pp., bibliography, illustrations, tables, charts; LC:71-141508.

Subjects: 1. Family Relationships and Dynamics / Family Relationships; 2. Aids for Theory and Research / Family Theory; 3. / Collected Works.

The articles in this edition attempt to define a Black family pathology.

1008 Staples, Robert E., comp. THE BLACK FAMILY: ESSAYS AND STUDIES. 2nd ed. Belmont, CA: Wadsworth Publishing Co., 1978. 282 pp., references, bibliography, tables, charts; ISBN:0-534-00557-8; LC:77-21417.

Subjects: 1. Family Relationships and Dynamics / Family Relationships; 2. Aids for Theory and Research / Family Theory; 3. / Collected Works.

The 39 articles in this edition "reflect the new trends and concerns in the sociology of the Black family..." The articles concentrate on the structure of the Black family rather than the issue of a Black family pathology. "Problems of the Black family are [presented] in a normative framework of Black culture." (From author's preface).

Notes: Bibliography: pp. 271-282.

1009 Staples, Robert E. "Black Sexuality." In SEXUALITY AND HUMAN VALUES: THE PERSONAL DIMENSION OF SEXUAL EXPERIENCE, edited by Mary Calderone, pp. 62-71. New York: Association Press, 1974. 10 pp.

Subjects: 1. Sexual Attitudes and Behavior / Sexual Attitudes and
   Behavior.

1010 Staples, Robert E. THE BLACK WOMAN IN AMERICA: SEX, MARRIAGE, AND
THE FAMILY. Chicago, IL: Nelson-Hall Publishing, 1973. 269 pp.,
references, bibliography, index; ISBN:0-911012-55-9; LC:72-95280.

Subjects: 1. Family Relationships and Dynamics / Women's Issues.

   The topics covered in this volume include the sexual life of black
   women, prostitution, marriage, motherhood, and women's liberation.

   Notes: Selected Bibliography: pp. 243-259.

1011 Staples, Robert E. "Race and Family Violence: The Internal
Colonialism Perspective." In CRIME AND ITS IMPACT ON THE BLACK
COMMUNITY, edited by Lawrence E. Gary and Lee Brown, P., pp. 85-96.
Washington, DC: Howard University. Institute for Urban Affairs and
Research, 1975. 12 pp.

Subjects: 1. Families with Special Problems / Family Violence.

1012 Staples, Robert E. "Strength and Inspiration: Black Families in
the United States." In ETHNIC FAMILIES IN AMERICA: PATTERNS AND
VARIATIONS, edited by Charles H. Mindel and Robert Wesley Habenstein,
pp. 222-247. New York: Elsevier North-Holland, Inc., 1976. 26 pp.

Subjects: 1. Trends and Change in Marriage and Family / Family Life in
   the United States; 2. Aids for Theory and Research / Family Theory.

1013 Staples, Robert E. "Toward a Sociology of Black Liberation." In
THE DEATH OF WHITE SOCIOLOGY, edited by Joyce A. Ladner, pp. 161-172.
New York: Vintage Books, 1973. 12 pp.

Subjects: 1. Psychology and Sociology / Sociology.

1014 Staples, Robert E. "Towards a Sociology and Methodological
Assessment." In A DECADE OF FAMILY RESEARCH AND ACTION, edited by
Carlfred Bartholomew Broderick, pp. 119-138. Minneapolis, MN: National
Council of Family Relations, 1971. 20 pp.

Subjects: 1. Psychology and Sociology / Sociology; 2. Aids for Theory
   and Research / Family Theory.

1015 Staples, Robert Eugene. "A Study of the Influence of Liberal-
Conservative Attitudes on the Premarital Sexual Standards of Different
Racial, Sex-Role and Social Class Groupings." (Ph.D. dissertation,
University of Minnesota, 1971.) DISSERTATION ABSTRACTS INTERNATIONAL,
32, 11, May 1972, 6573A. (University Microfilms No. 7214378.) 101 pp.

Subjects: 1. Family Relationships and Dynamics / Family Roles and Sex
   Roles; 2. Sexual Attitudes and Behavior / Premarital Sexual Behavior.

1016 Steady, Filomina Chioma, ed. THE BLACK WOMAN CROSS-CULTURALLY.
Cambridge, MA: Schenkman Publishing Co., 1981. 645 pp., bibliography,
illustrations; ISBN:0-87073-345-1; LC:80-17214.

Subjects: 1. Trends and Change in Marriage and Family / Family and
   Social Change; 2. Family Relationships and Dynamics / Women's Issues;
   3. Aids for Theory and Research / Collected Works.

   Notes: Bibliography: pp. 615-635

1017 Steckel, Richard H. "Slave Marriage and the Family." JOURNAL OF
FAMILY HISTORY 5, 4 (Winter 1980): 406-21. 16 pp., references,
bibliography.

Subjects: 1. Trends and Change in Marriage and Family / Family Life
   Prior to 1900; 2. Marriage and Divorce / Marriage Customs and Forms.

   This article contributes to the literature on slave marriage and the
   family by analyzing evidence from plantation records and Civil War
   pension files. The Civil War pension files contain information on the
   seasonal pattern of slave marriage. The marriage data are linked with
   the seasonal pattern of slave births available from plantation birth
   lists to suggest that marriage was an important institution to slaves.
   Similarly, some plantation birth lists systematically recorded the
   name of the father and permit measurement of the stability of slave
   unions. The data described here reveal seasonal patterns of marriage
   and birth, and the stability of slave unions, with   important
   consequences for an understanding of slave marriage and family in the
   antebellum South. (From author's text)

1018 Stein, P. and Hilty, R., eds. SINGLES AND SOCIETY. New York:
St. Martin's Press, 1981.

Subjects: 1. Family Relationships and Dynamics / Singles (Lifestyle).

1019 Stein, Peter J. SINGLE LIFE: UNMARRIED ADULTS IN SOCIAL CONTEXT.
New York: St. Martin's Press, 1981. 360 pp., references, tables,
charts, appendices; ISBN:0-312-72596-5; LC:80-52388.

Subjects: 1. Family Relationships and Dynamics / Singles (Lifestyle);
   2. Aids for Theory and Research / Collected Works.

1020 Stember, Charles Herbert. SEXUAL RACISM: THE EMOTIONAL BARRIER TO
AN INTEGRATED SOCIETY. New York: Eisevier Science Publishing Company,
Inc., 1976. 234 pp., bibliography, illustrations, index; ISBN:0-444-
99034-8; LC:76-26869.

Subjects: 1. Sexual Attitudes and Behavior / Sexual Attitudes and
   Behavior; 2. Psychology and Sociology / Sociology; 3. / Racial
   Attitudes.

   Notes: Bibliography: pp. 222-229.

1021 Sterling, Dorothy, ed. BLACK FOREMOTHERS: THREE LIVES. Women's
Lives/Women's Work. Old Westbury, NY: The Feminist Press/McGraw Hill
Book Company, 1979. 167 pp., bibliography, illustrations, index;
ISBN:0-07-020433-0; LC:78-8094.

Subjects: 1. Family Relationships and Dynamics / Women's Issues.

Notes: Bibliography: pp. 160-162. Introduction by Margaret Walker. Illustration by Judith Louise Hooper.

1022 Stevens, Joseph H., Jr. and Mathews, Marilyn, eds. MOTHER CHILD, FATHER CHILD RELATIONSHIPS. Washington, DC: National Association for the Education of Young Children, 1978. 258 pp., bibliography, illustrations; ISBN:0-912674-58-X; LC:77-95173.

Subjects: 1. Family Relationships and Dynamics / Mother-Child Relationships; 2. / Father-Child Relationships; 3. Family Counseling and Education / Child Development.

1023 Stewart, James B. "Perspectives on Black Families from Contemporary Soul Music: The Case of Millie Jackson." PHYLON 41, 1 (March 1980): 57-71. 15 pp., references.

Subjects: 1. Trends and Change in Marriage and Family / Family Life in the United States; 2. Family Counseling and Education / Media and the Family.

[Vocalist Millie Jackson's albums, "Caught Up"(1974) and "Still Caught Up"(1975) are concerned with the phenomenon of "man-sharing".] The two albums [therefore] constitute a saga involving a husband, a wife and a mistress. . .Millie Jackson typically emphasizes the sexual dimensions of sharing relationships, but it is also true that her female characters perceive moral contradictions arising from their participation in such liaisons. There is no indication that she views the underlying moral values as dysfunctional, rather her particularly graphic treatment of sexual instincts appears to be directed only at achieving a heightened realism in her presentation. Her presentations do not appear to advocate the liberation of black males and females from value orientations that limit the unrestrained formation of sharing relationships as some kind of expression of "black sexuality." Rather, her principal intent seems to be the examination of one implication of conflicting psychological, emotional, and physical needs among individuals in differing circumstances in contemporary society. Further research is clearly needed to determine the degree of similarity and dissimilarity among the psychological profiles of participants in sharing relationships to ascertain the net effects on community welfare of such relationships. (From author's text)

1024 Stewart, James B. and Scott, Joseph W. "The Institutional Decimation of Black American Males." THE WESTERN JOURNAL OF BLACK STUDIES 2, 2 (September 1978): 82-92. 11 pp., references, illustrations.

Subjects: 1. Trends and Change in Marriage and Family / Family and Social Change; 2. Family Relationships and Dynamics / Men's Issues; 3. Families with Special Problems / Family Disorganization.

[In the Black community the principal factor producing an imbalance in the sex ratio is that] Black males are the victims of the institutional decimation process. The process leads to the temporary and permanent removal of Black males from the civilian population through the operation of labor market mechanisms, the educational system, the health care delivery system, the public assistance complex, the subliminal institution of crime and vice, the penal correction system, and the military. The politico-socio-economic situation of the Black male in American society produces continuous economic frustration, and the responses of Black males to frustration facilitate their elimination from the population. The ineffectiveness of typical responses to economic frustration is structurally programmed. There is, then, no need for explicit conspiracies or ongoing monitoring of the system. (Authors' conclusion)

1025 Stewart, Phyllis Louise Albert. "A Study of Role Perceptions of Lower-Income Black Husbands in Black Families." (Ph.D. dissertation, United States International University, 1978.) DISSERTATION ABSTRACTS INTERNATIONAL, 40, 4, Oct. 1979, 1966B-1967B. (University Microfilms No. 7922709.) 152 pp.

Subjects: 1. Family Relationships and Dynamics / Family Roles and Sex Roles; 2. Aids for Theory and Research / Family Theory.

1026 Stimpson, Catherine. "Thy Neighbor's Wife, Thy Neighbor's Servants: Women's Liberation and Black Civil Rights." In WOMAN IN SEXIST SOCIETY: STUDIES IN POWER AND POWERLESSNESS, edited by Vivian Gornick and Barbara K. Moran, pp. 622-657. New York: Basic Books, Inc., 1971. 36 pp.

Subjects: 1. Family Relationships and Dynamics / Women's Issues; 2. Psychology and Sociology / Racial Attitudes.

1027 Stimson, Ardyth, Stimson, John and Kelton, Todd. "Interracial Dating: Willingness to Violate a Changing Norm." JOURNAL OF SOCIAL AND BEHAVIOR SCIENCES 25, 2 (Spring 1979): 36-45. 10 pp., references, tables.

Subjects: 1. Mate Selection / Dating, Courtship, and Romanticism.

1028 Stokes, C. Shannon, Crader, Kelly W. and Smith, Jack C. "Race, Education and Fertility: A Comparison of Black-White Reproductive Behavior." PHYLON 38, 2 (June 1977): 160-69. 10 pp., references, tables.

Subjects: 1. Issues Related to Reproduction / Fertility Rates.

[Based on research data from the 1971 Metropolitan Atlanta Family Planning Survey, conducted by the Family Planning Evaluation Activity Unit of the Center for Disease Control,] the major findings of the present study are congruent with the minority group status explanation of black-white fertility differentials. Overall, blacks in Atlanta have higher fertility than whites due in part to educational and demographic differences between these groups. However, these factors do not explain the lower fertility of better educated black women. The latter finding supports the view that the insecurities associated with minority status, coupled with the difficulty in rising in the educational and economic structure, promote lower fertility among well-educated blacks. . .Since blacks earn less money than whites of the same educational level, and the income differential is greatest among the college educated, their lower fertility may be due to economic pressure rather than (or in addition to) minority status. (From authors' text)

1029 Stuart, Irving R. and Abt, Lawrence Edwin, eds. INTERRACIAL
MARRIAGE: EXPECTATIONS AND REALITIES. New York: Grossman Publishers,
1973. 335 pp., bibliography; ISBN:0-670-40014-9; LC:72-77705.

Subjects: 1. Marriage and Divorce / Inter-marriage; 2. Aids for Theory
   and Research / Collected Works.

Notes: Bibliography: pp. 322-31.

1030 Stukes, Sandra Paulette. "A Comparative Analysis of Black and
White Urban Households and Help Seeking Behavior." (Ph.D. dissertation,
The University of Michigan, 1979.) DISSERTATION ABSTRACTS
INTERNATIONAL, 40, 2, Aug. 1979, 1104A-1105A. (University Microfilms
No. 7916823.) 165 pp.

Subjects: 1. Family Relationships and Dynamics / Extended Family and
   Kinship Groups; 2. Psychology and Sociology / Sociology.

1031 Sudarkasa, Niara. "African and Afro-American Family Structure: A
Comparison." BLACK SCHOLAR 11, 8 (November-December 1980): 37-60. 24
pp., references, bibliography, charts.

Subjects: 1. Trends and Change in Marriage and Family / Comparative
   Studies--International, Interclass, Sex, and Time Differences; 2.
   Family Relationships and Dynamics / Family Relationships.

   The purpose of the present paper is two-fold: (1) to analyze and
   interpret   the   structure   of   African   families, with the aim of
   clarifying the operation of the principles of consanguinity and
   conjugality in the formation and maintenance of these groups, and (2)
   to show how the data on African family structure point to a need for
   studying the process by which, in the changing socio-economic and
   political contexts of the United States, Afro-American   family
   organization evolved from the African patterns re-created by the first
   blacks brought here as slaves. (From author's text)

1032 Sudarkasa, Niara. "An Exposition on the Value Premises Underlying
Black Family Studies." JOURNAL OF THE NATIONAL MEDICAL ASSOCIATION 67,
3 (May 1975): 235-39. 5 pp.

Subjects: 1. Organizations and Services to Families / Education and the
   Family; 2. Aids for Theory and Research / Family Theory.

1033 Sudarkasa, Niara. "Interpreting the African Heritage in Afro-
American Family Organization." In BLACK FAMILIES, edited by Harriette
Pipes McAdoo, pp. 37-53. Beverly Hills, CA: Sage Publications, Inc.,
1981. 17 pp., references.

Subjects: 1. Trends and Change in Marriage and Family / Family Life in
   the United States; 2. / Family Life in Foreign Countries; 3. Aids for
   Theory and Research / Family Theory.

   This review seeks to show how an understanding of African family
   structure sheds light on the form and functioning of Black American
   family structure as it developed in the context of slavery and later
   periods. It seeks to elucidate African institutional arrangements and
   values that were manifest in the family organization of Blacks

enslaved in America, and suggests that some of these values and institutional arrangements continue to be recognizable in contemporary formations. (From author's introduction)

1034 Surlin, Stuart H. and Dominick, Joseph R. "Television's Function as a 'Third Parent' for Black and White Teenagers." JOURNAL OF BROADCASTING 15, 1 (Winter 1970-71): 55-64. 10 pp., references.

Subjects: 1. Family Counseling and Education / Children and Television.

1035 Swan, L. Alex. "Moynihan: A Methodological Note." JOURNAL OF AFRO-AMERICAN ISSUES 2, 1 (February 1974): 11-20. 10 pp., tables.

Subjects: 1. Aids for Theory and Research / Family Research Methodology.

1036 Sweet, James A. and Bumpass, Larry. "Differentials in Marital Instability of the Black Population 1970." PHYLON 35, 3 (September 1974): 323-31. 9 pp., references, tables.

Subjects: 1. Marriage and Divorce / Differential Marriage Rates; 2. Families with Special Problems / Family Disorganization.

1037 Sykes, Delores Roselle. "The Effects of a Marriage Education Course on the Attitudes toward Marriage and Cohabitation of Black American College Students." (Ph.D. dissertation, University of Maryland, 1980.) DISSERTATION ABSTRACTS INTERNATIONAL, 41, 9, March 1981, 4184A. (University Microfilms No. 8104973.) 178 pp.

Subjects: 1. Mate Selection / Cohabiting; 2. Marriage and Divorce / Marriage Satisfaction and Prediction Studies; 3. Family Counseling and Education / Education for Marriage.

1038 Tanner, Nancy. "Matrifocality in Indonesia and Africa and among Black Americans." In WOMAN, CULTURE, AND SOCIETY, edited by Michelle Zimbalist Rosaldo, Louise Lamphere and Joan Bamberger, pp. 129-156. Stanford, CA: Stanford University Press, 1974. 28 pp.

Subjects: 1. Trends and Change in Marriage and Family / Comparative Studies--International, Interclass, Sex, and Time Differences; 2. Family Relationships and Dynamics / Women's Issues; 3. Aids for Theory and Research / Family Theory.

This essay explores (1) the nature of matrifocality and (2) the special social and cultural features that characterize societies in which it occurs...[particularly among] the Javanese, Atjehnese, and Minangkaban (all Indonesian groups), the Igbo of West Africa, and the Black Americans. (From author's text)

1039 Taylor, Arnold H. TRAVAIL AND TRIUMPH: BLACK LIFE AND CULTURE IN THE SOUTH SINCE THE CIVIL WAR. Contributions in Afro-American and African Studies, No. 26. Westport, CT: Greenwood Press, 1976. 325 pp., bibliography, index; ISBN:0-8371-8912-8; LC:76-5264.

Subjects: 1. Trends and Change in Marriage and Family / Family and Social Change.

Notes: Bibliography: pp. 279-307.

1040   Taylor, Ronald L.   "Black Youth and Psychosocial Development."
JOURNAL OF BLACK STUDIES 6, 4 (June 1976): 353-72.   20 pp., references,
bibliography.

Subjects: 1. Family Counseling and Education / Adolescence.

The development of a relevant theoretical or conceptual framework is
essential   for   a   more thorough understanding and analysis of
psychosocial identity development among black youth. The purpose here
is to emphasize, through theoretical formulation and case study
analysis, the utility of the role model approach as a conceptual
framework for investigating the development of psychosocial identity
among black youth. More specifically, this paper focuses upon the ways
in which role models are selected and rendered useful by these youth
in their various attempts to cultivate features of their personal and
social identities. Such a focus allows observation of how the youth
shapes his own identity through his own actions, rather than being
acted upon by his social environment. While such an approach is
subject to certain limitations, it is clearly a useful strategy to
explore the theoretical possibilities opened up by considering the
function of role models in black psychosocial development. (From
author's text)

1041   Thomas, George Benjamin.   YOUNG BLACK ADULTS: LIBERATION AND
FAMILY ATTITUDES.   New York: Friendship Press, 1974.   95 pp.,
bibliography; ISBN:0-377-00002-7; LC:73-22204.

Subjects: 1. Family Relationships and Dynamics / Family Relationships;
   2. / Stages in Family Life Cycle; 3. Family Counseling and Education /
   Family Life Education.

A study commissioned by the Committee on Ministries with Black
Families of the National Council of the Churches of Christ in the USA.

Notes: Foreword by Olivia Pearl Stokes. Study questions and guide by
Robert O. Dulin, Jr. Bibliography: pp. 80-81.

1042   Thompson, Daniel Calbert.   SOCIOLOGY OF THE BLACK
EXPERIENCE. Contributions in Sociology, No. 14. Westport, CT: Greenwood
Press, 1974.   261 pp., bibliography; ISBN:0-8371-7336-1; LC:73-20974.

Subjects: 1. Family Relationships and Dynamics / Socialization; 2.
   Psychology and Sociology / Sociology; 3. / Racial Attitudes.

One chapter centers on the black family and the socialization of the
child in New Orleans, 1968-1969.

Notes: Bibliography: pp. 245-254

1043   Thompson, Kendrick S.   "A Comparison of Black and White
Adolescents' Belief about Having Children." JOURNAL OF MARRIAGE AND THE
FAMILY 42, 1 (February 1980): 133-39.   7 pp., references, bibliography,
tables.

Subjects: 1. Psychology and Sociology / General Attitudes; 2. Family
   Counseling and Education / Adolescence.

This research compares the beliefs, perceptions, and decisions of 150 black adolescents with those of 150 white adolescents as they are related to having children. Responses to a 35-item inventory were factor analyzed and subjected to MANOVA and ANOVA procedures. From the numerous findings, it was concluded that both black males and females expressed stonger beliefs than comparable white respondents that having children promotes greater marital success, personal security, and approval from others. Black respondents also expressed stronger beliefs that couples should have as many children as they wish. Females of both ethnic groups perceived themselves as exposed to stronger social pressures to have children than did males. Both black and white males placed more value on the having of children, a finding for males that has now been replicated in several studies. (Author's abstract)

1044 Thompson, Mary Lou, ed. VOICES OF THE NEW FEMINISM. Boston, MA: Beacon Press, Inc., 1970. 246 pp., references, bibliography; ISBN:0-8070-4175-0; LC:76-119679.

Subjects: 1. Family Relationships and Dynamics / Women's Issues; 2. Aids for Theory and Research / Collected Works.

Notes: Includes "Women: A Bibliography" by Lucinda Cisler on pp. 217-46.

1045 Tillman, Johnnie. "Welfare is a Women's Issue." In MARRIAGE AND THE FAMILY: A CRITICAL ANALYSIS AND PROPOSALS FOR CHANGE, edited by Carolyn Cummings Perrucci and Dena B. Targ, pp. 108-16. New York: David McKay Company, Inc., 1974. 9 pp.

Subjects: 1. Organizations and Services to Families / Social Welfare; 2. Family Relationships and Dynamics / Women's Issues.

1046 Tolnay, Stewart E. "Black Fertility in Decline: Urban Differentials in 1900." SOCIAL BIOLOGY 27, 4 (Winter 1980): 249-60. 12 pp., references, tables.

Subjects: 1. Trends and Change in Marriage and Family / Family Life 1900 to Present; 2. Issues Related to Reproduction / Fertility Rates.

1047 Tomeh, Aida K. "The Value of Voluntarism among Minority Groups." PHYLON 42, 1 (Spring 1981): 86-96. 11 pp., references.

Subjects: 1. Family Counseling and Education / Value Education; 2. Minority Groups / Ethnic Groups in the United States.

1048 Trader, Harriett Peat. "Welfare Policies and Black Families." SOCIAL WORK 24, 6 (November 1979): 548-52. 5 pp., references.

Subjects: 1. Trends and Change in Marriage and Family / Family Policy; 2. Organizations and Services to Families / Social Welfare.

1049 Trufant, Carol Ann. "The Effects of Familial Support Systems on Black Mothers' Childrearing Attitudes and Behaviors, and on Their Children's Competence." (Ph.D. dissertation, Michigan State University, 1977.) DISSERTATION ABSTRACTS INTERNATIONAL, 39, 1, July 1978, 450B-451B. (University Microfilms No. 7810126.) 161 pp.

Subjects: 1. Family Relationships and Dynamics / Family Relationships;
   2. / Parent-Child Relationships.

1050 Trussel, James and Steckel, Richard. "The Age of Slaves at
Menarche and Their First Birth." JOURNAL OF INTERDISCIPLINARY HISTORY
8, 3 (Winter 1978): 477-505. 29 pp., references, tables, charts.

Subjects: 1. Trends and Change in Marriage and Family / Family Life
   Prior to 1900; 2. Issues Related to Reproduction / Fertility Rates.

One of the main areas of controversy generated by the conclusions of
[Robert] Fogel and [Stanley] Engerman as reported in TIME ON THE CROSS
involves the degree of intrusion into the sexual behavior of slaves by
their owners. . . Criticisms have been leveled at both the methodology
and the interpretation of Fogel and Engerman. In this paper we analyze
the biases inherent in their methodological procedure, propose a new
method of estimation that avoids these biases, and comment on the
substantive issue of whether reproductive behavior was substantially
manipulated. Combining the estimates of mean age at menarche and
waiting time until the first birth, we see that if slaveowners
successfully manipulated the fertility of slave women by causing them
to bear as soon as possible, then the observed mean age at first birth
should not have exceeded 15 + 3 = 18 years. Since the observed mean is
in fact 20.6 or some 2.6 years later, we must conclude that slave
women did not bear children at the earliest possible age. More
reasonable estimates of the mean ages of menarche and waiting time
until the first birth indicate that successful manipulation would have
led to an observed mean age of first childbearing of from 16.5 to 17
years; such an estimate only reinforces our conclusion. (From authors'
text)

1051 Tuck, Samuel, Jr. "Working With Black Fathers." AMERICAN JOURNAL
OF ORTHOPSYCHIATRY 41, 3 (April 1971): 465-71. 7 pp.

Subjects: 1. Family Relationships and Dynamics / Father-Child
   Relationships; 2. Family Counseling and Education / Family Therapy.

1052 Tucker, Dorothy M. "The Effects of Internal/External Control as
Perceived by Black Couples in Interpersonal Conflict." JOURNAL OF
SOCIAL AND BEHAVIOR SCIENCES 25, 4 (Fall 1979): 126-131. 6 pp.,
references, tables.

Subjects: 1. Family Relationships and Dynamics / Conflict Resolution;
   2. / Premarital Couples.

The purpose of this study was to investigate the effects of internal-
external locus of control upon a black person's attribution of
responsibility to the black male or the black female member of a
couple involved in a conflictual situation. Using a sample of thirty
black males and thirty black females, 18 years of age or older and of
a relatively high educational level, the following tests were
administered: Rotter's I-E Locus of Control Scale to determine
internality and externality; three interpersonal vignette
questionnaires designed to ascertain responsibility for the
conflictual situation between the male and female couple; and a
demographic questionnaire. Because the Rotter I-E Locus of Control
Scale was found to be unproductive with respect to black cultural

distinctions, one of the recommendations of this study is that the Rotter I-E Scale be standardized on black populations of different socio-economic backgrounds; and that further research should be planned which will study the implications of black male-female interpersonal relations and the impact that this relationship has on black culture. (Author's abstract)

1053 Tufte, Virginia and Myerhoff, Barbara G., eds. CHANGING IMAGE OF THE FAMILY. New Haven and London, CT: Yale University Press, 1979. 403 pp., references, bibliography, illustrations; ISBN:0-300-02361-8; LC:79-537.

Subjects: 1. Trends and Change in Marriage and Family / Family and Social Change; 2. Aids for Theory and Research / Collected Works.

1054 Tulkin, Steven R. "Race, Class, Family and School Achievement." JOURNAL OF PERSONALITY AND SOCIAL PSYCHOLOGY 9, 1 (May 1968): 31-37. 7 pp., references, tables.

Subjects: 1. Families with Special Problems / Achievement and the Family; 2. Minority Groups / Family and Social Class.

1055 Turner, Barbara F. and McCaffrey, Joanne Hammar. "Socialization and Career Orientation among Black and White College Women." JOURNAL OF VOCATIONAL BEHAVIOR 5, 3 (1974): 307-19. 13 pp., references, tables, charts.

Subjects: 1. Family Relationships and Dynamics / Socialization; 2. Organizations and Services to Families / Dual Career Families.

In a study of career orientation among black and white college women, support was found for hypotheses derived from postulates of Rotter's Social Learning Theory. Compared to whites, (1) blacks were less likely to expect the level of work involvement preferred; (2) blacks expected more employment; and (3) blacks were more likely to prefer less employment than they realistically expected. Antecedents of career expectation were categorized as internal, external, or neutral. As hypothesized, variables expressive of external control predicted level of career expectation among blacks, whereas variables expressive of internal control predicted high career expectations among whites. (Authors' abstract)

1056 Turner, Barbara F. and Turner, Castellano B. "The Political Implications of Social Stereotyping of Women and Men among Black and White College Students." SOCIOLOGY AND SOCIAL RESEARCH 58, 2 (January 1974): 155-62. 8 pp., references, bibliography, tables.

Subjects: 1. Family Relationships and Dynamics / Socialization; 2. Psychology and Sociology / Sociology.

Semantic differential scales rating the concepts "Most women are. . ." and "Most men are. . ." were administered to black female, black male, white female, and white male university freshmen. White females were the only group to rate the opposite sex significantly more positively than their own sex. Black females did NOT share white females' tendency to idealize men. Black females rated men as more unreliable than did the other groups. Further, black females were the only group to rate men as significantly more unreliable than they rated women. Otherwise, black females' evaluations of men did not differ from those of male. (Authors' abstract)

1057 Turner, Castellano B. and Darity, William A.   "Black Family Design." In BLACK MARRIAGE AND FAMILY THERAPY, edited by Constance E. Obudho, pp. 151-165. Westport, CT: Greenwood Press, 1983. 15 pp.

Subjects: 1. Aids for Theory and Research / Family Theory.

1058 Turner, Castellano B. and Turner, Barbara F.   "Black Families, Social Evaluations and Future Marital Relationships." In BLACK MARRIAGE AND FAMILY THERAPY, edited by Constance E. Obudho, pp. 23-37. Westport, CT: Greenwood Press, 1983. 15 pp.

Subjects: 1. Family Relationships and Dynamics / Family Relationships; 2. Marriage and Divorce / Marriage Satisfaction and Prediction Studies.

1059 Turner, S. H. Regina. "Images of Black Women in the Plays of Black Female Playwrights, 1950-1975." (Ph.D. dissertation, Bowling Green State University, 1982.) DISSERTATION ABSTRACTS INTERNATIONAL, 43, 1, July 1982, 19A. (University Microfilms No. 8214438.) 404 pp.

Subjects: 1. Trends and Change in Marriage and Family / Family and Social Change; 2. Family Relationships and Dynamics / Women's Issues; 3. Psychology and Sociology / Sociology.

1060 Turner, William H.   "Black Men/White Women: A Philosophical View." In BLACK MALE/WHITE FEMALE: PERSPECTIVES ON INTERRACIAL MARRIAGE AND COURTSHIP, compiled by Doris Y. Wilkinson, pp. 170-174. Cambridge, MA: Schenkman Publishing Co., 1975. 5 pp.

Subjects: 1. Mate Selection / Mate Selection, Differential Patterns.

1061 U.S. Bureau of Labor Statistics. THE NEGRO IN THE WEST: SOME FACTS RELATING TO SOCIAL AND ECONOMIC CONDITIONS. VOL. 3: THE NEGRO FAMILY. San Francisco, CA: Bureau of Labor Statistics, 1967. 30 pp., references, illustrations, tables, charts; LC:L66-119.

Subjects: 1. Trends and Change in Marriage and Family / Family and Social Change; 2. Organizations and Services to Families / Economics and the Family.

1062 U.S. Bureau of the Census. THE SOCIAL AND ECONOMIC STATUS OF THE BLACK POPULATION IN THE UNITED STATES, 1971, by Nampeo D.R. McKenney. Current Population Reports. Special Studies (Series P-23), No. 42. Washington, DC: United States Government Printing Office, 1972. 164 pp.; LC:72-602571.

Subjects: 1. Trends and Change in Marriage and Family / Family and Social Change; 2. Organizations and Services to Families / Economics and the Family; 3. Aids for Theory and Research / Statistics.

1063 U.S. Bureau of the Census. THE SOCIAL AND ECONOMIC STATUS OF THE BLACK POPULATION IN THE UNITED STATES, 1974. Current Population Reports. Special Studies (Series P-23), No. 54. Washington, DC: United

States Government Printing Office, 1975.   195 pp., references, illustrations; LC:75-602784.

Subjects: 1. Organizations and Services to Families / Economics and the Family; 2. Minority Groups / Family and Social Class; 3. Aids for Theory and Research / Statistics.

1064 U.S. Bureau of the Census. THE SOCIAL AND ECONOMIC STATUS OF THE BLACK POPULATION IN THE UNITED STATES: AN HISTORICAL VIEW, 1790-1978, by Nampeo D.R. McKenney. Current Population Reports. Special Studies (Series P-23), No. 80. Washington, DC: United States Government Printing Office, 1979.   271 pp., references, tables, appendices; LC:79-607000.

Subjects: 1. Trends and Change in Marriage and Family / Family and Social Change; 2. Organizations and Services to Families / Economics and the Family; 3. Aids for Theory and Research / Statistics.

1065 U.S. Children's Bureau. Division of Research and Evaluation. Social Research Group. FAMILIES FOR BLACK CHILDREN: THE SEARCH FOR ADOPTIVE PARENTS, AN EXPERIENCE SURVEY, by Elizabeth Herzog. Washington, DC: United States Government Printing Office, 1971.   79 pp., references; LC:72-614239.

Subjects: 1. Organizations and Services to Families / Adoption and Adoption Services.

Notes: A cooperative report of the Division of Research and Evaluation, Children's Bureau, Office of Child Development and Social Research Group and George Washington University. Superintendent Document Number is HE 21:102:F21.

1066 U.S. Department of Health, Education and Welfare. WOMEN AND THEIR HEALTH: RESEARCH IMPLICATIONS FOR A NEW ERA. Washington, DC: United States Government Printing Office, 1975.

Subjects: 1. Organizations and Services to Families / Physical Health and the Family; 2. Family Relationships and Dynamics / Women's Issues; 3. Aids for Theory and Research / Family Research Methodology.

1067 U.S. Department of Health, Education and Welfare. Children's Bureau. Office of Child Development. Youth and Child Studies Branch.. BOYS IN FATHERLESS FAMILIES, by Elizabeth Herzog and Cecelia Sudia. DHEW Publication, No. 72-33. Washington, D.C.: United States Government Printing Office, 1971.   120 pp., bibliography; LC:72-602551.

Subjects: 1. Family Relationships and Dynamics / Single Parent Families; 2. / Father-Child Relationships; 3. / Family Roles and Sex Roles.

Notes: Bibliography: pp. 99-120.

1068 U.S. Department of Health, Education and Welfare. National Institute of Education. Career Education Program. ISSUES OF SEX BIAS AND SEX FAIRNESS IN CAREER INTEREST MEASUREMENT, edited by Esther E. Diamond. Washington, DC: United States Government Printing Office, 1975.   219 pp., bibliography, index; LC:75-603045.

Subjects: 1. Family Relationships and Dynamics / Family Roles and Sex
    Roles; 2. Sexual Attitudes and Behavior / Sexual Attitudes and
    Behavior; 3. Families with Special Problems / Achievement and the
    Family.

1069 U.S. Department of Health, Education and Welfare. Office of
Education. EQUALITY OF EDUCATIONAL OPPORTUNITY, by James Samuel
Coleman. Washington, DC: United States Government Printing Office,
1966. 548 pp., illustrations, tables, appendices; LC:HEW 66-127.

Subjects: 1. Organizations and Services to Families / Education and the
    Family.

    Notes: Co-authored by E. Q. Campbell, C. J. Hobson, J. McPartland, A.
    M. Mood, F. D. Weinfeld, and R. L. York. A publication of the National
    Center for Educational Statistics. Bound in 2 parts; the second part
    has special title page: Supplemental appendix to the survey; Section
    9.10 contains correlation tables.

1070 U.S. Department of Labor. Office of Policy Planning and Research.
THE NEGRO FAMILY: THE CASE FOR NATIONAL ACTION, by Daniel Patrick
Moynihan. Washington, DC: United States Government Printing Office,
1965. 78 pp., illustrations; LC:L65-80.

Subjects: 1. Trends and Change in Marriage and Family / Family and
    Social Change; 2. / Family Policy; 3. Organizations and Services to
    Families / Family Law.

    Notes: Bibliography: pp. 51-53.

1071 U.S. Task Force on Juvenile Delinquency. TASK FORCE REPORT:
JUVENILE DELINQUENCY AND YOUTH CRIME: REPORT ON JUVENILE JUSTICE AND
CONSULTANTS' PAPERS. Washington, DC: United States Government Printing
Office, 1967. 428 pp., bibliography, illustrations; LC:67-61654.

Subjects: 1. Organizations and Services to Families / Governmental Units
    and the Family; 2. Families with Special Problems / Families with
    Juvenile Delinquents.

1072 Udry, Richard J. "Marital Instability by Race, Sex, Education,
and Occupation Using 1960 Census Data." AMERICAN JOURNAL OF SOCIOLOGY
72, 2 (September 1966): 203-10. 8 pp.

Subjects: 1. Marriage and Divorce / Differential Marriage Rates; 2.
    Families with Special Problems / Family Disorganization.

1073 Uhlenberg, Peter. "Changing Family Patterns of Blacks, Chicanos,
and Whites: 1960-1970." RESEARCH PREVIEWS 21, 1 (1974): 1-7. 7 pp.

Subjects: 1. Trends and Change in Marriage and Family / Family and
    Social Change; 2. Minority Groups / Ethnic Groups in the United
    States.

1074 Uhlenberg, Peter. "Marital Instability among Mexican Americans:
Following the Patterns of Blacks?" SOCIAL PROBLEMS 20, 1 (Summer 1972):
49-56. 8 pp.

Subjects: 1. Marriage and Divorce / Marriage Satisfaction and Prediction
Studies; 2. Families with Special Problems / Family Disorganization;
3. Minority Groups / Ethnic Groups in the United States.

1075 Uhlenberg, Peter P. "Negro Fertility Patterns in the United
States." BERKELEY JOURNAL OF SOCIOLOGY 11, (1966): 54-65. 12 pp.,
references, tables, charts.

Subjects: 1. Issues Related to Reproduction / Fertility Rates.

1076 Umbarger, Carter Conrad. "Black and White Fathers: Their Impact
on the Idealized Models and Vocational Plans of their Adolescent
Sons." (Ph.D. dissertation, Brandeis University, 1969.) DISSERTATION
ABSTRACTS INTERNATIONAL, 30, 6, Dec. 1969, 2919B. (University
Microfilms No. 6920747.) 203 pp.

Subjects: 1. Organizations and Services to Families / Employment and the
Family; 2. Family Relationships and Dynamics / Father-Child
Relationships; 3. Family Counseling and Education / Adolescence.

1077 Valentine, Charles A. CULTURE AND POVERTY: CRITIQUE AND COUNTER-
PROPOSALS. Chicago, IL: University of Chicago Press, 1968. 216 pp.,
bibliography; ISBN:0-226-84545; LC:68-16718.

Subjects: 1. Trends and Change in Marriage and Family / Family and
Social Change; 2. Organizations and Services to Families / Economics
and the Family; 3. Aids for Theory and Research / Family Theory.

Critical discussion of the Frazierian Tradition and the study of the
Black family.

Notes: Bibliography: pp. 197-208.

1078 Verinis, J. Scott. "Maternal and Child Pathology in an Urban
Ghetto." JOURNAL OF CLINICAL PSYCHOLOGY 32, 1 (January 1976): 13-15.   3
pp., references.

Subjects: 1. Organizations and Services to Families / Physical Health
and the Family; 2. Family Relationships and Dynamics / Mother-Child
Relationships.

A group of 80 black, urban ghetto mothers, 40 with a behaviorally
disturbed child and 40 with no identified disturbed child, was
evaluated by the MMPI. The literature reports a relationship between
maternal pathology and child disturbance for middle- and working-class
families. The present study, however, showed no such relationship
between these two variables in ghetto families. (Author's summary)

1079 Vincent, Charles. "Aspects of the Family and Public Life of
Antoine Dubuclet: Louisiana's Black State Treasurer, 1868-1878."
JOURNAL OF NEGRO HISTORY 66, 1 (Spring 1981): 26-36. 11 pp.,
references.

Subjects: 1. Trends and Change in Marriage and Family / Family Life
Prior to 1900.

1080 Vincent, Clark E., Haney, C. Allen and Cochrane, Carl M.
"Familial and Generational Patterns of Illegitimacy." JOURNAL OF
MARRIAGE AND THE FAMILY 31, 4 (November 1969): 659-67. 9 pp., tables,
charts.

Subjects: 1. Issues Related to Reproduction / Illegitimacy.

1081 Wade-Gayles, Gloria. "She Who is Black and Mother: In Sociology
and Fiction, 1940-70." In THE BLACK WOMAN, edited by La Frances
Rodgers-Rose, pp. 89-106. Beverly Hills, CA: Sage Publications, Inc.,
1980. 18 pp., references.

Subjects: 1. Family Relationships and Dynamics / Mother-Child
   Relationships; 2. / Women's Issues; 3. Aids for Theory and Research /
   Critiques and Analyses of Family Research Literature.

   This chapter. . .[presents] an in-depth portrait of the Black mother
   in America as she is presented in selected novels and in selected
   sociological studies published between 1940 and 1970. The portrait
   highlights three features: (1) child-rearing posture, (2) maternal
   aspirations, and (3) maternal fulfillment. (From author's text.)

1082 Wade, Brenda Karon. "The Relationship between the Disciplinary
Styles of Black Parents and Preference for Mode of Family
Therapy." (Ph.D. dissertation, University of Washington, 1979.)
DISSERTATION ABSTRACTS INTERNATIONAL, 40, 12, June 1980, 5835B.
(University Microfilms No. 8013612.) 121 pp.

Subjects: 1. Family Relationships and Dynamics / Parent-Child
   Relationships; 2. Family Counseling and Education / Family Therapy.

1083 Wakin, Edward. AT THE EDGE OF HARLEM: PORTRAIT OF A MIDDLE-CLASS
NEGRO FAMILY. New York: William Morrow and Co., Inc., 1965. 127 pp.,
illustrations; LC:64-23581.

Subjects: 1. Trends and Change in Marriage and Family / Family and
   Social Change; 2. Family Relationships and Dynamics / Family
   Relationships; 3. Minority Groups / Family and Social Class.

   Notes: Photos by Edward Lettau. Text by Edward Wakin.

1084 Walberg, Herbert J., Yeh, Elaine Gee and Paton, Stephanie Mooney.
"Family Background, Ethnicity, and Urban Delinquency." JOURNAL OF
RESEARCH IN CRIME AND DELINQUENCY 11, 1 (January 1974): 80-87. 8 pp.,
bibliography, tables.

Subjects: 1. Minority Groups / Ethnic Groups in the United States; 2.
   Families with Special Problems / Families with Juvenile Delinquents.

   Four problems characterize much of the past research on the relation
   of social factors to juvenile delinquency: measurement of social
   background, one-dimensional indexes of delinquency, bias   in
   measurement of delinquency, and nonparametric statistical tests. These
   problems may be overcome in part by using specific, proximal measures
   of background; multiple indexes of delinquency; anonymous self-reports
   of delinquency incidence; and parametric statistics such as components
   analysis and regression or analysis of variance. The present paper

demonstrates the use of these methods in a pilot study of about 400 public high school students in Chicago. The components analysis shows the factor pattern of delinquency varies in samples of boys and girls; hence multiple rather than single indicators must be used. The regression analysis shows that different types of delinquency are functions of different combinations of family background, ethnicity, and sex; for example, boys, especially white boys, in the sample more often reported car thefts; and Negro girls reported more frequently than white girls of having engaged in gang fights. Several methodological implications are drawn from the findings for future research on delinquency. (Authors' abstract)

1085 Wallace, Joan S. and Wong, Samuel P. "Some Sociocultural Aspects of Growing Up Black." JOURNAL OF SOCIOLOGY AND SOCIAL WELFARE 2, 2 (Spring 1975): 345-57. 13 pp., references.

Subjects: 1. Family Relationships and Dynamics / Socialization.

1086 Wallace, Michele. BLACK MACHO AND THE MYTH OF THE SUPERWOMAN. New York: Dial Press, 1979. 182 pp.; ISBN:0-8037-0934-X; LC:78-12850.

Subjects: 1. Family Relationships and Dynamics / Socialization; 2. / Men's Issues; 3. / Women's Issues.

1087 Wallace, Phyllis A., Datcher, Linda and Malveaux, Julianne. BLACK WOMEN IN THE LABOR FORCE. Cambridge, MA: MIT Press, 1980., references, bibliography, tables, charts, appendices, index; ISBN:0-262-23103-4; LC:80-14175.

Subjects: 1. Organizations and Services to Families / Economics and the Family; 2. / Employment and the Family; 3. Family Relationships and Dynamics / Women's Issues.

A survey of economic literature on the employment status of black women. Chapter two focuses on a review of economic literature concerning labor force participation by Black women. The third chapter focuses on characteristics of Black women workers. Chapter four is a review of the impact of labor market policies; chapter five is an assessment of the black/white earning differentials from the perspective of Black women workers (contributed by Linda Datcher). The employment status of Black teenagers and female heads of families is reviewed in chapter six by Julianne Malveaux. In chapter seven, some research issues and policy suggestions are outlined and noted. (Extracted from Wallace's introduction)

1088 Washington, Ernest D. "Politicizing Black Children." BLACK SCHOLAR 4, 8/9 (May-June 1973): 2-7. 6 pp., bibliography.

Subjects: 1. Family Relationships and Dynamics / Socialization; 2. Family Counseling and Education / Child Development.

1089 Washington, Joseph R., Jr. MARRIAGE IN BLACK AND WHITE. Boston, MA: Beacon Press, Inc., 1970. 358 pp., references; ISBN:0-8070-4172-6; LC:77-121828.

Subjects: 1. Marriage and Divorce / Marriage Satisfaction and Prediction Studies; 2. / Inter-marriage; 3. Psychology and Sociology / Racial Attitudes.

1090 Wasserman, Herbert L. "A Comparative Study of School Performance among Boys from Broken and Intact Black Families." JOURNAL OF NEGRO EDUCATION 41, 2 (Spring 1972): 137-141. 5 pp., references, tables.

Subjects: 1. Organizations and Services to Families / Education and the Family; 2. Family Relationships and Dynamics / Father-Child Relationships; 3. Families with Special Problems / Achievement and the Family.

1091 Wasserman, Herbert Louis. "Father-Absent and Father-Present Lower Class Negro Families: A Comparative Study of Family Functioning." (Ph.D. dissertation, Brandeis University, 1968.) DISSERTATION ABSTRACTS INTERNATIONAL, 29, 12, June 1969, 4569A-4570A. (University Microfilms No. 6908919.) 241 pp.

Subjects: 1. Trends and Change in Marriage and Family / Family Life in the United States; 2. Family Relationships and Dynamics / Family Relationships; 3. / Father-Child Relationships.

1092 Weathers, Olethia Delmar and Bullock, Samuel C. "Therapeutic Group Home Care for Adolescent Girls: An Interagency Development." JOURNAL OF THE NATIONAL MEDICAL ASSOCIATION 70, 5 (May 1978): 331-34. 4 pp.

Subjects: 1. Issues Related to Reproduction / Teenage Pregnancy.

In the District of Columbia, because of inappropriate placement resources, crisis units in mental health centers are keeping children long after treatment evaluation has taken place. It was thought that disturbed adolescents might be served in a small family-type setting with live-in house parents, direct clinical services, and back-up from the mental health center. This paper discusses an attempt to provide services to some disturbed adolescents in an interagency therapeutic group home. The study experience is limited, but the design of the program and the problems encountered may be of some value to health and child care agencies. (Authors' abstract)

1093 Webb-Woodard, Linda Delores. "Selfhood: Discovery of Survival Values in Low Income Black Families in Hartford, Connecticut. Two Case Studies Using Family Systems Theory." (Ed.D. dissertation, University of Massachusetts, 1980.) DISSERTATION ABSTRACTS INTERNATIONAL, 41, 3, Sept. 1980, 950A-951A. (University Microfilms No. 8019499.) 266 pp.

Subjects: 1. Family Relationships and Dynamics / Extended Family and Kinship Groups; 2. Families with Special Problems / Family Stress; 3. Family Counseling and Education / Value Education.

1094 Webster, Staten W. "Some Correlates of Reported Academically Supportive Behaviors of Negro Mothers toward Their Children." JOURNAL OF NEGRO EDUCATION 34, 2 (Spring 1965): 114-20. 7 pp., references, tables.

Subjects: 1. Organizations and Services to Families / Education and the Family; 2. Family Relationships and Dynamics / Mother-Child Relationships.

1095 Wehrle, James Mark. "The Marriage Squeeze: Perceptions and Adaptations of Black Female Doctorates." (Ph.D. dissertation, Southern Illinois University at Carbondale, 1982.) DISSERTATION ABSTRACTS INTERNATIONAL, 43, 2, Aug. 1982, 559A. (University Microfilms No. 8215827.) 229 pp.

Subjects: 1. Organizations and Services to Families / Education and the Family; 2. Family Relationships and Dynamics / Women's Issues; 3. Mate Selection / Mate Selection, Differential Patterns.

1096 Weinberger, Andrew D. "Interracial Intimacy: Interracial Marriage--Its Statutory Prohibition, Genetic Import, and Incidence." JOURNAL OF SEX RESEARCH 2, 3 (November 1966): 157-68. 12 pp., references, charts.

Subjects: 1. Marriage and Divorce / Inter-marriage.

1097 Weisbord, Robert G. "Birth Control and the Black American: A Matter of Genocide." DEMOGRAPHY 10, 4 (November 1973): 571-90. 20 pp., references.

Subjects: 1. Issues Related to Reproduction / Birth Control.

During the 1960's and continuing into the 1970's, the charge that birth control and abortion are integral elements of a white genocidal conspiracy directed against Afro-Americans had been heard with increasing frequency and stridency in black communities. The genocide theory finds greatest acceptance among spokesmen for black nationalist and black revolutionary groups, but suspicion of family planning programs is not limited to them. An analysis of black leadership opinion on birth control is provided in this paper. The black debate over the desirability of population limitation is traced back approximately fifty years. It began with a dispute between those blacks who believed that in sheer numbers there was strength and those blacks, such as W. E. B. DuBois, who argued that among human races, among vegetables, quality and not quantity counted. An appreciation of the sexual exploitation of the chattel slave in the ante-bellum period, which did not end with emancipation, is also essential to an understanding of the roots and rationale of the genocide notion which are the foci of this paper. (Author's abstract)

1098 Weisbord, Robert G. GENOCIDE? BIRTH CONTROL AND THE BLACK AMERICAN. Westport, CT: Greenwood Press, 1975. 219 pp.; ISBN:0-8467-0069-7; LC:75-13531.

Subjects: 1. Issues Related to Reproduction / Birth Control.

1099 Weller, Leonard and Luchterhand, Elmer. "Effects of Improved Housing on the Family Functioning of Large, Low-Income Black Families." SOCIAL PROBLEMS 20, 3 (Winter 1973): 382-89. 8 pp., references, tables.

Subjects: 1. Family Relationships and Dynamics / Environment (Space/Housing).

To determine whether moving into decidedly better housing improves the functioning of large, low-income families, a comparison was made between such families who (as part of a demonstration program) had been relocated to subsidized private housing and two control groups: 1) similar families who were likewise forced to move but were not included in this housing program, and 2) matched families who continued living in deteriorating neighborhoods. Interviews were first conducted while all were still in their old apartments and again a year later. Family functioning showed no general improvement. (Authors' abstract)

1100 Weller, Robert H. "The Differential Attainment of Family Size Goals by Race." POPULATION STUDIES 33, 1 (March 1979): 157-64. 8 pp., references, tables.

Subjects: 1. Issues Related to Reproduction / Population Studies.

1101 Westoff, Leslie Aldridge and Westoff, Charles F. FROM NOW TO ZERO: FERTILITY, CONTRACEPTION AND ABORTION IN AMERICA. Boston, MA: Little, Brown and Company, 1971. 358 pp., bibliography; LC:73-149473.

Subjects: 1. Issues Related to Reproduction / Fertility Rates; 2. / Birth Control; 3. / Abortion.

1102 Wetherell, Charles. "Slave Kinship: A Case Study of the South Carolina Good Hope Plantation, 1835-1856." JOURNAL OF FAMILY HISTORY 6, 3 (Fall 1981): 294-308. 15 pp.

Subjects: 1. Trends and Change in Marriage and Family / Family Life Prior to 1900.

1103 Wheeler, Edward Lorenzo. "Uplifting the Race: The Black Minister in the New South, 1865-1902." (Ph.D. dissertation, Emory University, 1982.) DISSERTATION ABSTRACTS INTERNATIONAL, 43, 6, Dec. 1982, 2002A. (University Microfilms No. 8221542.) 273 pp.

Subjects: 1. Trends and Change in Marriage and Family / Family Life Prior to 1900; 2. Organizations and Services to Families / Religion and the Family.

1104 Whitaker, Barbara. "Breakdown in the Negro Family: Myth or Reality." NEW SOUTH 22, 4 (Fall 1967): 37-47. 11 pp., references.

Subjects: 1. Families with Special Problems / Family Disorganization; 2. Aids for Theory and Research / Critiques and Analyses of Family Research Literature.

1105 White, Deborah G. "Female Slaves: Sex Roles and Status in the Antebellum Plantation South." JOURNAL OF FAMILY HISTORY 8, 3 (Fall 1983): 248-261. 14 pp.

Subjects: 1. Trends and Change in Marriage and Family / Family Life Prior to 1900; 2. Family Relationships and Dynamics / Family Roles and Sex Roles.

This paper analyzes female slave life in the context of female slave interaction and familial roles. It looks at the bonded woman's work, her control of particular resources, her contribution to slave households, and her ability to cooperate with other women on a daily basis. It suggests that in relation to the slave family, too much emphasis has been placed on what men could not do rather than on what women could do and did. It finds that the bonded female made significant "economic" contributions to the slave family, that the slave's world was sex stratified so that the female slave world existed quite independently of the male slave world, and that slave families were matrifocal. (Author's abstract)

1106 White, Lynn K. "A Note on Racial Differences in the Effect of Female Economic Opportunity on Marriage Rates." DEMOGRAPHY 18, 3 (August 1981): 349-354. 6 pp.

Subjects: 1. Organizations and Services to Families / Employment and the Family; 2. Family Relationships and Dynamics / Women's Issues; 3. Marriage and Divorce / Differential Marriage Rates.

The previously observed aggregate relationship between marriage rates and female work opportunities is not found among black Americans. Alternative definitions of family formation which take illegitimacy into consideration are explored and also found to be unrelated to black females' economic opportunities. Although some of the difference may be attributed to measurement error, the significant disparity between the two populations probably reflects substantive differences. (Author's abstract)

1107 White, Patricia Elizabeth. "Patterns of Marriage among the Black Population: A Preliminary Analysis of the Black Female." (Ph.D. dissertation, The Ohio State University, 1980.) DISSERTATION ABSTRACTS INTERNATIONAL, 41, 2, Aug. 1980, 822A. (University Microfilms No. 8015936.) 197 pp.

Subjects: 1. Family Relationships and Dynamics / Singles (Lifestyle); 2. Mate Selection / Mate Selection, Differential Patterns.

1108 White, Priscilla and Scott, Patricia. "The Role of Black Women in Black Families: Teaching about Black Families on a Predominantly White Campus." In PERSPECTIVES ON AFRO-AMERICAN WOMEN, edited by Willa D. Johnson and Thomas L. Green, pp. 187-195. Washington, DC: Educational and Community Counselors Associates Publications, 1975. 9 pp.

Subjects: 1. Trends and Change in Marriage and Family / Family Life in the United States; 2. Family Relationships and Dynamics / Family Relationships; 3. Family Counseling and Education / Family Life Education.

1109 Whitehead, John. IDA'S FAMILY: ADAPTATIONS TO POVERTY IN A SUBURBAN GHETTO. Yellow Springs, OH: Antioch College, 1969.

Subjects: 1. Organizations and Services to Families / Economics and the Family; 2. Minority Groups / Family and Social Class.

Describes a low income black family in a Washington, D.C. ghetto.

1110 Whitehead, Tony L. "Residence, Kinship, and Mating as Survival Strategies: A West Indian Example." JOURNAL OF MARRIAGE AND THE FAMILY 40, 4 (November 1978): 817-28. 12 pp., references, tables.

Subjects: 1. Organizations and Services to Families / Economics and the Family; 2. Mate Selection / Mate Selection, Differential Patterns; 3. Minority Groups / Blacks in the Caribbean.

This paper is a contribution to a recent trend in the study of Afro-American behavior and social organization in which the emphasis is on adaptive strategies rather than social pathology. The paper explores the applicability of an adaptive model to an industrializing Jamaican town. The primary premise of the model is that economic marginality leads to certain adaptive responses in residential, kinship, and mating patterns. After demonstrating the model's applicability, the author concludes with a warning against the paper being taken as support for any particular school of thought. He then argues for more research using other theoretical approaches. (Author's abstract)

1111 Whiteman, Maxwell. "Black Genealogy." RQ: REFERENCE QUARTERLY 11, 4 (Summer 1972): 311-19. 9 pp., references.

Subjects: 1. Trends and Change in Marriage and Family / Family Life in the United States.

1112 Whitfield, Cynthia Elaine Bell. "Low Income Black and White Mothers' Verbal Communication Patterns with Their Preschool Children." (Ph.D. dissertation, Arizona State University, 1980.) DISSERTATION ABSTRACTS INTERNATIONAL, 41, 2, Aug. 1980, 527A. (University Microfilms No. 8018468.) 106 pp.

Subjects: 1. Family Relationships and Dynamics / Mother-Child Relationships; 2. / Communication in the Family; 3. Family Counseling and Education / Early Childhood Education.

1113 Whitted, Christine. "Supports in the Black Community: Black Unmarried Mothers Who Kept Their Babies and Achieved Their Educational and/or Professional Goals." (Ed.D. dissertation, Columbia University Teachers College, 1978.) DISSERTATION ABSTRACTS INTERNATIONAL, 39, 1, July 1978, 499A. (University Microfilms No. 7810906.) 346 pp.

Subjects: 1. Organizations and Services to Families / Education and the Family; 2. Issues Related to Reproduction / Illegitimacy.

1114 Whitten, Norman E., Jr. and Szwed, John F., eds. AFRO-AMERICAN ANTHOLOGY: CONTEMPORARY PERSPECTIVES. New York: The Free Press, 1970. 468 pp., bibliography, illustrations; LC:79-93109.

Subjects: 1. Trends and Change in Marriage and Family / Family and Social Change; 2. Aids for Theory and Research / Collected Works.

1115 Whittington, James Attison, Jr. "Kinship, Mating and Family in the Choco' of Colombia: An Afro-American Adaptation." (Ph.D. dissertation, Tulane University, 1971.) DISSERTATION ABSTRACTS INTERNATIONAL, 32, 11, May 1972, 6179B-6180B. (University Microfilms No. 7214209.) 395 pp.

Subjects: 1. Family Relationships and Dynamics / Parent-Child
  Relationships; 2. / Family Relationships; 3. Mate Selection / Mate
  Selection, Differential Patterns.

1116 Wilder, Katherine A. "Captain Paul Cuffee, Master Mariner of
Westport, Massachusetts, 1759-1817." OLD-TIME NEW ENGLAND 63, 3 (Winter
1973): 78-80. 3 pp.

Subjects: 1. Trends and Change in Marriage and Family / Family Life
  Prior to 1900.

1117 Wilkinson, Charles B. and O'Connor, William A. "Growing Up Male
in a Black Single-Parent Family." PSYCHIATRIC ANNALS 7, 7 (July 1977):
50-51,55-59. 6 pp., bibliography, tables.

Subjects: 1. Family Relationships and Dynamics / Single Parent Families;
  2. Families with Special Problems / Death, Bereavement and the Family.

The purpose of the study [of 101 metropolitan single-parent
households with a male child in which the mother has been the sole
parent since her son's infancy] is to investigate the relationships
between patterns of child rearing and the utilization of available
community resources by mothers and the community participation
patterns and competence reflected in the son's midadolescent
lifestyle. . .[T]he data. . .suggest that black female-headed
households can function effectively as family units and do not
necessarily reproduce the problems of poverty, delinquency, and mental
health so often confronted in the urban environment. The percentage of
black adolescent boys with delinquency or mental health contacts is
extremely small (less than 3 per cent). It is also apparent that
community resources can be identified and provided to such families in
order to help them function effectively. . .The active participation
of a parent within the community and the social competence and
adjustment skills that this participation may provide for children in
the family can be noted. . .[And]the absence of such social-
competency-learning opportunities appears to have negative effects.
(From authors' text)

1118 Wilkinson, Doris Y., comp. BLACK MALE/WHITE FEMALE: PERSPECTIVES
ON INTERRACIAL MARRIAGE AND COURTSHIP. Cambridge, MA: Schenkman
Publishing Co., 1975. 182 pp., bibliography; ISBN:0-87073-167-X; LC:73-
82382.

Subjects: 1. Family Relationships and Dynamics / Women's Issues; 2.
  Marriage and Divorce / Inter-marriage; 3. Aids for Theory and Research
  / Collected Works.

A collection of nineteen essays on the topic of interracial marriage
and interracial courtship.

Notes: Bibliography: pp. 175-182.

1119 Wilkinson, Doris Y. "Toward a Positive Frame of Reference for
Analysis of Black Families: A Selected Bibliography." JOURNAL OF
MARRIAGE AND THE FAMILY 40, 4 (November 1978): 707-708. 2 pp.,
bibliography.

Subjects: 1. Aids for Theory and Research / Critiques and Analyses of
Family Research Literature; 2. / Classified Bibliographies of Family
Literature.

1120 Wilkinson, Doris Yvonne and Taylor, Ronald Lewis, eds. THE BLACK
MALE IN AMERICA: PERSPECTIVES ON HIS STATUS IN CONTEMPORARY SOCIETY.
Chicago: Nelson-Hall Publishing, 1977. 375 pp., references,
bibliography, tables, index; ISBN:0-88229-227-7; LC:76-44310.

Subjects: 1. Trends and Change in Marriage and Family / Family Life in
the United States; 2. Family Relationships and Dynamics / Men's
Issues; 3. Psychology and Sociology / Psychology.

Notes: Bibliography: pp. 361-369.

1121 Williams, Charles Robert. "Adaptations of the Black-White Mixed
Racial Child." (Ed.D. dissertation, University of Northern Colorado,
1981.) DISSERTATION ABSTRACTS INTERNATIONAL, 42, 8, Feb. 1982, 3522A.
(University Microfilms No. 8202730.) 144 pp.

Subjects: 1. Trends and Change in Marriage and Family / Family and
Social Change; 2. Family Relationships and Dynamics / Socialization.

1122 Williams, J. Allen, Jr. and Stockton, Robert. "Black
Family Structures and Functions: An Empirical Examination of Some
Suggestions Made by Billingsley." JOURNAL OF MARRIAGE AND THE FAMILY
35, 1 (February 1973): 39-49. 11 pp., references, tables.

Subjects: 1. Family Relationships and Dynamics / Family Relationships;
2. Aids for Theory and Research / Critiques and Analyses of Family
Research Literature.

Andrew Billingsley in BLACK FAMILIES IN WHITE AMERICA has criticized
much of the previous research on the black family, saying that social
scientists have ignored the structural variation among families and
have focused on a very limited number of family functions. To correct
what he believes to be a distorted picture of the black family, he has
suggested a typology of family structures and a large number of family
functions which should be taken into consideration. This paper, based
upon data collected from 321 black households, uses Billingsley's
typology to examine the association between family structures and
functions. It is concluded that a few modifications of the typology
would expand its utility, that more detailed information about family
structure does reduce the chances of distortion and contribute to
greater understanding, and that Billingsley may have overemphasized
the capacity of many black families to deal with their functional
problems. (Authors' abstract)

1123 Williams, John E. and Morland, J. Kenneth. RACE, COLOR AND THE
YOUNG CHILD. Chapel Hill, NC: University of North Carolina Press, 1976.
360 pp., bibliography, illustrations, index; ISBN:0-8078-1261-7; LC:76-
812.

Subjects: 1. Psychology and Sociology / Psychology; 2. / Racial
Attitudes; 3. Family Counseling and Education / Child Development.

Notes: Bibliography: pp. 341-350

1124 Williams, Robert Lewis, ed. EBONICS: THE TRUE LANGUAGE OF BLACK
FOLKS. St. Louis, MO: The Institute of Black Studies, 1975. 144 pp.,
bibliography; LC:75-32291.

Subjects: 1. Family Relationships and Dynamics / Communication in the
  Family; 2. Aids for Theory and Research / Collected Works.

  Notes: "Selected from...papers submitted to a conference" held January
  1973 in St. Louis.(NUC)

1125 Williamson, Robert C. "Dating Frequency, Ethnicity, and
Adjustment in the High School: A Comparative Study." INTERNATIONAL
JOURNAL OF SOCIOLOGY OF THE FAMILY 7, 2 (July-December 1977): 157-69.
13 pp., references, tables.

Subjects: 1. Organizations and Services to Families / Education and the
  Family; 2. Mate Selection / Dating, Courtship, and Romanticism; 3.
  Family Counseling and Education / Adolescence.

  The present article focuses on one aspect of a larger study of the
  adjustment of 2,431 students in 14 high schools in eastern
  Pennsylvania, that is, the influence of dating frequency on the
  personal,   social, and school adjustment among black and white
  students. Among the findings was an indeterminate relation between
  dating frequency and school adjustment. Basically, daters showed a
  middle-class orientation in their choice of an academic tract and
  preference for an appropriate collar-career. As a reminder of the
  Coleman profile, daters were peer- rather than parent-oriented, and
  showed greater autonomy and flexibility in given attitudes. Although
  noticeable differences in the percentage of responses were found
  between blacks and whites, the basic findings generally held for both.
  The data were also affected by the larger proportion of daters among
  the upper grades who are also the ones who stay in school. (Author's
  abstract)

1126 Willie, Charles V. "Dominance in the Family: The Black and White
Experience." JOURNAL OF BLACK PSYCHOLOGY 7, 2 (February 1981): 91-97.
7 pp., references.

Subjects: 1. Family Relationships and Dynamics / Power in the Family.

1127 Willie, Charles V. "Population Policy and Growth: Perspectives
from the Black Community--A Position Paper." In MARRIAGE AND THE
FAMILY: A CRITICAL ANALYSIS AND PROPOSALS FOR CHANGE, edited by Carolyn
Cummings Perrucci and Dena B. Targ, pp. 250-56. New York: David McKay
Company, Inc., 1974. 7 pp.

Subjects: 1. Trends and Change in Marriage and Family / Family Policy;
  2. Issues Related to Reproduction / Abortion.

1128 Willie, Charles V. and Greenblatt, Susan L. "Four 'Classic'
Studies of Power Relationships in Black Families: A Review and Look to
the Future." JOURNAL OF MARRIAGE AND THE FAMILY 40, 4 (November 1978):
691-94. 4 pp., references.

Subjects: 1. Family Relationships and Dynamics / Husband-Wife
Relationships; 2. / Power in the Family; 3. Aids for Theory and
Research / Family Research Methodology.

Studies of black families in varying social classes are reviewed to
determine the prevailing power relationship between spouses.   In
general, black families appear to be more equalitarian than white
families; the middle-class black family is more equalitarian than any
other family type. Rigid role-differentiation for husbands and wives
most frequently occurs in middle-class white families according to
studies reviewed here. Social scientists are cautioned   against
projecting upon black families behavior more frequently observed in
their own race or social class group. (Authors' abstract)

1129 Willie, Charles Vert, comp. THE FAMILY LIFE OF BLACK PEOPLE.
Columbus, OH: Charles E. Merrill, 1970. 341 pp., references; ISBN:0-
675-09297-3; LC:79-127082.

Subjects: 1. Trends and Change in Marriage and Family / Family Life in
the United States; 2. Aids for Theory and Research / Collected Works.

A collection of articles that examine the Black family structure as a
functional system rather than a social problem. (From author's
introduction)

1130 Willie, Charles Vert. A NEW LOOK AT BLACK FAMILIES. New Bayside,
NY: General Hall, Inc., 1976. 211 pp., references, index; LC:76-9293.

Subjects: 1. Trends and Change in Marriage and Family / Family Life in
the United States.

1131 Willie, Charles Vert. A NEW LOOK AT BLACK FAMILIES. 2nd ed.
Bayside, NY: General Hall, Inc., 1981. 250 pp., references, appendices,
index; ISBN:0-930390-42-1; LC:81-82122 .

Subjects: 1. Trends and Change in Marriage and Family / Family Life in
the United States; 2. Aids for Theory and Research / Family Research
Methodology.

A revision of the 1976 edition with six new case studies of family
lifestyle added: 6 affluent, 6 working-class, and 6 poor families.
(From author's introduction)

1132 Willie, Charles Vert, Kramer, Bernard M. and Brown, Bertram S.,
eds. RACISM AND MENTAL HEALTH: ESSAYS. Pittsburgh, PA: University of
Pittsburgh Press, 1973. 604 pp., bibliography; ISBN:0-8229-3252-0;
LC:72-78933.

Subjects: 1. Organizations and Services to Families / Mental Health and
the Family; 2. Psychology and Sociology / Racial Attitudes; 3. Aids
for Theory and Research / Collected Works.

Notes: Based on a series of conferences at Syracuse University, 1970-
71 and conducted by the University's Department of Sociology. (NUC)

1133 Willis, Robert E. THE BLACK WOMAN. New York: Vantage Press,
1978.; ISBN:0-533-03807-3.

Subjects: 1. Family Relationships and Dynamics / Women's Issues.

1134 Wilson, Amos N. THE DEVELOPMENTAL PSYCHOLOGY OF THE BLACK CHILD.
New York: Africana Publications, 1978. 216 pp., references,
illustrations, tables, appendices; ISBN:0-686-24183-5.

Subjects: 1. Family Counseling and Education / Child Development.

1135 Wilson, Bobby M. "Church Participation: A Social Space Analysis
in a Community of Black In-Migrants." JOURNAL OF BLACK STUDIES 10, 2
(December 1979): 198-217. 20 pp., references, bibliography, tables,
charts.

Subjects: 1. Organizations and Services to Families / Religion and the
    Family.

1136 Wilson, Hugh. "Black Families and the Suburban Dream." In FAMILY
LIFE IN AMERICA, 1620-2000, edited by Mel Albin and Dominick Cavallo,
pp. 309-18. New York: Revisionary Press, 1981. 10 pp., references.

Subjects: 1. Family Relationships and Dynamics / Environment (Space/
    Housing).

1137 Wingate, Rosalee Ruth Martin. "A Life Cycle Approach to the Study
of Families Receiving 'Aid to Families with Dependent Children'." (Ph.D.
dissertation, The University of Texas at Austin, 1979.) DISSERTATION
ABSTRACTS INTERNATIONAL, 40, 3, Sept. 1979, 1704A. (University
Microfilms No. 7920241.) 307 pp.

Subjects: 1. Trends and Change in Marriage and Family / Family Policy;
    2. Organizations and Services to Families / Social Services and the
    Family; 3. Family Relationships and Dynamics / Stages in Family Life
    Cycle.

1138 Wood, Forrest G. BLACK SCARE: THE RACIST RESPONSE TO EMANCIPATION
AND RECONSTRUCTION. Berkeley, CA: University of California Press, 1968.
219 pp., bibliography, illustrations; LC:68-26066.

Subjects: 1. Psychology and Sociology / Racial Attitudes.

    Notes: Bibliography: pp. 193-210.

1139 Wright, Maggie Saxon. "Parent-Child Relations, Achievement
Motivation, and Sex-Role Attitudes among Black and White Professional
Women in Traditional and Pioneer Occupations." (Ph.D. dissertation,
State University of New York at Buffalo, 1981.) DISSERTATION ABSTRACTS
INTERNATIONAL, 42, 9, March 1982, 3875A. (University Microfilms
No. 8204137.) 238 pp.

Subjects: 1. Family Relationships and Dynamics / Parent-Child
    Relationships; 2. / Family Roles and Sex Roles; 3. Families with
    Special Problems / Achievement and the Family.

1140 Wyatt, Derrick. "The Social Security Rights of Migrant Workers
and Their Families." COMMON MARKET LAW REVIEW 14, Special Issue (1977):
411-33. 21 pp., references.

Subjects: 1. Organizations and Services to Families / Family Law; 2. / Social Services and the Family; 3. Minority Groups / Ethnic Groups in the United States.

1141 Wyatt, Gail Elizabeth. "Studying the Black Mother-Child Interaction: Issues and Alternatives." YOUNG CHILDREN 33, 1 (November 1977): 16-22. 7 pp., references, illustrations.

Subjects: 1. Family Relationships and Dynamics / Mother-Child Relationships.

1142 Wyatt, Gail Elizabeth, Strayer, Richard G. and Lobitz, W. Charles. "Issues in the Treatment of Sexually Dysfunctioning Couples of Afro-American Descent." PSYCHOTHERAPY: THEORY, RESEARCH, AND PRACTICE 13, 1 (Spring 1976): 44-50. 7 pp., references.

Subjects: 1. Sexual Attitudes and Behavior / Sexual Attitudes and Behavior; 2. Family Counseling and Education / Sex Therapy; 3. Aids for Theory and Research / Critiques and Analyses of Family Research Literature.

The present paper reviews the literature describing the myths of black sexuality and delineates the issues involved in the treatment of sexually dysfunctioning black couples by an interracial therapy team. A case history elucidating these factors is presented. . . In addition to descriptive research, there is a need for therapy outcome studies on sexual dysfunctions in black populations. In the present case, the black co-therapist facilitated resolution of several issues involving the interracial nature of therapy. The question remains as to how the race of the therapists affects the success of the treatment program. Systematic outcome research comparing white, black, and interracial therapy teams is required to provide a definitive answer. (From authors' text)

1143 Wyde, Janet Shibley and Rosenberg, B. G. HALF THE HUMAN EXPERIENCE. Lexington, Massachusetts: D. C. Heath Co., 1976.

Subjects: 1. Psychology and Sociology / Sociology.

1144 Wylan, Louise and Mintz, Norbett L. "Ethnic Differences in Family Attitudes towards Psychotic Manifestations, with Implications for Treatment Programmes." INTERNATIONAL JOURNAL OF SOCIAL PSYCHIATRY 22, 2 (Summer 1976): 86-95. 7 pp., references, tables.

Subjects: 1. Families with Special Problems / Families with Emotionally Disturbed; 2. Family Counseling and Education / Family Therapy; 3. Minority Groups / Ethnic Groups in the United States.

1145 Wylie, F. "Suicide among Black Families: A Case Study." In MENTAL AND PHYSICAL HEALTH PROBLEMS OF BLACK WOMEN, WASHINGTON, D.C., MARCH 29-30, 1974. PROCEEDINGS., by , pp. 121-125. Washington, D.C.: Black Women's Community Development Foundation, 1975. 5 pp.

Subjects: 1. Families with Special Problems / Suicide and the Family.

1146 Yellin, Joel. "Urban Population Distribution, Family Income, and Social Prejudice: The Long, Narrow City." JOURNAL OF URBAN ECONOMICS 1, 1 (January 1974): 21-47. 27 pp., references.

Subjects: 1. Organizations and Services to Families / Economics and the Family; 2. Issues Related to Reproduction / Population Studies; 3. Psychology and Sociology / Racial Attitudes.

1147 Young, Jean Childs. "International Year of the Child: Black America's Baby?" CRISIS 86, 1 (January 1979): 9-12. 4 pp., illustrations.

Subjects: 1. Family Counseling and Education / Early Childhood Education.

1148 Young, Virginia Heyer. "A Black American Socialization Pattern." AMERICAN ETHNOLOGIST 1, 2 (May 1974): 405-13. 9 pp.

Subjects: 1. Family Relationships and Dynamics / Socialization.

Based on observations of how welfare mothers structure the interaction with their children in an urban day care setting, it is suggested that these mothers are not so much concerned with teaching "conventions of behavior". Rather they are concerned with instilling in their children the techniques of adaptation to situations and persons of authority while at the same time maintaining a strong sense of an independent self. It is argued that this socialization pattern offers a new perspective for analyzing the "bicultural" position of Blacks who are dominated by the larger American society.

1149 Young, Virginia Heyer. "Family and Childhood in a Southern Negro Community." AMERICAN ANTHROPOLOGIST 72, 2 (April 1970): 269-88. 20 pp., references, tables.

Subjects: 1. Family Relationships and Dynamics / Family Relationships.

The American Negro family is generally interpreted, ethnocentrically, as an impoverished version of the American White family, in which deprivation has induced pathogenic and dysfunctional features. This concept of the family is assumed in studies of Negro personality formation, which furthermore have relied entirely on clinical methods of research. Fieldwork among Negro town-dwellers in the southeastern United States plus a reassessment of the literature yield a sharply contrasting portrait and interpretation of the American Negro family in which organizational strength and functionality are found. Observations of parent-child relations show highly distinctive behavioral styles, some of which have remained undiscovered by psychoanalytically oriented studies and others of which differ markedly from the extrapolations of clinical research. These forms and styles are viewed as aspects of an indigenous American Negro culture. Finally, the formative effect of an indigenous culture is argued as a corrective to the common viewpoint of deprivation as the prime cause of Negro behavior. (Author's abstract)

1150 Zegiob, Leslie E. and Forehand, Rex. "Maternal Interactive Behavior as a Function of Race, Socioeconomic Status, and Sex of the

Child." CHILD DEVELOPMENT 46, 2 (June 1975): 564-68.   5 pp.,
references, tables.

Subjects: 1. Family Relationships and Dynamics / Mother-Child
   Relationships.

An observational method was used to investigate the effects of race,
socioeconomic status, and the child's sex on maternal interactive
behavior. Both free-play and command periods were used. Of the 3
independent variables, socioeconomic status proved to be the most
significant in determining the nature of maternal behavior. Middle-
class mothers were less directive and displayed more social
interchange, particularly on a verbal level, with their children than
lower-class mothers. With regard to the racial factor, white mothers
exhibited more cooperative behavior than black mothers. Some
inconsistencies in the findings for the middle-class black group were
noted. Sex of child was rarely a significant factor in determining
maternal behavior. Finally, it is suggested that the command period,
which has not been used previously in parent-child interaction
studies, represented a more realistic sample of maternal behavior than
the free-play period. (Authors' abstract)

1151 Zimmerman, Carle C. "Family System of the Third World."
INTERNATIONAL JOURNAL OF SOCIOLOGY OF THE FAMILY 4, 1 (Spring 1974): 1-
10. 10 pp., references.

Subjects: 1. Trends and Change in Marriage and Family / Comparative
   Studies--International, Interclass, Sex, and Time Differences.

1152 Zollar, Ann Creighton. A MEMBER OF THE FAMILY: STRATEGIES FOR
BLACK FAMILY CONTINUITY. Chicago, IL: Nelson-Hall Publishing, 1985.
174 pp., bibliography, index; ISBN:0-8304-1031-7.

Subjects: 1. Family Relationships and Dynamics / Extended Family and
   Kinship Groups; 2. Aids for Theory and Research / Family Research
   Methodology.

Four intensive case studies of extended families (i.e., spanning many
generations and several households) in Urban Chicago, 1978-1982,
suggest among other things that: (1) 'black extended families [despite
their commonalities] are by no means identically organized nor are
they identically prepared to deal with adverse changes in their
political and economic environment' (p.11); and (2) 'it remains
necessary to debunk the myth which claims that black involvement with
the extended kin represents an adaptation to conditions of urban
poverty.' (From author's text)

Notes: Bibliography: pp. 165-69.

1153 Zwiebel, Sarah. "The Relation between Maternal Behaviors and
Aggression in Sons: Black and Puerto Rican Families." (D.S.W.
dissertation, Adelphi University, School of Social Work, 1979.)
DISSERTATION ABSTRACTS INTERNATIONAL, 40, 12, June 1980, 6430A.
(University Microfilms No. 8013689.) 218 pp.

Subjects: 1. Family Relationships and Dynamics / Mother-Child
Relationships; 2. Minority Groups / Ethnic Groups in the United
States.

CLASSIFIED INDEX WITH TITLES

Furstenberg, Frank F. Jr., Hershberg, Theodore and Modell, John. "The Origins of the Female-Headed Black Family: The Impact of the Urban Experience." (360)

Genovese, Eugene D. "Husbands, Fathers, Wives and Mothers During Slavery." (373)

Genovese, Eugene D. ROLL, JORDAN, ROLL: THE WORLD THE SLAVES MADE. (374)

Gilmore, Al-Tony, ed. REVISITING BLASSINGAME'S "THE SLAVE COMMUNITY": THE SCHOLARS RESPOND. (383)

Graham, Richard. "Slave Families on a Rural Estate in Colonial Brazil." (403)

Gudeman, Stephen. "Herbert Gutman's THE BLACK FAMILY IN SLAVERY AND FREEDOM, 1750-1925: An Anthropologist's View." (417)

Gutman, Herbert George. THE BLACK FAMILY IN SLAVERY AND FREEDOM: 1750-1925. (425)

Gutman, Herbert George. SLAVERY AND THE NUMBERS GAME: A CRITIQUE OF TIME ON THE CROSS. (426)

Harris, William. "Work and the Family in Black Atlanta, 1880." (466)

Higman, B. W. "Household Structure and Fertility on Jamaican Slave Plantations: A Nineteenth-Century Example." (504)

Higman, B. W. "The Slave Family and Household in the British West Indies, 1800-1834." (505)

Hine, Darlene C. "Female Slave Resistance: The Economics of Sex." (512)

Horton, James Oliver and Horton, Lois E. BLACK BOSTONIANS: FAMILY LIFE AND COMMUNITY STRUGGLE IN THE ANTEBELLUM NORTH. (523)

Huggins, Nathan Irvin, Kilson, Martin and Fox, Daniel M., eds. KEY ISSUES IN THE AFRO-AMERICAN EXPERIENCE. VOL 1.: TO 1877. (530)

Huggins, Nathan Irvin, Kilson, Martin and Fox, Daniel M., eds. KEY ISSUES IN THE AFRO-AMERICAN EXPERIENCE. VOL 2: SINCE 1865. (531)

Jones, Bobby Frank. "A Cultural Middle Passage: Slave Marriage and Family in the Antebellum South." (597)

Jones, Jacqueline. "'My Mother Was Much of A Woman': Black Women, Work, and the Family under Slavery." (599)

Jordan, Winthrop D. WHITE OVER BLACK: AMERICAN ATTITUDES TOWARD THE NEGRO, 1550-1812. (605)

Kulikoff, Allan. "The Beginnings of the Afro-American Family in Maryland." (627)

Labinjoh, Justin. "The Sexual Life of the Oppressed: An Examination of the Family Life of Antebellum Slaves." (632)

Lammermeier, Paul J. "The Urban Black Family of the 19th Century: A Study of Black Family Structure in the Ohio Valley, 1850-1880." (640)

Lantz, Herman R. and Hendrix, Lewellyn. "The Free Black Family at the Time of the U.S. Census: Some Implications." (643)

Lantz, Herman R. "A Research Note on the Free Black Family in Our Early History." (644)

Leashore, Bogart Raymond. "Interracial Households in 1850-1880 Detroit, Michigan." (647)

Lebsock, Suzanne. "Free Black Women and the Question of Matriarchy: Petersburg, Virginia, 1784-1820." (648)

Loewenberg, Bert and Bogin, Ruth, eds. BLACK WOMEN IN NINETEENTH CENTURY AMERICAN LIFE: THEIR WORDS, THEIR THOUGHTS, THEIR FEELINGS. (678)

Mackinlay, Peter W. "The New England Puritan Attitude toward Black Slavery." (690)

Meeker, Edward. "Freedom, Economic Opportunity, and Fertility: Black Americans, 1860-1910." (733)

Miller, Randall M., ed. "DEAR MASTER": LETTERS OF A SLAVE FAMILY. (742)

Mitchell, J. Marcus. "The Paul Family." (748)

Modell, John. "Herbert Gutman's THE BLACK FAMILY IN SLAVERY AND FREEDOM, 1750-1925: Demographic Perspectives." (751)

Owens, Leslie Howard. THIS SPECIES OF PROPERTY: SLAVE LIFE AND CULTURE IN THE OLD SOUTH. (815)

Parris, Percival J. "Pedro Tovookan Parris." (820)

Pleck, Elizabeth H. "The Two-Parent Household: Black Family Structure in Late Nineteenth-Century Boston." (843)

Powell, Frances LaJune Johnson. "A Study of the Structure of the Freed Black Family in Washington, D.C., 1850-1880." (855)

Rawick, George P., ed. THE AMERICAN SLAVE: A COMPOSITE AUTOBIOGRAPHY. VOL. 1: FROM SUNDOWN TO SUNUP: THE MAKING OF THE BLACK COMMUNITY. (871)

Ripley, C. Peter. "The Black Family in Transition: Louisiana, 1860-65." (881)

Sanderson, Warren C. "Herbert Gutman's THE BLACK FAMILY IN SLAVERY AND FREEDOM, 1750-1925: A Cliometric Reconsideration." (917)

Schweninger, Loren. "A Slave Family in the Antebellum South." (929)

Shifflet, Crandall A. "The Household Composition of Rural Black Families: Louisa County, Virginia, 1880." (953)

Smallwood, James. "Emancipation and the Black Family: A Case Study in Texas." (971)

Smith, Daniel Scott, Dahlin, Michel and Friedberger, Mark. "The Family Structure of the Older Black Population in the American South in 1880 and 1900." (972)

Steckel, Richard H. "Slave Marriage and the Family." (1017)

Trussel, James and Steckel, Richard. "The Age of Slaves at Menarche and Their First Birth." (1050)

Vincent, Charles. "Aspects of the Family and Public Life of Antoine Dubuclet: Louisiana's Black State Treasurer, 1868-1878." (1079)

Wetherell, Charles. "Slave Kinship: A Case Study of the South Carolina Good Hope Plantation, 1835-1856." (1102)

Wheeler, Edward Lorenzo. "Uplifting the Race: The Black Minister in the New South, 1865-1902." (1103)

White, Deborah G. "Female Slaves: Sex Roles and Status in the Antebellum Plantation South." (1105)

Wilder, Katherine A. "Captain Paul Cuffee, Master Mariner of Westport, Massachusetts, 1759-1817." (1116)

Family Life 1900 to Present

Albin, Mel and Cavallo, Dominick, eds. FAMILY LIFE IN AMERICA, 1620-2000. (12)

Henri, Florette. BLACK MIGRATION: MOVEMENT NORTH, 1890-1920. (495)

Huggins, Nathan Irvin, Kilson, Martin and Fox, Daniel M., eds. KEY ISSUES IN THE AFRO-AMERICAN EXPERIENCE. VOL 1.: TO 1877. (530)

Huggins, Nathan Irvin, Kilson, Martin and Fox, Daniel M., eds. KEY ISSUES IN THE AFRO-AMERICAN EXPERIENCE. VOL 2: SINCE 1865. (531)

Tolnay, Stewart E. "Black Fertility in Decline: Urban Differentials in 1900." (1046)

Family Life in the United States

Addison, Donald P. BLACK FAMILIES: A COMPREHENSIVE BIBLIOGRAPHY. (5)

Agbasegbe, Bamidele Ade. "The Role of Wife in the Black Extended Family: Perspectives from a Rural Community in the Southern United States." (6)

Aldridge, Delores P. "The Changing Nature of Interracial Marriage in Georgia: A Research Note." (15)

Allen, Walter R. and Stukes, Sandra. "Black Family Lifestyles and the Mental Health of Black Americans." (31)

Balkwell, Carolyn, Balswick, Jack and Balkwell, James W. "On Black and White Family Patterns in America: Their Impact on the Expressive Aspect of Sex-Role Socialization." (55)

Barnes, Ben E. and Gay, Kathlyn. THE RIVER FLOWS BACKWARD. (63)

Bernard, Jessie Shirley. MARRIAGE AND FAMILY AMONG NEGROES. (100)

Bethel, Elizabeth Rauh. PROMISELAND: A CENTURY OF LIFE IN A NEGRO COMMUNITY. (101)

Billingsley, Andrew. BLACK FAMILIES AND THE STRUGGLE FOR SURVIVAL. (108)

Billingsley, Andrew and Billingsley, Amy Tate. "Negro Family Life in America." (113)

Billingsley, Andrew and Greene, Marilyn Cynthia. "Family Life among the Free Black Population in the 18th Century." (115)

Broderick, Carlfred Bartholomew, ed. A DECADE OF FAMILY RESEARCH AND ACTION. (154)

Brunswick, Ann F. "What Generation Gap? A Comparison of Some Generational Differences among Blacks and Whites." (174)

Christian, Barbara. "Community and Nature: The Novels of Toni Morrison." (216)

Clarke, John Henrik, ed. BLACK FAMILIES IN THE AMERICAN ECONOMY. (226)

Clarke, John Henrik. "The Black Family in Historical Perspective." (227)

Comer, James P. THE BLACK FAMILY: AN ADAPTIVE PERSPECTIVE. (237)

Davis, Lenwood G. BLACK FAMILIES IN URBAN AREAS IN THE UNITED STATES: A BIBLIOGRAPHY OF PUBLISHED WORKS ON THE BLACK FAMILY IN URBAN AREAS IN THE UNITED STATES. (271)

Davis, Lenwood G. THE BLACK FAMILY IN THE UNITED STATES: A SELECTED BIBLIOGRAPHY OF ANNOTATED BOOKS, ARTICLES AND DISSERTATIONS ON BLACK FAMILIES IN AMERICA. (272)

Demerson, Bamidele Agbasegbe. "Some Aspects of Contemporary Rural Afro American Family Life in the Sea Islands of Southeastern United States." (282)

Dixon, Johanne C., comp. A SELECTED ANNOTATED BIBLIOGRAPHY ON BLACK FAMILIES. VOLUME 1. (291)

Dougherty, Molly Crocker. BECOMING A WOMAN IN RURAL BLACK CULTURE. (296)

Engerman, Stanley L. "Black Fertility and Family Structure in the U.S., 1880-1940." (313)

Engerrand, Steven W. "Black and Mulatto Mobility and Stability in Dallas, Texas, 1880-1910." (314)

English, Richard H. "Beyond Pathology: Research and Theoretical Perspectives on Black Families." (316)

Engram, Eleanor. SCIENCE, MYTH, REALITY: THE BLACK FAMILY IN ONE-HALF CENTURY OF RESEARCH. (317)

Farmer, James. "The Plight of Negro Children in America Today." (328)

Ferman, Louis A., Kornbluh, Joyce L. and Haber, Alan, eds. POVERTY IN AMERICA: A BOOK OF READINGS. (333)

Frazier, Edward Franklin. THE NEGRO FAMILY IN THE UNITED STATES. (351)

Gibson, William. FAMILY LIFE AND MORALITY: STUDIES IN BLACK AND WHITE. (379)

Goldstein, Rhoda L., ed. BLACK LIFE AND CULTURE IN THE UNITED STATES. (391)

Goode, William Josiah, ed. THE CONTEMPORARY AMERICAN FAMILY. (392)

Gutman, Herbert G. "Persistent Myths about the Afro-American
   Family." (424)
Gutman, Herbert George. THE BLACK FAMILY IN SLAVERY AND FREEDOM: 1750-
   1925. (425)
Haley, Alex. ROOTS: THE SAGA OF AN AMERICAN FAMILY. (431)
Harwood, Edwin. "Urbanism as a Way of Life." (471)
Heiss, Jerold. THE CASE OF THE BLACK FAMILY: A SOCIOLOGICAL
   INQUIRY. (485)
Herzog, Elizabeth. "Is There a 'Break-Down' of the Negro Family?" (500)
Iowa. State University of Science and Technology, Ames. College of Home
   Economics. FAMILIES OF THE FUTURE. (550)
Jackson, Jacquelyne J. "Family Organization and Ideology." (562)
Jones, Clarence B. "Perspective on the Black Family." (598)
Jones, Jacqueline. LABOR OF LOVE, LABOR OF SORROW: BLACK WOMEN, WORK,
   AND THE FAMILY FROM SLAVERY TO THE PRESENT. (600)
King, James R. "African Survivals in the Black American Family: Key
   Factors in Stability." (618)
Kushnick, Louis. "The Negro Family in the United States: A
   Review." (630)
Lee, Irene Kathy. "Intergenerational Interaction among Black Limited-
   Resource Middlescent Couples, Adult Children, Aging Parents." (649)
Martin, Elmer P. and Martin, Joanne Mitchell. THE BLACK EXTENDED
   FAMILY. (698)
McAdoo, Harriette Pipes, ed. BLACK FAMILIES. (709)
McCummings, Le Verne, comp. THE BLACK FAMILY: A CONSOLIDATION OF PAPERS
   PRESENTED TO THE NATIONAL CONFERENCE OF BLACK SOCIAL WORKERS, FEBRUARY
   21-23, 1969. (720)
McPherson, James M. et al. "The Black Family in Urban America." (728)
McQueen, Albert J. "The Adaptations of Urban Black Families: Trends,
   Problems and Issues." (731)
Miller, Elizabeth W. and Fisher, Mary L., comps. THE NEGRO IN AMERICA: A
   BIBLIOGRAPHY. (740)
Mogey, John M. "The Negro Family System in the United States." (752)
Moody, Anne. COMING OF AGE IN MISSISSIPPI. (762)
Munoz, Faye V. and Endo, Russell, eds. PERSPECTIVES ON MINORITY GROUP
   MENTAL HEALTH. (779)
Nobles, Wade and Nobles, Grady. "African Roots in Black Families: The
   Social-Psychological Dynamics of Black Family Life and the
   Implications for Health Care." (795)
Perrucci, Carolyn Cummings and Targ, Dena B., eds. MARRIAGE AND THE
   FAMILY: A CRITICAL ANALYSIS AND PROPOSALS FOR CHANGE. (832)
Peters, Marie F., ed. "Special Issue: Black Families." (835)
Rainwater, Lee. BEHIND GHETTO WALLS: BLACK FAMILIES IN A FEDERAL
   SLUM. (862)
Reiss, David and Hoffman, Howard A., eds. THE AMERICAN FAMILY: DYING OR
   DEVELOPING? (877)
Scanzoni, John H. THE BLACK FAMILY IN MODERN SOCIETY. (922)
Stack, Carol B. and Semmel, Herbert. "The Concept of Family in the Poor
   Black Community." (984)
Staples, Robert. "The Black American Family." (986)
Staples, Robert. "The Black Family Revisited: A Review and
   Preview." (988)
Staples, Robert. "The Myth of the Black Matriarchy." (997)
Staples, Robert E. "Strength and Inspiration: Black Families in the
   United States." (1012)
Stewart, James B. "Perspectives on Black Families from Contemporary Soul
   Music: The Case of Millie Jackson." (1023)

Sudarkasa, Niara. "Interpreting the African Heritage in Afro-American
  Family Organization." (1033)
Wasserman, Herbert Louis. "Father-Absent and Father-Present Lower Class
  Negro Families: A Comparative Study of Family Functioning." (1091)
White, Priscilla and Scott, Patricia. "The Role of Black Women in Black
  Families: Teaching about Black Families on a Predominantly White
  Campus." (1108)
Whiteman, Maxwell. "Black Genealogy." (1111)
Wilkinson, Doris Yvonne and Taylor, Ronald Lewis, eds. THE BLACK MALE IN
  AMERICA: PERSPECTIVES ON HIS STATUS IN CONTEMPORARY SOCIETY. (1120)
Willie, Charles Vert, comp. THE FAMILY LIFE OF BLACK PEOPLE. (1129)
Willie, Charles Vert. A NEW LOOK AT BLACK FAMILIES. (1130)
Willie, Charles Vert. A NEW LOOK AT BLACK FAMILIES. (1131)

Family Life in Foreign Countries

Burgest, David R. "Afrocircular Child in a Eurocircular Society." (180)
Enberg, Lila E. "Household Differentiation and Integration as Predictors
  of Child Welfare in a Ghanaian Community." (312)
Greenfield, Sidney M. ENGLISH RUSTICS IN BLACK SKIN: A STUDY OF MODERN
  FAMILY FORMS IN A PRE-INDUSTRIALIZED SOCIETY. (410)
Idusogie, E. O. "Role of Maternal Nutritional Health and Care in the
  Development and Personality of Children in Africa." (543)
Lesi, F. E. A. and Bassey, Expo E. E. "Family Study in Sickle Cell
  Disease in Nigeria." (654)
LeVine, Robert A. "Intergenerational Tensions and Extended
  Family Structures in Africa." (656)
Sudarkasa, Niara. "Interpreting the African Heritage in Afro-American
  Family Organization." (1033)

Family and Social Change

Agbasegbe, Bamidele Ade. "Social Change and Extended Family in the Black
  World: A Report on Research in Progress." (7)
Allen, Walter R. "Class, Culture, and Family Organization: The Effects
  of Class and Race on Family Structure in Urban America." (22)
Anderson, Claud and Cromwell, Rue L. "'Black is Beautiful' and the Color
  Preferences of Afro-American Youth." (36)
Avery, Reginald Stanley. "The Impact of Court-Ordered Busing on Black
  Families in Boston, Massachusetts." (48)
Barney, William L. "Patterns of Crisis: Alabama White Families and
  Social Change 1850-1870." (68)
Brigham, John C., Woodmansee, John J. and Cook, Stuart W. "Dimensions of
  Verbal Racial Attitudes: Interracial Marriage and Approaches to Racial
  Equality." (150)
Caldwell, John C. "Fertility and the Household Economy in
  Nigeria." (191)
Clark, Kenneth Bancroft. DARK GHETTO: DILEMMAS OF SOCIAL POWER. (220)
Dean, Dwight G., Braito, Rita, Powers, Edward A. and Bruton,
  Brent. "Cultural Contradictions and Sex Roles Revisited: A Replication
  and a Reassessment." (280)
Dougherty, Molly Crocker. BECOMING A WOMAN IN RURAL BLACK CULTURE. (296)
Elder, Glen H., Jr. "Approaches to Social Change and the Family." (311)
Epps, Edgar G. "Impact of School Desegregation on Aspirations, Self-
  Concepts and Other Aspects of Personality." (318)

Staples, Robert and Mirande, Alfredo. "Racial and Cultural Variations among American Families: A Decennial Review of the Literature on Minority Families." (1005)

Steady, Filomina Chioma, ed. THE BLACK WOMAN CROSS-CULTURALLY. (1016)

Stewart, James B. and Scott, Joseph W. "The Institutional Decimation of Black American Males." (1024)

Taylor, Arnold H. TRAVAIL AND TRIUMPH: BLACK LIFE AND CULTURE IN THE SOUTH SINCE THE CIVIL WAR. (1039)

Tufte, Virginia and Myerhoff, Barbara G., eds. CHANGING IMAGE OF THE FAMILY. (1053)

Turner, S. H. Regina. "Images of Black Women in the Plays of Black Female Playwrights, 1950-1975." (1059)

U.S. Bureau of Labor Statistics. THE NEGRO IN THE WEST: SOME FACTS RELATING TO SOCIAL AND ECONOMIC CONDITIONS. VOL. 3: THE NEGRO FAMILY. (1061)

U.S. Bureau of the Census. THE SOCIAL AND ECONOMIC STATUS OF THE BLACK POPULATION IN THE UNITED STATES, 1971, by Nampeo D.R. McKenney. (1062)

U.S. Bureau of the Census. THE SOCIAL AND ECONOMIC STATUS OF THE BLACK POPULATION IN THE UNITED STATES: AN HISTORICAL VIEW, 1790-1978, by Nampeo D.R. McKenney. (1064)

U.S. Department of Labor. Office of Policy Planning and Research. THE NEGRO FAMILY: THE CASE FOR NATIONAL ACTION, by Daniel Patrick Moynihan. (1070)

Uhlenberg, Peter. "Changing Family Patterns of Blacks, Chicanos, and Whites: 1960-1970." (1073)

Valentine, Charles A. CULTURE AND POVERTY: CRITIQUE AND COUNTER-PROPOSALS. (1077)

Wakin, Edward. AT THE EDGE OF HARLEM: PORTRAIT OF A MIDDLE-CLASS NEGRO FAMILY. (1083)

Whitten, Norman E., Jr. and Szwed, John F., eds. AFRO-AMERICAN ANTHOLOGY: CONTEMPORARY PERSPECTIVES. (1114)

Williams, Charles Robert. "Adaptations of the Black-White Mixed Racial Child." (1121)

Alternative Family Forms

Allen, Walter R. and Agbasegbe, Bamidele Ade. "A Comment on Scott's 'Black Polygamous Family Formation'." (30)

Cazenave, Noel, ed. "Black Alternative Lifestyles: Special Issue on Commentary and Reprise on Joseph Scott's Black Polygamous Family Formation." (197)

Cazenave, Noel A. "Alternative Intimacy, Marriage, and Family Lifestyles among Low-Income Black Americans." (198)

Cogswell, Betty E. and Sussman, Marvin B. "Changing Family and Marriage Forms: Complications for Human Service Systems." (231)

Ericksen, Julia A. "Race, Sex, and Alternative Lifestyle Choices." (323)

Ladner, Joyce A. "Mixed Families: White Parents and Black Children." (637)

Lenus, Jack, Jr. "Friendship: A Refutation." (652)

Mabrey, Wilbert Gene. "African-American Polygynous Relatedness: An Exploratory Study Utilizing Phenomenological Techniques." (686)

McAdoo, Harriette Pipes. "Commentary on Joseph Scott's 'Black Polygamous Family Formation'." (711)

Monahan, Thomas P. "Interracial Parentage as Revealed by Birth Records in the United States, 1970." (757)

Morin, Rita J. "Black Child, White Parents: A Beginning
Biography." (765)
Morris, Roger Baxter. "Strengths of the Black Community: An
Investigation of the Black Community and 'Broken Homes'." (767)
Savage, James E. Jr., Adair, Alvis V. and Friedman, Philip. "Community-
Social Variables Related to Black Parent-Absent Families." (919)
Scott, Joseph W. "Black Polygamous Family Formation: Case Studies of
Legal Wives and Consensual 'Wives'." (934)
Scott, Joseph W. "Conceptualizing and Researching American Polygyny--And
Critics Answered." (935)
Scott, Joseph W. "Polygamy: A Futuristic Family Arrangement for African-
Americans." (936)
Staples, Robert. "Beyond the Black Family: The Trend toward
Singlehood." (985)
Staples, Robert. "Intimacy Patterns among Black, Middle-Class
Single Parents." (991)

Futuristic Studies of the Family

Kilpatrick, Allie C. "Future Directions for the Black Family." (617)

Social Mobility as it Affects the Family

Goldenberg, Sheldon. "Kinship and Ethnicity Viewed as Adaptive Responses
to Location in the Opportunity Structure." (390)
McAdoo, Harriette P. "Stress Absorbing Systems in Black Families." (708)
McAdoo, Harriette Pipes. "Factors Related to Stability in
Upwardly Mobile Black Families." (713)
Safa, Helen Icken. AN ANALYSIS OF UPWARD MOBILITY IN LOW-INCOME
FAMILIES: A COMPARISON OF FAMILY AND COMMUNITY LIFE AMONG AMERICAN
NEGROES AND PUERTO RICAN POOR. (912)

Comparative Studies--International, Interclass, Sex, and Time Differences

Agbasegbe, Bamidele Ade. "Woman-to-Woman Marriages in Africa and
Afroamerica." (8)
Allen, Walter R. "Class, Culture, and Family Organization: The Effects
of Class and Race on Family Structure in Urban America." (22)
An, Judy Yi-Bii Li. "Marital Satisfaction: A Comparative Study of Black
and White College Students' Attitudes toward Marriage." (34)
Aronoff, Joel and Crano, William D. "A Re-examination of the Cross-
Cultural Principles of Task Segregation and Sex Role Differentiation
in the Family." (41)
Bartz, Karen W. and Levine, Elaine S. "Childrearing by Black Parents: A
Description and Comparison to Anglo and Chicano Parents." (70)
Beckett, Joyce O. "Racial Differences in Why Women Work." (83)
Bell, Robert R. "The Lower-Class Negro Family in the United States and
Great Britain: Some Comparisons." (91)
Bianchi, Suzanne M. "Racial Differences in Per Capita Income, 1960-76:
The Importance of Household Size, Headship and Labor Force
Participation." (102)
Biller, Henry B. "A Note on Father Absence and Masculine Development in
Lower-Class Negro and White Boys." (105)

Bortner, R.W., Bohn, Claudia J. and Hultsch, David F. "A Cross-Cultural Study of the Effects of Children on Parental Assessment of Past, Present and Future." (136)

Brooks, Robert. SEX--BLACK AND WHITE. (162)

Broude, Gwen J. "Extramarital Sex Norms in Cross-Cultural Perspective." (163)

Chandler, Susan Meyers. "Self-Perceived Competency in Cross-Cultural Counseling." (203)

deAlmeida, Eleanor Engram. "A Descriptive and Analytical Study of the Early Adult Roles of Black and White Women." (279)

Degler, Carl N. "Slavery in Brazil and the United States: An Essay in Comparative History." (281)

Dowdall, George W. "Intermetropolitan Differences in Family Income Inequality: An Ecological Analysis of Total White and Nonwhite Patterns in 1960." (297)

Duberman, Lucile, ed. GENDER AND SEX IN SOCIETY. (299)

Giovannoni, Jeanne M. and Billingsley, Andrew. "Child Neglect among the Poor: A Study of Parental Adequacy in Families of Three Ethnic Groups." (384)

Gump, Janice Porter. "Comparative Analysis of Black and White Women's Sex-Role Attitudes." (418)

Hale, Janice. "The Black Woman and Childrearing." (430)

Hare, Bruce R. Black Girls: A Comparative Analysis of Self-Perception and Achievement by Race, Sex and Socioeconomic Background. (451)

Harrell-Bond, Barbara E. "Stereotypes of Western and African Patterns of Marriage and Family Life." (460)

Hays, William C. and Mindel, Charles H. "Extended Kinship Relations in Black and White Families." (480)

Hempel, Donald J. "Family Buying Decisions: A Cross-Cultural Perspective." (488)

Hill, Herbert. "Of Blacks, Whites and Family Stability." (506)

Hunt, Larry L. and Hunt, Janet G. "Family Structure and Educational Attainment: Sex Differences among Urban Blacks." (534)

International Family Research Seminar, 9th, Tokyo, 1965. FAMILIES IN EAST AND WEST: SOCIALIZATION PROCESS AND KINSHIP TIES, edited by Reuben Hill and Rene Konig. (548)

Jackson, Agnes Durham. "Militancy and Black Women's Competitive Behavior in Competitive vs. Non-Competitive Conditions." (555)

Johnson, Leon Johanson, Sr. "A Comparative Study of the Womanhood Experiences of Black Young Adult Females and White Young Adult Females." (589)

Kamii, Constance K. and Radin, Norma L. "Class Differences in the Socialization Practices of Negro Mothers." (607)

Kanno, Nellie B. "Comparative Lifestyles of the Black Female in the United States and the Black Female in Lesotho." (610)

Lindsay, Beverly, ed. COMPARATIVE PERSPECTIVES OF THIRD WORLD WOMEN: THE IMPACT OF RACE, SEX, AND CLASS. (673)

Mack, Delores E. "The Power Relationship in Black Families and White Families." (688)

Miller, Kent S. and Dreger, Ralph Mason, eds. COMPARATIVE STUDIES OF BLACKS AND WHITES IN THE UNITED STATES. (741)

Nobles, Wade W. "African Root and American Fruit: The Black Family." (796)

Parron, Eugenia Mary. "Relationships of Black and White Golden Wedding Couples." (822)

Pope, Hallowell. "Negro-White Differences in Decisions Regarding Illegitimate Children." (847)

Scott, Mona Claire Vaughn. "Ethnic Differences in the Impact of Family
  Background Factors on Level of Education and College
  Completion." (938)
Shanas, Ethel and Streib, Gordon Franklin, eds. SYMPOSIUM ON THE FAMILY,
  INTERGENERATIONAL RELATIONS AND SOCIAL STRUCTURE. DUKE UNIVERSITY,
  1963. SOCIAL STRUCTURE AND THE FAMILY: GENERATIONAL RELATIONS. (948)
Siegel, Jacob S. "Estimates of Coverage of the Population by Sex, Race
  and Age in the 1970 Census." (958)
Staples, Robert. "The Matricentric Family System: A Cross-Cultural
  Exploration." (994)
Staples, Robert. "The Mexican-American Family: Its Modifications Over
  Time and Space." (995)
Sudarkasa, Niara. "African and Afro-American Family Structure: A
  Comparison." (1031)
Tanner, Nancy. "Matrifocality in Indonesia and Africa and among Black
  Americans." (1038)
Zimmerman, Carle C. "Family System of the Third World." (1151)

Family Policy

Barnett, Marguerite Ross and Hefner, James A., eds. PUBLIC POLICY FOR
  THE BLACK COMMUNITY: STRATEGIES AND PERSPECTIVES. (67)
Bell, Winifred. "Relatives' Responsibility: A Problem in Social
  Policy." (93)
Bianchi, Suzanne M. and Farley, Reynolds. "Racial Differences in Family
  Living Arrangements and Economic Well-Being: An Analysis of Recent
  Trends." (104)
Billingsley, Andrew. "Black Families and National Policy." (107)
Billingsley, Andrew. BLACK FAMILIES IN WHITE AMERICA. (110)
Blaydon, Colin C. and Stack, Carol B. "Income Support Policies and the
  Family." (129)
Clark, Candace. "Race, Motherhood, and Abortion." (219)
Gary, Lawrence E. "Policy Decisions in the Aid to Families with
  Dependent Children Program: A Comparative State Analysis." (365)
Hill, Robert Bernard. BLACK FAMILIES IN THE 1974-1975 DEPRESSION:
  SPECIAL POLICY REPORT. (508)
Institute of Society, Ethics and the Life Sciences. Research Group on
  Ethics and Population. POPULATION POLICY AND ETHICS: THE AMERICAN
  EXPERIENCE. A PROJECT OF THE RESEARCH GROUP ON ETHICS AND POPULATION
  OF THE INSTITUTE OF SOCIETY, ETHICS AND THE LIFE SCIENCES, edited by
  Robert M. Veatch. (546)
Jackson, Anthony W., ed. BLACK FAMILIES AND THE MEDIUM OF
  TELEVISION. (556)
Trader, Harriett Peat. "Welfare Policies and Black Families." (1048)
U.S. Department of Labor. Office of Policy Planning and Research. THE
  NEGRO FAMILY: THE CASE FOR NATIONAL ACTION, by Daniel Patrick
  Moynihan. (1070)
Willie, Charles V. "Population Policy and Growth: Perspectives from the
  Black Community--A Position Paper." (1127)
Wingate, Rosalee Ruth Martin. "A Life Cycle Approach to the Study of
  Families Receiving 'Aid to Families with Dependent Children'." (1137)

ORGANIZATIONS AND SERVICES TO FAMILIES

Governmental Units and the Family

Conference on Maryland History, 1st, Annapolis, 1974. LAW, SOCIETY, AND
POLITICS IN EARLY MARYLAND. PROCEEDINGS OF THE FIRST CONFERENCE ON
MARYLAND HISTORY, JUNE 14-15, 1974, edited by Aubrey C. Land, Loris
Green Carr and Edward C. Papenfuge. (240)
Cottle, Thomas J. BLACK CHILDREN, WHITE DREAMS. (244)
Greenberg, Edward S. "Black Children and the Political System." (408)
Karge, Bernadine. "Constitutional Law-Municipal Ordinance Limiting
Occupancy of Homeowners Dwelling to Certain Family Members Violative
of Fourteenth Amendment Due Process Clause: Moore v. City of East
Cleveland, Ohio." (612)
King, Mae C. "Oppression and Power: The Unique Status of the Black Woman
in the American Political System." (623)
Rainwater, Lee and Yancey, William L. "Black Families and the
White House." (864)
Rainwater, Lee and Yancey, William L., eds. THE MOYNIHAN REPORT AND THE
POLITICS OF CONTROVERSY: A TRANSACTION SOCIAL SCIENCE AND
PUBLIC POLICY REPORT. (865)
Scott, James F. "Police Authority and the Low-Income Black Family: An
Area Needed Research." (933)
Staples, Robert. "Public Policy and the Changing Status of Black
Families." (999)
U.S. Task Force on Juvenile Delinquency. TASK FORCE REPORT: JUVENILE
DELINQUENCY AND YOUTH CRIME: REPORT ON JUVENILE JUSTICE AND
CONSULTANTS' PAPERS. (1071)

Family Law

Moles, Oliver C. "Marital Dissolution and Public Assistance Payments:
Variations among American States." (753)
Scott, Patricia Bell and Weddle, Karen. "Bringing Outsiders into the
Legislative Process: A Brief Report from a Pilot Project in the Black
Community." (941)
Sickels, Robert J. RACE, MARRIAGE AND THE LAW. (956)
U.S. Department of Labor. Office of Policy Planning and Research. THE
NEGRO FAMILY: THE CASE FOR NATIONAL ACTION, by Daniel Patrick
Moynihan. (1070)
Wyatt, Derrick. "The Social Security Rights of Migrant Workers and Their
Families." (1140)

Military Families

Keller, Ella Tates. "Black Families in the Military System." (613)

Community Groups and the Family

Bankde, Faola. "The Strategy of the Black Father's Council." (59)
Barnes, Annie S. "An Urban Black Voluntary Association." (61)
Barnes, Annie Shaw. "The Black Family in Golden Towers." (62)

Barnes, Edward J. "The Black Community as the Source of Children: A
Theoretical Perspective." (64)

Billingsley, Andrew. "Family Functioning in the Low-Income Black
Community." (111)

Christian, Barbara. "Community and Nature: The Novels of Toni
Morrison." (216)

Gary, Lawrence E., ed. SOCIAL RESEARCH AND THE BLACK COMMUNITY: SELECTED
ISSUES AND PRIORITIES. A SELECTION OF PAPERS FROM A WORKSHOP ON
DEVELOPING RESEARCH PRIORITIES FOR THE BLACK COMMUNITY HELD AT
HOWARD UNIVERSITY IN WASHINGTON, D.C., JUNE 25-29, 1973. (366)

Gilbert, Gwendolyn Cynthia. "Patterns of Child Care among Black
Families." (381)

Grigg, Ernest C. "Save the Children." (413)

Hannerz, Ulf. SOULSIDE: INQUIRIES INTO GHETTO CULTURE AND
COMMUNITY. (447)

Hirsch, Carl. "Primary Group Supports among a Sample of Elderly Black
and White Ethnic Residents of Urban, Working-Class
Neighborhoods." (513)

Hopkins, Thomas J. "The Role of Community Agencies as Viewed by Black
Fathers." (519)

Hopkins, Thomas J. "The Role of the Agency in Supporting Black
Manhood." (520)

Irvine, Russell W. "The Black Family and Community: Some Problems in the
Development of Achievement Values." (551)

Johnson, Robert C. "The Black Family and Black Community
Development." (593)

Jones, Mary Elaine. "An Anthropological Assessment of Bonding:
Mother Infant Attachment Behavior in a Study of Forty Adolescent Black
and White Mothers from Delivery through Six Months." (601)

Kunkel, Peter H. and Kennard, Sara Sue. SPOUT SPRING: A BLACK
COMMUNITY. (628)

Mithun, Jacqueline S. "Cooperation and Solidarity as Survival
Necessities in a Black Urban Community." (750)

Morris, Roger Baxter. "Strengths of the Black Community: An
Investigation of the Black Community and 'Broken Homes'." (767)

Morrison, Toni. THE BLUEST EYE: A NOVEL. (768)

Perry, Lorraine. "Strategies of Black Community Groups." (833)

Phillips, Mona Taylor. "The Black Family and Community: Their Role in
the Formation of Positive Self-Concept of Working-Class Black
Youth." (839)

Proctor, Samuel D. "Stability of the Black Family and the Black
Community." (860)

Safa, Helen Icken. AN ANALYSIS OF UPWARD MOBILITY IN LOW-INCOME
FAMILIES: A COMPARISON OF FAMILY AND COMMUNITY LIFE AMONG AMERICAN
NEGROES AND PUERTO RICAN POOR. (912)

Religion and the Family

Cone, James H. "Black Theology and the Black College Student." (239)

Craggett, Foster T. "A Form Critical Approach to the Oral Traditions of
the Black Church as They Relate to the Celebration of Death." (245)

Edwards, Harry. "Black Muslim and Negro Christian Family
Relationships." (309)

Johnson, Otis Samuel. "The Social Welfare Role of the Black
Church." (592)

Kunz, Phillip R. "Black and Mormonism: A Social Distance Change." (629)

Lincoln, Charles Eric, ed. THE BLACK EXPERIENCE IN RELIGION. (671)
Long, Charles H. "Perspectives for a Study of Afro-American Religion in the United States." (680)
Wheeler, Edward Lorenzo. "Uplifting the Race: The Black Minister in the New South, 1865-1902." (1103)
Wilson, Bobby M. "Church Participation: A Social Space Analysis in a Community of Black In-Migrants." (1135)

Education and the Family

Albanese, Anthony Gerald. THE PLANTATION SCHOOL. (11)
Aldridge, Delores P. "Teaching about Black American Families." (18)
Avery, Reginald Stanley. "The Impact of Court-Ordered Busing on Black Families in Boston, Massachusetts." (48)
Bequer, Marta Maria. "The Relationship of Parent Participation and Selected Variables in Three Multi-Ethnic Elementary Schools in Dade County, Florida." (96)
Bernard, Jessie. "Note On Educational Homogamy in Negro-White and White-Negro Marriages, 1960." (99)
Black Child Development Institute. BLACK CHILDREN JUST KEEP ON GROWING: ALTERNATIVE CURRICULUM MODELS FOR YOUNG BLACK CHILDREN, edited by Madeleine Coleman. (121)
Brown, William Neal. "Strategies of Intervention with the Parents of 'Acting Out' Preschool Black Children." (173)
Burlew, Ann Kathleen. "Career Educational Choices Among Black Females." (182)
Cade, Tinina Quick. "Black Parents' Beliefs about Appropriate Child Behaviors Relating to White Teachers." (189)
Chappell, Earl Birges, III. "The Relationships between Socioeconomic Status, Sex, Self-Concept, Academic Achievement, and Course Selection of Urban Black Tenth-Grade Students." (206)
Chavis, William M. and Lyles, Gladys J. "Divorce Among Educated Black Women." (208)
Clark, Reginald M. FAMILY LIFE AND SCHOOL ACHIEVEMENT: WHY POOR BLACK CHILDREN SUCCEED OR FAIL. (221)
Clark, Reginald Milton. "Black Families as Educators: A Qualitative Inquiry." (222)
Creswell-Betsch, Carol. "Comparison of a Family Microtraining Program and a Reading Program to Enhance Empathic Communication by Black Parents with Young Children." (250)
Datcher, Linda. "Effects of Community, Family and Education on Earnings of Black and White Men." (263)
Epps, Edgar G. "Impact of School Desegregation on Aspirations, Self-Concepts and Other Aspects of Personality." (318)
Gerstman, Leslie Sue. "Withdrawal of Blacks and Whites from Public to Nonpublic Elementary Schools in Minneapolis." (376)
Gordon, Vivian Verdell, ed. LECTURES: BLACK SCHOLARS ON BLACK ISSUES. (396)
Graber, Anita Wine. "Imagining the World: The Reflections and Perceptions of Black Low-Income Mothers in Relation to Their Involvements in the Educational Lives of Their Children." (401)
Granger, Robert C. and Young, James C., eds. DEMYTHOLOGIZING THE INNER CITY CHILD: PAPERS. (404)
Higginbotham, Elizabeth Starr. "Educated Black Women: An Exploration into Life Chances and Choices." (503)

Williamson, Robert C. "Dating Frequency, Ethnicity, and Adjustment in
  the High School: A Comparative Study." (1125)

Social Services and the Family

Baldwin, Doris. "Poverty and the Older Woman: Reflections of a
  Social Worker." (53)
Burnett-Epps, Martha Alma. "The Perceptions of the Black Aged and Their
  Relatives toward the Receipt of Care Components at Contracting
  Socioeconomic Levels." (183)
Cogswell, Betty E. and Sussman, Marvin B. "Changing Family and Marriage
  Forms: Complications for Human Service Systems." (231)
Crumbley, Joseph. "A Descriptive Analysis of Black and White Families
  Reported for Child Maltreatment." (254)
Cutright, Phillips and Madras, Patrik. "AFDC and the Marital and Family
  Status of Ever Married Women Aged 15-44: United States, 1950-
  1970." (259)
Davis, Frank, G. "Impact of Social Security Taxes on the Poor." (269)
Dixon, Johanne C., comp. A SELECTED ANNOTATED BIBLIOGRAPHY ON BLACK
  FAMILIES. VOLUME 1. (291)
Frey, Cecile P. "The House of Refuge for Colored Children." (357)
Graves, Conrad. "Family and Community Support Networks and Their
  Utilization by the Black Elderly." (405)
Herson, Jay, Crocker, Cyril L. and Butts, Ernest. "Comprehensive Family
  Planning Services to an Urban Black Community." (499)
Kammeyer, Kenneth C., Yetman, Norman R. and McClendon, Mckee J. "Family
  Planning Services and the Distribution of Black Americans." (608)
Moore, William. THE VERTICAL GHETTO: EVERYDAY LIFE IN AN URBAN
  PROJECT. (763)
Savage, James E. Jr., Adair, Alvis V. and Friedman, Philip. "Community-
  Social Variables Related to Black Parent-Absent Families." (919)
Wingate, Rosalee Ruth Martin. "A Life Cycle Approach to the Study of
  Families Receiving 'Aid to Families with Dependent Children'." (1137)
Wyatt, Derrick. "The Social Security Rights of Migrant Workers and Their
  Families." (1140)

Foster Care

Harris, Clotiel J. "Alternative Planning for Foster Care and Treatment
  of Children and Adolescents in Crises." (462)
Hill, Robert Bernard. INFORMAL ADOPTION AMONG BLACK FAMILIES. (509)
Husbands, Ann. "The Developmental Task of the Black Foster Child." (538)
Perkowski, Stefan. "Some Observations Concerning Black Children Living
  in a Residential Care Agency." (831)

Social Welfare

Billingsley, Andrew and Giovannoni, Jeanne M. CHILDREN OF THE STORM:
  BLACK CHILDREN AND AMERICAN CHILD WELFARE. (114)
Durbin, Elizabeth. "The Vicious Cycle of Welfare: Problems of the
  Female-Headed Household in New York City." (304)
Enberg, Lila E. "Household Differentiation and Integration as Predictors
  of Child Welfare in a Ghanaian Community." (312)

Ferranti, David Marc de. "Tests of Seven Hypotheses on Welfare
Dependency and Family Disintegration." (334)

Ford, Beverly O. "Case Studies of Black Female Heads of Households in
the Welfare System: Socialization and Survival." (345)

Gary, Lawrence E. "Policy Decisions in the Aid to Families with
Dependent Children Program: A Comparative State Analysis." (365)

Iglitzin, Lynne B. "A Case Study in Patriarchal Politics: Women on
Welfare." (544)

Janowitz, Barbara S. "The Impact of AFDC on Illegitimate Birth
Rates." (574)

Jewell, K. Sue. "Use of Social Welfare Programs and the Disintegration
of the Black Nuclear Family." (580)

Johnson, Otis Samuel. "The Social Welfare Role of the Black
Church." (592)

Morisey, Patricia Garland. "Professional Advocacy, Community
Participation and Social Planning: The Case of the Unmarried Mother
from the 'Inside the Ghetto' Perspective." (766)

Presser, Harriet B. and Salsberg, Linda S. "Public Assistance and Early
Family Formation: Is There a Pronatulist Effect?" (857)

Solomon, Barbara Bryant and Mendes, Helen A. "Black Families: A Social
Welfare Perspective." (978)

Tillman, Johnnie. "Welfare is a Women's Issue." (1045)

Trader, Harriett Peat. "Welfare Policies and Black Families." (1048)

Social Work

Adams, Cora Marie Gaines. "The Black Family: Implications for
Social Work Education and Practice." (3)

Gilbert, Gwendolyn Cynthia. "Patterns of Child Care among Black
Families." (381)

Gilkes, Cheryl Louise Townsend. "Living and Working in a World of
Trouble: The Emergent Career of the Black Woman Community
Worker." (382)

Adoption and Adoption Services

Aldridge, Delores P. "Problems and Approaches to Black Adoptions." (17)

Anderson, David C. CHILDREN OF SPECIAL VALUE: INTERRACIAL ADOPTION IN
AMERICA. (37)

Bayerl, John Aloysius. "Transracial Adoption: White Parents Who Adopted
Black Children and White Parents Who Adopted White Children." (78)

Chestang, Leon. "The Dilemma of Biracial Adoption." (210)

Chimezie, Amuzie. "Black Identity and the Grow-Shapiro Study on
Transracial Adoption." (213)

Chimezie, Amuzie. "Transracial Adoption of Black Children." (214)

Cohen, Leland Bernard. "Interracial Families Adapt to Their Marginality:
Between Black and White." (232)

Day, Dawn. THE ADOPTION OF BLACK CHILDREN: COUNTERACTING INSTITUTIONAL
DISCRIMINATION. (278)

Fowler, Irving A. "The Urban Middle Class Negro and Adoption: Two Series
of Studies and Their Implications for Action." (347)

Grow, Lucille J. and Shapiro, Deborah. "Adoption of Black Children by
White Parents." (415)

Grow, Lucille J. and Shapiro, Deborah. BLACK CHILDREN--WHITE PARENTS: A
STUDY OF TRANSRACIAL ADOPTION. (416)

Howard, Alicia, Royse, David D. and Skerl, John A. "Transracial Adoption: The Black Community Perspective." (525)

Johnson, C. Lincoln. "Transracial Adoption: Victim of Ideology." (584)

Ladner, Joyce A. "Mixed Families: White Parents and Black Children." (637)

Lawder, Elizabeth A., Hoopes, Janet L., Andrews, Roberta G., Lower, Katherine D. and Perry, Susan Y. A STUDY OF BLACK ADOPTION FAMILIES: A COMPARISON OF A TRADITIONAL AND QUASI-ADOPTION PROGRAM. (645)

Madison, Bernice Q. and Schapiro, Michael. "Black Adoption-Issues and Policies: Review of the Literature." (691)

McRoy, Ruth Gail Murdock. "A Comparative Study of the Self-Concept of Transracially and Inracially Adopted Black Children." (732)

Morin, Rita J. "Black Child, White Parents: A Beginning Biography." (765)

Neilson, Jacqueline. "Tayari: Black Homes for Black Children." (791)

Nichols, Robert C. "Black Children Adopted by White Families." (792)

Pepper, Gerald Wesley. "Interracial Adoptions: Family Profile, Motivation and Coping Methods." (825)

Robertson, Diana Conway. "Parental Socialization Patterns in Interracial Adoption." (885)

Scarr, Sandra and Weinberg, Richard A. "I.Q. Test Performance of Black Children Adopted by White Families." (923)

Simon, Rita J. "Black Attitudes toward Transracial Adoption." (962)

Simon, Rita James and Altstein, Howard. TRANSRACIAL ADOPTION. (964)

U.S. Children's Bureau. Division of Research and Evaluation. Social Research Group. FAMILIES FOR BLACK CHILDREN: THE SEARCH FOR ADOPTIVE PARENTS, AN EXPERIENCE SURVEY, by Elizabeth Herzog. (1065)

Mental Health and the Family

Adams, Harold. "The Collective Black Family: Barriers to Community Mental Health Services." (4)

Allen, Walter R. and Stukes, Sandra. "Black Family Lifestyles and the Mental Health of Black Americans." (31)

Bass, Barbara Ann, Wyatt, Gail Elizabeth and Powell, Gloria Johnson, eds. THE AFRO-AMERICAN FAMILY: ASSESSMENT, TREATMENT, AND RESEARCH ISSUES. (71)

Calhoun, Princess Diane. "Family Factors in Black Adolescent Mental Health." (193)

English, Richard A. The Challenge for Mental Health Minorities and Their World Views. (315)

Gary, Lawrence E., ed. MENTAL HEALTH: A CHALLENGE TO THE BLACK COMMUNITY. (364)

Hendricks, Leo Edward, Jr. "The Effect of Family Size, Child Spacing and Family Density on Stress in Low Income Black Mothers and Their Preadolescent Children." (493)

Lawrence, Margaret Morgan. YOUNG INNER CITY FAMILIES: DEVELOPMENT OF EGO STRENGTH UNDER STRESS. (646) MENTAL AND PHYSICAL HEALTH PROBLEMS OF BLACK WOMEN, WASHINGTON, D.C., MARCH 29-30, 1974. PROCEEDINGS. (738)

Munoz, Faye V. and Endo, Russell, eds. PERSPECTIVES ON MINORITY GROUP MENTAL HEALTH. (779)

Sager, Clifford J., Brayboy, Thomas L. and Waxenberg, Barbara R. BLACK GHETTO FAMILY IN THERAPY: A LABORATORY EXPERIENCE. (913)

Spurlock, Jeanne. "Introduction: Children and Families -- Cultural Differences and Mental Health." (981)

Staples, Robert E. "Black Family Life and Development." (1006)

Willie, Charles Vert, Kramer, Bernard M. and Brown, Bertram S.,
eds. RACISM AND MENTAL HEALTH: ESSAYS. (1132)

Physical Health and the Family

Barnes, Jimmie Franklin, Jr. "Factors Related to Deviant Health-Care
Practices: A Study of Black Families in the Mississippi Delta." (65)

Bates, James E., Lieberman, Harry H. and Powell, Rodney N. "Provisions
for Health Care in the Ghetto: The Family Health Team." (72)

Borland, Barry L. and Rudolp, Joseph P. "Relative Effects of
Low Socioeconomic Status, Parental Smoking and Poor Scholastic
Performance on Smoking among High School Students." (135)

Closs, Elizabeth Lee. "Isokinetic Measurement of Strength in Black and
White University Women." (230)

Edmonds, Mary McKinney. "Social Class and the Functional Health Status
of the Aged Black Female." (308)

Frate, Dennis Anthony. "Family Functioning and Hypertension in a Black
Population." (350)

Havenstein, Louise S., Kasl, Stanislav V. and Harburg, Ernest. "Work
Status, Work Satisfaction, and Blood Pressure among Married Black and
White Women." (475)

Idusogie, E. O. "Role of Maternal Nutritional Health and Care in the
Development and Personality of Children in Africa." (543)

Jones, Reginald Lorrin. "The Impact of Newborn Sickle Cell Testing on
Maternal Attitudes toward Childrearing: A Simulation Study." (603)

Lesi, F. E. A. and Bassey, Expo E. E. "Family Study in Sickle Cell
Disease in Nigeria." (654)

Luckraft, Dorothy, ed. BLACK AWARENESS: IMPLICATIONS FOR BLACK PATIENT
CARE. (684)

MacDonald, Mairi T. and Stewart, J. B. "Nutrition and Low-Income
Families." (687)

Mays, Rose M. "Primary Health Care and the Black Family." (705) MENTAL
AND PHYSICAL HEALTH PROBLEMS OF BLACK WOMEN, WASHINGTON, D.C., MARCH
29-30, 1974. PROCEEDINGS. (738)

Monroe, Ben, III. "The Effects of Mode of Presentation on the
Comprehension of Sickle Cell Disease Information of Black
Parents." (761)

Nobles, Wade and Nobles, Grady. "African Roots in Black Families: The
Social-Psychological Dynamics of Black Family Life and the
Implications for Health Care." (795)

Pierre, Thelma. "The Relationship between Hypertension and Psychosocial
Functioning in Young Black Men." (841)

Robertson, Leon S., Kosa, John, Alpert, Joel J. and Heagarty, Margaret
C. "Race, Status and Medical Care." (886)

Rodman, Hyman. "Family and Social Pathology in the Ghetto." (890)

Smith, Virginia Ware. "The Impact of Selected Internal and External
Influences on Successful Coping among Mothers of Children with
Sickle Cell Disease." (974)

U.S. Department of Health, Education and Welfare. WOMEN AND THEIR
HEALTH: RESEARCH IMPLICATIONS FOR A NEW ERA. (1066)

Verinis, J. Scott. "Maternal and Child Pathology in an Urban
Ghetto." (1078)

Economics and the Family

Allen, Walter R. "Family Roles, Occupational Statuses, and
Achievement Orientations among Black Women in the United States." (24)

Allen, Walter R. "The Social and Economic Statuses of Black Women in the
United States." (29)

Baldwin, Doris. "Poverty and the Older Woman: Reflections of a
Social Worker." (53)

Barnett, Marguerite Ross and Hefner, James A., eds. PUBLIC POLICY FOR
THE BLACK COMMUNITY: STRATEGIES AND PERSPECTIVES. (67)

Bean, Frank D. and Wood, Charles H. "Ethnic Variations in the
Relationship between Income and Fertility." (81)

Bell, Duran Jr. "Indebtedness In Black And White Families." (89)

Bianchi, Suzanne M. "Racial Differences in Per Capita Income, 1960-76:
The Importance of Household Size, Headship and Labor Force
Participation." (102)

Bianchi, Suzanne M. and Farley, Reynolds. "Racial Differences in Family
Living Arrangements and Economic Well-Being: An Analysis of Recent
Trends." (104)

Blaydon, Colin C. and Stack, Carol B. "Income Support Policies and the
Family." (129)

Cazenave, Noel A. "Middle Income Black Fathers: An Analysis of the
Provider Role." (200)

Chilman, Catherine S. "Families in Poverty in the Early 1970's: Rates,
Associated Factors, Some Implications." (212)

Clarke, John Henrik, ed. BLACK FAMILIES IN THE AMERICAN ECONOMY. (226)

Datcher, Linda. "Effects of Community, Family and Education on Earnings
of Black and White Men." (263)

Gossett, Ruth. "Economics of Black Widowhood." (398)

Haney, C. Allen, Michielutte, Robert, Vincent, Clark E. and Cochrane,
Carl M. "Factors Associated with the Poverty of Black Women." (442)

Hemming, R. C. L. "The Net Resource Distribution of Two Parent
Low Income Families: A Regional Comparison." (487)

Hempel, Donald J. "Family Buying Decisions: A Cross-Cultural
Perspective." (488)

Hill, Robert Bernard. BLACK FAMILIES IN THE 1974-1975 DEPRESSION:
SPECIAL POLICY REPORT. (508)

Hu, Teh-Wei and Knaub, Norman. "Effects of Cash and In-Kind Welfare
Payments on Family Expenditures." (528)

Jeffers, Camille. LIVING POOR: A PARTICIPANT OBSERVER STUDY OF
PRIORITIES AND CHOICES. (576)

Levin, Herman. "Income Alternatives for Poor Families." (655)

Martindale, Melanie and Poston, Dudley L., Jr. "Variations in Veteran/
Nonveteran Earnings Patterns among WWII, Korea, and Vietnam War
Cohorts." (699)

Meeker, Edward. "Freedom, Economic Opportunity, and Fertility: Black
Americans, 1860-1910." (733)

Oliver, Mamie O. "Elderly Blacks and the Economy: Variables of Survival:
'Personal Integration', 'Style', 'Pride and Positive Spirit'." (808)

Reed, Fred W., Udry, J. Richard and Ruppert, Maxine. "Relative Income
and Fertility: The Analysis of Individuals' Fertility in a Biracial
Sample." (873)

Ross, Arthur Max and Hill, Herbert, eds. EMPLOYMENT, RACE AND
POVERTY. (899)

Scanzoni, John H. THE BLACK FAMILY IN MODERN SOCIETY. (922)

Stack, Carol B. ALL OUR KIN: STRATEGIES FOR SURVIVAL IN A BLACK
COMMUNITY. (982)

U.S. Bureau of Labor Statistics. THE NEGRO IN THE WEST: SOME FACTS
RELATING TO SOCIAL AND ECONOMIC CONDITIONS. VOL. 3: THE NEGRO
FAMILY. (1061)

U.S. Bureau of the Census. THE SOCIAL AND ECONOMIC STATUS OF THE BLACK
POPULATION IN THE UNITED STATES, 1971, by Nampeo D.R. McKenney. (1062)

U.S. Bureau of the Census. THE SOCIAL AND ECONOMIC STATUS OF THE BLACK
POPULATION IN THE UNITED STATES, 1974. (1063)

U.S. Bureau of the Census. THE SOCIAL AND ECONOMIC STATUS OF THE BLACK
POPULATION IN THE UNITED STATES: AN HISTORICAL VIEW, 1790-1978, by
Nampeo D.R. McKenney. (1064)

Valentine, Charles A. CULTURE AND POVERTY: CRITIQUE AND COUNTER-
PROPOSALS. (1077)

Wallace, Phyllis A., Datcher, Linda and Malveaux, Julianne. BLACK WOMEN
IN THE LABOR FORCE. (1087)

Whitehead, John. IDA'S FAMILY: ADAPTATIONS TO POVERTY IN A SUBURBAN
GHETTO. (1109)

Whitehead, Tony L. "Residence, Kinship, and Mating as Survival
Strategies: A West Indian Example." (1110)

Yellin, Joel. "Urban Population Distribution, Family Income, and Social
Prejudice: The Long, Narrow City." (1146)

Consumerism

Brown, George L. "Invisible Again: Blacks and the Energy Crisis." (167)

Jenkins, Clyde Elbert. "The Profile Analysis of Parent-Child Interaction
in Families' Purchasing Decisions: A Cross-Cultural Study." (577)

Dual Career Families

Bould, Sally. "Black and White Families: Factors Affecting the Wife's
Contribution to the Family Income Where the Husband's Income is Low to
Moderate." (137)

Turner, Barbara F. and McCaffrey, Joanne Hammar. "Socialization and
Career Orientation among Black and White College Women." (1055)

Employment and the Family

Aldous, Joan. "Wives' Employment Status and Lower-Class Men as Husband-
Fathers: Support for the Moynihan Thesis." (14)

Ashburn, Elizabeth Alexander. "Influences and Motivations for Black and
White Women to Attain Positions in a Male-Dominated Profession." (46)

Axelson, Leland, Jr. "The Working Wife: Differences in Perception among
Negro and White Males." (49)

Beckett, Joyce O. "Racial Differences in Why Women Work." (83)

Beckett, Joyce O. "Working Wives: A Racial Comparison." (84)

Beckett, Joyce Octavia. "Working Wives: A Racial Analysis." (85)

Bell, Duran. "Why Participation Rates of Black and White Wives
Differ." (88)

Bird, Caroline and Briller, Sara Welles. BORN FEMALE: THE HIGH COST OF
KEEPING WOMEN DOWN. (116)

Bird, Caroline and Briller, Sara Welles. BORN FEMALE: THE HIGH COST OF
KEEPING WOMEN DOWN. (117)

Bishop, John H. "Jobs, Cash Transfers and Marital Instability: A Review
and Synthesis of the Evidence." (118)

Branson, Nathaniel William. "An Investigation of the Effects of Work on the Families of Black, Female Registrants in the Baltimore City Win Program, A Pilot Study." (146)

Brook, Judith S., Whiteman, Martin, Peisach, Estelle and Deutsch, Martin. "Aspiration Levels of and for Children: Age, Sex, Race, Socioeconomic Correlates." (160)

Burroughs, Louise Vitiello. "Occupational Preferences and Expectations as Related to Locus of Control, Sex-Role Contingency Orientation, Race and Family History among College Women." (185)

Chermesh, Ran. "Internal Relations in Unemployed Families." (209)

Coley, Soraya Moore. "And Still I Rise: An Exploratory Study of Contemporary Black Private Household Workers." (235)

Dill, Bonnie Thornton. "Across the Boundaries of Race and Class: An Exploration of the Relationship between Work and Family among Black Female Domestic Servants." (289)

Dobbins, Margaret Powell and Mulligan, James. "Black Matriarchy: Transforming a Myth of Racism into a Class Model." (293)

Epstein, Cynthia Fuchs. "Women and Professional Careers: The Case of the Woman Lawyer." (320)

Fadayomi, Theophilus Oyeyemi. "Black Women in the Labor Force: An Investigation of Factors Affecting the Labor Force Participation of Black Women in the United States." (324)

Gackenbach, Jayne. "The Effect of Race, Sex and Career Goal Differences on Sex Role Attitudes at Home and at Work." (361)

George, Valerie Daring. "An Investigation of the Occupational Aspirations of Talented Black Adolescent Females." (375)

Gilkes, Cheryl Louise Townsend. "Living and Working in a World of Trouble: The Emergent Career of the Black Woman Community Worker." (382)

Golden, Susan, ed. WORK, FAMILY ROLES AND SUPPORT SYSTEMS. (389)

Gump, Janice Porter. "Reality and Myth: Employment and Sex Role Ideology in Black Women." (419)

Hahn, Andrew Barry. "The Voluntary Dimension in Work Effort: The Effects of Work and Leisure Orientations on the Work Patterns of Low Income Familyheads." (429)

Harris, William. "Work and the Family in Black Atlanta, 1880." (466)

Harwood, Edwin and Hodge, Claire C. "Jobs and the Negro Family: A Reappraisal." (472)

Havenstein, Louise. ATTITUDES OF MARRIED WOMEN TOWARD WORK AND FAMILY: COMPARISON BY STRESS LEVEL, RACE AND WORK STATUS. (474)

Havenstein, Louise S., Kasl, Stanislav V. and Harburg, Ernest. "Work Status, Work Satisfaction, and Blood Pressure among Married Black and White Women." (475)

Jones, Jacqueline. LABOR OF LOVE, LABOR OF SORROW: BLACK WOMEN, WORK, AND THE FAMILY FROM SLAVERY TO THE PRESENT. (600)

Landry, Bart and Jendrek, Margaret Platt. "The Employment of Wives in Middle-Class Black Families." (641)

Lloyd, Cynthia B., ed. SEX, DISCRIMINATION AND THE DIVISION OF LABOR. (677)

Love, Bette Bonder. "Self-Esteem in Women Related to Occupational Status: A Biracial Study." (682)

Macke, Anne Statham and Morgan, William R. "Maternal Employment, Race, and Work Orientation of High School Girls." (689)

Mortimer, Jeylan T. "Social Class, Work and the Family: Some Implications of the Father's Occupation for Familial Relationships and Sons' Career Decisions." (770)

Mott, Frank L. "Racial Differences in Female Labor-Force Participation: Trends and Implications for the Future." (771)

Mott, Frank L. and Sandell, Steven H. WOMEN, WORK AND FAMILY: DIMENSIONS OF CHANGE IN AMERICAN SOCIETY. (772)

Moynihan, Daniel Patrick. "Employment, Income, and the Ordeal of the Negro Family." (773)

Mueller, Charles W. and Campbell, Blair G. "Female Occupational Achievement and Marital Status: A Research Note." (774)

Mullings, Leith. "On Women, Work and Society." (776)

Nanjundappa, G. "Occupational Differences among Black Male Cross-Regional Migrants from and to the South." (790)

Norris, Wessie Lavon. "A Path Model for Feelings of Personal Efficacy for Black Employed Male and Female Familyheads, Employed Female Non-Familyheads, and Housewives." (802)

Painter, Dianne Holland. "Black Women and the Family." (816)

Patterson, Orlando. "Persistence, Continuity and Change in the Jamaican Working-Class Family." (823)

Preston, Samuel H. "Differential Fertility, Unwanted Fertility and Racial Trends in Occupational Achievement." (858)

Reed, Fred W. and Udry, J. Richard. "Female Work, Fertility and Contraceptive Use in a Biracial Sample." (872)

Rosenfeld, Rachel A. "Race and Sex Differences in Career Dynamics." (898)

Ross, Arthur Max and Hill, Herbert, eds. EMPLOYMENT, RACE AND POVERTY. (899)

Umbarger, Carter Conrad. "Black and White Fathers: Their Impact on the Idealized Models and Vocational Plans of their Adolescent Sons." (1076)

Wallace, Phyllis A., Datcher, Linda and Malveaux, Julianne. BLACK WOMEN IN THE LABOR FORCE. (1087)

White, Lynn K. "A Note on Racial Differences in the Effect of Female Economic Opportunity on Marriage Rates." (1106)

Working Mothers

Aldous, Joan. "Wives' Employment Status and Lower-Class Men as Husband-Fathers: Support for the Moynihan Thesis." (14)

Bould, Sally. "Black and White Families: Factors Affecting the Wife's Contribution to the Family Income Where the Husband's Income is Low to Moderate." (137)

Brookins, Geraldine Kearse. "Maternal Employment: Its Impact on the Sex Roles and Occupational Choices of Middle and Working Class Black Children." (161)

Brown, Alexander Lionel. "The Effects of Race, Intelligence and Maternal Employment Status of the Career/Occupational Role Stereotypes of Four-Year Old Girls." (165)

Dill, Bonnie Thornton. "'The Means to Put My Children Through': Childrearing Goals and Strategies among Black Female Domestic Servants." (288)

Harrison, Algea Othella and Minor, Joanne Holbert. "Interrole Conflict, Coping Strategies, and Satisfaction among Black Working Wives." (469)

King, Karl, Abernathy, Thomas J. and Chapman, Ann H. "Black Adolescents' Views of Maternal Employment as a Threat to the Marital Relationship, 1963-1973." (622)

Peters, Marie Ferguson. "Nine Black Families: A Study of Household
    Management and Childrearing in Black Families with Working
    Mothers." (837)

FAMILY RELATIONSHIPS AND DYNAMICS

Nuclear Family

Bianchi, Suzanne M. "Racial Differences in Per Capita Income, 1960-76:
    The Importance of Household Size, Headship and Labor Force
    Participation." (102)
Bianchi, Suzanne M. and Farley, Reynolds. "Racial Differences in Family
    Living Arrangements and Economic Well-Being: An Analysis of Recent
    Trends." (104)
Brody, Gene H. and Endsley, Richard C. "Researching Children and
    Families: Differences in Approaches of Child and Family
    Specialists." (157)
Jenkins, Clyde Elbert. "The Profile Analysis of Parent-Child Interaction
    in Families' Purchasing Decisions: A Cross-Cultural Study." (577)
Jewell, K. Sue. "Use of Social Welfare Programs and the Disintegration
    of the Black Nuclear Family." (580)
Lieberson, Stanley. "Generational Differences among Blacks in the
    North." (666)
Pleck, Elizabeth H. "The Two-Parent Household: Black Family Structure in
    Late Nineteenth-Century Boston." (843)
Powell, Frances LaJune Johnson. "A Study of the Structure of the Freed
    Black Family in Washington, D.C., 1850-1880." (855)
Snow, Jacquelyn E. "A Heuristic Study of Black Female Heads of
    Households and Black Females Who Are Not Heads of Households and Their
    Involvement with Their Children's Educational Development in Camden,
    New Jersey." (976)

Extended Family and Kinship Groups

Agbasegbe, Bamidele Ade. "The Role of Wife in the Black Extended Family:
    Perspectives from a Rural Community in the Southern United
    States." (6)
Agbasegbe, Bamidele Ade. "Social Change and Extended Family in the Black
    World: A Report on Research in Progress." (7)
Aschenbrenner, Joyce. "Extended Families among Black Americans." (42)
Aschenbrenner, Joyce. LIFELINES: BLACK FAMILIES IN CHICAGO. (43)
Aschenbrenner, Joyce and Carr, Carolyn Hameedah. "Conjugal Relationships
    in the Context of the Black Extended Family." (44)
Ball, Richard E., Warheit, George J., Vandiver, Joseph S. and Holzer,
    Charles E., III. "Friendship Networks: More Supportive of Low-Income
    Black Women?" (56)
Bankde, Faola. "The Strategy of the Black Father's Council." (59)
Bell, Winifred. "Relatives' Responsibility: A Problem in Social
    Policy." (93)
Brown, Waln K. "Black Gangs as Family Extensions." (172)
Calhoun, Princess Diane. "Family Factors in Black Adolescent Mental
    Health." (193)

Single Parent Families

Austin, Roy L. "Race, Father-Absence, and Female Delinquency." (47)

Blackburn, George and Ricards, Sherman L. "The Mother-Headed Family among Free Negroes in Charleston, South Carolina, 1850-1860." (122)

Bould, Sally. "Female-Headed Families: Personal Fate Control and the Provider Role." (138)

Cooney, Rosemary Santana. "Demographic Components of Growth in White, Black, and Puerto Rican Female-Headed Families: Comparison of the Cutright and Ross/Sawhill Methodologies." (243)

Dietrich, Katheryn Thomas. "A Reexamination of the Myth of Black Matriarchy." (287)

Dobbins, Margaret Powell and Mulligan, James. "Black Matriarchy: Transforming a Myth of Racism into a Class Model." (293)

Durbin, Elizabeth. "The Vicious Cycle of Welfare: Problems of the Female-Headed Household in New York City." (304)

Ford, Beverly O. "Case Studies of Black Female Heads of Households in the Welfare System: Socialization and Survival." (345)

Hetherington, E. Mavis. "Effects of Paternal Absence on Sex-Typed Behaviors in Negro and White Preadolescent Males." (501)

Hirsch, Seth Lewis. "Home Climate in the Black Single-Parent Mother-Led Family: A Social-Ecological Interactional Approach." (514)

Hyman, Herbert H. and Reed, John Shelton. "'Black Matriarchy' Reconsidered: Evidence from Secondary Analysis of Sample Surveys." (541)

Hynes, Winifred Joyce. "Single Parent Mothers and Distress: Relationships between Selected Social and Psychological Factors and Distress in Low-Income Single Parent Mothers." (542)

Josephson, Eric. "The Matriarchy: Myth and Reality." (606)

Kriesberg, Lewis. "Rearing Children for Educational Achievement in Fatherless Families." (625)

McAdoo, Harriette Pipes, proj. dir. EXTENDED FAMILY SUPPORT OF SINGLE BLACK MOTHERS: FINAL REPORT. (712)

McBroom, Patricia. "The Black Matriarchy: Healthy or Pathological?" (716)

Morris, Roger Baxter. "Strengths of the Black Community: An Investigation of the Black Community and 'Broken Homes'." (767)

Parker, Seymour and Kleiner, Robert J. "Characteristics of Negro Mothers in Single-Headed Households." (818)

Point, Velma De Vonne La. "A Descriptive Survey of Some Perceptions and Concerns of Black Female Single Parent Families in Lansing, Michigan." (845)

Pope, Hallowell. "Unwed Mothers and Their Sex Partners." (848)

Sanderson, P. Rhonne. "Black and White Single Parents' Attitudes toward Traditional Family Relations." (916)

Snow, Jacquelyn E. "A Heuristic Study of Black Female Heads of Households and Black Females Who Are Not Heads of Households and Their Involvement with Their Children's Educational Development in Camden, New Jersey." (976)

Staples, Robert. "Intimacy Patterns among Black, Middle-Class Single Parents." (991)

U.S. Department of Health, Education and Welfare. Children's Bureau. Office of Child Development. Youth and Child Studies Branch.. BOYS IN FATHERLESS FAMILIES, by Elizabeth Herzog and Cecelia Sudia. (1067)

Wilkinson, Charles B. and O'Connor, William A. "Growing Up Male in a Black Single-Parent Family." (1117)

Family Relationships

Adams, Cora Marie Gaines. "The Black Family: Implications for Social Work Education and Practice." (3)

Allen, Richard L. and Chaffee, Steven H. "Racial Differences in Family Communication Patterns." (20)

Allen, Walter R. "Class, Culture, and Family Organization: The Effects of Class and Race on Family Structure in Urban America." (22)

Allen, Walter R. "Race and Sex Differences in the Socialization of Male Children." (25)

Aschenbrenner, Joyce and Carr, Carolyn Hameedah. "Conjugal Relationships in the Context of the Black Extended Family." (44)

Babchuk, Nicholas and Ballweg, John A. "Black Family Structure and Primary Relations." (50)

Ball, Richard Everett. "Expressive Functioning and the Black Family: Life and Domain Satisfaction of Black Women." (57)

Baumer-Mulloy, Marjorie. "A Study of the Relationship of Certain Home Environmental Factors to High or Low Achievement in Reading among Black Primary School Age Pupils of Low Socioeconomic Status." (76)

Berger, Alan S. and Simon, William. "Black Families and the Moynihan Report: A Research Evaluation." (97)

Billingsley, Andrew. BLACK FAMILIES IN WHITE AMERICA. (110)

Billingsley, Andrew. "Family Functioning in the Low-Income Black Community." (111)

Billingsley, Andrew and Billingsley, Amy Tate. "Illegitimacy and Patterns of Negro Family Life." (112)

Blackburn, Regina Lynn. "Conscious Agents of Time and Self: The Lives and Styles of African-American Women as Seen through Their Autobiographical Writings." (123)

Braithwaite, Ronald L. "Interpersonal Relations between Black Males and Black Females." (145)

Cazenave, Noel A. "Alternative Intimacy, Marriage, and Family Lifestyles among Low-Income Black Americans." (198)

Chermesh, Ran. "Internal Relations in Unemployed Families." (209)

Chunn, Jay Carrington, II. "A Comparison of Two Measures of Socioeconomic Status and Familial Factors as They Relate to Self Concept in Two Samples of Black Third and Fourth Grade Children." (217)

Clark, Reginald Milton. "Black Families as Educators: A Qualitative Inquiry." (222)

Clarke, James W. "Family Structure and Political Socialization among Urban Black Children." (225)

Cramer, M. Richard. "Family Strength and Family Satisfaction: Some Racial Comparisons." (246)

Creighton-Zollar, Ann. "A Member of the Family: Strategies for Black Family Continuity." (249)

Davis, Elizabeth B. "The American Negro: From Family Membership to Personal and Social Identity." (268)

Duncan, Beverly I. and Duncan, Otis Dudley. "Family Stability and Occupational Success." (302)

Edwards, Harry. "Black Muslim and Negro Christian Family Relationships." (309)

Engerman, Stanley L. "Black Fertility and Family Structure in the U.S., 1880-1940." (313)

Ericksen, Julia A. "Race, Sex, and Alternative Lifestyle Choices." (323)

Farley, Reynolds and Hermalin, Albert I. "Family Stability: A Comparison of Trends between Blacks and Whites." (326)

Farmer, Bonnita May. "Black Family Structure and Its Effects on
  Adolescents." (327)
Fogel, Robert William and Engerman, Stanley L. "Recent Findings in the
  Slave Demography and Family Structure." (340)
Frazier, Edward Franklin. THE NEGRO FAMILY IN THE UNITED STATES. (351)
Genovese, Eugene D. "Husbands, Fathers, Wives and Mothers During
  Slavery." (373)
Gutman, Herbert George. THE BLACK FAMILY IN SLAVERY AND FREEDOM: 1750-
  1925. (425)
Haney, C. Allen, Michielutte, Robert, Vincent, Clark E. and Cochrane,
  Carl M. "Characteristics of Black Women in Male and Female Headed
  Households." (441)
Harper, D. Wood, Jr. and Garza, Joseph M. "Ethnicity, Family
  Generational Structure and Intergenerational Solidarity." (459)
Heiss, Jerold. THE CASE OF THE BLACK FAMILY: A SOCIOLOGICAL
  INQUIRY. (485)
Hill, Robert Bernard. THE STRENGTHS OF BLACK FAMILIES. (510)
Hirsch, Seth Lewis. "Home Climate in the Black Single-Parent Mother-Led
  Family: A Social-Ecological Interactional Approach." (514)
Houten, Warren D. Ten. "The Black Family: Myth and Reality." (524)
Hoffman, Louis Wladis and Manis, Jean Denby. "The Value of Children in
  U.S.: A New Approach to the Study of Fertility." (529)
Hunter, Virginia. "The Impact of Adolescent Parenthood on Black Teenage
  Mothers and Their Families and the Influence of Two Alternative Types
  of Child Care." (537)
Indiana University. Libraries. THE BLACK FAMILY AND THE BLACK WOMAN: A
  BIBLIOGRAPHY, edited by Phyllis Rauch Klotman and Wilmer H. Baatz.
  (545)
Jackson, Jacquelyne Johnson. "Comparative Lifestyles and Family and
  Friend Relationships among Older Black Women." (564)
Johnson, Shirley B. "The Impact of Women's Liberation on Marriage,
  Divorce and Family Lifestyles." (594)
Jones, Bobby Frank. "A Cultural Middle Passage: Slave Marriage and
  Family in the Antebellum South." (597)
Kennedy, Theodore R. YOU GOTTA DEAL WITH IT: BLACK FAMILY RELATIONS IN A
  SOUTHERN COMMUNITY. (615)
King, Jerry Glenn. "A Study of Strengths in Black Families." (619)
Kunkel, Peter H. and Kennard, Sara Sue. SPOUT SPRING: A BLACK
  COMMUNITY. (628)
Ladner, Joyce A. TOMORROW'S TOMORROW: THE BLACK WOMAN. (638)
Lefcowitz, Myron Jack. DIFFERENCES BETWEEN NEGRO AND WHITE WOMEN IN
  MARITAL STABILITY AND FAMILY STRUCTURE: A MULTIPLE REGRESSION
  ANALYSIS. (650)
Lewis, Hylan. "Culture, Class and Family Life among Low-Income Urban
  Negroes." (663)
McAdoo, Harriette Pipes, ed. BLACK FAMILIES. (709)
McAdoo, Harriette Pipes. "Minority Families." (714)
Mercer, Charles V. "Interrelations among Family Stability, Family
  Composition, Residence and Race." (739)
Morrow, Betty Hearn. "A Comparison of Eight-Year-Old Children Born to
  Young Black Adolescents and Those Born to Comparable Mothers in Their
  Early Twenties." (769)
Pinderhughes, Elaine B. "Family Functioning of Afro-Americans." (842)
Rainwater, Lee. "Crucible of Identity: The Negro Lower Class
  Family." (863)

Rao, V.V. Prakakasa and Rao, V. Nandini. "Alternatives in Intimacy, Marriage, and Family Lifestyles: Preferences of Black College Students." (867)

Reiss, David and Hoffman, Howard A., eds. THE AMERICAN FAMILY: DYING OR DEVELOPING? (877)

Rodgers-Rose, La Frances, ed. THE BLACK WOMAN. (889)

Rubin, Roger H. MATRICENTRIC FAMILY STRUCTURE AND THE SELF-ATTITUDES OF NEGRO CHILDREN. (908)

Sanderson, P. Rhonne. "Black and White Single Parents' Attitudes toward Traditional Family Relations." (916)

Scanzoni, John H. THE BLACK FAMILY IN MODERN SOCIETY. (922)

Shell, Juanita. "Familial, Situational, and Cognitive Determinants of Sharing Behavior in African American Children." (950)

Skerry, Peter. "The Black Family Revisited." (968)

Spaights, Ernest. "Some Dynamics of the Black Family." (979)

Spurlock, Jeanne. "Introduction: Children and Families -- Cultural Differences and Mental Health." (981)

Stack, Carol B. and Semmel, Herbert. "The Concept of Family in the Poor Black Community." (984)

Staples, Robert. "The Black Family in Evolutionary Perspective." (987)

Staples, Robert. "The Black Family Revisited: A Review and Preview." (988)

Staples, Robert. "The Matricentric Family System: A Cross-Cultural Exploration." (994)

Staples, Robert E., comp. THE BLACK FAMILY: ESSAYS AND STUDIES. (1007)

Staples, Robert E., comp. THE BLACK FAMILY: ESSAYS AND STUDIES. (1008)

Sudarkasa, Niara. "African and Afro-American Family Structure: A Comparison." (1031)

Thomas, George Benjamin. YOUNG BLACK ADULTS: LIBERATION AND FAMILY ATTITUDES. (1041)

Trufant, Carol Ann. "The Effects of Familial Support Systems on Black Mothers' Childrearing Attitudes and Behaviors, and on Their Children's Competence." (1049)

Turner, Castellano B. and Turner, Barbara F. "Black Families, Social Evaluations and Future Marital Relationships." (1058)

Wakin, Edward. AT THE EDGE OF HARLEM: PORTRAIT OF A MIDDLE-CLASS NEGRO FAMILY. (1083)

Wasserman, Herbert Louis. "Father-Absent and Father-Present Lower Class Negro Families: A Comparative Study of Family Functioning." (1091)

White, Priscilla and Scott, Patricia. "The Role of Black Women in Black Families: Teaching about Black Families on a Predominantly White Campus." (1108)

Whittington, James Attison, Jr. "Kinship, Mating and Family in the Choco' of Colombia: An Afro-American Adaptation." (1115)

Williams, J. Allen, Jr. and Stockton, Robert. "Black Family Structures and Functions: An Empirical Examination of Some Suggestions Made by Billingsley." (1122)

Young, Virginia Heyer. "Family and Childhood in a Southern Negro Community." (1149)

Mother-Child Relationships

Aschenbrenner, Joyce. LIFELINES: BLACK FAMILIES IN CHICAGO. (43)

Bell, Robert R. "Lower Class Negro Mothers and Their Children." (90)

Bell, Robert R. "Lower-Class Negro Mothers' Aspirations for Their Children." (92)

Biller, Henry B. and Meredith, Dennis. FATHER POWER. (106)

Brown, Josephine V., Bakeman, Roger, Snyder, Patricia A., Fredrickson, W. Timm, Morgan, Sharon T. and Hepler, Ruth. "Interactions of Black Inner-City Mothers with their Newborn Infants." (168)

Cranford, Sharon Anita Hill. "An Expanded Case Study of Family Interaction and Transaction Roles of Middle-Class Black Mothers." (247)

Davids, Anthony. "Self-Concept and Mother-Concept in Black and White Preschool Children." (265)

Graber, Anita Wine. "Imagining the World: The Reflections and Perceptions of Black Low-Income Mothers in Relation to Their Involvements in the Educational Lives of Their Children." (401)

Hale, Janice. "The Black Woman and Childrearing." (430)

Harris, Joan Ricks. "Black/White and Socioeconomic Status as Factors in Maternal Attitudes toward Childrearing Practices and the Use of Health Care in Families with and without an Educable Mentally Retarded Child." (463)

Jackson, Roberta H. "Some Aspirations of Lower Class Black Mothers." (569)

Jones, Mary Elaine. "An Anthropological Assessment of Bonding: Mother Infant Attachment Behavior in a Study of Forty Adolescent Black and White Mothers from Delivery through Six Months." (601)

Jones, Reginald Lorrin. "The Impact of Newborn Sickle Cell Testing on Maternal Attitudes toward Childrearing: A Simulation Study." (603)

Jordan, Ernest E. "A Study of the Social and Maternal Responsibility of a Group of Negro Unwed Mothers." (604)

McMillan, Sylvia R. "Aspirations of Low-Income Mothers." (726)

McQueen, Adele Bolden. "The Influence of Increased Parent-Child Verbal Interaction on the Language Facility of Preschool Inner-City Black Children." (730)

North, George E. and Buchanan, O. Lee. "Maternal Attitudes in a Poverty Area." (803)

Oppel, Wallace Churchill. "Illegitimacy: A Comparative Follow-Up Study. A Matched Group of 120 Six to Eight Year-Old Negro Illegitimate Children and Their Mothers Is Compared to a Group of 120 Legitimate Six to Eight Year-Old Negro Children and Their Mothers on Measures of Child Development and Mothering Behavior." (810)

Perry, Robert L. "The Black Matriarchy Controversy and Black Male Delinquency." (834)

Radin, Norma and Kamii, Constance K. "The Childrearing Attitudes of Disadvantaged Negro Mothers and Some Educational Implications." (861)

Richardson, Barbara Blayton. "Racism and Childrearing: A Study of Black Mothers." (878)

Rosen, Lawrence. "Matriarchy and Lower Class Negro Male Delinquency." (896)

Samuels, Douglas D. and Griffore, Robert. "Ethnic Differences in Mothers' Anxiety." (914)

Saunders, Marie Teresa. "Disciplinary Techniques of Black Mothers of Higher and Lower Socioeconomic Status: A Questionnaire and Interview Study." (918)

Sitgraves, Mary Elizabeth. "Recent Life Event Stress and Patterns of Mother-Son Interaction in High Risk Versus Low Risk Black Mothers." (967)

Stevens, Joseph H., Jr. and Mathews, Marilyn, eds. MOTHER CHILD, FATHER CHILD RELATIONSHIPS. (1022)

Verinis, J. Scott. "Maternal and Child Pathology in an Urban Ghetto." (1078)

Wade-Gayles, Gloria. "She Who is Black and Mother: In Sociology and
    Fiction, 1940-70." (1081)
Webster, Staten W. "Some Correlates of Reported Academically Supportive
    Behaviors of Negro Mothers toward Their Children." (1094)
Whitfield, Cynthia Elaine Bell. "Low Income Black and White Mothers'
    Verbal Communication Patterns with Their Preschool Children." (1112)
Wyatt, Gail Elizabeth. "Studying the Black Mother-Child Interaction:
    Issues and Alternatives." (1141)
Zegiob, Leslie E. and Forehand, Rex. "Maternal Interactive Behavior as a
    Function of Race, Socioeconomic Status, and Sex of the Child." (1150)
Zwiebel, Sarah. "The Relation between Maternal Behaviors and Aggression
    in Sons: Black and Puerto Rican Families." (1153)

Father-Child Relationships

Biller, Henry B. "A Note on Father Absence and Masculine Development in
    Lower-Class Negro and White Boys." (105)
Calhoun, Fred S. "Childrearing Practices of the Black Father." (192)
Clarke, James W. "Family Structure and Political Socialization among
    Urban Black Children." (225)
Dukes, Phyllis Jean Carmack. "The Relationship between Paternal
    Interaction Style and Infant Behavior as a Function of
    Social Economic Status and Sex of Infant." (301)
Hartnagel, Timothy F. "Father Absence and Self Conception among
    Lower Class White and Negro Boys." (470)
Hendricks, Leo E. "Black Unwed Adolescent Fathers." (490)
Hunt, Janet G. and Hunt, Larry L. "Race, Daughters and Father-Loss: Does
    Absence Make the Girl Grow Stronger?" (532)
Hunt, Larry L. and Hunt, Janet G. "Race and the Father-Son Connection:
    The Conditional Relevance of Father Absence for the Orientations and
    Identities of Adolescent Boys." (535)
Hunt, Larry L. and Hunt, Janet G. "Race, Father Identification and
    Achievement Orientation: The Subjective Side of the Father-Son
    Connection, A Research Note." (536)
Labrecque, Suzanne Volin. "Childrearing Attitudes and Observed Behaviors
    of Black Fathers with Kindergarten Daughters." (634)
Liebow, Elliot. "Fathers Without Children." (668)
Liebow, Elliot. TALLY'S CORNER: A STUDY OF NEGRO STREETCORNER MEN. (669)
McAdoo, John. "Black Father and Child Interactions." (715)
Mortimer, Jeylan T. "Social Class, Work and the Family: Some
    Implications of the Father's Occupation for Familial Relationships and
    Sons' Career Decisions." (770)
Nolle, David B. "Changes in Black Sons and Daughters: A Panel Analysis
    of Black Adolescents' Orientations toward Their Fathers." (801)
Price-Bonham, Sharon and Skeen, Patsy. "A Comparison of Black and White
    Fathers with Implications for Parent Education." (859)
Schulz, David A. "Variations in the Father Role in Complete Families of
    the Negro Lower Class." (926)
Sciara, Frank J. "Effects of Father Absence on the Educational
    Achievement of Urban Black Children." (930)
Sciara, Frank J. and Jantz, Richard K. "Father Absence and Its Apparent
    Effect on the Reading Achievement of Black Children from Low-Income
    Families." (931)
Simmons, Joe Louis. "A Study of the Relationship between Father-Absent
    Homes and Father-Present Homes and the Academic Performance and Social
    Adjustment of Black Middle School Students." (960)

Stevens, Joseph H., Jr. and Mathews, Marilyn, eds. MOTHER CHILD,
  FATHER CHILD RELATIONSHIPS. (1022)
Tuck, Samuel, Jr. "Working With Black Fathers." (1051)
U.S. Department of Health, Education and Welfare. Children's
  Bureau. Office of Child Development. Youth and Child Studies
  Branch.. BOYS IN FATHERLESS FAMILIES, by Elizabeth Herzog and Cecelia
  Sudia. (1067)
Umbarger, Carter Conrad. "Black and White Fathers: Their Impact on the
  Idealized Models and Vocational Plans of their Adolescent
  Sons." (1076)
Wasserman, Herbert L. "A Comparative Study of School Performance among
  Boys from Broken and Intact Black Families." (1090)
Wasserman, Herbert Louis. "Father-Absent and Father-Present Lower Class
  Negro Families: A Comparative Study of Family Functioning." (1091)

Husband-Wife Relationships

Aguirre, B. E. and Parr, W. C. "Husbands' Marriage Order and the
  Stability of First and Second Marriages of White and Black
  Women." (10)
Aldous, Joan. "Wives' Employment Status and Lower-Class Men as Husband-
  Fathers: Support for the Moynihan Thesis." (14)
Allen, Walter R. "Race Differences in Husband-Wife Interpersonal
  Relationships during the Middle Years of Marriage." (26)
Bould, Sally. "Black and White Families: Factors Affecting the Wife's
  Contribution to the Family Income Where the Husband's Income is Low to
  Moderate." (137)
Buehler, Marilyn H., Weigert, Andrew J. and Thomas, Darwin
  L. "Correlates of Conjugal Power: A Five Cultural Analysis of
  Adolescent Perceptions." (176)
Chapman, Jane Roberts and Gates, Margaret, eds. WOMEN INTO WIVES: THE
  LEGAL AND ECONOMIC IMPACT OF MARRIAGE. (204)
Genovese, Eugene D. "Husbands, Fathers, Wives and Mothers During
  Slavery." (373)
Hammond, Judith and Enoch, J. Rex. "Conjugal Power Relations among Black
  Working Class Families." (436)
Hampton, Robert L. "Husband's Characteristics and Marital Disruption in
  Black Families." (438)
Iglitzin, Lynne B. "A Case Study in Patriarchal Politics: Women on
  Welfare." (544)
Jacques, Jeffrey M. "Self-Esteem among Southeastern Black American
  Couples." (572)
Mabrey, Wilbert Gene. "African-American Polygynous Relatedness: An
  Exploratory Study Utilizing Phenomenological Techniques." (686)
Melton, Willie, III. "Self-Satisfaction and Marital Stability among
  Black Males: Socioeconomic and Demographic Antecedents." (737)
Peters, Marie Ferguson. "Nine Black Families: A Study of Household
  Management and Childrearing in Black Families with Working
  Mothers." (837)
Rutledge, Essie Manuel. "Marital Interaction Goals of Black Women:
  Strengths and Effects." (909)
Willie, Charles V. and Greenblatt, Susan L. "Four 'Classic' Studies of
  Power Relationships in Black Families: A Review and Look to the
  Future." (1128)

Parent-Child Relationships

Mahone, Jack Randall. "The Influence of Family Relations upon Socially
Desiring Behavior of Black and Caucasian Preschool Children." (692)

Malina, Robert M., Mueller, William H. and Holman, John D. "Parent-Child
Correlations and Heritability of Stature in Philadelphia Black and
White Children 6-12 Years of Age." (695)

Morrison, Toni. THE BLUEST EYE: A NOVEL. (768)

N'Namdi, George Richard. "Analysis of Parent-Child Interaction in the
Two-Child Black Family." (788)

Parron, Delores Louise. "Black Parents' Concept of Parenthood: A Study
of Parental Role Definition and Parenting Style." (821)

Peters, Marie Ferguson. "Nine Black Families: A Study of Household
Management and Childrearing in Black Families with Working
Mothers." (837)

Rosser, Pearl L. and Hamlin, Joyce Fite, eds. RESEARCH ON THE BLACK
CHILD AND FAMILY AT HOWARD UNIVERSITY: 1867-1978. (901)

Rowland, Glovioell Winsmore. "Early Effects of Postpartum Intervention
on Black Adolescent Mother-Infant Interaction." (902)

Rubin, Dorothy. "Parental Schemata of Negro Primary School
Children." (903)

Scott-Jones, Diane. "Family Variables Associated with School Achievement
in Low-Income Black First-Graders." (932)

Trufant, Carol Ann. "The Effects of Familial Support Systems on Black
Mothers' Childrearing Attitudes and Behaviors, and on Their Children's
Competence." (1049)

Wade, Brenda Karon. "The Relationship between the Disciplinary Styles of
Black Parents and Preference for Mode of Family Therapy." (1082)

Whittington, James Attison, Jr. "Kinship, Mating and Family in the
Choco' of Colombia: An Afro-American Adaptation." (1115)

Wright, Maggie Saxon. "Parent-Child Relations, Achievement Motivation,
and Sex-Role Attitudes among Black and White Professional Women in
Traditional and Pioneer Occupations." (1139)

Parent-Adolescent Relationships

Allen, Walter R. "Race, Family Setting and Adolescent
Achievement Orientation." (27)

Brook, Judith S., Lukoff, Irving F. and Whiteman, Martin. "Peer, Family,
and Personality Domains as Related to Adolescents' Drug
Behavior." (159)

Buehler, Marilyn H., Weigert, Andrew J. and Thomas, Darwin
L. "Correlates of Conjugal Power: A Five Cultural Analysis of
Adolescent Perceptions." (176)

Cummings, Scott. "Family Socialization and Fatalism among Black
Adolescents." (256)

Freeman, Janie Earlyn Andrews. "A Study of Black Middle-Class Feelings
and Attitudes on Male/Female Role Identifications." (356)

Goodlett, Carlton B. "The Crisis of Youth and Adult
Responsibility." (393)

Horton, Carrell P., Gray, Billie B. and Roberts, S. Oliver. "Attitudes
of Black Teenagers and Their Mothers toward Selected Contemporary
Issues." (522)

Kandel, Denise B. "Race, Maternal Authority and Adolescent
Aspiration." (609)

Littlefield, Robert P. "Self-Disclosure among Some Negro, White, and
Mexican American Adolescents." (676)

Sibling Relationships

Mitchell, Jacquelyn. "Strategies for Achieving One-Upsmanship: A Descriptive Analysis of Afro-American Siblings in Two Speech Events." (749)

Socialization

Allen, Walter R. "Race and Sex Differences in the Socialization of Male Children." (25)

Anderson, Claud and Cromwell, Rue L. "'Black is Beautiful' and the Color Preferences of Afro-American Youth." (36)

Aseltine, Gwendolyn Pamenter. "Family Socialization Perceptions among Black and White High School Students." (45)

Balkwell, Carolyn, Balswick, Jack and Balkwell, James W. "On Black and White Family Patterns in America: Their Impact on the Expressive Aspect of Sex-Role Socialization." (55)

Ball, Richard E., Warheit, George J., Vandiver, Joseph S. and Holzer, Charles E., III. "Friendship Networks: More Supportive of Low-Income Black Women?" (56)

Barnes, Annie Shaw. "The Black Family in Golden Towers." (62)

Barnes, Edward J. "The Black Community as the Source of Children: A Theoretical Perspective." (64)

Baumrind, Diana and Black, Allen E. "Socialization Practices Associated with Dimension of Competence in Preschool Boys and Girls." (77)

Blau, Zena Smith. "Exposure to Childrearing Experts: A Structural Interpretation of Class-Color Differences." (127)

Broderick, Carlfred B. "Social Heterosexual Development among Urban Negroes and Whites." (152)

Burgest, David R. "Afrocircular Child in a Eurocircular Society." (180)

Cade, Tinina Quick. "Black Parents' Beliefs about Appropriate Child Behaviors Relating to White Teachers." (189)

Cazenave, Noel A. and Strauss, Murray A. "Race, Class, Network Embeddedness and Family Violence: A Search for Potent Support Systems." (201)

Chunn, Jay I., ed. THE SURVIVAL OF BLACK CHILDREN AND YOUTH. (218)

Clark, Reginald Milton. "The Dance Party as a Socialization Mechanism for Black Urban Preadolescents and Adolescents." (223)

Clay, Phillip L. "The Process of Black Suburbanization." (228)

Cottle, Thomas J. BLACK CHILDREN, WHITE DREAMS. (244)

Cross, William E., Jr. "Black Family and Black Identity: A Literature Review." (253)

Cummings, Scott. "Family Socialization and Fatalism among Black Adolescents." (256)

Davids, Anthony. "Self-Concept and Mother-Concept in Black and White Preschool Children." (265)

Davis, Elizabeth B. "The American Negro: From Family Membership to Personal and Social Identity." (268)

Durrett, Mary Ellen, O'Bryant, Shirley and Pennebaker, James W. "Childrearing Reports of White, Black and Mexican-American Families." (305)

Epstein, Ralph and Komorita, S.S. "Prejudice among Negro Children as Related to Parental Ethnocentrism and Punitiveness." (321)

Eray, P. CHILDHOOD AND THE COSMOS: THE SOCIAL PSYCHOLOGY OF THE BLACK AFRICAN CHILD. (322)

Farmer, Bonnita May. "Black Family Structure and Its Effects on Adolescents." (327)

Farmer, James. "The Plight of Negro Children in America Today." (328)

Feinman, Saul. "Trends in Racial Self-Image of Black Children: Psychological Consequences of a Social Movement." (332)

Ford, Beverly O. "Case Studies of Black Female Heads of Households in the Welfare System: Socialization and Survival." (345)

Freeman, Howard E., Ross, J. Michael, Armor, David and Pettigrew, Thomas F. "Color Gradation and Attitudes among Middle-Income Negroes." (355)

Goodlett, Carlton B. "The Crisis of Youth and Adult Responsibility." (393)

Gunthorpe, Wayne West. "Skin Color Recognition, Preference and Identification in Interracial Children: A Comparative Study." (420)

Hammond, Boone E. and Ladner, Joyce. "Socialization into Sexual Behavior in a Negro Slum Ghetto." (435)

Hannerz, Ulf. "Roots of Black Manhood: Sex, Socialization and Culture in the Ghettos of American Cities." (446)

Hare, Bruce R. "Black and White Child Self-Esteem in Social Science: An Overview." (450)

Hare, Bruce R. "Racial and Socioeconomic Variations in Preadolescent Area-Specific and General Self-Esteem." (452)

Iscoe, Ira, Williams, Martha and Harvey, Jerry. "Age, Intelligence and Sex as Variables in the Conformity Behavior of Negro and White Children." (552)

Jackson, Jacquelyne Johnson. "Comparative Lifestyles and Family and Friend Relationships among Older Black Women." (564)

Jacob, Theodore, Fagin, Robert, Perry, Joseph and Dyke, Ruth Ann Van. "Social Class, Child Age, and Parental Socialization Values." (570)

Jacobs, James Harris. "Black/White Interracial Families: Marital Process and Identity Development in Young Children." (571)

Kamii, Constance K. and Radin, Norma L. "Class Differences in the Socialization Practices of Negro Mothers." (607)

Kokonis, Nicholas. "Three Wishes of Black American Children: Psychosocial Implications." (624)

Ladner, Joyce A. "Labeling Black Children: Social-Psychological Implications." (636)

Logan, Sadye L. "Race, Identity, and Black Children: A Developmental Perspective." (679)

Mahone, Jack Randall. "The Influence of Family Relations upon Socially Desiring Behavior of Black and Caucasian Preschool Children." (692)

McRoy, Ruth Gail Murdock. "A Comparative Study of the Self-Concept of Transracially and Inracially Adopted Black Children." (732)

Mithun, Jacqueline S. "Cooperation and Solidarity as Survival Necessities in a Black Urban Community." (750)

Myers, Hector F., Rana, Phyllis G. and Harris, Marcia, eds. BLACK CHILD DEVELOPMENT IN AMERICA: 1927-1977: AN ANNOTATED BIBLIOGRAPHY. (785)

Norris, Wessie Lavon. "A Path Model for Feelings of Personal Efficacy for Black Employed Male and Female Familyheads, Employed Female Non-Familyheads, and Housewives." (802)

Orive, Ruben and Gerard, Harold B. "Social Contact of Minority Parents and Their Children's Acceptance by Classmates." (811)

Parker, Maude I. "Growing Up Black." (817)

Robertson, Diana Conway. "Parental Socialization Patterns in Interracial Adoption." (885)

Samuels, Shirley C. "An Investigation into the Self-Concepts of Lower and Middle-Class Black and White Kindergarten Children." (915)

Savage, James E. Jr., Adair, Alvis V. and Friedman, Philip. "Community-Social Variables Related to Black Parent-Absent Families." (919)

Shannon, Lyle W. "The Changing World View of Minority Migrants in an Urban Setting." (949)

Silverstein, Barry and Krate, Ronald. CHILDREN OF THE DARK GHETTO: A DEVELOPMENTAL PSYCHOLOGY. (959)

Simon, Rita James and Altstein, Howard. TRANSRACIAL ADOPTION. (964)

Thompson, Daniel Calbert. SOCIOLOGY OF THE BLACK EXPERIENCE. (1042)

Turner, Barbara F. and McCaffrey, Joanne Hammar. "Socialization and Career Orientation among Black and White College Women." (1055)

Turner, Barbara F. and Turner, Castellano B. "The Political Implications of Social Stereotyping of Women and Men among Black and White College Students." (1056)

Wallace, Joan S. and Wong, Samuel P. "Some Sociocultural Aspects of Growing Up Black." (1085)

Wallace, Michele. BLACK MACHO AND THE MYTH OF THE SUPERWOMAN. (1086)

Washington, Ernest D. "Politicizing Black Children." (1088)

Williams, Charles Robert. "Adaptations of the Black-White Mixed Racial Child." (1121)

Young, Virginia Heyer. "A Black American Socialization Pattern." (1148)

Communication in the Family

Allen, Richard L. and Chaffee, Steven H. "Racial Differences in Family Communication Patterns." (20)

Brown, Delindus R. and Anderson, Wanda F. "A Survey of the Black Woman and the Persuasion Process: The Study of Strategies of Identification and Resistance." (166)

Folb, Edith A. RUNNING DOWN SOME LINES: THE LANGUAGE AND CULTURE OF BLACK TEENAGERS. (342)

Gaston, John Coy. "The Denver, Colorado Area Black Professional/Businesswoman's Perception of Her Communication with the Black Male." (369)

Hawkins, James L., Weisberg, Carol and Ray, Dixie L. "Marital Communication Style and Social Class." (479)

Orum, Anthony M., Cohen, Roberta S., Grasmuck, Sherri and Orum, Amy W. "Sex, Socialization and Politics." (812)

Whitfield, Cynthia Elaine Bell. "Low Income Black and White Mothers' Verbal Communication Patterns with Their Preschool Children." (1112)

Williams, Robert Lewis, ed. EBONICS: THE TRUE LANGUAGE OF BLACK FOLKS. (1124)

Conflict Resolution

Cromwell, Vicky L. and Cromwell, Ronald E. "Perceived Dominance in Decision-Making and Conflict Resolution among Anglo, Black, and Chicano Couples." (252)

Fowler, Dale Eugene. "An Exploratory Investigation of the Relationship between Locus of Control and Parenting Tasks among Lower Socioeconomic Status Black Mothers." (346)

Franklin, Clyde W., II. "White Racism as the Cause of Black Male/Black Female Conflict: A Critique." (349)

Goodlett, Carlton B. "The Crisis of Youth and Adult Responsibility." (393)

Harrell, Jules P. "Analyzing Black Coping Styles: A Supplemental
Diagnostic System." (461)
Tucker, Dorothy M. "The Effects of Internal/External Control as
Perceived by Black Couples in Interpersonal Conflict." (1052)

Power in the Family

Hammond, Judith and Enoch, J. Rex. "Conjugal Power Relations among Black
Working Class Families." (436)
Kandel, Denise B. "Race, Maternal Authority and Adolescent
Aspiration." (609)
Khalesi, Mohammad Reza. "Comparison of the Parenting Attitudes, Conflict
Management Styles, and Interpersonal Behavior Patterns of Anglo, Black
and Mexican-American Parents." (616)
King, Karl. "Adolescent Perception of Power Structure in the Negro
Family." (620)
King, Karl. "A Comparison of the Negro and White Family Structure in
Low Income Families." (621)
Mack, Delores E. "The Power Relationship in Black Families and White
Families." (688)
Maxwell, Joseph W. "Rural Negro Father Participation in Family
Activities." (703)
McBroom, Patricia. "The Black Matriarchy: Healthy or
Pathological?" (716)
Willie, Charles V. "Dominance in the Family: The Black and White
Experience." (1126)
Willie, Charles V. and Greenblatt, Susan L. "Four 'Classic' Studies of
Power Relationships in Black Families: A Review and Look to the
Future." (1128)

Decision Making

Andrew, Gwen. "Determinants of Negro Family Decisions in Management of
Retardation." (40)
Bayerl, John Aloysius. "Transracial Adoption: White Parents Who Adopted
Black Children and White Parents Who Adopted White Children." (78)
Dietrich, Katheryn Thomas. "A Reexamination of the Myth of Black
Matriarchy." (287)
Eigsti, Marilyn Ann H. "Interrelationships of Value Orientation,
Decision-Making Mode and Decision-Implementing Style of Selected
Low Socioeconomic Status Negro Homemakers." (310)
Floyd, Russell F. "Marital Adjustment and Decision Making among Stable
Black Married Couples." (338)
Gerstman, Leslie Sue. "Withdrawal of Blacks and Whites from Public to
Nonpublic Elementary Schools in Minneapolis." (376)
Jenkins, Clyde Elbert. "The Profile Analysis of Parent-Child Interaction
in Families' Purchasing Decisions: A Cross-Cultural Study." (577)
Keller, Ella Tates. "Black Families in the Military System." (613)
Mumbauer, Corrine C. and Gray, Susan W. "Resistance to Temptation in
Young Negro Children." (777)

Stages in Family Life Cycle

Baltes, Paul B. and Brim, Orville G., Jr., eds. LIFE-SPAN DEVELOPMENT AND BEHAVIOR. VOLUME 2. (58)

Bengston, Vern L., Furlong, Michael J. and Lauffer, Robert S. "Time, Aging and Continuity of Social Structure: Themes and Issues in Generational Analysis." (94) "Black Age Lauded." (119)

Golden, Herbert M. "Black Ageism." (388)

Hampton, Robert Lewis. "Marital Disruption among Blacks." (440)

Hareven, Tamara K., ed. TRANSITIONS: THE FAMILY AND THE LIFE COURSE IN HISTORICAL PERSPECTIVE. (457)

Hershey, Marjorie Randon. "Racial Differences in Sex-Role Identities and Sex Stereotyping: Evidence against a Common Assumption." (498)

Hutchinson, Ira W., III. "The Significance of Marital Status for Morale and Life Satisfaction among Lower-Income Elderly." (539)

Intons-Peterson, M. J. and Samuels, Arlene K. "The Cultural Halo Effect: Black and White Women Rate Black and White Men." (549)

Jackson, Jacquelyne Johnson. "The Plight of Older Black Women in the United States." (566)

Johnson, Cynthia Elaine. "Factors Influencing the Marital Stability of Older Black Couples." (586)

Kanno, Nellie B. "Comparative Lifestyles of the Black Female in the United States and the Black Female in Lesotho." (610)

McCord, William M. et al. LIFESTYLES IN THE BLACK GHETTO. (718)

Parron, Eugenia Mary. "Relationships of Black and White Golden Wedding Couples." (822)

Rathbone, McCuan Eloise. "Elderly Victims of Family Violence and Neglect." (870)

Thomas, George Benjamin. YOUNG BLACK ADULTS: LIBERATION AND FAMILY ATTITUDES. (1041)

Wingate, Rosalee Ruth Martin. "A Life Cycle Approach to the Study of Families Receiving 'Aid to Families with Dependent Children'." (1137)

Later Years and Aging

Baldwin, Doris. "Poverty and the Older Woman: Reflections of a Social Worker." (53)

Black Aged in the Future, San Juan, P.R., 1972. Proceedings. PROCEEDINGS OF 'BLACK AGED IN THE FUTURE'. (120)

Blau, Zena Smith, Oser, George T. and Stephens, Richard C. "Aging, Social Class, and Ethnicity: A Comparison of Anglo, Black and Mexican-American Texans." (128)

Burnett-Epps, Martha Alma. "The Perceptions of the Black Aged and Their Relatives toward the Receipt of Care Components at Contracting Socioeconomic Levels." (183)

Cazenave, Noel A. "Family Violence and Aging Blacks: Theoretical Perspectives and Research Possibilities." (199)

Chapman, Sabrina Coffey. "A Social-Psychological Analysis of Morale in a Selected Population: Low-Income Elderly Black Females." (205)

Creecy, Robert F and Wright, Roosevelt. "Morale and Informal Activity with Friends among Black and White Elderly." (248)

Dancy, Joseph, Jr. THE BLACK ELDERLY: A GUIDE FOR PRACTITIONERS: WITH COMPREHENSIVE BIBLIOGRAPHY. (261)

Dorsett-Robinson, Jean, ed. THE BLACK ELDERS: WORKSHOP AND CONFERENCE PROCEEDINGS. CONDUCTED BY THE COMMUNITY SERVICES PROGRAM TO PROVIDE QUALITY CARE TO THE AGED. (295)

Edmonds, Mary McKinney. "Social Class and the Functional Health Status of the Aged Black Female." (308)

Gibson, Rose C. "Blacks at Middle and Late Life: Resources and Coping." (378)

Graves, Conrad. "Family and Community Support Networks and Their Utilization by the Black Elderly." (405)

Harris, Roland Arsville, Jr. "A Study of Black Aged Persons." (465)

Hawkins, Brin D. "Formal and Informal Support Systems for the Black Elderly." (476)

Hirsch, Carl. "Primary Group Supports among a Sample of Elderly Black and White Ethnic Residents of Urban, Working-Class Neighborhoods." (513)

Jackson, Jacquelyn. MINORITIES AND AGING. (558)

Jackson, Jacquelyn Johnson, ed. AGING BLACK WOMEN: SELECTED READINGS FOR NCBA. (559)

Jackson, Jacquelyn Johnson. RESEARCH CONFERENCE ON MINORITY GROUP AGED IN THE SOUTH, DURHAM, NC, 1971. PROCEEDINGS. (560)

Jackson, Jacquelyn Johnson, Childs, Faith Hampton and Ficker, Robin, eds. AGING BLACK WOMEN: SELECTED READINGS FOR NCBA. (561)

Jackson, Jacquelyne Johnson. "Comparative Lifestyles and Family and Friend Relationships among Older Black Women." (564)

Jackson, Jacquelyne Johnson. "Marital Life among Aging Blacks." (565)

Jackson, Maurice and Wood, James. IMPLICATIONS FOR THE BLACK AGED. (568)

Johnson, Cynthia Elaine. "Factors Influencing the Marital Stability of Older Black Couples." (586)

Lee, Irene Kathy. "Intergenerational Interaction among Black Limited-Resource Middlescent Couples, Adult Children, Aging Parents." (649)

Linn, Margaret W., Hunter, Kathleen I. and Perry, Priscilla R. "Differences by Sex and Ethnicity in the Psychosocial Adjustment of the Elderly." (674)

Oliver, Mamie O. "Elderly Blacks and the Economy: Variables of Survival: 'Personal Integration', 'Style', 'Pride and Positive Spirit'." (808)

Rubin, Isador. SEXUAL LIFE IN THE LATER YEARS. (904)

Shanas, Ethel. "Family-Kin Networks and Aging in Cross-Cultural Perspective." (947)

Shanas, Ethel and Streib, Gordon Franklin, eds. SYMPOSIUM ON THE FAMILY, INTERGENERATIONAL RELATIONS AND SOCIAL STRUCTURE. DUKE UNIVERSITY, 1963. SOCIAL STRUCTURE AND THE FAMILY: GENERATIONAL RELATIONS. (948)

Middle Years

Allen, Walter R. "Race Differences in Husband-Wife Interpersonal Relationships during the Middle Years of Marriage." (26)

Gibson, Rose C. "Blacks at Middle and Late Life: Resources and Coping." (378)

Premarital Couples

Hare, J. and Hare, Nathan. "Coping with Male/Female Alienation in the Coming of Bad Years." (454)

Mahoney, E. R. "Premarital Coitus and the Southern Black: A Comment." (693)

Semaj, Leahcim Tufani. "Meaningful Male/Female Relationships in a State of Declining Sex-Ratio." (945)

Tucker, Dorothy M. "The Effects of Internal/External Control as
Perceived by Black Couples in Interpersonal Conflict." (1052)

Singles (Lifestyle)

Jackson, Lorraine B. "The Attitudes of Black Females toward Upper and
Lower Class Black Males." (567)
Staples, Robert. "Beyond the Black Family: The Trend toward
Singlehood." (985)
Staples, Robert. "Black Singles in America." (990)
Staples, Robert. "The New Majority: Black Singles in America." (998)
Staples, Robert. THE WORLD OF BLACK SINGLES: CHANGING PATTERNS OF MALE/
FEMALE RELATIONS. (1004)
Stein, P. and Hilty, R., eds. SINGLES AND SOCIETY. (1018)
Stein, Peter J. SINGLE LIFE: UNMARRIED ADULTS IN SOCIAL CONTEXT. (1019)
White, Patricia Elizabeth. "Patterns of Marriage among the Black
Population: A Preliminary Analysis of the Black Female." (1107)

Family Roles and Sex Roles

Agbasegbe, Bamidele Ade. "The Role of Wife in the Black Extended Family:
Perspectives from a Rural Community in the Southern United
States." (6)
Allen, Walter R. "Family Roles, Occupational Statuses, and
Achievement Orientations among Black Women in the United States." (24)
Almquist, Elizabeth M. "Untangling the Effects of Race and Sex: The
Disadvantaged Status of Black Women." (32)
An, Judy Yi-Bii Li. "Marital Satisfaction: A Comparative Study of Black
and White College Students' Attitudes toward Marriage." (34)
Aronoff, Joel and Crano, William D. "A Re-examination of the Cross-
Cultural Principles of Task Segregation and Sex Role Differentiation
in the Family." (41)
Badaines, Joel. "Identification, Imitation, and Sex-Role Preference in
Father-Present and Father-Absent Black and Chicano Boys." (51)
Balkwell, Carolyn, Balswick, Jack and Balkwell, James W. "On Black and
White Family Patterns in America: Their Impact on the Expressive
Aspect of Sex-Role Socialization." (55)
Baumer-Mulloy, Marjorie. "A Study of the Relationship of Certain Home
Environmental Factors to High or Low Achievement in Reading among
Black Primary School Age Pupils of Low Socioeconomic Status." (76)
Benjamin, Rommel. FACTORS RELATED TO CONCEPTIONS OF THE MALE FAMILIAL
ROLE BY BLACK YOUTH. (95)
Bonner, Florence B. "Black Women and White Women: Comparative Analysis
of Perceptions of Sex Roles for Self, Ideal Self and the Ideal
Male." (134)
Bould, Sally. "Female-Headed Families: Personal Fate Control and the
Provider Role." (138)
Bowser, Benjamin P. "The Contribution of Blacks to Sociological
Knowledge: A Problem of Theory and Role to 1950." (140)
Braxton, B. WOMEN, SEX AND RACE: A REALISTIC VIEW OF SEXISM AND
RACISM. (147)
Brookins, Geraldine Kearse. "Maternal Employment: Its Impact on the
Sex Roles and Occupational Choices of Middle and Working Class Black
Children." (161)

Brown, Prudence, Perry, Lorraine and Harburg, Ernest. "Sex Role Attitudes and Psychological Outcomes for Black and White Women Experiencing Marital Dissolution." (169)

Burroughs, Louise Vitiello. "Occupational Preferences and Expectations as Related to Locus of Control, Sex-Role Contingency Orientation, Race and Family History among College Women." (185)

Butler, Cynthia and Doster, Joseph A. "Sex-Role Learning in the Black Male: Research and Clinical Implications." (188)

Cazenave, Noel A. "Middle Income Black Fathers: An Analysis of the Provider Role." (200)

Cole, O. Jackson. "Scale Construction in the Assessment of Sex-Role Stereotypes among Minorities." (233)

Cranford, Sharon Anita Hill. "An Expanded Case Study of Family Interaction and Transaction Roles of Middle-Class Black Mothers." (247)

Davis, Angela. "Reflections on the Black Woman's Role in the Community of Slaves." (266)

Davis, Maria Susanne. "Sex-Role Factors in the Career Development of Black Female High School Students." (275)

deAlmeida, Eleanor Engram. "A Descriptive and Analytical Study of the Early Adult Roles of Black and White Women." (279)

Dean, Dwight G., Braito, Rita, Powers, Edward A. and Bruton, Brent. "Cultural Contradictions and Sex Roles Revisited: A Replication and a Reassessment." (280)

Duberman, Lucile, ed. GENDER AND SEX IN SOCIETY. (299)

Epstein, Cynthia Fuchs. "Positive Effects of the Multiple Negative: Explaining the Success of Black Professional Women." (319)

Freeman, Harvey R., Schockett, Melanie R. and Freeman, Evelyn B. "Effects of Gender and Race on Sex-Role Preferences of Fifth-Grade Children." (354)

Freeman, Janie Earlyn Andrews. "A Study of Black Middle-Class Feelings and Attitudes on Male/Female Role Identifications." (356)

Gackenbach, Jayne. "The Effect of Race, Sex and Career Goal Differences on Sex Role Attitudes at Home and at Work." (361)

Golden, Susan, ed. WORK, FAMILY ROLES AND SUPPORT SYSTEMS. (389)

Gump, Janice Porter. "Comparative Analysis of Black and White Women's Sex-Role Attitudes." (418)

Gump, Janice Porter. "Reality and Myth: Employment and Sex Role Ideology in Black Women." (419)

Hacker, Helen M. "Class and Race Differences in Gender Roles." (428)

Harris, Richard J. "An Examination of the Effects of Ethnicity, Socioeconomic Status and Generation on Familism and Sex Role Orientation." (464)

Harrison, Algea Othella and Minor, Joanne Holbert. "Interrole Conflict, Coping Strategies, and Satisfaction among Black Working Wives." (469)

Iglitzin, Lynne B. "A Case Study in Patriarchal Politics: Women on Welfare." (544)

Johnson, Leanor Boulin and Staples, Robert E. "Family Planning of the Young Minority Male: A Pilot Project." (588)

Jordan, Ernest E. "A Study of the Social and Maternal Responsibility of a Group of Negro Unwed Mothers." (604)

Ladner, Joyce Ann. "On Becoming a Woman in the Ghetto: Modes of Adaptation." (639)

Lewis, Diane K. "The Black Family: Socialization and Sex Roles." (658)

Liebow, Elliot. "Attitudes toward Marriage and Family among Black Males in Tally's Corner." (667)

Lowry, Waldra Greene. "Sex-Role Attitudes and Stereotypes among Black College Students." (683)

McConahay, Shirley A. and McConahay, John B. "Sexual Permissiveness, Sex Role Rigidity, and Violence Across Cultures." (717)

McCurdy, Paula Carol Kresser. "Sex Role, Decision Making Practices, Marital Satisfaction and Family Problems with Economically Disadvantaged Anglo, Black, and Chicano Couples." (721)

Oberle, Wayne H. "Role Models of Black and White Rural Youth at Two States of Adolescence." (805)

Orum, Anthony M., Cohen, Roberta S., Grasmuck, Sherri and Orum, Amy W. "Sex, Socialization and Politics." (812)

Osmond, Marie Withers. "Marital Organization in Low-Income Families: A Cross-Race Comparison." (813)

Parker, Seymour and Kleiner, Robert J. "Social and Psychological Dimensions of the Family Role Performance of the Negro Male." (819)

Pepper, Gerald Wesley. "Interracial Adoptions: Family Profile, Motivation and Coping Methods." (825)

Rao, V.V. Prakakasa and Rao, V. Nandini. "Family Size and Sex Preferences of Children: A Biracial Comparison." (868)

Romer, Nancy and Cherry, Debra. "Ethnic and Social Class Differences in Children's Sex-Role Concepts." (893)

Scanzoni, John. "Sex Roles, Economic Factors, and Marital Solidarity in Black and White Marriages." (920)

Scanzoni, John and Fox, Greer Litton. "Sex Roles, Family and Society: The Seventies and Beyond." (921)

Schulz, David A. "Variations in the Father Role in Complete Families of the Negro Lower Class." (926)

Schulz, David Allen. COMING UP BLACK: PATTERNS OF GHETTO SOCIALIZATION. (927)

Scott, Patricia Bell. "Sex Roles Research and Black Families: Some Comments on the Literature." (939)

Stack, Carol B. "Sex Roles and Survival Strategies in an Urban Black Community." (983)

Staples, Robert. BLACK MASCULINITY: THE BLACK MALE'S ROLE IN AMERICAN SOCIETY. (989)

Staples, Robert Eugene. "A Study of the Influence of Liberal-Conservative Attitudes on the Premarital Sexual Standards of Different Racial, Sex-Role and Social Class Groupings." (1015)

Stewart, Phyllis Louise Albert. "A Study of Role Perceptions of Lower-Income Black Husbands in Black Families." (1025)

U.S. Department of Health, Education and Welfare. Children's Bureau. Office of Child Development. Youth and Child Studies Branch.. BOYS IN FATHERLESS FAMILIES, by Elizabeth Herzog and Cecelia Sudia. (1067)

U.S. Department of Health, Education and Welfare. National Institute of Education. Career Education Program. ISSUES OF SEX BIAS AND SEX FAIRNESS IN CAREER INTEREST MEASUREMENT, edited by Esther E. Diamond. (1068)

White, Deborah G. "Female Slaves: Sex Roles and Status in the Antebellum Plantation South." (1105)

Wright, Maggie Saxon. "Parent-Child Relations, Achievement Motivation, and Sex-Role Attitudes among Black and White Professional Women in Traditional and Pioneer Occupations." (1139)

Birth Order Differences

Dixon, Richard D. "The Absence of Birth Order Correlations among Unwed and Married Black First-Conceptors." (292)

Men's Issues

Anderson, Elijah. A PLACE ON THE CORNER. (38)

Axelson, Leland, Jr. "The Working Wife: Differences in Perception among Negro and White Males." (49)

Bayless, Vaurice G. "Selected Research Studies and Professional Literature Dealing with Physiological, Socioeconomic, Psychological, and Cultural Differences between Black and White Males with Reference to the Performance of Athletic Skills." (79)

Biller, Henry B. and Meredith, Dennis. FATHER POWER. (106)

Braithwaite, Ronald L. "Interpersonal Relations between Black Males and Black Females." (145)

Buehler, Marilyn H., Weigert, Andrew J. and Thomas, Darwin L. "Correlates of Conjugal Power: A Five Cultural Analysis of Adolescent Perceptions." (176)

Cazenave, Noel A. "Middle Income Black Fathers: An Analysis of the Provider Role." (200)

Cromwell, Vicky L. and Cromwell, Ronald E. "Perceived Dominance in Decision-Making and Conflict Resolution among Anglo, Black, and Chicano Couples." (252)

Datcher, Linda. "Effects of Community, Family and Education on Earnings of Black and White Men." (263)

Gary, Lawrence E., ed. BLACK MEN. (363)

Hannerz, Ulf. "Growing Up Male in a Black Ghetto." (445)

Hannerz, Ulf. "Roots of Black Manhood: Sex, Socialization and Culture in the Ghettos of American Cities." (446)

Hannerz, Ulf. "What Ghetto Males Are Like: Another Look." (448)

Hempel, Donald J. "Family Buying Decisions: A Cross-Cultural Perspective." (488)

Hendricks, Leo E. "Sexual Knowledge, Attitudes, and Practices of Black Unwed Fathers." (491)

Hendricks, Leo E. Unmarried Adolescent Fathers: Problems They Face and the Ways They Cope with Them. Final Report. (492) "Homicide among Black Males: Highlights of the Symposium Sponsored by the Alcohol, Drug Abuse, and Mental Health Administration, Washington, D.C. May 13-14, 1980." (517)

Hopkins, Thomas J. "The Role of Community Agencies as Viewed by Black Fathers." (519)

Hopkins, Thomas J. "The Role of the Agency in Supporting Black Manhood." (520)

Jones, Bobby Frank. "A Cultural Middle Passage: Slave Marriage and Family in the Antebellum South." (597)

Liebow, Elliot. "Fathers Without Children." (668)

Maxwell, Joseph W. "Rural Negro Father Participation in Family Activities." (703)

Melton, Willie, III. "Self-Satisfaction and Marital Stability among Black Males: Socioeconomic and Demographic Antecedents." (737)

Misra, B. D. "Correlates of Males Attitudes toward Family Planning." (747)

Oliver, William. "Black Males and the Tough Guy Image: A Dysfunctional Compensatory Adaptation." (809)

Pierre, Thelma. "The Relationship between Hypertension and Psychosocial Functioning in Young Black Men." (841)

Staples, Robert. BLACK MASCULINITY: THE BLACK MALE'S ROLE IN AMERICAN SOCIETY. (989)

Staples, Robert. "Masculinity and Race: The Dual Dilemma of Black Men." (993)

Staples, Robert. "The Myth of Black Macho: A Response to Angry Black Feminists." (996)

Stewart, James B. and Scott, Joseph W. "The Institutional Decimation of Black American Males." (1024)

Wallace, Michele. BLACK MACHO AND THE MYTH OF THE SUPERWOMAN. (1086)

Wilkinson, Doris Yvonne and Taylor, Ronald Lewis, eds. THE BLACK MALE IN AMERICA: PERSPECTIVES ON HIS STATUS IN CONTEMPORARY SOCIETY. (1120)

Environment (Space/Housing)

Baldassare, Mark. "The Effects of Household Density on Subgroups." (52)

Bianchi, Suzanne M., Farley, Reynolds and Spain, Daphne. "Racial Inequalities in Housing: An Examination of Recent Trends." (103)

Brown, George L. "Invisible Again: Blacks and the Energy Crisis." (167)

Bullard, Robert D. "Housing and the Quality of Life in the Urban Community: A Focus on the Dynamic Factor Affecting Blacks in the Housing Market." (177)

Bullard, Robert D. and Tryman, Donald L. "Competition for Decent Housing: A Focus on Housing Discrimination Complaints in a Sunbelt City." (178)

Demerson, Bamidele Agbasegbe. "Some Aspects of Contemporary Rural Afro American Family Life in the Sea Islands of Southeastern United States." (282)

Hawkins, Homer C. "Urban Housing and the Black Family." (477)

Jack, Lenus, Jr. "Kinship and Residential Propinquity: A Case Study of a Black Extended Family in New Orleans." (553)

Jones, Allan P. and Demaree, R. G. "Family Disruption, Social Indices, and Problem Behavior: A Preliminary Study." (596)

Kapsis, Robert E. "Black Streetcorner Districts." (611)

Karge, Bernadine. "Constitutional Law-Municipal Ordinance Limiting Occupancy of Homeowners Dwelling to Certain Family Members Violative of Fourteenth Amendment Due Process Clause: Moore v. City of East Cleveland, Ohio." (612)

Moore, William. THE VERTICAL GHETTO: EVERYDAY LIFE IN AN URBAN PROJECT. (763)

Neilson, Jacqueline. "Tayari: Black Homes for Black Children." (791)

Nobles, Wade W. and Goddard, Lawford V. "Consciousness, Adaptability and Coping Strategies. Socioeconomic Characteristics and Ecological Issues in Black Families." (800)

Polgar, Steven and Hiday, Virginia A. "The Effect of an Additional Birth on Low-Income Urban Families." (846)

Rainwater, Lee. BEHIND GHETTO WALLS: BLACK FAMILIES IN A FEDERAL SLUM. (862)

Sims, Edward, Jr. and Snowden, Thomas Gayle. BLACK NOMADS IN THE URBAN CENTERS: THE EFFECTS OF RACISM AND URBANISM ON THE BLACK FAMILY. (965)

Weller, Leonard and Luchterhand, Elmer. "Effects of Improved Housing on the Family Functioning of Large, Low-Income Black Families." (1099)

Wilson, Hugh. "Black Families and the Suburban Dream." (1136)

Women's Issues

Allen, Walter R. "The Social and Economic Statuses of Black Women in the
United States." (29)

Ball, Richard E., Warheit, George J., Vandiver, Joseph S. and Holzer,
Charles E., III. "Friendship Networks: More Supportive of Low-Income
Black Women?" (56)

Banks, William and Walker, Shelia, eds. AND AIN'T I A WOMAN
TOO! INTERACTION OF SEX AND ETHNICITY IN BLACK WOMEN. (60)

Beckett, Joyce O. "Racial Differences in Why Women Work." (83)

Beckett, Joyce Octavia. "Working Wives: A Racial Analysis." (85)

Bell, Duran. "Why Participation Rates of Black and White Wives
Differ." (88)

Bird, Caroline and Briller, Sara Welles. BORN FEMALE: THE HIGH COST OF
KEEPING WOMEN DOWN. (116)

Bird, Caroline and Briller, Sara Welles. BORN FEMALE: THE HIGH COST OF
KEEPING WOMEN DOWN. (117)

Blackburn, Regina Lynn. "Conscious Agents of Time and Self: The Lives
and Styles of African-American Women as Seen through Their
Autobiographical Writings." (123)

Bracey, John H., Meier, August and Rudwick, Elliott, eds. BLACK
MATRIARCHY: MYTH OR REALITY? (143)

Braxton, B. WOMEN, SEX AND RACE: A REALISTIC VIEW OF SEXISM AND
RACISM. (147)

Brent, Linda, ed. INCIDENTS IN THE LIFE OF A SLAVE GIRL. (149)

Brown, Delindus R. and Anderson, Wanda F. "A Survey of the Black Woman
and the Persuasion Process: The Study of Strategies of Identification
and Resistance." (166)

Burgest, David R. and Bower, Joanna. "Erroneous Assumptions Black Women
Make about Black Men." (181)

Burlew, Ann Kathleen. "Career Educational Choices Among Black
Females." (182)

Burwell, Sherri Lynn. "The Soul of Black Women: The Hermeneutical Method
of Analysis as Applied to the Novel 'Corregidora'." (186)

Cade, Toni, comp. THE BLACK WOMAN: AN ANTHOLOGY. (190)

Carrington, Christine Hardy. "A Comparison of Cognitive and Analytically
Oriented Brief Treatment Approaches to Depression in Black
Women." (195)

Carson, Josephine. SILENT VOICES: THE SOUTHERN NEGRO WOMAN TODAY. (196)

Closs, Elizabeth Lee. "Isokinetic Measurement of Strength in Black and
White University Women." (230)

Coleman, Willie Mae. "Keeping the Faith and Disturbing the Peace. Black
Women: From Anti-Slavery to Women's Suffrage." (234)

Cranford, Sharon Anita Hill. "An Expanded Case Study of Family
Interaction and Transaction Roles of Middle-Class Black
Mothers." (247)

Davis, Angela Y. WOMEN, RACE AND CLASS. (267)

Davis, Lenwood G. THE BLACK WOMAN IN AMERICAN SOCIETY: A SELECTED
ANNOTATED BIBLIOGRAPHY. (274)

deAlmeida, Eleanor Engram. "A Descriptive and Analytical Study of the
Early Adult Roles of Black and White Women." (279)

Dill, Bonnie Thornton. "Across the Boundaries of Race and Class: An
Exploration of the Relationship between Work and Family among Black
Female Domestic Servants." (289)

Dill, Bonnie Thornton. "The Dialectics of Black Womanhood." (290)

Dougherty, Molly Crocker. BECOMING A WOMAN IN RURAL BLACK CULTURE. (296)

Johnson, Audrey Louise. "The Perceptions and Social Characteristics
   Related to Occupational Mobility of Black Women and Intraracial
   Assimilation of Blacks in America." (583)
Johnson, Leon Johanson, Sr. "A Comparative Study of the Womanhood
   Experiences of Black Young Adult Females and White Young Adult
   Females." (589)
Johnson, Shirley B. "The Impact of Women's Liberation on Marriage,
   Divorce and Family Lifestyles." (594)
Johnson, Willa D. and Green, Thomas L., eds. PERSPECTIVES ON AFRO-
   AMERICAN WOMEN. (595)
Jones, Jacqueline. "'My Mother Was Much of A Woman': Black Women, Work,
   and the Family under Slavery." (599)
Jones, Jacqueline. LABOR OF LOVE, LABOR OF SORROW: BLACK WOMEN, WORK,
   AND THE FAMILY FROM SLAVERY TO THE PRESENT. (600)
Kanno, Nellie B. "Comparative Lifestyles of the Black Female in the
   United States and the Black Female in Lesotho." (610)
King, Mae C. "Oppression and Power: The Unique Status of the Black Woman
   in the American Political System." (623)
Ladner, Joyce A. TOMORROW'S TOMORROW: THE BLACK WOMAN. (638)
Ladner, Joyce Ann. "On Becoming a Woman in the Ghetto: Modes of
   Adaptation." (639)
Lebsock, Suzanne. "Free Black Women and the Question of Matriarchy:
   Petersburg, Virginia, 1784-1820." (648)
Lefcowitz, Myron Jack. DIFFERENCES BETWEEN NEGRO AND WHITE WOMEN IN
   MARITAL STABILITY AND FAMILY STRUCTURE: A MULTIPLE REGRESSION
   ANALYSIS. (650)
Lerner, Gerda, comp. BLACK WOMEN IN WHITE AMERICA: A DOCUMENTARY
   HISTORY. (653)
Lewis, Diane K. "A Response to Inequality: Black Women, Racism, and
   Sexism." (659)
Lindsay, Beverly, ed. COMPARATIVE PERSPECTIVES OF THIRD WORLD WOMEN: THE
   IMPACT OF RACE, SEX, AND CLASS. (673)
Lloyd, Cynthia B., ed. SEX, DISCRIMINATION AND THE DIVISION OF
   LABOR. (677)
Loewenberg, Bert and Bogin, Ruth, eds. BLACK WOMEN IN NINETEENTH CENTURY
   AMERICAN LIFE: THEIR WORDS, THEIR THOUGHTS, THEIR FEELINGS. (678)
Lorde, Audre. "Scratching the Surface: Some Notes on Barriers to Women
   and Loving." (681)
Love, Bette Bonder. "Self-Esteem in Women Related to Occupational
   Status: A Biracial Study." (682)
Mayo, Julia. "The New Black Feminism: A Minority Report." (704)
McAdoo, Harriette Pipes. "Black Women and the Extended Family Support
   Network." (710)
McAdoo, Harriette Pipes. "Commentary on Joseph Scott's 'Black Polygamous
   Family Formation'." (711)
McGuigan, Dorothy G., ed. NEW RESEARCH ON WOMEN AND SEX ROLES AT THE
   UNIVERSITY OF MICHIGAN: PAPERS. (724) MENTAL AND PHYSICAL HEALTH
   PROBLEMS OF BLACK WOMEN, WASHINGTON, D.C., MARCH 29-30, 1974.
   PROCEEDINGS. (738)
Mott, Frank L. and Sandell, Steven H. WOMEN, WORK AND FAMILY: DIMENSIONS
   OF CHANGE IN AMERICAN SOCIETY. (772)
Mullings, Leith. "On Women, Work and Society." (776)
Murray, Pauli. "The Liberation of Black Women." (780)
Myers, Lena Wright. BLACK WOMEN: DO THEY COPE BETTER? (786)
Myers, Lena Wright. "On Marital Relations: Perceptions of Black
   Women." (787)

MATE SELECTION

Dating, Courtship, and Romanticism

Dickinson, George E. "Dating Behavior of Black and White Adolescents Before and After Desegregation." (286)

Hare, J. and Hare, Nathan. "Coping with Male/Female Alienation in the Coming of Bad Years." (454)

Lorde, Audre. "Scratching the Surface: Some Notes on Barriers to Women and Loving." (681)

Peretti, Peter O. "'Woman-Lady' Concept in the Dating Process among Black College Youth." (827)

Porter, John R. DATING HABITS OF YOUNG BLACK AMERICANS: AND ALMOST EVERYBODY ELSE'S TOO. (851)

Sebald, Hans. "Patterns of Interracial Dating and Sexual Liaison of White and Black College Men." (944)

Semaj, Leahcim Tufani. "Meaningful Male/Female Relationships in a State of Declining Sex-Ratio." (945)

Staples, Robert. "Intimacy Patterns among Black, Middle-Class Single Parents." (991)

Stimson, Ardyth, Stimson, John and Kelton, Todd. "Interracial Dating: Willingness to Violate a Changing Norm." (1027)

Williamson, Robert C. "Dating Frequency, Ethnicity, and Adjustment in the High School: A Comparative Study." (1125)

Mate Selection, Differential Patterns

Aschenbrenner, Joyce. LIFELINES: BLACK FAMILIES IN CHICAGO. (43)

Braithwaite, Ronald L. "Interpersonal Relations between Black Males and Black Females." (145)

Clark, Reginald Milton. "The Dance Party as a Socialization Mechanism for Black Urban Preadolescents and Adolescents." (223)

Gaston, John C. "The Acculturation of the First-Generation Black Professional Woman: A Denver, Colorado Area Study." (368)

Hare, Nathan, ed. (455)

Intons-Peterson, M. J. and Samuels, Arlene K. "The Cultural Halo Effect: Black and White Women Rate Black and White Men." (549)

Jackson, Jacquelyne Johnson. "But Where Are the Men?" (563)

Jackson, Lorraine B. "The Attitudes of Black Females toward Upper and Lower Class Black Males." (567)

Kelley, Michael Robert. "Some Psychological and Sociological Factors Influencing Motivation for Interracial Marriage." (614)

Melton, Willie and Thomas, Darwin. "Instrumental and Expressive Values in Mate Selection of Black and White College Students." (736)

Mueller, William H. and Malina, Robert M. "Differential Contribution of Stature Phenotypes to Assortative Mating in Parents of Philadelphia Black and White School Children." (775)

Nobbe, Charles E., Ebanks, G. Edward and George, P. M. "A Re-exploration of the Relationship between Types of Sex Unions and Fertility: The Barbadian Case." (793)

Rao, V.V. Prakakasa and Rao, V. Nandini. "Instrumental and Expressive Values in Mate Selection among Black College Students." (869)

Snell, Dee. HOW TO GET AND HOLD YOUR BLACK MAN IN SPITE OF WOMEN'S LIB. (975)

Staples, Robert. "Male/Female Sexual Variations: Functions of Biology or Culture." (992)

Staples, Robert. "The Myth of Black Macho: A Response to Angry Black Feminists." (996)

Staples, Robert. THE WORLD OF BLACK SINGLES: CHANGING PATTERNS OF MALE/FEMALE RELATIONS. (1004)

Turner, William H. "Black Men/White Women: A Philosophical View." (1060)
Wehrle, James Mark. "The Marriage Squeeze: Perceptions and Adaptations of Black Female Doctorates." (1095)
White, Patricia Elizabeth. "Patterns of Marriage among the Black Population: A Preliminary Analysis of the Black Female." (1107)
Whitehead, Tony L. "Residence, Kinship, and Mating as Survival Strategies: A West Indian Example." (1110)
Whittington, James Attison, Jr. "Kinship, Mating and Family in the Choco' of Colombia: An Afro-American Adaptation." (1115)

Cohabiting

Clayton, Richard R. and Voss, Harwin L. "Shacking Up: Cohabitation in the 1970's." (229)
Mahoney, E. R. "Premarital Coitus and the Southern Black: A Comment." (693)
McAdoo, Harriette Pipes. "Commentary on Joseph Scott's 'Black Polygamous Family Formation'." (711)
Sykes, Delores Roselle. "The Effects of a Marriage Education Course on the Attitudes toward Marriage and Cohabitation of Black American College Students." (1037)

MARRIAGE AND DIVORCE

Marriage Satisfaction and Prediction Studies

Aguirre, B. E. and Parr, W. C. "Husbands' Marriage Order and the Stability of First and Second Marriages of White and Black Women." (10)
An, Judy Yi-Bii Li. "Marital Satisfaction: A Comparative Study of Black and White College Students' Attitudes toward Marriage." (34)
Ball, Richard Everett. "Expressive Functioning and the Black Family: Life and Domain Satisfaction of Black Women." (57)
Bernard, Jessie. "Marital Stability and Patterns of Status Variables." (98)
Bernard, Jessie Shirley. MARRIAGE AND FAMILY AMONG NEGROES. (100)
Bishop, John H. "Jobs, Cash Transfers and Marital Instability: A Review and Synthesis of the Evidence." (118)
Chapman, Jane Roberts and Gates, Margaret, eds. WOMEN INTO WIVES: THE LEGAL AND ECONOMIC IMPACT OF MARRIAGE. (204)
Conwill, William Louis. "A Conceptual Analysis of Black Family Instability." (241)
Eberstein, Isaac W. and Frisbie, W. Parker. "Differences in Marital Instability among Mexican Americans, Blacks, and Anglos: 1960 and 1970." (307)
Floyd, Russell F. "Marital Adjustment and Decision Making among Stable Black Married Couples." (338)
Glick, Paul C. "Marriage and Marital Stability among Blacks." (386)
Hampton, Robert L. "Husband's Characteristics and Marital Disruption in Black Families." (438)
Hampton, Robert Lewis. "Marital Disruption among Blacks." (440)
Hardy, Kenneth Vandelle. "Attitudes toward Marriage Counseling: A Study of Middle and Lower Class Blacks." (449)

Heiss, Jerold. "On the Transmission of Marital Instability in Black
   Families." (486)
Hutchinson, Ira W., III. "The Significance of Marital Status for Morale
   and Life Satisfaction among Lower-Income Elderly." (539)
International Conference on Love and Attraction. Swansea, Wales,
   1977. LOVE AND ATTRACTION: AN INTERNATIONAL CONFERENCE, edited by Mark
   Cook and Glenn Wilson. (547)
Jackson, Jacquelyne Johnson. "Marital Life among Aging Blacks." (565)
Johnson, Cynthia Elaine. "Factors Influencing the Marital Stability of
   Older Black Couples." (586)
Johnson, Shirley B. "The Impact of Women's Liberation on Marriage,
   Divorce and Family Lifestyles." (594)
King, Jerry Glenn. "A Study of Strengths in Black Families." (619)
King, Karl, Abernathy, Thomas J. and Chapman, Ann H. "Black Adolescents'
   Views of Maternal Employment as a Threat to the Marital Relationship,
   1963-1973." (622)
Lefcowitz, Myron Jack. DIFFERENCES BETWEEN NEGRO AND WHITE WOMEN IN
   MARITAL STABILITY AND FAMILY STRUCTURE: A MULTIPLE REGRESSION
   ANALYSIS. (650)
Liebow, Elliot. "Attitudes toward Marriage and Family among Black Males
   in Tally's Corner." (667)
Matthews, Basil. CRISIS OF THE WEST INDIAN FAMILY: A SAMPLE STUDY. (702)
McCurdy, Paula Carol Kresser. "Sex Role, Decision Making Practices,
   Marital Satisfaction and Family Problems with Economically
   Disadvantaged Anglo, Black, and Chicano Couples." (721)
Melton, Willie and Otto, Lothen B. "Antecedents of Self-Satisfaction and
   Marital Stability among Black Males." (735)
Melton, Willie, III. "Self-Satisfaction and Marital Stability among
   Black Males: Socioeconomic and Demographic Antecedents." (737)
Mueller, Charles W. and Campbell, Blair G. "Female Occupational
   Achievement and Marital Status: A Research Note." (774)
Myers, Lena Wright. "On Marital Relations: Perceptions of Black
   Women." (787)
Obudho, Constance E., ed. BLACK MARRIAGE AND FAMILY THERAPY. (806)
Painter, Dianne Holland. "Black Women and the Family." (816)
Parron, Eugenia Mary. "Relationships of Black and White Golden Wedding
   Couples." (822)
Perrucci, Carolyn Cummings and Targ, Dena B., eds. MARRIAGE AND THE
   FAMILY: A CRITICAL ANALYSIS AND PROPOSALS FOR CHANGE. (832)
Pope, Hallowell and Mueller, Charles W. "The Intergenerational
   Transmission of Marital Instability: Comparisons by Race and
   Sex." (849)
Rooks, Evelyn and King, Karl. "A Study of the Marriage Role Expectations
   of Black Adolescents." (894)
Rutledge, Essie Manuel. "Marital Interaction Goals of Black Women:
   Strengths and Effects." (909)
Scanzoni, John. "Sex Roles, Economic Factors, and Marital Solidarity in
   Black and White Marriages." (920)
Sykes, Delores Roselle. "The Effects of a Marriage Education Course on
   the Attitudes toward Marriage and Cohabitation of Black American
   College Students." (1037)
Turner, Castellano B. and Turner, Barbara F. "Black Families, Social
   Evaluations and Future Marital Relationships." (1058)
Uhlenberg, Peter. "Marital Instability among Mexican Americans:
   Following the Patterns of Blacks?" (1074)
Washington, Joseph R., Jr. MARRIAGE IN BLACK AND WHITE. (1089)

Divorce and Separation

Brown, Prudence, Perry, Lorraine and Harburg, Ernest. "Sex Role Attitudes and Psychological Outcomes for Black and White Women Experiencing Marital Dissolution." (169)

Bryant, Barbara Huddleston. "The Postdivorce Adjustment of Middle Class Black Women." (175)

Chavis, William M. and Lyles, Gladys J. "Divorce Among Educated Black Women." (208)

Moles, Oliver C. "Marital Dissolution and Public Assistance Payments: Variations among American States." (753)

Custody and Child Support

Liebow, Elliot. "Fathers Without Children." (668)

Inter-marriage

Aldridge, Delores P. "The Changing Nature of Interracial Marriage in Georgia: A Research Note." (15)

Aldridge, Delores P. "Interracial Marriages: Empirical and Theoretical Considerations." (16)

Barnett, Larry D. "Research on International and Interracial Marriages." (66)

Barron, Milton Leon, ed. THE BLENDING AMERICA: PATTERNS OF INTERMARRIAGE. (69)

Bean, Frank D. and Aiken, Linda H. "Intermarriage and Unwanted Fertility in the United States." (80)

Bernard, Jessie. "Note On Educational Homogamy in Negro-White and White-Negro Marriages, 1960." (99)

Brigham, John C., Woodmansee, John J. and Cook, Stuart W. "Dimensions of Verbal Racial Attitudes: Interracial Marriage and Approaches to Racial Equality." (150)

Cohen, Leland Bernard. "Interracial Families Adapt to Their Marginality: Between Black and White." (232)

Day, Beth Feagles. SEXUAL LIFE BETWEEN BLACKS AND WHITES: THE ROOTS OF RACISM. (277)

Furlong, William Berry. "Intermarriage is a Sometime Thing." (359)

Halsell, Grace. BLACK/WHITE SEX. (434)

Heer, David M. "Negro-White Marriage in the United States." (482)

Heer, David M. "Negro-White Marriage in the United States." (483)

Heer, David M. "The Prevalence of Black-White Marriage in the United States, 1960 and 1970." (484)

Hernton, Calvin C. SEX AND RACISM IN AMERICA. (497)

Jacobs, James Harris. "Black/White Interracial Families: Marital Process and Identity Development in Young Children." (571)

Kelley, Michael Robert. "Some Psychological and Sociological Factors Influencing Motivation for Interracial Marriage." (614)

Leashore, Bogart Raymond. "Interracial Households in 1850-1880 Detroit, Michigan." (647)

Monahan, Thomas P. "Are Interracial Marriages Really Less Stable?" (755)

Monahan, Thomas P. "Interracial Parentage as Revealed by Birth Records in the United States, 1970." (757)

Monahan, Thomas P. "Marriage Across Racial Lines in Indiana." (758)

Monahan, Thomas P. "The Occupational Class of Couples Entering into Interracial Marriages." (759)
Monahan, Thomas P. "An Overview of Statistics on Interracial Marriage in the United States with Data on Its Extent from 1963-1970." (760)
Peres, Yochanan and Schrift, Ruth. "Intermarriage and Interethnic Relations: A Comparative Study." (826)
Porterfield, Ernest. BLACK AND WHITE MIXED MARRIAGES. (853)
Sickels, Robert J. RACE, MARRIAGE AND THE LAW. (956)
Stuart, Irving R. and Abt, Lawrence Edwin, eds. INTERRACIAL MARRIAGE: EXPECTATIONS AND REALITIES. (1029)
Washington, Joseph R., Jr. MARRIAGE IN BLACK AND WHITE. (1089)
Weinberger, Andrew D. "Interracial Intimacy: Interracial Marriage--Its Statutory Prohibition, Genetic Import, and Incidence." (1096)
Wilkinson, Doris Y., comp. BLACK MALE/WHITE FEMALE: PERSPECTIVES ON INTERRACIAL MARRIAGE AND COURTSHIP. (1118)

Marriage Customs and Forms

Agbasegbe, Bamidele Ade. "Woman-to-Woman Marriages in Africa and Afroamerica." (8)
Allen, Walter R. and Agbasegbe, Bamidele Ade. "A Comment on Scott's 'Black Polygamous Family Formation'." (30)
Cogswell, Betty E. and Sussman, Marvin B. "Changing Family and Marriage Forms: Complications for Human Service Systems." (231)
Greenfield, Sidney M. ENGLISH RUSTICS IN BLACK SKIN: A STUDY OF MODERN FAMILY FORMS IN A PRE-INDUSTRIALIZED SOCIETY. (410)
Harrell-Bond, Barbara E. "Stereotypes of Western and African Patterns of Marriage and Family Life." (460)
Lenus, Jack, Jr. "Friendship: A Refutation." (652)
Mabrey, Wilbert Gene. "African-American Polygynous Relatedness: An Exploratory Study Utilizing Phenomenological Techniques." (686)
Rao, V.V. Prakakasa and Rao, V. Nandini. "Alternatives in Intimacy, Marriage, and Family Lifestyles: Preferences of Black College Students." (867)
Scott, Joseph W. "Black Polygamous Family Formation: Case Studies of Legal Wives and Consensual 'Wives'." (934)
Scott, Joseph W. "Conceptualizing and Researching American Polygyny--And Critics Answered." (935)
Steckel, Richard H. "Slave Marriage and the Family." (1017)

Differential Marriage Rates

Blood, Robert O., Jr. and Wolfe, Donald M. "Negro-White Differences in Blue-Collar Marriages in a Northern Metropolis." (130)
Chauhan, Shri J.S. "Age at Marriage: A Study of 400 Mothers Obtaining Maternity Services at a Metropolitan Teaching Hospital." (207)
Reed, Julia. "Marriage and Fertility in Black Female Teachers." (874)
Sweet, James A. and Bumpass, Larry. "Differentials in Marital Instability of the Black Population 1970." (1036)
Udry, Richard J. "Marital Instability by Race, Sex, Education, and Occupation Using 1960 Census Data." (1072)
White, Lynn K. "A Note on Racial Differences in the Effect of Female Economic Opportunity on Marriage Rates." (1106)

ISSUES RELATED TO REPRODUCTION

Family Planning

Bogue, Donald J. "Family Planning in the Negro Ghettos of
Chicago." (131)
Brodber, Erma and Wagner, Nathaniel N. "The Black Family, Poverty, and
Family Planning: Anthropological Impressions." (151)
Gustavus, Susan O. and Mommsen, Kent G. "Black-White Differentials in
Family Size Preferences among Youth." (423)
Herson, Jay, Crocker, Cyril L. and Butts, Ernest. "Comprehensive Family
Planning Services to an Urban Black Community." (499)
Johnson, Leanor Boulin and Staples, Robert E. "Family Planning of the
Young Minority Male: A Pilot Project." (588)
Kammeyer, Kenneth C., Yetman, Norman R. and McClendon, Mckee J. "Family
Planning Services and the Distribution of Black Americans." (608)
Misra, B. D. "Correlates of Males Attitudes toward Family
Planning." (747)
Murray, Robert F., Jr. "The Ethical and Moral Values of Black Americans
and Population Policy." (781)
Scott, Ralph and Kobes, David A. "The Influence of Family Size on
Learning Readiness Patterns of Socioeconomically Disadvantaged
Preschool Blacks." (943)
Smith, Larry J. BLACK-WHITE REPRODUCTIVE BEHAVIOR: AN ECONOMIC
INTERPRETATION. (973)

Population Studies

Farley, Reynolds. GROWTH OF THE BLACK POPULATION: A STUDY OF DEMOGRAPHIC
TRENDS. (325)
Haney, C. Allen, Michielutte, Robert, Vincent, Clark E. and Cochrane,
Carl M. "The Value Stretch Hypothesis: Family Size Preferences in a
Black Population." (444)
Institute of Society, Ethics and the Life Sciences. Research Group on
Ethics and Population. POPULATION POLICY AND ETHICS: THE AMERICAN
EXPERIENCE. A PROJECT OF THE RESEARCH GROUP ON ETHICS AND POPULATION
OF THE INSTITUTE OF SOCIETY, ETHICS AND THE LIFE SCIENCES, edited by
Robert M. Veatch. (546)
Markides, Kyriakos S. and Hazuda, Helen P. "Ethnicity and Infant
Mortality in Texas Counties." (694)
Rao, V.V. Prakakasa and Rao, V. Nandini. "Family Size and Sex
Preferences of Children: A Biracial Comparison." (868)
Weller, Robert H. "The Differential Attainment of Family Size Goals by
Race." (1100)
Yellin, Joel. "Urban Population Distribution, Family Income, and Social
Prejudice: The Long, Narrow City." (1146)

Fertility Rates

Anderson, John E. and Smith, Jack C. "Planned and Unplanned Fertility in
a Metropolitan Area: Black and White Differences." (39)
Bean, Frank D. and Aiken, Linda H. "Intermarriage and Unwanted Fertility
in the United States." (80)

Bean, Frank D. and Wood, Charles H. "Ethnic Variations in the Relationship between Income and Fertility." (81)

Blair, Annie. "A Comparison of Negro and White Fertility Attitudes." (124)

Caldwell, John C. "Fertility and the Household Economy in Nigeria." (191)

Chauhan, Shri J.S. "Age at Marriage: A Study of 400 Mothers Obtaining Maternity Services at a Metropolitan Teaching Hospital." (207)

Cutright, Phillips and Jaffe, Frederick S. "Family Planning Program Effects on the Fertility of Low-Income U.S. Women." (258)

Engerman, Stanley L. "Black Fertility and Family Structure in the U.S., 1880-1940." (313)

Gupta, Prithwis, Dasi. "A Period Analysis of Parity Distribution among White and Nonwhite Women in the United States, 1940-1974." (421)

Higman, B. W. "Household Structure and Fertility on Jamaican Slave Plantations: A Nineteenth-Century Example." (504)

Hoffman, Louis Wladis and Manis, Jean Denby. "The Value of Children in U.S.: A New Approach to the Study of Fertility." (529)

Jiobu, J. and Marshall, H. "Minority Status and Family Size: A Comparison of Explanations." (581)

John, Craig St. "Race Differences in Age at First Birth and the Pace of Subsequent Fertility: Implications for the Minority Group Status Hypothesis." (582)

Meeker, Edward. "Freedom, Economic Opportunity, and Fertility: Black Americans, 1860-1910." (733)

Nobbe, Charles E., Ebanks, G. Edward and George, P. M. "A Re-exploration of the Relationship between Types of Sex Unions and Fertility: The Barbadian Case." (793)

Pohlmann, Vernon C. and Walsh, Robert H. "Black Minority Racial Status and Fertility in the United States, 1970." (844)

Polgar, Steven and Hiday, Virginia A. "The Effect of an Additional Birth on Low-Income Urban Families." (846)

Preston, Samuel H. "Differential Fertility, Unwanted Fertility and Racial Trends in Occupational Achievement." (858)

Reed, Fred W. and Udry, J. Richard. "Female Work, Fertility and Contraceptive Use in a Biracial Sample." (872)

Reed, Fred W., Udry, J. Richard and Ruppert, Maxine. "Relative Income and Fertility: The Analysis of Individuals' Fertility in a Biracial Sample." (873)

Reed, Julia. "Marriage and Fertility in Black Female Teachers." (874)

Rindfuss, Ronald R. "Minority Status and Fertility Revisited Again: A Comment on Johnson." (880)

Ritchey, P. Neal. "The Effect of Minority Group Status on Fertility: A Re-examination of Concepts." (882)

Smith, Larry J. BLACK-WHITE REPRODUCTIVE BEHAVIOR: AN ECONOMIC INTERPRETATION. (973)

Stokes, C. Shannon, Crader, Kelly W. and Smith, Jack C. "Race, Education and Fertility: A Comparison of Black-White Reproductive Behavior." (1028)

Tolnay, Stewart E. "Black Fertility in Decline: Urban Differentials in 1900." (1046)

Trussel, James and Steckel, Richard. "The Age of Slaves at Menarche and Their First Birth." (1050)

Uhlenberg, Peter P. "Negro Fertility Patterns in the United States." (1075)

Westoff, Leslie Aldridge and Westoff, Charles F. FROM NOW TO ZERO: FERTILITY, CONTRACEPTION AND ABORTION IN AMERICA. (1101)

Childlessness

Bortner, R.W., Bohn, Claudia J. and Hultsch, David F. "A Cross-Cultural
Study of the Effects of Children on Parental Assessment of Past,
Present and Future." (136)

Grindstaff, Carl F. "Trend and Incidence of Childlessness by Race:
Indicators of Black Progress Over Three Decades." (414)

Birth Control

Bauman, Karl E. and Udry, Richard J. "The Difference in Unwanted Births
between Blacks and Whites." (74)

Bauman, Karl E. and Udry, Richard J. "Powerlessness and Regularity of
Contraception in an Urban Negro Male Sample: A Research Note." (75)

Bogue, Donald J. "A Long-Term Solution to the AFDC Problem: Prevention
of Unwanted Pregnancy." (132)

Bogue, Donald Joseph, ed. SOCIOLOGICAL CONTRIBUTIONS TO FAMILY PLANNING
RESEARCH. (133)

Clark, Samuel D. "Sex, Contraception and Parenthood: Experience and
Attitudes among Urban Black Young Men." (224)

Graves, William L. and Bradshaw, Barbara R. "Early Reconception and
Contraceptive Use among Black Teenage Girls After an Illegitimate
Birth." (406)

Gray, Naomi. "Sterilization and the Black Family: An Historical
Perspective." (407)

Herson, Jay, Crocker, Cyril L. and Butts, Ernest. "Comprehensive Family
Planning Services to an Urban Black Community." (499)

Reed, Fred W. and Udry, J. Richard. "Female Work, Fertility and
Contraceptive Use in a Biracial Sample." (872)

Weisbord, Robert G. "Birth Control and the Black American: A Matter of
Genocide." (1097)

Weisbord, Robert G. GENOCIDE? BIRTH CONTROL AND THE BLACK
AMERICAN. (1098)

Westoff, Leslie Aldridge and Westoff, Charles F. FROM NOW TO ZERO:
FERTILITY, CONTRACEPTION AND ABORTION IN AMERICA. (1101)

Abortion

Clark, Candace. "Race, Motherhood, and Abortion." (219)

McCormick, E. Patricia. ATTITUDES TOWARD ABORTION: EXPERIENCES OF
SELECTED BLACK AND WHITE WOMEN. (719)

Westoff, Leslie Aldridge and Westoff, Charles F. FROM NOW TO ZERO:
FERTILITY, CONTRACEPTION AND ABORTION IN AMERICA. (1101)

Willie, Charles V. "Population Policy and Growth: Perspectives from the
Black Community--A Position Paper." (1127)

Illegitimacy

Bauman, Karl E. and Udry, Richard J. "The Difference in Unwanted Births
between Blacks and Whites." (74)

Billingsley, Andrew and Billingsley, Amy Tate. "Illegitimacy and
Patterns of Negro Family Life." (112)

Fischer, Ann, Beasley, Joseph D. and Harter, Carl L. "Occurrence of the Extended Family at the Origin of the Family of Procreation: A Developmental Approach to Negro Family Structure." (335)

Haney, C. Allen, Michielutte, Robert, Cochrane, Carl M. and Vincent, Clark E. "Some Consequences of Illegitimacy in a Sample of Black Women." (443)

Janowitz, Barbara S. "The Impact of AFDC on Illegitimate Birth Rates." (574)

Jordan, Ernest E. "A Study of the Social and Maternal Responsibility of a Group of Negro Unwed Mothers." (604)

Ladner, Joyce A. TOMORROW'S TOMORROW: THE BLACK WOMAN. (638)

Monahan, Thomas P. "Illegitimacy by Race and Mixture of Race." (756)

Morisey, Patricia Garland. "Professional Advocacy, Community Participation and Social Planning: The Case of the Unmarried Mother from the 'Inside the Ghetto' Perspective." (766)

Oppel, Wallace Churchill. "Illegitimacy: A Comparative Follow-Up Study. A Matched Group of 120 Six to Eight Year-Old Negro Illegitimate Children and Their Mothers Is Compared to a Group of 120 Legitimate Six to Eight Year-Old Negro Children and Their Mothers on Measures of Child Development and Mothering Behavior." (810)

Pope, Hallowell. "Negro-White Differences in Decisions Regarding Illegitimate Children." (847)

Roberts, Robert W., ed. THE UNWED MOTHER. (884)

Schulz, David Allen. COMING UP BLACK: PATTERNS OF GHETTO SOCIALIZATION. (927)

Vincent, Clark E., Haney, C. Allen and Cochrane, Carl M. "Familiar and Generational Patterns of Illegitimacy." (1080)

Whitted, Christine. "Supports in the Black Community: Black Unmarried Mothers Who Kept Their Babies and Achieved Their Educational and/or Professional Goals." (1113)

Pregnancy and Child Birth

Clark, Candace. "Race, Motherhood, and Abortion." (219)

Frankel, Barbara. CHILDBIRTH IN THE GHETTO: FOLK BELIEFS OF NEGRO WOMEN IN A NORTH PHILADELPHIA HOSPITAL WARD. (348)

McLaughlin, Clara J., Frisby, Donald R., McLaughlin, Richard A. and Williams, Melvin W. THE BLACK PARENTS HANDBOOK: A GUIDE TO HEALTHY PREGNANCY, BIRTH AND CHILD CARE. (725)

Teenage Pregnancy

Burgess, Rebecca Bahr. "Effects of Attitudes about Premarital Sex on Contraceptive Risk-Taking among Low-Income Unmarried Teenagers." (179)

Graves, William L. and Bradshaw, Barbara R. "Early Reconception and Contraceptive Use among Black Teenage Girls After an Illegitimate Birth." (406)

Hendricks, Leo E. "Black Unwed Adolescent Fathers." (490)

Hendricks, Leo E. Unmarried Adolescent Fathers: Problems They Face and the Ways They Cope with Them. Final Report. (492)

Hunter, Virginia. "The Impact of Adolescent Parenthood on Black Teenage Mothers and Their Families and the Influence of Two Alternative Types of Child Care." (537)

Johnson, Clara L. "Adolescent Pregnancy: Intervention into the Poverty Cycle." (585)

Jones, Mary Elaine. "An Anthropological Assessment of Bonding: Mother Infant Attachment Behavior in a Study of Forty Adolescent Black and White Mothers from Delivery through Six Months." (601)

Morrow, Betty Hearn. "A Comparison of Eight-Year-Old Children Born to Young Black Adolescents and Those Born to Comparable Mothers in Their Early Twenties." (769)

O'Connell, Martin. "Comparative Estimates of Teenage Illegitimacy in the United States, 1940-44 to 1970-74." (804)

Pettapiece, Mervyn Arthur. "Interpersonal Relationships and Affection Needs of Black, Teenage, Inner-City, Unwed Mothers." (838)

Reiner, Beatrice Simcox. "The Real World of the Teenage Negro Mother." (876)

Roberts, Robert W., ed. THE UNWED MOTHER. (884)

Rowland, Glovioell Winsmore. "Early Effects of Postpartum Intervention on Black Adolescent Mother-Infant Interaction." (902)

Scott, Joseph W. "Black Polygamous Family Formation: Case Studies of Legal Wives and Consensual 'Wives'." (934)

Weathers, Olethia Delmar and Bullock, Samuel C. "Therapeutic Group Home Care for Adolescent Girls: An Interagency Development." (1092)

SEXUAL ATTITUDES AND BEHAVIOR

Sexual Attitudes and Behavior

American Psychopathological Association. CONTEMPORARY SEXUAL BEHAVIOR: CRITICAL ISSUES IN THE 1970'S, edited by Joseph Zubin and John Money. (33)

Broderick, Carlfred B. "Social Heterosexual Development among Urban Negroes and Whites." (152)

Broderick, Carlfred B. and Bernard, Jesse, eds. THE INDIVIDUAL, SEX AND SOCIETY. (153)

Brody, Eugene B., Ottey, Frank and Lagranade, Janet. "Early Sex Education in Relationship Behavior: Evidence from Jamaican Women." (156)

Brooks, Robert. SEX--BLACK AND WHITE. (162)

Brown, Steven E. "Sexuality and the Slave Community." (171)

Clark, Samuel D. "Sex, Contraception and Parenthood: Experience and Attitudes among Urban Black Young Men." (224)

Day, Beth Feagles. SEXUAL LIFE BETWEEN BLACKS AND WHITES: THE ROOTS OF RACISM. (277)

Derbyshire, Robert L. "The Uncompleted Negro Family: Suggested Research into the Hypotheses Regarding the Effect of the Negro's Outcaste Conditions upon His Own and Other American Sexual Attitudes and Behavior." (284)

Gochros, Harvey L. and Gochros, Jean S., eds. THE SEXUALLY OPPRESSED. (387)

Gump, Janice Porter. "Comparative Analysis of Black and White Women's Sex-Role Attitudes." (418)

Halsell, Grace. BLACK/WHITE SEX. (434)

Hammond, Boone E. and Ladner, Joyce. "Socialization into Sexual Behavior in a Negro Slum Ghetto." (435)

Hendricks, Leo E. "Sexual Knowledge, Attitudes, and Practices of Black Unwed Fathers." (491)

Hernton, Calvin C. SEX AND RACISM IN AMERICA. (497)

Hetherington, E. Mavis. "Effects of Paternal Absence on Sex-Typed Behaviors in Negro and White Preadolescent Males." (501)

Hopper, Columbus B. SEX IN PRISON: THE MISSISSIPPI EXPERIMENT WITH CONJUGAL VISITING. (521)

Hunt, Janet G. and Hunt, Larry L. "The Sexual Mystique: A Common Dimension of Racial and Sexual Stratification." (533)

International Conference on Love and Attraction. Swansea, Wales, 1977. LOVE AND ATTRACTION: AN INTERNATIONAL CONFERENCE, edited by Mark Cook and Glenn Wilson. (547)

Johnson, Leonor Bonlin. "The Sexual Oppression of Blacks." (590)

Kapsis, Robert E. "Black Streetcorner Districts." (611)

Ladner, Joyce Ann. "On Becoming a Woman in the Ghetto: Modes of Adaptation." (639)

Mayo, Julia. "The New Black Feminism: A Minority Report." (704)

McConahay, Shirley A. and McConahay, John B. "Sexual Permissiveness, Sex Role Rigidity, and Violence Across Cultures." (717)

McGuigan, Dorothy G., ed. NEW RESEARCH ON WOMEN AND SEX ROLES AT THE UNIVERSITY OF MICHIGAN: PAPERS. (724)

Rao, V.V. Prakakasa and Rao, V. Nandini. "Alternatives in Intimacy, Marriage, and Family Lifestyles: Preferences of Black College Students." (867)

Rubin, Isadore. SEXUAL LIFE IN THE LATER YEARS. (904)

Rubin, Isadore and Kirkendall, Lester A., comps. SEX IN THE ADOLESCENT YEARS. (905)

Sebald, Hans. "Patterns of Interracial Dating and Sexual Liaison of White and Black College Men." (944)

SIECUS Conference on Religion and Sexuality, St. Louis, 1971. SEXUALITY AND HUMAN VALUES: THE PERSONAL DIMENSION OF SEXUAL EXPERIENCE, edited by Mary Calderone. (957)

Slovenko, Ralph, ed. SEXUAL BEHAVIOR AND THE LAW. (970)

Staples, Robert. "Male/Female Sexual Variations: Functions of Biology or Culture." (992)

Staples, Robert. "The Sexuality of Black Women." (1002)

Staples, Robert E. "Black Sexuality." (1009)

Stember, Charles Herbert. SEXUAL RACISM: THE EMOTIONAL BARRIER TO AN INTEGRATED SOCIETY. (1020)

U.S. Department of Health, Education and Welfare. National Institute of Education. Career Education Program. ISSUES OF SEX BIAS AND SEX FAIRNESS IN CAREER INTEREST MEASUREMENT, edited by Esther E. Diamond. (1068)

Wyatt, Gail Elizabeth, Strayer, Richard G. and Lobitz, W. Charles. "Issues in the Treatment of Sexually Dysfunctioning Couples of Afro-American Descent." (1142)

Extramarital Sexual Behavior

Broude, Gwen J. "Extramarital Sex Norms in Cross-Cultural Perspective." (163)

Scott, Joseph W. "The Sociology of the Other Woman." (937)

Premarital Sexual Behavior

Broude, Gwen J. "Norms of Premarital Sexual Behavior: A Cross-Cultural Study." (164)

Burgess, Rebecca Bahr. "Effects of Attitudes about Premarital Sex on
Contraceptive Risk-Taking among Low-Income Unmarried Teenagers." (179)

Christensen, Harold T. and Johnson, Leanor B. "Premarital Coitus and the
Southern Black: A Comparative View." (215)

Dixon, Richard D. "The Absence of Birth Order Correlations among Unwed
and Married Black First-Conceptors." (292)

Pope, Hallowell. "Unwed Mothers and Their Sex Partners." (848)

Staples, Robert. "Race, Liberalism-Conservatism and Premarital Sexual
Permissiveness: A Biracial Comparison." (1000)

Staples, Robert Eugene. "A Study of the Influence of Liberal-
Conservative Attitudes on the Premarital Sexual Standards of Different
Racial, Sex-Role and Social Class Groupings." (1015)

Homosexuality and the Family

Agbasegbe, Bamidele Ade. "Woman-to-Woman Marriages in Africa and
Afroamerica." (8)

Chambers, Andrew Wade. "A Comparative Study of Black and White
Homosexuals." (202)

Fitzgerald, William A. "Pseudoheterosexuality in Prison and Out: A Study
of the Lower Class Black Lesbian." (337)

Prostitution

Kapsis, Robert E. "Black Streetcorner Districts." (611)

Milner, Christina and Milner, Richard. BLACK PLAYERS: THE SECRET WORLD
OF BLACK PIMPS. (743)

FAMILIES WITH SPECIAL PROBLEMS

Family Disorganization

Conwill, William Louis. "A Conceptual Analysis of Black
Family Instability." (241)

Eberstein, Isaac W. and Frisbie, W. Parker. "Differences in
Marital Instability among Mexican Americans, Blacks, and Anglos: 1960
and 1970." (307)

Engerrand, Steven W. "Black and Mulatto Mobility and Stability in
Dallas, Texas, 1880-1910." (314)

Farley, Reynolds and Hermalin, Albert I. "Family Stability: A Comparison
of Trends between Blacks and Whites." (326)

Ferranti, David Marc de. "Tests of Seven Hypotheses on Welfare
Dependency and Family Disintegration." (334)

Giovannoni, Jeanne M. and Billingsley, Andrew. "Child Neglect among the
Poor: A Study of Parental Adequacy in Families of Three Ethnic
Groups." (384)

Hampton, Robert L. "Husband's Characteristics and Marital Disruption in
Black Families." (438)

Hampton, Robert L. "Institutional Decimation, Marital Exchange, and
Disruption in Black Families." (439)

Hampton, Robert Lewis. "Marital Disruption among Blacks." (440)

Heiss, Jerold. "On the Transmission of Marital Instability in Black
  Families." (486)
Hill, Herbert. "Of Blacks, Whites and Family Stability." (506)
Jones, Allan P. and Demaree, R. G. "Family Disruption, Social Indices,
  and Problem Behavior: A Preliminary Study." (596)
Pavenstedt, Eleanor, ed. THE DRIFTERS: CHILDREN OF DISORGANIZED LOWER-
  CLASS FAMILIES, BY CHARLES A. MALONE AND OTHERS. (824)
Pope, Hallowell and Mueller, Charles W. "The Intergenerational
  Transmission of Marital Instability: Comparisons by Race and
  Sex." (849)
Stewart, James B. and Scott, Joseph W. "The Institutional Decimation of
  Black American Males." (1024)
Sweet, James A. and Bumpass, Larry. "Differentials in
  Marital Instability of the Black Population 1970." (1036)
Udry, Richard J. "Marital Instability by Race, Sex, Education, and
  Occupation Using 1960 Census Data." (1072)
Uhlenberg, Peter. "Marital Instability among Mexican Americans:
  Following the Patterns of Blacks?" (1074)
Whitaker, Barbara. "Breakdown in the Negro Family: Myth or
  Reality." (1104)

Child Abuse

Crumbley, Joseph. "A Descriptive Analysis of Black and White Families
  Reported for Child Maltreatment." (254)
Duhon, Rose Marie. "An Analysis of Curriculum Offerings and Services
  Related to Child Abuse and Neglect in Early Childhood Teacher
  Preparation Programs at Historically Black Colleges and
  Universities." (300)
Faulkes, Yolanda. "Child Abuse in the Black Community." (329)

Drug Abuse

Brook, Judith S., Lukoff, Irving F. and Whiteman, Martin. "Peer, Family,
  and Personality Domains as Related to Adolescents' Drug
  Behavior." (159)
Cuffaro, Sara Todd. "A Discriminant Analysis of Sociocultural,
  Motivation, and Personality Differences among Black, Anglo and Chicana
  Female Drug Abusers in a Medium Security Prison." (255)
Nail, Richard L., Gunderson, Eric and Arthur, Ransom J. "Black-White
  Differences in Social Background and Military Drug Abuse
  Patterns." (789)

Runaways

Brennan, Tim, Huizinga, David and Elliot, Delbert S. THE
  SOCIAL PSYCHOLOGY OF RUNAWAYS. (148)

Suicide and the Family

Bedrosian, Richard C. and Beck, Aaron T. "Premature Conclusions
  Regarding Black and White Suicide Attempters: A Reply to Steele." (86)

Davis, Robert. "Suicide among Young Blacks: Trend and
    Perspectives." (276)
Hendin, Herbert. BLACK SUICIDE. (489)
Wylie, F. "Suicide among Black Families: A Case Study." (1145)

Family Violence

Cazenave, Noel A. "Family Violence and Aging Blacks: Theoretical
    Perspectives and Research Possibilities." (199)
Cazenave, Noel A. and Strauss, Murray A. "Race, Class, Network
    Embeddedness and Family Violence: A Search for Potent
    Support Systems." (201)
Curtis, Lynn A. VIOLENCE, RACE AND CULTURE. (257)
Gary, Lawrence E. and Brown, Lee, P., eds. CRIME AND ITS IMPACT ON THE
    BLACK COMMUNITY. (367)
Gelles, Richard J. "Violence in the Family: A Review of Research in the
    Seventies." (372)
McConahay, Shirley A. and McConahay, John B. "Sexual Permissiveness,
    Sex Role Rigidity, and Violence Across Cultures." (717)
Poussaint, Alvin F. WHY BLACKS KILL BLACKS. (854)
Rathbone, McCuan Eloise. "Elderly Victims of Family Violence and
    Neglect." (870)
Staples, Robert. "Race, Stress and Family Violence." (1001)
Staples, Robert E. "Race and Family Violence: The Internal Colonialism
    Perspective." (1011)

Family Stress

Avery, Reginald Stanley. "The Impact of Court-Ordered Busing on Black
    Families in Boston, Massachusetts." (48)
Brodber, Erma and Wagner, Nathaniel N. "The Black Family, Poverty, and
    Family Planning: Anthropological Impressions." (151)
Chilman, Catherine S. "Families in Poverty in the Early 1970's: Rates,
    Associated Factors, Some Implications." (212)
Driskell, Judy A. and Price, Claudia S. "Nutritional Status of
    Preschoolers from Low-Income Alabama Families." (298)
Frate, Dennis Anthony. "Family Functioning and Hypertension in a Black
    Population." (350)
Gibson, Rose C. "Blacks at Middle and Late Life: Resources and
    Coping." (378)
Glasser, Paul H. and Glasser, Lois N., eds. FAMILIES IN CRISIS. (385)
Haney, C. Allen, Michielutte, Robert, Vincent, Clark E. and Cochrane,
    Carl M. "Factors Associated with the Poverty of Black Women." (442)
Hare, J. and Hare, Nathan. "Coping with Male/Female Alienation in the
    Coming of Bad Years." (454)
Harrell, Jules P. "Analyzing Black Coping Styles: A Supplemental
    Diagnostic System." (461)
Harrison, Algea Othella and Minor, Joanne Holbert. "Interrole Conflict,
    Coping Strategies, and Satisfaction among Black Working Wives." (469)
Hendricks, Leo Edward, Jr. "The Effect of Family Size, Child Spacing and
    Family Density on Stress in Low Income Black Mothers and Their
    Preadolescent Children." (493)
Henry, Sheila E. "Family Structures, Social Class and Cultural
    Values." (496)

Hiday, Virginia Aldige. "Parity and Well-Being among Low-Income Urban Families." (502)

Hill, Robert Bernard. THE STRENGTHS OF BLACK FAMILIES. (510)

Holly, Ellen. "The Role of Media in the Programming of an Underclass." (516)

Hynes, Winifred Joyce. "Single Parent Mothers and Distress: Relationships between Selected Social and Psychological Factors and Distress in Low-Income Single Parent Mothers." (542)

Kutner, Nancy G. "The Poor Vs. the Non-poor: An Ethnic and Metropolitan-Non-metropolitan Comparison." (631)

Lawrence, Margaret Morgan. YOUNG INNER CITY FAMILIES: DEVELOPMENT OF EGO STRENGTH UNDER STRESS. (646)

Levin, Herman. "Income Alternatives for Poor Families." (655)

McAdoo, Harriette P. "Stress Absorbing Systems in Black Families." (708)

Mirowsky, John, II and Ross, Catherine E. "Minority Status, Ethnic Culture, and Distress: A Comparison of Blacks, Whites, Mexicans, and Mexican Americans." (746)

Mithun, Jacqueline S. "Cooperation and Solidarity as Survival Necessities in a Black Urban Community." (750)

Molofed, Martin. COLLOQUIUM ON STRESS AND CRIME. (754)

Nobles, Wade W. and Goddard, Lawford V. "Consciousness, Adaptability and Coping Strategies. Socioeconomic Characteristics and Ecological Issues in Black Families." (800)

Sitgraves, Mary Elizabeth. "Recent Life Event Stress and Patterns of Mother-Son Interaction in High Risk Versus Low Risk Black Mothers." (967)

Smith, Virginia Ware. "The Impact of Selected Internal and External Influences on Successful Coping among Mothers of Children with Sickle Cell Disease." (974)

Stack, Carol B. ALL OUR KIN: STRATEGIES FOR SURVIVAL IN A BLACK COMMUNITY. (982)

Stack, Carol B. "Sex Roles and Survival Strategies in an Urban Black Community." (983)

Staples, Robert. "Race, Stress and Family Violence." (1001)

Webb-Woodard, Linda Delores. "Selfhood: Discovery of Survival Values in Low Income Black Families in Hartford, Connecticut. Two Case Studies Using Family Systems Theory." (1093)

Families with Mentally Retarded

Andrew, Gwen. "Determinants of Negro Family Decisions in Management of Retardation." (40)

Harris, Joan Ricks. "Black/White and Socioeconomic Status as Factors in Maternal Attitudes toward Childrearing Practices and the Use of Health Care in Families with and without an Educable Mentally Retarded Child." (463)

Hauser, Stuart T. BLACK AND WHITE IDENTITY FORMATION: STUDIES IN THE PSYCHOSOCIAL DEVELOPMENT OF LOWER SOCIOECONOMIC CLASS ADOLESCENT BOYS. (473)

Families with Emotionally Disturbed

Harris, Clotiel J. "Alternative Planning for Foster Care and Treatment of Children and Adolescents in Crises." (462)

Wylan, Louise and Mintz, Norbett L. "Ethnic Differences in Family
Attitudes towards Psychotic Manifestations, with Implications for
Treatment Programmes." (1144)

Families with Depressives

Carrington, Christine Hardy. "A Comparison of Cognitive and Analytically
Oriented Brief Treatment Approaches to Depression in Black
Women." (195)

Families with Juvenile Delinquents

Austin, Roy L. "Race, Father-Absence, and Female Delinquency." (47)
Brown, Waln K. "Black Gangs as Family Extensions." (172)
Perry, Robert L. "The Black Matriarchy Controversy and Black Male
Delinquency." (834)
Robins, Lee N., West, Patricia A. and Herjanie, Barbara L. "Arrests and
Delinquency in Two Generations: A Study of Black Urban Families and
Their Children." (887)
Rodman, Hyman and Crams, Paul. "Juvenile Delinquency and the Family: A
Review and Discussion in the United States President's Commission on
Law Enforcement and Administration of Justice." (892)
Rosen, Lawrence. "Matriarchy and Lower Class Negro Male
Delinquency." (896)
U.S. Task Force on Juvenile Delinquency. TASK FORCE REPORT: JUVENILE
DELINQUENCY AND YOUTH CRIME: REPORT ON JUVENILE JUSTICE AND
CONSULTANTS' PAPERS. (1071)
Walberg, Herbert J., Yeh, Elaine Gee and Paton, Stephanie
Mooney. "Family Background, Ethnicity, and Urban Delinquency." (1084)

Families with Criminal Offenders

Braithwaite, Ronald. "A Paired Study of Self-Disclosure of Black and
White Inmates." (144)
Curtis, Lynn A. VIOLENCE, RACE AND CULTURE. (257)
Fitzgerald, William A. "Pseudoheterosexuality in Prison and Out: A Study
of the Lower Class Black Lesbian." (337)
Gary, Lawrence E. and Brown, Lee, P., eds. CRIME AND ITS IMPACT ON THE
BLACK COMMUNITY. (367)
Hopper, Columbus B. SEX IN PRISON: THE MISSISSIPPI EXPERIMENT WITH
CONJUGAL VISITING. (521)
Molofed, Martin. COLLOQUIUM ON STRESS AND CRIME. (754)
Schneller, Donald P. "Prisoners' Families: A Study of Some Social and
Psychological Effects of Incarceration on the Families of Negro
Prisoners." (925)
Slovenko, Ralph, ed. SEXUAL BEHAVIOR AND THE LAW. (970)
Spain, Johnny. "The Black Family and the Prisons." (980)

Death, Bereavement and the Family

Badaines, Joel. "Identification, Imitation, and Sex-Role Preference in
Father-Present and Father-Absent Black and Chicano Boys." (51)

Craggett, Foster T. "A Form Critical Approach to the Oral Traditions of
the Black Church as They Relate to the Celebration of Death." (245)
D'Andrade, Roy G. "Father Absence, Identification, and Identity." (260)
Furstenberg, Frank F. Jr., Hershberg, Theodore and Modell, John. "The
Origins of the Female-Headed Black Family: The Impact of the Urban
Experience." (360)
Geerken, Michael and Gove, Walter R. "Race, Sex, and Marital Status:
Their Effect on Mortality." (370)
Gossett, Ruth. "Economics of Black Widowhood." (398)
Gossett, Ruth R. "Black Widows." (399)
Gossett, Ruth Ross. "So Few Men: A Study of Black Widowhood." (400)
"Homicide among Black Males: Highlights of the Symposium Sponsored by
the Alcohol, Drug Abuse, and Mental Health Administration, Washington,
D.C. May 13-14, 1980." (517)
Hunt, Janet G. and Hunt, Larry L. "Race, Daughters and Father-Loss: Does
Absence Make the Girl Grow Stronger?" (532)
Hunt, Larry L. and Hunt, Janet G. "Race and the Father-Son Connection:
The Conditional Relevance of Father Absence for the Orientations and
Identities of Adolescent Boys." (535)
Markides, Kyriakos S. and Hazuda, Helen P. "Ethnicity and Infant
Mortality in Texas Counties." (694)
Markides, Kyriakos S. "Mortality among Minority Populations: A Review of
Recent Patterns and Trends." (697)
Wilkinson, Charles B. and O'Connor, William A. "Growing Up Male in a
Black Single-Parent Family." (1117)

Achievement and the Family

Allen, Walter R. "The Family Antecedents of Adolescent Mobility
Aspirations." (23)
Allen, Walter R. "Family Roles, Occupational Statuses, and
Achievement Orientations among Black Women in the United States." (24)
Allen, Walter R. "Race, Family Setting and Adolescent
Achievement Orientation." (27)
Baumer-Mulloy, Marjorie. "A Study of the Relationship of Certain Home
Environmental Factors to High or Low Achievement in Reading among
Black Primary School Age Pupils of Low Socioeconomic Status." (76)
Baumrind, Diana and Black, Allen E. "Socialization Practices Associated
with Dimension of Competence in Preschool Boys and Girls." (77)
Borland, Barry L. and Rudolp, Joseph P. "Relative Effects of
Low Socioeconomic Status, Parental Smoking and Poor Scholastic
Performance on Smoking among High School Students." (135)
Brook, Judith S., Whiteman, Martin, Peisach, Estelle and Deutsch,
Martin. "Aspiration Levels of and for Children: Age, Sex, Race,
Socioeconomic Correlates." (160)
Brown, Alexander Lionel. "The Effects of Race, Intelligence and Maternal
Employment Status of the Career/Occupational Role Stereotypes of Four-
Year Old Girls." (165)
Chappell, Earl Birges, III. "The Relationships between Socioeconomic
Status, Sex, Self-Concept, Academic Achievement, and Course Selection
of Urban Black Tenth-Grade Students." (206)
Clark, Reginald M. FAMILY LIFE AND SCHOOL ACHIEVEMENT: WHY POOR BLACK
CHILDREN SUCCEED OR FAIL. (221)
Darity, Evangeline Royall. "A Comparison of Fear-Of-Success Imagery
between Black Male and Female Undergraduates." (262)

FAIRNESS IN CAREER INTEREST MEASUREMENT, edited by Esther E. Diamond. (1068)

Wasserman, Herbert L. "A Comparative Study of School Performance among Boys from Broken and Intact Black Families." (1090)

Wright, Maggie Saxon. "Parent-Child Relations, Achievement Motivation, and Sex-Role Attitudes among Black and White Professional Women in Traditional and Pioneer Occupations." (1139)

Family and Geographic Mobility

Clay, Phillip L. "The Process of Black Suburbanization." (228)

Creighton-Zollar, Ann. "A Member of the Family: Strategies for Black Family Continuity." (249)

Henri, Florette. BLACK MIGRATION: MOVEMENT NORTH, 1890-1920. (495)

Munick, Warren A. and Sullivan, Dennis. "Race, Age, and Family Status Differentials in Metropolitan Migration of Households." (778)

Shannon, Lyle W. "The Changing World View of Minority Migrants in an Urban Setting." (949)

Shin, Eui Hang. "Correlates of Intercounty Variations in Net Migration Rates of Blacks in the Deep South, 1960-1970." (955)

PSYCHOLOGY AND SOCIOLOGY

Psychology

Adams, Harold. "The Collective Black Family: Barriers to Community Mental Health Services." (4)

Baldwin, Joseph A. "Theory and Research Concerning the Notion of Black Self-Hatred: A Review and Reinterpretation." (54)

Bass, Barbara Ann, Wyatt, Gail Elizabeth and Powell, Gloria Johnson, eds. THE AFRO-AMERICAN FAMILY: ASSESSMENT, TREATMENT, AND RESEARCH ISSUES. (71)

Baughman, Emmett Earl. BLACK AMERICANS: A PSYCHOLOGICAL ANALYSIS. (73)

Boykin, A. Wade, Franklin, Anderson J. and Yates, Jacques Frank, eds. RESEARCH DIRECTIONS OF BLACK PSYCHOLOGISTS. (142)

Braithwaite, Ronald. "A Paired Study of Self-Disclosure of Black and White Inmates." (144)

Brennan, Tim, Huizinga, David and Elliot, Delbert S. THE SOCIAL PSYCHOLOGY OF RUNAWAYS. (148)

Brody, Eugene B. et al. MINORITY GROUP ADOLESCENTS IN THE UNITED STATES. (155)

Burwell, Sherri Lynn. "The Soul of Black Women: The Hermeneutical Method of Analysis as Applied to the Novel 'Corregidora'." (186)

Calhoun, Princess Diane. "Family Factors in Black Adolescent Mental Health." (193)

Carrington, Christine Hardy. "A Comparison of Cognitive and Analytically Oriented Brief Treatment Approaches to Depression in Black Women." (195)

Comer, James P. BEYOND BLACK AND WHITE. (236)

Cuffaro, Sara Todd. "A Discriminant Analysis of Sociocultural, Motivation, and Personality Differences among Black, Anglo and Chicana Female Drug Abusers in a Medium Security Prison." (255)

Davis, George. LOVE, BLACK LOVE. (270)

Epps, Edgar G. "Impact of School Desegregation on Aspirations, Self-Concepts and Other Aspects of Personality." (318)

Eray, P. CHILDHOOD AND THE COSMOS: THE SOCIAL PSYCHOLOGY OF THE BLACK AFRICAN CHILD. (322)

Frazier, Edward Franklin. NEGRO YOUTH AT THE CROSSWAYS, THEIR PERSONALITY DEVELOPMENT IN THE MIDDLE STATES. (352)

Grier, William H. and Cobbs, Price M. BLACK RAGE. (411)

Griffin, Don Quincy. "Personality Competence in Black Adolescents." (412)

Gunthorpe, Wayne West. "Skin Color Recognition, Preference and Identification in Interracial Children: A Comparative Study." (420)

Hauser, Stuart T. BLACK AND WHITE IDENTITY FORMATION: STUDIES IN THE PSYCHOSOCIAL DEVELOPMENT OF LOWER SOCIOECONOMIC CLASS ADOLESCENT BOYS. (473)

Hays, William C. and Mindel, Charles H. "Parental Perceptions for Children: A Comparison of Black and White Families." (481)

Hendin, Herbert. BLACK SUICIDE. (489)

Hyde, Janet Shibley and Rosenberg, Benjamin George. HELP THE HUMAN EXPERIENCE: THE PSYCHOLOGY OF WOMEN. (540)

Jackson, Agnes Durham. "Militancy and Black Women's Competitive Behavior in Competitive vs. Non-Competitive Conditions." (555)

Jacobs, James Harris. "Black/White Interracial Families: Marital Process and Identity Development in Young Children." (571)

Jones, Reginald Lanier, ed. BLACK PSYCHOLOGY. (602)

Jordan, Winthrop D. WHITE OVER BLACK: AMERICAN ATTITUDES TOWARD THE NEGRO, 1550-1812. (605)

Lawrence, Margaret Morgan. YOUNG INNER CITY FAMILIES: DEVELOPMENT OF EGO STRENGTH UNDER STRESS. (646)

Lindblad, Marion Barr. "A Study of the Relationships between Family Interaction Patterns and Imaginativeness in Disadvantaged Preschool Children." (672)

Myers, Lena Wright. BLACK WOMEN: DO THEY COPE BETTER? (786)

Norris, Wessie Lavon. "A Path Model for Feelings of Personal Efficacy for Black Employed Male and Female Familyheads, Employed Female Non-Familyheads, and Housewives." (802)

Perkins, Eugene. HOME IS A DIRTY STREET: THE SOCIAL OPPRESSION OF BLACK CHILDREN. (828)

Porter, Judith D. R. BLACK CHILD, WHITE CHILD: THE DEVELOPMENT OF RACIAL ATTITUDES. (852)

Poussaint, Alvin F. WHY BLACKS KILL BLACKS. (854)

Prather, Jeffrey Lynn. A MERE REFLECTION: THE PSYCHODYNAMICS OF BLACK AND HISPANIC PSYCHOLOGY. (856)

Ramirez, Manuel, III and Price-Williams, Douglas R. "Cognitive Styles of Children of Three Ethnic Groups in the United States." (866)

Robins, Lee N. and Wish, Eric. "Childhood Deviance as a Development Process: A Study of 223 Urban Black Men from Birth to 18." (888)

Rosenberg, Morris and Simmons, Roberta G. BLACK AND WHITE SELF-ESTEEM: THE URBAN SCHOOL CHILD. (897)

Shade, Barbara J. "Regional Differences in Personality of Afro-American Children." (946)

Shell, Juanita. "Familial, Situational, and Cognitive Determinants of Sharing Behavior in African American Children." (950)

Sherman, Julia A. and Denmark, Florence L., eds. THE PSYCHOLOGY OF WOMEN: FUTURE DIRECTIONS IN RESEARCH. (951)

Wilkinson, Doris Yvonne and Taylor, Ronald Lewis, eds. THE BLACK MALE IN AMERICA: PERSPECTIVES ON HIS STATUS IN CONTEMPORARY SOCIETY. (1120)

Williams, John E. and Morland, J. Kenneth. RACE, COLOR AND THE YOUNG
CHILD. (1123)

Sociology

Bogue, Donald Joseph, ed. SOCIOLOGICAL CONTRIBUTIONS TO FAMILY PLANNING
RESEARCH. (133)
Bowser, Benjamin P. "The Contribution of Blacks to Sociological
Knowledge: A Problem of Theory and Role to 1950." (140)
Chapman, Sabrina Coffey. "A Social-Psychological Analysis of Morale in a
Selected Population: Low-Income Elderly Black Females." (205)
Dill, Bonnie Thornton. "Across the Boundaries of Race and Class: An
Exploration of the Relationship between Work and Family among Black
Female Domestic Servants." (289)
Eigsti, Marilyn Ann H. "Interrelationships of Value Orientation,
Decision-Making Mode and Decision-Implementing Style of Selected
Low Socioeconomic Status Negro Homemakers." (310)
Hannerz, Ulf. SOULSIDE: INQUIRIES INTO GHETTO CULTURE AND
COMMUNITY. (447)
Heiss, Jerold. THE CASE OF THE BLACK FAMILY: A SOCIOLOGICAL
INQUIRY. (485)
Johnson, Audrey Louise. "The Perceptions and Social Characteristics
Related to Occupational Mobility of Black Women and Intraracial
Assimilation of Blacks in America." (583)
Ladner, Joyce A., ed. THE DEATH OF WHITE SOCIOLOGY. (635)
Lefever, Harry G. "'Playing the Dozens': A Mechanism for Social
Control." (651)
Levitt, Morris. "Negro Student Rebellion against Parental Political
Beliefs." (657)
Lewis, Diane K. "A Response to Inequality: Black Women, Racism, and
Sexism." (659)
Peters, Marie Ferguson. "The Black Family--Perpetuating the Myths: An
Analysis of Family Sociology Textbook Treatment of Black
Families." (836)
Pinderhughes, Elaine B. "Family Functioning of Afro-Americans." (842)
Roberts, Joan I., ed. SCHOOL CHILDREN IN THE URBAN SLUM: READINGS IN
SOCIAL SCIENCE RESEARCH. (883)
Shin, Eui Hang. "Correlates of Intercounty Variations in Net Migration
Rates of Blacks in the Deep South, 1960-1970." (955)
Staples, Robert. "Towards a Sociology of the Black Family: A Theoretical
and Methodological Assessment." (1003)
Staples, Robert E. "Toward a Sociology of Black Liberation." (1013)
Staples, Robert E. "Towards a Sociology and Methodological
Assessment." (1014)
Stember, Charles Herbert. SEXUAL RACISM: THE EMOTIONAL BARRIER TO AN
INTEGRATED SOCIETY. (1020)
Stukes, Sandra Paulette. "A Comparative Analysis of Black and White
Urban Households and Help Seeking Behavior." (1030)
Thompson, Daniel Calbert. SOCIOLOGY OF THE BLACK EXPERIENCE. (1042)
Turner, Barbara F. and Turner, Castellano B. "The Political Implications
of Social Stereotyping of Women and Men among Black and White
College Students." (1056)
Turner, S. H. Regina. "Images of Black Women in the Plays of Black
Female Playwrights, 1950-1975." (1059)
Wyde, Janet Shibley and Rosenberg, B. G. HALF THE HUMAN
EXPERIENCE. (1143)

Racial Attitudes

Yellin, Joel. "Urban Population Distribution, Family Income, and Social Prejudice: The Long, Narrow City." (1146)

Self-Esteem

Ball, Richard Everett. "Expressive Functioning and the Black Family: Life and Domain Satisfaction of Black Women." (57)

Beglis, Jeanne F. and Sheikh, Anees A. "Development of the Self-Concept in Black and White Children." (87)

Blackburn, Regina Lynn. "Conscious Agents of Time and Self: The Lives and Styles of African-American Women as Seen through Their Autobiographical Writings." (123)

Branson, Nathaniel William. "An Investigation of the Effects of Work on the Families of Black, Female Registrants in the Baltimore City Win Program, A Pilot Study." (146)

Chambers, Andrew Wade. "A Comparative Study of Black and White Homosexuals." (202)

Chandler, Susan Meyers. "Self-Perceived Competency in Cross-Cultural Counseling." (203)

Chappell, Earl Birges, III. "The Relationships between Socioeconomic Status, Sex, Self-Concept, Academic Achievement, and Course Selection of Urban Black Tenth-Grade Students." (206)

Chunn, Jay Carrington, II. "A Comparison of Two Measures of Socioeconomic Status and Familial Factors as They Relate to Self Concept in Two Samples of Black Third and Fourth Grade Children." (217)

Darity, Evangeline Royall. "A Comparison of Fear-Of-Success Imagery between Black Male and Female Undergraduates." (262)

Farmer, Bonnita May. "Black Family Structure and Its Effects on Adolescents." (327)

Freeman, Howard E., Ross, J. Michael, Armor, David and Pettigrew, Thomas F. "Color Gradation and Attitudes among Middle-Income Negroes." (355)

Frey, Cecile P. "The House of Refuge for Colored Children." (357)

Fu, Victoria R. "A Longitudinal Study of the Self-Concepts of Euro-American, Afro-American, and Mexican American Preadolescent Girls." (358)

Gordon, Chad. LOOKING AHEAD: SELF CONCEPTIONS, RACE AND FAMILY AS DETERMINANTS OF ADOLESCENT ORIENTATION TO ACHIEVEMENT. (394)

Greenberg, Edward S. "Black Children, Self-Esteem, and the Liberation Movement." (409)

Gurin, Patricia and Epps, Edgar. BLACK CONSCIOUSNESS, IDENTITY AND ACHIEVEMENT: A STUDY OF STUDENTS IN HISTORICALLY BLACK COLLEGES. (422)

Hammond, Lavinia Grace. "Differential Use of Reward and Punishment as a Function of Need Achievement and of Fear of Failure in Black Mothers." (437)

Hare, Bruce R. "Black and White Child Self-Esteem in Social Science: An Overview." (450)

Hare, Bruce R. Black Girls: A Comparative Analysis of Self-Perception and Achievement by Race, Sex and Socioeconomic Background. (451)

Jacques, Jeffrey M. "Self-Esteem among Southeastern Black American Couples." (572)

King, Jerry Glenn. "A Study of Strengths in Black Families." (619)

Love, Bette Bonder. "Self-Esteem in Women Related to Occupational Status: A Biracial Study." (682)

McDonald, Robert L. and Gynther, Malcolm D. "Relationship of Self and Ideal-Self: Descriptions with Sex, Race and Class in Southern Adolescents." (722)

McRoy, Ruth Gail Murdock. "A Comparative Study of the Self-Concept of Transracially and Inracially Adopted Black Children." (732)

Phillips, Mona Taylor. "The Black Family and Community: Their Role in the Formation of Positive Self-Concept of Working-Class Black Youth." (839)

Rosenberg, Morris and Simmons, Roberta G. BLACK AND WHITE SELF-ESTEEM: THE URBAN SCHOOL CHILD. (897)

Rubin, Roger H. MATRICENTRIC FAMILY STRUCTURE AND THE SELF-ATTITUDES OF NEGRO CHILDREN. (908)

Samuels, Shirley C. "An Investigation into the Self-Concepts of Lower and Middle-Class Black and White Kindergarten Children." (915)

Simmons, Roberta G., Brown, Leslie, Bush, Diane Mitsch and Blyth, Dale A. "Self-Esteem and Achievement of Black and White Adolescents." (961)

General Attitudes

Davis, Elizabeth B. "The American Negro: From Family Membership to Personal and Social Identity." (268)

Ericksen, Julia A. "Race, Sex, and Alternative Lifestyle Choices." (323)

Hirsch, Seth Lewis. "Home Climate in the Black Single-Parent Mother-Led Family: A Social-Ecological Interactional Approach." (514)

Horton, Carrell P., Gray, Billie B. and Roberts, S. Oliver. "Attitudes of Black Teenagers and Their Mothers toward Selected Contemporary Issues." (522)

Jackson, Lorraine B. "The Attitudes of Black Females toward Upper and Lower Class Black Males." (567)

Linn, Margaret W., Hunter, Kathleen I. and Perry, Priscilla R. "Differences by Sex and Ethnicity in the Psychosocial Adjustment of the Elderly." (674)

North, George E. and Buchanan, O. Lee. "Maternal Attitudes in a Poverty Area." (803)

Point, Velma De Vonne La. "A Descriptive Survey of Some Perceptions and Concerns of Black Female Single Parent Families in Lansing, Michigan." (845)

Staples, Robert. "The Myth of Black Macho: A Response to Angry Black Feminists." (996)

Staples, Robert. "Race, Liberalism-Conservatism and Premarital Sexual Permissiveness: A Biracial Comparison." (1000)

Thompson, Kendrick S. "A Comparison of Black and White Adolescents' Belief about Having Children." (1043)

FAMILY COUNSELING AND EDUCATION

Adolescence

Allen, Walter R. "The Family Antecedents of Adolescent Mobility Aspirations." (23)

Anderson, Claud and Cromwell, Rue L. "'Black is Beautiful' and the Color Preferences of Afro-American Youth." (36)

Aseltine, Gwendolyn Pamenter. "Family Socialization Perceptions among Black and White High School Students." (45)

Benjamin, Rommel. FACTORS RELATED TO CONCEPTIONS OF THE MALE FAMILIAL ROLE BY BLACK YOUTH. (95)

Brennan, Tim, Huizinga, David and Elliot, Delbert S. THE SOCIAL PSYCHOLOGY OF RUNAWAYS. (148)

Brody, Eugene B. et al. MINORITY GROUP ADOLESCENTS IN THE UNITED STATES. (155)

Clark, Reginald Milton. "The Dance Party as a Socialization Mechanism for Black Urban Preadolescents and Adolescents." (223)

Comer, James P. and Poussaint, Alvin F., Jr. BLACK CHILD CARE: HOW TO BRING UP A HEALTHY BLACK CHILD IN AMERICA. A GUIDE TO EMOTIONAL AND PSYCHOLOGICAL DEVELOPMENT. (238)

Folb, Edith A. RUNNING DOWN SOME LINES: THE LANGUAGE AND CULTURE OF BLACK TEENAGERS. (342)

Frazier, Edward Franklin. NEGRO YOUTH AT THE CROSSWAYS, THEIR PERSONALITY DEVELOPMENT IN THE MIDDLE STATES. (352)

Fu, Victoria R. "A Longitudinal Study of the Self-Concepts of Euro-American, Afro-American, and Mexican American Preadolescent Girls." (358)

George, Valerie Daring. "An Investigation of the Occupational Aspirations of Talented Black Adolescent Females." (375)

Gilbert, Gwendolyn C. "Counseling Black Adolescent Parents." (380)

Gordon, Chad. LOOKING AHEAD: SELF CONCEPTIONS, RACE AND FAMILY AS DETERMINANTS OF ADOLESCENT ORIENTATION TO ACHIEVEMENT. (394)

Griffin, Don Quincy. "Personality Competence in Black Adolescents." (412)

Harris, Clotiel J. "Alternative Planning for Foster Care and Treatment of Children and Adolescents in Crises." (462)

Hauser, Stuart T. BLACK AND WHITE IDENTITY FORMATION: STUDIES IN THE PSYCHOSOCIAL DEVELOPMENT OF LOWER SOCIOECONOMIC CLASS ADOLESCENT BOYS. (473)

Hendricks, Leo E. "Black Unwed Adolescent Fathers." (490)

Hetherington, E. Mavis. "Effects of Paternal Absence on Sex-Typed Behaviors in Negro and White Preadolescent Males." (501)

Horton, Carrell P., Gray, Billie B. and Roberts, S. Oliver. "Attitudes of Black Teenagers and Their Mothers toward Selected Contemporary Issues." (522)

Jackman, Norman and Dodson, Jack. "Negro Youth and Direct Action." (554)

James, W. F. Bernell, James, Pauline M. and Walker, Edgar. "Some Problems of Sexual Growth in Adolescent Underprivileged Unwed Black Girls." (573)

King, Karl. "Adolescent Perception of Power Structure in the Negro Family." (620)

King, Karl, Abernathy, Thomas J. and Chapman, Ann H. "Black Adolescents' Views of Maternal Employment as a Threat to the Marital Relationship, 1963-1973." (622)

Macke, Anne Statham and Morgan, William R. "Maternal Employment, Race, and Work Orientation of High School Girls." (689)

McDonald, Robert L. and Gynther, Malcolm D. "Relationship of Self and Ideal-Self: Descriptions with Sex, Race and Class in Southern Adolescents." (722)

Nolle, David B. "Changes in Black Sons and Daughters: A Panel Analysis of Black Adolescents' Orientations toward Their Fathers." (801)

Oberle, Wayne H. "Role Models of Black and White Rural Youth at Two States of Adolescence." (805)

Pierce, Chester M. "Problems of the Negro Adolescent in the Next Decade." (840)

Porter, John R. DATING HABITS OF YOUNG BLACK AMERICANS: AND ALMOST EVERYBODY ELSE'S TOO. (851)

Rooks, Evelyn and King, Karl. "A Study of the Marriage Role Expectations of Black Adolescents." (894)

Schab, Fred. "Work Ethic of Gifted Black Adolescents." (924)

Scott, Patricia Bell and McKenry, Patrick C. "Some Suggestions for Teaching about Black Adolescence." (940)

Taylor, Ronald L. "Black Youth and Psychosocial Development." (1040)

Thompson, Kendrick S. "A Comparison of Black and White Adolescents' Belief about Having Children." (1043)

Umbarger, Carter Conrad. "Black and White Fathers: Their Impact on the Idealized Models and Vocational Plans of their Adolescent Sons." (1076)

Williamson, Robert C. "Dating Frequency, Ethnicity, and Adjustment in the High School: A Comparative Study." (1125)

Value Education

Anders, Sarah F. "New Dimensions in Ethnicity and Childrearing Attitudes." (35)

Brown, Raeford. "The Relationship of Moral Conscience, Discipline and Culture among Black Children." (170)

Chapman, Sabrina Coffey. "A Social-Psychological Analysis of Morale in a Selected Population: Low-Income Elderly Black Females." (205)

Dole, Arthur A. "Aspirations of Blacks and Whites for Their Children." (294)

Gibson, William. FAMILY LIFE AND MORALITY: STUDIES IN BLACK AND WHITE. (379)

Hare, Bruce R. "Racial and Socioeconomic Variations in Preadolescent Area-Specific and General Self-Esteem." (452)

Henry, Sheila E. "Family Structures, Social Class and Cultural Values." (496)

Hutchinson, Ira W., III. "The Significance of Marital Status for Morale and Life Satisfaction among Lower-Income Elderly." (539)

Jacob, Theodore, Fagin, Robert, Perry, Joseph and Dyke, Ruth Ann Van. "Social Class, Child Age, and Parental Socialization Values." (570)

Johnson, Leanor B. "The Search for Values in Black Family Research." (587)

Mumbauer, Corrine C. and Gray, Susan W. "Resistance to Temptation in Young Negro Children." (777)

Tomeh, Aida K. "The Value of Voluntarism among Minority Groups." (1047)

Webb-Woodard, Linda Delores. "Selfhood: Discovery of Survival Values in Low Income Black Families in Hartford, Connecticut. Two Case Studies Using Family Systems Theory." (1093)

Child Development

Alden, Lynn, Rappaport, Julian and Seidman, Edward. "College Students as Interventionists for Primary-Grade Children: A Comparison of Structured Academic and Companionship Programs for Children from Low-Income Families." (13)

Beglis, Jeanne F. and Sheikh, Anees A. "Development of the Self-Concept in Black and White Children." (87)

Black Child Development Institute. BLACK CHILDREN JUST KEEP ON GROWING: ALTERNATIVE CURRICULUM MODELS FOR YOUNG BLACK CHILDREN, edited by Madeleine Coleman. (121) CHILD DEVELOPMENT FROM A BLACK PERSPECTIVE-- CONFERENCE, JUNE 10-13, 1970, WASHINGTON, DC. (211)

Chunn, Jay I., ed. THE SURVIVAL OF BLACK CHILDREN AND YOUTH. (218)

Comer, James P. and Poussaint, Alvin F., Jr. BLACK CHILD CARE: HOW TO BRING UP A HEALTHY BLACK CHILD IN AMERICA. A GUIDE TO EMOTIONAL AND PSYCHOLOGICAL DEVELOPMENT. (238)

Cottle, Thomas J. BLACK CHILDREN, WHITE DREAMS. (244)

Eray, P. CHILDHOOD AND THE COSMOS: THE SOCIAL PSYCHOLOGY OF THE BLACK AFRICAN CHILD. (322)

Feinman, Saul. "Trends in Racial Self-Image of Black Children: Psychological Consequences of a Social Movement." (332)

Harrison-Ross, Phyllis and Wyden, Barbara. THE BLACK CHILD: A PARENT'S GUIDE TO RAISING HAPPY AND HEALTHY CHILDREN. (468)

Husbands, Ann. "The Developmental Task of the Black Foster Child." (538)

Idusogie, E. O. "Role of Maternal Nutritional Health and Care in the Development and Personality of Children in Africa." (543)

Logan, Sadye L. "Race, Identity, and Black Children: A Developmental Perspective." (679)

Mahone, Jack Randall. "The Influence of Family Relations upon Socially Desiring Behavior of Black and Caucasian Preschool Children." (692)

Morrison, Toni. THE BLUEST EYE: A NOVEL. (768)

Myers, Hector F., Gabriel-Rana, Phyllis, Harris-Epps, Ronee and Jones, Rhonda J., comps. RESEARCH IN BLACK CHILD DEVELOPMENT: DOCTORAL DISSERTATION ABSTRACTS, 1927-1979. (784)

Myers, Hector F., Rana, Phyllis G. and Harris, Marcia, eds. BLACK CHILD DEVELOPMENT IN AMERICA: 1927-1977: AN ANNOTATED BIBLIOGRAPHY. (785)

N'Namdi, George Richard. "Analysis of Parent-Child Interaction in the Two-Child Black Family." (788)

Parker, Maude I. "Growing Up Black." (817)

Perkins, Eugene. HOME IS A DIRTY STREET: THE SOCIAL OPPRESSION OF BLACK CHILDREN. (828)

Perkins, Useni Eugene, ed. (829)

Perkins, Useni Eugene, ed. (830)

Porter, Judith D. R. BLACK CHILD, WHITE CHILD: THE DEVELOPMENT OF RACIAL ATTITUDES. (852)

Robins, Lee N. and Wish, Eric. "Childhood Deviance as a Development Process: A Study of 223 Urban Black Men from Birth to 18." (888)

Rosenberg, Morris and Simmons, Roberta G. BLACK AND WHITE SELF-ESTEEM: THE URBAN SCHOOL CHILD. (897)

Rubin, Isadore and Kirkendall, Lester A., comps. SEX IN THE CHILDHOOD YEARS: EXPERT GUIDANCE FOR PARENTS, COUNSELORS AND TEACHERS. (906)

Scott-Jones, Diane. "Family Variables Associated with School Achievement in Low-Income Black First-Graders." (932)

Shade, Barbara J. "Regional Differences in Personality of Afro-American Children." (946)

Shell, Juanita. "Familial, Situational, and Cognitive Determinants of Sharing Behavior in African American Children." (950)

Slaughter, Diana T. "The Black Child: Issues and Priorities." (969)

Stevens, Joseph H., Jr. and Mathews, Marilyn, eds. MOTHER CHILD, FATHER CHILD RELATIONSHIPS. (1022)

Washington, Ernest D. "Politicizing Black Children." (1088)

Williams, John E. and Morland, J. Kenneth. RACE, COLOR AND THE YOUNG CHILD. (1123)

Wilson, Amos N. THE DEVELOPMENTAL PSYCHOLOGY OF THE BLACK CHILD. (1134)

Early Childhood Education

Abramson, Paul R. and Abramson, Seth D. "A Factorial Study of a
Multidimensional Approach to Aggressive Behavior in Black Preschool
Age Children." (1)

Alden, Lynn, Rappaport, Julian and Seidman, Edward. "College Students as
Interventionists for Primary-Grade Children: A Comparison of
Structured Academic and Companionship Programs for Children from Low-
Income Families." (13)

Bowie, Geraldine Robert Basley. "A Comparative Analysis of Vocabulary
Diversity, Syntactic Maturity, and the Communicative and Cognitive
Function of the Language of Black Four-Year-Old Children at Two
Socioeconomic Levels." (139)

Brown, Alexander Lionel. "The Effects of Race, Intelligence and Maternal
Employment Status of the Career/Occupational Role Stereotypes of Four-
Year Old Girls." (165)

Duhon, Rose Marie. "An Analysis of Curriculum Offerings and Services
Related to Child Abuse and Neglect in Early Childhood Teacher
Preparation Programs at Historically Black Colleges and
Universities." (300)

McQueen, Adele Bolden. "The Influence of Increased Parent-Child Verbal
Interaction on the Language Facility of Preschool Inner-City Black
Children." (730)

Scott, Ralph and Kobes, David A. "The Influence of Family Size on
Learning Readiness Patterns of Socioeconomically Disadvantaged
Preschool Blacks." (943)

Whitfield, Cynthia Elaine Bell. "Low Income Black and White Mothers'
Verbal Communication Patterns with Their Preschool Children." (1112)

Young, Jean Childs. "International Year of the Child: Black America's
Baby?" (1147)

Family Life Education

Adams, Cora Marie Gaines. "The Black Family: Implications for
Social Work Education and Practice." (3)

Aldridge, Delores P. "Teaching about Black American Families." (18)

Brody, Gene H. and Endsley, Richard C. "Researching Children and
Families: Differences in Approaches of Child and Family
Specialists." (157)

Dynneson, Thomas L. "A Cross-Cultural Approach to Learning about the
Family." (306)

Gilbert, Gwendolyn Cynthia. "Patterns of Child Care among Black
Families." (381)

Hampton, Robert L. "Institutional Decimation, Marital Exchange, and
Disruption in Black Families." (439)

Johnson, Leanor Boulin and Staples, Robert E. "Family Planning of the
Young Minority Male: A Pilot Project." (588)

Peters, Marie Ferguson. "The Black Family--Perpetuating the Myths: An
Analysis of Family Sociology Textbook Treatment of Black
Families." (836)

Point, Velma De Vonne La. "A Descriptive Survey of Some Perceptions and
Concerns of Black Female Single Parent Families in Lansing,
Michigan." (845)

Rubin, Roger H. "Matriarchal Themes in Black Family Literature:
Implications for Family Life Education." (907)

Scott, Patricia Bell and McKenry, Patrick C. "Some Suggestions for
Teaching about Black Adolescence." (940)

Thomas, George Benjamin. YOUNG BLACK ADULTS: LIBERATION AND FAMILY
ATTITUDES. (1041)

White, Priscilla and Scott, Patricia. "The Role of Black Women in Black
Families: Teaching about Black Families on a Predominantly White
Campus." (1108)

Education for Marriage

Sykes, Delores Roselle. "The Effects of a Marriage Education Course on
the Attitudes toward Marriage and Cohabitation of Black American
College Students." (1037)

Education for Parenthood

Blau, Zena Smith. "Exposure to Childrearing Experts: A Structural
Interpretation of Class-Color Differences." (127)

Busse, Thomas V. and Seraydarian, Louisa. "Desirability of First Names,
Ethnicity and Parental Education." (187)

Creswell-Betsch, Carol. "Comparison of a Family Microtraining Program
and a Reading Program to Enhance Empathic Communication by Black
Parents with Young Children." (250)

Fowler, Dale Eugene. "An Exploratory Investigation of the Relationship
between Locus of Control and Parenting Tasks among Lower Socioeconomic
Status Black Mothers." (346)

Gilbert, Gwendolyn C. "Counseling Black Adolescent Parents." (380)

Harrison-Ross, Phyllis and Wyden, Barbara. THE BLACK CHILD: A PARENT'S
GUIDE TO RAISING HAPPY AND HEALTHY CHILDREN. (468)

Hays, William C. and Mindel, Charles H. "Parental Perceptions for
Children: A Comparison of Black and White Families." (481)

Hobbs, Daniel F., Jr. and Wimbish, Jane Maynard. "Transition to
Parenthood by Black Couples." (515)

Hunter, Virginia. "The Impact of Adolescent Parenthood on Black Teenage
Mothers and Their Families and the Influence of Two Alternative Types
of Child Care." (537)

Kokonis, Nicholas. "Three Wishes of Black American Children:
Psychosocial Implications." (624)

Ladner, Joyce A. "Labeling Black Children: Social-Psychological
Implications." (636)

McLaughlin, Clara J., Frisby, Donald R., McLaughlin, Richard A. and
Williams, Melvin W. THE BLACK PARENTS HANDBOOK: A GUIDE TO HEALTHY
PREGNANCY, BIRTH AND CHILD CARE. (725)

Morgan, Elizabeth Ruth Pryor. "The Process of Parenting among Twenty-
Four Black Families in Berkeley, California." (764)

Parron, Delores Louise. "Black Parents' Concept of Parenthood: A Study
of Parental Role Definition and Parenting Style." (821)

Price-Bonham, Sharon and Skeen, Patsy. "A Comparison of Black and White
Fathers with Implications for Parent Education." (859)

Rubin, Dorothy. "Parental Schemata of Negro Primary School
Children." (903)

Sex Education

Brody, Eugene B., Ottey, Frank and Lagranade, Janet. "Early
  Sex Education in Relationship Behavior: Evidence from Jamaican
  Women." (156)
James, W. F. Bernell, James, Pauline M. and Walker, Edgar. "Some
  Problems of Sexual Growth in Adolescent Underprivileged Unwed Black
  Girls." (573)
Parker, Maude I. "Growing Up Black." (817)
Rubin, Isadore. SEXUAL LIFE IN THE LATER YEARS. (904)
Rubin, Isadore and Kirkendall, Lester A., comps. SEX IN THE ADOLESCENT
  YEARS. (905)
Rubin, Isadore and Kirkendall, Lester A., comps. SEX IN THE CHILDHOOD
  YEARS: EXPERT GUIDANCE FOR PARENTS, COUNSELORS AND TEACHERS. (906)
SIECUS Conference on Religion and Sexuality, St. Louis, 1971. SEXUALITY
  AND HUMAN VALUES: THE PERSONAL DIMENSION OF SEXUAL EXPERIENCE, edited
  by Mary Calderone. (957)

Sex Therapy

Wyatt, Gail Elizabeth, Strayer, Richard G. and Lobitz, W. Charles.
  "Issues in the Treatment of Sexually Dysfunctioning Couples of Afro-
  American Descent." (1142)

Children and Television

Jackson, Anthony W., ed. BLACK FAMILIES AND THE MEDIUM OF
  TELEVISION. (556)
Surlin, Stuart H. and Dominick, Joseph R. "Television's Function as a
  'Third Parent' for Black and White Teenagers." (1034)

Media and the Family

Holly, Ellen. "The Role of Media in the Programming of an
  Underclass." (516)
Stewart, James B. "Perspectives on Black Families from Contemporary Soul
  Music: The Case of Millie Jackson." (1023)

Marriage Counseling and Therapy

Hardy, Kenneth Vandelle. "Attitudes toward Marriage Counseling: A Study
  of Middle and Lower Class Blacks." (449)

Family Therapy

Boyd, Nancy Jeanne. "Clinicians' Perceptions of Black Families in
  Therapy." (141)
Foley, Vincent D. "Can a White Therapist Deal with Black
  Families?" (343)
Foley, Vincent D. "Family Therapy with Black, Disadvantaged Families:
  Some Observations on Roles, Communication and Technique." (344)

Hallowitz, David. "Counseling and Treatment of the Poor Black
  Family." (432)
Lyles, Michael R. and Carter, James H. "Myths and Strengths of the Black
  Family: A Historical and Sociological Contribution to Family
  Therapy." (685)
McAdoo, Harriette. "Family Therapy in the Black Community." (706)
McAdoo, Harriette P. "A Review of the Literature Related to Family
  Therapy in the Black Community." (707)
McFadden, Johnnie. "Stylistic Counseling of the Black Family." (723)
Meggerson-Moore, Joyce Ann. "A Survey of a Sample of Black Families'
  Views of the Counseling Profession." (734)
Obudho, Constance E., ed. BLACK MARRIAGE AND FAMILY THERAPY. (806)
Sager, Clifford J., Brayboy, Thomas L. and Waxenberg, Barbara R. BLACK
  GHETTO FAMILY IN THERAPY: A LABORATORY EXPERIENCE. (913)
Tuck, Samuel, Jr. "Working With Black Fathers." (1051)
Wade, Brenda Karon. "The Relationship between the Disciplinary Styles of
  Black Parents and Preference for Mode of Family Therapy." (1082)
Wylan, Louise and Mintz, Norbett L. "Ethnic Differences in Family
  Attitudes towards Psychotic Manifestations, with Implications for
  Treatment Programmes." (1144)

Marital and Family Enrichment

Chandler, Susan Meyers. "Self-Perceived Competency in Cross-Cultural
  Counseling." (203)
McFadden, Johnnie. "Stylistic Counseling of the Black Family." (723)
Scott, Ralph. "Home Start: Family-Centered Preschool Enrichment for
  Black and White Children." (942)

MINORITY GROUPS

Ethnic Groups in the United States

Badaines, Joel. "Identification, Imitation, and Sex-Role Preference in
  Father-Present and Father-Absent Black and Chicano Boys." (51)
Bean, Frank D. and Wood, Charles H. "Ethnic Variations in the
  Relationship between Income and Fertility." (81)
Blau, Zena Smith, Oser, George T. and Stephens, Richard C. "Aging,
  Social Class, and Ethnicity: A Comparison of Anglo, Black and Mexican-
  American Texans." (128)
Busse, Thomas V. and Seraydarian, Louisa. "Desirability of First Names,
  Ethnicity and Parental Education." (187)
Cooney, Rosemary Santana. "Changing Labor Force Participation of
  Mexican American Wives: A Comparison with Anglos and Blacks." (242)
Cooney, Rosemary Santana. "Demographic Components of Growth in White,
  Black, and Puerto Rican Female-Headed Families: Comparison of the
  Cutright and Ross/Sawhill Methodologies." (243)
Cromwell, Ronald E., Vaughn, C. Edwin and Mindel, Charles H. "Ethnic
  Minority Family Research in an Urban Setting: A Process of
  Exchange." (251)
Cromwell, Vicky L. and Cromwell, Ronald E. "Perceived Dominance in
  Decision-Making and Conflict Resolution among Anglo, Black, and
  Chicano Couples." (252)

Cuffaro, Sara Todd. "A Discriminant Analysis of Sociocultural, Motivation, and Personality Differences among Black, Anglo and Chicana Female Drug Abusers in a Medium Security Prison." (255)

Eberstein, Isaac W. and Frisbie, W. Parker. "Differences in Marital Instability among Mexican Americans, Blacks, and Anglos: 1960 and 1970." (307)

Fisher, Jerilyn Beth. "The Minority Woman's Voice: A Cultural Study of Black and Chicana Fiction." (336)

Giovannoni, Jeanne M. and Billingsley, Andrew. "Child Neglect among the Poor: A Study of Parental Adequacy in Families of Three Ethnic Groups." (384)

Graham, Lawrence O. "Behind the Mask." (402)

Khalesi, Mohammad Reza. "Comparison of the Parenting Attitudes, Conflict Management Styles, and Interpersonal Behavior Patterns of Anglo, Black and Mexican-American Parents." (616)

Lindsay, Beverly, ed. COMPARATIVE PERSPECTIVES OF THIRD WORLD WOMEN: THE IMPACT OF RACE, SEX, AND CLASS. (673)

Littlefield, Robert P. "Self-Disclosure among Some Negro, White, and Mexican American Adolescents." (676)

Markides, Kyriakos S. and Hazuda, Helen P. "Ethnicity and Infant Mortality in Texas Counties." (694)

McCurdy, Paula Carol Kresser. "Sex Role, Decision Making Practices, Marital Satisfaction and Family Problems with Economically Disadvantaged Anglo, Black, and Chicano Couples." (721)

Mindel, Charles H. and Habenstein, Robert Wesley, eds. ETHNIC FAMILIES IN AMERICA: PATTERNS AND VARIATIONS. (744)

Mindel, Charles H. and Habenstein, Robert Wesley, eds. ETHNIC FAMILIES IN AMERICA: PATTERNS AND VARIATIONS. (745)

Mirowsky, John, II and Ross, Catherine E. "Minority Status, Ethnic Culture, and Distress: A Comparison of Blacks, Whites, Mexicans, and Mexican Americans." (746)

Monahan, Thomas P. "Illegitimacy by Race and Mixture of Race." (756)

Peres, Yochanan and Schrift, Ruth. "Intermarriage and Interethnic Relations: A Comparative Study." (826)

Prather, Jeffrey Lynn. A MERE REFLECTION: THE PSYCHODYNAMICS OF BLACK AND HISPANIC PSYCHOLOGY. (856)

Simon, Rita James and Altstein, Howard. TRANSRACIAL ADOPTION. (964)

Staples, Robert. "The Mexican-American Family: Its Modifications Over Time and Space." (995)

Staples, Robert and Mirande, Alfredo. "Racial and Cultural Variations among American Families: A Decennial Review of the Literature on Minority Families." (1005)

Tomeh, Aida K. "The Value of Voluntarism among Minority Groups." (1047)

Uhlenberg, Peter. "Changing Family Patterns of Blacks, Chicanos, and Whites: 1960-1970." (1073)

Uhlenberg, Peter. "Marital Instability among Mexican Americans: Following the Patterns of Blacks?" (1074)

Walberg, Herbert J., Yeh, Elaine Gee and Paton, Stephanie Mooney. "Family Background, Ethnicity, and Urban Delinquency." (1084)

Wyatt, Derrick. "The Social Security Rights of Migrant Workers and Their Families." (1140)

Wylan, Louise and Mintz, Norbett L. "Ethnic Differences in Family Attitudes towards Psychotic Manifestations, with Implications for Treatment Programmes." (1144)

Zwiebel, Sarah. "The Relation between Maternal Behaviors and Aggression in Sons: Black and Puerto Rican Families." (1153)

Blacks in the Caribbean

Higman, B. W. "Household Structure and Fertility on Jamaican Slave
Plantations: A Nineteenth-Century Example." (504)

Higman, B. W. "The Slave Family and Household in the British
West Indies, 1800-1834." (505)

Matthews, Basil. CRISIS OF THE WEST INDIAN FAMILY: A SAMPLE STUDY. (702)

Patterson, Orlando. "Persistence, Continuity and Change in the Jamaican
Working-Class Family." (823)

Rodman, Hyman. LOWER-CLASS FAMILIES: THE CULTURE OF POVERTY IN NEGRO
TRINIDAD. (891)

Whitehead, Tony L. "Residence, Kinship, and Mating as Survival
Strategies: A West Indian Example." (1110)

Family and Social Class

Anderson, Elijah. A PLACE ON THE CORNER. (38)

Bell, Robert R. "Lower-Class Negro Mothers' Aspirations for Their
Children." (92)

Bernard, Jessie. "Marital Stability and Patterns of Status
Variables." (98)

Blau, Zena Smith. "Exposure to Childrearing Experts: A Structural
Interpretation of Class-Color Differences." (127)

Blau, Zena Smith, Oser, George T. and Stephens, Richard C. "Aging,
Social Class, and Ethnicity: A Comparison of Anglo, Black and Mexican-
American Texans." (128)

Borland, Barry L. and Rudolp, Joseph P. "Relative Effects of
Low Socioeconomic Status, Parental Smoking and Poor Scholastic
Performance on Smoking among High School Students." (135)

Brook, Judith S., Whiteman, Martin, Peisach, Estelle and Deutsch,
Martin. "Aspiration Levels of and for Children: Age, Sex, Race,
Socioeconomic Correlates." (160)

Desai, S. R. and Mehta, N. R. "The Impact of Health Education on
Acceptance of Family Planning Methods for Spacing by
Lower Socioeconomic Primiparous Urban Women." (285)

Eigsti, Marilyn Ann H. "Interrelationships of Value Orientation,
Decision-Making Mode and Decision-Implementing Style of Selected
Low Socioeconomic Status Negro Homemakers." (310)

Engerrand, Steven W. "Black and Mulatto Mobility and Stability in
Dallas, Texas, 1880-1910." (314)

Ferman, Louis A., Kornbluh, Joyce L. and Haber, Alan, eds. POVERTY IN
AMERICA: A BOOK OF READINGS. (333)

Geismar, Ludwig L. and Gerhart, Ursula C. "Social Class, Ethnicity, and
Family Functioning: Exploring Some Issues Raised by the Moynihan
Report." (371)

Goldenberg, Sheldon. "Kinship and Ethnicity Viewed as Adaptive Responses
to Location in the Opportunity Structure." (390)

Harris, Joan Ricks. "Black/White and Socioeconomic Status as Factors in
Maternal Attitudes toward Childrearing Practices and the Use of
Health Care in Families with and without an Educable Mentally Retarded
Child." (463)

Harris, Richard J. "An Examination of the Effects of Ethnicity,
Socioeconomic Status and Generation on Familism and Sex Role
Orientation." (464)

Hawkins, Ioma LaNell. "Achievement Motivation, Race, and Social Class
Influences upon Female Attributions." (478)

Hawkins, James L., Weisberg, Carol and Ray, Dixie L. "Marital Communication Style and Social Class." (479)

Henry, Sheila E. "Family Structures, Social Class and Cultural Values." (496)

Higginbotham, Elizabeth Starr. "Educated Black Women: An Exploration into Life Chances and Choices." (503)

Jacob, Theodore, Fagin, Robert, Perry, Joseph and Dyke, Ruth Ann Van. "Social Class, Child Age, and Parental Socialization Values." (570)

Jeffers, Camille. LIVING POOR: A PARTICIPANT OBSERVER STUDY OF PRIORITIES AND CHOICES. (576)

Jones, Allan P. and Demaree, R. G. "Family Disruption, Social Indices, and Problem Behavior: A Preliminary Study." (596)

Kamii, Constance K. and Radin, Norma L. "Class Differences in the Socialization Practices of Negro Mothers." (607)

Kronus, Sidney J. THE BLACK MIDDLE CLASS. (626)

Lewis, Hylan. "Childrearing among Low-Income Families." (662)

Lewis, Hylan. "Culture, Class and Family Life among Low-Income Urban Negroes." (663)

Little, Monroe H. "Class and Culture: A Reassessment of E. Franklin Frazier's Black Experience." (675)

Martineau, William H. "Informal Social Ties among Urban Black Americans: Some New Data and a Review of the Problem." (700)

McAdoo, Harriette Pipes. "Factors Related to Stability in Upwardly Mobile Black Families." (713)

Monahan, Thomas P. "The Occupational Class of Couples Entering into Interracial Marriages." (759)

Morrow, Betty Hearn. "A Comparison of Eight-Year-Old Children Born to Young Black Adolescents and Those Born to Comparable Mothers in Their Early Twenties." (769)

Mortimer, Jeylan T. "Social Class, Work and the Family: Some Implications of the Father's Occupation for Familial Relationships and Sons' Career Decisions." (770)

Munick, Warren A. and Sullivan, Dennis. "Race, Age, and Family Status Differentials in Metropolitan Migration of Households." (778)

Orive, Ruben and Gerard, Harold B. "Social Contact of Minority Parents and Their Children's Acceptance by Classmates." (811)

Osmond, Marie Withers. "Marital Organization in Low-Income Families: A Cross-Race Comparison." (813)

Osmond, Marie Withers and Martin, Patricia Yancey. "A Contingency Model of Marital Organization in Low Income Families." (814)

Pavenstedt, Eleanor, ed. THE DRIFTERS: CHILDREN OF DISORGANIZED LOWER-CLASS FAMILIES, BY CHARLES A. MALONE AND OTHERS. (824)

Pohlmann, Vernon C. and Walsh, Robert H. "Black Minority Racial Status and Fertility in the United States, 1970." (844)

Ritchey, P. Neal. "The Effect of Minority Group Status on Fertility: A Re-examination of Concepts." (882)

Rodman, Hyman. LOWER-CLASS FAMILIES: THE CULTURE OF POVERTY IN NEGRO TRINIDAD. (891)

Romer, Nancy and Cherry, Debra. "Ethnic and Social Class Differences in Children's Sex-Role Concepts." (893)

Ross, Joel A. "Influence of Expert and Peer upon Negro Mothers of Low Socioeconomic Status." (900)

Ryan, Vernon and Warland, Rex H. "Race and the Effect of Family Status among Male Agricultural Laborers." (910)

Schwartz, Michael. "The Northern United States Negro Matriarchy: Status Versus Authority." (928)

Tulkin, Steven R. "Race, Class, Family and School Achievement." (1054)
U.S. Bureau of the Census. THE SOCIAL AND ECONOMIC STATUS OF THE BLACK
  POPULATION IN THE UNITED STATES, 1974. (1063)
Wakin, Edward. AT THE EDGE OF HARLEM: PORTRAIT OF A MIDDLE-CLASS NEGRO
  FAMILY. (1083)
Whitehead, John. IDA'S FAMILY: ADAPTATIONS TO POVERTY IN A SUBURBAN
  GHETTO. (1109)

AIDS FOR THEORY AND RESEARCH

Family Research Methodology

Allen, Walter R. "Black Family Research in the United States: A Review,
  Assessment and Extension." (21)
Anders, Sarah F. "New Dimensions in Ethnicity and Childrearing
  Attitudes." (35)
Anderson, Elijah. A PLACE ON THE CORNER. (38)
Bengston, Vern L., Furlong, Michael J. and Lauffer, Robert S. "Time,
  Aging and Continuity of Social Structure: Themes and Issues in
  Generational Analysis." (94)
Billingsley, Andrew and Billingsley, Amy Tate. "Illegitimacy and
  Patterns of Negro Family Life." (112)
Boykin, A. Wade, Franklin, Anderson J. and Yates, Jacques Frank,
  eds. RESEARCH DIRECTIONS OF BLACK PSYCHOLOGISTS. (142)
Brody, Gene H. and Endsley, Richard C. "Researching Children and
  Families: Differences in Approaches of Child and Family
  Specialists." (157)
Brown, William Neal. "Strategies of Intervention with the Parents of
  'Acting Out' Preschool Black Children." (173)
Butler, Cynthia and Doster, Joseph A. "Sex-Role Learning in the Black
  Male: Research and Clinical Implications." (188)
Cazenave, Noel A. "Family Violence and Aging Blacks: Theoretical
  Perspectives and Research Possibilities." (199)
Christensen, Harold T. and Johnson, Leanor B. "Premarital Coitus and the
  Southern Black: A Comparative View." (215)
Cole, O. Jackson. "Scale Construction in the Assessment of Sex-Role
  Stereotypes among Minorities." (233)
Cooney, Rosemary Santana. "Demographic Components of Growth in White,
  Black, and Puerto Rican Female-Headed Families: Comparison of the
  Cutright and Ross/Sawhill Methodologies." (243)
Craggett, Foster T. "A Form Critical Approach to the Oral Traditions of
  the Black Church as They Relate to the Celebration of Death." (245)
Dean, Dwight G., Braito, Rita, Powers, Edward A. and Bruton,
  Brent. "Cultural Contradictions and Sex Roles Revisited: A Replication
  and a Reassessment." (280)
Derbyshire, Robert L. "The Uncompleted Negro Family: Suggested Research
  into the Hypotheses Regarding the Effect of the Negro's Outcaste
  Conditions upon His Own and Other American Sexual Attitudes and
  Behavior." (284)
Dietrich, Katheryn Thomas. "A Reexamination of the Myth of Black
  Matriarchy." (287)
Dixon, Richard D. "The Absence of Birth Order Correlations among Unwed
  and Married Black First-Conceptors." (292)

Willie, Charles V. and Greenblatt, Susan L. "Four 'Classic' Studies of
Power Relationships in Black Families: A Review and Look to the
Future." (1128)
Willie, Charles Vert. A NEW LOOK AT BLACK FAMILIES. (1131)
Zollar, Ann Creighton. A MEMBER OF THE FAMILY: STRATEGIES FOR BLACK
FAMILY CONTINUITY. (1152)

Kinship Terminology

Kunkel, Peter H. and Kennard, Sara Sue. SPOUT SPRING: A BLACK
COMMUNITY. (628)

Family Theory

Aldridge, Delores P. "Interracial Marriages: Empirical and Theoretical
Considerations." (16)
Allen, Walter R. "Race and Sex Differences in the Socialization of Male
Children." (25)
Allen, Walter R. "The Search for Applicable Theories of Black Family
Life." (28)
Aschenbrenner, Joyce and Carr, Carolyn Hameedah. "Conjugal Relationships
in the Context of the Black Extended Family." (44)
Baldwin, Joseph A. "Theory and Research Concerning the Notion of Black
Self-Hatred: A Review and Reinterpretation." (54)
Barnes, Edward J. "The Black Community as the Source of Children: A
Theoretical Perspective." (64)
Beatt, Barbara Hamby and Wahlstrom, Barbara Berg. "A Developmental
Approach to Understanding Families." (82)
Bernard, Jessie Shirley. MARRIAGE AND FAMILY AMONG NEGROES. (100)
Billingsley, Andrew. BLACK FAMILIES IN WHITE AMERICA. (110)
Boyd, Nancy Jeanne. "Clinicians' Perceptions of Black Families in
Therapy." (141)
Bracey, John H., Meier, August and Rudwick, Elliott, eds. BLACK
MATRIARCHY: MYTH OR REALITY? (143)
Burr, Wesley R., Hill, Reuben, Nye, F. I. and Reiss, Ira L. CONTEMPORARY
THEORIES ABOUT THE FAMILY: VOLUME 1. RESEARCH-BASED THEORIES. (184)
Cazenave, Noel A. "Alternative Intimacy, Marriage, and Family Lifestyles
among Low-Income Black Americans." (198)
Dennis, Rutledge M. "Theories of the Black Family: The Weak-Family and
Strong-Family Schools as Competing Ideologies." (283)
Elder, Glen H., Jr. "Approaches to Social Change and the Family." (311)
Floyd, Russell F. "Marital Adjustment and Decision Making among Stable
Black Married Couples." (338)
Gibson, William. FAMILY LIFE AND MORALITY: STUDIES IN BLACK AND
WHITE. (379)
Gilmore, Al-Tony, ed. REVISITING BLASSINGAME'S "THE SLAVE COMMUNITY":
THE SCHOLARS RESPOND. (383)
Hare, Bruce R. "Racial and Socioeconomic Variations in Preadolescent
Area-Specific and General Self-Esteem." (452)
Herzog, Elizabeth. "Is There a 'Break-Down' of the Negro Family?" (500)
Hill, Robert Bernard. THE STRENGTHS OF BLACK FAMILIES. (510)
Jackson, Jacquelyne J. "Family Organization and Ideology." (562)
Josephson, Eric. "The Matriarchy: Myth and Reality." (606)
Kilpatrick, Allie C. "Future Directions for the Black Family." (617)

Critiques and Analyses of Family Research Literature

Aldridge, Delores P. "Toward an Understanding of Black Male/Female Relationships." (19)

Allen, Walter R. "Black Family Research in the United States: A Review, Assessment and Extension." (21)

Allen, Walter R. "The Search for Applicable Theories of Black Family Life." (28)

Allen, Walter R. and Agbasegbe, Bamidele Ade. "A Comment on Scott's 'Black Polygamous Family Formation'." (30)

Barnett, Larry D. "Research on International and Interracial Marriages." (66)

Bayless, Vaurice G. "Selected Research Studies and Professional Literature Dealing with Physiological, Socioeconomic, Psychological, and Cultural Differences between Black and White Males with Reference to the Performance of Athletic Skills." (79)

Berger, Alan S. and Simon, William. "Black Families and the Moynihan Report: A Research Evaluation." (97)

Billingsley, Andrew. "Black Families and White Social Science." (109)

Bowser, Benjamin P. "The Contribution of Blacks to Sociological Knowledge: A Problem of Theory and Role to 1950." (140)

Broderick, Carlfred Bartholomew, ed. A DECADE OF FAMILY RESEARCH AND ACTION. (154)

Burr, Wesley R., Hill, Reuben, Nye, F. I. and Reiss, Ira L. CONTEMPORARY THEORIES ABOUT THE FAMILY: VOLUME 1. RESEARCH-BASED THEORIES. (184)

Cazenave, Noel, ed. "Black Alternative Lifestyles: Special Issue on Commentary and Reprise on Joseph Scott's Black Polygamous Family Formation." (197)

Clarke, John Henrik. "The Black Family in Historical Perspective." (227)

Comer, James P. THE BLACK FAMILY: AN ADAPTIVE PERSPECTIVE. (237)

Cromwell, Ronald E., Vaughn, C. Edwin and Mindel, Charles H. "Ethnic Minority Family Research in an Urban Setting: A Process of Exchange." (251)

Cross, William E., Jr. "Black Family and Black Identity: A Literature Review." (253)

Davis, Robert. "Suicide among Young Blacks: Trend and Perspectives." (276)

Dill, Bonnie Thornton. "The Dialectics of Black Womanhood." (290)

English, Richard H. "Beyond Pathology: Research and Theoretical Perspectives on Black Families." (316)

Engram, Eleanor. SCIENCE, MYTH, REALITY: THE BLACK FAMILY IN ONE-HALF CENTURY OF RESEARCH. (317)

Gary, Lawrence E., ed. SOCIAL RESEARCH AND THE BLACK COMMUNITY: SELECTED ISSUES AND PRIORITIES. A SELECTION OF PAPERS FROM A WORKSHOP ON DEVELOPING RESEARCH PRIORITIES FOR THE BLACK COMMUNITY HELD AT HOWARD UNIVERSITY IN WASHINGTON, D.C., JUNE 25-29, 1973. (366)

Gelles, Richard J. "Violence in the Family: A Review of Research in the Seventies." (372)

Gilmore, Al-Tony, ed. REVISITING BLASSINGAME'S "THE SLAVE COMMUNITY": THE SCHOLARS RESPOND. (383)

Gordon, Vivian V. "The Methodologies of Black Self-Concept Research: A Critique." (395)

Gutman, Herbert G. "Persistent Myths about the Afro-American Family." (424)

Hare, Nathan. "What Black Intellectuals Misunderstand about the Black Family." (456)

Harris, William G. "Research on the Black Family: Mainstream and
  Dissenting Perspectives." (467)
Houten, Warren D. Ten. "The Black Family: Myth and Reality." (524)
Hoffman, Louis Wladis and Manis, Jean Denby. "The Value of Children in
  U.S.: A New Approach to the Study of Fertility." (529)
Johnson, Leanor B. "The Search for Values in Black Family
  Research." (587)
Johnson, Nan E. "A Response to Rindfuss." (591)
Kushnick, Louis. "The Negro Family in the United States: A
  Review." (630)
Lenus, Jack, Jr. "Friendship: A Refutation." (652)
Lyles, Michael R. and Carter, James H. "Myths and Strengths of the Black
  Family: A Historical and Sociological Contribution to Family
  Therapy." (685)
Madison, Bernice Q. and Schapiro, Michael. "Black Adoption-Issues and
  Policies: Review of the Literature." (691)
Martineau, William H. "Informal Social Ties among Urban Black Americans:
  Some New Data and a Review of the Problem." (700)
McAdoo, Harriette P. "A Review of the Literature Related to Family
  Therapy in the Black Community." (707)
Myers, Hector F. "Research on the Black Family: A Critical
  Review." (783)
Peters, Marie F., ed. "Special Issue: Black Families." (835)
Rubin, Roger H. "Matriarchal Themes in Black Family Literature:
  Implications for Family Life Education." (907)
Scott, James F. "Police Authority and the Low-Income Black Family: An
  Area Needed Research." (933)
Scott, Patricia Bell. "Sex Roles Research and Black Families: Some
  Comments on the Literature." (939)
Sherman, Roger Holmes. "Portraits of Family and Kinship Relations among
  Black Americans: A Study in the Properties, Structures and Functions
  of Primary Groups." (952)
Staples, Robert. "The Black Family Revisited: A Review and
  Preview." (988)
Staples, Robert. "Towards a Sociology of the Black Family: A Theoretical
  and Methodological Assessment." (1003)
Staples, Robert and Mirande, Alfredo. "Racial and Cultural Variations
  among American Families: A Decennial Review of the Literature on
  Minority Families." (1005)
Wade-Gayles, Gloria. "She Who is Black and Mother: In Sociology and
  Fiction, 1940-70." (1081)
Whitaker, Barbara. "Breakdown in the Negro Family: Myth or
  Reality." (1104)
Wilkinson, Doris Y. "Toward a Positive Frame of Reference for Analysis
  of Black Families: A Selected Bibliography." (1119)
Williams, J. Allen, Jr. and Stockton, Robert. "Black Family Structures
  and Functions: An Empirical Examination of Some Suggestions Made by
  Billingsley." (1122)
Wyatt, Gail Elizabeth, Strayer, Richard G. and Lobitz, W. Charles.
  "Issues in the Treatment of Sexually Dysfunctioning Couples of Afro-
  American Descent." (1142)

Classified Bibliographies of Family Literature

Addison, Donald P. BLACK FAMILIES: A COMPREHENSIVE BIBLIOGRAPHY. (5)

Davis, Lenwood G. BLACK FAMILIES IN URBAN AREAS IN THE UNITED STATES: A
BIBLIOGRAPHY OF PUBLISHED WORKS ON THE BLACK FAMILY IN URBAN AREAS IN
THE UNITED STATES. (271)

Davis, Lenwood G. THE BLACK FAMILY IN THE UNITED STATES: A SELECTED
BIBLIOGRAPHY OF ANNOTATED BOOKS, ARTICLES AND DISSERTATIONS ON BLACK
FAMILIES IN AMERICA. (272)

Davis, Lenwood G. THE BLACK FAMILY IN URBAN AREAS IN THE UNITED STATES:
A BIBLIOGRAPHY OF PUBLISHED WORKS ON THE BLACK FAMILY IN URBAN AREAS
OF THE UNITED STATES. (273)

Davis, Lenwood G. THE BLACK WOMAN IN AMERICAN SOCIETY: A SELECTED
ANNOTATED BIBLIOGRAPHY. (274)

Dixon, Johanne C., comp. A SELECTED ANNOTATED BIBLIOGRAPHY ON BLACK
FAMILIES. VOLUME 1. (291)

Dunmore, Charlotte J. BLACK CHILDREN AND THEIR FAMILIES: A
BIBLIOGRAPHY. (303)

Hill, Robert B. and Godley, Carol J. AN INVENTORY OF SELECTED NATIONAL
DATA SOURCES ON THE SOCIAL AND ECONOMIC CHARACTERISTICS OF BLACK
FAMILIES. (507)

Howard, Cleopatra S., comp. A RESOURCE GUIDE ON BLACK FAMILIES IN
AMERICA. (526)

Indiana University. Libraries. THE BLACK FAMILY AND THE BLACK WOMAN: A
BIBLIOGRAPHY, edited by Phyllis Rauch Klotman and Wilmer H. Baatz.
(545)

McPherson, James M., Holland, Lawrence B., Banner, James M., Jr., Weiss,
Nancy J., Bell, Michael D. et al. BLACKS IN AMERICA: BIBLIOGRAPHIC
ESSAYS. (729)

Miller, Elizabeth W. and Fisher, Mary L., comps. THE NEGRO IN AMERICA: A
BIBLIOGRAPHY. (740)

Myers, Hector F., Gabriel-Rana, Phyllis, Harris-Epps, Ronee and Jones,
Rhonda J., comps. RESEARCH IN BLACK CHILD DEVELOPMENT: DOCTORAL
DISSERTATION ABSTRACTS, 1927-1979. (784)

Myers, Hector F., Rana, Phyllis G. and Harris, Marcia, eds. BLACK CHILD
DEVELOPMENT IN AMERICA: 1927-1977: AN ANNOTATED BIBLIOGRAPHY. (785)

Porter, Dorothy B. "Family Records, A Major Resource for Documenting the
Black Experience in New England." (850)

Rosser, Pearl L. and Hamlin, Joyce Fite, eds. RESEARCH ON THE BLACK
CHILD AND FAMILY AT HOWARD UNIVERSITY: 1867-1978. (901)

Sims, Janet L., comp. THE PROGRESS OF AFRO-AMERICAN WOMEN: A SELECTED
BIBLIOGRAPHY AND RESOURCE GUIDE. (966)

Wilkinson, Doris Y. "Toward a Positive Frame of Reference for Analysis
of Black Families: A Selected Bibliography." (1119)

Statistics

Abramson, Paul R. and Abramson, Seth D. "A Factorial Study of a
Multidimensional Approach to Aggressive Behavior in Black Preschool
Age Children." (1)

Clark, Samuel D. "Sex, Contraception and Parenthood: Experience and
Attitudes among Urban Black Young Men." (224)

Farley, Reynolds. GROWTH OF THE BLACK POPULATION: A STUDY OF DEMOGRAPHIC
TRENDS. (325)

Fogel, Robert William and Engerman, Stanley L. "Recent Findings in the
Slave Demography and Family Structure." (340)

Hill, Robert B. and Godley, Carol J. AN INVENTORY OF SELECTED NATIONAL
DATA SOURCES ON THE SOCIAL AND ECONOMIC CHARACTERISTICS OF BLACK
FAMILIES. (507)

Hill, Robert Bernard. BLACK FAMILIES IN THE 1974-1975 DEPRESSION: SPECIAL POLICY REPORT. (508)

Linn, Margaret W., Hunter, Kathleen I. and Perry, Priscilla R. "Differences by Sex and Ethnicity in the Psychosocial Adjustment of the Elderly." (674)

Mercer, Charles V. "Interrelations among Family Stability, Family Composition, Residence and Race." (739)

Monahan, Thomas P. "An Overview of Statistics on Interracial Marriage in the United States with Data on Its Extent from 1963-1970." (760)

Rao, V.V. Prakakasa and Rao, V. Nandini. "Family Size and Sex Preferences of Children: A Biracial Comparison." (868)

Shin, Eui Hang. "Correlates of Intercounty Variations in Net Migration Rates of Blacks in the Deep South, 1960-1970." (955)

Siegel, Jacob S. "Estimates of Coverage of the Population by Sex, Race and Age in the 1970 Census." (958)

U.S. Bureau of the Census. THE SOCIAL AND ECONOMIC STATUS OF THE BLACK POPULATION IN THE UNITED STATES, 1971, by Nampeo D.R. McKenney. (1062)

U.S. Bureau of the Census. THE SOCIAL AND ECONOMIC STATUS OF THE BLACK POPULATION IN THE UNITED STATES, 1974. (1063)

U.S. Bureau of the Census. THE SOCIAL AND ECONOMIC STATUS OF THE BLACK POPULATION IN THE UNITED STATES: AN HISTORICAL VIEW, 1790-1978, by Nampeo D.R. McKenney. (1064)

Collected Works

Barnett, Marguerite Ross and Hefner, James A., eds. PUBLIC POLICY FOR THE BLACK COMMUNITY: STRATEGIES AND PERSPECTIVES. (67)

Barron, Milton Leon, ed. THE BLENDING AMERICA: PATTERNS OF INTERMARRIAGE. (69)

Bass, Barbara Ann, Wyatt, Gail Elizabeth and Powell, Gloria Johnson, eds. THE AFRO-AMERICAN FAMILY: ASSESSMENT, TREATMENT, AND RESEARCH ISSUES. (71)

Black Aged in the Future, San Juan, P.R., 1972. Proceedings. PROCEEDINGS OF 'BLACK AGED IN THE FUTURE'. (120)

Bogue, Donald Joseph, ed. SOCIOLOGICAL CONTRIBUTIONS TO FAMILY PLANNING RESEARCH. (133)

Bracey, John H., Meier, August and Rudwick, Elliott, eds. BLACK MATRIARCHY: MYTH OR REALITY? (143)

Broderick, Carlfred B. and Bernard, Jesse, eds. THE INDIVIDUAL, SEX AND SOCIETY. (153)

Broderick, Carlfred Bartholomew, ed. A DECADE OF FAMILY RESEARCH AND ACTION. (154)

Brody, Eugene B. et al. MINORITY GROUP ADOLESCENTS IN THE UNITED STATES. (155)

Bromley, David G. and Longino, Charles F., Jr., eds. WHITE RACISM AND BLACK AMERICANS. (158)

Burr, Wesley R., Hill, Reuben, Nye, F. I. and Reiss, Ira L. CONTEMPORARY THEORIES ABOUT THE FAMILY: VOLUME 1. RESEARCH-BASED THEORIES. (184)

Cade, Toni, comp. THE BLACK WOMAN: AN ANTHOLOGY. (190)

Chapman, Jane Roberts and Gates, Margaret, eds. WOMEN INTO WIVES: THE LEGAL AND ECONOMIC IMPACT OF MARRIAGE. (204) CHILD DEVELOPMENT FROM A BLACK PERSPECTIVE--CONFERENCE, JUNE 10-13, 1970, WASHINGTON, DC. (211)

Chunn, Jay I., ed. THE SURVIVAL OF BLACK CHILDREN AND YOUTH. (218)

Clark, Kenneth Bancroft. DARK GHETTO: DILEMMAS OF SOCIAL POWER. (220)

Clarke, John Henrik, ed. BLACK FAMILIES IN THE AMERICAN ECONOMY. (226)

Conference on Maryland History, 1st, Annapolis, 1974. LAW, SOCIETY, AND
POLITICS IN EARLY MARYLAND. PROCEEDINGS OF THE FIRST CONFERENCE ON
MARYLAND HISTORY, JUNE 14-15, 1974, edited by Aubrey C. Land, Loris
Green Carr and Edward C. Papenfuge. (240)
Dorsett-Robinson, Jean, ed. THE BLACK ELDERS: WORKSHOP AND CONFERENCE
PROCEEDINGS. CONDUCTED BY THE COMMUNITY SERVICES PROGRAM TO PROVIDE
QUALITY CARE TO THE AGED. (295)
Duberman, Lucile, ed. GENDER AND SEX IN SOCIETY. (299)
Frazier, Edward Franklin, ed. ON RACE RELATIONS: SELECTED
WRITINGS. (353)
Gary, Lawrence E., ed. BLACK MEN. (363)
Gary, Lawrence E. and Brown, Lee, P., eds. CRIME AND ITS IMPACT ON THE
BLACK COMMUNITY. (367)
Glasser, Paul H. and Glasser, Lois N., eds. FAMILIES IN CRISIS. (385)
Gochros, Harvey L. and Gochros, Jean S., eds. THE SEXUALLY
OPPRESSED. (387)
Goldstein, Rhoda L., ed. BLACK LIFE AND CULTURE IN THE UNITED
STATES. (391)
Gordon, Vivian Verdell, ed. LECTURES: BLACK SCHOLARS ON BLACK
ISSUES. (396)
Gornick, Vivian and Moran, Barbara K., eds. WOMAN IN SEXIST SOCIETY:
STUDIES IN POWER AND POWERLESSNESS. (397)
Granger, Robert C. and Young, James C., eds. DEMYTHOLOGIZING THE
INNER CITY CHILD: PAPERS. (404)
Gwaltney, John Langston, ed. DRYLONGSO: A SELF-PORTRAIT OF BLACK
AMERICA. (427)
Hareven, Tamara K., ed. TRANSITIONS: THE FAMILY AND THE LIFE COURSE IN
HISTORICAL PERSPECTIVE. (457)
Harley, Sharon and Terborg-Penn, Rosalyn, eds. THE AFRO-AMERICAN WOMAN:
STRUGGLES AND IMAGES. (458)
Huggins, Nathan Irvin, Kilson, Martin and Fox, Daniel M., eds. KEY
ISSUES IN THE AFRO-AMERICAN EXPERIENCE. VOL 1.: TO 1877. (530)
Huggins, Nathan Irvin, Kilson, Martin and Fox, Daniel M., eds. KEY
ISSUES IN THE AFRO-AMERICAN EXPERIENCE. VOL 2: SINCE 1865. (531)
Institute of Society, Ethics and the Life Sciences. Research Group on
Ethics and Population. POPULATION POLICY AND ETHICS: THE AMERICAN
EXPERIENCE. A PROJECT OF THE RESEARCH GROUP ON ETHICS AND POPULATION
OF THE INSTITUTE OF SOCIETY, ETHICS AND THE LIFE SCIENCES, edited by
Robert M. Veatch. (546)
International Conference on Love and Attraction. Swansea, Wales,
1977. LOVE AND ATTRACTION: AN INTERNATIONAL CONFERENCE, edited by Mark
Cook and Glenn Wilson. (547)
International Family Research Seminar, 9th, Tokyo, 1965. FAMILIES IN
EAST AND WEST: SOCIALIZATION PROCESS AND KINSHIP TIES, edited by
Reuben Hill and Rene Konig. (548)
Iowa. State University of Science and Technology, Ames. College of Home
Economics. FAMILIES OF THE FUTURE. (550)
Jackson, Anthony W., ed. BLACK FAMILIES AND THE MEDIUM OF
TELEVISION. (556)
Jackson, Jacquelyne Johnson, ed. AGING BLACK WOMEN: SELECTED READINGS
FOR NCBA. (559)
Jackson, Jacquelyne Johnson, Childs, Faith Hampton and Ficker, Robin,
eds. AGING BLACK WOMEN: SELECTED READINGS FOR NCBA. (561)
Jones, Reginald Lanier, ed. BLACK PSYCHOLOGY. (602)
Lerner, Gerda, comp. BLACK WOMEN IN WHITE AMERICA: A DOCUMENTARY
HISTORY. (653)

KEY WORD INDEX

A Discriminant Analysis of Sociocultural, Motivation, and Personality
   Differences among Black, Anglo and Chicana Female Drug Abusers in a
   Medium Security Prison (255)
Differences in Marital Instability among Mexican Americans, Blacks,
   and Anglos: 1960 and 1970 (307)
Comparison of the Parenting Attitudes, Conflict Management Styles, and
   Interpersonal Behavior Patterns of Anglo, Black and Mexican-American
   Parents (616)
Sex Role, Decision Making Practices, Marital Satisfaction and Family
   Problems with Economically Disadvantaged Anglo, Black, and Chicano
   Couples (721)
ANGRY
The Myth of Black Macho: A Response to Angry Black Feminists (996)
ANTEBELLUM
The Slave Community: Plantation Life in the Antebellum South (125)
The Slave Community: Plantation Life in the Antebellum South (126)
Culture, Conflict and Community: The Meaning of Power on an Antebellum
   Plantation (330)
Black Bostonians: Family Life and Community Struggle in the Antebellum
   North (523)
A Cultural Middle Passage: Slave Marriage and Family in the Antebellum
   South (597)
The Sexual Life of the Oppressed: An Examination of the Family Life of
   Antebellum Slaves (632)
A Slave Family in the Antebellum South (929)
Female Slaves: Sex Roles and Status in the Antebellum Plantation South
   (1105)
ANTECEDENTS
The Family Antecedents of Adolescent Mobility Aspirations (23)
Antecedents of Self-Satisfaction and Marital Stability among Black
   Males (735)
Self-Satisfaction and Marital Stability among Black Males:
   Socioeconomic and Demographic Antecedents (737)
ANTHROPOLOGICAL, ANTHROPOLOGIST
The Black Family, Poverty, and Family Planning: Anthropological
   Impressions (151)
Herbert Gutman's THE BLACK FAMILY IN SLAVERY AND FREEDOM, 1750-1925:
   An Anthropologist's View (417)
An Anthropological Assessment of Bonding: Mother Infant Attachment
   Behavior in a Study of Forty Adolescent Black and White Mothers from
   Delivery through Six Months (601)
ANTI SLAVERY
Keeping the Faith and Disturbing the Peace. Black Women: From Anti-
   Slavery to Women's Suffrage (234)
ANXIETY
Ethnic Differences in Mothers' Anxiety (914)
ARITHMETIC
Does Living with a Female Head of Household Affect the Arithmetic
   Achievement of Black Fourth-Grade Pupils? (575)
ARRESTS
Arrests and Delinquency in Two Generations: A Study of Black Urban
   Families and Their Children (887)
ASPIRATION(S)
The Family Antecedents of Adolescent Mobility Aspirations (23)
Lower-Class Negro Mothers' Aspirations for Their Children (92)
Aspiration Levels of and for Children: Age, Sex, Race, Socioeconomic
   Correlates (160)

Attitudes toward Marriage Counseling: A Study of Middle and
    Lower Class Blacks (449)
Black/White and Socioeconomic Status as Factors in Maternal Attitudes
    toward Childrearing Practices and the Use of Health Care in Families
    with and without an Educable Mentally Retarded Child (463)
Attitudes of Married Women toward Work and Family: Comparison by
    Stress Level, Race and Work Status (474)
Sexual Knowledge, Attitudes, and Practices of Black Unwed Fathers
    (491)
Attitudes of Black Teenagers and Their Mothers toward Selected
    Contemporary Issues (522)
The Attitudes of Black Females toward Upper and Lower Class Black
    Males (567)
The Impact of Newborn Sickle Cell Testing on Maternal Attitudes toward
    Childrearing: A Simulation Study (603)
White Over Black: American Attitudes toward the Negro, 1550-1812 (605)
Comparison of the Parenting Attitudes, Conflict Management Styles, and
    Interpersonal Behavior Patterns of Anglo, Black and Mexican-American
    Parents (616)
Childrearing Attitudes and Observed Behaviors of Black Fathers with
    Kindergarten Daughters (634)
Attitudes toward Marriage and Family among Black Males in Tally's
    Corner (667)
The New England Puritan Attitude toward Black Slavery (690)
Sex-Role Attitudes and Stereotypes among Black College Students (683)
Attitudes toward Abortion: Experiences of Selected Black and White
    Women (719)
Correlates of Males Attitudes toward Family Planning (747)
Maternal Attitudes in a Poverty Area (803)
Black Child, White Child: The Development of Racial Attitudes (852)
The Childrearing Attitudes of Disadvantaged Negro Mothers and Some
    Educational Implications (861)
Black and White Single Parents' Attitudes toward Traditional Family
    Relations (916)
Black Attitudes toward Transracial Adoption (962)
A Study of the Influence of Liberal-Conservative Attitudes on the
    Premarital Sexual Standards of Different Racial, Sex-Role and
    Social Class Groupings (1015)
The Effects of a Marriage Education Course on the Attitudes toward
    Marriage and Cohabitation of Black American College Students (1037)
Young Black Adults: Liberation and Family Attitudes (1041)
The Effects of Familial Support Systems on Black Mothers' Childrearing
    Attitudes and Behaviors, and on Their Children's Competence (1049)
Parent-Child Relations, Achievement Motivation, and Sex-Role Attitudes
    among Black and White Professional Women in Traditional and Pioneer
    Occupations (1139)
Ethnic Differences in Family Attitudes towards Psychotic
    Manifestations, with Implications for Treatment Programmes (1144)
AUTHORITY
Race, Maternal Authority and Adolescent Aspiration (609)
The Northern United States Negro Matriarchy: Status Versus Authority
    (928)
Police Authority and the Low-Income Black Family: An Area Needed
    Research (933)
AUTOBIOGRAPHICAL, AUTOBIOGRAPHY
Conscious Agents of Time and Self: The Lives and Styles of African-
    American Women as Seen through Their Autobiographical Writings (123)

Changes in Black Sons and Daughters: A Panel Analysis of Black
  Adolescents' Orientations toward Their Fathers (801)
Persistence, Continuity and Change in the Jamaican Working-Class
  Family (823)
Marriage and the Family: A Critical Analysis and Proposals for Change
  (832)
The Changing World View of Minority Migrants in an Urban Setting (949)
Public Policy and the Changing Status of Black Families (999)
The World of Black Singles: Changing Patterns of Male/Female Relations
  (1004)
Interracial Dating: Willingness to Violate a Changing Norm (1027)
Changing Image of the Family (1053)
Changing Family Patterns of Blacks, Chicanos, and Whites: 1960-1970
  (1073)
CHARACTERISTICS
Husband's Characteristics and Marital Disruption in Black Families
  (438)
Characteristics of Black Women in Male and Female Headed Households
  (441)
An Inventory of Selected National Data Sources on the
  Social and Economic Characteristics of Black Families (507)
The Perceptions and Social Characteristics Related to Occupational
  Mobility of Black Women and Intraracial Assimilation of Blacks in
  America (583)
Childhood Characteristics of Black College Graduates Reared in Poverty
  (642)
Consciousness, Adaptability and Coping Strategies. Socioeconomic
  Characteristics and Ecological Issues in Black Families (800)
Characteristics of Negro Mothers in Single-Headed Households (818)
CHARACTERS
To Make a Woman Black: A Critical Analysis of the Women Characters in
  the Fiction and Folklore of Zora Neale Hurston (578)
CHARLESTON
The Mother-Headed Family among Free Negroes in Charleston,
  South Carolina, 1850-1860 (122)
CHICAGO
Lifelines: Black Families in Chicago (43)
Family Planning in the Negro Ghettos of Chicago (131)
CHICANA, CHICANO(S)
Identification, Imitation, and Sex-Role Preference in Father-Present
  and Father-Absent Black and Chicano Boys (51)
Childrearing by Black Parents: A Description and Comparison to Anglo
  and Chicano Parents (70)
Perceived Dominance in Decision-Making and Conflict Resolution among
  Anglo, Black, and Chicano Couples (252)
A Discriminant Analysis of Sociocultural, Motivation, and Personality
  Differences among Black, Anglo and Chicana Female Drug Abusers in a
  Medium Security Prison (255)
The Minority Woman's Voice: A Cultural Study of Black and Chicana
  Fiction (336)
Sex Role, Decision Making Practices, Marital Satisfaction and Family
  Problems with Economically Disadvantaged Anglo, Black, and Chicano
  Couples (721)
Changing Family Patterns of Blacks, Chicanos, and Whites: 1960-1970
  (1073)
CHILD   See also: Children
Children of the Storm: Black Children and American Child Welfare (114)

CHILD CARE
  Black Child Care: How to Bring Up a Healthy Black Child in America. A
    Guide to Emotional and Psychological Development (238)
  Patterns of Child Care among Black Families (381)
  The Impact of Adolescent Parenthood on Black Teenage Mothers and Their
    Families and the Influence of Two Alternative Types of Child Care
    (537)
  The Black Parents Handbook: A Guide to Healthy Pregnancy, Birth and
    Child Care (725)
CHILDBIRTH
  Childbirth in the Ghetto: Folk Beliefs of Negro Women in a North
    Philadelphia Hospital Ward (348)
CHILDHOOD
  An Analysis of Curriculum Offerings and Services Related to Child
    Abuse and Neglect in Early Childhood Teacher Preparation Programs at
    Historically Black Colleges and Universities (300)
  Childhood and the Cosmos: The Social Psychology of the Black African
    Child (322)
  Childhood Characteristics of Black College Graduates Reared in Poverty
    (642)
  Childhood Deviance as a Development Process: A Study of 223 Urban
    Black Men from Birth to 18 (888)
  Sex in the Childhood Years: Expert Guidance for Parents, Counselors
    and Teachers (906)
  Family and Childhood in a Southern Negro Community (1149)
CHILDLESSNESS
  Trend and Incidence of Childlessness by Race: Indicators of Black
    Progress Over Three Decades (414)
CHILDREARING
  New Dimensions in Ethnicity and Childrearing Attitudes (35)
  Childrearing by Black Parents: A Description and Comparison to Anglo
    and Chicano Parents (70)
  Exposure to Childrearing Experts: A Structural Interpretation of
    Class-Color Differences (127)
  Childrearing Practices of the Black Father (192)
  'The Means to Put My Children Through': Childrearing Goals and
    Strategies among Black Female Domestic Servants (288)
  Childrearing Reports of White, Black and Mexican-American Families
    (305)
  The Black Woman and Childrearing (430)
  Black/White and Socioeconomic Status as Factors in Maternal Attitudes
    toward Childrearing Practices and the Use of Health Care in Families
    with and without an Educable Mentally Retarded Child (463)
  The Ecology of Childrearing Patterns of Low to Moderate Income Black
    Families: The Development of Sociobehavioral Competencies in Black
    Children (494)
  The Impact of Newborn Sickle Cell Testing on Maternal Attitudes toward
    Childrearing: A Simulation Study (603)
  Childrearing Attitudes and Observed Behaviors of Black Fathers with
    Kindergarten Daughters (634)
  Childrearing among Low-Income Families (662)
  Nine Black Families: A Study of Household Management and Childrearing
    in Black Families with Working Mothers (837)
  The Childrearing Attitudes of Disadvantaged Negro Mothers and Some
    Educational Implications (861)
  Racism and Childrearing: A Study of Black Mothers (878)

The Effects of Familial Support Systems on Black Mothers' Childrearing
   Attitudes and Behaviors, and on Their Children's Competence (1049)
CHILDREN   See also: AFDC(Aid to Families with Dependent Children)
A Factorial Study of a Multidimensional Approach to Aggressive
   Behavior in Black Preschool Age Children (1)
College Students as Interventionists for Primary-Grade Children: A
   Comparison of Structured Academic and Companionship Programs for
   Children from Low-Income Families (13)
Race and Sex Differences in the Socialization of Male Children (25)
Children of Special Value: Interracial Adoption in America (37)
The Black Community as the Source of Children: A Theoretical
   Perspective (64)
Transracial Adoption: White Parents Who Adopted Black Children and
   White Parents Who Adopted White Children (78)
Development of the Self-Concept in Black and White Children (87)
Lower Class Negro Mothers and Their Children (90)
Lower-Class Negro Mothers' Aspirations for Their Children (92)
Children of the Storm: Black Children and American Child Welfare (114)
Black Children Just Keep on Growing: Alternative Curriculum Models for
   Young Black Children (121)
A Cross-Cultural Study of the Effects of Children on Parental
   Assessment of Past, Present and Future (136)
A Comparative Analysis of Vocabulary Diversity, Syntactic Maturity,
   and the Communicative and Cognitive Function of the Language of
   Black Four-Year-Old Children at Two Socioeconomic Levels (139)
Researching Children and Families: Differences in Approaches of Child
   and Family Specialists (157)
Aspiration Levels of and for Children: Age, Sex, Race, Socioeconomic
   Correlates (160)
Maternal Employment: Its Impact on the Sex Roles and Occupational
   Choices of Middle and Working Class Black Children (161)
The Relationship of Moral Conscience, Discipline and Culture among
   Black Children (170)
Strategies of Intervention with the Parents of "Acting Out" Preschool
   Black Children (173)
Transracial Adoption of Black Children (214)
A Comparison of Two Measures of Socioeconomic Status and Familial
   Factors as They Relate to Self Concept in Two Samples of Black Third
   and Fourth Grade Children (217)
The Survival of Black Children and Youth (218)
Family Life and School Achievement: Why Poor Black Children Succeed or
   Fail (221)
Family Structure and Political Socialization among Urban Black
   Children (225)
Black Children, White Dreams (244)
Comparison of a Family Microtraining Program and a Reading Program to
   Enhance Empathic Communication by Black Parents with Young Children
   (250)
Self-Concept and Mother-Concept in Black and White Preschool Children
   (265)
The Adoption of Black Children: Counteracting Institutional
   Discrimination (278)
'The Means to Put My Children Through': Childrearing Goals and
   Strategies among Black Female Domestic Servants (288)
Aspirations of Blacks and Whites for Their Children (294)
Black Children and Their Families: A Bibliography (303)

Prejudice among Negro Children as Related to Parental Ethnocentrism
and Punitiveness (321)
The Plight of Negro Children in America Today (328)
Trends in Racial Self-Image of Black Children: Psychological
Consequences of a Social Movement (332)
Effects of Gender and Race on Sex-Role Preferences of Fifth-Grade
Children (354)
The House of Refuge for Colored Children (357)
Imagining the World: The Reflections and Perceptions of Black Low-
Income Mothers in Relation to Their Involvements in the Educational
Lives of Their Children (401)
Black Children and the Political System (408)
Black Children, Self-Esteem, and the Liberation Movement (409)
Save the Children (413)
Adoption of Black Children by White Parents (415)
Black Children--White Parents: A Study of Transracial Adoption (416)
Skin Color Recognition, Preference and Identification in Interracial
Children: A Comparative Study (420)
Alternative Planning for Foster Care and Treatment of Children and
Adolescents in Crises (462)
The Black Child: A Parent's Guide to Raising Happy and Healthy
Children (468)
Parental Perceptions for Children: A Comparison of Black and White
Families (481)
The Effect of Family Size, Child Spacing and Family Density on Stress
in Low Income Black Mothers and Their Preadolescent Children (493)
The Ecology of Childrearing Patterns of Low to Moderate Income Black
Families: The Development of Sociobehavioral Competencies in Black
Children (494)
The Value of Children in U.S.: A New Approach to the Study of
Fertility (529)
Role of Maternal Nutritional Health and Care in the Development and
Personality of Children in Africa (543)
Age, Intelligence and Sex as Variables in the Conformity Behavior of
Negro and White Children (552)
Black/White Interracial Families: Marital Process and Identity
Development in Young Children (571)
Three Wishes of Black American Children: Psychosocial Implications
(624)
Rearing Children for Educational Achievement in Fatherless Families
(625)
Labeling Black Children: Social-Psychological Implications (636)
Mixed Families: White Parents and Black Children (637)
Intergenerational Interaction among Black Limited-Resource Middlescent
Couples, Adult Children, Aging Parents (649)
Fathers Without Children (668)
A Study of the Relationships between Family Interaction Patterns and
Imaginativeness in Disadvantaged Preschool Children (672)
Race, Identity, and Black Children: A Developmental Perspective (679)
The Influence of Family Relations upon Socially Desiring Behavior of
Black and Caucasian Preschool Children (692)
Parent-Child Correlations and Heritability of Stature in Philadelphia
Black and White Children 6-12 Years of Age (695)
The Influence of Increased Parent-Child Verbal Interaction on the
Language Facility of Preschool Inner-City Black Children (730)
A Comparative Study of the Self-Concept of Transracially and
Inracially Adopted Black Children (732)

A Comparison of Eight-Year-Old Children Born to Young Black
Adolescents and Those Born to Comparable Mothers in Their Early
Twenties (769)
Differential Contribution of Stature Phenotypes to Assortative Mating
in Parents of Philadelphia Black and White School Children (775)
Resistance to Temptation in Young Negro Children (777)
Tayari: Black Homes for Black Children (791)
Black Children Adopted by White Families (792)
Illegitimacy: A Comparative Follow-Up Study. A Matched Group of 120
Six to Eight Year-Old Negro Illegitimate Children and Their Mothers
Is Compared to a Group of 120 Legitimate Six to Eight Year-Old Negro
Children and Their Mothers on Measures of Child Development and
Mothering Behavior (810)
Social Contact of Minority Parents and Their Children's Acceptance by
Classmates (811)
The Drifters: Children of Disorganized Lower-Class Families, by
Charles A. Malone and Others (824)
Home is a Dirty Street: The Social Oppression of Black Children (828)
Some Observations Concerning Black Children Living in a Residential
Care Agency (831)
Negro-White Differences in Decisions Regarding Illegitimate Children
(847)
Cognitive Styles of Children of Three Ethnic Groups in the United
States (866)
Family Size and Sex Preferences of Children: A Biracial Comparison
(868)
School Children in the Urban Slum: Readings in Social Science Research
(883)
Arrests and Delinquency in Two Generations: A Study of Black Urban
Families and Their Children (887)
Ethnic and Social Class Differences in Children's Sex-Role Concepts
(893)
Parental Schemata of Negro Primary School Children (903)
Matricentric Family Structure and the Self-Attitudes of Negro Children
(908)
An Investigation into the Self-Concepts of Lower and Middle-Class
Black and White Kindergarten Children (915)
I.Q. Test Performance of Black Children Adopted by White Families
(923)
Effects of Father Absence on the Educational Achievement of Urban
Black Children (930)
Father Absence and Its Apparent Effect on the Reading Achievement of
Black Children from Low-Income Families (931)
Home Start: Family-Centered Preschool Enrichment for Black and White
Children (942)
Regional Differences in Personality of Afro-American Children (946)
Familial, Situational, and Cognitive Determinants of Sharing Behavior
in African American Children (950)
Children of the Dark Ghetto: A Developmental Psychology (959)
An Assessment of Racial Awareness, Preference, and Self-Identity among
White and Adopted Non-White Children (963)
The Impact of Selected Internal and External Influences on Successful
Coping among Mothers of Children with Sickle Cell Disease (974)
A Heuristic Study of Black Female Heads of Households and Black
Females Who Are Not Heads of Households and Their Involvement with
Their Children's Educational Development in Camden, New Jersey (976)

An Analysis of Curriculum Offerings and Services Related to Child
Abuse and Neglect in Early Childhood Teacher Preparation Programs at
Historically Black Colleges and Universities (300)
Black Consciousness, Identity and Achievement: A Study of Students in
Historically Black Colleges (422)
Race, SES Contexts and Fulfillment of College Aspirations (633)
"Woman-Lady" Concept in the Dating Process among Black College Youth
(827)
Ethnic Differences in the Impact of Family Background Factors on Level
of Education and College Completion (938)
Patterns of Interracial Dating and Sexual Liaison of White and Black
College Men (944)
Socialization and Career Orientation among Black and White College
Women (1055)
COLLEGE GRADUATES
Childhood Characteristics of Black College Graduates Reared in Poverty
(642)
COLLEGE STUDENT(S)
College Students as Interventionists for Primary-Grade Children: A
Comparison of Structured Academic and Companionship Programs for
Children from Low-Income Families (13)
Marital Satisfaction: A Comparative Study of Black and White
College Students' Attitudes toward Marriage (34)
Black Theology and the Black College Student (239)
Black Consciousness, Identity and Achievement: A Study of Students in
Historically Black Colleges (422)
Negro Student Rebellion against Parental Political Beliefs (657)
Sex-Role Attitudes and Stereotypes among Black College Students (683)
The Relationship of Family--Non-Family Support to the Academic
Performance of Urban Black Disadvantaged College Students (696)
Instrumental and Expressive Values in Mate Selection of Black and
White College Students (736)
Alternatives in Intimacy, Marriage, and Family Lifestyles: Preferences
of Black College Students (867)
Instrumental and Expressive Values in Mate Selection among Black
College Students (869)
The Effects of a Marriage Education Course on the Attitudes toward
Marriage and Cohabitation of Black American College Students (1037)
The Political Implications of Social Stereotyping of Women and Men
among Black and White College Students (1056)
COLOMBIA
Kinship, Mating and Family in the Choco' of Colombia: An Afro-American
Adaptation (1115)
COLONIAL, COLONIALISM
Slave Families on a Rural Estate in Colonial Brazil (403)
Race and Family Violence: The Internal Colonialism Perspective (1011)
COLOR
"Black is Beautiful" and the Color Preferences of Afro-American Youth
(36)
Color Gradation and Attitudes among Middle-Income Negroes (355)
Skin Color Recognition, Preference and Identification in Interracial
Children: A Comparative Study (420)
Race, Color and the Young Child (1123)
COLORADO
The Acculturation of the First-Generation Black Professional Woman: A
Denver, Colorado Area Study (368)

COMPARATIVE
  Marital Satisfaction: A Comparative Study of Black and White
    College Students' Attitudes toward Marriage (34)
  Black Women and White Women: Comparative Analysis of. Perceptions of
    Sex Roles for Self, Ideal Self and the Ideal Male (134)
  A Comparative Analysis of Vocabulary Diversity, Syntactic Maturity,
    and the Communicative and Cognitive Function of the Language of
    Black Four-Year-Old Children at Two Socioeconomic Levels (139)
  A Comparative Study of Black and White Homosexuals (202)
  Premarital Coitus and the Southern Black: A Comparative View (215)
  Slavery in Brazil and the United States: An Essay in Comparative
    History (281)
  A Comparative Study on the Assertiveness of Black and White Women at
    the University Level (362)
  Policy Decisions in the Aid to Families with Dependent Children
    Program: A Comparative State Analysis (365)
  Comparative Analysis of Black and White Women's Sex-Role Attitudes
    (418)
  Skin Color Recognition, Preference and Identification in Interracial
    Children: A Comparative Study (420)
  Black Girls: A Comparative Analysis of Self-Perception and Achievement
    by Race, Sex and Socioeconomic Background (451)
  Comparative Lifestyles and Family and Friend Relationships among Older
    Black Women (564)
  A Comparative Study of the Womanhood Experiences of Black Young Adult
    Females and White Young Adult Females (589)
  Comparative Lifestyles of the Black Female in the United States and
    the Black Female in Lesotho (610)
  Comparative Perspectives of Third World Women: The Impact of Race,
    Sex, and Class (673)
  A Comparative Study of the Self-Concept of Transracially and
    Inracially Adopted Black Children (732)
  Comparative Studies of Blacks and Whites in the United States (741)
  Comparative Estimates of Teenage Illegitimacy in the United States,
    1940-44 to 1970-74 (804)
  Illegitimacy: A Comparative Follow-Up Study. A Matched Group of 120
    Six to Eight Year-Old Negro Illegitimate Children and Their Mothers
    Is Compared to a Group of 120 Legitimate Six to Eight Year-Old Negro
    Children and Their Mothers on Measures of Child Development and
    Mothering Behavior (810)
  Intermarriage and Interethnic Relations: A Comparative Study (826)
  A Comparative Analysis of Black and White Urban Households and Help
    Seeking Behavior (1030)
  A Comparative Study of School Performance among Boys from Broken and
    Intact Black Families (1090)
  Father-Absent and Father-Present Lower Class Negro Families: A
    Comparative Study of Family Functioning (1091)
  Dating Frequency, Ethnicity, and Adjustment in the High School: A
    Comparative Study (1125)
COMPENSATORY
  Black Males and the Tough Guy Image: A Dysfunctional Compensatory
    Adaptation (809)
COMPETENCE, COMPETENCIES, COMPETENCY
  Socialization Practices Associated with Dimension of Competence in
    Preschool Boys and Girls (77)
  Self-Perceived Competency in Cross-Cultural Counseling (203)
  Personality Competence in Black Adolescents (412)

CONTROL
  Female-Headed Families: Personal Fate Control and the Provider Role
    (138)
  "Playing the Dozens": A Mechanism for Social Control (651)
  The Effects of Internal/External Control as Perceived by Black Couples
    in Interpersonal Conflict (1052)
  Birth Control and the Black American: A Matter of Genocide (1097)
  Genocide? Birth Control and the Black American (1098)
COOPERATION
  Cooperation and Solidarity as Survival Necessities in a Black Urban
    Community (750)
COPE, COPING
  Blacks at Middle and Late Life: Resources and Coping (378)
  Coping with Male/Female Alienation in the Coming of Bad Years (454)
  Analyzing Black Coping Styles: A Supplemental Diagnostic System (461)
  Interrole Conflict, Coping Strategies, and Satisfaction among Black
    Working Wives (469)
  Unmarried Adolescent Fathers: Problems They Face and the Ways They
    Cope with Them. Final Report (492)
  Black Women: Do They Cope Better? (786)
  Consciousness, Adaptability and Coping Strategies. Socioeconomic
    Characteristics and Ecological Issues in Black Families (800)
  Interracial Adoptions: Family Profile, Motivation and Coping Methods
    (825)
  The Impact of Selected Internal and External Influences on Successful
    Coping among Mothers of Children with Sickle Cell Disease (974)
CORREGIDORA
  The Soul of Black Women: The Hermeneutical Method of Analysis as
    Applied to the Novel "Corregidora" (186)
CORRELATES, CORRELATIONS
  Aspiration Levels of and for Children: Age, Sex, Race, Socioeconomic
    Correlates (160)
  Correlates of Conjugal Power: A Five Cultural Analysis of Adolescent
    Perceptions (176)
  The Absence of Birth Order Correlations among Unwed and Married Black
    First-Conceptors (292)
  Parent-Child Correlations and Heritability of Stature in Philadelphia
    Black and White Children 6-12 Years of Age (695)
  Correlates of Males Attitudes toward Family Planning (747)
  Correlates of Intercounty Variations in Net Migration Rates of Blacks
    in the Deep South, 1960-1970 (955)
  Some Correlates of Reported Academically Supportive Behaviors of Negro
    Mothers toward Their Children (1094)
COSMOS
  Childhood and the Cosmos: The Social Psychology of the Black African
    Child (322)
COUNSELING, COUNSELORS
  Self-Perceived Competency in Cross-Cultural Counseling (203)
  Counseling Black Adolescent Parents (380)
  Counseling and Treatment of the Poor Black Family (432)
  Attitudes toward Marriage Counseling: A Study of Middle and
    Lower Class Blacks (449)
  Stylistic Counseling of the Black Family (723)
  A Survey of a Sample of Black Families' Views of the Counseling
    Profession (734)
  Sex in the Childhood Years: Expert Guidance for Parents, Counselors
    and Teachers (906)

COUNTIES, COUNTY
  The First Decades of Freedom: Black Families in a Southern County,
    1870 and 1885 (9)
  Ethnicity and Infant Mortality in Texas Counties (694)
  The Household Composition of Rural Black Families: Louisa County,
    Virginia, 1880 (953)
COUPLES
  Perceived Dominance in Decision-Making and Conflict Resolution among
    Anglo, Black, and Chicano Couples (252)
  Marital Adjustment and Decision Making among Stable Black Married
    Couples (338)
  Transition to Parenthood by Black Couples (515)
  Self-Esteem among Southeastern Black American Couples (572)
  Factors Influencing the Marital Stability of Older Black Couples (586)
  Intergenerational Interaction among Black Limited-Resource Middlescent
    Couples, Adult Children, Aging Parents (649)
  Sex Role, Decision Making Practices, Marital Satisfaction and Family
    Problems with Economically Disadvantaged Anglo, Black, and Chicano
    Couples (721)
  The Occupational Class of Couples Entering into Interracial Marriages
    (759)
  Relationships of Black and White Golden Wedding Couples (822)
  The Effects of Internal/External Control as Perceived by Black Couples
    in Interpersonal Conflict (1052)
  Issues in the Treatment of Sexually Dysfunctioning Couples of Afro-
    American Descent (1142)
COURSE
  The Relationships between Socioeconomic Status, Sex, Self-Concept,
    Academic Achievement, and Course Selection of Urban Black Tenth-
    Grade Students (206)
  Transitions: The Family and the Life Course in Historical Perspective
    (457)
  The Effects of a Marriage Education Course on the Attitudes toward
    Marriage and Cohabitation of Black American College Students (1037)
COURTSHIP
  Black Male/White Female: Perspectives on Interracial Marriage and
    Courtship (1118)
CRIME
  Crime and Its Impact on the Black Community (367)
  Colloquium on Stress and Crime (754)
  Task Force Report: Juvenile Delinquency and Youth Crime: Report on
    Juvenile Justice and Consultants' Papers (1071)
CRISES, CRISIS
  Patterns of Crisis: Alabama White Families and Social Change 1850-1870
    (68)
  Invisible Again: Blacks and the Energy Crisis (167)
  Families in Crisis (385)
  The Crisis of Youth and Adult Responsibility (393)
  Alternative Planning for Foster Care and Treatment of Children and
    Adolescents in Crises (462)
  Crisis of the West Indian Family: A Sample Study (702)
CROSS CULTURAL, CROSS CULTURALLY
  A Re-examination of the Cross-Cultural Principles of Task Segregation
    and Sex Role Differentiation in the Family (41)
  A Cross-Cultural Study of the Effects of Children on Parental
    Assessment of Past, Present and Future (136)
  Extramarital Sex Norms in Cross-Cultural Perspective (163)

DECISION IMPLEMENTING
  Interrelationships of Value Orientation, Decision-Making Mode and
    Decision-Implementing Style of Selected Low Socioeconomic Status
    Negro Homemakers (310)
DECISION MAKING
  Perceived Dominance in Decision-Making and Conflict Resolution among
    Anglo, Black, and Chicano Couples (252)
  Interrelationships of Value Orientation, Decision-Making Mode and
    Decision-Implementing Style of Selected Low Socioeconomic Status
    Negro Homemakers (310)
  Marital Adjustment and Decision Making among Stable Black Married
    Couples (338)
  Sex Role, Decision Making Practices, Marital Satisfaction and Family
    Problems with Economically Disadvantaged Anglo, Black, and Chicano
    Couples (721)
DECISIONS
  Determinants of Negro Family Decisions in Management of Retardation
    (40)
  Policy Decisions in the Aid to Families with Dependent Children
    Program: A Comparative State Analysis (365)
  Family Buying Decisions: A Cross-Cultural Perspective (488)
  The Profile Analysis of Parent-Child Interaction in Families'
    Purchasing Decisions: A Cross-Cultural Study (577)
  Social Class, Work and the Family: Some Implications of the Father's
    Occupation for Familial Relationships and Sons' Career Decisions
    (770)
  Negro-White Differences in Decisions Regarding Illegitimate Children
    (847)
DEFICIT
  Cumulative Deficit: A Testable Hypothesis (579)
DELINQUENCY
  Race, Father-Absence, and Female Delinquency (47)
  The Black Matriarchy Controversy and Black Male Delinquency (834)
  Arrests and Delinquency in Two Generations: A Study of Black Urban
    Families and Their Children (887)
  Juvenile Delinquency and the Family: A Review and Discussion in the
    United States President's Commission on Law Enforcement and
    Administration of Justice (892)
  Matriarchy and Lower Class Negro Male Delinquency (896)
  Task Force Report: Juvenile Delinquency and Youth Crime: Report on
    Juvenile Justice and Consultants' Papers (1071)
  Family Background, Ethnicity, and Urban Delinquency (1084)
DEMOGRAPHIC, DEMOGRAPHY
  Demographic Components of Growth in White, Black, and Puerto Rican
    Female-Headed Families: Comparison of the Cutright and Ross/Sawhill
    Methodologies (243)
  Growth of the Black Population: A Study of Demographic Trends (325)
  Recent Findings in the Slave Demography and Family Structure (340)
  Self-Satisfaction and Marital Stability among Black Males:
    Socioeconomic and Demographic Antecedents (737)
  Herbert Gutman's THE BLACK FAMILY IN SLAVERY AND FREEDOM, 1750-1925:
    Demographic Perspectives (751)
DENSITY
  The Effects of Household Density on Subgroups (52)
  The Effect of Family Size, Child Spacing and Family Density on Stress
    in Low Income Black Mothers and Their Preadolescent Children (493)

Research in Black Child Development: Doctoral Dissertation Abstracts, 1927-1979 (784)

Black Child Development in America: 1927-1977: An Annotated Bibliography (785)

Illegitimacy: A Comparative Follow-Up Study. A Matched Group of 120 Six to Eight Year-Old Negro Illegitimate Children and Their Mothers Is Compared to a Group of 120 Legitimate Six to Eight Year-Old Negro Children and Their Mothers on Measures of Child Development and Mothering Behavior (810)

Black Child, White Child: The Development of Racial Attitudes (852)

Childhood Deviance as a Development Process: A Study of 223 Urban Black Men from Birth to 18 (888)

Children of the Dark Ghetto: A Developmental Psychology (959)

A Heuristic Study of Black Female Heads of Households and Black Females Who Are Not Heads of Households and Their Involvement with Their Children's Educational Development in Camden, New Jersey (976)

Black Family Life and Development (1006)

Black Youth and Psychosocial Development (1040)

Therapeutic Group Home Care for Adolescent Girls: An Interagency Development (1092)

The Developmental Psychology of the Black Child (1134)

DEVIANCE, DEVIANT

Factors Related to Deviant Health-Care Practices: A Study of Black Families in the Mississippi Delta (65)

Childhood Deviance as a Development Process: A Study of 223 Urban Black Men from Birth to 18 (888)

DIFFER, DIFFERENCE(S), DIFFERENT

Planned and Unplanned Fertility in a Metropolitan Area: Black and White Differences (39)

The Working Wife: Differences in Perception among Negro and White Males (49)

The Difference in Unwanted Births between Blacks and Whites (74)

Selected Research Studies and Professional Literature Dealing with Physiological, Socioeconomic, Psychological, and Cultural Differences between Black and White Males with Reference to the Performance of Athletic Skills (79)

Why Participation Rates of Black and White Wives Differ (88)

Exposure to Childrearing Experts: A Structural Interpretation of Class-Color Differences (127)

Negro-White Differences in Blue-Collar Marriages in a Northern Metropolis (130)

Researching Children and Families: Differences in Approaches of Child and Family Specialists (157)

A Discriminant Analysis of Sociocultural, Motivation, and Personality Differences among Black, Anglo and Chicana Female Drug Abusers in a Medium Security Prison (255)

Intermetropolitan Differences in Family Income Inequality: An Ecological Analysis of Total White and Nonwhite Patterns in 1960 (297)

Differences in Marital Instability among Mexican Americans, Blacks, and Anglos: 1960 and 1970 (307)

The Effect of Race, Sex and Career Goal Differences on Sex Role Attitudes at Home and at Work (361)

Differences between Negro and White Women in Marital Stability and Family Structure: A Multiple Regression Analysis (650)

Differences by Sex and Ethnicity in the Psychosocial Adjustment of the Elderly (674)

DUKE UNIVERSITY
  Symposium on the Family, Intergenerational Relations and Social
    Structure. Duke University, 1963. Social Structure and the Family:
    Generational Relations (948)
DURHAM
  Research Conference on Minority Group Aged in the South, Durham, NC,
    1971. Proceedings (560)
DYING
  The American Family: Dying or Developing? (877)
DYNAMIC(S)
  Housing and the Quality of Life in the Urban Community: A Focus on the
    Dynamic Factor Affecting Blacks in the Housing Market (177)
  African Roots in Black Families: The Social-Psychological Dynamics of
    Black Family Life and the Implications for Health Care (795)
  Race and Sex Differences in Career Dynamics (898)
  Some Dynamics of the Black Family (979)
DYSFUNCTIONAL, DYSFUNCTIONING
  Black Males and the Tough Guy Image: A Dysfunctional Compensatory
    Adaptation (809)
  Issues in the Treatment of Sexually Dysfunctioning Couples of Afro-
    American Descent (1142)
EARNINGS
  Effects of Community, Family and Education on Earnings of Black and
    White Men (263)
  Variations in Veteran/Nonveteran Earnings Patterns among WWII, Korea,
    and Vietnam War Cohorts (699)
EBONICS
  Ebonics: The True Language of Black Folks (1124)
ECOLOGICAL, ECOLOGY
  Intermetropolitan Differences in Family Income Inequality: An
    Ecological Analysis of Total White and Nonwhite Patterns in 1960
    (297)
  The Ecology of Childrearing Patterns of Low to Moderate Income Black
    Families: The Development of Sociobehavioral Competencies in Black
    Children (494)
  Consciousness, Adaptability and Coping Strategies. Socioeconomic
    Characteristics and Ecological Issues in Black Families (800)
ECONOMIC, ECONOMICALLY, ECONOMICS, ECONOMY
  Racial Differences in Family Living Arrangements and Economic Well-
    Being: An Analysis of Recent Trends (104)
  Fertility and the Household Economy in Nigeria (191)
  Women into Wives: The Legal and Economic Impact of Marriage (204)
  Black Families in the American Economy (226)
  Time on the Cross: The Economics of American Negro Slavery (341)
  Economics of Black Widowhood (398)
  Female Slave Resistance: The Economics of Sex (512)
  Sex Role, Decision Making Practices, Marital Satisfaction and Family
    Problems with Economically Disadvantaged Anglo, Black, and Chicano
    Couples (721)
  Elderly Blacks and the Economy: Variables of Survival: "Personal
    Integration", "Style", "Pride and Positive Spirit" (808)
  Sex Roles, Economic Factors, and Marital Solidarity in Black and White
    Marriages (920)
  Black-White Reproductive Behavior: An Economic Interpretation (973)
ECONOMIC OPPORTUNITY
  Freedom, Economic Opportunity, and Fertility: Black Americans, 1860-
    1910 (733)

EXPRESSIVE
   On Black and White Family Patterns in America: Their Impact on the
      Expressive Aspect of Sex-Role Socialization (55)
   Expressive Functioning and the Black Family: Life and Domain
      Satisfaction of Black Women (57)
   Instrumental and Expressive Values in Mate Selection of Black and
      White College Students (736)
   Instrumental and Expressive Values in Mate Selection among Black
      College Students (869)
EXTENDED
   The Role of Wife in the Black Extended Family: Perspectives from a
      Rural Community in the Southern United States (6)
   Social Change and Extended Family in the Black World: A Report on
      Research in Progress (7)
   Extended Families among Black Americans (42)
   Conjugal Relationships in the Context of the Black Extended Family
      (44)
   Occurrence of the Extended Family at the Origin of the Family of
      Procreation: A Developmental Approach to Negro Family Structure
      (335)
   Extended Kinship Relations in Black and White Families (480)
   The Black Extended Family Revisited (511)
   Kinship and Residential Propinquity: A Case Study of a Black Extended
      Family in New Orleans (553)
   Intergenerational Tensions and Extended Family Structures in Africa
      (656)
   The Black Extended Family (698)
   Black Women and the Extended Family Support Network (710)
   Extended Family Support of Single Black Mothers: Final Report (712)
   The Extended Family in Black Societies (954)
EXTENSIONS
   Black Gangs as Family Extensions (172)
EXTERNAL
   The Impact of Selected Internal and External Influences on Successful
      Coping among Mothers of Children with Sickle Cell Disease (974)
   The Effects of Internal/External Control as Perceived by Black Couples
      in Interpersonal Conflict (1052)
EXTRAMARITAL
   Extramarital Sex Norms in Cross-Cultural Perspective (163)
EYE
   The Bluest Eye: A Novel (768)
FACILITY
   The Influence of Increased Parent-Child Verbal Interaction on the
      Language Facility of Preschool Inner-City Black Children (730)
FACTOR(S)
   Factors Related to Deviant Health-Care Practices: A Study of Black
      Families in the Mississippi Delta (65)
   A Study of the Relationship of Certain Home Environmental Factors to
      High or Low Achievement in Reading among Black Primary School Age
      Pupils of Low Socioeconomic Status (76)
   Factors Related to Conceptions of the Male Familial Role by Black
      Youth (95)
   Black and White Families: Factors Affecting the Wife's Contribution to
      the Family Income Where the Husband's Income is Low to Moderate
      (137)
   Housing and the Quality of Life in the Urban Community: A Focus on the
      Dynamic Factor Affecting Blacks in the Housing Market (177)

Familial, Situational, and Cognitive Determinants of Sharing Behavior
  in African American Children (950)
The Effects of Familial Support Systems on Black Mothers' Childrearing
  Attitudes and Behaviors, and on Their Children's Competence (1049)
FAMILIAR
Familiar and Generational Patterns of Illegitimacy (1080)
FAMILISM
An Examination of the Effects of Ethnicity, Socioeconomic Status and
  Generation on Familism and Sex Role Orientation (464)
FAMILY CENTERED
Home Start: Family-Centered Preschool Enrichment for Black and White
  Children (942)
FAMILY INSTABILITY   See also: Family Stability
A Conceptual Analysis of Black Family Instability (241)
FAMILY KIN
Family-Kin Networks and Aging in Cross-Cultural Perspective (947)
FAMILY ROLES
Family Roles, Occupational Statuses, and Achievement Orientations
  among Black Women in the United States (24)
Work, Family Roles and Support Systems (389)
FAMILY SIZE
Black-White Differentials in Family Size Preferences among Youth (423)
The Value Stretch Hypothesis: Family Size Preferences in a Black
  Population (444)
The Effect of Family Size, Child Spacing and Family Density on Stress
  in Low Income Black Mothers and Their Preadolescent Children (493)
Minority Status and Family Size: A Comparison of Explanations (581)
Family Size and Sex Preferences of Children: A Biracial Comparison
  (868)
The Influence of Family Size on Learning Readiness Patterns of
  Socioeconomically Disadvantaged Preschool Blacks (943)
The Differential Attainment of Family Size Goals by Race (1100)
FAMILY STABILITY   See also: Family Instability
Family Stability and Occupational Success (302)
Family Stability: A Comparison of Trends between Blacks and Whites
  (326)
Of Blacks, Whites and Family Stability (506)
Interrelations among Family Stability, Family Composition, Residence
  and Race (739)
FAMILY STRUCTURE(S)
Class, Culture, and Family Organization: The Effects of Class and Race
  on Family Structure in Urban America (22)
Black Family Structure and Primary Relations (50)
Family Structure and Political Socialization among Urban Black
  Children (225)
Black Fertility and Family Structure in the U.S., 1880-1940 (313)
Black Family Structure and Its Effects on Adolescents (327)
Occurrence of the Extended Family at the Origin of the Family of
  Procreation: A Developmental Approach to Negro Family Structure
  (335)
Recent Findings in the Slave Demography and Family Structure (340)
Family Structures, Social Class and Cultural Values (496)
Family Structure and Educational Attainment: Sex Differences among
  Urban Blacks (534)
A Comparison of the Negro and White Family Structure in Low Income
  Families (621)

FUNCTIONAL, FUNCTIONING

Expressive Functioning and the Black Family: Life and Domain
Satisfaction of Black Women (57)

Family Functioning in the Low-Income Black Community (111)

Social Class and the Functional Health Status of the Aged Black Female
(308)

Family Functioning and Hypertension in a Black Population (350)

Social Class, Ethnicity, and Family Functioning: Exploring Some Issues
Raised by the Moynihan Report (371)

Kin Family Network: Overheralded Structure in Past Conceptualizations
of Family Functioning (377)

The Relationship between Hypertension and Psychosocial Functioning in
Young Black Men (841)

Family Functioning of Afro-Americans (842)

Father-Absent and Father-Present Lower Class Negro Families: A
Comparative Study of Family Functioning (1091)

Effects of Improved Housing on the Family Functioning of Large, Low-
Income Black Families (1099)

FUTURE, FUTURISTIC

Proceedings of 'Black Aged in the Future' (120)

A Cross-Cultural Study of the Effects of Children on Parental
Assessment of Past, Present and Future (136)

Families of the Future (550)

Future Directions for the Black Family (617)

Racial Differences in Female Labor-Force Participation: Trends and
Implications for the Future (771)

Polygamy: A Futuristic Family Arrangement for African-Americans (936)

The Psychology of Women: Future Directions in Research (951)

Black Families, Social Evaluations and Future Marital Relationships
(1058)

Four "Classic" Studies of Power Relationships in Black Families: A
Review and Look to the Future (1128)

GAME

Slavery and the Numbers Game: A Critique of TIME ON THE CROSS (426)

GANGS

Black Gangs as Family Extensions (172)

GAP

What Generation Gap? A Comparison of Some Generational Differences
among Blacks and Whites (174)

GENDER

Gender and Sex in Society (299)

Effects of Gender and Race on Sex-Role Preferences of Fifth-Grade
Children (354)

Class and Race Differences in Gender Roles (428)

GENEALOGY

Black Genealogy (1111)

GENERATION, GENERATIONAL, GENERATIONS

Time, Aging and Continuity of Social Structure: Themes and Issues in
Generational Analysis (94)

What Generation Gap? A Comparison of Some Generational Differences
among Blacks and Whites (174)

Ethnicity, Family Generational Structure and Intergenerational
Solidarity (459)

An Examination of the Effects of Ethnicity, Socioeconomic Status and
Generation on Familism and Sex Role Orientation (464)

Arrests and Delinquency in Two Generations: A Study of Black Urban
Families and Their Children (887)

A Heuristic Study of Black Female Heads of Households and Black
    Females Who Are Not Heads of Households and Their Involvement with
    Their Children's Educational Development in Camden, New Jersey (976)
HEALTH, HEALTHY
    The Collective Black Family: Barriers to Community Mental Health
        Services (4)
    Black Family Lifestyles and the Mental Health of Black Americans (31)
    Provisions for Health Care in the Ghetto: The Family Health Team (72)
    Family Factors in Black Adolescent Mental Health (193)
    Black Child Care: How to Bring Up a Healthy Black Child in America. A
        Guide to Emotional and Psychological Development (238)
    The Impact of Health Education on Acceptance of Family Planning
        Methods for Spacing by Lower Socioeconomic Primiparous Urban Women
        (285)
    Social Class and the Functional Health Status of the Aged Black Female
        (308)
    The Challenge for Mental Health Minorities and Their World Views (315)
    Mental Health: A Challenge to the Black Community (364)
    The Black Child: A Parent's Guide to Raising Happy and Healthy
        Children (468)
    Homicide among Black Males: Highlights of the Symposium Sponsored by
        the Alcohol, Drug Abuse, and Mental Health Administration,
        Washington, D.C. May 13-14, 1980 (517)
    Role of Maternal Nutritional Health and Care in the Development and
        Personality of Children in Africa (543)
    The Black Matriarchy: Healthy or Pathological? (716)
    The Black Parents Handbook: A Guide to Healthy Pregnancy, Birth and
        Child Care (725)
    Mental and Physical Health Problems of Black Women, Washington, D.C.,
        March 29-30, 1974. Proceedings. (738)
    Perspectives on Minority Group Mental Health (779)
    Introduction: Children and Families -- Cultural Differences and Mental
        Health (981)
    Women and Their Health: Research Implications for a New Era (1066)
    Racism and Mental Health: Essays (1132)
HEALTH CARE
    Factors Related to Deviant Health-Care Practices: A Study of Black
        Families in the Mississippi Delta (65)
    Provisions for Health Care in the Ghetto: The Family Health Team (72)
    Black/White and Socioeconomic Status as Factors in Maternal Attitudes
        toward Childrearing Practices and the Use of Health Care in Families
        with and without an Educable Mentally Retarded Child (463)
    Primary Health Care and the Black Family (705)
    African Roots in Black Families: The Social-Psychological Dynamics of
        Black Family Life and the Implications for Health Care (795)
HERITABILITY, HERITAGE
    Parent-Child Correlations and Heritability of Stature in Philadelphia
        Black and White Children 6-12 Years of Age (695)
    Interpreting the African Heritage in Afro-American Family Organization
        (1033)
HERMENEUTICAL
    The Soul of Black Women: The Hermeneutical Method of Analysis as
        Applied to the Novel "Corregidora" (186)
HETEROSEXUAL
    Social Heterosexual Development among Urban Negroes and Whites (152)

HEURISTIC
  A Heuristic Study of Black Female Heads of Households and Black
    Females Who Are Not Heads of Households and Their Involvement with
    Their Children's Educational Development in Camden, New Jersey (976)
HIGH SCHOOL
  Maternal Employment, Race, and Work Orientation of High School Girls
    (689)
  Dating Frequency, Ethnicity, and Adjustment in the High School: A
    Comparative Study (1125)
HIGH SCHOOL STUDENTS
  Family Socialization Perceptions among Black and White
    High School Students (45)
  Relative Effects of Low Socioeconomic Status, Parental Smoking and
    Poor Scholastic Performance on Smoking among High School Students
    (135)
  Sex-Role Factors in the Career Development of Black Female
    High School Students (275)
HISPANIC
  A Mere Reflection: The Psychodynamics of Black and Hispanic Psychology
    (856)
HISTORICAL, HISTORICALLY, HISTORIOGRAPHY, HISTORY
  Occupational Preferences and Expectations as Related to
    Locus of Control, Sex-Role Contingency Orientation, Race and Family
    History among College Women (185)
  The Black Family in Historical Perspective (227)
  Law, Society, and Politics in Early Maryland. Proceedings of the First
    Conference on Maryland History, June 14-15, 1974 (240)
  Reckoning with Slavery: A Critical Study in the Quantitative History
    of American Negro Slavery (264)
  Slavery in Brazil and the United States: An Essay in Comparative
    History (281)
  An Analysis of Curriculum Offerings and Services Related to Child
    Abuse and Neglect in Early Childhood Teacher Preparation Programs at
    Historically Black Colleges and Universities (300)
  Cliometrics and Culture: Some Recent Developments in the
    Historiography of Slavery (339)
  Sterilization and the Black Family: An Historical Perspective (407)
  Black Consciousness, Identity and Achievement: A Study of Students in
    Historically Black Colleges (422)
  Transitions: The Family and the Life Course in Historical Perspective
    (457)
  A Research Note on the Free Black Family in Our Early History (644)
  Black Women in White America: A Documentary History (653)
  Myths and Strengths of the Black Family: A Historical and Sociological
    Contribution to Family Therapy (685)
  Beautiful, Also, Are the Souls of My Black Sisters: A History of the
    Black Woman in America (794)
  The Social and Economic Status of the Black Population in the United
    States: An Historical View, 1790-1978 (1064)
HOME, HOMEMAKERS, HOMEOWNERS, HOMES
  A Study of the Relationship of Certain Home Environmental Factors to
    High or Low Achievement in Reading among Black Primary School Age
    Pupils of Low Socioeconomic Status (76)
  Interrelationships of Value Orientation, Decision-Making Mode and
    Decision-Implementing Style of Selected Low Socioeconomic Status
    Negro Homemakers (310)

Instrumental and Expressive Values in Mate Selection among Black
  College Students (869)
INTACT
  A Comparative Study of School Performance among Boys from Broken and
    Intact Black Families (1090)
INTEGRATED, INTEGRATION
  Household Differentiation and Integration as Predictors of Child
    Welfare in a Ghanaian Community (312)
  Elderly Blacks and the Economy: Variables of Survival: "Personal
    Integration", "Style", "Pride and Positive Spirit" (808)
  Perceptions of Black Parents in an Undesegregated Subdistrict of an
    Integrated School System (977)
  Sexual Racism: The Emotional Barrier to an Integrated Society (1020)
INTELLECTUALS
  What Black Intellectuals Misunderstand about the Black Family (456)
INTELLIGENCE
  The Effects of Race, Intelligence and Maternal Employment Status of
    the Career/Occupational Role Stereotypes of Four-Year Old Girls
    (165)
  Age, Intelligence and Sex as Variables in the Conformity Behavior of
    Negro and White Children (552)
INTERACTION, INTERACTIONAL, INTERACTIONS, INTERACTIVE
  And Ain't I a Woman Too! Interaction of Sex and Ethnicity in Black
    Women (60)
  Interactions of Black Inner-City Mothers with their Newborn Infants
    (168)
  An Expanded Case Study of Family Interaction and Transaction Roles of
    Middle-Class Black Mothers (247)
  The Relationship between Paternal Interaction Style and Infant
    Behavior as a Function of Social Economic Status and Sex of Infant
    (301)
  Home Climate in the Black Single-Parent Mother-Led Family: A Social-
    Ecological Interactional Approach (514)
  The Profile Analysis of Parent-Child Interaction in Families'
    Purchasing Decisions: A Cross-Cultural Study (577)
  Intergenerational Interaction among Black Limited-Resource Middlescent
    Couples, Adult Children, Aging Parents (649)
  A Study of the Relationships between Family Interaction Patterns and
    Imaginativeness in Disadvantaged Preschool Children (672)
  Black Father and Child Interactions (715)
  The Influence of Increased Parent-Child Verbal Interaction on the
    Language Facility of Preschool Inner-City Black Children (730)
  Analysis of Parent-Child Interaction in the Two-Child Black Family
    (788)
  Early Effects of Postpartum Intervention on Black Adolescent Mother-
    Infant Interaction (902)
  Marital Interaction Goals of Black Women: Strengths and Effects (909)
  Recent Life Event Stress and Patterns of Mother-Son Interaction in
    High Risk Versus Low Risk Black Mothers (967)
  Studying the Black Mother-Child Interaction: Issues and Alternatives
    (1141)
  Maternal Interactive Behavior as a Function of Race, Socioeconomic
    Status, and Sex of the Child (1150)
INTERAGENCY
  Therapeutic Group Home Care for Adolescent Girls: An Interagency
    Development (1092)

A Study of the Influence of Liberal-Conservative Attitudes on the
  Premarital Sexual Standards of Different Racial, Sex-Role and
  Social Class Groupings (1015)
LIBERATION
  The Impact of Women's Liberation on Marriage, Divorce and Family
    Lifestyles (594)
  The Liberation of Black Women (780)
  How to Get and Hold Your Black Man in Spite of Women's Lib (975)
  Toward a Sociology of Black Liberation (1013)
  Thy Neighbor's Wife, Thy Neighbor's Servants: Women's Liberation and
    Black Civil Rights (1026)
  Young Black Adults: Liberation and Family Attitudes (1041)
LIBERATION MOVEMENT
  Black Children, Self-Esteem, and the Liberation Movement (409)
LIFE SPAN
  Life-Span Development and Behavior. Volume 2 (58)
LIFELINES
  Lifelines: Black Families in Chicago (43)
LIFESTYLE(S)
  Black Family Lifestyles and the Mental Health of Black Americans (31)
  Black Alternative Lifestyles: Special Issue on Commentary and Reprise
    on Joseph Scott's Black Polygamous Family Formation (197)
  Alternative Intimacy, Marriage, and Family Lifestyles among Low-Income
    Black Americans (198)
  Race, Sex, and Alternative Lifestyle Choices (323)
  Comparative Lifestyles and Family and Friend Relationships among Older
    Black Women (564)
  The Impact of Women's Liberation on Marriage, Divorce and Family
    Lifestyles (594)
  Comparative Lifestyles of the Black Female in the United States and
    the Black Female in Lesotho (610)
  Lifestyles in the Black Ghetto (718)
  Alternatives in Intimacy, Marriage, and Family Lifestyles: Preferences
    of Black College Students (867)
LIMITED RESOURCE
  Intergenerational Interaction among Black Limited-Resource Middlescent
    Couples, Adult Children, Aging Parents (649)
LITERATURE
  Selected Research Studies and Professional Literature Dealing with
    Physiological, Socioeconomic, Psychological, and Cultural
    Differences between Black and White Males with Reference to the
    Performance of Athletic Skills (79)
  Black Family and Black Identity: A Literature Review (253)
  Black Adoption-Issues and Policies: Review of the Literature (691)
  A Review of the Literature Related to Family Therapy in the Black
    Community (707)
  Matriarchal Themes in Black Family Literature: Implications for Family
    Life Education (907)
  Sex Roles Research and Black Families: Some Comments on the Literature
    (939)
  Racial and Cultural Variations among American Families: A Decennial
    Review of the Literature on Minority Families (1005)
LOCATION
  Kinship and Ethnicity Viewed as Adaptive Responses to Location in the
    Opportunity Structure (390)

Culture, Class and Family Life among Low-Income Urban Negroes (663)

Nutrition and Low-Income Families (687)

Aspirations of Low-Income Mothers (726)

Marital Organization in Low-Income Families: A Cross-Race Comparison (813)

A Contingency Model of Marital Organization in Low Income Families (814)

The Effect of an Additional Birth on Low-Income Urban Families (846)

An Analysis of Upward Mobility in Low-Income Families: A Comparison of Family and Community Life among American Negroes and Puerto Rican Poor (912)

Father Absence and Its Apparent Effect on the Reading Achievement of Black Children from Low-Income Families (931)

Family Variables Associated with School Achievement in Low-Income Black First-Graders (932)

Police Authority and the Low-Income Black Family: An Area Needed Research (933)

A Study of Role Perceptions of Lower-Income Black Husbands in Black Families (1025)

Selfhood: Discovery of Survival Values in Low Income Black Families in Hartford, Connecticut. Two Case Studies Using Family Systems Theory (1093)

Effects of Improved Housing on the Family Functioning of Large, Low-Income Black Families (1099)

Low Income Black and White Mothers' Verbal Communication Patterns with Their Preschool Children (1112)

LOW SOCIOECONOMIC, LOWER SOCIOECONOMIC

A Study of the Relationship of Certain Home Environmental Factors to High or Low Achievement in Reading among Black Primary School Age Pupils of Low Socioeconomic Status (76)

Relative Effects of Low Socioeconomic Status, Parental Smoking and Poor Scholastic Performance on Smoking among High School Students (135)

The Impact of Health Education on Acceptance of Family Planning Methods for Spacing by Lower Socioeconomic Primiparous Urban Women (285)

Interrelationships of Value Orientation, Decision-Making Mode and Decision-Implementing Style of Selected Low Socioeconomic Status Negro Homemakers (310)

An Exploratory Investigation of the Relationship between Locus of Control and Parenting Tasks among Lower Socioeconomic Status Black Mothers (346)

Black and White Identity Formation: Studies in the Psychosocial Development of Lower Socioeconomic Class Adolescent Boys (473)

Influence of Expert and Peer upon Negro Mothers of Low Socioeconomic Status (900)

Disciplinary Techniques of Black Mothers of Higher and Lower Socioeconomic Status: A Questionnaire and Interview Study (918)

LOWER CLASS

Wives' Employment Status and Lower-Class Men as Husband-Fathers: Support for the Moynihan Thesis (14)

Lower Class Negro Mothers and Their Children (90)

The Lower-Class Negro Family in the United States and Great Britain: Some Comparisons (91)

Lower-Class Negro Mothers' Aspirations for Their Children (92)

Characteristics of Black Women in Male and Female Headed Households (441)

Growing Up Male in a Black Ghetto (445)

What Ghetto Males Are Like: Another Look (448)

Coping with Male/Female Alienation in the Coming of Bad Years (454)

Effects of Paternal Absence on Sex-Typed Behaviors in Negro and White Preadolescent Males (501)

Homicide among Black Males: Highlights of the Symposium Sponsored by the Alcohol, Drug Abuse, and Mental Health Administration, Washington, D.C. May 13-14, 1980 (517)

The Attitudes of Black Females toward Upper and Lower Class Black Males (567)

Family Planning of the Young Minority Male: A Pilot Project (588)

Attitudes toward Marriage and Family among Black Males in Tally's Corner (667)

Antecedents of Self-Satisfaction and Marital Stability among Black Males (735)

Self-Satisfaction and Marital Stability among Black Males: Socioeconomic and Demographic Antecedents (737)

Correlates of Males Attitudes toward Family Planning (747)

Occupational Differences among Black Male Cross-Regional Migrants from and to the South (790)

A Path Model for Feelings of Personal Efficacy for Black Employed Male and Female Familyheads, Employed Female Non-Familyheads, and Housewives (802)

Black Males and the Tough Guy Image: A Dysfunctional Compensatory Adaptation (809)

Social and Psychological Dimensions of the Family Role Performance of the Negro Male (819)

The Black Matriarchy Controversy and Black Male Delinquency (834)

Matriarchy and Lower Class Negro Male Delinquency (896)

Race and the Effect of Family Status among Male Agricultural Laborers (910)

Meaningful Male/Female Relationships in a State of Declining Sex-Ratio (945)

Black Masculinity: The Black Male's Role in American Society (989)

Male/Female Sexual Variations: Functions of Biology or Culture (992)

The World of Black Singles: Changing Patterns of Male/Female Relations (1004)

The Institutional Decimation of Black American Males (1024)

Growing Up Male in a Black Single-Parent Family (1117)

Black Male/White Female: Perspectives on Interracial Marriage and Courtship (1118)

The Black Male in America: Perspectives on His Status in Contemporary Society (1120)

MALE DOMINATED

Influences and Motivations for Black and White Women to Attain Positions in a Male-Dominated Profession (46)

MALONE

The Drifters: Children of Disorganized Lower-Class Families, by Charles A. Malone and Others (824)

MALTREATMENT

A Descriptive Analysis of Black and White Families Reported for Child Maltreatment (254)

MANAGEMENT

Determinants of Negro Family Decisions in Management of Retardation (40)

MARITAL INSTABILITY
  Jobs, Cash Transfers and Marital Instability: A Review and Synthesis
    of the Evidence (118)
  Differences in Marital Instability among Mexican Americans, Blacks,
    and Anglos: 1960 and 1970 (307)
  On the Transmission of Marital Instability in Black Families (486)
  The Intergenerational Transmission of Marital Instability: Comparisons
    by Race and Sex (849)
  Differentials in Marital Instability of the Black Population 1970
    (1036)
  Marital Instability by Race, Sex, Education, and Occupation Using 1960
    Census Data (1072)
  Marital Instability among Mexican Americans: Following the Patterns of
    Blacks? (1074)
MARITAL STABILITY   See also: Marriage
  Marital Stability and Patterns of Status Variables (98)
  Marriage and Marital Stability among Blacks (386)
  Factors Influencing the Marital Stability of Older Black Couples (586)
  Differences between Negro and White Women in Marital Stability and
    Family Structure: A Multiple Regression Analysis (650)
  Antecedents of Self-Satisfaction and Marital Stability among Black
    Males (735)
  Self-Satisfaction and Marital Stability among Black Males:
    Socioeconomic and Demographic Antecedents (737)
MARKET
  Housing and the Quality of Life in the Urban Community: A Focus on the
    Dynamic Factor Affecting Blacks in the Housing Market (177)
MARRIAGE(S), MARRIED   See also: Unmarried
  Woman-to-Woman Marriages in Africa and Afroamerica (8)
  Husbands' Marriage Order and the Stability of First and Second
    Marriages of White and Black Women (10)
  The Changing Nature of Interracial Marriage in Georgia: A Research
    Note (15)
  Interracial Marriages: Empirical and Theoretical Considerations (16)
  Race Differences in Husband-Wife Interpersonal Relationships during
    the Middle Years of Marriage (26)
  Marital Satisfaction: A Comparative Study of Black and White
    College Students' Attitudes toward Marriage (34)
  Research on International and Interracial Marriages (66)
  Note On Educational Homogamy in Negro-White and White-Negro Marriages,
    1960 (99)
  Marriage and Family among Negroes (100)
  Negro-White Differences in Blue-Collar Marriages in a Northern
    Metropolis (130)
  Dimensions of Verbal Racial Attitudes: Interracial Marriage and
    Approaches to Racial Equality (150)
  Alternative Intimacy, Marriage, and Family Lifestyles among Low-Income
    Black Americans (198)
  Women into Wives: The Legal and Economic Impact of Marriage (204)
  Age at Marriage: A Study of 400 Mothers Obtaining Maternity Services
    at a Metropolitan Teaching Hospital (207)
  Changing Family and Marriage Forms: Complications for Human Service
    Systems (231)
  AFDC and the Marital and Family Status of Ever Married Women Aged 15-
    44: United States, 1950-1970 (259)
  The Absence of Birth Order Correlations among Unwed and Married Black
    First-Conceptors (292)

MARYLAND
  Law, Society, and Politics in Early Maryland. Proceedings of the First
    Conference on Maryland History, June 14-15, 1974 (240)
  The Beginnings of the Afro-American Family in Maryland (627)
MASCULINE, MASCULINITY
  A Note on Father Absence and Masculine Development in Lower-Class
    Negro and White Boys (105)
  Black Masculinity: The Black Male's Role in American Society (989)
  Masculinity and Race: The Dual Dilemma of Black Men (993)
MASK
  Behind the Mask (402)
MASSACHUSETTS
  The Impact of Court-Ordered Busing on Black Families in Boston,
    Massachusetts (48)
  Captain Paul Cuffee, Master Mariner of Westport, Massachusetts, 1759-
    1817 (1116)
MATE
  Instrumental and Expressive Values in Mate Selection of Black and
    White College Students (736)
  Instrumental and Expressive Values in Mate Selection among Black
    College Students (869)
MATERNAL
  Maternal Employment: Its Impact on the Sex Roles and Occupational
    Choices of Middle and Working Class Black Children (161)
  The Effects of Race, Intelligence and Maternal Employment Status of
    the Career/Occupational Role Stereotypes of Four-Year Old Girls
    (165)
  Black/White and Socioeconomic Status as Factors in Maternal Attitudes
    toward Childrearing Practices and the Use of Health Care in Families
    with and without an Educable Mentally Retarded Child (463)
  Role of Maternal Nutritional Health and Care in the Development and
    Personality of Children in Africa (543)
  The Impact of Newborn Sickle Cell Testing on Maternal Attitudes toward
    Childrearing: A Simulation Study (603)
  A Study of the Social and Maternal Responsibility of a Group of Negro
    Unwed Mothers (604)
  Race, Maternal Authority and Adolescent Aspiration (609)
  Black Adolescents' Views of Maternal Employment as a Threat to the
    Marital Relationship, 1963-1973 (622)
  Maternal Employment, Race, and Work Orientation of High School Girls
    (689)
  Maternal Attitudes in a Poverty Area (803)
  Maternal and Child Pathology in an Urban Ghetto (1078)
  Maternal Interactive Behavior as a Function of Race, Socioeconomic
    Status, and Sex of the Child (1150)
  The Relation between Maternal Behaviors and Aggression in Sons: Black
    and Puerto Rican Families (1153)
MATERNITY
  Age at Marriage: A Study of 400 Mothers Obtaining Maternity Services
    at a Metropolitan Teaching Hospital (207)
MATING
  Differential Contribution of Stature Phenotypes to Assortative Mating
    in Parents of Philadelphia Black and White School Children (775)
  Residence, Kinship, and Mating as Survival Strategies: A West Indian
    Example (1110)
  Kinship, Mating and Family in the Choco' of Colombia: An Afro-American
    Adaptation (1115)

The Relationship between Hypertension and Psychosocial Functioning in Young Black Men (841)
Childhood Deviance as a Development Process: A Study of 223 Urban Black Men from Birth to 18 (888)
Patterns of Interracial Dating and Sexual Liaison of White and Black College Men (944)
Masculinity and Race: The Dual Dilemma of Black Men (993)
The Political Implications of Social Stereotyping of Women and Men among Black and White College Students (1056)
Black Men/White Women: A Philosophical View (1060)
MENARCHE
The Age of Slaves at Menarche and Their First Birth (1050)
MENTAL, MENTALLY
The Collective Black Family: Barriers to Community Mental Health Services (4)
Black Family Lifestyles and the Mental Health of Black Americans (31)
Family Factors in Black Adolescent Mental Health (193)
The Challenge for Mental Health Minorities and Their World Views (315)
Mental Health: A Challenge to the Black Community (364)
Black/White and Socioeconomic Status as Factors in Maternal Attitudes toward Childrearing Practices and the Use of Health Care in Families with and without an Educable Mentally Retarded Child (463)
Homicide among Black Males: Highlights of the Symposium Sponsored by the Alcohol, Drug Abuse, and Mental Health Administration, Washington, D.C. May 13-14, 1980 (517)
Mental and Physical Health Problems of Black Women, Washington, D.C., March 29-30, 1974. Proceedings. (738)
Perspectives on Minority Group Mental Health (779)
Introduction: Children and Families -- Cultural Differences and Mental Health (981)
Racism and Mental Health: Essays (1132)
METROPOLIS, METROPOLITAN
Planned and Unplanned Fertility in a Metropolitan Area: Black and White Differences (39)
Negro-White Differences in Blue-Collar Marriages in a Northern Metropolis (130)
Age at Marriage: A Study of 400 Mothers Obtaining Maternity Services at a Metropolitan Teaching Hospital (207)
The Poor Vs. the Non-poor: An Ethnic and Metropolitan-Non-metropolitan Comparison (631)
Race, Age, and Family Status Differentials in Metropolitan Migration of Households (778)
MEXICAN AMERICAN(S)
Aging, Social Class, and Ethnicity: A Comparison of Anglo, Black and Mexican-American Texans (128)
Changing Labor Force Participation of Mexican American Wives: A Comparison with Anglos and Blacks (242)
Childrearing Reports of White, Black and Mexican-American Families (305)
Differences in Marital Instability among Mexican Americans, Blacks, and Anglos: 1960 and 1970 (307)
A Longitudinal Study of the Self-Concepts of Euro-American, Afro-American, and Mexican American Preadolescent Girls (358)
Comparison of the Parenting Attitudes, Conflict Management Styles, and Interpersonal Behavior Patterns of Anglo, Black and Mexican-American Parents (616)

MIGRANT(S)
  Occupational Differences among Black Male Cross-Regional Migrants from
    and to the South (790)
  The Changing World View of Minority Migrants in an Urban Setting (949)
  The Social Security Rights of Migrant Workers and Their Families
    (1140)
MIGRATION
  Black Migration: Movement North, 1890-1920 (495)
  Race, Age, and Family Status Differentials in Metropolitan Migration
    of Households (778)
  Correlates of Intercounty Variations in Net Migration Rates of Blacks
    in the Deep South, 1960-1970 (955)
MILITANCY, MILITARY
  Militancy and Black Women's Competitive Behavior in Competitive vs.
    Non-Competitive Conditions (555)
  Black Families in the Military System (613)
  Black-White Differences in Social Background and Military Drug Abuse
    Patterns (789)
MINISTER
  Uplifting the Race: The Black Minister in the New South, 1865-1902
    (1103)
MINNEAPOLIS
  Withdrawal of Blacks and Whites from Public to Nonpublic
    Elementary Schools in Minneapolis (376)
MINORITIES
  Scale Construction in the Assessment of Sex-Role Stereotypes among
    Minorities (233)
  The Challenge for Mental Health Minorities and Their World Views (315)
  Minorities and Aging (558)
MINORITY
  Minority Group Adolescents in the United States (155)
  Ethnic Minority Family Research in an Urban Setting: A Process of
    Exchange (251)
  The Minority Woman's Voice: A Cultural Study of Black and Chicana
    Fiction (336)
  Research Conference on Minority Group Aged in the South, Durham, NC,
    1971. Proceedings (560)
  Minority Status and Family Size: A Comparison of Explanations (581)
  Race Differences in Age at First Birth and the Pace of Subsequent
    Fertility: Implications for the Minority Group Status Hypothesis
    (582)
  Family Planning of the Young Minority Male: A Pilot Project (588)
  Mortality among Minority Populations: A Review of Recent Patterns and
    Trends (697)
  The New Black Feminism: A Minority Report (704)
  Minority Families (714)
  Minority Status, Ethnic Culture, and Distress: A Comparison of Blacks,
    Whites, Mexicans, and Mexican Americans (746)
  Perspectives on Minority Group Mental Health (779)
  Social Contact of Minority Parents and Their Children's Acceptance by
    Classmates (811)
  Black Minority Racial Status and Fertility in the United States, 1970
    (844)
  Minority Status and Fertility Revisited Again: A Comment on Johnson
    (880)
  The Effect of Minority Group Status on Fertility: A Re-examination of
    Concepts (882)

Parent-Child Relations, Achievement Motivation, and Sex-Role Attitudes
among Black and White Professional Women in Traditional and Pioneer
Occupations (1139)

MOYNIHAN

Wives' Employment Status and Lower-Class Men as Husband-Fathers:
Support for the Moynihan Thesis (14)

Black Families and the Moynihan Report: A Research Evaluation (97)

Social Class, Ethnicity, and Family Functioning: Exploring Some Issues
Raised by the Moynihan Report (371)

The Moynihan Report and the Politics of Controversy: A Transaction
Social Science and Public Policy Report (865)

Moynihan: A Methodological Note (1035)

MULATTO

Black and Mulatto Mobility and Stability in Dallas, Texas, 1880-1910
(314)

MULTI ETHNIC

The Relationship of Parent Participation and Selected Variables in
Three Multi-Ethnic Elementary Schools in Dade County, Florida (96)

MULTIDIMENSIONAL

A Factorial Study of a Multidimensional Approach to Aggressive
Behavior in Black Preschool Age Children (1)

MUSIC

Perspectives on Black Families from Contemporary Soul Music: The Case
of Millie Jackson (1023)

MUSLIM

Black Muslim and Negro Christian Family Relationships (309)

MYTH(S)

Black Matriarchy: Myth or Reality? (143)

A Reexamination of the Myth of Black Matriarchy (287)

Black Matriarchy: Transforming a Myth of Racism into a Class Model
(293)

Science, Myth, Reality: The Black Family in One-Half Century of
Research (317)

Reality and Myth: Employment and Sex Role Ideology in Black Women
(419)

Persistent Myths about the Afro-American Family (424)

The Black Family: Myth and Reality (524)

The Matriarchy: Myth and Reality (606)

Myths and Strengths of the Black Family: A Historical and Sociological
Contribution to Family Therapy (685)

The Black Family--Perpetuating the Myths: An Analysis of Family
Sociology Textbook Treatment of Black Families (836)

The Myth of Black Macho: A Response to Angry Black Feminists (996)

The Myth of the Black Matriarchy (997)

Black Macho and the Myth of the Superwoman (1086)

Breakdown in the Negro Family: Myth or Reality (1104)

NAMES

Desirability of First Names, Ethnicity and Parental Education (187)

NATIONALIST

Adelaide Casely Hayford: Cultural Nationalist and Feminist (807)

NCBA (National Caucus on the Black Aged)

Aging Black Women: Selected Readings for NCBA. (559)

Aging Black Women: Selected Readings for NCBA (561)

NEED(S)

Differential Use of Reward and Punishment as a Function of Need
Achievement and of Fear of Failure in Black Mothers (437)

Role of Maternal Nutritional Health and Care in the Development and
Personality of Children in Africa (543)
Regional Differences in Personality of Afro-American Children (946)
PERSUASION
A Survey of the Black Woman and the Persuasion Process: The Study of
Strategies of Identification and Resistance (166)
PETERSBURG
Free Black Women and the Question of Matriarchy: Petersburg, Virginia,
1784-1820 (648)
PHENOMENOLOGICAL
African-American Polygynous Relatedness: An Exploratory Study
Utilizing Phenomenological Techniques (686)
PHENOTYPES
Differential Contribution of Stature Phenotypes to Assortative Mating
in Parents of Philadelphia Black and White School Children (775)
PHILADELPHIA
Childbirth in the Ghetto: Folk Beliefs of Negro Women in a North
Philadelphia Hospital Ward (348)
Parent-Child Correlations and Heritability of Stature in Philadelphia
Black and White Children 6-12 Years of Age (695)
Differential Contribution of Stature Phenotypes to Assortative Mating
in Parents of Philadelphia Black and White School Children (775)
PHYSICAL
Mental and Physical Health Problems of Black Women, Washington, D.C.,
March 29-30, 1974. Proceedings. (738)
PHYSIOLOGICAL
Selected Research Studies and Professional Literature Dealing with
Physiological, Socioeconomic, Psychological, and Cultural
Differences between Black and White Males with Reference to the
Performance of Athletic Skills (79)
PIMPS
Black Players: The Secret World of Black Pimps (743)
PIONEER
Parent-Child Relations, Achievement Motivation, and Sex-Role Attitudes
among Black and White Professional Women in Traditional and Pioneer
Occupations (1139)
PLACE
A Place on the Corner (38)
PLANNED, PLANNING, PLANS
Planned and Unplanned Fertility in a Metropolitan Area: Black and
White Differences (39)
Family Planning in the Negro Ghettos of Chicago (131)
Sociological Contributions to Family Planning Research (133)
The Black Family, Poverty, and Family Planning: Anthropological
Impressions (151)
Family Planning Program Effects on the Fertility of Low-Income U.S.
Women (258)
The Impact of Health Education on Acceptance of Family Planning
Methods for Spacing by Lower Socioeconomic Primiparous Urban Women
(285)
Alternative Planning for Foster Care and Treatment of Children and
Adolescents in Crises (462)
Comprehensive Family Planning Services to an Urban Black Community
(499)
Family Planning of the Young Minority Male: A Pilot Project (588)
Family Planning Services and the Distribution of Black Americans (608)
Correlates of Males Attitudes toward Family Planning (747)

POLITICIZING, POLITICS
  Law, Society, and Politics in Early Maryland. Proceedings of the First
    Conference on Maryland History, June 14-15, 1974 (240)
  A Case Study in Patriarchal Politics: Women on Welfare (544)
  Sex, Socialization and Politics (812)
  The Moynihan Report and the Politics of Controversy: A Transaction
    Social Science and Public Policy Report (865)
  Politicizing Black Children (1088)
POLYGAMOUS, POLYGAMY
  A Comment on Scott's "Black Polygamous Family Formation" (30)
  Black Alternative Lifestyles: Special Issue on Commentary and Reprise
    on Joseph Scott's Black Polygamous Family Formation (197)
  Commentary on Joseph Scott's "Black Polygamous Family Formation" (711)
  Black Polygamous Family Formation: Case Studies of Legal Wives and
    Consensual "Wives" (934)
  Polygamy: A Futuristic Family Arrangement for African-Americans (936)
POLYGYNOUS, POLYGYNY
  African-American Polygynous Relatedness: An Exploratory Study
    Utilizing Phenomenological Techniques (686)
  Conceptualizing and Researching American Polygyny--And Critics
    Answered (935)
POOR   See also: Poverty
  Relative Effects of Low Socioeconomic Status, Parental Smoking and
    Poor Scholastic Performance on Smoking among High School Students
    (135)
  Family Life and School Achievement: Why Poor Black Children Succeed or
    Fail (221)
  Impact of Social Security Taxes on the Poor (269)
  Child Neglect among the Poor: A Study of Parental Adequacy in Families
    of Three Ethnic Groups (384)
  Counseling and Treatment of the Poor Black Family (432)
  Living Poor: A Participant Observer Study of Priorities and Choices
    (576)
  The Poor Vs. the Non-poor: An Ethnic and Metropolitan-Non-metropolitan
    Comparison (631)
  Income Alternatives for Poor Families (655)
  An Analysis of Upward Mobility in Low-Income Families: A Comparison of
    Family and Community Life among American Negroes and Puerto Rican
    Poor (912)
  The Concept of Family in the Poor Black Community (984)
POPULATION(S)
  Family Life among the Free Black Population in the 18th Century (115)
  A Social-Psychological Analysis of Morale in a Selected Population:
    Low-Income Elderly Black Females (205)
  Growth of the Black Population: A Study of Demographic Trends (325)
  Family Functioning and Hypertension in a Black Population (350)
  The Value Stretch Hypothesis: Family Size Preferences in a Black
    Population (444)
  Population Policy and Ethics: The American Experience. A Project of
    the Research Group on Ethics and Population of the Institute of
    Society, Ethics and the Life Sciences (546)
  Mortality among Minority Populations: A Review of Recent Patterns and
    Trends (697)
  The Ethical and Moral Values of Black Americans and Population Policy
    (781)
  Estimates of Coverage of the Population by Sex, Race and Age in the
    1970 Census (958)

The Family Structure of the Older Black Population in the American
    South in 1880 and 1900 (972)
Differentials in Marital Instability of the Black Population 1970
    (1036)
The Social and Economic Status of the Black Population in the United
    States, 1971 (1062)
The Social and Economic Status of the Black Population in the United
    States, 1974 (1063)
The Social and Economic Status of the Black Population in the United
    States: An Historical View, 1790-1978 (1064)
Patterns of Marriage among the Black Population: A Preliminary
    Analysis of the Black Female (1107)
Population Policy and Growth: Perspectives from the Black Community--A
    Position Paper (1127)
Urban Population Distribution, Family Income, and Social Prejudice:
    The Long, Narrow City (1146)
POSTDIVORCE
The Postdivorce Adjustment of Middle Class Black Women (175)
POSTPARTUM
Early Effects of Postpartum Intervention on Black Adolescent Mother-
    Infant Interaction (902)
POVERTY
Poverty and the Older Woman: Reflections of a Social Worker (53)
The Black Family, Poverty, and Family Planning: Anthropological
    Impressions (151)
Families in Poverty in the Early 1970's: Rates, Associated Factors,
    Some Implications (212)
Poverty in America: A Book of Readings (333)
Factors Associated with the Poverty of Black Women (442)
Adolescent Pregnancy: Intervention into the Poverty Cycle (585)
Childhood Characteristics of Black College Graduates Reared in Poverty
    (642)
Maternal Attitudes in a Poverty Area (803)
Lower-Class Families: The Culture of Poverty in Negro Trinidad (891)
Employment, Race and Poverty (899)
Culture and Poverty: Critique and Counter-Proposals (1077)
Ida's Family: Adaptations to Poverty in a Suburban Ghetto (1109)
POWER
Father Power (106)
Correlates of Conjugal Power: A Five Cultural Analysis of Adolescent
    Perceptions (176)
Dark Ghetto: Dilemmas of Social Power (220)
Culture, Conflict and Community: The Meaning of Power on an Antebellum
    Plantation (330)
Woman in Sexist Society: Studies in Power and Powerlessness (397)
Conjugal Power Relations among Black Working Class Families (436)
Adolescent Perception of Power Structure in the Negro Family (620)
Oppression and Power: The Unique Status of the Black Woman in the
    American Political System (623)
The Power Relationship in Black Families and White Families (688)
Four "Classic" Studies of Power Relationships in Black Families: A
    Review and Look to the Future (1128)
POWERLESSNESS
Powerlessness and Regularity of Contraception in an Urban Negro Male
    Sample: A Research Note (75)
Woman in Sexist Society: Studies in Power and Powerlessness (397)

A Study of the Influence of Liberal-Conservative Attitudes on the
  Premarital Sexual Standards of Different Racial, Sex-Role and
  Social Class Groupings (1015)
PREMATURE
  Premature Conclusions Regarding Black and White Suicide Attempters: A
    Reply to Steele (86)
PRESCHOOL(S)
  A Factorial Study of a Multidimensional Approach to Aggressive
    Behavior in Black Preschool Age Children (1)
  Socialization Practices Associated with Dimension of Competence in
    Preschool Boys and Girls (77)
  Strategies of Intervention with the Parents of "Acting Out" Preschool
    Black Children (173)
  Self-Concept and Mother-Concept in Black and White Preschool Children
    (265)
  Nutritional Status of Preschoolers from Low-Income Alabama Families
    (298)
  A Study of the Relationships between Family Interaction Patterns and
    Imaginativeness in Disadvantaged Preschool Children (672)
  The Influence of Family Relations upon Socially Desiring Behavior of
    Black and Caucasian Preschool Children (692)
  The Influence of Increased Parent-Child Verbal Interaction on the
    Language Facility of Preschool Inner-City Black Children (730)
  Home Start: Family-Centered Preschool Enrichment for Black and White
    Children (942)
  The Influence of Family Size on Learning Readiness Patterns of
    Socioeconomically Disadvantaged Preschool Blacks (943)
  Low Income Black and White Mothers' Verbal Communication Patterns with
    Their Preschool Children (1112)
PRESSURE
  Work Status, Work Satisfaction, and Blood Pressure among Married Black
    and White Women (475)
PREVALENCE
  The Prevalence of Black-White Marriage in the United States, 1960 and
    1970 (484)
PREVENTION
  A Long-Term Solution to the AFDC Problem: Prevention of Unwanted
    Pregnancy (132)
PRIDE
  Elderly Blacks and the Economy: Variables of Survival: "Personal
    Integration", "Style", "Pride and Positive Spirit" (808)
PRIMARY GRADE
  College Students as Interventionists for Primary-Grade Children: A
    Comparison of Structured Academic and Companionship Programs for
    Children from Low-Income Families (13)
PRIMARY SCHOOL
  A Study of the Relationship of Certain Home Environmental Factors to
    High or Low Achievement in Reading among Black Primary School Age
    Pupils of Low Socioeconomic Status (76)
  Parental Schemata of Negro Primary School Children (903)
PRIMIPAROUS
  The Impact of Health Education on Acceptance of Family Planning
    Methods for Spacing by Lower Socioeconomic Primiparous Urban Women
    (285)

PRISON, PRISONERS, PRISONS
  A Discriminant Analysis of Sociocultural, Motivation, and Personality
    Differences among Black, Anglo and Chicana Female Drug Abusers in a
    Medium Security Prison (255)
  Pseudoheterosexuality in Prison and Out: A Study of the Lower Class
    Black Lesbian (337)
  Sex in Prison: The Mississippi Experiment with Conjugal Visiting (521)
  Prisoners' Families: A Study of Some Social and Psychological Effects
    of Incarceration on the Families of Negro Prisoners (925)
  The Black Family and the Prisons (980)
PROCREATION
  Occurrence of the Extended Family at the Origin of the Family of
    Procreation: A Developmental Approach to Negro Family Structure
    (335)
PROFESSIONAL
  Selected Research Studies and Professional Literature Dealing with
    Physiological, Socioeconomic, Psychological, and Cultural
    Differences between Black and White Males with Reference to the
    Performance of Athletic Skills (79)
  Positive Effects of the Multiple Negative: Explaining the Success of
    Black Professional Women (319)
  Women and Professional Careers: The Case of the Woman Lawyer (320)
  The Acculturation of the First-Generation Black Professional Woman: A
    Denver, Colorado Area Study (368)
  The Denver, Colorado Area Black Professional/Businesswoman's
    Perception of Her Communication with the Black Male (369)
  Professional Advocacy, Community Participation and Social Planning:
    The Case of the Unmarried Mother from the "Inside the Ghetto"
    Perspective (766)
  Supports in the Black Community: Black Unmarried Mothers Who Kept
    Their Babies and Achieved Their Educational and/or Professional
    Goals (1113)
  Parent-Child Relations, Achievement Motivation, and Sex-Role Attitudes
    among Black and White Professional Women in Traditional and Pioneer
    Occupations (1139)
PROFILE
  The Profile Analysis of Parent-Child Interaction in Families'
    Purchasing Decisions: A Cross-Cultural Study (577)
  Interracial Adoptions: Family Profile, Motivation and Coping Methods
    (825)
PROHIBITION
  Interracial Intimacy: Interracial Marriage--Its Statutory Prohibition,
    Genetic Import, and Incidence (1096)
PROMISELAND
  Promiseland: A Century of Life in a Negro Community (101)
PRONATULIST
  Public Assistance and Early Family Formation: Is There a Pronatulist
    Effect? (857)
PROPERTIES
  Portraits of Family and Kinship Relations among Black Americans: A
    Study in the Properties, Structures and Functions of Primary Groups
    (952)
PROPERTY
  This Species of Property: Slave Life and Culture in the Old South
    (815)

PROPINQUITY
  Kinship and Residential Propinquity: A Case Study of a Black Extended
    Family in New Orleans (553)
PROVIDER
  Female-Headed Families: Personal Fate Control and the Provider Role
    (138)
  Middle Income Black Fathers: An Analysis of the Provider Role (200)
PSEUDOHETEROSEXUALITY
  Pseudoheterosexuality in Prison and Out: A Study of the Lower Class
    Black Lesbian (337)
PSYCHODYNAMICS
  A Mere Reflection: The Psychodynamics of Black and Hispanic Psychology
    (856)
PSYCHOLOGICAL, PSYCHOLOGISTS, PSYCHOLOGY
  Black Americans: A Psychological Analysis (73)
  Selected Research Studies and Professional Literature Dealing with
    Physiological, Socioeconomic, Psychological, and Cultural
    Differences between Black and White Males with Reference to the
    Performance of Athletic Skills (79)
  Research Directions of Black Psychologists (142)
  Sex Role Attitudes and Psychological Outcomes for Black and White
    Women Experiencing Marital Dissolution (169)
  Black Child Care: How to Bring Up a Healthy Black Child in America. A
    Guide to Emotional and Psychological Development (238)
  Trends in Racial Self-Image of Black Children: Psychological
    Consequences of a Social Movement (332)
  Help the Human Experience: The Psychology of Women (540)
  Single Parent Mothers and Distress: Relationships between Selected
    Social and Psychological Factors and Distress in Low-Income
    Single Parent Mothers (542)
  Black Psychology (602)
  Some Psychological and Sociological Factors Influencing Motivation for
    Interracial Marriage (614)
  Social and Psychological Dimensions of the Family Role Performance of
    the Negro Male (819)
  A Mere Reflection: The Psychodynamics of Black and Hispanic Psychology
    (856)
  Prisoners' Families: A Study of Some Social and Psychological Effects
    of Incarceration on the Families of Negro Prisoners (925)
  The Psychology of Women: Future Directions in Research (951)
  Children of the Dark Ghetto: A Developmental Psychology (959)
  The Developmental Psychology of the Black Child (1134)
PSYCHOSOCIAL
  Black and White Identity Formation: Studies in the Psychosocial
    Development of Lower Socioeconomic Class Adolescent Boys (473)
  Three Wishes of Black American Children: Psychosocial Implications
    (624)
  Differences by Sex and Ethnicity in the Psychosocial Adjustment of the
    Elderly (674)
  The Relationship between Hypertension and Psychosocial Functioning in
    Young Black Men (841)
  Black Youth and Psychosocial Development (1040)
PSYCHOTIC
  Ethnic Differences in Family Attitudes towards Psychotic
    Manifestations, with Implications for Treatment Programmes (1144)

PUBLIC
  Withdrawal of Blacks and Whites from Public to Nonpublic
    Elementary Schools in Minneapolis (376)
  Aspects of the Family and Public Life of Antoine Dubuclet: Louisiana's
    Black State Treasurer, 1868-1878 (1079)
PUBLIC ASSISTANCE
  Marital Dissolution and Public Assistance Payments: Variations among
    American States (753)
  Public Assistance and Early Family Formation: Is There a Pronatulist
    Effect? (857)
PUBLIC POLICY
  Public Policy for the Black Community: Strategies and Perspectives
    (67)
  The Moynihan Report and the Politics of Controversy: A Transaction
    Social Science and Public Policy Report (865)
  Public Policy and the Changing Status of Black Families (999)
PUERTO RICAN
  Demographic Components of Growth in White, Black, and Puerto Rican
    Female-Headed Families: Comparison of the Cutright and Ross/Sawhill
    Methodologies (243)
  An Analysis of Upward Mobility in Low-Income Families: A Comparison of
    Family and Community Life among American Negroes and Puerto Rican
    Poor (912)
  The Relation between Maternal Behaviors and Aggression in Sons: Black
    and Puerto Rican Families (1153)
PUNISHMENT, PUNITIVENESS
  Prejudice among Negro Children as Related to Parental Ethnocentrism
    and Punitiveness (321)
  Differential Use of Reward and Punishment as a Function of Need
    Achievement and of Fear of Failure in Black Mothers (437)
PUPILS
  A Study of the Relationship of Certain Home Environmental Factors to
    High or Low Achievement in Reading among Black Primary School Age
    Pupils of Low Socioeconomic Status (76)
  Does Living with a Female Head of Household Affect the Arithmetic
    Achievement of Black Fourth-Grade Pupils? (575)
PURCHASING
  The Profile Analysis of Parent-Child Interaction in Families'
    Purchasing Decisions: A Cross-Cultural Study (577)
PURITAN
  The New England Puritan Attitude toward Black Slavery (690)
QUALITY OF LIFE
  Housing and the Quality of Life in the Urban Community: A Focus on the
    Dynamic Factor Affecting Blacks in the Housing Market (177)
QUASI ADOPTION
  A Study of Black Adoption Families: A Comparison of a Traditional and
    Quasi-Adoption Program (645)
RACE   See also: Racial
  Class, Culture, and Family Organization: The Effects of Class and Race
    on Family Structure in Urban America (22)
  Race and Sex Differences in the Socialization of Male Children (25)
  Race, Family Setting and Adolescent Achievement Orientation (27)
  Untangling the Effects of Race and Sex: The Disadvantaged Status of
    Black Women (32)
  Race, Father-Absence, and Female Delinquency (47)
  Women, Sex and Race: A Realistic View of Sexism and Racism (147)

Aspiration Levels of and for Children: Age, Sex, Race, Socioeconomic
  Correlates (160)
The Effects of Race, Intelligence and Maternal Employment Status of
  the Career/Occupational Role Stereotypes of Four-Year Old Girls
  (165)
Occupational Preferences and Expectations as Related to
  Locus of Control, Sex-Role Contingency Orientation, Race and Family
  History among College Women (185)
Race, Class, Network Embeddedness and Family Violence: A Search for
  Potent Support Systems (201)
Race, Motherhood, and Abortion (219)
Violence, Race and Culture (257)
Women, Race and Class (267)
Across the Boundaries of Race and Class: An Exploration of the
  Relationship between Work and Family among Black Female Domestic
  Servants (289)
Race, Sex, and Alternative Lifestyle Choices (323)
On Race Relations: Selected Writings (353)
Effects of Gender and Race on Sex-Role Preferences of Fifth-Grade
  Children (354)
The Effect of Race, Sex and Career Goal Differences on Sex Role
  Attitudes at Home and at Work (361)
Race, Sex, and Marital Status: Their Effect on Mortality (370)
Looking Ahead: Self Conceptions, Race and Family as Determinants of
  Adolescent Orientation to Achievement (394)
Trend and Incidence of Childlessness by Race: Indicators of Black
  Progress Over Three Decades (414)
Black Girls: A Comparative Analysis of Self-Perception and Achievement
  by Race, Sex and Socioeconomic Background (451)
Attitudes of Married Women toward Work and Family: Comparison by
  Stress Level, Race and Work Status (474)
Achievement Motivation, Race, and Social Class Influences upon Female
  Attributions (478)
Race, Daughters and Father-Loss: Does Absence Make the Girl Grow
  Stronger? (532)
Race and the Father-Son Connection: The Conditional Relevance of
  Father Absence for the Orientations and Identities of Adolescent
  Boys (535)
Race, Father Identification and Achievement Orientation: The
  Subjective Side of the Father-Son Connection, A Research Note (536)
Race, Maternal Authority and Adolescent Aspiration (609)
Race, SES Contexts and Fulfillment of College Aspirations (633)
Comparative Perspectives of Third World Women: The Impact of Race,
  Sex, and Class (673)
Race, Identity, and Black Children: A Developmental Perspective (679)
Maternal Employment, Race, and Work Orientation of High School Girls
  (689)
Relationship of Self and Ideal-Self: Descriptions with Sex, Race and
  Class in Southern Adolescents (722)
Interrelations among Family Stability, Family Composition, Residence
  and Race (739)
Illegitimacy by Race and Mixture of Race (756)
Race, Age, and Family Status Differentials in Metropolitan Migration
  of Households (778)
The Intergenerational Transmission of Marital Instability: Comparisons
  by Race and Sex (849)
Race, Status and Medical Care (886)

Father Absence and Its Apparent Effect on the Reading Achievement of
Black Children from Low-Income Families (931)

REARED, REARING
Rearing Children for Educational Achievement in Fatherless Families
(625)
Childhood Characteristics of Black College Graduates Reared in Poverty
(642)

REBELLION
Negro Student Rebellion against Parental Political Beliefs (657)

RECOGNITION
Skin Color Recognition, Preference and Identification in Interracial
Children: A Comparative Study (420)

RECONCEPTION
Early Reconception and Contraceptive Use among Black Teenage Girls
After an Illegitimate Birth (406)

RECONSTRUCTION
The Black Family During Reconstruction (2)
Black Scare: The Racist Response to Emancipation and Reconstruction
(1138)

REFUGE
The House of Refuge for Colored Children (357)

REGISTRANTS
An Investigation of the Effects of Work on the Families of Black,
Female Registrants in the Baltimore City Win Program, A Pilot Study
(146)

REGULARITY
Powerlessness and Regularity of Contraception in an Urban Negro Male
Sample: A Research Note (75)

RELATEDNESS
African-American Polygynous Relatedness: An Exploratory Study
Utilizing Phenomenological Techniques (686)

RELATIONS
Black Family Structure and Primary Relations (50)
Interpersonal Relations between Black Males and Black Females (145)
Internal Relations in Unemployed Families (209)
On Race Relations: Selected Writings (353)
Conjugal Power Relations among Black Working Class Families (436)
Extended Kinship Relations in Black and White Families (480)
You Gotta Deal With It: Black Family Relations in a Southern Community
(615)
The Influence of Family Relations upon Socially Desiring Behavior of
Black and Caucasian Preschool Children (692)
On Marital Relations: Perceptions of Black Women (787)
Intermarriage and Interethnic Relations: A Comparative Study (826)
Black and White Single Parents' Attitudes toward Traditional Family
Relations (916)
Symposium on the Family, Intergenerational Relations and Social
Structure. Duke University, 1963. Social Structure and the Family:
Generational Relations (948)
Portraits of Family and Kinship Relations among Black Americans: A
Study in the Properties, Structures and Functions of Primary Groups
(952)
The World of Black Singles: Changing Patterns of Male/Female Relations
(1004)
Parent-Child Relations, Achievement Motivation, and Sex-Role Attitudes
among Black and White Professional Women in Traditional and Pioneer
Occupations (1139)

RELATIONSHIP(S)

A Study of the Relationship between Father-Absent Homes and Father-
Present Homes and the Academic Performance and Social Adjustment of
Black Middle School Students (960)
Mother Child, Father Child Relationships (1022)
Black Families, Social Evaluations and Future Marital Relationships
(1058)
The Relationship between the Disciplinary Styles of Black Parents and
Preference for Mode of Family Therapy (1082)
Four "Classic" Studies of Power Relationships in Black Families: A
Review and Look to the Future (1128)
RELATIVES
Relatives' Responsibility: A Problem in Social Policy (93)
The Perceptions of the Black Aged and Their Relatives toward the
Receipt of Care Components at Contracting Socioeconomic Levels (183)
RELIGION
The Black Experience in Religion (671)
Perspectives for a Study of Afro-American Religion in the United
States (680)
REPRODUCTIVE
Black-White Reproductive Behavior: An Economic Interpretation (973)
Race, Education and Fertility: A Comparison of Black-White
Reproductive Behavior (1028)
RESIDENCE, RESIDENTIAL, RESIDENTS
Primary Group Supports among a Sample of Elderly Black and White
Ethnic Residents of Urban, Working-Class Neighborhoods (513)
Kinship and Residential Propinquity: A Case Study of a Black Extended
Family in New Orleans (553)
Interrelations among Family Stability, Family Composition, Residence
and Race (739)
Some Observations Concerning Black Children Living in a Residential
Care Agency (831)
Residence, Kinship, and Mating as Survival Strategies: A West Indian
Example (1110)
RESISTANCE
A Survey of the Black Woman and the Persuasion Process: The Study of
Strategies of Identification and Resistance (166)
Female Slave Resistance: The Economics of Sex (512)
Resistance to Temptation in Young Negro Children (777)
RESOLUTION
Perceived Dominance in Decision-Making and Conflict Resolution among
Anglo, Black, and Chicano Couples (252)
RESOURCE(S)
Blacks at Middle and Late Life: Resources and Coping (378)
The Net Resource Distribution of Two Parent Low Income Families: A
Regional Comparison (487)
A Resource Guide on Black Families in America (526)
Agenda Paper No. V: The Family: Resources for Change-Planning Session
for the White House Conference 'To Fulfill These Rights' (660)
Family Records, A Major Resource for Documenting the Black Experience
in New England (850)
The Progress of Afro-American Women: A Selected Bibliography and
Resource Guide (966)
RESPONSIBILITY
Relatives' Responsibility: A Problem in Social Policy (93)
The Crisis of Youth and Adult Responsibility (393)
A Study of the Social and Maternal Responsibility of a Group of Negro
Unwed Mothers (604)

This Species of Property: Slave Life and Culture in the Old South
  (815)
The American Slave: A Composite Autobiography. Vol. 1: From Sundown to
  Sunup: The Making of the Black Community (871)
A Slave Family in the Antebellum South (929)
Slave Marriage and the Family (1017)
The Age of Slaves at Menarche and Their First Birth (1050)
Slave Kinship: A Case Study of the South Carolina Good Hope
  Plantation, 1835-1856 (1102)
Female Slaves: Sex Roles and Status in the Antebellum Plantation South
  (1105)
SLAVERY
Reckoning with Slavery: A Critical Study in the Quantitative History
  of American Negro Slavery (264)
Slavery in Brazil and the United States: An Essay in Comparative
  History (281)
Cliometrics and Culture: Some Recent Developments in the
  Historiography of Slavery (339)
Time on the Cross: The Economics of American Negro Slavery (341)
Husbands, Fathers, Wives and Mothers During Slavery (373)
Herbert Gutman's THE BLACK FAMILY IN SLAVERY AND FREEDOM, 1750-1925:
  An Anthropologist's View (417)
The Black Family in Slavery and Freedom: 1750-1925 (425)
Slavery and the Numbers Game: A Critique of TIME ON THE CROSS (426)
"My Mother Was Much of A Woman": Black Women, Work, and the Family
  under Slavery. (599)
Labor of Love, Labor of Sorrow: Black Women, Work, and the Family from
  Slavery to the Present (600)
The New England Puritan Attitude toward Black Slavery (690)
Herbert Gutman's THE BLACK FAMILY IN SLAVERY AND FREEDOM, 1750-1925:
  Demographic Perspectives (751)
Herbert Gutman's THE BLACK FAMILY IN SLAVERY AND FREEDOM, 1750-1925: A
  Cliometric Reconsideration (917)
SLUM
Socialization into Sexual Behavior in a Negro Slum Ghetto (435)
Behind Ghetto Walls: Black Families in a Federal Slum (862)
School Children in the Urban Slum: Readings in Social Science Research
  (883)
SMOKING
Relative Effects of Low Socioeconomic Status, Parental Smoking and
  Poor Scholastic Performance on Smoking among High School Students
  (135)
SOCIAL
Relatives' Responsibility: A Problem in Social Policy (93)
Time, Aging and Continuity of Social Structure: Themes and Issues in
  Generational Analysis (94)
Social Heterosexual Development among Urban Negroes and Whites (152)
Dark Ghetto: Dilemmas of Social Power (220)
The American Negro: From Family Membership to Personal and Social
  Identity (268)
Social Research and the Black Community: Selected Issues and
  Priorities. A Selection of Papers from a Workshop on Developing
  Research Priorities for the Black Community held at
  Howard University in Washington, D.C., June 25-29, 1973 (366)
Single Parent Mothers and Distress: Relationships between Selected
  Social and Psychological Factors and Distress in Low-Income
  Single Parent Mothers (542)

Conscious Agents of Time and Self: The Lives and Styles of African-
American Women as Seen through Their Autobiographical Writings (123)
Time on the Cross: The Economics of American Negro Slavery (341)
Slavery and the Numbers Game: A Critique of TIME ON THE CROSS (426)
The Free Black Family at the Time of the U.S. Census: Some
Implications (643)
The Mexican-American Family: Its Modifications Over Time and Space
(995)
TOGETHER
"Together" Black Women (875)
TOMORROW
Tomorrow's Tomorrow: The Black Woman (638)
TOUGH
Black Males and the Tough Guy Image: A Dysfunctional Compensatory
Adaptation (809)
TRADITIONAL, TRADITIONS
A Form Critical Approach to the Oral Traditions of the Black Church as
They Relate to the Celebration of Death (245)
A Study of Black Adoption Families: A Comparison of a Traditional and
Quasi-Adoption Program (645)
Black and White Single Parents' Attitudes toward Traditional Family
Relations (916)
Parent-Child Relations, Achievement Motivation, and Sex-Role Attitudes
among Black and White Professional Women in Traditional and Pioneer
Occupations (1139)
TRANSACTION
An Expanded Case Study of Family Interaction and Transaction Roles of
Middle-Class Black Mothers (247)
The Moynihan Report and the Politics of Controversy: A Transaction
Social Science and Public Policy Report (865)
TRANSFERS
Jobs, Cash Transfers and Marital Instability: A Review and Synthesis
of the Evidence (118)
TRANSITION(S)
Transitions: The Family and the Life Course in Historical Perspective
(457)
Transition to Parenthood by Black Couples (515)
The Black Family in Transition: Louisiana, 1860-65 (881)
TRANSMISSION
On the Transmission of Marital Instability in Black Families (486)
The Intergenerational Transmission of Marital Instability: Comparisons
by Race and Sex (849)
TRANSRACIAL, TRANSRACIALLY
Transracial Adoption: White Parents Who Adopted Black Children and
White Parents Who Adopted White Children (78)
Black Identity and the Grow-Shapiro Study on Transracial Adoption
(213)
Transracial Adoption of Black Children (214)
Black Children--White Parents: A Study of Transracial Adoption (416)
Transracial Adoption: The Black Community Perspective (525)
Transracial Adoption: Victim of Ideology (584)
A Comparative Study of the Self-Concept of Transracially and
Inracially Adopted Black Children (732)
Black Attitudes toward Transracial Adoption (962)
Transracial Adoption (964)

VETERAN
  Variations in Veteran/Nonveteran Earnings Patterns among WWII, Korea,
    and Vietnam War Cohorts (699)
VICTIM(S)
  Transracial Adoption: Victim of Ideology (584)
  Elderly Victims of Family Violence and Neglect (870)
  Blaming the Victim (911)
VIETNAM
  Variations in Veteran/Nonveteran Earnings Patterns among WWII, Korea,
    and Vietnam War Cohorts (699)
VIOLENCE
  Family Violence and Aging Blacks: Theoretical Perspectives and
    Research Possibilities (199)
  Race, Class, Network Embeddedness and Family Violence: A Search for
    Potent Support Systems (201)
  Violence, Race and Culture (257)
  Violence in the Family: A Review of Research in the Seventies (372)
  Sexual Permissiveness, Sex Role Rigidity, and Violence Across Cultures
    (717)
  Elderly Victims of Family Violence and Neglect (870)
  Race, Stress and Family Violence (1001)
  Race and Family Violence: The Internal Colonialism Perspective (1011)
VIRGINIA
  Free Black Women and the Question of Matriarchy: Petersburg, Virginia,
    1784-1820 (648)
  The Household Composition of Rural Black Families: Louisa County,
    Virginia, 1880 (953)
VOCABULARY
  A Comparative Analysis of Vocabulary Diversity, Syntactic Maturity,
    and the Communicative and Cognitive Function of the Language of
    Black Four-Year-Old Children at Two Socioeconomic Levels (139)
VOCATIONAL
  Black and White Fathers: Their Impact on the Idealized Models and
    Vocational Plans of their Adolescent Sons (1076)
VOICE(S)
  Silent Voices: The Southern Negro Woman Today (196)
  The Minority Woman's Voice: A Cultural Study of Black and Chicana
    Fiction (336)
  Voices of the New Feminism (1044)
VOLUNTARISM, VOLUNTARY
  An Urban Black Voluntary Association (61)
  The Voluntary Dimension in Work Effort: The Effects of Work and
    Leisure Orientations on the Work Patterns of Low Income Familyheads
    (429)
  The Value of Voluntarism among Minority Groups (1047)
WAR   See also: Civil War, WWII
  Variations in Veteran/Nonveteran Earnings Patterns among WWII, Korea,
    and Vietnam War Cohorts (699)
WASHINGTON
  Child Development from a Black Perspective--Conference, June 10-13,
    1970, Washington, DC (211)
  Social Research and the Black Community: Selected Issues and
    Priorities. A Selection of Papers from a Workshop on Developing
    Research Priorities for the Black Community held at
    Howard University in Washington, D.C., June 25-29, 1973 (366)

A Comparison of Cognitive and Analytically Oriented Brief Treatment Approaches to Depression in Black Women (195)
Women into Wives: The Legal and Economic Impact of Marriage (204)
Divorce Among Educated Black Women (208)
Isokinetic Measurement of Strength in Black and White University Women (230)
Keeping the Faith and Disturbing the Peace. Black Women: From Anti-Slavery to Women's Suffrage (234)
Family Planning Program Effects on the Fertility of Low-Income U.S. Women (258)
AFDC and the Marital and Family Status of Ever Married Women Aged 15-44: United States, 1950-1970 (259)
Women, Race and Class (267)
A Descriptive and Analytical Study of the Early Adult Roles of Black and White Women (279)
The Impact of Health Education on Acceptance of Family Planning Methods for Spacing by Lower Socioeconomic Primiparous Urban Women (285)
Positive Effects of the Multiple Negative: Explaining the Success of Black Professional Women (319)
Women and Professional Careers: The Case of the Woman Lawyer (320)
Black Women in the Labor Force: An Investigation of Factors Affecting the Labor Force Participation of Black Women in the United States (324)
Childbirth in the Ghetto: Folk Beliefs of Negro Women in a North Philadelphia Hospital Ward (348)
A Comparative Study on the Assertiveness of Black and White Women at the University Level (362)
Comparative Analysis of Black and White Women's Sex-Role Attitudes (418)
Reality and Myth: Employment and Sex Role Ideology in Black Women (419)
A Period Analysis of Parity Distribution among White and Nonwhite Women in the United States, 1940-1974 (421)
Characteristics of Black Women in Male and Female Headed Households (441)
Factors Associated with the Poverty of Black Women (442)
Some Consequences of Illegitimacy in a Sample of Black Women (443)
Attitudes of Married Women toward Work and Family: Comparison by Stress Level, Race and Work Status (474)
Work Status, Work Satisfaction, and Blood Pressure among Married Black and White Women (475)
Educated Black Women: An Exploration into Life Chances and Choices (503)
Ain't I a Woman: Black Women and Feminism (518)
Help the Human Experience: The Psychology of Women (540)
A Case Study in Patriarchal Politics: Women on Welfare (544)
The Cultural Halo Effect: Black and White Women Rate Black and White Men (549)
Militancy and Black Women's Competitive Behavior in Competitive vs. Non-Competitive Conditions (555)
Aging Black Women: Selected Readings for NCBA. (559)
Aging Black Women: Selected Readings for NCBA (561)
Comparative Lifestyles and Family and Friend Relationships among Older Black Women (564)
The Plight of Older Black Women in the United States (566)

CO-AUTHOR / CO-EDITOR INDEX

About the Editors

WALTER R. ALLEN is Associate Professor of Sociology and Director of the Center for Afro-American Studies at the University of Michigan. He is a co-editor of *Beginnings: The Social and Affective Development of Black Children* and co-author of *The Color-Line and the Quality of Life*. He has contributed articles to the *Annual Review of Sociology*, the *Journal of Negro Education*, *Phylon*, *Sociological Quarterly*, and the *Journal of Comparative Family Studies*.

RICHARD A. ENGLISH is Dean of the School of Social Work and Professor at Howard University, Washington, D.C. He is a co-editor of *Human Service Organizations* and has published articles and essays in *Things That Matter*, *Issues in Race and Ethnic Relations*, *Integrateducation*, *Individual Change Through Group Methods*, and *Social Research and the Black Community*.

JO ANNE HALL is an Assistant Librarian at the University of Michigan's Center for Afro-American Studies. She has contributed to *RQ*.